JAMES W. VANDER ZANDEN, Ph.D., University of North Carolina, is Associate Professor of Sociology at The Ohio State University. He previously taught at Duke University. Professor Vander Zanden is the author of *Sociology— A Systematic Approach*, Second Edition, also published by The Ronald Press Company, as well as three other books in the area of sociology.

AMERICAN MINORITY RELATIONS

JAMES W. VANDER ZANDEN
THE OHIO STATE UNIVERSITY

THIRD EDITION

THE RONALD PRESS COMPANY • NEW YORK

Preface

This third edition of a widely-used and successful textbook is designed for the course in minority relations. In the past decade a deluge of new materials has appeared treating American minority relations. Indeed, it has reached a point where many a specialist in the area feels overwhelmed. Although in truth a good deal of the material has had a journalistic and impressionistic quality, it nonetheless has generally contained useful insights into various facets of minority-dominant relations. In addition, there has been a significant proliferation in sophisticated empirical studies, often encompassing and cutting across disciplines—sociology, psychology, biology, anthropology, political science, and history.

Students in race relations courses should have access to this knowledge in some convenient, manageable form—and in a form that is relevant to the contemporary world in which they live. And that is the purpose of this text. It aims to be home base for the student, providing him with a solid, sound foundation. While thorough and comprehensive, it is intentionally compact so that the instructor can additionally, if he so chooses, select from the vast array of current supplementary titles.

In treating the vast amount of data and theory within the field, I have attempted to strike a judicious balance between theory and description. This approach avoids the disadvantages of a mere descriptive rundown of each of the minority groups, on the one hand, and a too ambitious theoretical and conceptual approach, on the other. The former, it seems to me, fails to provide a firm grounding in theory or to give the reader an understanding of the considerable dimensions and processes involved in intergroup relations, while the latter strikes me as presumptuous and unsatisfactory in terms of our understanding of human behavior in general and of religious, ethnic, and race relations in particular.

Part I of the book sets the stage for the consideration of American minority relations in treating a number of key concepts and analyzing some of the facts and myths revolving about race. Part II examines the sources of racism, considering a number of variables that typically come into play in the emergence and initial stabilization of racism. It shows how racism is maintained by becoming deeply embedded in the social and cultural fabric—indeed how it becomes institutionalized. The last chapter in Part II deals with the personality bulwarks of racism. Part III considers four processes of intergroup relations—conflict, segregation, stratification, and assimilation—particularly in terms of recent developments in these areas.

Next, Part IV examines the reactions of minorities to their disadvantaged status, which are discussed primarily in terms of acceptance or aggression and avoidance or assimilation. This approach permits a study of assimilationist-oriented minorities and an extensive analytical consideration of the Black "Revolution," including a treatment of Black Power. Finally, Part V focuses upon the fact that dominant-minority relations are anything but static and that social change is an inescapable fact of social existence. The concluding chapter examines that body of sociological literature dealing with means by which democratic goals may be advanced and racism combated.

JAMES W. VANDER ZANDEN

Columbus, Ohio
February, 1972

Contents

I INTRODUCTION

1 THE NATURE OF MINORITY RELATIONS   3

Science and the Study of Minority Relations. Minorities. Additional
Concepts. Summary.

2 RACE: FACT AND MYTH   30

What Is Race? Are There Superior Races? Are There "Racial"
Personalities and Temperaments? Is There a "Racial" Morality?
Interracial Mixture. How Are Races Formed? Summary.

II SOURCES OF RACISM

3 ORIGINS OF RACISM   67

Contact. Social Visibility. Ethnocentrism. Competition. Unequal
Power. Summary.

4 MAINTENANCE OF RACISM   97

The Role of Culture. Reference Groups and Racism. The Thomas
Theorem. Acquiring Prejudice. Summary.

5 PERSONALITY BULWARKS OF RACISM   124

Frustration and Aggression. Projection. The Prejudiced Personality.
Summary.

III INTERGROUP RELATIONS WITHIN AMERICA

6 CONFLICT   157

Conflict and the Social Order. Social Violence in the United States.
Some Other Forms of Conflict. Arousal and Resolution of Conflict.
Summary.

7 SEGREGATION   185

American Indians. Blacks. Puerto Ricans. Chicanos. Chinese.
Japanese. Jews. Summary.

8 STRATIFICATION   221

Class, Ethnic, and Racial Stratification. Patterns of Stratification.
Mobility. Controversial Issues. Summary.

9 ASSIMILATION   258

The Nature of Assimilation. Differing Conceptions of Assimilation.
A Natural History of Race Relations? The Rate of Assimilation.
Marginality. Intergroup Marriage. Assimilation Within Hawaii.
Minimum Assimilation: The Amish. Summary.

IV MINORITY REACTIONS TO DOMINANCE

10 RESPONDING BY ACCEPTANCE   305

The Case of the Rural South. The Case of Evacuated West Coast
Japanese. Apathy and Reform Movements. Variables Affecting
the Response of Minority-Group Members. Summary.

11 RESPONDING BY AGGRESSION   330

The Expression of Hostility. Protest. Variables Affecting the Response of Minority-Group Members. Summary.

12 RESPONDING BY ASSIMILATION   351

European Immigrant Groups. Passing. The Black Protest—1955–
1965: Aggression–Assimilation. Variables Affecting the Response
of Minority-Group Members. Summary.

13   RESPONDING BY AVOIDANCE   377

Insulation. Migration. Separatism. Variables Affecting the Response of Minority-Group Members. Summary.

V   SOCIAL CHANGE

14   MINORITY-DOMINANT PATTERNS IN TRANSITION   409

The Early Years. Segregation in the South. Racial Integration in a
Northern Transition Community. Trends in Desegregation. Summary.

15   TOWARD LESSENING RACISM   446

Some Preliminary Considerations. Propaganda. Education. Contact. Psychological Techniques. The Legal Approach. Summary.

AUTHOR INDEX   483

SUBJECT INDEX   491

1

INTRODUCTION

1

The Nature of Minority Relations

Our domestic well-being and the dictates of our world position have compelled us as a nation to focus increasing attention upon our racial and ethnic relations. Indeed, many Americans believe that our nation's racial crisis is second in gravity only to, and perhaps even equal to, the threat of nuclear war. A widely heralded report by a Presidential Commission on Civil Disorders concludes:

Our nation is moving toward two societies, one black, one white—separate and unequal. . . . Discrimination and segregation have long permeated much of American life; they now threaten the future of every American.

This deepening racial division is not inevitable. The movement apart can be reversed. Choice is still possible. . . .

To pursue our present course will involve the continuing polarization of the American community and, ultimately, the destruction of basic democratic values.[1]

On the world scene American racial and ethnic patterns, both North and South, have assumed considerable importance. Joseph Modupe Johnson, a Nigerian leader, notes:

If the government only knew how much damage was being done they would not continue this costly indulgence. For every penny of aid poured into Africa, America continues to lose tons of goodwill because of the racial discrimination in this country. Something drastic must be done, fast, before it is too late.[2]

[1] *Report of the National Advisory Commission on Civil Disorders* (New York: Bantam Books, 1968), 1.
[2] Arnold H. Lubasch, "Racial Strife Pictured as Losing Friends for U.S. in Africa," *New York Times*, May 20, 1964.

3

Within this context the scientific study of minority relations assumes the greatest gravity.

SCIENCE AND THE STUDY OF MINORITY RELATIONS

The Pursuit of Objectivity

Sociology undertakes to examine minority relations with a scientific orientation characterized by *a rigorous, disciplined pursuit of objectivity*. Underlying this approach is the assumption that there is a "real world"—that something exists "out there," something that is divorced from the individual himself, and that this something is empirically knowable. Thus, whether calculated by an American, a Russian, or an Indonesian, or by a Communist, a Methodist, or a Hindu spiritualist, two plus two nonetheless equals four.

Put still another way, there are such things as *facts*—certain empirically verifiable observations—and hence we can make reliable statements regarding what *is*. People, however, do not necessarily regard "what is" as desirable, as the way things *ought* to be. Hence we find it useful to distinguish between facts and *values*. Values are conceptions regarding the desirability or undesirability of things (their beauty, merit, worth, etc.)—in brief, notions of what "ought" to be. Science, be it chemistry or sociology, can only ascertain facts; it cannot tell us whether these facts are good or bad—whether it is ethically desirable or undesirable that every chemical compound contains unvarying proportions of its constituent elements (the Law of Constant Composition) or that Black–White relations within the United States have been characterized by discrimination and segregation.

That science should concern itself only with "what is" is of course an ideal; in practice, things do not work out quite this way, for science involves *human* activity, carried on by individual people and by groups of people. It is this element that injects subjectivity into the picture. All human beings have values, and to the extent to which we are human, we cannot be completely objective. Even at our best, we find values subtly invading our work. Indeed, the very fact of studying human behavior reveals concern with it, and the decision to focus upon social rather than biological, psychological, or other factors betrays an implicit belief that the social factor is somehow "more significant." Similarly, values shape our selec-

tion of research problems (e.g., race relations rather than the structure of business enterprise), our preference for certain hypotheses,
and our neglect of others.

What we have been saying adds up to this. Sociology, as a science, is not characterized by the absolute absence of values but by
a *rigorous, disciplined* attempt to look as objectively as is humanly
possible upon the phenomena that it studies. As such, sociologists
are enjoined to avoid such emotional involvement in their work
that they cannot adopt a new approach or reject an old answer when
their findings indicate that this is required. Further, sociologists
are enjoined not to turn their back on facts or distort them simply
because they do not like them.[3] Much of sociological education
beyond the bachelor's degree is oriented toward fostering this kind
of commitment and developing those skills whereby valid, reliable
knowledge can be realized. And there is the additional check—
indeed, social pressure—provided by the scientist's peers. Having
published his work in professional publications, other scientists, not
necessarily sharing his biases, come to scrutinize and criticize his
work.[4]

Sociological Controversy

Over the past decade considerable controversy has been generated
within sociological circles over the questions of "knowledge for
what?" and "sociology for whom?" Let us consider these matters.

Knowledge for What? A good many nineteenth-century American sociologists were personally interested in social reform, and
viewed sociology as a potentially powerful instrument for relieving
human suffering and guiding man in the search for a better future.
And Hinkle and Hinkle point to the prevalence of rural and religious
backgrounds and the deep concern with ethical matters among
leading sociologists in the first decades of this century—indeed, a
surprising number launched their careers as Protestant ministers.[5]
In succeeding decades, despite changes in the philosophical and
social climate, sociology has secured many of its recruits from among

---

[3] In this regard see: Tamotsu Shibutani and Kian M. Kwan, *Ethnic Stratification*
(New York: The Macmillan Company, 1965), 11–20.

[4] Alan P. Bates, *The Sociological Enterprise* (Boston: Houghton Mifflin Company, 1967).

[5] R. C. Hinkle, Jr., and G. J. Hinkle, *The Development of Modern Sociology*
(New York: Random House, Inc., 1954), 3.

highly idealistic youth, those who hope for the solution of man's problems in the scientific study of society.

During its formative years, however, sociology struggled to gain respectability and acceptance within the scientific community (Harvard, for instance, did not establish a department of sociology until 1930 and Princeton not until 1960). Partly as a response to this, another theme arose that asserted sociology should remain aloof from involvement with social problems and concern itself strictly with the enlargement of sociological knowledge. This was the dominant position of the profession during the 1940s, 1950s, and 1960s. It was associated with such men as Talcott Parsons and George A. Lundberg who advocated a neutral, amoral sociology— one in which sociologists were bound to the tenet: "Thou shall not commit a value judgment." [6] Robert Bierstedt, a prominent sociologist of this period, expressed the view as follows:

> Sociology is a pure science, not an applied science. The immediate goal of sociology is the acquisition of knowledge about human society, not the utilization of that knowledge. Physicists do not build bridges, physiologists do not treat people afflicted with pneumonia, and chemists do not fill prescriptions at the corner drugstore. Similarly, sociologists do not determine questions of public policy, do not tell legislators what laws should be passed or repealed, and do not dispense relief to the ill, the lame, the blind, or the poor. . . . Sociology . . . stands in the same relation to administration, legislation, diplomacy, teaching, supervision, social work, and citizenship, as physics does to engineering, physiology to medicine, jurisprudence to law, astronomy to navigation, chemistry to pharmacy, and biology to plant and animal husbandry.[7]

Bierstedt concedes that sociological knowledge can be used for solving some of the world's problems, but insists that this application is not the job of sociologists. Rather, he maintains, a division of labor operates in which the individuals who acquire sociological knowledge are not necessarily the ones who undertake to apply it.

Brewton Berry outlines a somewhat similar position for the study of race relations. Responding to those who accuse sociologists of "fiddling about leisurely" studying race problems in the face of urgent calls for remedial social engineering, Berry writes:

> We fully appreciate the seriousness and urgency of the situation, but we believe that knowledge and understanding are prerequisites for wise and effective action. We are sympathetic, for instance, with the medical research

---

[6] In this regard see: Alvin W. Gouldner, "Anti-Minotaur: The Myth of a Value-Free Sociology," *Social Problems,* 9 (1962), 199.

[7] Robert Bierstedt, *The Social Order,* 2nd ed. (New York: McGraw-Hill Book Co., 1963), 12–13.

scientists who work away in their laboratories while an epidemic rages in the community. Why, some will say, do they not do something immediately useful? Why not put into practical use such knowledge and skill as they have, imperfect though it be? Why waste their efforts on research when the times demand action? It is our opinion that, in the long run, the research scientists will relieve more suffering by their investigations than by abandoning their study and devoting themselves to therapy.[8]

But sociology has hardly enjoyed unanimity on this matter.[9] For several decades a minority voice critical of the value-free position struggled to make itself heard. Dan W. Dodson exemplifies this tradition:

. . . we [sociologists] are of necessity reformers. If we are not reformers, we have no place in relations and other areas where groups have unequal opportunities. Ours is the task of restructuring intergroup relations to the end that basic human rights are translated into civil rights, i.e., undergirded by law, and that the total society is brought to respect equality of relationships between us.[10]

Critics of the ethically-neutral stance of Bierstedt and Berry argue that the apostles of sociological "neutrality" are remiss in their public and civic responsibilities, that they come to champion moral insenitivity—a crass disregard for such things as the suffering of the poor and minority groups, the destructiveness of war, and the high social costs of crime and delinquency. To ignore values, they maintain, is to usher in an era of spiritless technicians, individuals capable of crippling mankind with a sociological atomic bomb—not an idle threat in a world where already prisoners of war are systematically brainwashed and where housewives' buying habits are systematically molded through sophisticated advertising campaigns. Before Hiroshima, physicists also liked to talk about their value-free science but today many of them are no longer quite sure that this can or should be the case.[11]

[8] Brewton Berry, *Race and Ethnic Relations,* 3rd ed. (Boston: Houghton Mifflin Company, 1965), 18.

[9] In this regard see: Gouldner, *op. cit.,* 199–213; David J. Gray, "Value-Free Sociology: A Doctrine of Hypocrisy and Irresponsibility," *The Sociological Quarterly,* 9 (1968), 176–185; Martin Nicolaus, "Remarks at ASA Convention," *The American Sociologist,* 4 (1969), 154–156; and "Some Radical Perspectives in Sociology," *Sociological Inquiry,* 40 (Winter, 1970). This issue of *Sociological Inquiry* contains seven articles by the Sociology Liberation Movement (since renamed the Union of Radical Sociologists).

[10] Dan W. Dodson, "The Creative Role of Conflict Reexamined," *The Journal of Intergroup Relations,* 1 (Winter, 1959–1960), 5.

[11] Gouldner, *op. cit.,* 212. For a further elaboration of this thesis see Alvin W. Gouldner, *The Coming Crisis of Western Sociology* (New York: Basic Books, Inc., 1970).

A value-free sociology, the critics assert, is a sterile, irrelevant sociology and they point an accusing finger at the established sociological journals for the "inconsequential trivia" that allegedly appear within their pages. They insist that the strong ethic of social concern that characterized many early sociologists must be resurrected and that sociology concern itself with human suffering and its alleviation. They criticize as "inward-looking" those sociologists who relegate social betterment to a secondary place and accuse them of being more concerned with the betterment of the occupational group than with the larger society that they ultimately serve. Moreover, these "new breed" sociologists ask why a man's professional status as a sociologist should set him aside from other men. Accordingly, they seek to establish bridges between sociology and what they view as the larger hopes, aspirations, and purposes of mankind. This latter orientation has become increasingly popular during the past decade, especially among recent Ph.D. graduates.

Sociology for Whom?   Another question increasingly being raised, especially by younger sociologists, is: "Sociology for whom?" Those asking this question generally note that the sociologist is as much a social being as the people he studies, and he is not free of the social demands of colleagues, research organizations and government granting agencies, political systems, university administrators, students, or friends. In brief, a variety of individuals and groups act as influences on the sociologist's conduct. Moreover, values do not exist in a vacuum or in the abstract. Rather values are found within groups and serve the interests of groups. Since a conflict of values and interests often characterizes differing groups, it is argued that the choice for the sociologist becomes a choice of whose interests shall be served by his work.

Critics of contemporary American sociology contend that the ideology of ethical neutrality actually serves to mask a very definite commitment: ". . . the choice that has generally been made by sociologists is to put their skills at the service of the 'establishment,' that is to say, of groups who wield a great deal of economic and political power in the society." [12] They insist that a "non-committed" sociology is the handmaiden of the status quo—"a gentleman's promise that boats will not be rocked." [13] Indeed, "to do

[12] Arturo Biblarz, "On the Question of Objectivity in Sociology," *Et Al.,* 2 (Fall, 1969), 4.
[13] Gouldner, "Anti-Minotaur: The Myth of a Value-Free Sociology," 201.

nothing in today's world is as political in its effect as to do something; to assent is as political as to dissent." [14] Hence proponents of this view argue that the alternatives are not "neutrality" and "advocacy"; rather, "to be uncommited is not to be neutral but to be committed—consciously or not—to the *status quo*." [15] Accordingly, sociologists are increasingly being asked, "Which side are you on?" —the implication being, for example, that one stands either for or against a racist society.

Is a Resolution of the Divergent Views Possible? Much of the controversy that we have considered revolves about the uses of science, and in particular of sociology.[16] Traditionally many scientists have assessed scientific work in terms of its contribution to knowledge as opposed to its use on grounds that only in this manner can science remain fairly autonomous and free. Conversely, they argue, if practical utility becomes the sole measure of significance, then science becomes only a handmaiden—of business, the church, the state, the party, or the "movement." In truth there is a basic duality in science: it can provide greater understanding of how things operate and occur and it can also provide understanding that enables man to change things and to move toward given goals. And as with most dualities in life, this one has given rise to ambivalent attitudes. Further, since people generally find ambivalence difficult to tolerate, scientists have historically dealt with their indecision by periodically swinging violently to one extreme position or the other—in the process tending to deny the worth of the other alternative.

Perhaps we can be a little more relaxed about these matters if we realize that we need not be addicted to either position—that sociology is *nothing but* self-contained knowledge, entirely insulated from the world of social action, or that sociology is *nothing but* a guide to action. In truth, sociology is both. Some sociologists no doubt—by temperament or capacity—are more comfortable or better suited in one or the other paths of inquiry, and some move back

[14] Gerald D. Berreman, "Speech to Council," *Newsletter of the American Anthropological Association*, 12 (January, 1971), 19.

[15] Douglas Dowd, "Thorstein Veblen and C. Wright Mills: Social Science and Social Criticism," in Irving Horowitz, ed., *The New Sociology* (New York: Oxford University Press, 1964), 63.

[16] The discussion that follows is in large measure adapted from Robert K. Merton, "Social Problems and Sociological Theory," in Robert K. Merton and Robert A. Nisbet, eds., *Contemporary Social Problems*, 2nd ed. (New York: Harcourt, Brace Jovanovich, 1966), 755–778.

and forth between paths. In brief, then, we need not see a hard-and-fast boundary separating pure from applied science.

Finally, it needs to be understood that science does not call upon sociologists to give up their moral convictions or biases; indeed, such a demand would be humanly unrealistic and impossible. But by the same token our discussion should not be taken as a recommendation for license to offer value judgments at random, resulting in a "this I believe"-type sociology. Rather, regardless of the path the sociologist takes—be it in the direction of pure or applied science—it is nonetheless incumbent upon him rigorously to cultivate a disciplined approach to the phenomena that he studies so that he might determine facts as they are and not as he might wish them to be.[17]

MINORITIES

The Concept

In approaching human behavior, tools of analysis are crucial—concepts with which the vast array of social phenomena may be examined. The term *minority* is one such concept. What is a minority? Probably the most satisfactory answer to this question is that suggested by Wagley and Harris, who single out five definitive features.[18] Let us examine each of these in turn:

1. *A minority is a social group whose members experience at the hands of another social group various disabilities in the form of prejudice, discrimination, segregation, or persecution (or any combination of these).* Where two groups are unequal in power—by virtue of superior technology (especially weapons); control of critical economic, political, and social institutions; etc.—the more powerful group is able to actualize its claim to an unequal and larger share of the socially defined "good" things (unless prevented by norms that restrain exploitation of the weaker by the more powerful). In other words, unequal interaction occurs between two groups. While the interaction between individuals and groups may continue to be reciprocal, involving a two-way interchange, the reciprocity is unequal and uneven. Action on one side of the interaction equation

---

[17] In this regard see: Walter R. Gove, "Should the Sociology Profession Take Moral Stands on Political Issues?" *The American Sociologist*, 5 (1970), 221–223.

[18] Charles Wagley and Marvin Harris, *Minorities in the New World* (New York: Columbia University Press, 1964), 4–11.

is effective and decisive to a degree greater than that found on the other side in that one group is better able than the other to translate what it defines as its just dessert into actuality.[19] The advantaged group is generally referred to as the *dominant group.*

The term *minority*, however, does not necessarily have any numerical connotation. Despite its literal meaning, a minority is *not* a statistical category. Although minority groups are generally of smaller size than the dominant group, this is not always the case. Within the Union of South Africa and some areas of our southern states, Blacks constitute a majority of the population. Moreover, at least until recently, a limited number of Europeans dominated "minority" peoples in Indonesia, in the Congo, and other former colonial areas. Yet despite the fact that they are a numerical majority in such settings, the minority occupies a disadvantaged position and experiences various disabilities.

2. *The disabilities experienced by minorities are related to special characteristics that its members share, either physical or cultural or both, which the dominant group holds in low esteem.* The disapproval ranges from ridicule or mere suspicion to hate. Most frequently the special traits distinguishing the minority from the dominant group are differences in physical appearances (for example, skin color within the United States) or in language, religion, or some other cultural traits (for example, Jews). Groups identified on cultural grounds are commonly referred to as *ethnic* minorities; those identified on physical grounds, as *racial* minorities.

3. *Minorities are self-conscious social units; they are characterized by a consciousness of kind.* The individuals making up a minority recognize the fact of their membership and this recognition affects their behavior. Minority members are aware of something that they share in common with others like themselves—that is, "I am one of them." The common traits that they share often form the basis of an *esprit de corps,* an in-group feeling, a sense of belonging to a group distinct from the dominant group. Wagley and Harris note:

In addition to whatever special traits they share, their sense of isolation, of common suffering, and of a common burden makes most minorities self-conscious groups apart from all others in their society. It is often this self-consciousness, this awareness of common problems, that keeps a minority intact. A person who no longer practices the traditional Jewish religion and who is completely acculturated to the dominant culture patterns and language

---

[19] R. A. Schermerhorn, "Power as a Primary Concept in the Study of Minorities," *Social Forces,* 35 (1956), 53–54.

of his society, often continues to identify himself as a Jew. Individuals whose physical features are mainly Caucasoid identify themselves as Negroes in the United States because of their feelings for their group.[20]

4. *Generally a person does not become a member of a minority voluntarily; he or she is born into it.* Members of a minority usually (but not always) conceive of themselves as being alike by virtue of their common ancestry. At any rate, and this is critical, by virtue of their real or presumed ancestry, members of the dominant group ascribe minority group status to them. At times but one parent (father or mother) is sufficient to insure the membership of a child in a minority, and in certain cases, a single grandparent or great-grandparent suffices. Within the United States an individual who is physically indistinguishable from the dominant White group but who has a known Black grandparent is defined as a Black. In Nazi Germany it was of no avail that a "Jew" looked like German non-Jews, had been converted to Christianity, and had taken a Christian spouse—he was still, according to the Nazis, a "Jew."

5. *Members of a minority group, by choice or necessity, tend to marry within their own group (endogamy).* In-group marriage is sometimes enforced by the dominant group, sometimes by the minority, and frequently by both. Within some areas of the United States, for example, White-Black marriage is barred by the White group, but informally is also discouraged by the Black group. The rule of endogamy functions to perpetuate the physical and cultural differences between the dominant and minority groups as well as inequalities in status.

Robin M. Williams, Jr., captures the core of the above five features in this summary definition: *"Minorities . . . are any culturally or physically distinctive and self-conscious social aggregates, with hereditary membership and a high degree of endogamy, which are subject to political, or economic, or social discrimination by a dominant segment of an environing political society."* [21]

The Relativity of Minority Membership

A given racial, nationality, or religious group may be dominant in one area and a minority in another. Jews constitute the dominant

---

[20] Wagley and Harris, *op. cit.*, 6–7.
[21] Robin M. Williams, Jr., *Strangers Next Door* (Englewood Cliffs, N.J.: Prentice-Hall, Inc., 1964), 304.

group in Israel, while Arabs represent a minority group. In the Arab nations the situation is reversed. Roman Catholics are a dominant group within Spain and Italy but a minority within Norway. Chinese exercise dominance over Tibetans and the various nationality groups within contemporary China but constitute a minority throughout most other areas of the world. In various historical periods the dominant-minority relationship may also be altered or, in fact in some instances, reversed. During the Nazi occupation of Czechoslovakia, the Sudeten Germans secured a position of dominance over the Czechs among whom they previously had been a minority.

Furthermore, dominant and minority group memberships are not necessarily mutually exclusive. As Barron points out, it is possible for an individual to have dominant and minority roles simultaneously.[22] This possibility derives from the fact that within the United States the minority-dominant group classification has a threefold basis: race, religion, and nationality. Roman Catholics are members of a prominent religious minority, yet many of their members may simultaneously be Whites and thus racially grouped with the dominant group. Blacks on the other hand, are racially grouped with a minority, yet in terms of religion may be members of the dominant Protestant group. Norwegians in some areas of the Midwest, by virtue of their national descent, are accorded minority status, although they are members of the dominant White race and the dominant Protestant religion.

Minorities on the World Scene

Western scholars and laymen alike generally conceive of *society* as a culturally distinctive and politically sovereign entity that enjoys specific geographical frontiers. We commonly think of *cultural distinctiveness* in terms of a population whose members possess a considerable degree of homogeneity in customs, often minimally taken to be a population whose members speak a common language.[23] We usually take *political sovereignity* to mean self-sufficiency, a condition in which a population has original and definitive jurisdic-

[22] Milton L. Barron, *American Minorities* (New York: Alfred A. Knopf, Inc., 1957), 4-5.
[23] Melvin Ember, "The Relationship between Economic and Political Development in Non-Industrialized Societies," *Ethnology*, 2 (1963), 236.

tion in the main spheres of social life (it enjoys functional autonomy in decision-making).[24] And we view the matter of *geographical frontiers* in terms of territoriality—a population that occupies a definable piece of the earth's surface. In practice the most typical referent of society is taken to be the nation-state: "Mostly, then, when we look for a society we find the political unit, and when speaking of the former we mean in effect that latter." [25] In this Westernized view all states are sovereign and every piece of the earth's surface can appropriately be divided up in terms of the legal possession of this or that people so that, at least in theory, there are not any blank spaces on the map or overlap between the territories of two states.[26]

Western legal and constitutional definitions of society are one thing; practice is still another. Take Europe. Almost every territory of Europe has combined at some time or other with almost every one of its neighbors. Indeed, the territories covered by European nation-states have never been, and could not possibly be, exactly the same as the territories inhabited by various ethnic nationality groups. Frequently such groups occupy small pieces of territory or are dispersed by residence and place of occupation throughout the territory of the dominant group. Hence political self-determination for one nationality has often been quite incompatible with political self-determination for another. Thus a large number of European nation-states contain multiple nationality groups, including Great Britain (Scotch, Welsh, and English), Belgium (Flemish and Walloons), Czechoslovakia (Czechs and Slovaks), and Switzerland (Germans, French, and Italians).[27] Seldom do we find the formula, "one nation, one state," realized within Europe.

The story was not too dissimilar in pre-colonial "Burma" where the "frontiers" that separated the petty political units were not clearly demarcated lines but zones of mutual interests in which there prevailed interpenetrating networks of relationships. "Fron-

---

[24] See: G. E. Swanson, *The Birth of the Gods* (Ann Arbor: University of Michigan Press, 1960), 20, and George P. Murdock, "Ethnographic Atlas," *Ethnology,* 2 (1962), 249–253.

[25] S. F. Nadel, *The Foundation of Social Anthropology* (New York: The Free Press of Glencoe, Inc., 1957, 187.

[26] Edmund R. Leach, "The Frontiers of 'Burma,'" *Comparative Studies in Society and History,* 3 (1960), 49.

[27] Arnold Rose, *Race Prejudice and Discrimination* (New York: Alfred A. Knopf, Inc., 1951), 3.

tier" zones were occupied by people who were not an integral part of some larger whole, although they may have been involved as tributaries, as raiders, or sometimes as furnishers of forest products. Local and regional groups politically and culturally graded into and overlapped with one another so that it was often impossible to state where the lines of cleavage ran; people at times even had recourse to more than one ethnic "identity"; and in some cases, as in highland "Burma," whole villages or communities shifted their ethnic "identity," for instance, where Kachin became Shan.[28]

In truth, "societies" in much of the world, be they termed tribes, nations, national minorities, or ethnic groups, are in part the artificial constructs of Western social scientists and colonial administrators who carved up areas, who drew boundaries, with little regard for ethnic distributions. In many areas of the world we seldom find sharp boundaries but rather continuous variation and/or interpenetration so that it is next to impossible to say where one population begins and another ends. Fortes and Evans-Pritchard note this situation for some areas of Africa:

This overlapping and interlocking of societies is largely due to the fact that the point at which political relations, narrowly defined in terms of military action and legal sanctions, end is not the point at which all social relations cease. The social structure of a people stretches beyond their political system, so defined, for there are always social relations of one kind or another between peoples of different autonomous political groups. Clans, age-sets, ritual associations, relations of affinity and of trade, and social relations of other kinds unite people of different political units. Common language or closely related languages, similar customs and beliefs, and so on, also unite them. Hence a strong feeling of community may exist between groups which do not acknowledge a single ruler or units for specific political purposes. Community of language and culture . . . does not necessarily give rise to political unity, any more than linguistic and cultural dissimilarity prevents political unity.[29]

Even to use political terms for delimiting a "society" ignores the common phenomenon of intermediate zones in which relations between different political units are not covered by the formula, "war without and law within." Such a formula is not applicable to the

---

[28] Edmund R. Leach, *Political Systems of Highland Burma* (Cambridge, Mass.: Harvard University Press, 1954) and F. K. Lehman, "Ethnic Categories in Burma and the Theory of Social Systems," in Peter Kunstadter, ed., *Southeast Asian Tribes, Minorities, and Nations* (Princeton, N.J.: Princeton University Press, 1967), Vol. 1, 93–124.

[29] M. Fortes and E. E. Evans-Pritchard, *African Political Systems* (London: Oxford University Press, 1940), 23. By permission.

Nuba peoples of the African Sudan, and one gains a not too different picture from some other areas of Africa.[30]

In a very real sense, Western social scientists and colonial administrators often created "minority problems" by imposing European legal and constitutional definitions of a national state upon the peoples of much of Africa and Southeast Asia. The problem of national minorities arises from a conceptual scheme of what the most inclusive social unit *ought* to be—an ideal of *fashioning* a political entity that includes some and excludes others. Hence, national minority status is not a condition inherent in relationships—it is a property conferred on a relationship, a matter of social definition emanating from a conception of what a "society" (i.e., nation-state) is. Of equal significance, the dominant group, by virtue of its superior power, is able in considerable measure to translate its definition of "society" into actuality.

Put still another way, "society-ness" or "group-ness" derives from varying levels of "entity" awareness (of "consciousness of kind"), images in which some are included and others are excluded from certain flows of social interaction. Thus "American Indian," "White," "Black," "Irish," "Mexican," and the like are essentially subjective phenomena. But this does not mean that such "groups" are not real. They are real because people define them as real; because people *attribute* to certain relationships the properties of thinghood, that is, they define certain perceived regularities in social interaction in "entity" (i.e., group) terms. In brief, we order and classify the information we obtain from our sense organs and *impose* a structure upon it. The consequence of this fact for the subject matter of this book is, as we have noted, that man creates minority-dominant group "problems"—such "problems" themselves do not inhere in the mere existence of human or group differences.

Types of Minorities

As Louis Wirth suggests, minorities can be classified in any number of ways.[31] Among these are (1) the number and size of the

---

[30] S. F. Nadel, *The Nuba* (London: Oxford University Press, 1947). Also see: Jack Goody, *Death, Property and the Ancestors* (Stanford, Calif.: Stanford University Press, 1962), 3–7; I. Schapera, *Government and Politics in Tribal Societies* (London: Watts, 1956); and Colin M. Turnbull, *The Forest People* (New York: Simon & Schuster, 1961 and *Wayward Servants* (Garden City, N.Y.: The Natural History Press, 1965).

[31] Louis Wirth, "The Problem of Minority Groups," in Ralph Linton, ed., *The Science of Man in the World Crisis* (New York: Columbia University Press, 1945), 347–372.

minorities within the society, (2) the degree to which minority status involves friction and discrimination, (3) the nature of the social arrangement governing the interaction between the minority and dominant groups, and (4) the goals toward which the minority and dominant groups are striving. In view of the contemporary world setting, Wirth feels that the last criterion is the most meaningful and satisfactory. Accordingly, he distinguishes between four types of minorities: (1) pluralistic, (2) assimilationist, (3) secessionist, and (4) militant.

A *pluralistic minority* desires to live peacefully side-by-side with the dominant group. It seeks tolerance for its differences. But while craving tolerance for various of its cultural idiosyncrasies, a pluralistic minority also seeks to maintain its cultural identity against dominant-group absorption. Switzerland provides an example of a culturally pluralistic nation. A majority of the Swiss speak a variety of German known as *Schwyzertütsch;* about 20 per cent speak French; another 6 per cent, Italian; and slightly more than 1 per cent speak an ancient language known as Romansh. Within the various cantons, there are notable differences in costume, dialect, and patterns of life. Although a majority of the people are Protestant, there is a sizable Catholic population. Within this setting, Switzerland officially recognizes all four languages, although only German, French, and Italian have been declared "official languages" into which all federal documents are translated. Although religious and ethnic prejudice is by no means non-existent, the Swiss have learned to live harmoniously with their differences.[32]

Whereas a pluralistic minority seeks to maintain its group integrity, an *assimilationist minority* expects to be absorbed within an emergent common culture that is the product of the blending of divergent racial and ethnic strains. Assimilation is viewed as a two-way process in which, through a fusion of the differing racial stocks and cultural traditions, a new people and culture emerge. This has been the prevailing orientation among the various European immigrant groups within the United States.

The *secessionist minority* repudiates both assimilation and cultural pluralism. Although desiring to maintain their own cultural identity, they are not satisfied, as are the cultural pluralists, with mere toleration or cultural autonomy. The aim of the secessionists is statehood—full political self-determination. Frequently the seces-

[32] Kurt Mayer, "Cultural Pluralism and Linguistic Equilibrium in Switzerland," *American Sociological Review,* 16 (1951), 157–163.

sionist minority enjoyed national sovereignty at an earlier period
and cultivates among its members the romantic sentiments associated with it. No matter how archaic the cultural patterns, strong
emphasis is placed upon the revival of the language, lore, literature,
and ceremonial institutions associated with the group's prior independence. The Irish, Czech, Polish, Lithuanian, Estonian, Latvian,
and Finnish nationalistic movements that culminated in the establishment of independent nations at the end of World War I are illustrative of secessionist movements. The Jewish Zionist movement
and the Garveyite movement among Blacks in the 1920s are other
examples.

A *militant minority* goes far beyond the demand for equality, or
even cultural and political autonomy, and insists upon reversing the
statuses. Domination over others is set as its goal. Such a group
is frequently convinced of its own superiority. The Sudeten Germans, aided and abetted by the Nazis, made claims upon the Czech-
oslovakian republic which in effect would have reduced the Czechs
to minority status.[33]

Wirth's types have not gone without criticism. The fourth type,
"militant," is not the same kind of concept as the others, dealing as
it does with tactics. Similarly, there is no reason why some of the
other types may not also be "militant" in their tactics. Still another
effort to classify minorities has been undertaken by Oliver C. Cox,
who distinguishes between the differing kinds of situations which
characterize dominant-minority relations:

1. Situations in which the non-White is a stranger in a White society,
   such as a Hindu in the United States or a Black in many parts of
   Canada and in Argentina—the stranger situation.
2. Situations of original White contact in which the culture of the
   Colored group is very simple, such as the conquistadors and Indians
   in the West Indies, and the Dutch and Hottentots in South Africa—
   the original contact situation.
3. Situations of Colored enslavement in which a small aristocracy of
   Whites exploits large quantities of natural resources (as in plantation settings) with forced Colored labor, raised or purchased like
   capital in a slave market, such as that in the pre-Civil War South
   and in Jamaica before 1834—the slavery situation.
4. Situations in which a small minority of Whites in a Colored society
   is bent upon maintaining a ruling-class status, such as the pre-World
   War II British in the West Indies or the Dutch in Indonesia—the
   ruling-class situation.

[33] Wirth, *op. cit.*, 354–363.

5. Situations where there are large proportions of both Colored and White persons seeking to live in the same area, with Whites insisting that the society is a "White man's country," for instance, United States and South Africa—the bipartite situation.
6. Situations where Colored-and-White amalgamation is far advanced and in which a White ruling class is not established, as for example in Brazil—the amalgamative situation.
7. Situations where a minority of Whites has been subdued by a dominantly Colored population, as that which occurred in Haiti during the turn of the eighteenth century, or the expulsion of the Whites from Japan in 1638—the nationalistic situation.[34]

It is not always clear, however, as to which variable Cox is using in his classificatory approach: the nature of the original contact, the degree of cultural contrast, the proportionate size of the minority, or some other.

ADDITIONAL CONCEPTS

Prejudice

The term prejudice has taken on so many unfavorable connotations that today people are quick to disassociate themselves from it. "I'm not prejudiced," is a frequently heard comment. "In fact, one of my best friends is a Jew. But, you know, I just can't stand most of 'em! They're just full of gall!" It is difficult to examine dispassionately and objectively something that is so widely condemned yet simultaneously so prevalent. Many college students afford a good illustration of this. When they denounce the "racist" university or "racist" American society, we have little doubt as to what they are referring. Generally, such students have litle difficulty recognizing the bigotry of a lower-middle class policeman toward a ghetto Black or of a lower-middle class mayor toward a "rioter." But the prejudice is generally not viewed in the same perspective as the bigotry of an upper-middle class peace matron toward a lower-middle class mayor or of an upper class university student toward an Italian, a Pole, or a National Guardsman from Cicero, Illinois; the violence of the ghetto is patronized since it is "understood" and forgiven, while the violence of a Cicero racist convinced that Blacks

[34] Adapted from Oliver Cromwell Cox, *Caste, Class, and Race* (New York: Doubleday & Co., 1948), 353–354.

threaten his lawn, house, and powerboat is detested without being "understood." Yet in truth the two bigotries are quite similar.[35]

The term *prejudice* is used with somewhat differing meanings by various individuals. Prejudice is commonly taken to mean a "pre-judgment" about a person or group without bothering to verify the opinion or to examine the merits of the judgment. Implicit in this definition is the assumption that prejudice involves a hasty or premature appraisal of individuals or groups. If this is the case, knowledge and experience should be all that is necessary to dispel prejudice. In truth, however, considerable evidence is available which suggests that knowledge and experience frequently have little impact upon prejudice. Furthermore, some of the prevalent beliefs about particular groups, although containing many half-truths and distortions, may in some instances have a "kernel of truth" to them. Thus this definition of prejudice as a "pre-judgment" is *not* adequate or satisfactory.

Probably one of the most common failures in examining prejudice is the tendency to view it as a unitary phenomenon. Actually prejudice is not one thing but, rather, many things. Kramer makes a useful distinction between three major levels of orientation toward any minority group: (1) the cognitive, (2) the emotional, and (3) the action levels.[36] Research testifies to the fact that these three levels constitute analytically distinct aspects of prejudice and that the levels are not necessarily interrelated.[37] Let us examine each of these levels in turn.

The *cognitive* level of orientation refers to the individual's picture of the minority group. It deals with how an individual perceives a minority, what he believes about it, and what common traits he attributes to its members. An individual's "picture" of Blacks may be that they fight and brawl, have criminal instincts, live like animals, and are mentally inferior, lazy, slow, unimaginative, and sloppy. Jews may be pictured as possessing unbounded power and control in money matters, as sticking together, as conniving to outwit Gentiles, and as pursuing unscruplous, ruthless, and unpatriotic activities.

[35] Michael Lerner, "Elite Bigotry—'Stinking and Covered,'" *Wall Street Journal*, December 30, 1969, p. 12.

[36] Bernard M. Kramer, "Dimensions of Prejudice," *The Journal of Psychology*, 27 (1949), 389–451.

[37] See, for example, John H. Mann, "The Relationship between Cognitive, Affective, and Behavioral Aspects of Racial Prejudice," *Journal of Social Psychology*, 49 (1959), 223–228.

The *emotional* level of orientation refers to the emotions—the feelings—that the actual or symbolic stimulus of the minority evokes within the individual. Fear, sympathy, pity, hate, anger, love, contempt, and envy are among the emotional responses that may be experienced by individuals within the context of racial interaction or when confronted with the prospect of such interaction. The idea of patronizing a washroom, of eating at the same restaurant, or of shaking hands with a Jew or Black may excite horror or disgust within some individuals. Black movement into a previously all-White neighborhood may produce fear and anxiety among many Whites. The social standing of a prominent Jewish businessman or doctor may elicit envy among some Gentiles. Identification with the persecuted may lead some Whites to experience sympathy for Blacks, and to desire that a Black win in a prize fight with a White. It should be noted that although the emotional level is distinct from that of the cognitive, the two may appear together—one may overlay the other.

The *action* level of orientation refers to the tendency or disposition to act in certain ways toward a minority group. Here the emphasis is upon tendencies to act, not upon the actions themselves. Whites may desire to keep Blacks out of their circle of friends and may be disposed to reject any direct personal relations with them. Similarly, Whites may favor barring Blacks from their social clubs, athletic organizations, and business and professional associations. They may prefer segregated schools, parks, buses, washrooms, lunch counters, and waiting rooms. Accordingly, they may be viewed as disposed toward discriminatory behavior.

We shall conceive of *prejudice as a system of negative conceptions, feeling, and action-orientations regarding the members of a particular group*. This definition reflects the three major levels of an attitude system: the cognitive, the emotional, and the predisposition to act in a given fashion.

Stereotypes

We have observed that prejudice is a state of mind. Further, we noted that one aspect of this state of mind is the cognitive level of orientation—the image or picture we carry in our heads concerning a people, for instance, the "fighting" Irish, the "inscrutable" Orientals, the "stolid" Swedes, the "grasping" Jews, the "emotional" Italians, and the "shiftless" Blacks. Walter Lippmann, a distinguished American journalist and author, dubbed "these pictures in our heads" *stereotypes*. He indicated that the world is filled with "so much subtley, so much variety, so many permutations and combinations . . . we have to reconstruct it on a simpler model before we can manage with it."[38] In other words, we find it almost impossible to weigh every reaction of every person, minute-by-minute in terms of its individual meanings. Instead, we type individuals and groups in snap-judgment style. Without stereotypes we would find it necessary to interpret each new situation as if we had never met anything of the kind before. Stereotypes are convenient and have the virtue of efficiency although not always of accuracy.

We may define stereotypes as "the unscientific and hence unreliable generalizations that people make about other people either as persons or groups."[39] They constitute *beliefs* about people. Such beliefs, however, overlook the differences found among a people with regard to a trait; stereotypes would have us believe that all people in the group are identical—fighting, inscrutable, stolid, or grasping. Moreover, they overlook the fact that people have a great many traits; in stereotyping, people are "sized up" in terms of only one or a limited number of characteristics.

It is often suggested that stereotypes are rigid, firm, and unchanging. Evidence, however, indicates that, while some stereotypes are relatively stable, others do change through time. Studies of stereotypes among Princeton undergraduates are revealing. In 1932, in a pioneer investigation of stereotypes, Katz and Braly asked Princeton undergraduates to select out of a list of eighty-four attributes five that they thought were most characteristic of each of the following: Americans, English, Germans, Jews, "Negroes," Japanese, Italians, Chinese, Irish, and Turks.[40] After a lapse of nearly twenty years, Gilbert repeated the study;[41] then, in 1967, Karlins, Coffman, and Walters again replicated the work with still a third generation of Princeton students.[42]

---

[38] Walter Lippmann, *Public Opinion* (New York: Harcourt, Brace Jovanovich, 1922), 16.

[39] Emory S. Bogardus, "Stereotypes Versus Sociotypes," *Sociology and Social Research*, 34 (1950), 287.

[40] D. Katz and K. W. Braly, "Racial Stereotypes of 100 College Students," *Journal of Abnormal and Social Psychology*, 28 (1933), 280–290.

[41] G. M. Gilbert, "Stereotype Persistence and Change Among College Students," *Journal of Abnormal and Social Psychology*, 46 (1951), 245–254.

[42] Marvin Karlins, Thomas L. Coffman, and Gary Walters, "On the Fading of Social Stereotypes: Studies in Three Generations of College Students," *Journal of Personality and Social Psychology*, 13 (1969), 1–16.

Evidence for the *persistence* of ethnic and racial stereotypes is contained in the fact that the characteristics checked most frequently by the 1951 and 1967 students were, for the most part, the ones most frequently checked in 1932. But perhaps of greatest interest is that the apparent "fading" of stereotypes noted by Gilbert in 1951 is not upheld as an overall trend in the 1967 study. Where many of the 1932 assignments have declined in frequency they have, in the long run, been *replaced* by others, resulting again in 1967 in a high degree of stereotype uniformity. Further, the "new" stereotypes *resemble* previous ones. The hot-tempered image of the Italian, for instance, is still reflected in the temperamental cluster—"passionate" (44%), "impulsive" (28%), and "quick-tempered" (28%)—and is supplemented by "pleasure loving" (33%) and "sensual" (26%). The findings of these studies are summarized in Table 1-1.

Also of considerable interest is the reluctance of the 1951 and 1967 students to engage in stereotyping at all. Many expressed sentiments indicating they felt it was unreasonable to force them to make generalizations about people. Some were especially concerned with the fact that they were asked to characterize people with whom they had never been in contact. One wrote:

I refuse to be a part of a childish game like this. It seems to me that the Psych. Dept. at Princeton, at least, ought to recognize the intelligence of students who choose courses in this department. As far as I have come into contact with these so-called ethnic groups I can think of no distinguishing charactertisics which will apply to any group as a whole.

Stereotyping runs counter to the image of the American "thinking man" who is not "supposed" to fall into such stylized modes of thought. If a person labels, there is a tendency to think of him as prejudiced, as thinking irrationally and contrary to an American idealized way of making choices.[43] Apparently the image of the "thinking man" took its toll of students who were prepared to stereotype, or at least to *admit* to stereotyping. Hence, caution is in order. Indeed, although the character of the new stereotypes is consistent with the more liberal attitudes found in most contemporary college communities,[44] the most outstanding aspect of the recent stereo-

[43] Forrest La Violette and K. H. Silvert, "A Theory of Stereotypes," *Social Forces,* 29 (1951), 257–262 and Harold Sigall and Richard Page, "Current Stereotypes: A Little Fading, a Little Faking," *Journal of Personality and Social Psychology,* 18 (1971), 247–255.

[44] In this regard also see: "H. C. Triandis and V. Vassilious," "Frequency of Contact and Stereotyping," *Journal of Personality and Social Psychology,* 7 (1967), 316–328.

TABLE 1-1 Stereotypes in Three Generations of Princeton Undergraduates

Trait	% Checking Trait			Trait	% Checking Trait		
	1933	1951	1967		1933	1951	1967
AMERICANS				GERMANS			
Industrious	48	30	23	Scientifically minded	78	62	47
Intelligent	47	32	20	Industrious	65	50	59
Materialistic	33	37	67	Stolid	44	10	9
Ambitious	33	21	42	Intelligent	32	32	19
Progressive	27	5	17	Methodical	31	20	21
Pleasure loving	26	27	28	Extremely nationalistic	24	50	43
Alert	23	7	7	Progressive	16	3	13
Efficient	21	9	15	Efficient	16	—	46
Aggressive	20	8	15	Jovial	15	—	5
Straightforward	19	—	9	Musical	13	—	4
Practical	19	—	12	Persistent	11	—	4
Sportsmanlike	19	—	9	Practical	11	—	9
Individualistic [a]	—	26	15	Aggressive [a]	—	27	30
Conventional [b]	—	—	17	Arrogant [a]	—	23	18
Scientifically minded [b]	—	—	15	Ambitious [b]	—	—	15
Ostentatious [b]	—	—	15	IRISH			
				Pugnacious	45	24	13
CHINESE				Quick tempered	39	35	43
				Witty	38	16	7
Superstitious	34	18	8	Honest	32	11	17
Sly	29	4	6	Very religious	29	30	27
Conservative	29	14	15	Industrious	21	8	8
Tradition loving	26	26	32	Extremely nationalistic	21	20	41
Loyal to family ties	22	35	50	Superstitious	18	—	11
Industrious	18	18	23	Quarrelsome	14	—	5
Meditative	19	—	21	Imaginative	13	—	3
Reserved	17	18	15	Aggressive	13	—	5
Very religious	15	—	6	Stubborn	13	—	23
Ignorant	15	—	7	Tradition loving [b]	—	—	25
Deceitful	14	—	5	Loyal to family ties [b]	—	—	23
Quiet	13	19	23	Argumentative [b]	—	—	20
Courteous [b]	—	—	20	Boastful [b]	—	—	17
Extremely nationalistic [b]	—	—	19	ITALIANS			
Humorless [b]	—	—	17				
Artistic [b]	—	—	15	Artistic	53	28	30
				Impulsive	44	19	28
ENGLISH				Passionate	37	25	44
				Quick tempered	35	15	28
Sportsmanlike	53	21	22	Musical	32	22	9
Intelligent	46	29	23	Imaginative	30	20	7
Conventional	34	25	19	Very religious	21	33	25
Tradition loving	31	42	21	Talkative	21	23	23
Conservative	30	22	53	Revengeful	17	—	0
Reserved	29	39	40	Physically dirty	13	—	4
Sophisticated	27	37	47	Lazy	12	—	0
Courteous	21	17	17	Unreliable	11	—	3
Honest	20	11	17	Pleasure loving [a]	—	28	33
Industrious	18	—	17	Loyal to family ties [b]	—	—	26
Extremely nationalistic	18	—	7	Sensual [b]	—	—	23
Humorless	17	—	11	Argumentative [b]	—	—	19
Practical [b]	—	—	25				

TABLE 1–1 (Continued)

Trait	% Checking Trait			Trait	% Checking Trait		
	1933	1951	1967		1933	1951	1967
JAPANESE				NEGROES			
				Superstitious	84	41	13
				Lazy	75	31	26
Intelligent	45	11	20	Happy-go-lucky	38	17	27
Industrious	43	12	57	Ignorant	38	24	11
Progressive	24	2	17	Musical	26	33	47
Shrewd	22	13	7	Ostentatious	26	11	25
Sly	20	21	3	Very religious	24	17	8
Quiet	19	—	14	Stupid	22	10	4
Imitative	17	24	22	Physically dirty	17	—	3
Alert	16	—	11	Naive	14	—	4
Suave	16	—	0	Slovenly	13	—	5
Neat	16	—	7	Unreliable	12	—	6
Treacherous	13	17	1	Pleasure loving [a]	—	19	26
Aggressive	13	—	19	Sensitive [b]	—	—	17
Extremely nationalistic [a]	—	18	21	Gregarious [b]	—	—	17
Ambitious [b]	—	—	33	Talkative [b]	—	—	14
Efficient [b]	—	—	27	Imitative [b]	—	—	13
Loyal to family ties [b]	—	—	23	TURKS			
Courteous [b]	—	—	22	Cruel	47	12	9
JEWS				Very religious	26	6	7
				Treacherous	21	3	13
				Sensual	20	4	9
Shrewd	79	47	30	Ignorant	15	7	13
Mercenary	49	28	15	Physically dirty	15	7	14
Industrious	48	29	33	Deceitful	13	—	7
Grasping	34	17	17	Sly	12	7	7
Intelligent	29	37	37	Quarrelsome	12	—	9
Ambitious	21	28	48	Revengeful	12	—	6
Sly	20	14	7	Conservative	12	—	11
Loyal to family ties	15	19	19	Superstitious	11	—	5
Persistent	13	—	9	Aggressive [b]	—	—	17
Talkative	13	—	3	Quick tempered [b]	—	—	13
Aggressive	12	—	23	Impulsive [b]	—	—	12
Very religious	12	—	7	Conventional [b]	—	—	10
Materialistic [b]	—	—	46	Pleasure loving [b]	—	—	11
Practical [b]	—	—	19	Slovenly [b]	—	—	10

[a] Indicates the additional traits reported by Gilbert (1951).

[b] Indicates the new traits needed in 1967 to account for the 10 most frequently selected traits today.

Source: Marvin Karlins, Thomas L. Coffman, and Gary Walters, "On the Fading of Social Stereotypes: Studies in Three Generations of College Students," *Journal of Personality and Social Psychology*, 13 (1969), Table 1, pp. 4–5. By permission.

types is nevertheless still their uniformity. In brief, the students' protestations against being asked to classify various groups as an irrelevant task should not have been accompanied by such highly standardized impressions of the groups in question if indeed they were not prone to stereotyping.

Discrimination

Earlier we observed that prejudice is a state of mind—a psychological phenomenon. It involves attitudes and feelings. But attitudes and feelings are not to be equated with overt action. The former constitute merely a predisposition to act, a predilection for certain kinds of behavior, but not the actual response itself. Overt action, on the other hand, involves the actual response or series of responses that an individual makes. Feelings and attitudes are not necessarily correlated with actual behavior. A student may feel considerable antipathy for his professor, yet he may take great pains to hide his feelings and to act instead in a very personable, friendly, and ingratiating manner. His failure to act out his genuine feelings in hostile, aggressive, and antagonistic actions may be the product of fear lest his professor retaliate and lower his grade. By the same token, a student may bear warm, friendly, and sympathetic attitudes and feelings toward a professor, yet engage in cool, ritualistic, and formalized responses. His failure to act out his friendly feelings may be the product of concern lest his fellow students consider him an "oddball" or an "apple polisher."

Similarly with prejudice. A White businessman may bear considerable prejudice toward Blacks yet nevertheless display friendly responses toward Black customers in order to gain their goodwill. Thus his negative sentiments are not translated into overt action. On the other hand, a businessman who lacks prejudice may refuse to accept Black customers, because he believes their presence would injure his business. In this instance, he fails to translate his nonprejudiced outlook into overt action. Accordingly, it is necessary to distinguish between *prejudice*, which is a state of mind, and *discrimination*, which entails overt action in which members of a group are accorded unfavorable treatment on the basis of their religious, ethnic, or racial membership.

We have seen, then, that discrimination is not simply the result —the acting-out—of prejudice. Discrimination occurs without prejudice and prejudice without discrimination. Overall, however, a correlation exists between prejudice and discrimination such that the more prejudiced are also more likely to practice discrimination. Yet there are numerous occasions in real life when there is far from a one-to-one relation between them. In the 1930s, for instance, a sociologist, Richard T. LaPiere traveled throughout the United States with a Chinese couple. In the course of the trip, LaPiere and the Chinese couple asked for service in hundreds of hotels, auto camps, tourist homes, and restaurants. They were refused service only once. Six months later, LaPiere wrote each of the establishments and asked if Chinese guests were welcome. Over 90 per cent replied that they would *not* accommodate Chinese, clearly in contradiction to their actions. Here is a clear case of verbal prejudice combined with no actual face-to-face discrimination.[45]

DeFleur and Westie conducted a study that bears directly on this question of attitude versus action. They attempted to find out how willing a number of college students were to be photographed with members of another race. First, they gave the students a verbal test that measured their attitudes toward Blacks. Then the students were asked to sign a series of "releases," indicating that they were willing to be photographed with Blacks and that they would allow these photographs to be widely publicized. DeFleur and Westie found that many of the students were inconsistent: one-third of those who had revealed liberal attitudes balked at signing the releases. Finally, each of the students was asked why he had signed, or refused to sign, the releases. From the answers it appeared that most of the students were greatly influenced by social pressure—by whether they thought certain groups that they respected (for instance, parents and friends) would approve or disapprove of their signing.[46] In still later studies, researchers placed subjects in other types of controlled situations where they were given "behavioral opportunities" to act in accord with their known attitudes.[47] These studies similarly revealed that there is no simple way in which actions toward an individual can be accurately predicted from knowledge of relevant attitudes alone.

[45] Richard T. LaPiere, "Attitudes vs. Actions," *Social Forces,* 13 (1934), 230–237.

[46] Melvin L. DeFleur and Frank R. Westie, "Verbal Attitudes and Overt Acts," *American Sociological Review,* 23 (1958), 667–673.

[47] Lawrence S. Linn, "Verbal Attitudes and Overt Behavior: A Study of Racial Discrimination," *Social Forces,* 43 (1965), 353–364; James M. Fendrich, "Perceived Reference Group Support: Racial Attitudes and Overt Behavior," *American Sociological Review,* 32 (1967), 969–970; and Lyle G. Warner and Melvin L. DeFleur, "Attitude as an Interactional Concept: Social Constraint and Social Distance as Intervening Variables between Attitudes and Action," *American Sociological Review,* 34 (1969), 153–169. In this regard, also see Gordon H. DeFriese and W. Scott Ford, "Verbal Attitudes, Overt Acts, and the Influence of Social Constraint in Interracial Behavior," *Social Problems,* 16 (1969), 493–505, and Lyle G. Warner and Rutledge M. Dennis, "Prejudice Versus Discrimination: An Empirical Example and Theoretical Extension," *Social Forces,* 48 (1970), 473–484.

Structural Racism

The concepts prejudice and discrimination tend to have an *individual* emphasis—for instance, an individual White's attitude or action toward an individual Black or group of Blacks. Such an approach is of course useful, but it leaves much to be desired in studying the ways in which people of one racial or ethnic group are systematically oppressed and/or exploited by the institutions of a society controlled by another racial or ethnic group. Carmichael and Hamilton make the point in these terms:

> When white terrorists bomb a black church and kill five black children, that is an act of individual racism, widely deplored by most segments of the society. But when in the same city—Birmingham, Alabama—five hundred black babies die each year because of the lack of proper food, shelter and medical facilities, and thousands more are destroyed and maimed physically, emotionally and intellectually because of conditions of poverty and discrimination in the black community, that is a function of institutional racism. When a black family moves into a home in a white neighborhood and is stoned, burned or routed out, they are victims of an overt act of individual racism which many people will condemn—at least in words. But it is institutional racism that keeps black people locked in dilapidated slum tenements, subject to the daily prey of exploitative slumlords, merchants, loan sharks and discriminatory real estate agents.[48]

The term *structural racism* (sometimes also referred to as *institutional racism*) is often employed to refer to the type of phenomenon described by Carmichael and Hamilton. It calls our attention to the fact that one or more of the institutions of a society functions to impose more burdens and give less benefits on an on-going basis to the members of one racial or ethnic group than to another. According to Friedman:

> This means (in the American context) that decisions are made, agendas structured, issues defined, beliefs, values, and attitudes promulgated and enshrined, commitments entered into, and/or resources allocated, in such a way that non-whites are systematically deprived or exploited. It should be emphasized that . . . the intentions of the actors, or the formal statements of the relevant norms, laws, and values, are irrelevant to the question of whether an institution is acting in a structurally racist manner. What counts is whether its actions in fact distribute burdens and rewards in a racially biased fashion or defends or supports other actors who are making biased distributions.[49]

[48] Stokely Carmichael and Charles V. Hamilton, *Black Power* (New York: Random House, Inc., 1967), 4.
[49] Samuel Friedman, "How Is Racism Maintained?" *Et Al.*, 2 (Fall, 1969), 19.

Viewed from this perspective, then, prejudice is not a little demon that emerges in people simply because they are depraved (because they have, for instance, some psychological "hang-up"), but because society itself is structured in a racist fashion. Institutions structure —they shape and restrict—the experiences that people will have. Prejudices, accordingly, are learned; they do not grow out of a social vacuum but out of concrete social experiences in a racist social order. And it follows that discrimination is not primarily an expression of prejudice but rather a byproduct of purposive striving to attain or hold social, economic, and political advantages and privileges. Hence, within the United States, Whites and Blacks for the most part are residentially, occupationally, and socially segregated; the two racial divisions frequently operate parallel but separate and distinctive organizations, and the Black community characteristically remains economically depressed and dependent on the wealthier and more powerful White community.

In this text, we shall make periodic reference to *racism*. We shall employ the term as an inclusive concept that embraces the notion of prejudice, discrimination, and structural racism.

SUMMARY

In this chapter we have presented an overview of minority-dominant group relations that provides a foundation for the material that follows in later chapters. We noted that sociology, as a science, is not characterized by the absolute absence of values but by a *rigorous, disciplined* attempt to look as objectively as is humanly possible upon the phenomena that it studies. Increasingly sociologists are raising the questions, "knowledge for what?" and "knowledge for whom?"

In examining human behavior, tools of analysis are crucial—concepts with which the vast array of social phenomena may be approached. Hence we looked at a number of key concepts: minority, prejudice, stereotype, discrimination, structural racism, and racism. Since these concepts will be employed extensively in the chapters that follow, the reader may wish to review their definitions.

2

Race: Fact and Myth

No treatment of minority relations would be complete without a consideration of "race." By virtue of the ignorance, superstition, and prejudice that have surrounded the matter for generations, we have postponed this consideration until we could thoroughly examine it. Various questions need to be dealt with: What is race? Are there "pure" races? Are Jews a "race"? Are there intellectually superior races? Are there "racial" personalities and temperaments? Is there a "racial" morality? Is racial interbreeding harmful? How are races formed? Although myths of one sort or another have clouded these basic human questions, scientific evidence can help to dispel some of the mystery and confusion.

WHAT IS RACE?

We of course all know—scientist and layman alike—that people in various parts of the world differ in certain hereditary features, in such things as skin color, hair texture, various facial features, stature, and head shape. It is equally true that the number of features that man everywhere shares in common is very much larger and of considerably greater importance than his divergent features. Nonetheless, differences do exist and are readily evident. We encounter little difficulty, for instance, distinguishing *groups* of Swedes, Japanese, and Congolese from one another. The concept "race" has often been employed to refer to this fact—*to populations differing in the incidence of certain traits.* Considerable controversy, however, surrounds the concept of race.

Conceptions of Race

We can identify three schools of thought regarding race: the "fixed type," the "breeding population," and the "no-race" traditions. Let us examine each of these more closely.

The Fixed Type School. The fixed type approach to race enjoyed primacy in the period between 1850 and 1950, although it continues to appear in the writings of some East European scholars [1] and shades of it periodically emerge in the works of the American anthropologist, Carleton S. Coon.[2] And among laymen in the United States the fixed type view still occupies a preeminent position. According to this notion, races are relatively fixed and immutable hereditary groupings that reach back into antiquity. Scholars of this tradition (such men as Joseph Deniker, William Z. Ripley, Egon von Eickstedt, and Earnest A. Hooton) [3] typically began by distinguishing a number of more or less "pure," ancestral races and then in turn a number of "mixed" populations. The number three was popular for the identification of "pure" races (Mongoloids, Caucasoids, and Negroids) though a few scholars suggested that perhaps a fourth or fifth "oid" might advisedly also be added; and then there were also those who took a more microscopic view, and liked to talk about Nordics, Alpines, Baltics, Keltics, Mediterraneans, and perhaps thirty or a hundred more "races." The typology of the late Earnest A. Hooton, Harvard University physical anthropologist, is illustrative, and is summarized in Figure 2–1.

[1] See: Jan Czekanowski, "The Theoretical Assumptions of Polish Anthropology and the Morphological Facts," *Current Anthropology,* 3 (1962), 481–494; and Andrzej Wiercinski, "The Racial Analysis of Human Populations in Relation to Their Ethnogenesis," *Current Anthropology,* 3 (1962), 9–20, "Comments," *Current Anthropology,* 4 (1963), 201–204, and "Comments," *Current Anthropology,* 5 (1964), 318–319.

[2] Carleton S. Coon, *The Origin of Races* (New York: Alfred A. Knopf, 1962), and *The Living Races of Man* (New York: Alfred A. Knopf, 1965). Coon denies that he takes this sort of position in the study of race, but Buettner-Janusch makes a good case for a contrary interpretation. See: John Buettner-Janusch, "Review of The Living Races of Man," *American Journal of Physical Anthropology,* 25 (1966), 182–188, and Carleton S. Coon, "Reply to Buettner-Janusch," *American Journal of Physical Anthropology,* 26 (1967), 359–360.

[3] Joseph Deniker, *The Races of Man* (New York: Charles Scribner and Sons, 1912); William Z. Ripley, *The Races of Europe* (New York: Appleton-Century-Crofts, 1899); Egon von Eickstedt, *Rassenkunde and Rassengeschechte der Menschheit* (Stuttgart: Gustav Fisher Verlag, 1934); and Earnest A. Hooton, *Up from the Ape,* rev. ed. (New York: The Macmillan Co., 1946).

PRIMARY RACE (a great division of mankind)	WHITE RACE	NEGROID RACE	MONGOLOID RACE
Primary Subraces (formed by evolutionary processes within a primary race)	Mediterranean Ainu Keltic Nordic Alpine East Baltic	African Negro Nilotic Negro Negrito	Classic Mongoloid Arctic Mongoloid
Composite Subraces (stabilized blends due to interbreeding of primary subraces of a primary race)	Armenoid Dinaric		
Residual Mixed Types (interbreeds)	Nordic-Alpine Nordic-Mediterranean		

COMPOSITE RACE (formed by the stabilization of blends of two or more primary races)	PREDOMINANTLY WHITE	PREDOMINANTLY NEGROID	PREDOMINANTLY MONGOLOID
Secondary Subraces (formed by evolutionary processes within a secondary race)	Australian Indo-Dravidian Polynesian	Tasmanian Melanesian-Papuan Bushman-Hottentot Melanesian Papuan Bushman Hottentot	American Indian Indonesian-Mongoloid Malay-Mongoloid Indonesian

Fig. 2–1. Earnest A. Hooton's Typology of the Races of Man. *Source:* Adapted from Earnest A. Hooton, *Up from the Ape,* rev. ed. (New York: The Macmillan Co., 1948), Part V.

Fixed type scholars saw the task of science as one of identifying and describing "original races" and in turn of *separating* present-day populations into the various ancestral components. Viewed in this fashion, race is a combination of characteristics that is discernible in *individuals*. Illustrative is the Hooton-Dupertuis study of the population of Ireland which was based on a representative sample of Irish males on whom Dupertuis made more than 80 measurements, indices, and morphological observations (e.g., chest breadth, sitting height, cephalic index, nasal index, extent of lip eversion, and inner arm skin color).[4] Using Hooton's typology of the "White" race, the researchers undertook to fish individuals (as types) out of the Irish sample through the use of their *precast* racial criteria (see Table 2–1). In essence, the "racial types" realized in this manner

TABLE 2–1   Hooton's Typology of Irish Racial Types

Sub-Racial Types	Sorting Criteria	Percentage of Total Series
Nordic Mediterranean	Long-headed; short stature; mixed hair; mixed eyes	28.9
Keltic	Long-headed; darkish or red hair; blue-eyed	25.3
Dinaric	Round-headed; long, hooked noses; mixed hair; mixed eyes	18.6
Nordic Alpine	Round-headed; mixed hair; mixed eyes	18.4
Predominantly Nordic	Long-headed; "near blonds"; either blue or mixed eyes	6.8
East Baltic	Round-headed; blond or red-headed; either light or mixed eyes	1.1
Pure Nordic	Long-headed; fair-haired; blue-eyed	0.6
Pure Mediterranean	Long-headed; brunet hair; dark eyes	0.3

Source: Adapted from Earnest A. Hooton and C. Wesley Dupertuis, *The Physical Anthropology of Ireland* (Cambridge, Mass.: Peabody Museum of Archaeology and Ethnology, Harvard University, 1955), 141–143.

reflected the typological guesses made at the start of the study, and hence entailed full-circle reasoning. In truth, such "races" constituted artificial assemblages that were arrived at through intuition.

[4] Earnest A. Hooton and C. Wesley Dupertuis, *The Physical Anthropology of Ireland* (Cambridge, Mass.: Peabody Museum of Archaeology and Ethnology, Harvard University, 1955).

The fixed type approach has by now become largely discredited. Fixed type scholars observed, for instance, that in Sweden there are a good many tall, blond, and blue-eyed people, and hence they inferred the existence of an ancestral "Nordic" race. What they failed to note was that there are also a good many short, dark-haired, and brown-eyed Swedes, and still more Swedes with various combinations of stature, hair shading, and eye color. Interestingly enough, if Swedish pre-military induction records are to be believed, only 11 per cent of Swedish young men are of the "pure" Nordic type with tall stature, blond hair, blue eyes, and long skulls.[5]

Further, while individuals as "types" clearly exist—for instance, tall, blond, blue-eyed men and women—the inference that they recapitulate ancestral strains (e.g., a "Nordic" race) is nonsense. Individual "types" are merely chance combinations of genetically independent traits. Since traits are independent, and "segregate" out separately, such types prove nothing about the appearance of ancestral groups. Blue eyes and blond hair are no more proof for an original "Nordic" race than are short hair and heavy beards evidence for an ancestral race of Trolls, or red hair and freckles for an original Rufous race. The search for racial types is premised upon the notion that traits are transmitted as complexes, that somehow they are linked together to constitute some sort of Caucasian, Nordic, or Mediterranean "package." Such a notion is pre-Mendelian and unscientific.

Fixed type scholars commonly compounded their difficulties by viewing various contemporary populations as simply mixtures, in varying degrees, of a few "original races." It is not surprising that of the many racial classifications premised upon this mistaken notion, all found their nemeis in certain people who defied placement, such people as the Bushmen, the Polynesians, the Veddas, the Lapps, the Australian aborigines, the Ainus of northern Japan, and many others.

Take the Polynesians. Their skin color ranges from almost white to dark brown; some are roundheads, others are longheads; their noses may be slender and high, or broad, short, and concave; their hair is prevailingly wavy but sometimes straight and even frizzly. Some fixed type scholars, in their search for simplicity, were inclined to label the Polynesians "Caucasians." Others were more cautious, and like Hooton preferred to view the Polynesians as a "composite

---

[5] H. Lundborg and F. J. Linders, *The Racial Character of the Swedish Nation* (Uppsala and Stockholm: Swedish State Institute for Race Biology, 1926).

race." Yet, in truth, no possible combination of Caucasoid, Negroid and Mongoloid (ill-defined as the terms are) could produce the Polynesian. The blood group distributions in Polynesia could hardly be explained in terms of some sort of Caucasoid-Negroid-Mongoloid admixture. Still other fixed type scholars preferred to add another "oid." But this really did not help matters for it simply shifted the problem to a lower level—in turn there were some "Polynesian" groups that did not quite fit, and so where was the multiplication of races to stop?

The Breeding Population School. A more recent view conceives of race as a "breeding population" within a species (identified with such men as William C. Boyd, Theodosius Dobzhansky, Stanley M. Garn, and Marshall T. Newman).[6] While still searching for "types," these scholars focus their attention upon *groups* characterized by sets of average tendencies—the frequencies of given genes within particular groups (e.g., the relative prevalence of the ABO, MNS, Diego, Duffy, and sickle-cell genes) and the "commonness" of particular phenotypic traits (e.g., the prevalence of "inner" eyefolds, body hair, and male pattern balding). This school generally provides us with an abbreviated statement of average tendencies within various populations ("races").

Breeding population scholars typically seek to identify and describe "natural units" of man that constitute taxonomic units below the species level—geographically-delimited populations that have more or less finite and known breeding limits. They stress the view that social barriers (associated with language, religion, caste, and class) and geographical barriers (associated with mountain ranges, deserts, oceans, and territorial distance) operate as reproductive barriers. Viewed from this perspective, mankind is divided into mating groups or reproductive communities—termed demes or Mendelian populations—the members of which are more likely to interbreed among themselves than with other populations. In brief, there arise through such mechanisms as isolation, mutation, natural

6 William C. Boyd, *Genetics and the Races of Man* (Boston: Little, Brown and Company, 1950); Theodosius Dobzhansky, *Mankind Evolving* (New Haven: Yale University Press, 1962) and *Evolution, Genetics, and Man* (New York: John Wiley & Sons, Inc., 1963); Stanley M. Garn, "Comment," *Current Anthropology,* 4 (1963), 197–198, "Comment," *Current Anthropology,* 5 (1964), 316, and *Human Races,* 2nd ed. (Springfield, Ill.: Charles C Thomas, 1965); Marshall T. Newman, "Geographic and Microgeographic Races," *Current Anthropology,* 4 (1963), 189–192.

selection, and genetic drift more or less stable, differentiated gene pools among mankind—people who have a common genetic heritage.

There is a difference of opinion among the scholars commonly identified with this school as to just how finite "races" are. Garn— who recognizes nine major "geographical races" and 32 "local races" —speaks of races as "discrete groupings" [7] and "natural units, reproductively isolated from each other and with separate evolutionary histories through time." [8] The impression unmistakenly conveyed by Garn is that he views his taxonomic races as mirroring nature in being more or less discretely delimited divisions of mankind.[9]

In contrast with Garn, Theodosius Dobzhansky, a distinguished geneticist, argues that "if races have to be 'discrete units,' then there are no races" and that racial classification "is a matter of convenience and hence of judgment" [10]—even a matter of "common sense." [11] But he also insists:

. . . it does not follow that races are arbitrary and "mere" inventions of the classifiers; some authors have talked themselves into denying that the human species has any races at all! Let us make very clear what is and what is not arbitrary about races. Race *differences* are facts of nature which can, given sufficient study, be ascertained objectively: Mendelian populations of any kind, from small tribes to inhabitants of countries and continents, may differ in frequencies of some genetic variants or they may not. If they so differ, they are racially distinct.[12]

According to this view, race is both a real biological phenomenon and a category of classification.[13]

The No-Race School. The "no-race" school denies that "races" are real if viewed as relatively discrete biological entities "out there" in nature and as units of evolution (it includes such men as Ashley Montagu and Frank B. Livingstone).[14] For the most part it builds its case upon the following two premises:

[7] Garn, *Human Races, op. cit.,* 3.
[8] *Ibid.,* 82.
[9] Garn, *Current Anthropology, op. cit.,* 1963, 1964.
[10] Theodosius Dobzhansky, "Comment on Livingstone's Paper," *Current Anthropology,* 3 (1962), 279–280.
[11] Dobzhansky, *Evolution, Genetics, and Man, op. cit.,* 160–161.
[12] Dobzhansky, *Mankind Evolving, op. cit.,* 367.
[13] Theodosius Dobzhansky, "Introduction," in Margaret Mead, Theodosius Dobzhansky, Ethel Tobach, and Robert E. Light, eds., *Science and the Concept of Race* (New York: Columbia University Press, 1968), 77–79.
[14] Ashley Montagu, "What Is Remarkable About Varieties of Man Is Likenessnesses, Not Differences," *Current Anthropology,* 4 (1963), 361–364 and *The Concept of Race* (New York: The Free Press of Glencoe, 1964); and Frank B. Livingstone, "On the Non-Existence of Human Races," *Current Anthropology,* 3 (1962), 279–281.

1. *The absence of boundaries between populations.* Most people recognize that Scandinavians such as the Swedes manifest a series of physical characteristics that differentiate them from Mediterranean peoples such as the Italians. Swedes are often classified within the Caucasian sub-race of Nordics; Italians within the Caucasian sub-race of Mediterraneans. Between the Nordics and the Mediterraneans in the central zone of Europe are the Alpine sub-race. Yet among what people or where geographically in Europe can one say with definitive authority, "Here Nordics end and Alpines start"? Or, "Here Alpines end and Mediterraneans begin?"? Or, for that matter, why distinguish between merely Nordics, Alpines, and Mediterraneans? Why not five or nine or some other number of sub-races? Might not one classificatory system have as much merit as another? Moreover, if one studies, district by district, the inhabitants of Germany, France, or northern and central Italy, one finds Nordic, Alpine, and Mediterranean types and every conceivable intermediate type.

On a larger scale one might ask, "Where and among what people in Africa can one with justice to the evidence indicate that here and among these people Caucasians cease and there and among those people Negroids start?" The problem is readily seen. It stems from the fact that most racial differences are *continuous* rather than *discrete*. With regard to skin color, hair form, stature, head shape, and the like, populations often show no sharp distinctions. Variations on the contrary are gradual and continuous. Blood types, however, are discrete. An individual's blood is either A, B, AB, or O, never a mixture or a shading of all four. Yet here too populations generally differ not so much in the presence or absence of a given blood type gene, but in its frequency—for instance, most populations merely differ in the relative prevalence of the ABO blood groups (although there are a few exceptions including the apparent absence of blood group B among a number of American Indian tribes and certain groups of Australian aborigines). See Table 2–2. In sum, "races" are not characterized by fixed clear-cut differences but by fluid, continuous differences; it is next to impossible to say where one population ends and another begins.

2. *Trait distributions tend to be discordant.* Peoples throughout the world differ in a great many traits, but variations are largely independent (they do not necessarily vary together). Since the inheritance of blood group systems follows Mendelian rules (for instance, the ABO, MSN, Rh, Duffy, Kidd, and Diego systems), they

**TABLE 2–2 Percentage of Individuals of the Four Blood Groups
Among Certain Populations**

	O	A	B	AB
AMERICA				
Utes (Montana)	97.4	2.6	—	—
Navaho (New Mexico)	77.7	22.5	—	—
Blackfeet (Montana)	23.5	76.5	—	—
Eskimos (Cape Farewell)	41.1	53.8	3.5	1.4
Toba (Argentina)	98.5	1.5	—	—
Bororo (Brazil)	100.0	—	—	—
AUSTRALIA				
Aborigines (West Australia)	48.1	51.9	—	—
Aborigines (South Australia)	42.6	57.4	—	—
Aborigines (Queensland)	58.6	37.8	3.6	—
ASIA				
Kirghiz (USSR)	31.6	27.4	32.2	8.8
Hindu (Bombay)	31.8	29.2	28.3	10.8
Chinese (Peking)	30.7	25.1	34.2	10.0
Japanese (Tokyo)	30.1	38.4	21.9	9.7
Bogobos (Philippines)	53.6	16.9	26.5	3.0
Micronesians (Saipan)	50.5	33.8	14.0	1.7
AFRICA				
Egyptians (Cairo)	27.3	38.5	25.5	8.8
Kikuyu (Kenya)	60.4	18.7	19.8	1.1
Bembe (Brazzaville)	50.0	25.7	20.3	4.1
Bushman (Kun-Bechuanaland)	37.0	53.4	5.5	4.1
Bushman (Magon-Bechuanaland)	61.1	34.7	4.2	—
Hottentot (Vaal River)	26.4	44.8	24.7	4.0
Zulu (South Africa)	51.8	24.6	21.6	2.0
EUROPE				
Irish (Dublin)	55.2	31.1	12.1	1.7
English (London)	47.9	42.4	8.3	1.4
Swedes (Stockholm)	37.9	46.1	9.5	6.5
French (Paris)	39.8	42.3	11.8	6.1
Hungarians (Budapest)	36.1	41.8	15.9	6.2
Russian (Moscow)	33.3	37.4	22.8	6.5

constitute some of our best material for studying population diver-
gence at the genetic level. Maps showing the patterns of distribution of various blood group systems reveal no more than partial
coincidence and are sometimes strikingly discordant.[15] Moreover,
considerable juggling is necessary to make serological taxonomies
coincide with so-called "natural populations." [16]

[15] Nigel A. Barnicot, "Taxonomy and Variation in Modern Man," in Montagu,
The Concept of Race, op. cit., 208ff. Also see the materials in Paul T. Baker and
J. S. Weiner, eds., *The Biology of Human Adaptability* (New York: Oxford Univer-
sity Press, 1966).

[16] Garn, *Human Races, op. cit.,* 50.

Hence, if we take blood groups to be a valid guide to overall genetic similarities, it appears unlikely that "African Negroids" and "Oceanic Negroids" (populations in Melanesia) are at all closely related and to approximate them taxonomically because of their similar hair form may be fallacious. On the other hand "Mongoloid" peoples, generally characterized among other things by straight hair, may well be a more closely interrelated group; however, there is much regional variation in other characteristics—for instance, considerable variation with respect to the major serological factors—and hence what is really meant by the term "Mongoloid" is by no means clear.[17] Nor, contrary to many popular myths, do classifications based on skin color yield the same results as those based on some other characteristic—there is not even a necessary direct correlation between skin color and hair form as is shown by the presence of extremely kinky hair among the only moderately pigmented Bushmen of South Africa and the presence of straight or wavy hair among some otherwise dark-pigmented peoples of southern India.

Conclusion. Humans do not lend themselves easily to cut-and-dried "racial" classifications and neat labels. Where two or more people come into contact, populations are usually found that are intermediate or combine the traits of the different stocks. The longer the time over which such contacts occur, the more widely spread are the intermediate populations and the more blurred the "divisions." In time there unfolds a situation such as in contemporary Europe where one or a multiple number of "sub-races" can be identified according to one's own predilections.

The world "racial" panorama is complex and varied, and no two people would probably classify "races" in the same way. Here we will not attempt the task at all. As we have seen, present-day scientists are far from agreement in making a division of human "races." Indeed, the number of "races" one identifies depends upon the purpose of the classification, and hence is a matter of convenience and judgment. By necessity any classification of "races" is almost entirely arbitrary, and depends upon the particular characteristics on which one chooses to base it. Any number of "racial" classifications of the same populations but based on different gene frequencies may be equally valid and useful. The concept "race" merely enables us to place a "handle" upon a phenomenon, to look at, to describe, and

[17] See: *Ibid.*, 133, and Barnicot, *op. cit.*, 201.

to analyze it. Classification and systematization are tools employed to make diversity intelligible and manageable. But this need not bar us from recognizing the shortcomings or relative nature of our tools.

In itself color (or some other trait) is meaningless. It is not important in itself as an optical phenomenon but rather as a bearer of a message. In brief, it stands as a "sign" or "mark" of a social status or role. Hence, whether races are real in a biological sense is not the chief issue for this text. Race *is* real in a social sense. As W. I. Thomas once observed, "If men define situations as real, they are real in their consequences." [18] In other words, what people believe affects their behavior, whether the beliefs are true or not. Hence, although there are no such things as elves, some people have a firm image as to what they are like and what they do. If people believe in elves—and the notion is not an uncommon one in folklore —people then are likely to take them into account in their behavior. And if man believes there are races, then he too acts on the basis of such beliefs—the results often being prejudice, discrimination, and structural racism. And it is these latter matters that are the focus of this text.

Are Jews a Race?

There are a good many people who assert that Jews constitute a "race." They go on to claim that they can identify a Jew from other people simply on the basis of appearance. The distinguishing physical traits are allegedly short to medium stature, black hair, a long hooked nose, greasy skin, a dark complexion, and a tendency for the women to be somewhat hefty. We are then faced with the question, "Do Jews possess a complex of physical characteristics which makes them a distinct racial group?" Science answers the question with an unequivocal "No." In fact even the Nazis implicitly answered the question negatively, as they required Jews to display on their clothing the Star of David or yellow armbands so that "Aryans" might identify them. Apparently, in the absence of such insignia, the "Aryans" were having difficulty distinguishing the Jews.

Jews have a wide distribution throughout the world. During the Babylonian captivity in the sixth century B.C., they intermingled and

[18] W. I. Thomas, "The Relation of Research to the Social Process," in *Essays on Research in the Social Science* (Washington, D.C.: The Brookings Institution, 1931), 189.

intermixed with the Mesopotamian peoples. During the Hellenistic period they followed Alexander the Great into Egypt, Syria, Asia Minor, and other regions. At the time of the Maccabees, in the second century B.C., the Jews moved to the farthest corners of the Roman Empire, including Spain, Italy, France, and the Rhineland of Germany. With the coming of the First Crusade in the eleventh century and the persecution of the Jews by Christian knights, Rhineland Jews migrated to present-day Poland, Russia, and the Ukraine.[19] Likewise, there are Chinese Jews who are identical in Mongoloid traits with other Chinese; there are Abyssinian and American Negroids who are Jews; and in Italy there is a Jewish community of ex-Catholics. Jewish settlements are found in Transcaucasia, Syria, Turkistan, Persia, Afghanistan, Morocco, and Algeria.

Obviously it is not possible here to present the detailed statistics demonstrating the considerable variability in physical characteristics among the misnamed "Jewish race." The type usually regarded as typically "Jewish" is actually prevalent among the peoples of the eastern Mediterranean area, most of whom are not Jews and never have been. Thus Turks, Greeks, Syrians, and others are often mistaken for Jews by those who claim to be able to identify Jews by their appearance. Actually the Jews involved in the widespread migrations just described tended through time to interbreed with the inhabitants of the new lands. Accordingly, they frequently became indistinguishable from the aboriginal groups. By way of illustration, it is calculated that in Germany, between 1921 and 1925, for every 100 Jewish marriages, there were 58 all-Jewish and 42 mixed marriages. In 1926, in Berlin, there were 861 all-Jewish and 554 mixed marriages.[20] In the light of such evidence it is not surprising to note that a census of schoolchildren taken in Germany during the nineteenth century revealed that among 75,000 Jewish children, 32 per cent had light hair and 46 per cent light eyes.

Other evidence likewise points to the fact that different populations of Jews at one time or another have intermixed with the various populations among whom they were living. Among Jews in Yemen 100 per cent had dark eyes and dark hair. But among Jews in Baden (part of Germany), the dark-eyed Jews were in the minority (48.8 per cent), although nearly 85 per cent had dark hair, while 2.3 per

[19] Ashley Montagu, *Man's Most Dangerous Myth: The Fallacy of Race* (New York: Columbia University Press, 1942), 221–222.
[20] Juan Comas, *Racial Myths* (Paris: UNESCO, 1951), 30.

cent had red hair. Some 51.2 per cent had light eyes and 12.8 per cent had fair or blond hair. A significant number of Baden Jews, accordingly, had the so-called "Aryan" traits. Similarly, in Lithuania 34.8 per cent of the Jews had light eyes and 29.0 per cent had fair or blond hair. When head shape is considered, Jews in different regions of the world show considerable differences from one another. Jews residing in the Daghestan Caucasus are predominantly round-headed; those in North Africa and especially those in Yemen Arabia are predominantly long-headed; and those in Europe tend to be of all varieties with the intermediate types predominating.

Quite clearly Jews are not of a uniform physical type. Even the hooked nose, ostensibly so characteristic of Jews, was shown by one study to be prevalent among only 44 per cent of the Jews of one group, while straight noses were found in 40 per cent, the "Roman" nose in 9 per cent, and the tip-tilted nose in 7 per cent. A trip to the new nation of Israel testifies to the absence of a Jewish "race." The flow of Jews into Israel, over a million and a half in the last thirty years, has come in two main streams, the first ("Western" or "Euro-pean" Jews) from eastern and central Europe, the second ("Eastern" or "Oriental" Jews) from the West Asian or North African countries —Yemen, Egypt, Tunisia, Iraq, Morocco, Algeria. In fact these two disparate traditions have been termed "the two Israels." This in-gathering of the long-wandering tribes of Israel dramatically reveals the extent to which Jews have become not only the cultural but also the physical products of the cultures and peoples among whom they lived as "outsiders" for so long. Jews seeking to regain homogeneity in Israel now not only have to bridge all the great differences of culture that separate peoples of industrialized and non-industrialized societies, but also have to close the gap of color.

In summary, the existence among Jews of Caucasian, Mongoloid, and Negroid types, the presence of blonds and brunets, of hooked and Roman noses, of round, long, and intermediate heads, etc., is demonstrable evidence of the non-existence of a Jewish "race." Those emotional and temperamental reactions which may charac-terize some Jews, such as distinctive facial expressions, bodily pos-turings and mannerisms, styles of speaking and intonation can be traced to Jewish cultural traditions and to the treatment Jews re-ceived at the hands of the non-Jews. Who then is a Jew? We need to resort to a *social* definition. A Jew is an individual who is defined as a Jew by the community-at-large or by Jews or both. Perhaps

Jean-Paul Sartre put it best of all, "A Jew is a man whom other men call a Jew."

ARE THERE SUPERIOR RACES?

Notions of Racial Intellectual Superiority

In the field of minority relations probably few other aspects have attracted as much attention as the question of whether certain racial or ethnic groups enjoy an inherent intellectual superiority over others. The notion of racial and ethnic superiority and inferiority has had wide currency in the modern age. It formed a cornerstone of official government policy in Nazi Germany, and traditionally provided a firm ideological foundation in defense of the southern segregated order.

With the development in 1905 of the first tests to quantitatively measure intelligence, developed by Alfred Binet, a noted French psychologist, seemingly a scientific instrument was at hand to substantiate the doctrine of White intellectual superiority. Early authorities alleged that the Binet scale was a true test of inborn intelligence, relatively free of the disturbing influences of environment. Investigations based upon the Binet and related tests revealed that racial and ethnic groups differed markedly from one another in innate intelligence. In the various studies of Black children by means of the Binet test, the intelligence quotient (IQ) ranged from 83 to 99, with an average around 90. A score of about 100 was considered normal for the population at large, thus Blacks performed at a lower-than-average level. With American Indians, IQ scores were also low, the majority ranging between 70 and 90. Mexicans did only slightly better. Chinese and Japanese, however, showed relatively little difference from Whites, the scores ranging from 85 to 114, with an average only slightly below 100. Among European immigrant groups, Italians ranged from 76 to 100, with an average about 87, and the Poles did equally poorly. On the other hand, immigrants from Great Britain, Holland, Germany, and the Scandinavian countries were superior to others in test performance.

Contemporary intelligence testing, employing a variety of tests, tends to corroborate the earlier findings of differential racial and ethnic group performance on IQ tests. As part of the Civil Rights Act of 1964, Congress ordered the United States Commissioner of

Education to conduct a survey of educational opportunities in the nation. The result was the "Coleman Report" (named after James S. Coleman, a prominent sociologist who had the prime responsibility for planning and carrying out the survey).[21] The report was based on a sample of some 4,000 schools, 605,000 students, and 60,000 teachers. As part of the survey, achievement tests were administered to students at various grade levels. Attention was paid to six racial and ethnic groups: Blacks, American Indians, Oriental Americans, Puerto Ricans living in the continental United States, Mexican-Americans, and Whites other than Mexican-Americans and Puerto Ricans. Coleman and his associates used these terms of identification not in a biological or genetic sense, but as reflecting social categories by which people identified themselves and were identified by others. The results for 12th grade students, indicated in Figure 2–2, are representative, and reveal sharp difference among the various racial and ethnic groups. The Whites' average score tended to be above those of the other groups, followed in order by Orientals, Indians, Mexican-Americans, Puerto Ricans, and Blacks. Results from the Armed Forces Qualification Test (AFQT), administered to all draftees and enlistees before entering the military services, similarly reveals that Whites on the average, do better than Blacks (the AFQT test covers four subject areas: vocabulary, arithmetic, spatial relationships, and mechanical ability).[22] See Table 2–3.

TABLE 2–3 Estimated Percentage Distribution of Draftees by Mental Group, by Race, 1966

Mental Group	White	Black	Total
I	7.6%	0.3%	6.7%
II	32.1	3.3	28.8
III	34.6	18.2	32.8
IV	16.0	38.2	18.5
V	9.1	37.1	12.3

Source: Adapted from Richard de Neufville and Caryl Conner, "How Good Are Our Schools?" American Education, 2 (October, 1966), 5.

21 James S. Coleman et al., Equality of Educational Opportunity (Washington, D.C.: U. S. Government Printing Office, 1966).
22 Richard de Neufville and Caryl Conner, "How Good Are Our Schools?" American Education, 2 (October, 1966), 1–9, and Supplement to Health of the Army: Results of the Examination of Youths for Military Service, 1966 (Washington, D.C.: Office of the Surgeon General, United States Army, 1967).

Any number of scholars have interpreted these and other findings as indicating White intellectual superiority and Black inferiority. In recent years, a group of "new hereditarians," such men as Dwight J. Ingle, professor of physiology at the University of Chicago, William Shockley, a Nobel Prize-winning physicist at Stanford University, and Arthur R. Jensen, University of California (Berkeley) educational psychologist, have argued that hereditary factors have a major influence on "racial" differences in intelligence.[23] Ingle and Shockley go so far as to imply that genetic research aimed at "positive eugenics" might be needed if Blacks are to achieve "true equality" (indeed, Shockley calls for a "voluntary, sterilization bonus" plan for low IQ Blacks).

Jensen's work in particular has commanded a good deal of interest and generated considerable controversy, in part because his paper appeared in the prestigious *Harvard Educational Review*. Jensen believes that hereditary factors are primarily responsible for the fact that Blacks average 15 points below Whites on IQ tests. Blacks, he argues, are disadvantaged when it comes to "cognitive" or "conceptual" learning—the capacity for abstract reasoning and problem-solving (the key to higher mental functions) while tending to do well in tasks involving rote learning—memorizing mainly through repetition. He views the influence of environment as limited by the "threshold" effect—that is, below a certain threshold of environmental adequacy, deprivation does have a marked depressing effect on IQ, but above that threshold, remedial action does little to raise intelligence. Hence, "compensatory" education is doomed to failure for Black children so long as the emphasis falls upon "cognitive" learning; rather, Jensen insists, education needs to gear itself to accord with different and unequal racial patterns of native ability.[24]

What assessment can we make of the view that racial and ethnic groups differ in native intelligence? How might we appraise the position of Jensen and other "new hereditarians"? In coming to

[23] Dwight J. Ingle, "Racial Differences and the Future," *Science*, 146 (October 16, 1964), 375–379 and "The Need to Investigate Average Biological Differences among Racial Groups," in Mead *et al.*, *op. cit.*, 113–121; William Shockley, "Possible Transfer of Metallurgical and Astronomical Approaches to the Problem of Environment Versus Ethnic Heredity," unpublished presentation at the Regional Meeting of the National Academy of Science, 1966, and "Proposed Research to Reduce Racial Aspects of the Environment–Hereditary Uncertainty," *Science* (April 26, 1968), 443; and Arthur R. Jensen, "How Much Can We Boost IQ and Scholastic Achievement?," *Harvard Educational Review*, 39 (1969), 1–123.

[24] For a critique of Jensen's paper see the papers in the Spring, 1969, and Summer, 1969, issues of the *Harvard Educational Review* (Vol. 39).

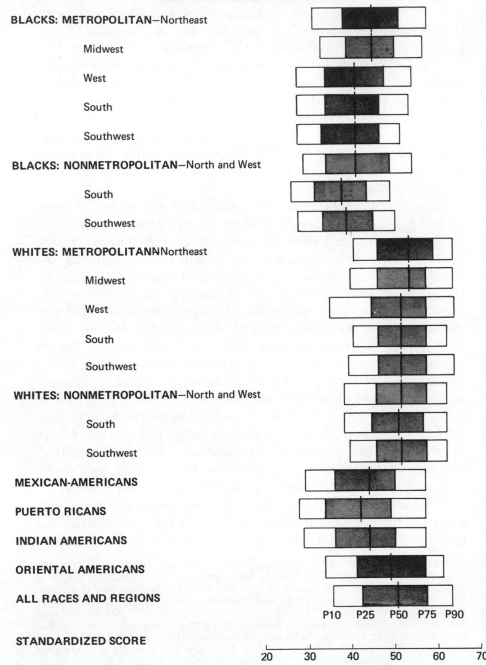

Fig. 2–2. Achievement Test Scores, National Sample of 12th Grade Stu-
points at the first and last deciles (10 and 90 percentage points) and showing
percentage points). *Source: James S. Coleman et al., Equality of Educational*
ures 3.11.24, 3.11.25, and 3.11.31, pages 244, 245, and 251.

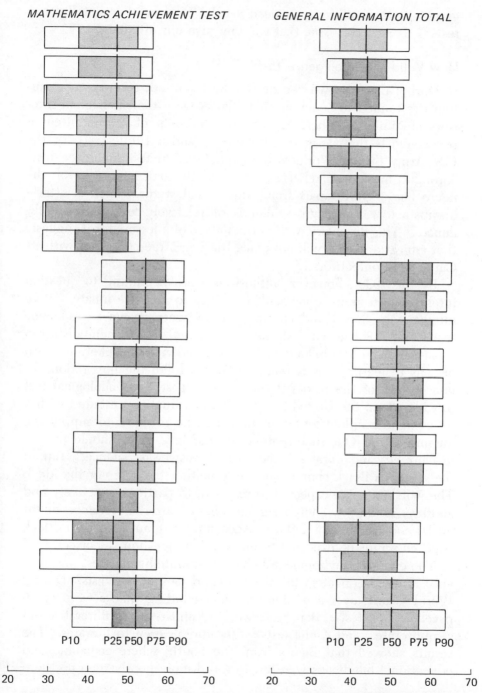

MATHEMATICS ACHIEVEMENT TEST   *GENERAL INFORMATION TOTAL*

P10   P25 P50 P75 P90   P10   P25   P50   P75   P90

20   30   40   50   60   70   20   30   40   50   60   70

dents, 1965. Each bar indicates the distribution of test scores having its end-
also the location of the median and the first and third quartiles (25 and 75
Opportunity (Washington, D.C.: U. S. Government Printing Office, 1966), Fig-

grips with these matters, we need to ask, "How valid are intelligence tests?" It is to this issue that we now turn our attention.

How Valid Are Intelligence Tests?

During the first two decades of the twentieth century, most authorities tended to conclude that Blacks were the intellectual inferiors of Whites. Robert M. Yerkes, chairman of a committee of psychologists that designed intelligence and aptitude tests for the U.S. Army during World War I, concluded that intelligence tests "brought into clear relief . . . the intellectual inferiority of the negro [sic]. Quite apart from educational status, which is utterly unsatisfactory, the negro soldier is of relatively low grade intelligence." This discovery was "in the nature of a lesson, for it suggests that education alone will not place the negro race on a par with its Caucasian competitors." [25]

By the 1930s, however, authorities were beginning to question intelligence tests in terms of their ability to measure innate, native intelligence. Social and cultural factors were shown to influence test results. Social scientists came to recognize that membership in a particular culture influences what the individual is likely to learn or fails to learn. This is reflected in the following illustration: In one portion of the National Intelligence Test, a psychological test in wide use in the United States, the individual is presented with a series of incomplete sentences in which he is asked to supply the missing word. One such sentence reads, "_____ should prevail in churches and libraries"; the correct answer is "silence." But in the southern Black church, silence is neither the rule nor the ideal. The worshipers are expected to respond, to participate actively and audibly; in fact, a church service characterized by silence might well be considered a failure. Accordingly, many southern Black children might be expected to answer this question "incorrectly." [26]

The effect of environmental changes on intelligence-test performance also led educators to take a second look at the tests. During World War I, over a million recruits including Blacks were given psychological tests. Beta tests were administered to illiterates and semi-literates, and Alpha tests were administered to literates. The results showed that Blacks from the South, where economic and educational handicaps were greater, did more poorly than northern

25 Robert M. Yerkes, "Psychological Examining in the United States Army," National Academy of Sciences, *Memoir*, 15 (1921), 870.
26 Otto Klineberg, *Race and Psychology* (Paris: UNESCO, 1951), 11.

Blacks. But most striking perhaps of all was that Blacks from some *northern* states turned out scores averaging higher than *Whites* from some *southern* states. It has been suggested that the superior performance of northern Blacks was due to selective migration, i.e., Blacks with superior intelligence, energy, and initiative would leave the South, leaving behind Blacks with lesser intelligence. But the evidence in this connection for a theory of selective migration is slim. Klineberg, on the basis of a careful search through school records in several southern cities and a detailed statistical comparison of the school marks obtained by the migrants and non-migrants, found no differences between the two groups. Apparently the environmental opportunities of northern Blacks were the crucial factor.[27]

This conclusion regarding the operation of environmental factors is strengthened by other studies. Klineberg made tests in New York City which demonstrated that IQ scores of Blacks in that city increased with length of residence. This would hardly be the case if such tests exclusively measured innate intelligence. Everett S. Lee confirmed the Klineberg findings in an analysis of intelligence tests given by the Philadelphia school system. There was a steady upward trend in the average IQ scores of the Black migrants, so that, by the time all were in the ninth grade, those who came in at the first grade were less than a point below those born in the city.[28]

As was already noted, the test scores of American Indians are among the lowest of the groups examined in the United States. But Rohrer found that the performance of the Osage Indians was comparable to that of Whites. The noteworthy point here, however, is that these Indians are exceptional in that they live under conditions which are similar to those of the Whites with whom they were compared. Oil had been discovered on their reservation, enabling them to acquire an economic position and a social and environmental condition far superior to those of most American-Indian communities. On two different tests—one a non-language test, the second depending on language—they obtained average IQ scores of 104 and 100, respectively.[29]

[27] Otto Klineberg, *Negro Intelligence and Selective Migration* (New York: Columbia University Press, 1935).

[28] Everett S. Lee, "Negro Intelligence and Selective Migration: A Philadelphia Test of the Klineberg Hypothesis," *American Sociological Review*, 16 (1951), 227–233.

[29] John H. Rohrer, "The Test Intelligence of Osage Indians," *Journal of Social Psychology*, 16 (1942), 99–105.

The net result of all the research relating to intelligence testing indicates that as yet a "non-cultural" and "non-environmental" test has not been devised. Indeed, a "non-cultural (culture-free)" test is a misnomer, since there is no more reason to expect a culture-free intelligence than a diet-free stature. It is known that environmental factors account for large differences in measured intelligence performance, and that minority groups are usually disadvantaged in terms of favoring environmental conditions. Thus studies have repeatedly shown that Black children taken as a group, especially those who come from segregated schools, do not enjoy educational and related opportunities commensurate with those of Whites.

Moreover, it is not sufficient to divide the variance with respect to a behavioral trait into genetic and environmental variance, for in this way we lose what in many cases is the most important part of the variance, the *interaction* between genetic and environmental factors. In truth, the issue posed by the "new hereditarians" (Ingle, Shockley, Jensen)—the relationship between "racial" hereditary factors and intelligence—has its roots in the old nature-nurture controversy; the kinds of questions they ask reveal a preoccupation with "either/or" and "how much of which" strategies; they give no or insufficient attention to development and process, to the dynamic interplay between nature and environment.[30] Indeed, in learning, *the human organism modifies itself by responding* (consider, for instance, some of the work currently in progress in neurobiology that suggests that ribonucleic acid [RNA] may weave the molecular memory structure of the brain in accordance with social experience).

Still other questions have been raised regarding racist interpretations of differences in Black and White IQ scores. Any research that seriously attempts to make comparisons between or among "races" must sooner or later grapple with the questions, "What constitutes a race?" and "How do we go about classifying an individual or a group of people in terms of race?" Yet as we have already observed, these remain unsettled matters. Most racial comparisons rest upon *social* definitions of race. The distinctive genetic background of the individuals being tested is generally assumed rather than demonstrated; in a scientific sense, it is uncontrolled. Curiously, "racial" studies of intelligence revert to lay conceptions of race; most commonly the racial sorting is done on the basis of the subject's self-

[30] Ernst Caspari, "Genetic Endowment and Environment in the Determination of Human Behavior," *American Educational Research Journal*, 5 (1968), 43–55.

classification or on the opinion of the researcher. The sole or dominant criterion is usually skin color. Nor do racial comparisons allow for the considerable penetration of Caucasian genes among Black Americans, a penetration that renders any discussion of pure races invalid and any suspicion of massive genetic distinctions between Black and White Americans unlikely.[31]

In conclusion, any claims regarding innate differences between Blacks and Whites with regard to intelligence cannot be substantiated unless three conditions are met:

1. Adequate tests of native intelligence, uncontaminated by environmental influences, and with proved reliability and validity will have to be developed.
2. The environment—the social and cultural backgrounds—of the Blacks and Whites being tested must be fully equal.
3. The distinctive *genetic* homogeneity of the Black group being tested, as well as that of the White group, must be *demonstrated*, not assumed.[32]

To date, none of these conditions has been met. Hence, it cannot be definitively asserted that innate, native differences in intelligence exist between racial and ethnic groups. Nor, on the other hand, can it be definitively stated that *no* differences exist between racial and ethnic groups in innate, native intelligence. On the basis of what evidence is currently available, however, most contemporary authorities are of the opinion that notions of appreciable inborn differences in intelligence between various racial and ethnic groups simply cannot be supported.[33] Moreover, should such differences be found in the future, they are unlikely to be of major consequence or to have any great importance for social participation.

[31] See R. M. Dreger and K. S. Miller, "Comparative Psychological Studies of Negroes and Whites in the United States," *Psychological Bulletin*, 57 (1960), 361–401.
[32] See: Melvin M. Tumin, *Race and Intelligence* (New York: Anti-Defamation League of B'nai B'rith, 1963), 9.
[33] A few psychologists, however, challenge this point of view. See: Henry E. Garrett, "The Equalitarian Dogma," *Mankind Quarterly*, 1 (1961), 253–257; Audrey Shuey, *The Testing of Negro Intelligence* (New York: Social Science Press, 1966); Frank McGurk, "Psychological Tests: A Scientist's Report on Race Differences," *U.S. News and World Report*, September 21, 1956, 92–96; and Ernest Van Den Haag, "Intelligence or Prejudice?," *National Review*, December 1, 1964. However, these psychologists have won little support. Their conclusions have come under attack by the Society for the Psychological Study of Social Issues, a division of the American Psychological Association; the Society for the Study of Social Problems; the American Anthropological Association; as well as a number of other professional associations.

ARE THERE "RACIAL" PERSONALITIES AND TEMPERAMENTS?

The Subjective Nature of Many Appraisals

The same exaggeration of the role of biological forces may also be noted in popular notions regarding differences in personality and temperament. Jews are alleged to be shrewd, sly, and mercenary; Blacks, happy-go-lucky, lazy, and superstitious; Italians, impulsive, passionate, and quick-tempered; American Indians, unshrinking, stalwart, and brave; etc. Such traits are supposedly the products of inborn, genetic properties. Here we have much the same situation and much the same scientific support that we found regarding innate intellectual differences. Often, the alleged traits are fictitious and change with the times. In 1935 most Americans thought of Japanese as "progressive," "intelligent," and "industrious"; by 1942 they were "cunning" and "treacherous"; and by 1950 the image had changed again. When there was a need for Chinese laborers in California, they were portrayed as "frugal," "sober," and "law-abiding"; when labor was plentiful and they competed with White workers, they became "dirty," "repulsive," "unassimilable," and "dangerous." Much the same situation existed in India, where American troops found the natives "dirty" and "uncivilized," whereas Hindu intellectuals found Americans "boorish," "materialistic," "unintellectual," and "uncivilized." Accordingly, such appraisals often rest on subjective evaluation. This is not to deny that peoples may differ, but such differences are inconsistent and appear related to social and environmental factors, not to biology.

Rorschach-Test Results

One useful technique for determining personality characteristics is the Rorschach Test. The subject is shown an inkblot and is asked what he "sees" in the configuration. The individual gives his responses to each of ten inkblots. It is assumed that he portrays a "total action" picture of his state of adjustment without realizing that he is revealing his frustrations, hostilities, or emotional status. No matter what his interpretations—whether he sees a volcano, a bear, individuals bowing to each other, a genital organ, or a woman's face in the shadows—the subject is believed to be projecting his general personality pattern. Abel and Hsu administered the Rorschach Test to a group of Chinese born in China and a group of

Chinese who had lived their entire life in the United States. Had the general personality pattern of the Chinese been biological, one would expect their responses to be similar. Yet the study revealed some striking differences in the personality pattern of the two groups. The authors of the study concluded that the reason for the divergences was the merging of the Chinese Americans within the American way of life.[34] In a word, environmental forces were responsible.

Such findings are supported by other evidence. As Montagu notes, the alleged "expansive and rhythm-loving" Black reared in England becomes as composed, phlegmatic, and awkward rhythmically as the average Englishman.[35] And, despite the fact that between the sixteenth and nineteenth centuries there were no new invasions of England nor any major genetic infusions from the outside, the boisterous joy of life of the Elizabethan period gave way to the prudish Victorian age, while the rationalism of the eighteenth century gave way to the romanticism of the nineteenth century. Similarly, Australians, New Zealanders, Canadians, and South Africans show different typical personality structures from one another and from their English ancestors. Clearly such phenomena as these would seem incapable of interpretation in strictly biological terms. Yet any final, definitive conclusion would be premature, as science as yet lacks adequate tests for the measurement of personality characteristics.[36]

IS THERE A "RACIAL" MORALITY?

The Image of the Italian as a Gangster

Closely related to other racial myths is the notion that there is an association between races and ethical standards. Not infrequently, a nationality group is erroneously equated with a racial group. Thus blanket assertions are sometimes heard that some immigrant groups, most notably the Italians, are "racially" predisposed toward crime, racketeering, and acts of violence. Questioned, the proponent of this viewpoint is likely to respond with considerable indignation and recite a list of Italian names including Capone, Luciano, Costello,

[34] Klineberg, *Race and Psychology, op. cit.*, 35–36.
[35] Ashley Montagu, *Statement on Race* (New York: Abelard-Schuman, Ltd., 1951), 102.
[36] See Dreger and Miller, *op. cit.*, 374–381.

Fischetti, and those of many other notorious gangsters. It is always interesting to note that such infamous "bad men" of the 1930s as Dillinger, Van Meter, Floyd, Nelson, Barker, and Kelly—all with traditional old American names—are conveniently forgotten. Actually the rate of criminal convictions among foreign-born Italians was approximately the same as that for other foreign-language groups and less than that for native-born whites. Although crimes against the person were higher, other crimes had a much lower incidence, including those of drunkenness, forgery, and disorderly conduct.

The prevalence of crimes against the person within the total criminal behavior of Italian immigrants is sometimes attributed to their "hair-trigger" disposition. Some insist that Italians are easily offended at trifles and respond with violence. Yet closer analysis reveals some important flaws in this theory. Root and Giardini demonstrate that American-born sons of Italians, though involved in predatory crimes, are not usually violent in their offenses. In short, this supposed inborn Italian predisposition passes in a single generation. This phenomenon is inconsistent with our present knowledge of genetics. Rather, a social explanation appears more in order. Traditionally the lack of a strong government in southern Italy promoted the practice of self-defense. A "true" man would not go to court; he would draw his stiletto at the slightest imagined affront. But his American-born son has become "Americanized" in his crimes. He loses much of his father's alleged hair-trigger temperament and seeks financial gain from crime, not personal honor.[37]

Criminality Among Blacks

Crime reports in America consistently show that the percentage of Blacks caught within the meshes of the machinery of crime repression is out of proportion to their percentage in the total population. Blacks tend to rank disproportionately high as compared with Whites in arrests for gambling, aggravated assault, murder, carrying weapons, narcotics, robbery, and prostitution (with the exception of robbery, 60 to 70 per cent of the victims of Black crime are Black). On the other hand, Blacks rank disproportionately low in arrests for forgery, driving while intoxicated, auto theft, embezzlement, and manslaughter by negligence (Blacks understandably would be found ranking low in "white-collar crime" such as forgery and embezzle-

[37] See: Donald R. Taft, *Criminology*, 3d ed. (New York: The Macmillan Co., 1956), 101–102.

ment, owing to their less advantaged position and limited access to white-collar occupations). One point of view attributes the high incidence of Black homicide and assault to frustrations engendered by racism—unequal opportunity and discrimination, overcrowding and blight within urban ghettos, and demoralizing conditions within a racist social order—that find expression in explosive assaults or in repeated acts of predatory crime.[38]

Not all sociologists, however, agree that a high Black crime rate is a response to racial discrimination. Green, for example, on the basis of his examination of crime records in Ypsilanti, Michigan, challenges the classical interpretation and instead singles out a number of demographic and socioeconomic factors.[39] He analyzes the Black–White arrest differential with respect to age, sex, and such socioeconomic variables as employment status, occupation, and migration and concludes that

the higher official rate of crime for Negroes compared with whites results predominantly from the wider distribution among Negroes of lower social class characteristics associated with crime. The findings . . . show, for both white and Negro, disproportionately high arrest rates for males, youths age 17 to 24, persons in low income occupations (semi-skilled and unskilled workers), the unemployed, and persons not native to the State, predominantly Southern-ers. . . .

Even for serious crimes of violence including robbery, with a greater pre-ponderance of Negro over white arrests than any other major category of crimes, migrant whites incur substantially higher arrest rates than native-born (Michigan) Negroes at each occupational level. This difference reflects the effect of the southern regional culture pattern which the southern migrant transplants to his new abode in the urban industrial center [homicide and felonious assault rates are regularly higher in the South than in the rest of the nation].[40]

In evaluating statistics of Black crime, we should realize that Blacks are more liable to be suspected of crime than Whites. They are more liable to be arrested.[41] After arrest, they are less likely to secure bail, and accordingly are more liable to be counted in jail statistics. They are more liable to be indicted and less likely to

[38] See, for instance, Thomas F. Pettigrew, *A Profile of the American Negro* (Princeton, N.J.: Van Nostrand Reinhold Co., 1964), 150–156, and R. M. Stephenson and F. R. Scarpatti, "Negro–White Differentials and Delinquency," *Journal of Research in Crime and Delinquency*, 5 (1968), 122–123.

[39] Edward Green, "Race, Social Status, and Criminal Arrest," *American Sociological Review*, 35 (1970), 476–490.

[40] *Ibid.*, 489–490.

[41] One study, however, contradicts this conclusion. See: Donald J. Black, "Production of Crime Rates," *American Sociological Review*, 35 (1970), 744–746.

have their cases dismissed. If tried, Blacks are more likely than Whites to be convicted. If convicted, they are less likely to be given probation. Such factors would increase their proportion among prisoners.[42] We should also note in evaluating statistics of Black crime that when the homicide rate for Whites is found to be four times higher in Georgia than in Massachusetts, the difference is explained in terms of the surrounding cultural and socioeconomic conditions. But when the crime rate of Blacks is found to be generally four times higher than the rate for Whites, some racist-minded persons are quick to invent a genetic interpretation of the difference.[43]

There is no foundation for a biological interpretation of the higher incidence of some types of crimes among Blacks. If there were such a biological predisposition, we would expect to find among *all* groups of Blacks, regardless of social or economic circumstances, a similar incidence in criminal behavior. But this is not the case. Shaw and McKay, in a study of juvenile delinquency in Chicago, found that the rate of delinquency among Blacks as among Whites varied in relation to the organization or disorganization of the residential area. The rate of Black delinquency declined from 42.8 per 100 boys, ten to seventeen years, in the First Zone to 1.4 per 100 in the Seventh Zone. The First Zone was a deteriorated area in the center of Chicago; the Seventh Zone was in an area in which there was a marked increase in the proportion of Blacks in professional and business occupations.[44] Similarly, there is relatively little crime among Blacks in rural areas where Blacks are the dominant population group. Mound Bayou, Mississippi, is a case in point. Mound Bayou is an all-Black community of some 8,000 Blacks where for years no jail existed and no major crime was reported.

[42] Taft, *op. cit.*, 134; Sidney Axelrod, "Negro and White Institutionalized Delinquents," *American Journal of Sociology*, 57 (1952), 569–574); Irving Piliavin and Scott Briar, "Police Encounters with Juveniles," *American Journal of Sociology*, 70 (1964), 206–214; Thomas F. Pettigrew and Rosalind B. Spier, "The Ecological Structure of Negro Homicide," *American Journal of Sociology*, 67 (1962), 621–629; Theodore N. Ferdinand and Elmer G. Luchterhand, "Inner-City Youth, The Police, The Juvenile Court, and Justice," *Social Problems*, 17 (1970), 510–527; and Haywood Burns, "Can A Black Man Get A Fair Trial in This Country? *New York Times Magazine*, July 12, 1970, pp. 5, 38, 44–46. For a somewhat contrary view see: W. J. Chambliss and R. H. Nagasawa, "On the Validity of Official Statistics— A Comparative Study of White, Black, and Japanese High-School Boys," *Journal of Research in Crime and Delinquency*, 6 (1969), 71–77.

[43] Marvin E. Wolfgang, *Crime and Race: Conceptions and Misconceptions* (New York: Institute of Human Relations Press, 1964), 16.

[44] Clifford R. Shaw and Henry D. McKay, *Juvenile Delinquency and Urban Areas* (Chicago: University of Chicago Press, 1942).

There is no scientific evidence available that demonstrates that such a phenomenon as a "racial" morality exists. As we will see in Chapter 4, morality and ethical standards are cultural in nature and origin. Peoples throughout the world show a vast range in their evaluations of any particular type of behavior as "good" or "bad," "right" or "wrong." No demonstrable, consistent correlation occurs between racial groups and culture, nor between racial groups and "moral" patterns. If biology were at work, such correlations would exist. Similarly, from one generation to the next a people may demonstrate a considerable shift in ethical judgments and values. This is seen among groups converted to Christianity or communism, or groups assimilating a new culture, such as is true of immigrant Americans. Nor need the reader be reminded of the gulf that often exists between himself and his parents or grandparents in judgments of "appropriate" or "inappropriate" behavior. Clearly a biological interpretation would be erroneous.

INTERRACIAL MIXTURE

Closely related to the doctrine of inborn racial superiority and inferiority is the notion that interbreeding, or crossing, between races results in the mental and physical deterioration of the groups involved. According to a popular superstition, the offspring of interracial unions inherit most of the bad and few of the good qualities of the parental stocks. In turn these bad qualities are allegedly passed on to future generations, while the good qualities are further sifted out through continued interracial unions. Human degeneration is supposed to be the net result. A pamphlet of the pro-segregationist southern Citizens Councils asserts, "the intermingling of breeding stock results invariably in the production of 'scrubs' or mongrel types, and the downgrading of the whole herd. The same principle applies with equal force to the process of human development." [45]

For the proponents of this position, the consequences of race mixture are not merely academic, but of vast consequence to the fate of civilization. Hitler, writing on the issue in *Mein Kampf*, declares, "It is outstandingly evident from history that when the Aryan has mixed his blood with that of the inferior peoples, the result of the

[45] *A Christian View on Segregation,* pamphlet of the Mississippi Association of Citizens Councils (Greenwood, Miss., n.d.), 5.

miscegenation has invariably been the ruin of the civilizing races."
Similarly, U.S. Senator Herman E. Talmadge of Georgia writes,
"history shows that nations composed of a mongrel race lose their
strength and become weak, lazy and indifferent. They become
easy preys to outside nations." [46] And Mississippi Judge Tom P.
Brady declares:

> Whenever and wherever the white man has drunk the cup of black hem-
> lock, whenever and wherever his blood has been infused with the blood of
> the negro, the white man, his intellect and his culture have died. It is as true
> as two plus two equals four. The proof is that Egypt, India, the Mayan
> civilization, Babylon, Persia, Spain and all the others, have never and can
> never rise again.[47]

Scientists reject all these notions regarding the harmful consequences of racial interbreeding. Available evidence suggests that
race mixing has been going on from the earliest of times, having
been a common occurrence when peoples of differing genetic heritage have come into continuous contact. We have already pointed
out the fallacious character of the doctrine concerning "pure"
races. Most social scientists agree, Hitler, Senator Talmadge, and
Judge Brady not withstanding, that it was precisely the fact that
divergent peoples met—in the process often biologically and culturally fusing—which contributed the impetus for the emergence
of the Egyptian, Mesopotamian, Greek, Mayan, and Inca civilizations. Apparently it was not the mixing of genes per se that
produced the result, but ensuing cultural cross-fertilization resulting from the contact of divergent ways of life. A look at a world
map will demonstrate that the advance of civilization was most
marked, not on the peripheries of continents, but precisely where
continents joined. It was the Indians in Central America and its
margins that attained the highest advances in civilization, not those
to the far south or north. Likewise, it was near the juncture of three
continents, Asia, Europe, and Africa, that the Egyptian, Greek, and
Mesopotamian civilizations arose.

There are a number of traits, however, such as Rh-negative blood
types, sickle-cell anemia, and thalassemia, that apparently can be
transmitted through race crossings. While some groups possess the
traits, others do not. Accordingly, where crossing takes place, the

[46] H. E. Talmadge, *You and Segregation* (Birmingham: The Vulcan Press, Inc.,
1955), 44–45.
[47] Tom P. Brady, *Black Monday* (Winona, Miss.: Association of Citizens' Councils, 1954), 7.

genes for these conditions will be distributed among populations who either do not possess them or possess them in low frequencies. In the case of blood types, an Rh-negative mother mating with an Rh-positive male may have a number of babies who, by virtue of the consequent action of antibodies, may die either before or after birth (if untreated). Eight per cent of American Blacks carry the gene, as do about 16 per cent of the Whites, while Mongoloids are free of the condition. Sickle-cell anemia is usually a fatal condition in which the red cells of the body take on an irregular curved shape which is likened to a sickle. It is found exclusively in Negroids or individuals with Negroid ancestry. Thalassemia is also a disease affecting the blood, and is found primarily among Mediterranean peoples and their descendants within the United States.

HOW ARE RACES FORMED?

We have observed that people in various parts of the world differ in certain hereditary features, in such things as skin color, hair texture, various facial features, stature, and head shape. This raises the question, "How did the various people get the way they are?"— in short, "How are races formed?" A statement on race issued under UNESCO auspices answers the question in these terms:

Scientists have reached general agreement in recognizing that mankind is one: that all men belong to the same species, Homo sapiens. It is further generally agreed among scientists that all men are probably derived from the same common stock; and that such differences as exist between different groups of mankind are due to the operation of evolutionary factors of differentiation such as isolation, the drift and random fixation of the material particles which control heredity (the genes), changes in the structure of these particles, hybridization, and natural selection. In these ways groups have arisen of varying stability and degree of differentiation which have been classified in different ways for different purposes.

Mutations

If men are of a common stock, we must look at the mechanism by which they become differentiated. In short, how do new genes appear? The process is referred to as *mutation*. Mutation involves physical change in the chemical structure or position of the gene in relation to other genes. The exact cause or causes of mutation are not known. Various hair forms, for instance, have been the product of mutation. It is known, for example, that among swine, mice, rats, and rabbits curly hair has appeared spontaneously through mutation. Similarly, although kinky or woolly hair is a normal character-istic of Negroids, such hair has occurred as a mutation among Whites of exclusively White ancestry. On record are three Nor-wegian families in which such a mutation appeared.

Mutations constitute the raw materials of evolutionary change and racial differentiation. Some authorities assert that at least one mutation occurs in every human sometime between conception and death. Most mutations, perhaps as many as 99 per cent, are harm-ful. Hemophilia, or "bleeder's disease," characterized by a defect in the clotting power of blood, is a case in point. Estimates suggest that 1 in every 100,000 individuals in the English-speaking world today has the hemophilia gene, which came into being in each case quite spontaneously. England's Queen Victoria apparently arose from such a cell; at any rate, she transmitted the gene through her daughters and granddaughters to the royalty of Russia and Spain.[48]

Natural Selection

Occasionally a mutation appears that has a selective survival value. Among rabbits, for example, in a territory where the ground is covered with snow half the year, mutations in favor of a seasonal shift of coat color to white would be of adaptive value in lessening their chance of being killed by natural enemies. They would tend to possess an advantage over brown rabbits whose coats remained unchanged. Through the action of environment, the mutant rabbits would tend to be preserved so that they would tend to leave more offspring behind than the unchanging brown rabbits. And, through time, as would be expected, the mutant rabbits would flourish in comparison with the brown rabbits. This phenomenon is the process of *natural selection.*

It appears that some distinctive traits among human populations may have arisen in this manner. A case in point is the sickle-cell gene which in its heterozygous state (where the gene is present in one but not the other parent) apparently confers relative immunity to certain kinds of malaria (in the homozygous state—where the gene is inherited from both parents—it produces serious symptoms and often fatal anemia). The heterozygous carriers of the gene possess the greatest fitness in a population living in an area where malaria is prevalent. Another gene, which when homozygous pro-duces thalassemia (Mediterranean anemia) seemingly also confers

[48] L. C. Dunn and Theodore Dobzhansky, *Heredity, Race and Society* (New York: The New American Library of World Literature, Inc., 1959), 78.

immunity to malaria in the heterozygous state. It appears that the combined distribution of the sickle-cell and the thalassemia genes in the tropics of the Old World resembles that of fasciparum malaria —although there are exceptions associated with migrations and population mixtures.[49]

Coon, Garn, and Birdsell have taken the argument even further and have suggested that natural selection operated to produce distinct races. Body form among some populations is a case in point. Desert people, including the Tuareg of the Sahara and the Somalis of the Horn of Africa, are tall, lean, skinny people, with long arms and legs, shallow bodies, and narrow hands and feet. According to Coon, Garn, and Birdsell such a build is adaptive to dry desert heat. The skin surface area among such people is great in proportion to their volume and weight. The crucial factor seems to be that such a build presents the maximum skin surface area (in proportion to mass and weight) to the external environment, thus permitting a maximum of cooling surface for evaporation. Since roughly 50 per cent of the body's blood is inside of the legs at any one time, a long, pipelike leg is an excellent radiator. It exposes much more cooling surface than a short, barrel-like one.[50]

On the other hand, among people in the Arctic Circle, the opposite condition tends to prevail. In contrast to the inhabitants of desert areas, Arctic people present the least possible skin surface area to the environment in proportion to volume and weight. The Eskimo and Chukchi peoples are built to radiate as little heat as possible. Their bodies are thickset and chunky, their chests thick and wide, their legs short and thick, their fingers and toes short, and their wrists and ankles small and fat-covered. Likewise, Arctic-dwelling peoples often are at the door of starvation. Selection would favor those who could store and utilize fat, as "obesity" would have survival value where food is scarce.[51]

Coon, Garn, and Birdsell view the Mongoloid face as a piece of

[49] Anthony C. Allison, "Protection Afforded by Sickle Cell Trait against Subtertian Malarial Infection," *British Medical Journal*, 1 (1954), 290–292, "Notes on Sickle Cell Polymorphism," *Annals Human Genetics*, 19 (1954), 39–54, "Aspects of Polymorphism in Man," *Cold Spring Harbor Symposia on Quantitative Biology*, 20 (1955), 239–255, and "Metabolic Polymorphisms in Mammals and Their Bearing on Problems of Biochemical Genetics," *American Naturalist*, 93 (1959), 5–19; and Frank B. Livingstone, "Anthropological Implications of Sickle Cell Gene Distribution in West Africa," *American Anthropologist*, 60 (1958), 533–562.

[50] Carleton S. Coon, Stanley M. Garn, and Joseph B. Birdsell, *Races: A Study of the Problems of Race Formation in Man* (Springfield, Ill.: Charles C Thomas, 1950), 36–40.

[51] *Ibid.*, 41–45.

adaptive thermal "engineering." They argue that the presence of the world's most Mongoloid people in the coldest inhabited parts of the world, in Siberia and the Yukon, suggests that Mongoloids are adapted to cold. A man with thin, bony features, especially a narrow, prominent nose, would be in danger of freezing his face. On the other hand, a man with a flat face, padded with fat, and with a sparse beard would be well adapted. This is the Mongoloid face in its extreme form. Likewise, epicanthic folds (giving the appearance of slanting eyes) protect the eyeball with fatty layers of padding, bringing the lids close to one another. Whiskers are also a disadvantage, as moisture from the individual's breath freezes on the hair, and soon the face underneath freezes too.[52]

Such theories, however, are quite speculative. We lack experimental evidence for testing their validity. Indeed, the critics have dealt rather harshly with Coon, Garn, and Birdsell. Washburn, for instance, observes that large numbers of Mongoloids currently live in the hot, moist tropics, and many of them have lived for thousands of years under conditions that have been anything but cold. Moreover, Washburn fails to find the types of correlations that would support the Coon, Garn, and Birdsell position:

If one follows the form of the nose, in Europe, as one moves north, narrow noses are correlated with cold climate; in Eastern Asia low noses are correlated with cold climate. In neither case is there the slightest evidence that the difference in the form of the nose has anything whatsoever to do with warming the air that comes into the face.[53]

Washburn insists that the Mongoloid face has nothing to do with adaptation to the cold. He argues that it constitutes a complex structural pattern related to the teeth, and hence is primarily the result of large masseter (chewing) muscles and the bones from which these muscles arise. Superficially a very similar pattern may be seen among the African Bushmen whose facial form can hardly be attributed to thermal engineering. Caution, then, is called for in attempting to ascertain the role played by natural selection in race formation.

Isolation

Mutations having adaptive value would have tended to become established among early man, as populations were characteristically small. The land mass of Asia, Africa, and Europe is considerable,

[52] *Ibid.*, 65–75.
[52] Sherwood L. Washburn, "The Study of Race," in Tumin, *op. cit.*, 51.

and early man was frequently isolated from other groups of humans over considerable periods of history. Accordingly, breeding took place largely or entirely within isolated groups. Such natural factors as mountain ranges, rivers, forests, deserts, seas, and distance served to reinforce isolation. Thus, in time, no matter how much alike all peoples had initially been, groups isolated from one another would soon become different by virtue of the differing mutations among them. Isolation, then, is another factor contributing to racial differentiation.

Genetic Drift

Genetic drift may also bring about differences in gene frequencies between populations. Assuming that early man was periodically found in relatively isolated bands or tribes—in brief, groups characterized by *small* populations—abrupt and unpredictable shifts of gene frequencies might occur over several generations by *chance*.[54] The principles of genetic drift can readily be understood by analogy: Suppose that a person with a name as rare and unusual as the author's raises a family with five sons. If this family lives in New York City the name will still be rare, but if the family happens to live in a country hamlet, in a few generations the name may become relatively frequent. Conversely, one family by the name of Smith, by moving out of the hamlet, may eliminate the name from the community, whereas one Smith family leaving New York would make no appreciable difference in the frequency of Smiths in that city.[55] Small populations may also come to differ from the populations of their origin for still another reason, the "founder effect." When a new colony is established by a few individuals, it cannot be fully and proportionately representative of the gene pool from which it is drawn—in short, the new colony comes to differ because it initially received a somewhat different genetic repertory.[56]

[54] Bentley Glass, "Genetic Changes in Human Populations, Especially Those Due to Gene Flow and Genetic Drift," *Advances in Genetics*, 6 (1954), 95–139; J. B. Birdsell, "Some Implications of the Genetical Concept of Race in Terms of Spatial Analysis," *Cold Spring Harbor Symposia on Quantitative Biology*, 15 (1950), 259–314; Gabriel W. Lasker, "Mixture and Genetic Drift in Ongoing Human Evolution," *American Anthropologist*, 54 (1952), 433–436; Sewall Wright, "Classification of the Factors of Evolution," *Cold Spring Harbor Symposia on Quantitative Biology*, 20 (1955), 16–24.

[55] Dobzhansky, *Mankind Evolving, op. cit.*, 281.

[56] Bentley Glass, Milton S. Sacks, Elsa F. Jahn, and Charles Hess, "Genetic Drift in a Religious Isolate: An Analysis of the Causes of Variation in Blood Group and Other Gene Frequencies in a Small Population, *American Naturalist*, 86 (1952), 145–159.

Hybridization

The role of hybridization has been discussed in the earlier treatment of racial crossing. Hybridization involves crossings between individuals and populations differing in genetic characteristics. Such intercrossings increase the range of the recombinations of genes. Allowing for the action of selection, isolation, genetic drift, etc., one can see that an entirely new physical type can be formed. New "races" are emerging in Latin America (alloys of Indian, Mediterranean White, and Black), in Hawaii (Polynesians, Whites, and Mongoloids), in parts of the United States (Blacks and Whites), and elsewhere, the product of hybridization.

SUMMARY

Human races do not lend themselves easily to cut-and-dried classifications and neat labels. Racial and ethnic groups often display differences in certain physical features, in performance on intelligence, aptitude, and personality tests, in the incidence of certain types of crime and diseases, and in a good many other characteristics as well. Race bigots contend that these group differences reflect differences in genetic capacities. And from this they argue that certain peoples are inherently inferior to still others, usually themselves. Those who find such notions abhorrent have at times gone too far to the other side in their protest: They have insisted that all people are as similar in their abilities and potentialities as identical twins. In all candor we must confess that scientists cannot at this point definitively assert either that there are or that there are not native differences between various racial or ethnic groups in certain capacities or potentialities. None of the essential conditions for making such a scientific statement has as yet been met. However, on the basis of contemporary evidence most authorities are of the opinion that if in the future such differences should be established, they are unlikely to be of major consequence or to have any great importance for social participation.

SOURCES OF RACISM

3

Origins of Racism

How does racism arise? Admittedly, our knowledge on this matter is limited, although there is no shortage of theories that purport to supply us with explanations. The evidence we do have suggests that the processes involved are complex and that no single sequence of processes holds for all cases. Nonetheless, we do encounter a number of ingredients that typically come into play in the emergence and initial stabilization of racism: (1) contact; (2) social visibility; (3) ethnocentrism; (4) competition; and (5) unequal power.[1] Let us examine each of these variables in turn.

CONTACT

Contact between differing racial and ethnic groups is probably a development that is as old as man himself. Skeletal fossils from the third interglacial—estimated to be between 50,000 and 150,000 years ago—suggest that Cro Magnons and Neanderthals coexisted and interbred in the Palestinian caves of Mount Carmel. Archaeological evidence also affords indisputable evidence that, long before the dawn of history, primitive man was often on the move, invading the territory of others and borrowing ideas from his enemies and from strangers. Similarly, ancient folklore recounts such migrations —the Aztecs, for instance, told stories of their origin "in the North," of their invasion of Mexico, and of their conquest of the native tribes they found there, and the Bible recounts the migrations of the early

[1] In this regard see: Donald L. Noel, "A Theory of the Origin of Ethnic Stratification," *Social Problems*, 16 (1968), 157–172.

Hebrews. And as philologists have amply demonstrated, languages provide considerable evidence for the prevalence of population movements.[2]

If migration were not a common practice, if people were content to live among their own kind in communities that were more or less isolated from one another, racial and ethnic prejudice would be virtually unknown. In considering migration, it is useful to distinguish between a number of different types of movement. Petersen[3] provides us with a convenient framework by which to classify migrations:

1. *Primitive migration.* The movement of primitive peoples appears related to their inability to cope with forces of nature. By virtue of their limited technological level, primitive people exercise little control over their subsistence. The resources available within one locality are generally inadequate to support a food-gathering or hunting people. Instead they must range over a wider area, frequently moving haphazardly or back and forth over their traditional territory. Although a herding people generally have greater control over their food supply than do gathering and hunting peoples, they too need to migrate for new grazing lands. Similarly an agrarian people may migrate when there is a sharp disparity between the produce from the land and the number of people subsisting upon it. The disparity may come about suddenly, as by drought or an attack of locusts, or by the steady Malthusian pressure of an increasing population on land that is limited in extent or fertility. Within their new settings, the migrants typically seek to resume their previous way of life. In the modern period, however, the more usual destination for migrants has been the city, where new ways of thinking and acting are demanded of them.[4]

2. *Forced and impelled migrations.* In forced migrations it is the state or a functionally similar institution that has served as the activating agent for the migration. Petersen distinguishes between impelled migration, where the migrants retain some power to decide whether or not to leave, and forced migration, where they lack this power. The early Nazi policy of encouraging Jewish emigration by

---

[2] In this regard see: Brewton Berry, *Race and Ethnic Relations,* 3rd ed. (Boston: Houghton Mifflin Co., 1965), 68–73.

[3] William Petersen, "A General Typology of Migration," *American Sociological Review,* 23 (1958), 256–266.

[4] *Ibid.,* 259–260.

various anti-Semitic measures is illustrative of impelled migration, whereas their later policy of herding Jews into cattle trains and transporting them to concentration camps is an example of forced migration.

Impelled migration frequently takes the form of flight. As a new people moves into a territory, it may drive before it the weaker former occupants. This apparently was the case during the early centuries of the Christian era, when invaders from the East made their way into Europe. In the modern period, the mass flight of East Germans to West Germany had so undermined the East German Communist regime that in the summer of 1961 the Soviet Union precipitated a Berlin crisis and unilaterally closed the border between East and West Berlin.

Forced migration has assumed considerable importance since the turn of the twentieth century, with millions of people forcibly uprooted and transferred from their homelands. The separation of Pakistan from India was accompanied by the migration of more than 12 million Moslems and Hindus, in part induced by terrorism and in part arranged under government auspices. During World War II, the Soviet Union, on the claim that they were "disloyal nationalities," resorted to the forced deportation from their homelands of the Volga Germans, the Chechen-Ingush, the Crimean Tartars, and the Kalmuks, a movement involving more than two million people. The overseas shipment of Africans during the mercantile age—involving some 10 to 20 million Blacks—similarly constituted a forcible movement of people.

3. *Free migration.* In primitive migration the activating force is primarily the lack of means to satisfy physiological needs, and in forced migration the migrants are largely passive. In free migration, on the other hand, the decisive element is the will of the migrants. The overseas migration of Europeans to the New World during the nineteenth century affords an important illustration of this type of migration. The numbers involved in the free migration were not large—they were pioneers who helped to break the ice and clear the way for later mass migrations. The pioneers were often adventurers or intellectuals who were motivated by their ideals. Their letters home and their accounts in European newspapers encouraged others to follow them to the New World.[5]

5 *Ibid.*, 263.

4. *Mass migration.* The pioneers blazed the trails that others followed. Migration soon became the style. Once it began, it stimulated still further migration. Emigration became a *social* pattern, and it can be largely understood in term of the mechanisms of collective behavior. In various parts of Europe there developed what became known as "America fever": Emigration became an important aspect in the atmosphere of the times. In Sweden, children were "educated to emigrate"; they followed a tradition that made emigration the "natural" thing to do. In fact, the failure to emigrate may actually have posed difficulties for the individual, in terms of the expectations that had been set for him.[6]

Whatever the motivating factor or factors, migration serves to bring people of differing racial or ethnic backgrounds into contact with one another. But racial or cultural differences in and of themselves do not *ipso facto* produce a distinct categorization; such characteristics become factors of group differentiation only through *social definition* (for example, within the United States, we tend to ignore moles, circumcision, and ear lobe contour as features having "social" significance).[7] In brief, group differences provide a convenient peg upon which to hang the argument of deeper inferiority —to activate and sanction prejudice, discrimination, and structural racism. It is to this matter of social differentiation and visibility that we now turn our attention.

SOCIAL VISIBILITY

Categories are necessary to social life. They enable us to group things into "classes" or "pigeonholes," and to respond to them in terms of this placement rather than in terms of their uniqueness. In this manner we reduce the complexity of our world through subsuming the diverse under the general. In life, we not only have categories for such things as animals, plants, and minerals, but also for people. Hence, by virtue of any number of historical circumstances, people evolve categories for classifying their fellow men (for instance, they are slaves, newcomers, foreigners, or heathens). Certain traits with high social visibility serve as identifying symbols of the category.[8]

---

[6] *Ibid.*, 263–264.

[7] E. K. Francis, "Variables in the Formation of So-Called 'Minority Groups,'" *American Journal of Sociology,* 60 (1954), 7.

[8] Robin M. Williams, Jr., *Strangers Next Door* (Englewood Cliffs, N.J.: Prentice-Hall, Inc., 1964), 18.

At times groups of people can be distinguished on the basis of certain hereditary physical traits, for instance, Japanese, Mexicans, Indians, Blacks, and Whites within the United States. Cultural traits likewise provide identifying clues. Names, language, accents, mannerisms, dress, gestures, typical facial expressions, food habits, religious practices, and various types of folk behavior supply "marks," or "signs," of ethnic membership. The evidence of ethnic membership may be quite apparent in terms of dress as among many Amish and Puerto Ricans. Then again, the identifying traits may be less readily apparent. In most respects, Catholics are undifferentiated from the great mass of Protestant Americans. Yet clues to Catholic membership are frequently discernible. The individual who attaches a statue of the Virgin Mary to his car's dashboard, who indicates he goes to Mass, or who has attended and whose children attend a Catholic parochial school is customarily identified as a Catholic.

The identifying "marks," or "signs," of group membership are sometimes perceptible by senses other than sight. Language and accent involve audibility. Odors, the product of differing hygienic or dietary practices, may provide evidence of ethnic membership. Yet olfactory hallucinations are not uncommon. Individuals may associate garlic with Italians and cheap perfume with immigrants, and accordingly, even in the objective absence of the particular odor, "smell" garlic when they meet Italians, and cheap perfume when they are in contact with immigrants. Association may also provide clues of group membership—individuals who are frequently found in the company of known Jews are often identified as Jews; similarly, with individuals in frequent association with Blacks.

Individuals who decide to escape from their membership in particular racial or ethnic groups may undertake to diminish or to eliminate their "visibility." Blacks may employ hair straighteners and bleach; Jews may change their names from "Cohen," "Blumberg," and "Finkelstein" to Anglicized names and display crosses as jewelry. Where visibility is so minute as to make it impossible to detect by simple observation who is a member of the minority group and who is a member of the dominant group, the minority may be compelled to display some identifying symbol. In Nazi Germany Jews were required to wear the Star of David or a yellow armband. Pope Innocent III, unable to distinguish Christian from heretics, decreed that the latter dress in a distinctive manner. Such evidence points to the fact that a dominant-minority relationship requires some visible and conspicuous feature or features by which the members of the two groups can be differentiated and identified. In the absence of such traits, the boundaries between the in-group and the out-group could not be maintained.

By employing cues deriving from racial or cultural traits we are able to sort individuals into the relevant categories of social life ("White," "Black," "Jew," "Gentile," "Indian")—to "place" or "locate" them within one or more institutional structures. On the basis of such information we come to define the situation; we activate within our minds a map, so to speak, that guides us in identifying the mutual set of expectations that will operate within the relationship (what we can expect of another person and what he can expect of us)—for instance, what a "White" can expect of a "Black" and what a "Black" can expect of a "White."

By virtue of categories, we "size up" people in terms of only one or a limited number of characteristics. One consequence of categorization is that it can deter "personalistic" encounters; it tends to foster *object* relations as opposed to *person-centered* relations. Rather than being viewed as a unique individual, the person who is marked as an exemplar of a group becomes an object. He tends to be identified first of all as a Jew, a Black, or a White—in brief, the person so typed becomes an *It* rather than a *Thou*.[9] Hence, in a very real sense categories not only serve to systematize our experiences, but they influence what we experience as well.

ETHNOCENTRISM

Contact and social visibility are obvious requisites of racism, but they are equally requisites of equalitarian intergroup relations.[10] Ethnic and racial groups can interact and form stable patterns of relations without racism. Lindgren, for instance, on the basis of her anthropological field work in northwestern Manchuria, reports that the Tungus and Cossacks—two racially and culturally unlike peoples —lived together, trading and associating with each other, for generations yet nonetheless managed to avoid conflict and racist notions.[11]

---

[9] Kenneth J. Gergen, "The Significance of Skin Color in Human Relations," *Daedalus*, 96 (Spring, 1967), 401. 145–159.

[10] Noel, *op. cit.*, 157.

[11] Ethel John Lindgren, "An Example of Culture Contact Without Conflict: Reindeer Tungus and Cossacks of Northwestern Manchuria," *American Anthropologist*, 40 (1938), 605–621.

Contact and social visibility set the stage, so to speak, upon which other variables come to operate in the development of racism.[12] One of these is *ethnocentrism*.

The Nature of Ethnocentrism

William Graham Sumner, who coined the word, described ethnocentrism as "this view of things in which one's own group is the center of everything, and all others are scaled and rated with reference to it." [13] In other words, ethnocentrism means the tendency of group members to appraise peoples of other cultures by the standards of judgment prevailing in their own culture. This use of in-group standards in judging out-groups implies that the members of the ethnocentric group *project* their own values onto the behavior of other people, that is, they assume that in *the nature of things* other people should be organized according to the same assumptions as prevail within their own group.[14] Ethnocentrism entails strong *positive* feelings toward an in-group. It is often, although not inevitably, accompanied by prejudice—*negative* conceptions, feelings, and action orientations regarding the members of an out-group.

Notions that one's own group is superior to other groups are not new to mankind. It is not uncommon for men anywhere in the world to believe that they, and they alone, belong to the "best people." As Ruth Benedict points out, "The formula 'I belong to the Elect' has a far longer history than has modern racism." [15] Among even the most primitive peoples this formula is an integral part of their whole life experience.[16] Prior to mass contact with outside groups, they were prone to look upon themselves grandiosely as "*the* human beings," as "Men." The designation applied exclusively to

[12] For an inventory of propositions (some of them contradicting others) appearing in the literature on ethnocentrism and nationalism, see: Paul C. Rosenblatt, "Origin and Effects of Group Ethnocentrism and Nationalism," *Journal of Conflict Resolution*, 8 (1964), 131–146.

[13] William Graham Sumner, *Folkways* (Boston: Ginn and Co., 1906), 13.

[14] William R. Catton, Jr., "The Functions and Dysfunctions of Ethnocentrism: A Theory," *Social Problems*, 8 (1960), 203.

[15] Ruth Benedict, *Race: Science and Politics* (New York: Modern Age Books, 1940), 155.

[16] There are exceptions to this, especially where a group is totally overshadowed by the technical superiority of a colonial power. See: Marc J. Swartz, "Negative Ethnocentrism," *Journal of Conflict Resolution*, 5 (1961), 75–81. Swartz provides us with an illustration of this: the Romónum people of the Truk atoll. Peter A. Munch also gives us a fascinating account of self-hatred and self-depreciation among the inhabitants of the remote island of Tristan de Cunha. See: Peter A. Munch, "Cultural Contacts in an Isolated Community—Tristan de Cunha," *American Journal of Sociology*, 53 (1947), 1.9.

their own group. Zuñi, Déné, Kiowa, and the rest were tribal names by which primitive people knew themselves, and these terms were equated with "mankind." Outside of their own closed group, human beings in the true sense did not exist. Other peoples were seen within this highly provincial outlook:

> They were not people with whom my own tribe had common cause. God did not create them of the same clay, or they did not spring out of the same water jar, or they did not come up through the same hole in the ground. But my own little group was under the special providence of God; he gave it the middle place in the "world" and he foretold that if ever it was wiped out, the world would perish. To my tribe alone he gave the ceremonies which preserve the world.[17]

Ethnocentrism and Assumptions of Belief Dissimilarity

One factor that apparently fosters ethnocentrism is the tendency of people to be attracted to others who hold beliefs and attitudes similar to their own; similarly they tend to experience an aversion toward people with dissimilar beliefs and attitudes. Rokeach, on the basis of his research, maintains that White Americans are motivated to reject Blacks less by racism than by assumed belief and value differences—in brief, Whites generally perceive Blacks as holding contrasting beliefs, and it is this perception and not race *per se* that leads to rejection. Indeed, a variety of studies have revealed that Whites typically accept in a social situation a Black with beliefs that are similar to their own over a White with different beliefs.[18]

An illustration of this is a study undertaken by Rokeach using 24

[17] Benedict, *op. cit.*, 156.
[18] See: Milton Rokeach, ed., *The Open and Closed Mind* (New York: Basic Books, Inc., 1960); D. Byrne and T. J. Wong, "Racial Prejudice, Interpersonal Attraction, and Assumed Dissimilarity of Attitudes," *Journal of Abnormal and Social Psychology*, 65 (1962), 246–253; David D. Stein, Jane Allyn Hardyck, and M. Brewster Smith, "Race and Belief: An Open and Shut Case," *Journal of Personality and Social Psychology*, 1 (1965), 281–289; Carole R. Smith, L. Williams, and R. H. Willis, "Race, Sex and Belief as Determinants of Friendship Acceptance," *Journal of Personality and Social Psychology*, 5 (1967), 127–137; David D. Stein, "The Influence of Belief Systems on Interpersonal Preference," *Psychological Monographs*, 80 (1966), Whole No. 616; C. C. Anderson and A. D. J. Côté, "Belief Dissonance as a Source of Disaffection between Ethnic Groups," *Journal of Personality and Social Psychology*, 4 (1966), 447–453; Clyde Hendrick, V. Edwin Bixenstine, and Gayle Hawkins, "Race versus Belief Similarity as Determinants of Attraction," *Journal of Personality and Social Psychology*, 17 (1971), 250–258; and Louis Mezei, "Perceived Social Pressure as an Explanation of Shifts in the Relative Influence of Race and Belief on Prejudice across Social Interactions," *Journal of Personality and Social Psychology*, 19 (1971), 69–81.

White and 26 Black subjects that was carried out in the setting of the personnel offices of two state mental hospitals near Detroit. The subjects were applying for jobs as janitors, attendants, laundry-workers, etc. Each subject completed an application and provided a statement regarding his opinions on how to deal with difficult mental patients. These opinions were classified as "harsh" or "permissive." The subject was then sent to a waiting-room occupied by four other "interviewees," in reality confederates of the experimenter. Two of the four men already in the waiting-room were White, and two were Black. These four men initiated a discussion with each of the subjects as to how to handle mental patients, two advocating a "harsh" solution and two a "permissive" one. Later the subject was asked which one of these four men he would like to work with in his future job. The fifty subjects overwhelmingly selected as work-mates those individuals who held the same kind of opinions—"harsh" or "permissive"—about patient handling as themselves, *regardless* of the race of the work-mate.[19] This tendency of people to organize the world of human beings in terms of the principle of *belief congruence* appears to be an important factor feeding ethnocentric tendencies. Further, ethnocentrism, once established in one group, tends to beget ethnocentrism (indeed, even hostility) in other groups with which it interacts.[20]

The Out-Group Viewed as Deviant

Where a people are strongly ethnocentric, it is not difficult for them to perceive the out-group as an object for loathing. The out-group is "a symbol of strangeness, evil, and danger to the community as a whole. His existence disturbs the order of life in the sense in which order is understood and experienced by the in-group. His customs are scandalous, his rites sacrilegious. His laws are incomprehensible, so that he appears to be lawless. His gods are false gods." [21] In brief, *the out-group often appears to be engaged in deviant acts.*

[19] Milton Rokeach and Louis Mezei, "Race and Shared Belief as Factors in Social Choice," *Science*, 151 (January 14, 1966), 167–172.

[20] See: William R. Catton, Jr. and Sung Chick Hong, "Apparent Minority Ethnocentrism and Majority Antipathy," *American Sociological Review*, 27 (1962), 178–191, and Willem Doise, "Intergroup Relations and Polarization of Individual and Collective Judgments," *Journal of Personality and Social Psychology*, 12 (1969), 136–143.

[21] Hans Speier, "The Social Types of War," *American Journal of Sociology*, 46 (1941), 445.

We have suggested, then, that it is not difficult for the in-group to perceive the out-group—when judged by in-group standards—as being somehow ridiculous, evil, scandalous, sacrilegious, or the like. We find numerous illustrations of this. The Gusii of East Africa ridicule uncircumcised children for their childishness and accuse an older boy still uncircumcised of cowardice. This view provides the basis for a similar image of their uncircumcising Luo neighbors. By the same token, the Gusii child-rearing emphasis on modesty regarding nudity and elimination provides a familiar association base for their view of both Luo and Kipsigis, since both differ from the Gusii in these practices.[22] Bruner describes a similar situation in the Dakotas, between the Hidatsa Indians and the local ranchers of European extraction. As described by Bruner, the moral requirement of immediate sharing was fully imperative for the Hidatsa as was the imperative to thrift and providence among the White ranchers. Both viewed the behavior of the out-group as evil.[23]

In-Group Virtues Become Out-Group Vices

The above discussion deals with characteristics on which groups differ. We note similar effects for certain traits on which groups are similar, but in which the behavior of the out-group is *perceived* in a *different* context than comparable behavior within the in-group. It is often alleged, for instance, that Jews are disliked because they are ambitious, aggressive, and materialistic, a view that rests on the assumption that these traits are viewed as undesirable, regardless of the group to which they are applied. Yet a study by Saenger and Flowerman of 292 college students reveals that this is not the case. Only 28 per cent of the students viewed materialistic behavior as undesirable; 25 per cent disapproved of aggressiveness; 17 per cent, of emotionality; and 3 per cent, of ambitiousness, the trait most frequently ascribed to Jews. Further, the students described *both* Americans and Jews as aggressive, ambitious, industrious, materialistic, efficient, practical, and intelligent. And interestingly enough, there was one group to whom the students ascribed an even greater proportion of "typically" Jewish characteristics: businessmen.[24]

[22] R. A. LeVine and B. B. Le Vine, *Nyansongo, a Gusii Community in Kenya* (New York: John Wiley & Sons, Inc., 1966).

[23] Edward M. Bruner, "Primary Group Experience and the Process of Acculturation," *American Anthropologist*, 58 (1956), 605–623.

[24] Gerhart Saenger and Samuel Flowerman, "Stereotypes and Prejudicial Attitudes," *Human Relations*, 7 (1954), 217–238.

These findings are summarized in Table 3–1. Thus ethnocentrism makes in-group virtues into out-group vices.

TABLE 3–1   Stereotypes Considered Most Typical of Jews, Americans, and Businessmen *

Stereotype	Jews		Americans		Businessmen	
	Per Cent	Rank	Per Cent	Rank	Per Cent	Rank
Ambitious	71	1	67	1	82	1
Industrious	57	2	62	2	68	4
Intelligent	57	3	44	8	67	6
Aggressive	53	4	44	7	65	7
Shrewd	53	5	18	15	59	8
Materialistic	39	6	56	3	67	5
Efficient	37	7	49	5	69	3
Practical	36	8	48	6	77	2
Liberal	36	9	31	9	7	15
Mercenary	31	10	24	12	38	9

* The table is based on 292 cases and arranged in declining rank order of the stereotypes ascribed to Jews. The rank order relates to 26 stereotypes given to the subjects in a checklist.

Source: Gerhart Saenger and Samuel Flowerman, "Stereotypes and Prejudicial Attitudes," *Human Relations*, 1 (1954), 220. By permission.

Robert K. Merton also notes how the very same behavior may undergo a complete change of evaluation in its transition from the in-group to the out-group:

Did Lincoln work far into the night? This testifies that he was industrious, resolute, perseverant, and eager to realize his capacities to the full. Do the out-group Jews or Japanese keep these same hours? This only bears witness to their sweatshop mentality, their ruthless undercutting of American standards, their unfair competitive practices. Is the in-group hero frugal, thrifty, and sparing? Then the out-group villain is stingy, miserly and penny-pinching. All honor is due the in-group Abe for his having been smart, shrewd, and intelligent and, by the same token, all contempt is owing the out-group Abes for their being sharp, cunning, crafty, and too clever by far.[25]

Connotative Meanings of Color Names

In considering the part ethnocentrism played in the rise of racism, it is instructive to consider the initial English confrontation with and impressions of Africans.[26] Apparently English voyagers did not

[25] Robert K. Merton, *Social Theory and Social Structure*, rev. ed. (New York: The Free Press of Glencoe, Inc., 1957), 428. By permission of the publishers.

[26] The discussion that follows is in part adapted from Winthrop D. Jordan, *White Over Black* (Chapel Hill: The University of North Carolina Press, 1968), Chapter 1.

touch upon the shores of West Africa until after 1550, virtually a century after Prince Henry the Navigator had launched a sustained Portuguese thrust southward around Africa in route to the Orient. The English found the peoples of Africa very different from themselves, differences that they tended to view in an ethnocentric fashion: their religion was un-Christian ("heathen"); their manner of living was anything but English ("savage"); and they seemed to be a sexually "lustful" and "uninhibited" people.

Color, however, was for the English the most arresting characteristic of the Africans. The English actually described Africans as *black*, an exaggerated term itself suggesting that the African's complexion had a powerful impact upon English perceptions. In England prior to African contacts, perhaps more than among southern European nations, the concept of blackness was already loaded with intense ethnocentric meaning. The *Oxford English Dictionary* describes the meaning of "black" before the sixteenth century in these terms:

Deeply stained with dirt; soiled, dirty, foul. . . . Having dark or deadly purposes, malignant; pertaining to or involving death, deadly; baneful, disastrous, sinister. . . . Foul, iniquitous, atrocious, horrible, wicked. . . . Indicating disgrace, censure, liability to punishment, etc.

Black, then, was an emotionally partisan color, denoting baseness, evil, danger, and repulsion. In direct opposition was the concept of "whiteness"; no other colors were so frequently employed to denote polarization: white and black implied purity and filthiness, virginity and sin, virtue and baseness, beauty and ugliness, beneficence and evil, God and the devil.[27]

These early connotative meanings of color names persist in the modern period. A cursory examination of *Webster's New Collegiate Dictionary* reveals the adverse implications attached to the word *black:* blackball, blackbook, blackguard, black-letter, blacklist, blackmail, black dog, black sheep, etc.[28] Moreover, Williams found that the connotative meanings of the various color names (presented in a nonracial context) are strikingly different and that they are relatively stable across both regional and racial lines: the connotative

[27] For an excellent discussion of "Negro" as a contrast conception see Lewis C. Copeland, "The Negro as a Contrast Conception," in Edgar T. Thompson, ed., *Race Relations and the Race Problem* (Durham, N.C.: Duke University Press, 1939), 152–179. Also see: Roger Bastide, "Color, Racism, and Christianity," *Daedalus*, 96 (Spring, 1967), 312–327.

[28] Simon Podain, "Language and Prejudice toward Negroes," *Phylon*, 17 (1956), 390–394.

meaning of the color name *white* is "good," "active," and "weak," while the color name *black* is "bad," "passive," and "strong." [29] In still another study among Caucasian college students from both the South and Midwest, Williams discovered that racial concepts (e.g., Negro, Caucasian) have connotative meanings similar to the color names with which they are linked by the color-coding custom. He suggests that such color connotations are learned early in childhood and may influence the subsequent development of racial attitudes. Among Black students, however, Williams found an emerging resistance to the color-coding practice with its connotative significance; this tendency is most apparent in the efforts of the Black Muslims and certain other Black nationalist groups to reverse the conventional symbolism by associating black with goodness and white with badness.[30]

But are the emotional reactions and associations triggered by various colors generalized to people? Will, for instance, individuals who have a negative emotional reaction to black also experience negative feelings for people whose skins are dark? In theory, such a possibility seems highly plausible. Artists, for instance, have long used to advantage the assumption that colors have the capacity to elicit directly certain types of feelings or emotions.[31] Further, research by Harbin and Williams also reveals that emotions generated by color can be generalized to objects continuously paired with color.[32]

COMPETITION

By itself ethnocentrism need not lead to intergroup conflict or racism.[33] The Cossacks and Tungus—the former a Caucasian, agri-

[29] John E. Williams, "Connotations of Color Names among Negroes and Caucasians," *Perceptual & Motor Skills,* 18 (1964), 721–731.

[30] John E. Williams, "Connotations of Racial Concepts and Color Names," *Journal of Personality and Social Psychology,* 3 (1966), 531–540 and John E. Williams, Richard D. Tucker, and Frances Y. Dunham, "Changes in the Connotations of Color Names among Negroes and Caucasians: 1963–1969," *Journal of Personality and Social Psychology,* 19 (1971), 222–228. A replication of the research among German students revealed that the above findings are not specific to American culture (and language systems) but have greater generality within Western culture. See: John E. Williams and Dorothy Jean Carter, "Connotations of Racial Concepts and Color Names in Germany," *Journal of Social Psychology,* 72 (1967), 19–26.

[31] Gergen, *op. cit.,* 395–397.

[32] S. P. Harbin and J. E. Williams, "Conditioning of Color Connotations," *Perceptual and Motor Skills,* 22 (1966), 217–218.

[33] Noel, *op. cit.,* 159.

cultural, and sedentary people; the latter, a Mongoloid, reindeer-herding, nomadic people—lived in peace for several generations in northwestern Manchuria as independent but economically interdependent societies. Each group was characterized by a general ethnocentric preference for the in-group and its customs. Apparently the conflict potential was neutralized by low population density, outside foreign pressures that drew the two peoples together, economic and cultural complementarity, and the *absence* of competition.[34] It is this latter matter, competition, to which we now turn our attention.

Within any social system people act in relation to certain values that can be shared by everyone. These values are not scarce in the sense that one individual's sharing in them reduces or interferes with others' enjoyment. Religious salvation and national prestige are conspicuous illustrations of this. The adherents of a religious faith can all participate in a great many of its values, for example, salvation, without detracting from the participation of others. By the same token, all Americans tend to share in any increase or decrease in national prestige. National prestige as such is "participated in" rather than "divided up."[35] On the other hand, there are some values within any society that are scarce and divisible, such values as *wealth, power,* and *status.* In each instance, the more there is for the one, the less there is for others.[36]

People typically seek to improve their outcome with regard to those things that they define as good, worthwhile, and desirable. Where the outcomes of two distinct groups are perceived to be mutually exclusive and legitimate, so that each can realize what it defines as a rightful outcome only at the expense of the other, competition will ensue.[37] In other words, if two groups both believe they have a just claim upon the same scarce, divisible "good" things, their relationship will be characterized by competition—even conflict. Generally speaking, the attitudes that the members of a group evolve toward an out-group tend to be consistent with their perceptions of the relationships they have with the out-group. Hence *where the relations between two groups are perceived as competi-*

[34] Lindgren, *op. cit.,* 605–621.
[35] Robin M. Williams, Jr., *The Reduction of Intergroup Tensions* (New York: Social Science Research Council, 1947), 55.
[36] *Ibid.,* 55.
[37] The condition "all other things being equal" should be understood here. Since "other conditions" are rarely "equal," this is a rigorous limitation on the generalization.

tive, negative attitudes—prejudice—will be generated toward the out-group.

The hypothesis that intergroup competition for scarce values begets prejudice, discrimination, and racism is one that abounds in race relations literature.[38] Several studies lend support to this hypothesis. Experiments by Sherif, for instance, have shown that in the absence of institutionalized control, boys' groups normally develop very hostile, discriminatory relationships after a relatively short period of competition in sports and games.[39] Similarly, Blake and Manton, on the basis of their experiments dealing with competition, suggest that a loss in competition leads to hostility toward the winning group. Even though the members of the competing groups reported that they understood the competitor's view as well as they understood those of their own group, they in fact, did not. In all groups, the members knew their own group's position best and were inclined toward distortion in their comprehension of the other group's position.[40] Further, research suggests that winners and losers in competition feel uncomfortable in one another's presence, and that the resulting difficulties in interpersonal encounters can contribute to intergroup prejudice.[41]

Hamblin, using quota samples of White adults in St. Louis, also found some support for the competition hypothesis.[42] His study found (1) a correlation of .41 between frustration experienced by Whites in *past* competition with Blacks and the tendency of Whites to discriminate against Blacks and (2) a correlation of .62 between a *fear* of equal status competition with Blacks (the prospect of *future* competition) and the tendency of Whites to discriminate against Blacks.

Thus far in our consideration we have not differentiated between wealth, power, or status factors. It has probably occurred to some

---

[38] See, for instance: Hubert M. Blalock, Jr., *Toward a Theory of Minority-Group Relations* (New York: John Wiley & Sons, Inc., 1967), 49, and R. A. Schermerhorn, *Comparative Ethnic Relations* (New York: Random House, 1970), 245.

[39] Muzafer Sherif, "Experiments in Group Conflict," *Scientific American*, 195 (1956), 54–58. See Chapter 6 of this book for a lengthy review of this study.

[40] Robert R. Blake and Jane S. Manton, "Comprehension of Own and of Out-group Positions under Intergroup Competition," *Journal of Conflict Resolution*, 5 (1961), 309.

[41] Jacob M. Rabbie and Murray Horowitz, "Arousal of Ingroup-Outgroup Bias by a Chance Win or Loss," *Journal of Personality and Social Psychology*, 13 (1969), 269–277.

[42] Robert J. Hamblin, "The Dynamics of Racial Discrimination," *Social Problems*, 10 (1962), 103–120.

readers that a favorable position with regard to either wealth, power, or status tends to be associated with a favorable position with regard to the other two. Although often true, however, it is not always the case. By way of illustration, the sheriff of many rural counties may possess considerable political power but be ranked low in economic wealth or status. Similarly, a member of one of the aristocratic "old" families of the South may enjoy considerable status but have little in the way of power or wealth. And the "new rich" may have wealth but lack comparable power or status, as in the case of some Texas oil barons. Since some writers tend to stress the role of one variable over the others, let us focus our attention upon each variable in turn.

Economic Competition

We have noted that there appears to be some foundation to the notion that groups in competition for scarce values often develop prejudice toward one another. Some writers argue that economic competition plays a particularly critical role. Donald Young notes that within American history there is a direct correlation between peaks of agitation against minorities and the valleys of economic depression. The major "anti-foreign" movements—the Native American Party in the 1830s, the Know-Nothing Party of the 1850s, the American Protective Association of the late nineteenth century, and the post-World War I Ku Klux Klan—won their largest following in hard times. Various regional movements—against Chinese, Japanese, and Filipinos on the West Coast, Italians in Louisiana, and French Canadians in New England—have similarly coincided with economic difficulties in these areas.[43] At least two forces appear to operate in such settings. First, hard times have been associated with widespread unemployment that has intensified intergroup competition for jobs. Second, the frustrations associated with unemployment may breed hostile and aggressive impulses that are vented upon minority groups.

Race riots and violence have often been associated with intense intergroup competition. The 1919 Chicago race riot centered in two areas: the area about the stockyards, where Blacks had entered the meat packing industry in thousands and were accused of taking White men's jobs while the Whites were away in the army; and in

[43] Donald Young, *Research Memorandum on Minority Peoples in the Depression* (New York: Social Science Research Council, 1937), 133–141.

the Hyde Park area, where the chief grievance was the financial loss to White owners in Black residence areas, allegedly through depreciation of property values. In the Atlanta riot of 1906 one of the chief incitements of violence was the circulation of cards showing Black carpenters and bricklayers building houses, thus menacing the economic security of White craftsmen.[44] And in the 1943 Detroit riot, Blacks were in sharp competition with Whites for housing accommodations in the areas surrounding the Black ghetto of Paradise Valley, while competition for other goods and services, already scarce in the wartime economy, intensified antagonisms.[45] Further, in a comparative study of racial violence in the United States, Grimshaw found that, except during the peak of rioting, the incidence of violence was greatest in contested urban areas where Blacks and Whites were directly competing for housing and other accommodations.[46]

Power Gains

Power may be broadly defined as the ability to control or influence the behavior of others. Striving for power, of course, can be quite normal. In the normal person, feelings of power may be born of the realization of his own superior strength, whether it be physical strength, mental capacities, maturity, or wisdom. Striving for power, however, may also involve compensation for what are experienced as psychological shortcomings—the product of anxiety, hatred, and feelings of inferiority. In a word, normal striving for power is born of strength; the compensatory, of weakness. Many Americans may choose the route of power-striving precisely because within our society power is associated with security.[47] The striving for power can serve a number of functions for the individual. In the first place, it functions as a protection against helplessness, which is one of the basic elements in anxiety. In the second place, it functions as a protection against the danger of feeling, or being regarded as, insignificant.[48] Power-striving, then, may not only be derived from cultural, but also from personality sources.

[44] Charles S. Johnson, "Race Relations and Social Change," in Edgar T. Thompson, ed., *Race Relations and the Race Problem* (Durham, N.C.: Duke University Press, 1939), 271–303.
[45] Alfred McClung Lee and Norman D. Humphrey, *Race Riot* (New York: Holt, Rinehart, & Winston, Inc., 1943).
[46] Allen D. Grimshaw, "Urban Racial Violence in the United States," *American Journal of Sociology*, 64 (1960), 114–115.
[47] Karen Horney, *The Neurotic Personality of Our Time* (New York: W. W. Norton & Co., Inc., 1937), 162–163.
[48] *Ibid.*, 166–167.

Evidence points to the fact that high levels of prejudice may be associated with power-seeking personalities.[49] Power may be sought as an end in itself. Since power is commonly equated with the dominant racial or ethnic group, weakness—the absence of power— can be overcome through gaining a sense of participation in the dominant group. The power which one lacks but strives for can be realized, or so it seems, from identification with a powerful group, e.g., "the White race." The minority group is seen as weak and in- effective. Its weakness invites attack from the would-be powerful. It becomes a means to assert, "I am powerful." But, being weak— helpless and insignificant—the individual realizes by this means a power that is not genuine in that it is not rooted in the personality itself. Accordingly the power has to be repeatedly asserted and demonstrated in hopes of proving to oneself and the world that one actually is powerful. But the constant and excessive reassertion of prejudicial attitudes via statements, jokes and jibes, and prejudicial behavior betrays the precarious status of the individual's sense of adequacy and strength. On the other hand, the weakness of the minority serves to outrage the would-be powerful by reminding the individual of his own weakness. Thus, the minority must be at- tacked, even destroyed.

Racism, anti-Semitism, and prejudice in general may also be used and exploited by political leaders in the pursuit of power. By attrib- uting evils and difficulties to an out-group, members of the in-group can escape feelings of blame for their own failures or for failures in cherished institutions. It is painful to admit and to recognize such failure. How much more convenient and comforting it is to place the responsibility upon another! Thus political leaders throughout history have found it expedient to divert the hostility and aggressiveness of the in-group to out-groups. Hitler and Goeb- bels were masters at the art. The German people—frustrated by defeat in World War I, plagued by economic chaos, disgruntled by the problems of life in general—were given the Jews, Reds, and in- ternational bankers as targets upon which to vent their rage. Rus- sians and Chinese—restless under the failure of dreams for a "new world" and a "new life" to materialize and by the inevitable frus- trations of life—are presented with "Yankees," "foreign imperialists," and "Wall Street capitalists" as permissible targets for hate and

[49] T. W. Adorno *et al., The Authoritarian Personality* (New York: Harper & Row, Inc., 1950).

aggression. In ancient Rome, it was the Christian minority that was used as the target to divert attention from the problems, failures, and corruption within the Roman state. Tertullian observed, "If the Tiber rose to the walls of the city, if the inundation of the Nile failed to give the fields enough water, if the heavens did not send rain, if an earthquake occurred, if famine threatened, if pestilence raged, the cry resounded: 'Throw the Christians to the lions.'"

Political leaders need not create racial or ethnic prejudices; there is no hard evidence to suggest that they do. They may, however, capitalize upon incipient or marked tendencies toward prejudice among the in-group and exploit and intensify these tendencies. The late V. O. Key, Jr., an authority on southern politics, stressed the view that for decades Whites of the "Black Belt" counties constituted the core and backbone of the political South.[50] Historically the Black Belt made up only a small part of the area of the South, although it was here that large-scale-plantation or multiple-unit agriculture prevailed. And it was here that were located most of the large agricultural operators who oversaw the work of many tenants, sharecroppers, and laborers, most of whom were Black. Although the Black Belt Whites were few in number (Blacks constituted a majority of the population of the Black Belt), Key argued that their unity and political skill enabled them "to run a shoestring into decisive power at critical junctures in southern political history."[51] It was this group of Whites who were the prime movers in the fight to protect slave property and in the establishment of the Confederate States. Later, with conservative allies in the cities, they put down the radical Populist movement. And through the propagation of the racist position, they impressed on the entire South a philosophy agreeable to their needs and succeeded for decades in maintaining a regional unity in national politics to defend these necessities.[52] Their major vehicle for decades was the Democratic party.

In recent years some politicians have resorted to campaign "code words" with racial implications. The Fair Campaign Practices Committee has noted that new forms of racial smear have developed that are much more difficult to handle than earlier more blatant appeals to racism. Among the suspect euphemisms are "crime in the streets" and "law and order." The Committee has suggested that the oblique

[50] V. O. Key, Jr., *Southern Politics* (New York: Alfred A. Knopf, Inc., 1950).
[51] *Ibid.*, 6.
[52] *Ibid.*, 5–11.

appeals to racial prejudice are not limited to the South and South-west:

In fact, candidates who would never use the word "nigger" nor any of its slurring variations, are using other terms which apparently carry a similar connotation. They are using the racial shorthand in areas of the country where an outright expression of racism would bring immediate social—and political— ostracism. These forms suggest, rather than state, the campaigner's intent. For instance, instead of saying he is opposed to open housing, the sophisticated racist proclaims, "your home is your castle," and leaves the rest unsaid.[53]

Hence, the exploitation of racism by politicians in pursuit of political power persists.

Status Gains

Most of us enjoy the feeling that we are not just average but per-haps, at least to some degree, special and important. We like to identify with a winning football team, the "best" school, fraternity, or community, and so it goes. Indeed, our American culture places considerable emphasis upon status. Yet not all Americans are able to realize the status that they desire.[54] For members of the dominant group, however, status is acquired simply through the fact that they are a White or a Gentile. By virtue of one's dominant group mem-bership, an individual can acquire a sense of status that his own achievements might not command. Dollard asserts in his study of a southern town:

In the North a man may have a prestige position because he has money, or is learned, or is old; the novelty in the South is that one has prestige solely because one is white. The gain here is very simple. It consists in the fact that a member of the white caste has an automatic right to demand forms of behavior from Negroes which serve to increase his own self-esteem. To put it another way, it consists of an illumination of the image of the self, an expansive feeling of being something special and valuable. It might be com-pared to the illusion of greatness that comes with early stages of alcoholization, except that prestige is not an illusion but a steadily repeated fact.[55]

Membership, then, in the dominant group can take on enormous emotional significance for status-starved individuals. Thus South-ern "Jim Crow" (segregation) laws have provided numerous func-

[53] "Campaign Smears Held More Subtle," *New York Times,* September 18, 1968, p. 3.
[54] Robert K. Merton, *op. cit.,* 121–194.
[55] John Dollard, *Caste and Class in a Southern Town,* 3d ed. (New York: Double-day & Co., Inc., 1957), 174. Some authorities feel that this characterization by Dollard represents a gross overstatement of the situation.

tions for Whites, especially those whose statuses are comparable to those of minority Blacks. As Woodward has carefully documented, the passage of most "Jim Crow" legislation took place at the turn of the twentieth century when poor Whites were gaining political leverage, while remaining economically little better off than Blacks.[56] The symbolic value of these various forms of segregation seemingly are highest for those whose status claims are otherwise negligible.[57] By the same token, Whites may refuse to interact socially with Blacks because they fear they would *lose* status merely by associating with a low-status person.[58]

Status concerns have played a part in the slow, at times imperceptible, progress made in eliminating *de facto* school segregation. Middle class parents seek to pass on to their children a status at least as good as their own. College professors are a case in point. Although often strong advocates of equality, they nonetheless want for their children "equality-plus." They generally attempt to give their children an elite education of the sort required by their own occupation, and this proves difficult in class-heterogeneous schools. They prefer token integration of students, but not enough to interfere with the skills essential to an educational elite. It is not so much that they are anti-Black as pro-middle class. Moreover, people learn fashionable circumlocutions far faster than they change their racist habits. Any number of New York mothers recite liberal platitudes in one breath and in the next declare that "New York City schools are impossible," which is the reason they give for moving to Scarsdale. Yet they remain tactfully vague about *why* the schools are impossible.[59]

The status gains derived by dominant group members may often be complex. A consideration of the post-1954 (following the Supreme Court's school desegregation ruling) Ku Klux Klan is most revealing. The author was able to locate the names and occupations

[56] C. Vann Woodward, *The Stranger Career of Jim Crow*, rev. ed. (New York: Oxford University Press, 1957).

[57] Paradoxically, it was these very symbolic forms of segregation (for instance, at lunchcounters and on buses) that were given a high priority in the original Black "sit-in" and boycott movements; symbolic barriers can be especially irksome to a minority group since they serve as continuous reminders of thear subordinate status. Blalock, *op. cit.*, 165.

[58] *Ibid.*, 61–70. Especially helpful are the propositions Blalock provides on pages 67–70.

[59] John Finley Scott and Lois Heyman Scott, "They Are Not So Much Anti-Negro as Pro-Middle Class," *The New York Times Magazine*, March 24, 1968, pages 46–47, 107, 109, 110, 117, 119–120.

of 153 Klansmen.[60] They could be classified in four occupational groupings: (1) skilled workers (e.g., garage mechanics, machinists, carpenters, and stonemasons), (2) marginal small businessmen (e.g., small building-trade contractors and proprietors of food markets, grills, and gasoline stations), (3) marginal white-collar workers (e.g., grocery-store clerks, service-station attendants, policemen, and salesmen), and (4) transportation workers (primarily truck drivers) and unskilled and semi-skilled workers in the textile, construction, automotive, aircraft, coal, and steel industries. The sample was of unknown representativeness, and it was undoubtedly biased, yet it probably reflected the occupational breadth of the Klan's membership.

Two-thirds of the Klansmen were found in the first three categories. These positions—skilled workers, marginal businessmen, and marginal white-collar workers—are commonly ranked within the status hierarchy in the upper rungs of the working class and the lower rungs of the middle class. They occupy an intermediate position in the social structure between clear-cut "blue-collar" manual jobs and "white-collar" jobs—between the "working class" and the "middle class"—positions that are somewhat hazy and vague in their placement in one or the other of the socioeconomic class divisions. American society, with its emphasis upon success, its belief in an open class system, and its high valuation of middle-class status, places such individuals in a difficult position. Their status ranking tends to be nebulous and ambiguous. At best they have a toe hold within the middle class; at worst, middle-class status seems almost —but not quite—within their grasp. As a consequence their status tends to be insecure and they are anxious concerning their placement in the status hierarchy. Torn between the status America says they *ought* to have and what they in fact *actually* have, they feel disgruntled, discontented, and frustrated.

They tend to be "status starved." The Rev. James W. (Catfish") Cole told newsmen, after his group was routed by Lumbee Indians in an episode gaining national headlines, "I don't care what you write. Just be sure you write it. The name is easy to remember. The initials are J. C. as in Jesus Christ." Society gives such individuals a way out. They are still White, and they are still Americans,

---

[60] James W. Vander Zanden, "The Klan Revival," *American Journal of Sociology*, LXV (1960), 456–462.

in a region where such things are most important. They seize upon those status elements which are available to them, but elevate and magnify them out of proportion to their place in the social order. They *overconform* to the institutionalized caste pattern of the South and to patriotic identification with America. Judged by White group standards, their adherence to the dominant White racial values and Americanism is excessive. This leads to conflict with other values, most particularly the sanctity of the individual and of private property.

This exaggerated magnification of values commonly esteemed in America is reflected in this statement appearing in the handbook of the U.S. Klans, Knights of the Ku Klux Klan:

> We invite all men who can qualify to become citizens of the Invisible Empire, to approach the portal of our beneficient domain, join us in our noble work of extending its boundaries, and in disseminating the gospel of Klankraft, thereby encouraging, conserving, protecting and making vital the fraternal relationship in the presence of an honorable clannishness; to share with us the sacred duty of protecting womanhood; to maintain forever the God-given supremacy of the White Race; to commemorate the holy and chivalric achievement of our fathers; to safeguard the sacred rights, privileges and institutions of our civil government; to bless mankind and to keep eternally ablaze the sacred fire of a fervent devotion to a pure Americanism.

Secrecy plays a role similar to exaggerated conformity. The strongly emphasized exclusion of all outsiders makes for a feeling of possession. That which is secret and mysterious has a quality of importance and essentiality. By the possession of such secrets, the Klansman secures prestige. Similarly, Klan secrets give the Klansman a highly tangible and explicit group identification, since they set him apart from the amorphous mass of humanity. Without secure anchorage in the class structure, he compensates via the anchorage afforded by Klan membership.

Lacking prestive-giving symbols in the world-at-large, Klansmen establish their own world, an "Invisible Empire." It is a world with its own esteemed symbols—its grotesque, differentially valued purple, red, green and white gowns, its elaborate honorific insignia, and its exaggerated status-exalting nomenclature of Imperial Wizard, Grand Dragon, Grand Titan, Grand Giant, and Exalted Cyclops. Likewise, questions of power and staus had been a major source of Klan factionalism and splintering. The Klan, then, may afford any number of status gains for its members.

Vested Interests

Closely associated with the hypothesis that intergroup competition breeds racism is another hypothesis: a racial or ethnic group that commands a disproportionate advantage over another group in access to wealth, power, and/or status evolves and employs prejudice and discrimination as instruments for defending its position of privilege and advantage. One of the clearest formulations of a vested interest approach is suggested by Herbert Blumer, who views prejudice and discrimination as arising from a sense of "group position." [61] The dominant group, Blumer asserts, comes to view itself as being entitled to certain rights and privileges. These rights and privileges may include the ownership of choice property, the right to certain jobs, occupations, and professions, the claim to certain positions of power, the right to exclusive membership in particular institutions including schools, churches, and recreation facilities, the claim to certain positions of social prestige and to the display of the symbols associated with these positions, and the claim to certain areas of intimacy and privacy.

In Blumer's view, race prejudice arises from a fear that the minority threatens or will threaten the advantaged position of the dominant group:

> The source of race prejudice lies in a felt challenge to this sense of group position. The challenge, one must recognize, may come in many different ways. It may be in the form of an affront to feelings of group superiority; it may be in the form of attempts at familiarity or transgressing the boundary line of group exclusiveness; it may be in the form of encroachment at countless points of proprietary claim; it may be a challenge to power and privilege; it may take the form of economic competition. Race prejudice is a defensive reaction to such challenging of the sense of group position. It consists of the disturbed feelings, usually of marked hostility, that are thereby aroused. As such, race prejudice is a protective device. It functions, however shortsightedly, to preserve the integrity and the position of the dominant group.[62]

Prejudices arises, Blumer asserts, through a collective process. It operates chiefly through the media of mass communication in which spokesmen for a racial or ethnic group—public figures of prominence, leaders of powerful organizations, and intellectual and social elites—publicly characterize another group. Such spokesmen foster feelings

---

[61] Herbert Blumer, "Race Prejudice as a Sense of Group Position," in Jitsuichi Masuoka and Preston Valien, eds., *Race Relations* (Chapel Hill: The University of North Carolina Press, 1961), 215–227.
[62] *Ibid.*, 222.

of racial superiority, racial distance, and a claim to certain rights and privileges. Other members of the dominant group, although often having different views and feelings, fall into line lest they be subjected to in-group ostracism. In this fashion a sense of group position—with its encompassing matrix of prejudice—becomes a general kind of orientation. It is a hypothesis, then, that views the dominant group as having a vested interest in another group's subordination; the dominant group has a stake in preserving an order characterized by privilege and advantage. Prejudice becomes an instrument for defending this privilege and advantage.

In keeping with this hypothesis, some writers emphasize the part that the economic factor played in the appearance of racism. The emergence and elaboration of racist ideas were closely associated in time with the advent and development of Black slavery. An integral aspect of slavery was the economic gain realized by White slaveowners. Accordingly, it has been concluded by some and implicitly implied by others that the racist dogma evolved primarily as a means to excuse and sanction the institution of slavery in general and the economic exploitation of slaves in particular.

Initially, Black slavery in America was explained primarily on religious grounds—the Black was a heathen and a barbarian, a descendant of Noah's son Ham, cursed by God and doomed to be a servant forever as the price of an ancient sin. With the passing of time and the conversion of Blacks to Christianity, the heathen or infidel buttress no longer constituted a satisfactory defense of slavery. Gradually, then, the biological argument came into prominence. The Black's physical appearance was increasingly made the foundation for the assignment to him of a fundamental physical, mental, and moral inferiority.[63]

In the present period there is evidence that some Whites benefit occupationally from the presence and low status of Blacks. The primary beneficiaries apparently are White workers in proprietary, managerial, sales, and upper-level manual occupations. Many

[63] See: Winthrop D. Jordon, "Modern Tensions and the Origins of American Slavery," *Journal of Southern History*, 28 (1962), 18–30, and *White Over Black* (Chapel Hill: The University of North Carolina Press, 1968); Carl N. Degler, "Slavery and the Genesis of American Race Prejudice," *Comparative Studies in Society and History*, 2 (1959), 49–66; Oscar and Mary Handlin, "The Origins of the Southern Labor System," *William and Mary Quarterly*, 3rd Series, VII (April, 1950), 199–222; David Brion Davis, *The Problem of Slavery in Western Culture* (Ithaca: Cornell University Press, 1966); and William Sumner Jenkins, *Pro-Slavery Thought in the Old South* (Chapel Hill: The University of North Carolina Press, 1935).

Whites in these occupations enjoy what have been termed "White bonus jobs"—positions filled by Whites that would be filled by Blacks if Blacks were not subordinated and that would not exist if Blacks were not present. The Kerner Commission estimates, for instance, that 1.3 million non-White men would have to be upgraded occupationally in order to make the Black job distribution roughly equal to the White; this would in turn jeopardize the privileged position of 1.3 million White workers. Other beneficiaries of Black subordination are White housewives who employ Black domestic workers. And there are those White professionals who carry out the "dirty work" of administering the lives of the ghetto poor: social workers, school teachers, urban development people, and police. These Whites, then, have a stake—a vested interest—in Black subordination; the racist ideology is congruent with their economic interests.[64]

UNEQUAL POWER

As we observed in Chapter 1, inequality of power is a defining characteristic of dominant-minority group relationships. Where two groups are unequal in power, the more powerful group is able to actualize its claim to an unequal and larger share of the socially defined "good" things (unless prevented by norms that restrain exploitation of the weaker by the more powerful as in the case of Quaker settlers in Pennsylvania). While the interaction between dominant and minority groups is never a one-way street, nevertheless the interchange that occurs is unequal and uneven. Power is the vehicle by which subordination and superordination are effected.

Within human affairs force constitutes the final court of appeals; there is no appeal from force except the exercise of superior force. H. Rap Brown, a Black militant, makes the point in these terms:

Look what the brothers did in Plainfield [New Jersey]. The brothers got their stuff. They got 46 automatic weapons. Then they went back to their community . . . and they told the peckerwood cop: "Don't come in my community." He didn't come. And the only reason he didn't come was 'cause he

---

[64] For papers dealing with this matter and statistical procedures for measuring white gains, see: Norval D. Glenn, "Occupational Benefits to Whites from the Subordination of Negroes," *American Sociological Review*, 28 (1963), 443–448; "Reply to Cutright on Negro Subordination," *American Sociological Review*, 30 (1965), 416; "White Gains from Negro Subordination," *Social Problems*, 14 (1966), 159–178; and Phillips Cutright, "Negro Subordination and White Gains," *American Sociological Review*, 30 (1965), 110–112.

didn't want to get killed. And the brothers had the material to do it. They had 46 carbines down there. That's what he respects—power. He respects that kind of power.[65]

Clearly the ability to take life—to effect physical violence—can constitute an important instrument of social control as well as an instrument for challenging that same social control.

To be effective, however, force need not be implemented; it need merely remain in the wings, so to speak, ready at any moment to make its appearance. Many sociologists, in recognition of this fact, distinguish between force and power. *Force* refers to the *application* of sanctions; it is the implementation of coercive remedies. *Power*, in contrast, entails the *capacity* or *ability* to introduce force within a social situation; it is the potential for instituting force but *not* the actual implementation of force itself.[66]

European "expansion," beginning in the fifteenth and sixteenth centuries and resting largely upon power and force deriving from superior weaponry, brought with it a variety of outcomes. Where the native population consisted of small, sparsely settled, nomadic groups (as, for instance, in Brazil, the United States, and the Western Cape in South Africa), the characteristic pattern of contact was frontier expansion of the Whites punctuated by sporadic skirmishes, raids, and guerrilla warfare. Generally the outcome was virtual genocide of the natives or encapsulation of their scattered remnants on reservations. Where, in contrast, the European conquerors encountered large, densely settled, politically centralized, agricultural, and even urban nation-states (as in Mexico), the outcome was quite different:

Military conquest was not accompanied by extermination but by subjugation. The dominant group established its control either by "beheading" the indigenous societies and substituting itself as a new aristocracy, or by using the ruling class of the defeated peoples and ruling through it. In both situations the native masses became politically subordinate and economically exploited through some form of serfdom, forced or "contract" labor, debt peonage, or share-cropping tenancy.[67]

Lieberson likewise points to the part differential power plays in determining whether conflict or assimilation ensue when groups

[65] Quoted: Martin Oppenheimer, *The Urban Querrilla* (Chicago: Quadrangle Books, 1969).

[66] Robert Bierstedt, "An Analysis of Social Power," *American Sociological Review*, 15 (1950), 733.

[67] Pierre L. van den Berghe, *Race and Racism* (New York: John Wiley & Sons, Inc., 1967), 125.

come into contact.[68] Most situations of intergroup contact involve at least one indigenous group (a group native to and already established in an area) and at least one group migrating to the area. Either the indigenous or the migrant group may enjoy the power advantage, and hence Lieberson distinguishes between *migrant superordination* and *indigenous superordination.*

Migrant superordination generally occurs when the population migrating to a new contact situation is superior in technology (especially weapons) and is more tightly organized than the indigenous group. These conditions enable the migrant group to impose its political and economic institutions upon the indigenous population. Through its political and economic dominance, the migrant group can effectively cultivate its own cultural practices and maintain its distinct social institutions (educational, family, religious, and so on). In this setting warfare often accompanies the early contacts between the two groups. Even where the initial contact is friendly, conflict is generated as the migrants begin to interfere with the natives' established order. Price notes the following consequences of White invasion and subordination of the indigenous populations of Australia, Canada, New Zealand, and the United States:

> During an opening period of pioneer invasion on moving frontiers the whites decimated the natives with their diseases; occupied their lands by seizure or pseudo-purchase; slaughtered those who resisted; intensified tribal warfare by supplying white weapons; ridiculed and disrupted native religions, society and culture, and generally reduced the unhappy peoples to a state of despondency under which they neither desired to live, nor to have children to undergo similar conditions.[69]

With the passage of time the subordinated indigenous people begins to participate in the economy introduced by the migrant group, a fact that often accentuates the disruption of their native institutions. This, in turn, has frequently fostered both nationalism and a greater sense of racial unity. In many African states, where Blacks were subdivided in tribal groups prior to White contact, racial consciousness and unity among Africans were actually created by White European colonialism. Contact characterized by migrant

---

[68] Stanley Lieberson, "A Societal Theory of Race and Ethnic Relations," *American Sociological Review,* 26 (1961), 902–910. For still another effort to develop a general theory of race relations see R. A. Schermerhorn, "Toward a General Theory of Minority Groups," *Phylon,* 25 (1964), 238–246.

[69] A. Grenfell Price, *White Settlers and Native Peoples* (Melbourne: Georgian House, 1950), 1.

superordination is especially likely to breed a high incidence of racial and ethnic turmoil—in brief, *conflict*.

In contrast with migrant superordination, indigenous superordination entails the political and economic domination of the migrants by the indigenous population. When a population migrates to a subordinate position, Lieberson argues, considerably less conflict results. The movement of many European and Oriental populations to the United States, for example, did not give rise to warfare, nationalism, or long-term conflict. The occasional labor and racial strife marking the history of immigration to the United States is not on the same level as efforts to eliminate or revolutionize a particular social order.

In appraising differences in the effects of migrant and indigenous subordination, it is necessary to consider the options available to the migrants:

> Irish migrants to the United States in the 1840's, for example, although clearly subordinate to native whites of other origins, fared better economically than if they had remained in their mother country. Further, the option of returning to the homeland often exists for populations migrating to subordinate situations. . . . Finally, when contacts between racial and ethnic groups are under the control of the indigenous population, threats of demographic and institutional imbalance are reduced since the superordinate populations can limit the numbers and groups entering. For example, when Oriental migration to the United States threatened whites, sharp cuts were executed in the quotas.[70]

In indigenous superordination, then, conflict is likely to be limited and sporadic, while considerable emphasis is placed upon the *assimilation* of migrants. The history of migration to the United States provides a classic example. Hence, the consequences ensuing from indigenous superordination are in marked contrast to those of migrant superordination.

SUMMARY

The processes involved in the rise of racism are complex and no single sequence of processes holds for all cases. Nonetheless, a number of variables typically come into play in the emergence and initial stabilization of racism: (1) contact; (2) social visibility; (3) ethnocentrism; (4) competition; and (5) unequal power. Contact and social visibility set the stage, so to speak, upon which the

[70] Lieberson, *op. cit.*, 905–906.

other variables come into operation. Contact brings differing peoples into interaction with one another while social visibility provides the clues whereby individuals can be sorted into the categories that underlie such interaction.

Ethnocentrism involves the tendency of group members to appraise peoples of other cultures by the standards of judgment prevailing in their own culture; they assume that in the nature of things other people should be organized according to the same assumptions as prevail within their own group. From this perspective it is not difficult to view the members of the out-group as individuals engaging in deviant acts (e.g., in "savage," "heathen," "lustful" behavior); in brief, it is not difficult to view the out-group as an object for loathing.

Competition is still another ingredient that commonly contributes to the rise of racism. Within any social system some values are scarce and divisible. Where the outcomes of two distinct groups are perceived as mutually exclusive and legitimate, so that each can realize what it defines as a rightful outcome only at the expense of the other, competition (even conflict) ensues. Generally speaking, the attitudes that the members of a group evolve toward an out-group tend to be consistent with their perceptions of the relationships they have with the out-group. Hence where the relations between two groups are perceived as competitive, negative attitudes (prejudice) will be generated toward the out-group.

Inequality of power is a defining characteristic of dominant-minority group relationships. Where two groups are unequal in power, the more powerful group is able to actualize its claim to a larger and unequal share of the socially defined "good" things. Power is the instrument by which superordination and subordination are effected.

4

Maintenance of Racism

In the previous chapter we examined a number of variables that typically come into play in the emergence and initial stabilization of racism. Once racism has arisen within a society, it may continue even when the initial sources contributing to its origin disappear or become minimized. Racism may become deeply embedded in the social and cultural fabric—indeed, in a very real sense it may become *institutionalized* in the manner of other social institutions. It is this matter that is the focus of the chapter.

THE ROLE OF CULTURE

Peoples throughout the world exhibit markedly different patterns of behavior. In part the reason for this is their *culture*. Culture may be thought of as a "set of ready-made definitions of the situation which each participant only slightly retailors in his own idiomatic way."[1] It is a "set of blueprints for action."[2] Thus culture provides us with guideposts or a kind of map for all of life's activities. It tells us how to think and act. It gives us our moral values indicating what is "good" and "bad," "right" and "wrong." Americans "know" that suicide is "evil," "immoral," and "cowardly." But, for

[1] Clyde Kluckhohn and William H. Kelly, "The Concept of Culture," in Ralph Linton, ed., *The Science of Man in the World Crisis* (New York: Columbia University Press, 1945), 91.
[2] *Ibid.*, 97.

the Japanese, death by suicide can be "good," "moral," and "coura-geous." Such considerations are not simply matters of behavior, of overt action; they elicit strong emotional feelings—in this case, con-trasting feelings. Knowing a person's culture tells us countless things about him.

Social Conformity and Intergroup Relations

Culture provides guideposts for intergroup relations. The inter-action between members of dominant and minority groups is mapped out, patterned, by culture. The guideposts of the culture are *norms*. Norms constitute generally accepted, sanctioned prescriptions for, or prohibitions against, various types of behavior. They tell us what we *should, ought,* and *must* do, as well as what we *should not, ought not,* and *must not* do. They are expectations shared by the mem-bers of the society-at-large or by the members of particular groups within the society. A large part of our behavior can be understood in terms of the operation of the norms of our society or of groups of which we are a member. This does not mean, however, that we are necessarily conscious of our cultural norms. Ralph Linton, an anthropologist, notes:

It has been said that the last thing which a dweller in the deep sea would be likely to discover would be water. He would become conscious of its ex-istence only if some accident brought him to the surface and introduced him to air. Man, throughout most of his history, has been only vaguely conscious of the existence of culture and has owed even this consciousness to contrasts between the customs of his own society and those of some other with which he happened to be brought into contact.[3]

Hence, we tend to take our culture for granted; it is more or less second nature to us.

Norms tell the dominant-group member how he is expected to think, act, and feel toward a minority-group member; similarly, they tell the minority-group how he is expected to think, act, and feel toward a dominant-group member. They may spell out, for ex-ample, the "proper" racial etiquette. The Black in many rural areas of the South is "supposed" to go to the back door of the White's home, to knock on the door, to retreat down the steps to the ground level, and, with the appearance of the White, to remove his hat. He

---

[3] Ralph Linton, *The Cultural Background of Personality* (New York: Appleton-Century-Crofts, Inc., 1945), 125.

is "expected" to speak with deference, attempting to please the White, and to intersperse his speech with frequent expressions of "sir," "yes, boss," and "sho 'nuff." The White is "expected" to call the Black by his first name, to avoid the use of "Mr." in reference to the Black, and to tell, not ask, the Black what to do.

Some authorities explain prejudice and discrimination on the basis of the operation of norms. Black and Atkins argue:

> "May it not be," we asked ourselves, "that what is often taken for prejudice in the Southerner may be just a 'learned-by-rote' set of definitions and rules regarding his relationship to a certain object (the Negro), much as we all learn by rote a certain set of definitions and rules regarding our relationship to the flag of our country?" By what metaphysical twist of logic is the one to be regarded as being prejudiced while the other is not? [4]

Black and Atkins go on to suggest that not eating with a Black may be as "natural" to the southerner as is saluting the flag to most Americans.

Evidence confirming this type of interpretation is supplied by Pettigrew in a study of anti-Black prejudice among Whites in the southern United States and South Africa. Pettigrew first measured the degree of prejudice against Blacks by an attitude scale. He then administered another questionnaire scaled to measure conformity to norms independent of prejudice (the items differed for the two nations and were selected with a view toward each nation's distinct cultural heritage). In both South Africa and the southern United States, where prejudice and discrimination against Blacks is a norm, those who showed the most conformity to norms were also the most prejudiced. [5]

The part that norms play in discriminatory behavior was also revealed by Warner and DeFleur in a recent study conducted among students in a border state university. They found that even the least-prejudiced students became vulnerable to participation in discriminatory behavior when asked to behave favorably toward Blacks in

[4] Percy Black and Ruth Davidson Atkins, "Conformity Versus Prejudice as Exemplified in White-Negro Relations in the South: Some Methodological Considerations," *The Journal of Psychology*, 30 (July, 1950), 111. Also see: Harry H. L. Kitano, "Passive Discrimination in the Normal Person," *Journal of Social Psychology*, 70 (1966), 23–31.

[5] Thomas F. Pettigrew, "Personality and Sociocultural Factors in Intergroup Attitudes: A Cross-National Comparison," *Journal of Conflict Resolution*, 2 (1958), 29–42.

situations where their behavior would be in violation of norms and open to surveillance by others.[6]

Social Distance

One index of the role of culture in patterning prejudice is the degree of *similarity* that exists in the responses of a society's members to various racial and ethnic groups. If members rank the various groups within a society in a similar fashion, one concludes that this is the product of the operation of norms. A familiar technique, devised by Emory S. Bogardus, seeks to measure the *social distance* at which members of one group hold another group and its members. Bogardus formulated a list of statements representing varying degrees of social intimacy or distance. He asked his subjects to mark those classifications to which they would willingly admit members of a given group. The scale of statements is

> To close kinship by marriage (1 point)
> To my club as personal chums (2 points)
> To my street as neighbors (3 points)
> To employment in my occupation (4 points)
> To citizenship in my country (5 points)
> As visitors only to my country (6 points)
> Would exclude from my country (7 points)

In 1926, Bogardus secured the responses of 1,725 Americans to forty racial and ethnic groups. The individuals were aged from eighteen to thirty-five, of which approximately half were college students and half were college graduates who were employed but were taking one or more post-graduate courses. The study was conducted among respondents from thirty-two well-distributed areas in the United States and included Blacks who constituted 10 per cent of the participants. Bogardus obtained a racial distance score for each racial and ethnic group employing a scale from 1.00 (the lowest possible distance score) to 7.00 (the highest possible distance score). The results of the 1926 study and similar studies in 1946 (with 1,950 subjects), 1956 (with 2,053 subjects), and 1966 (with 2,605 subjects) are indicated in Table 4–1. Near the top of the preference-ranking scale are English, native White Americans, and other northern Europeans; then Spaniards, Italians, and generally southern and eastern Europeans; near the bottom, Orientals and Blacks.

[6] Lyle G. Warner and Melvin L. DeFleur, "Attitude as an Interactional Concept: Social Constraint and Social Distance as Intervening Variables between Attitudes and Action," *American Sociological Review*, 34 (1969), 153–169.

TABLE 4–1 Changes in Racial Distance Indices

Rank	I — Racial Distance Indices Given Racial Groups in 1926 by 1,725 Selected Persons throughout the U.S.		II — Racial Distance Indices Given Racial Groups in 1946 by 1,950 Selected Persons throughout the U.S.		III — Racial Distance Indices Given Racial Groups in 1956 by 2,053 Selected Persons throughout the U.S.		IV — Racial Distance Indices Given Racial Groups in 1966 by 2,605 Selected Persons throughout the U.S.	
1	English	1.06	Americans (U.S. white)	1.04	Americans (U.S. white)	1.08	Americans (U.S. white)	1.07
2	Americans (U.S. white)	1.10	Canadians	1.11	Canadians	1.16	English	1.14
3	Canadians	1.13	English	1.13	English	1.23	Canadians	1.15
4	Scots	1.13	Irish	1.24	French	1.47	French	1.36
5	Irish	1.30	Scots	1.26	Irish	1.56	Irish	1.40
6	French	1.32	French	1.31	Swedish	1.57	Swedish	1.42
7	Germans	1.46	Norwegians	1.35	Scots	1.60	Norwegians	1.50
8	Swedish	1.54	Hollanders	1.37	Germans	1.61	Italians	1.51
9	Hollanders	1.56	Swedish	1.40	Hollanders	1.63	Scots	1.53
10	Norwegians	1.59	Germans	1.59	Norwegians	1.66	Germans	1.54
11	Spanish	1.72	Finns	1.63	Finns	1.80	Hollanders	1.54
12	Finns	1.83	Czechs	1.76	Italians	1.89	Finns	1.67
13	Russians	1.88	Russians	1.83	Poles	2.07	Greeks	1.82
14	Italians	1.94	Poles	1.84	Spanish	2.08	Spanish	1.93
15	Poles	2.01	Spanish	1.94	Greeks	2.09	Jews	1.97
16	Armenians	2.06	Italians	2.28	Jews	2.15	Poles	1.98
17	Czechs	2.08	Armenians	2.29	Czechs	2.22	Czechs	2.02
18	Indians (American)	2.38	Greeks	2.29	Armenians	2.33	Indians (American)	2.12
19	Jews	2.39	Jews	2.32	Japanese Americans	2.34	Japanese Americans	2.14
20	Greeks	2.47	Indians (American)	2.45	Indians (American)	2.35	Armenians	2.18
21	Mexicans	2.69	Chinese	2.50	Filipinos	2.46	Filipinos	2.31
22	Mexican Americans	—	Mexican Americans	2.52	Mexican Americans	2.51	Chinese	2.34
23	Japanese	2.80	Filipinos	2.76	Turks	2.52	Mexican Americans	2.37
24	Japanese Americans	3.00	Mexicans	2.89	Russians	2.56	Russians	2.38
25	Filipinos	3.28	Turks	2.89	Chinese	2.68	Japanese	2.41
26	Negroes	3.30	Japanese Americans	2.90	Japanese	2.70	Turks	2.48
27	Turks	3.36	Koreans	3.05	Negroes	2.74	Koreans	2.51
28	Chinese	3.60	Indians (from India)	3.43	Mexicans	2.79	Mexicans	2.56
29	Koreans	3.91	Negroes	3.60	Indians (from India)	2.80	Negroes	2.56
30	Indians (from India)	—	Japanese	3.61	Koreans	2.83	Indians (from India)	2.62
	Arithmetic Mean of 48,300 Racial Reactions	2.14	Arithmetic Mean of 58,500 Racial Reactions	2.12	Arithmetic Mean of 61,590 Racial Reactions	2.08	Arithmetic Mean of 78,150 Racial Reactions	1.92
	Spread in Distance	2.85	Spread in Distance	2.57	Spread in Distance	1.75	Spread in Distance	1.56

Source: Emory S. Bogardus, "Comparing Racial Distance in Ethiopia, South, and the United States," *Sociology and Social Research,* 52 (1968), 152. By permission of Emory S. Bogardus and *Sociology and Social Research;* University of Southern Calif.; Los Angeles, California 90007.

It is of interest to note that through the years an overall decline occurred in distance reactions.[7]

Social scientists within the United States have been checking the social distance positions of various groups by this means for over forty years. The most striking of their findings is that the pattern of preference is found across the nation, varying little with income, region, education, occupation, or even with ethnic group. With a few minor shifts, the relative positions of the groups remain substantially constant. Thus a quite similar social distance ranking has been found from such diverse parts of the nation as Florida, New York, Illinois, Kansas, Nebraska, and Washington.[8] Meltzer, studying attitudes of schoolchildren of varying socioeconomic classes in St. Louis, found preferences very similar to those of college students.[9] Hartley found that girls in Bennington College, Vermont, had for the most part the same attitudes toward various minority groups as did Black students at Howard University, in Washington, D.C. Hartley concluded, "Let us accept, then, the conclusion that there is a standardized pattern of preferences or prejudices prevalent in the United States."[10]

To a considerable extent the social distance rankings of minority-group members are quite similar to those of dominant-group members. There is, however, one important difference. While the minority-group members tend to retain the standardized pattern, they move their own group up from its lower position to one near the top of the scale. Thus Bogardus found that Blacks placed Blacks at the top of their racial preferences, while Jews similarly put their own group on top.[11] In summary, the evidence generally points to the

[7] Emory S. Bogardus, *Social Distance* (Yellow Springs, Ohio: Antioch Press, 1959), chapter 6; and "Comparing Racial Distance in Ethiopia, South Africa, and the United States," *Sociology and Social Research*, 52 (1968), 149–156. For a more recent and modified version of the Bogardus Social Distance Scale see: Harry S. Triandis and Leigh Minturn Triandis, "Race, Social Class, Religion, and Nationality as Determinants of Social Distance," *Journal of Abnormal and Social Psychology*, 61 (1960), 110–118. For a methodological evaluation of the Bogardus Social Distance Scale see: Richard G. Ames and Arline F. Sakuma, "Criteria for Evaluating Others: A Re-Examination of the Bogardus Social Distance Scale," *Sociology and Social Research*, 54 (1969), 5–24.

[8] J. P. Guilford, "Racial Preference of a Thousand American University Students," *Journal of Social Psychology*, 2 (1931), 179–204.

[9] H. Meltzer, "Group Differences in Nationality and Race Preference of Children," *Sociometry*, 2 (1939), 86–105.

[10] Eugene Hartley, *Problems in Prejudice* (New York: King's Crown Press, 1946), 23.

[11] Bogardus, *Social Distance*, 26–29.

fact that the distance at which various ethnic and racial groups are held is relatively consistent within the United States. This consistency suggests that culture, more particularly norms, is a crucial factor in understanding prejudice and discrimination.

Perception and Culture

We never really "see" the physical world about us. Rather the world we "see" is the product of the interaction between our anatomy, the physical aspects of the universe, and what we have learned from our past experience. Thus our perception is never a photographic image of the physical world. Men differ considerably in the world they "see." Many variables enter into our perception of the world about us, one of which is culture. Hallowell gives an interesting example of the relation of culture to perception. He was discussing with a group of students the differing names that various peoples have given to the constellation Ursa Major (dipper, bear, otter, plow, etc.) and the influence that the assignment of such names has had upon the perception of these stars. When he finished, feeling he had made the point, one student spoke up, asserting, "But it *does* look like a dipper." As Hallowell's remarks indicate, it probably *does* look like a plow to those who use that label rather than a dipper.[12]

Bagby formulated an interesting experiment that demonstrates the part culture plays in our perception of the world about us.[13] Mexicans and Americans constituted the subjects in the study. Bagby set up ten pairs of slides to be viewed through a stereoscope. On one side he mounted pictures of objects familiar to most Mexicans, for example, a matador, a dark-haired girl, and a peon. On the other side he mounted a similar picture of objects familiar to most Americans, for example, a baseball player, a blonde girl, and a farmer. The corresponding photographs resembled one another in contour, texture, and the distribution of light and shadows. Most Americans saw only those objects that were already familiar to them (e.g., the baseball players rather than the matador), and most Mexicans likewise saw only those objects placed within the context of their culture (e.g., the matador rather than the baseball player). To

[12] A. Irving Hallowell, "Cultural Factors in the Structuralization of Perception," in J. H. Rohrer and M. Sherif, eds., *Social Psychology at the Crossroads* (New York: Harper & Row, 1951), 171–172.

[13] James W. Bagby, "A Cross-Cultural Study of Perceptual Predominance in Binocular Rivalry," *Journal of Abnormal and Social Psychology,* 54 (1957), 331–334.

a surprising extent, then, our selection and interpretation of the sensory cues reaching us from our environment rests upon cultural definitions and standards. The world we see is a world heavily colored and impregnated with cultural connotations.

Perception is not merely selective; it may also be distorted by cultural definitions. Eugene and Ruth Horowitz demonstrated this fact in an experiment involving southern White children. They briefly showed the children a picture of a large apartment building fronted by a well-kept lawn, taken in brilliant sunlight. After the picture was removed, they asked the children: "Who was at the window?," "What was she or he doing?," "Who was cleaning up the grounds?" Actually, no figures of people had been in the picture. Nevertheless, most of the children readily described some individual in answer to each of the questions calling for such a response. When the children responded that they had seen a Black woman at the window, they almost invariably attributed to her a menial activity, for instance, cleaning the window. The answer to the question "Who was cleaning up the grounds?" was usually "A colored man." [14]

Another interesting study indicating how cultural definitions can affect perceptions was made by Gregory Razran. One hundred college students and fifty non-college men were shown pictures of thirty young women, all strangers to them. They were asked to rank each photograph on a five-point scale that would indicate their general liking for the girl, her beauty, her character, her intelligence, her ambition, and her "entertainingness." Two months later the same group was again shown the identical photographs but with surnames added. For some of the photographs Jewish names were given, such as Finkelstein and Cohen; to others, Irish surnames such as O'Shaughnessy and McGillicuddy; to others, Italian surnames such as Valenti and Scadano; and to others, old American surnames such as Davis and Clark. The labeling of the photographs with the surnames had a definite effect upon the manner in which they were perceived. The addition of Jewish and Italian names resulted in a substantial drop in general liking and a smaller drop in the judgment of beauty and character. The falling of likability of the "Jewish girls" was twice as great as for "Italians" and five times as great as for "Irish." On the other hand, it also resulted in a gen-

[14] Eugene L. Horowitz and Ruth E. Horowitz, "Development of Social Attitudes in Children," *Sociometry*, 1 (1938), 301–338.

eral rise in the ratings in ambition and intelligence for the girls with Jewish surnames. Clearly, cultural definitions had a marked effect upon the perception of the photographs and upon the judgment of the characteristics assigned to the girls.[15]

The role of cultural definitions in influencing perception can be seen in other contexts. If we meet an Irishman at a social event and do not know his ethnic membership, we look at him with a more or less open mind. When someone tells us he is an Irishman, our perception is altered. We may expect him to be witty, quick-tempered, and quick to use his fists. If his anger flares, we say, "Aha! How like an Irishman!" But, if a non-Irishman shows the same traits, we say "Things have gone hard with him recently," "He has had one too many drinks," or "His health has been bothering him lately." We remember those Irish who are witty and quick-tempered; we tend to overlook and forget those who are not. Similarly with Jews. If we are in the supermarket and someone nearby is quite loud, we may turn and see it is a Jewish acquaintance. "Aha," we say to ourselves, "a typical Jew." But, if the individual were non-Jewish, we would say, "Boy, has that person got a loud mouth! How irritating!" The attribute is merely associated with the individual as an individual, and no larger ethnic category is involved. Subdued and quiet Jews we tend to overlook. They just do not "register." But let a Jew speak loudly and act aggressively, and we conclude, "You might know, a Jew!" He registers!

Prejudice and superstition resemble each other in some respects. Take, for instance, the superstition that if a black cat crosses our path, some misfortune will befall us. The consequence of this superstition is that it makes black cats, *but only black cats*, highly visible. We hardly notice non-black cats, since the superstition implies that they do not pose a danger. Indeed, the very logic of a superstitious belief discourages disconfirmation. We overlook the fact that misfortune sometimes occurs when a non-black cat crosses our path; but when a black cat crosses our path, we find it easy to find some instance of misfortune, no matter how slight or delayed in time.[16]

---

[15] Gregory Razran, "Ethnic Dislike and Stereotypes: A Laboratory Study," *Journal of Abnormal and Social Psychology*, 45 (1950), 7–27.

[16] Gertrude J. Selznick and Stephen Steinberg, *The Tenacity of Prejudice* (New York: Harper & Row, 1969), 127.

REFERENCE GROUPS AND RACISM

Reference Groups and Attitudes

Our American society is organized about an almost infinite variety of functioning social groups. Each individual may be simultaneously a member of a surprisingly large number of such groups. In appraising an individual's attitudes or behavior, it is necessary to know which of the many groups is the actual referent for the individual within the given situation. The group providing the standards and anchorage regulating his behavior within the given context is called the *reference group*. He may be a member of the group, relating himself psychologically to it, or he may be a non-member who aspires to membership, achieving the relation through psychological identification.[17] In any event, the individual uses the group as a model for his behavior. In the broadest sense, a reference group can even be an individual. Here we are concerned with the relationship between reference groups and attitudes.

Considerable research has been conducted on the relationship between the attitudes an individual holds and the reference groups of which he is a member. The research has ranged from attitude studies of the American soldier to studies of attitude shifts occurring with changing reference groups among Roman Catholic and Bennington College students. These studies demonstrate the close relationship between an individual's attitudes and his reference group. This general finding has been confirmed in studies dealing with attitudes toward racial and ethnic minorities.

Schlesinger, for instance, devised an experimental situation where college students were exposed to information that they believed to represent the opinions of their fellow students regarding Jews (but information that in fact had been designed by Schlesinger). After exposure to the "peer" information, the students were asked individually to answer a variety of questions regarding their attitudes toward Jews. The answers to these questions were compared with the results of an anti-Semitism attitude test that the students had completed two weeks before the experiment. Schlesinger found that as a result of exposure to "peer" information, the students' expression of agreement or disagreement with favorable or unfavorable

[17] Muzafer Sherif and Carolyn W. Sherif, *Groups in Harmony and Tension* (New York: Harper & Row, 1953), 167.

assertions about Jews changed in the direction of conformity with perceived peer opinion. Schlesinger concluded that most of the students were highly suggestible, tending to conform to supposed peer opinion, whether this was pro- or anti-Semitic, and almost regardless of their prior levels of prejudice.[18]

Leonard Pearlin conducted still another study investigating the role of reference groups among students at a southern women's college. The majority of the students experienced at the college a climate of opinion with respect to Blacks that was more favorable than that to which they had been exposed prior to their coming to college. Thus many of the students came into contact with norms and attitudes that were inconsistent or in conflict with those they had previously experienced.[19]

The data from the Pearlin study indicate that the least prejudiced students were those who had experienced a weakening of ties to pre-college membership groups, while the more prejudiced were those who had retained firm affiliations with such groups. Likewise, the least prejudiced students were those who most strongly referred themselves to college groups, while the more prejudiced were those who referred themselves less strongly to campus groups. Thus the shift toward favorable attitudes toward Blacks was in part the product of a double-edged process. On the one hand, there occurred a weakening of ties to pre-college groups. This weakening of ties was accompanied by a decrease in the effectiveness of the pre-college groups in regulating the individual's attitudes in an unfavorable direction toward Blacks. On the other hand, it was not sufficient that one simply "drift away" from previously established social relationships. Of equal importance in the modification of attitudes was the establishment of strong identification with those groups possessing attitudes favorable toward Blacks. By virtue of identifying with new reference groups, one shifts his attitudes in accordance with those harbored by the new groups.

The process of acquiring more favorable attitudes toward Blacks, then, involves both *disattachment* and *attachment:* disattachment from previous reference groups unfavorable to Blacks and attachment to new reference groups favorable to Blacks. Attitude changes

[18] Lawrence E. Schlesinger, "The Influence of Exposure to Peer Group Opinions on the Expressions of Attitudes toward a Minority Group" (unpublished doctoral dissertation, Boston University, Boston, 1955).

[19] Leonard I. Pearlin, "Shifting Group Attachments and Attitudes Toward Negroes," *Social Forces,* 33 (1954), 47–50.

cannot be reckoned solely in terms of exposure to new attitudes. Not all the students underwent a modification of their attitudes toward Blacks although they had been exposed to the new ideas. Whether or not an individual undergoes a modification of his attitudes depends to a considerable extent upon the nature of his relationship to groups holding the opposing sentiments. Generally, where a shift in attitudes occurs, there will be found a detachment from those groups from which one initially derived and found support for one's attitudes. Correspondingly, the shift in attitude will be in the direction of the sentiments of those groups with which one develops the firmest attachments and identifications.

In summary, stereotypes and attitudes are group-anchored. Individuals view themselves as being members in good standing within certain groups or as wishing to become members in good standing. Within these groups various favorable and unfavorable attitudes toward minorities are found. The individual tends to accept the prevalent attitudes as part of his acceptance of the group and identifies himself with these attitudes so as to be accepted by the group. The group's views tend to become his views.

Reference Groups and Overt Behavior

Attitudes and overt behavior are not to be equated. Attitudes involve a *predisposition* to act, think, perceive, or feel; they constitute merely a predilection and not the actual response or series of responses that an individual makes. This is, of course, the distinction between prejudice and discrimination, a distinction that is important in our consideration of the role of reference groups. We have already noted the close relationship between reference groups and attitudes. We have also noted that an individual is a "member" of multiple groups. These multiple groups may make conflicting demands upon an individual in terms of the behavior expected of him. Accordingly, an individual's behavior may appear to be inconsistent. These inconsistencies in reaction frequently can be understood as the product of membership in diverse reference groups. When operating within the framework of one reference group he may behave one way; he may behave in quite a contradictory manner when operating within the framework of another reference group.

This analysis can be applied to the contradictory behavior of

White union members during the Detroit race riots in 1943. These workers were members of unions with staunch anti-segregation policies. Blacks were members of the unions. The norms set by the unions were those fostering non-prejudiced behavior. Had these union men been *nothing but* good union members, they would not have engaged in the race riots. But they were also members of other reference groups including neighborhood and ethnic groups that directly and indirectly reminded the union men of "race." When they interacted within the context of these latter groups, their feelings were aroused as staunch members of their "racial" group. They followed the dictates of being "regular guys" in this situation no matter how contradictory such dictates were to the union role.

The inconsistency in the union members' reactions can be explained in part on the basis of the operation of differing reference groups within differing contexts. Thus as good union members these men participated in campaigns for equal job rights for Blacks. But they were many things at the same time. They had conflicting loyalties. When acting as participants in a race riot they were acting in conformity with their loyalties as members of a particular neighborhood and "racial" group. Still, on the job they could act on the basis of union loyalties in a non-discriminatory fashion toward Blacks.[20]

Considerable research has shown that new reference groups may serve to bring about conformity to new norms despite contrary and well-established practices and attitudes. Southern White migrants to Chicago reveal considerable antipathy to Blacks. They express strong attitudes and feelings of preference for southern race patterns, and they deplore the fact that Blacks are "taking over Chicago." But in most of their behavior they make a peaceful, if reluctant, accommodation to the Chicago patterns. This is not to imply that there is an absence of discrimination in Chicago, but the pattern of interracial interaction is of a type different from that customarily found in the South. Killian found, for instance, that while the South generally continued to be the reference group for White migrant attitudes, Chicago functioned as the reference group for their behavior. Similarly, as patrons of a "hillbilly" tavern these White migrants would be more likely to beat up a Black than to permit him to be served. But within the context of a different

[20] Muzafer Sherif, "The Problem of Inconsistency in Intergroup Relations," *Journal of Social Issues*, 5 (1949), 32–37.

reference group, the non-segregated restaurant next door, of which they were regular patrons, they ate lunch on a non-segregated basis.[21] And many of them not only worked in plants with Blacks, but shared the same rest rooms and dressing rooms.[22] Conformity to the interracial normative order in Chicago was realized despite contrary and well-established attitudes.

Similarly, in Panama there are places where one side of a street falls in the American Canal Zone, and the other side of the street falls in Panamanian territory. Biesanz and Smith found that Black Panamanians tend to conform to discriminatory practices when they go to the Zone side of the street; White Americans tend to adjust to non-discriminatory practices when they go to the Panamanian side.[23]

Hence, a good deal of accumulating research points to the fact that an individual's attitudes and feelings toward various racial and ethnic groups are not simple and straight-forward, but rather diverse, complex, and often *contradictory*.[24] It appears that the *situation* in which the individual finds himself does much to determine which of his *heterogeneous* attitudes and feelings about a minority will be brought into open play. Individuals, then, come into situations of contact with minority groups prepared to respond to them in a number of different ways, some favorable, others unfavorable. *Which responses an individual in fact brings forth depends to a considerable extent upon which of his many reference groups is functioning within the situation to provide him with behavioral standards.*

Some sociologists, such as Lohman and Reitzes, go so far as to suggest that "individual behavior is, for all practical purposes, made a fiction." [25] They believe that the individual's personal attitude

21 Lewis M. Killian, "The Adjustment of Southern White Migrants to Northern Urban Norms," *Social Forces,* 33 (October, 1953), 66–69.

22 Lewis M. Killian, "The Effects of Southern White Workers on Race Relations in Northern Plants," *American Sociological Review,* 17 (1952), 327–331.

23 John Biesanz and Luke M. Smith, "Race Relations in Panama and the Canal Zone," *American Journal of Sociology,* 57 (1951), 7–14.

24 In this regard see: Melvin M. Tumin, *An Inventory and Appraisal of Research on American Anti-Semitism* (New York: Freedom Books, 1961), Chapter 3; Richard Christie, "Authoritarianism Re-Examined," in Richard Christie and Marie Jahoda, eds., *Studies in the Scope and Method of the Authoritarian Personality* (New York: The Free Press of Glencoe, Inc., 1954), 152; Robin M. Williams, Jr., *Strangers Next Door* (Englewood Cliffs, N.J.: Prentice-Hall, Inc., 1964), 66–68; and John M. Orbell and Kenneth S. Sherrill, "Racial Attitudes and the Metropolitan Context: A Structural Analysis," *Public Opinion Quarterly,* 33 (1969), 46–54.

25 Joseph D. Lohman and Dietrich C. Reitzes, "Note on Race Relations in a Mass Society," *American Journal of Sociology,* 58 (1952), 242.

toward minorities is of little consequence in explaining his actual behavior. "The reality is the social fact: the key to the situation and the individual's action is the collectivity, and in our time the collectivity is increasingly of the nature of a deliberately organized interest group." [26] Most authorities would probably not concur in such an extreme statement of group determinism. Nevertheless, the role of reference groups in patterning behavior toward minorities is undoubtedly considerable and accepted by most authorities.

Conformity to the norms of the group is the product of both external and internal forces. The group itself exerts pressure for conformity to its norms by positive and negative means. Conformity is rewarded, encouraged, and approved. Non-conformity is responded to by corrective and coercive means including ridicule, scorn, warnings, ostracism, rejection, and even physical punishment. Conformity may also be the product of internal forces operating within the individual. In accepting the group definition of the situation, the individual develops self conceptions that in effect regulate conduct in accordance with the norms of the group. The individual may not see conformity as an act of coercion coming from the outside. Rather, through conformity the individual achieves pride, self-identity, a sense of security—products of belonging to a group. It is *his* group, *his* norm. He conforms because he has internalized his roles which are in accordance with the norms of the group.[27]

THE THOMAS THEOREM

The Self-fulfilling Prophecy

A number of decades ago, W. I. Thomas, a prominent American sociologist, noted, "If men define . . . situations as real, they are real in their consequences." [28] Thomas was pointing to the fact that men respond not only to the objective features of a situation, but also to the *meaning* the situation has for them.[29] Once the meaning has been assigned, it serves to determine not only men's be-

[26] *Ibid.*, 242.

[27] Sherif and Sherif, *Groups in Harmony and Tension*, 184–190.

[28] W. I. Thomas, "The Relation of Research to the Social Process," in *Essays on Research in the Social Sciences* (Washington, D.C.: The Brookings Institution, 1931), 189.

[29] Robert K. Merton, *Social Theory and Social Structure* (New York: The Free Press of Glencoe, 1957), 421–422.

havior, but also some of the consequences of that behavior. Accordingly, the act of making the definition is also an act of making a prophecy. The fact that the definition is made creates conditions whereby the prophecy will be realized. Thus the definition is a "self-fulfilling prophecy," a self-fulfilling anticipation.

Daily life provides numerous illustrations of the workings of this theorem. A student with ability adequate to pass an examination is convinced that he is destined to fail. Anxious, the student devotes more time to worry than to study, his mind preoccupied with thoughts of failing the examination. In turn he takes the examination and fails. What has happened? Initially the student was in a situation in which he was objectively capable of passing the examination. But he defined the examination as one which he could not pass. He defined the situation as real, and accordingly the situation was real in its consequences. By virtue of his definition, his behavior was influenced in such a manner that it brought about the very result anticipated; he failed. His prophecy was self-fulfilling.

In the beginning the self-fulfilling prophecy is a false *definition of the situation.* The resulting consequences never would have come into being in the absence of the false definition or prophecy. But, after acceptance of the false definition, new behavior is evoked that makes the originally false state of affairs come true. One of the most difficult points to grasp in this connection is that there is no conspiracy to make the definition come true. Rather the fulfillment occurs unintentionally by virtue of individuals acting as if it were true, that is, in accordance with their beliefs.

The operation of the self-fulfilling prophecy can be seen in the realm of race relations. Many Whites define Blacks as inferior. The definition is accepted as gospel, as actual reality. Such a definition is not intended by the Whites to accomplish Black inferiority; it is accepted as fact. But flowing from such a definition are a series of consequences. Whites, through the control of power resources, allocate to Blacks a lesser share in the privileges and opportunities of the society, since they believe Blacks to be "inferior." They believe it would be senseless to provide Blacks with more in the way of privileges and opportunities, as it would be of no avail. But in so doing the Whites do not give Blacks a chance to prove or disprove the point. Rather the consequences are built into the White behavior. It results in the very inferiority that was alleged in the initial definition. Whites then see Black in menial jobs, with limited education, in poor housing, and with various health problems, and find it easy to conclude that Blacks *are* inferior. Although there is no scientific support for the notion of Black inferiority, Whites, believing the notion, serve to bring about a disadvantaged state for the great mass of Blacks. Indeed it then appears to them that Blacks are "inferior." The prophecy is self-fulfilling. The fact of having made the definition creates the conditions whereby the prophecy is realized.

Such an interpretation is useful in understanding the southern segregationist credo. White southerners holding such beliefs are not necessarily dishonest or engaged in deliberate deceit. Their ideas conform in part to their personal experience and observation, selective as these may be. The Blacks' living standards, though rising, are still low; rates of tuberculosis and venereal disease, and of crimes against persons and property are considerably higher among Blacks than among Whites; and results of standardized, national I.Q., achievement, reading and related tests from Virginia to Texas show consistently lower scores for Black than for White children when taken as a racial group. The average southern White is not aware of the multitude of social and cultural facts and forces that have fostered these situations. He does not understand the operation of the self-fulfilling prophecy or of his role in its operation. Rather he associates such traits with the visible physical characteristics of the Black and concludes that the Black is inherently inferior or at the very least "different." Hence, the scars of discrimination come to feed and justify continued discrimination.

The Vicious Circle

The self-fulfilling prophecy may or may not be circular in character. If a self-fulfilling prophecy is circular, *the end is again the beginning*, the reassertion of the beginning, perhaps in a strengthened form. The student failing an examination is a case in point. Having failed one examination, the student's self-confidence may be further undermined, his anxiety intensified, such that his studying for subsequent examinations may be further impaired. Accordingly, he fails those examinations as well. Once set in motion the vicious-circle process goes on and on of its own momentum. This is seen historically in the typical case of international armament: "armament in country A→fear in country B→armament in country B→fear in country A→armament in country A, and so on *ad infinitum*—or *ad bellum*.[30]

Myrdal, in his study of American race relations, speaks of the "self-perpetuating color bar" and concludes that "discrimination breeds discrimination."[31] White prejudice and discrimination keep the Black low in standards of living, health, and education. This in turn gives support to White prejudice. White prejudice and Black standards thus mutually "cause" each other.[32] In this sense, discrimination begets discrimination. This can be depicted as follows: "discrimination→lower income level→lower standard of living→lower education→lower earning capacity→discrimination."[33]

The discriminating group begins with an advantage. It possesses greater power and usually other means by which to assert its advantaged position, and which enable it to discriminate. Through discrimination it cuts the other group off from a wide range of economic and social privileges and opportunities. The state and process of discriminating give the advantaged group a new consciousness of its superiority, reinforcing the discriminatory pattern. Such discrimination is in turn ratified by the factual evidences of inferiority that accompany the lack of opportunity and by the disadvantaged state of those who live and breed in poverty, who suffer repeated frustration, who have little incentive to improve their lot, and who feel themselves to be the outcasts of society. Accordingly, discrimination evokes both attitudes and modes of life favorable to its perpetuation in both the group discriminating and the group discriminated against.[34]

Myrdal suggests that by this means a vicious circle can ensue. On the one hand, the Blacks' plane of living is kept down by discrimination from the side of the Whites. On the other hand, the Whites' reason for discrimination is partly dependent upon the Blacks' plane of living. The Blacks' poverty and health deficiencies stimulate and feed the antipathy of Whites for them.[35] Their antipathy intensified, the Whites increase their discrimination. As a consequence, the Blacks' plane of living suffers, and White antipathy is fed even more. Thus, through time, there occurs a progressive, cumulative intensification of prejudice and discrimination.

30 R. M. MacIver, *The More Perfect Union* (New York: The Macmillan Co., 1948), 63.
31 Gunnar Myrdal, *An American Dilemma* (New York: Harper & Row, 1944).
32 *Ibid.*, 75.
33 MacIver, *op. cit.*, 64.
34 *Ibid.*, 67–68.
35 Myrdal, *op. cit.*, 1066.

Myrdal sees the Blacks' "plane of living," however, as a composite entity which includes levels of Black employment, wages, housing, nutrition, clothing, health, education, stability in family relations, law observance, and so on. The vicious-circle hypothesis can also work in the reverse direction. A movement in any of the Black variables in the direction toward the corresponding White level will tend to decrease White prejudice and discrimination. Furthermore, a rise in any single one of the Black variables, Myrdal asserts, will tend to raise all the other Black variables. Thus, a rise in employment will tend to increase earnings, raise standards of living, and improve health, and education; similarly, a better education is assumed to raise the chances of a higher-salaried job.[36]

Such formulations, however, must be carefully interpreted or they may mislead. Social systems are not indefinitely plastic. There are limits to the variation which occurs within them. The endless cumulation of effects is checked by such factors as the need for a certain amount of order, beyond which a system cannot proceed without disruption. Likewise, each variable in the situation is sustained by the others. If one is changed, there will be the pull and push of the others to bring it back into line. Furthermore, a given line of development may have one series of consequences at one stage and different or even opposite effects at later stages. Thus, Whites may go along with Black advancement in employment while such advancement is minimal or moderate, but, as the more crucial ingredients in the caste employment picture are approached, Whites may respond with an intense reaction that may eventuate in a reversion to previous patterns. There is still another limitation to the vicious-circle interpretation. The support of "the facts" is not essential to prejudice, as has been shown by the elaborate cultural equipment for prejudice that most Americans share even when they know no facts or when they have had no contact with the people toward whom the prejudice refers.

ACQUIRING PREJUDICE

Racial Awareness

A popular legend has it that a White baby will cry if it sees a Black face, thus demonstrating instinctive aversion. Actually babies pass through a period in their development when they will cry when

[36] *Ibid.*, 1066–1067.

they see any strange face including grandma's or even dad's if the latter has been absent long. In fact, in the South, Black nurses are frequently the ones to whom the child gives his first attachment. There is no evidence to suggest that prejudice and prejudiced behavior represent an instinctive response to minority groups. Nevertheless, many southerners believe that an instinctive repugnance for Blacks exists among Whites. The gradual increase in prejudice among children tends to discredit this notion. If it were the product of "instinct," we would expect to find prejudice existing at birth or expressing itself suddenly during a specific stage in maturation. This is not the case.

A significant number of studies have been conducted in an effort to determine the ages at which children become aware of race. These studies show that children as young as three and four are capable of making distinctions between the physical characteristics of Blacks and Whites. With advancing age, the frequency of such distinctions increases.[37] Morland's study of 454 nursery-school children in Lynchburg, Virginia, is representative of these studies. The measuring instrument consisted of a set of eight pictures about which the children were asked to make racial identifications. The ability to recognize racial differences was scored in terms of "high," "medium," or "low," depending on how many times the pictures of Blacks and Whites were identified correctly. Each child had sixteen chances to do this, two for each picture. He was scored "high" if he missed none or one out of the sixteen; "medium" if he missed two or three; and "low" if he missed more than three. Table 4–2 indicates the results of the study by the age of the children. Among the three-year-olds tested, fewer than two out of ten scored "high,"

[37] R. B. Ammons, "Reactions in a Projective Doll-Play Interview of White Males Two to Six Years of Age to Differences in Skin Color and Facial Features," *The Journal of Genetic Psychology*, 76 (1950), 323–341); Harold W. Stevenson and Edward C. Steward, "A Developmental Study of Racial Awareness in Young Children," *Child Development*, 29 (1958), 399–409; M. E. Goodman, *Race Awareness in Young Children* (Reading, Mass.: Addison-Wesley Publishing Co., Inc., 1952); and J. Kenneth Morland, "Racial Recognition by Nursery School Children in Lynchburg, Virginia," *Social Forces*, 37 (1958), 132–137. For related studies see: J. Kenneth Morland, "A Comparison of Race Awareness in Northern and Southern Children," *American Journal of Orthopsychiatry*, 36 (1966), 22–31 and "Race Awareness among American and Hong Kong Chinese Children," *American Journal of Sociology*, 75 (1969), 360–374; A. James Gregor and D. Angus McPherson, "Racial Attitudes among White and Negro Children in a Deep-South Standard Metropolitan Area," *The Journal of Social Psychology*, 68 (1966), 95–106; and Raymond G. Taylor, Jr., "Racial Stereotypes in Young Children," *The Journal of Psychology*, 64 (1966), 137–142.

TABLE 4–2　Ability of 454 Children, by Age, To Identify Pictures of Negroes and Whites

Ability	3 years old		4 years old		5 years old		6 years old	
	No.	%	No.	%	No.	%	No.	%
High	15	14.7	97	61.0	120	78.4	37	92.5
Medium	21	20.6	25	15.7	21	13.7	2	5.0
Low	66	64.7	37	23.3	12	7.8	1	2.5
Total	102	100.0	159	100.0	153	99.9	40	100.0

Chi Square = 119.1856; P less than .001.

Source: J. Kenneth Morland, "Racial Recognition by Nursery School Children in Lynchburg, Virginia," *Social Forces*, 37 (1958), 134. By permission.

while among the six-year-olds, more than nine out of ten scored "high." A regular progression in recognition ability by age occurs, with the most rapid spurt appearing during the fourth year.[38]

Yet racial awareness is one thing. Prejudice is quite another. Although children may be conscious of racial differences, this does not necessarily mean that they are prejudiced—that is, that they possess a system of negative conceptions, feelings, and action-orientations regarding the members of a particular group. We are confronted, then, with this question: At what age do children manifest prejudice? Our evidence is inconclusive and even somewhat contradictory. Horowitz, using three picture tests, sought to determine the racial preferences of White grammar school children in New York City schools and in segregated schools in Georgia and Tennessee. He found an overall preference for Whites over Blacks in all grammar school grades in both northern and southern schools.[39]

Radke, Sutherland, and Rosenberg, in a study of lower socioeconomic class children in Pittsburgh, grades 2 through 6, found that on the wish level *both* Black and White children tended to prefer Whites. But, interesting enough, when confronted with situation-bound sociometric and projective contexts, the results were somewhat different. In questions phrasing the context as the classroom, interracial choices were common. On the other hand, in questions phrasing the context as the neighborhood (the larger community), interracial choices were less common. Further, when asked in sit-

---

[38] Morland, "Racial Recognition," *op. cit.*, 132–137.
[39] Eugene L. Horowitz, "Development of Attitudes toward Negroes," *Archives of Psychology*, 28 (1936).

uation-bound contexts (i.e., with reference to the classroom and neighborhood situations), the Black children did not show greater preference for Whites.[40] Yet this and the Horowitz study do not necessarily demonstrate that prejudice is channeling the children's racial choices. Indeed, in both studies the children were quite aware of what was expected of them in each situation (norms were operative) and they may well have responded accordingly.

Westie, in a study of Indianapolis grade school children, found that children in the early grades, for the most part, are unprejudiced and, in general, incapable of coherent, consistent stereotyping. He concludes:

> The vast majority of the 232 grade school children . . . were as incoherent about their out-group preferences and images as children are about almost any other social phenomenon. It is one thing to demonstrate that prejudice and stereotyping *can,* in some cases, develop in young children; it is quite another to say that they are characteristic of children.[41]

Further, Westie is of the opinion that stereotyping develops considerably later in children than prejudice.

In conclusion, it appears that children develop racial awareness at an early age. Prejudice, however, seems to be a later development, but at just what age children commonly develop prejudice is not clear. More research is clearly needed on this matter.

The Transmission of Racial Attitudes

Learning that one is a "White" or a "Black" is part of the process of acquiring one's self-identity. The child learns his racial role in much the manner in which he learns other roles. He acquires the symbols and expectations appropriate to his racial role, and in the process is achieving the answer to the question "Who am I?" Society provides him with the answer; it is defined for him in terms of a variety of situations. In answering the question "Who am I?" the child needs to answer its corollary "And who are all those?" The answers to these questions are already contained in the culture of the society and are transmitted to him through the intermediaries of parents and peers.

Olive Westbrooke Quinn's study of the transmission of racial atti-

---

[40] Marian J. Radke, Jean Sutherland, and Pearl Rosenberg, "Racial Attitudes of Children," *Sociometry,* 13 (1950), 151–171.

[41] Frank R. Westie, "Race and Ethnic Relations," in R. E. L. Faris, ed., *Handbook of Modern Sociology* (Chicago: Rand McNally and Company, 1964), 591.

tudes among southern Whites sheds additional light on the process. She interviewed high-school and college youths in Tennessee, Arkansas, and Mississippi.[42] Direct instruction played a relatively unimportant role in the transmission to them of racial attitudes. Even the most perceptive and self-analytical of the young people interviewed had difficulty producing any memories of the direct teaching of such attitudes. For the most part, verbal instruction had been avoided. There was, however, one exception. Repeatedly these youths told of explicit parental instructions in the use of the word "lady": "I remember when I learned that lesson. I told Mother the wash lady was here. She said to say 'woman,' and I asked why. Mother explained that you never say 'Negro lady.' She said 'lady' was a term of respect applied to few white ladies and to no Negroes at all." [43]

Racial attitudes were largely acquired indirectly. When verbal instructions were given, they were generally preceded by some incident where the child violated the racial norms: "One time when I was leaving to go to kindergarten, I kissed my nurse. Father waited until I was in the car with him, and then he told me not to. I asked why, but Father was very domineering, and he told me I was too young to understand and that I'd just have to do as he said."

While direct verbal instruction was seldom used, indirect verbal instruction was not avoided. Indirect verbal instruction, given by the simple expedient of letting the child "overhear" adult conversation, constituted a major means of transmitting racial attitudes. As Quinn suggests, it is probably not accidental, except in a few cases, when parents permit their children to overhear adult conversation. Ordinarily, parents exercise care that their children will not hear things about which they are considered "too young" to know. However, when adults freely discuss sexual "looseness" and "immorality" among Blacks in the presence of children but maintain a strict silence on the subject of White sexual irregularities, it is difficult to escape the conclusion that they are not averse to their children hearing such talk:

I knew Alma [a Black] lived with men. It's funny, I never heard much talk about the morals of white people; it came to me as a decided shock that

---

[42] Olive Westbrooke Quinn, "The Transmission of Racial Attitudes among White Southerners," *Social Forces*, 33 (1954), 41–47. Also see: Ruth C. Schaffer and Albert Schaffer, "Socialization and the Development of Attitudes Toward Negroes in Alabama," *Phylon*, 27 (1966), 274–285.

[43] Quinn, *op. cit.*, 42.

white people are often sexually immoral, but I have always known—or nearly always—that colored people are not hampered by morals. I never heard any tales of sexual immorality involving white people until I was considered grown.[44]

The shortcomings and deficiences of Black employees are freely paraded before children, and stereotyped images of Black behavior are related. The following excerpts from a diary kept by Quinn is revealing on this point:

Tonight I went to Bea's for the evening. She and her mother were very much elated that at last they had found a Negro woman who had agreed to come to the house and do the laundry. All of us were sitting on the front porch, Bea, her mother, Sue and I. Mrs. White was laying plans for the morrow. "Bea," she said, "remind me to lock up the silver tomorrow. We don't know a thing about this nigger." Then she turned to me, "You know, you can't trust any of them. I always lock up my good silver." [45]

These remarks of Mrs. White were not addressed to her grand-daughter, Sue, but they did not escape her. By listening to the casual conversation of adults, she had again had the lesson driven home that Blacks were untrustworthy. In the process of growing up, children identify with their parents. A common expression of this identification is found in imitative behavior; the child "tries on" the behavior of the adult. In this manner, he assimilates and internalizes the norms of the world about him. They become a part of his very existence, an integral part of his being. The child, witnessing White adults' behavior toward Blacks, is likely to carry this pattern over into his own interaction with Blacks.

Another indirect means by which racial attitudes are communicated to children is through instructing them not to make disparaging remarks about Blacks; rather, they are told that they must not let the Black know their genuine feelings. But implicit within such instruction rests the assumption of Black inferiority, the underlying premise of which appears as an unquestioned fact within this context. The child may be instructed to respect Black feelings and rights, yet the overtone is unmistakably present that the Black is helpless, servile, and inferior.[46] Furthermore, such instruction may have an additional impact as reflected in this observation by one youth: "You know, I think from the fact that I was told so often that I must treat colored people with consideration, I got the idea that I

44 *Ibid.*, 43.
45 *Ibid.*, 44.
46 *Ibid.*, 44.

could mistreat them if I wanted to." [47] In short, this youth had come to view his parent's admonitions as an invitation to engage in the contrary behavior. When a parent seems excessive in his warnings, the fact may not escape the child. The child interprets the parent's words as in effect saying, "I don't really believe this myself. That is why I keep repeating it. I keep saying it over and over to convince *both* you and myself that I genuinely mean it. But I really have considerable inner doubt. That is why I can't be satisfied with just saying it once or twice. I need to constantly assert it. So don't take me seriously."

A Black employee, having accepted his role, may also actively train the child to engage in the expected White behavior. Furthermore, the child who is treated with deference by members of a racial or ethnic minority subtly picks up the fact that he "must" be "superior" to members of the minority group. If in acquiring his roles he can evoke deference by imitating the behavior of his parents, the conception is reinforced.

Indeed, the entire social setting in which the White child finds himself is often saturated with evidences of Black social inferiority. He does not have to be told that Blacks are "inferior." The fact is only too apparent. He is part of the White community and as such he behaves within the context of its patterns:

It is not just that his parents use a different rest room than do the Negroes. *He* uses a different rest room than the Negroes. *He* sits in the white section of the bus. *He* behaves towards them as social inferiors, and naturally comes to accept them as social inferiors. . . . By the time a child is told for the first time that "Negroes are inferior," he is already convinced of it. On the other hand, by the time he is told for the first time that "Negroes are *not* inferior" it is already often too late.[48]

A child takes on his society's "people habits" in much the same fashion he takes on its food habits. Just as all foods are not regarded as equally palatable, all peoples are not regarded as equally acceptable. The child soon learns which foods are "good" and which foods are "not so good"; he learns which people are "good" and which people are "not so good." [49]

In conclusion, there are numerous indirect means by which atti-

[47] *Ibid.* 44.
[48] Earl Raab and Seymour Martin Lipset, "The Prejudiced Society," in Earl Raab, ed., *American Race Relations Today* (New York: Doubleday & Company, Inc., 1962), 49–52.
[49] Westie, *op. cit.*, 583.

tudes toward minorities are communicated to children. Cues are constantly given the children as to appropriate and inappropriate behavior. A general atmosphere may prevail of racial or ethnic antagonism, an atmosphere of which the child is not unaware. From parental actions and inactions—big and small—their gestures, facial expressions, tone of voice, rapidity of speech, muscular movement, speed and rhythm of breathing, and other cues, sentiments are communicated. Parents are usually under the impression that they are not the ones responsible for teaching their children prejudice. Often they are not doing so consciously, but unconsciously cues are being emitted by them. Parents may actually seek to avoid the topic, "We don't discuss race in front of him." But the very failure to openly discuss race suggests to the child that perhaps the parents feel "uncomfortable" on the subject, itself a significant cue.

SUMMARY

Once racism has arisen within a society, it may continue even when the initial sources contributing to its origin disappear or become minimized. Racism may become deeply embedded in the social and cultural fabric—it becomes institutionalized in the manner of other social institutions. Culture provides us with guideposts for life's activities that includes a blueprint, so to speak, for interaction between dominant and minority group members. These guideposts are norms, and as with other norms, groups bring pressure upon their members to conform with them. One index of the role of culture in patterning racism is the social distance scale. Cultural definitions, moreover, serve both to select and distort our perceptions of our own and other groups.

The group that provides the standards and anchorage regulating our behavior in a given context is called a reference group. Reference groups serve to pattern and channel our attitudes and overt behavior. By virtue of the fact that we have many reference groups, our attitudes, feelings, and behavior toward various racial and ethnic groups are not simple and straight-forward, but rather diverse, complex, and often contradictory. Which responses an individual brings forth depends to a considerable extent upon which of his many reference groups is functioning within the situation to provide him with behavioral standards.

Racism may also be maintained through the operation of the Thomas theorem: If men define situations as real, they are real in their consequences. This is the self-fulfilling prophecy. Whites define Blacks as inferior, and, by virtue of greater access to our society's power resources, produce the very inferiority that is contained in the initial definition. When the self-fulfilling prophecy is circular, so that the end is again the beginning, we have a vicious circle.

Apparently children develop racial awareness during the pre-school period. Yet racial awareness is one thing, prejudice quite another. But at just what age children develop prejudice is not clear. Learning that one is a "White" or a "Black" is part of the process of acquiring one's self-identity. Racial attitudes are transmitted directly and subtly. Indeed, a child takes on his society's "people habits" in much the same fashion he takes on its food habits.

5

Personality Bulwarks
of Racism

The various factors of racism that we have considered in the past two chapters have dealt primarily with man's relation to man and to groups of men. In contrast to these "group-centered" orientations are those that are "personality-centered." Rather than focusing upon what occurs *between* people, "personality-centered" theories stress what occurs *within* people. These latter theories interpret dominant-minority relations primarily in personality terms. Since prejudice is a state of mind, and as such is "carried" in specific individuals, some social scientists insist that we look for the sources of prejudice within the individual personality. These social scientists are often quite critical of "group-centered" social scientists who they feel view individuals as "interchangeable specimens of gutless creatures."[1] In turn, "group-centered" social scientists accuse their "personality-centered" counterparts of depicting prejudice as some sort of individual disorder, ignoring the fact that society is organized in such a manner as to manufacture and stimulate intergroup hostility.

For the most part, "personality-centered" theories tell us little about the origins of racism, for instance, how and why one group is singled out while others are not. They are helpful, however, in understanding how racism may be maintained and even intensified,

[1] Theodore M. Newcomb, "Sociology and Psychology," in John Gillin, ed., *For a Science of Social Man* (New York: The Macmillan Co., 1954), 237.

that is, they provide us with insights into various personality bulwarks of racism.

FRUSTRATION AND AGGRESSION

The Scapegoat Theory of Prejudice

One of the most, if not *the* most, popular of the various theories of prejudice is the scapegoat theory.[2] The major postulates of the theory are the following:

1. *Needs.* An individual experiences a variety of needs, be they induced biologically (hunger, thrist, sex, sleep, etc.) or socially (various rewards, rights, privileges, etc.).

2. *Frustration.* For one reason or another an individual often finds himself blocked from realizing his needs or desires. In a word, the individual is *frustrated*.

3. *Aggression.* A frustrated individual experiences anger which disposes him toward aggressive actions. Blocked in realizing his needs or desires (especially where the blockage is repeated and persistent), he becomes enraged; he wants to strike out, to destroy, to tear to pieces.

4. *Displacement.* An enraged person needs to vent his emotions and it makes little or no difference against whom he directs his aggressive feelings. If some specific person is guilty of contributing to his frustration, he will tend to direct his aggression against him. But at times this is not possible. It may be dangerous to attack another, especially if the person is a powerful figure. Thus a child frustrated by his parents or a student thwarted by a professor cannot generally strike back at the source; it would be too dangerous. Similarly frustration may stem not only from identifiable persons but from some impersonal events, "fate," pervasive source, or even one's own acts or thoughts of commission and omission. In such circumstances, there is no direct external source against whom one can retaliate. Nevertheless, the impulse to vent anger persists. Under

[2] As examples of the scapegoat approach, see: John Dollard, *et al., Frustration and Aggression* (New Haven: Yale University Press, 1939); Talcott Parsons, "The Sociology of Modern Anti-Semitism," in Isacque Graeber and S. H. Britt, eds., *Jews in a Gentile World* (New York: The Macmillan Co., 1942), 101–122; Ellis Freeman, "The Motivation of Jew-Gentile Relationships," *Ibid.*, 149–178; Leonard Berkowitz, *Aggression: A Social Psychological Analysis* (New York: McGraw-Hill Book Co., Inc., 1962), chapter 6; and Aubrey J. Yates, *Frustration and Conflict* (London: Methuen & Co. Ltd., 1962), chapter 3.

such circumstances people unconsciously, at times consciously, tend to seek out a person, group, or object on which to "take out" their feelings, to find a "scapegoat." [3] When hostilities are removed from the source or sources of frustration and discharged upon a scapegoat, the process is referred to as *displacement*. Displacement appears to be a common practice—for example, more than one person has complained to a frustrated friend after receiving an unwarranted attack from him, "Don't take it out on me."

5. *Weak Victims.* Some sources for the displacement of hostile aggression are preferable to others, namely, those people who are too weak or defenseless to strike back, who are incapable of returning aggression with retaliatory aggression. They become the innocent victims of aggression. The student enraged by a poor grade, unable to retaliate against the professor, may respond to a trivial remark or act of a roommate with harsh, angry, and abusive words. The husband who encounters difficulties and irritations at work comes home in the evening ready, upon the slightest provocation, to snap at family members and vent his anger. Family members learn to watch for cues of such feelings, to "soft-pedal" requests, and to behave under such circumstances as unobtrusively as possible.

Aggression may also be deflected toward minorities, since they are generally portrayed as too weak or defenseless to strike back. The southern White reaction to Blacks following the Civil War is taken by some writers as a case in point. The post-war upsurge in racism is attributed by some writers to displaced hostility that derived from southern social disorganization and resentment toward the victorious North. In brief, after the bloody Civil War, the South turned its spent and fruitless hostility to the Blacks. Since White southerners could not avenge themselves directly against the North, they turned their aggression against the Blacks for whom the North had fought. To punish the Blacks represented a kind of deflected expression of hostility toward the victors, who had won the actual war but who could not win the fight for Black freedom. Blacks and Yankees tend to become associated in the mind of the White southerner. Northern pressure upon the South has historically often been

---

[3] Eisenman presents evidence suggesting that scapegoating may also serve to enforce social control and hence he concludes that it may well have integrative as well as disruptive consequences for society. Russell Eisenman, "Scapegoating and Social Control," *The Journal of Psychology*, 61 (1965), 203–209.

followed by increased southern pressure on the Black rather than by melioration of the Black's lot.[4]

6. *Rationalization.* Generally the expression of hostile impulses toward one's fellow men is discouraged, even prohibited by moral and ethical considerations, by norms. To "take out" one's feelings upon an *innocent* individual or group would conflict even more with such norms. Given the democratic creed of America, such behavior would bespeak rank injustice, hatred, and irrationality. It would tend to offend one's feelings of self-pride, morality, and intelligence. If one is to avoid feelings of self-condemnation, of guilt, it is essential that some excuse be available to sanction such behavior. In brief, the behavior, otherwise immoral, must be made to appear both rational and acceptable morally. Humans are quite ingenious in coming up with excuses for their behavior. This process is referred to as *rationalization.* Individuals justify their behavior by finding some convincing reason why they can hate and discriminate against a minority group. Accordingly, a racist ideology tends to be evolved. People can then rationalize: "I hate Blacks because they are criminally inclined, dirty, immoral, lazy, and irresponsible." In this manner they can feel justified for their feelings.

Experimental Evidence of Scapegoating

Any number of studies have been conducted in an attempt to test the scapegoating hypothesis experimentally. One of the earliest of these was undertaken by Miller and Bugelski.[5] The subjects of the experiment were thirty-one young men between the ages of eighteen and twenty, working at a CCC camp. The researchers learned that the young men were about to experience a frustrating situation. As part of the educational program of the camp, they were going to be required to take a long, uninteresting test, a test promising to be so difficult that everyone was bound to fail miserably. Furthermore, the test would run far overtime so that the young men would miss what they had looked forward to as the most interesting event of the otherwise dull week: bank night at the local theater. This event

---

[4] John Dollard, *Caste and Class in a Southern Town,* 3d ed. (New York: Doubleday & Co., Inc., 1957), 59.

[5] Neal E. Miller and Richard Bugelski, "Minor Studies of Aggression: II. The Influence of Frustrations Imposed by the In-Group on Attitudes Expressed Toward Out-Groups," *Journal of Psychology,* 25 (1948), 437–442.

was awaited with special eagerness, as the previous week one member of the group had won $200.

Accordingly, two frustrating experiences were awaiting the men. To the extent to which they were motivated to succeed on the tests, they were bound to experience frustration by virtue of failure. To the extent to which they were motivated to attend bank night, they were bound to experience frustration by the interference of the testing program. The frustration and aggressive feelings that the experimenters anticipated under these circumstances were confirmed. Before and after the frustrating situation, the young men were tested as to their attitudes toward a number of minority groups. It was found that after the frustrating situations there was a definite decrease in the number of favorable items checked. The experimenters concluded that aggression aroused by the in-group authorities in blocking the desires of these young men were generalized and displaced to the out-group minorities. The production of generalized feelings of hostility appears to be particularly great when the frustration experienced is unreasonable, unjust, and unnecessary.[6]

Although a number of studies have tended to confirm the scapegoating hypothesis,[7] still others have contradicted it.[8] Apparently the predictive value of the hypothesis has been limited by its focus on the motivational states of the individual, while overlooking a number of other relevant factors or variables. Let us examine a few of these:

[6] N. Pastore, "A Neglected Factor in the Frustration-Aggression Hypothesis: A Comment," *Journal of Psychology*, 25 (1948), 271–279, and Ralph Epstein, "Authoritarianism, Displaced Aggression, and Social Status of the Target," *Journal of Personality and Social Psychology*, 2 (1965), 588.

[7] See: Emory Cowen, Judah Landes, and Donald E. Schaet, "The Effects of Mild Frustration on the Expression of Prejudiced Attitudes," *Journal of Abnormal and Social Psychology*, 58 (1959), 33–38; Seymour Feshbach and Robert Singer, "The Effects of Personal and Shared Threats upon Social Prejudice," *Journal of Abnormal and Social Psychology*, 54 (1957), 411–416; Donald Weatherley, "Anti-Semitism and the Expression of Fantasy Aggression," *Journal of Abnormal and Social Psychology*, 62 (1961), 454–457; and George Stricker, "Scapegoating: An Experimental Investigation," *Journal of Abnormal and Social Psychology*, 67 (1963), 125–131; and Leonard Berkowitz, *op. cit.*, Chapter 6.

[8] See: Bohdan Zawadzki, "Limitations of the Scapegoat Theory of Prejudice," *Journal of Abnormal and Social Psychology*, 43 (1948), 127–141; Gardner Lindzey, "Differences Between the High and Low in Prejudice and Their Implications for a Theory of Prejudice," *Journal of Personality*, 19 (1950), 16–40; Nancy C. Morse and Floyd H. Allport, "The Causation of Anti-Semitism: An Investigation of Seven Hypotheses," *Journal of Psychology*, 34 (1953), 197–233; Ross Stagner and Clyde S. Congdon, "Another Failure to Demonstrate Displacement of Aggression," *Journal of Abnormal and Social Psychology*, 51 (1955), 659–696; and Epstein; *op. cit.*, 585–589.

1. *The Personality of the Displacer.* Berkowitz holds that highly prejudiced individuals will displace aggression more than non-prejudiced individuals when confronted with equally frustrating situations. In other words, whether or not displacement occurs depends not merely upon the objective fact of frustration or upon the availability of objects for displacement, but also upon the personality of the individual. Berkowitz's experiment involved female college students that had scored either very high or very low on an anti-Semitism attitude scale. These students were individually subjected either to an annoying, frustrating treatment by the experimenter or to a more neutral, non-frustrating experience with him. After this treatment, the girls were given a topic to discuss with another girl, but unknown to them this girl was actually the experimenter's confederate. A questionnaire rating by the confederate immediately after the conclusion of the discussion constituted the hostility index. In comparison with the nonfrustrated, highly anti-Semitic girls, the frustrated highly anti-Semitic girls gave evidence of increased unfriendliness toward their peer (in reality the confederate). On the other hand, tolerant coeds who received the harsh treatment displayed greater friendliness to the other girls. For the highly anti-Semitic girls, then, the hostility engendered by the frustrating experimenter presumably displaced to the neutral bystander; this displacement did not occur in the less prejudiced group. Similar results were obtained when the confederate was given a "Jewish" name. Hence, Berkowitz concludes that highly prejudiced individuals are more prone to scapegoating than less prejudiced individuals.[9]

Similarly individuals differ in how they handle frustration. Not all people respond to frustration by aggression. An individual may respond with some new or added effort by which to realize his goal. Or he may substitute a different goal. Then, again, he may respond with regression, a lowering of his level of performance, an evasion of the situation by leaving it or "going out of the field," or by apathy and resignation. The reaction to frustration varies according to the circumstances and the individual's perception of them.[10]

[9] Berkowitz, *op. cit.*, 143–144. Also see: Brendan Gail Rule, "Anti-Semitism, Stress, and Judgments of Strangers," *Journal of Personality and Social Psychology*, 3 (1966), 132–134.

[10] H. Himmelweit, "Frustration and Aggression: A Review of Recent Experimental Work," in T. H. Pear, ed., *Psychological Factors of Peace and War* (New York: Philosophical Library, Inc., 1950).

Even should frustration foster aggressive impulses, aggression need not be displaced. Some individuals are intrapunitive—they direct their aggressive impulses inward against themselves rather than outward against the outside world. Such individuals tend to "bottle up" their rage—to take their rage out on themselves—a fact that symtomatically may express itself in headaches, ulcers, psychological depression, and so on. Ackerman and Jahoda indicate that among their anti-Semitic patients they failed to find any cases of deep depression, a fact that they attribute to the tendency of anti-Semites to handle rage through attacks upon others (extrapunitiveness) as opposed to intrapunitive reactions.[11]

2. *The Kind of Frustration Involved.* A number of social scientists have suggested that people are more likely to scapegoat in response to some kinds of frustration than others. Feshbach and Singer investigated this possibility in differing responses to personal and shared threats.[12] While a personal threat poses a danger primarily to the individual himself, a shared threat constitutes a danger to the larger society of which an individual is a part. Feshbach and Singer randomly assigned the members of introductory psychology classes to six groups: three personal threat groups (marital failure, mental illness, and severe personal injury), two shared threat groups (the danger of flood and hurricane and the possibility of atomic war), and a control group (a group that was exposed to none of the threats and to which the other five groups were later compared).

Tests measuring attitudes toward Blacks were administered to the students. Four weeks later five of the groups (but not the control group) were asked to discuss mimeographed statements about one of the five threats (each group receiving statements concerning a different threat). After the discussions, attitudes toward Blacks were again measured in each of the five groups and the control group. All three of the personal threat groups gained significantly in prejudice beyond the change in the control group. On the other hand, the flood and hurricane group experienced an appreciable decline in prejudice toward Blacks. Feshbach and Singer suggest that this was perhaps a result of a sense of shared fate. The group discussing the threat of an atomic war, however, displayed a gain

---

[11] Nathan W. Ackerman and Marie Jahoda, *Anti-Semitism and Emotional Disorder* (New York: Harper & Row, 1950), 243. Also see Gerald S. Lesser, "Extrapunitiveness and Ethnic Attitude," *Journal of Abnormal and Social Psychology*, 56 (1958), 281–282.

[12] Feshbach and Singer, *op. cit.*, 411–416.

in prejudice. It is conceivable that the frequent linkage of atomic war with the Soviet Union resulted in hostility to Russians, which the students in turn then displaced upon Blacks. In conclusion, this study by Feshbach and Singer suggests that some kinds of frustration are more likely to produce scapegoating than others.

3. *The Perceived Qualities of Potential Targets.* Critics of the scapegoat hypothesis have noted that aggression is not always displaced upon an innocent victim or upon the safest available target. The hypothesis fails to explain, for instance, why at times minorities displace their hostilities against dominant groups. For some minorities the dominant group is not a defenseless target; in fact, it may be quite powerful. Further, evidence suggests that individuals of the political "left" may engage in scapegoating against groups that appear economically privileged or powerful.[13] The scapegoat, then, may not always be a "safe goat" as the theory would lead us to believe.[14]

The fact that aggression is not always displaced upon an innocent victim or upon the safest available target has led some social scientists to raise this question: Are some groups commonly perceived in such a fashion that they constitute particularly vulnerable or susceptible targets for the displacement of aggression? Berkowitz and his associates answer the question in the affirmative. Experimentally they have demonstrated that hostility will be displaced from the frustrater to another individual in direct ratio to the degree of dislike for this latter person.

In their experiments Berkowitz and his associates administered shocks to individuals who were working as partners on a common task. The subjects believed the shocks were applied by their partner and hence they acquired a dislike for him. Later the subjects were frustrated by one of the experimenters. The frustrated subjects were then presented with a task involving two potential targets for their hostility: the person they had been trained to dislike and a neutral individual. The study revealed that the frustrated subject directed considerably more aggression against the disliked person than against the neutral person. Berkowitz concludes that

[13] E. A. Shils, "Authoritarianism: Right and Left," in Richard Christie and Marie Jahoda, eds., *Studies in the Scope and Method of the Authoritarian Personality* (New York: The Free Press of Glencoe, 1954), 24–29, and Epstein, "Authoritarianism, Displaced Aggression, and Social Status of the Target," *op. cit.*, 585–589.

[14] Zawadzki, *op. cit.*, 127–141 and Gordon W. Allport, *The Nature of Prejudice* (Boston: Beacon Press, Inc., 1954), 351.

groups used as scapegoats are groups that individuals for one reason or another have *already* learned to dislike.

Berkowitz suggests still another point. A disliked group can be associated with an immediate frustrater, permitting the transfer of hostility aroused by the latter to the former. Hence, an industrial worker may become more hostile to the Jews in his community after receiving a cut in pay if he associates the disliked Jews with the non-Jewish factory owners. The worker may regard both the factory owners and Jews as rich and unscrupulous. Frustrated, he identifies Jews with the immediate frustrater (the factory owner), and displaces his rage from the factory owners to Jews.[15]

4. *The Role of Culture.* Whether or not an individual displays open aggression depends in part on the degree to which his culture or subculture *permits* aggression. In some societies, aggressive behavior may be viewed as the mark of a "real man" and hence be encouraged and rewarded, for example, the Kwakiutl of the Pacific Northwest. In still other societies aggression may be regarded as an evil force that disrupts group harmony, for example, the Zuni of the American Southwest. Among some groups within the United States—sailors, marines, soldiers, lumberjacks, longshoremen, and oil field workers—a "he-man" subgroup actively fosters violent interpersonal aggression. The man who exclaims, "I don't believe in fighting" wins no popularity contests. Similarly, Cash describes the "one-hell-of-a-fellow" complex among Southern males.[16] Such males, more rare today than in former times, idealize violence and interpersonal aggression. In contrast, some groups define overt aggression and fighting as sinful or at least ungentlemanly and uncivilized. Many Christians define Christ's Sermon on the Mount as suggesting that aggression in any form is evil:

In brief, there are varieties of cultural settings in which aggression is expressed and even encouraged and others in which aggression is defined as improper or immoral. Whether or not one expresses his aggressions is not simply a consequence of the degree of psychological frustration. The definitions of appropriate behavior provided by the groups in which one acts are equally important in determining the outcome of frustration.[17]

[15] Berkowitz, *op. cit.*, 152–164. Also see: Ralph Epstein, "Aggression Toward Outgroups as a Function of Authoritarianism and Imitation of Aggressive Models," *Journal of Personality and Social Psychology*, 3 (1966), 374–379.

[16] W. J. Cash, *The Mind of the South* (New York: Doubleday & Co., Inc., 1954).

[17] Frank R. Westie, "Race and Ethnic Relations," in R. E. L. Faris, ed., *Handbook of Modern Sociology* (Chicago: Rand McNally & Company, 1964), 610.

Our observations suggest that scapegoating is a more complex phenomenon than early formulations of the hypothesis led us to believe. We need to take into account a variety of other factors and variables. Further, it is important to note that the hypothesis tends to overlook the possibility of realistic social conflict. What may appear to be displacement in some instances may be aggression directed against the true source of the frustration.[18] This is especially the case where economic, power, or status competition occurs.

PROJECTION

Projection involves the tendency of people to attribute to others motives or traits which they sense within themselves but which would be painful to acknowledge. It is a mechanism by which attitudes and behavior that cannot be accepted in the self are attributed to others. In brief, one sees others as he is himself. To the alcoholic it may be the other fellow who drinks too much; to the failing student it may be the teacher who is incompetent; to the football player making a stupid play it may be the quarterback who was in error; to the hostile and aggressive boy it may be the other lad who started the fight. For the businessman the thought that "I'm going to ruin this Jew and run him out of business" is one that generally evokes feelings of guilt and shame. In projection it becomes, "The Jews are trying to ruin me and run me out of business." Aggression against the Jew then becomes justified self-defense. The Jew is portrayed in such a manner that he "deserves" to be ruined for his "unethical" practices. Projection is a prevalent mechanism in dominant-minority relations.

The Cultural Heritage and Projection

Projection seems to play a central role in the frequent assignment to minorities of traits characterized by inordinate sexual desire. Within American life strong overtones of disapproval have traditionally existed toward sex. Sexual desire is often viewed as "dirty," "filthy," "nasty," even as "sinful." The Fathers of the Christian Church contributed in no small way to the hostility of our modern culture toward sex. The ideal was developed that celibacy was su-

[18] Allport, *op. cit.*, 351–352.

perior to marriage. Paul declared, "But I say to the unmarried and to widows, it is good for them if they abide even as I. But if they have not continency, let them marry: for it is better to marry than to burn." [19] The mother of Christ, the Virgin Mary, was honored in part for her virginity, a cornerstone of her purity, since sex was seen as defiling and degrading. With time came the ascetic cults, the founding of monasteries, and the establishment of celibacy as a requirement for the clergy. Augustine in his *City of God* drew a distinction between the city of God and the city of the devil, implying a dichotomy and an antithesis between the flesh and the spirit. Christian leaders made frequent comments upon fleshy lust as being intrinsically evil.[20]

Given this cultural heritage that sexual desire is wrong, the feeling of such desire is often seen as a terrible thing, to be shunned at all costs. Yet it is an inevitable aspect of physical functioning; it cannot be entirely avoided—sexual desire makes itself felt. Many individuals are thus placed in a dilemma. On the one hand, they cannot deny the existence of the feeling; on the other hand, they cannot admit that they themselves harbor such feelings, feelings that by definition are "lustful" and "sinful." Unable to repress awareness of sexual desire, they instead repress the recognition of its origin within themselves, and the lustfulness is projected outside of themselves upon others. The mechanism can be stated in these terms: "I may feel sexual desire, but I am not responsible for it. You are. I am aware of lustful feelings. But it is *your* lust, *not mine*, that I am seeing."

Projection and Notions of Inordinate Black Sexuality

Some authorities suggest that the projection of sexual desire is of considerable aid in helping us to understand the preoccupation of southern Whites with Black sexuality and the fear of Black sexual attack. Discussions of the race issue with southern Whites usually boil down to the question, "Would you want your sister (daughter) to marry a Black?" But why such concern with this issue? As it takes two to make a legal marriage, supposedly the White sister or daughter could refuse a Black suitor. On the conscious level the

[19] Bible, I Cor. 7:8–9.
[20] Clifford Kirkpatrick, *The Family: As Process and Institution* (New York: The Ronald Press Co., 1955), 100–101.

question does not make sense. It does, however, make sense if there is a repressed, that is, unconscious, feeling of sexual attraction among Whites for Blacks.[21] A clear implication of the question is that White women would have no hesitation in marrying a Black, and, in fact, would readily do so once there is genuine social equality between Whites and Blacks.

There may be some foundation for the belief that there exists among Whites an unconscious feeling of sexual attraction toward Blacks. It is probably no accident that prejudiced people call tolerant people "niggerlovers." The very choice of the word suggests that perhaps they are fighting the feeling of attraction themselves.[22] White stereotypes depict Blacks as uninhibited, rhythmic, and passionate. In a word, the Black becomes an image—a symbol—for free and passionate sex. Experiencing sexual desire, White Americans, by virtue of their puritanical traditions (traditions which are particularly prevalent within the South), are often required to repress their feelings. But, in repressing them, it becomes easy to externalize them—to project these feelings upon the Black. It is the Black who is uninhibited, rhythmic, and passionate—the very qualities many Whites would themselves like to express. Such projection is facilitated by the less stringent sex codes found among lower-socioeconomic-class Blacks. Accordingly, many Whites do not find it difficult to embellish upon the theme of Black sexuality.

By virtue of projection, the Black becomes sexually tempting and attractive. The Black has sex appeal, *plus*—even a good many Whites agree to this! [23] Black women are commonly depicted in jokes, stories, and folklore as especially voluptuous, sensual, and passionate, and, accordingly, implicitly desirable as sexual partners. Dollard indicates that the image of the Black woman in southern White man's talk and fantasy was that of a seducing, accessible person dominated by sexual feeling and, so far as straight-out sexual gratification goes, desirable. In jokes the Black woman was represented as a crude, direct person, with little suppression or veiling of her sexual interest.[24] The remark was current in Southerntown that

[21] See: Dollard, *op. cit.*, 334; I. D. MacCrone, *Race Attitudes in South Africa* (London: Oxford University Press, 1937); and Calvin C. Hernton, *Sex and Racism in America* (New York: Doubleday & Company, Inc., 1965).

[22] See: Allport, *op. cit.*, 372–377.

[23] Hernton, *op. cit.*, 53. Also see: Louis J. West, "On Racial Violence," *Northwest Medicine*, 64 (1965), 679–682, and Frantz Fanon, *Black Skin; White Masks*, trans. by Charles Lam Markmann (New York: Grove Press, Inc., 1967), Chapter 6.

[24] Dollard, *op. cit.*, 137.

a man did not know what sexual experience was until he had had a Black woman.

Similarly, the Black male is viewed as especially virile and capable. Dollard indicates that the idea seemed prevalent that Black males were more like savages than humans and that their sexual appetites were more vigorous and ungoverned than those of White men. There was a belief in Southerntown that the genitals of Black males were larger than those of Whites: "One planter, for example, said he had had visual opportunity to confirm the fact; he had gone to one of his cabins, and on entering without warning, found a Negro man preparing for intercourse. Informant expressed surprise at the size of the penis and gave an indication by his arm and clenched fist of its great length and diameter." [25] Several authorities have noted, however, that there is no evidence to confirm the belief that the genitals of Black males are larger than those of White males.[26] The interesting point here is that Whites believe this to be true. Accordingly, it is not difficult to conclude on an unconscious level that one's daughter or sister may actually find Black men attractive as husbands—for do not women generally find virile, capable men attractive? Simultaneously such projection permits vicarious gratification of forbidden desires. By focusing thoughts upon and telling stories of Black immorality, the White can compensate in part for his inability or failure to implement his own desires.

The White image of the Black, then, is such as to make the Black sexually attractive. But such sentiments cannot be reckoned with openly—they are "disgraceful" and even "sinful." Although repressed —unconscious—they make their presence known in the preoccupation that many Whites have with Black sexuality, betraying sexual attraction. Thus, psychologists and psychiatrists note what many laymen have also observed, namely, those people who make vehement but unnecessary protestations of their innocence of, or of their horror at, certain types of behavior reveal their own attraction to the behavior. It is not unusual to find in life the ex-prostitute who is a militant, fanatical crusader against vice or the ex-Communist

[25] *Ibid.*, 160–161. Also see, 324–325.

[26] It appears that Whites may be imputing to Blacks not only their own sexual desires, but a wish for exaggerated potency as well. On the other hand, William Montague Cobb, "Physical Anthropology of the American Negro," *American Journal of Physical Anthropology,* 29 (1942), 158–159, cites five studies indicating that the penis of the Black is on average larger than that of the White and indicates that his own observations substantiate this. Social scientists, in contrast, have almost universally asserted that this notion has little or no basis in fact.

who is a militant leader in the fight against Communism. A similar principle operates with the White who constantly argues, "Would you want your daughter (sister) to marry a Black?"

Dr. Robert Seidenberg indicates an interesting case illustrating this general principle. One of his White patients inquired of him, "Is it true that Negroes have extra long penises and that they are erect all the time? Wouldn't it be disgusting to have intercourse with a Negro?" Later in therapy it was revealed that this woman could experience sexual pleasure with her husband only when she fantasied that a "large black Negro" was trying to rape her. In a word, her preoccupation with the issue and disavowal of it betrayed her own attraction to Black males.[27]

The matter is intensified by the fact that historically it was White males, not Black males, who most frequently transgressed the caste line and sexually engaged women of the other racial group. If White men can find Black women so titillating why then may not White women find Black men exciting? And if Black men are especially accomplished copulators—indeed sexual athletes—White women may like them especially well. This final blow to the White man's pride in his masculinity has to be avoided at all costs. And it has been avoided at the cost of all Blacks who have ever been lynched under the faintest suspicion of intercourse with a White woman.

Projection and Fear of Black Rape

The mechanism of projection is of value in understanding the agitating question of rape of White women by Black men. The Black man is held to possess an inordinate desire for White women, and southern communities have traditionally credited the slightest suspicious that such contacts have occurred. Although rapes do occur, the southern White's fear seem quite out of proportion to the actual danger. If the analysis thus far has some validity, the fear becomes comprehensible. Many Whites unconsciously find the Black sexually attractive. But such thoughts are too painful to acknowledge. They become permissible only when attributed to others, in this case the Black male. The Black male then appears as the aggressor.

[27] Robert Seidenberg, "The Sexual Basis of Social Prejudice," *Psychoanalytic Review*, 39 (1952), 90–95.

The situation is similar to that of the supermoral, sexually frustrated "old maid" who bars her door against fancied male aggressors. The old maid's sexual impulses, impulses she denies yet which are nevertheless real, are projected outside of herself upon fantasied male attackers. Indeed, "Methinks the lady doth protest too much." The projection to Black men of large genitals makes the fear of rape seem all the more realistic and menacing. Furthermore, White men crossing the caste line for sexual liaison with Black women tend to project to Black men a similar desire on the part of the latter for White women. Within the South there is the constant possibility of aggressive sexual behavior by White men against Black women; it is easy to believe—to project—that Black men must constantly wish to retaliate against White women.[28]

Notions of Inordinate Sexuality Among Other Minorities

An inordinate sexual desire has also been attributed to various minority groups other than Blacks, probably stemming from somewhat similar mechanisms of projection. In the decades preceding the Civil War a rash of anti-Catholic books appeared as "convent disclosures." Later evidence exposed these "disclosures" as frauds, but not before intense anti-Catholic sentiment had been aroused by them. Nuns and priests were vividly depicted as engaging in licentious practices and infanticide.[29] Dark tales of sexual debauchery have long been a stand-by among Catholic-haters.

Among the more scurrilous of these attacks were those launched against the Catholic clergy after the turn of the twentieth century by the ex-Populist leader and United States senator from Georgia Tom Watson. In Watson's magazine, the confessional was depicted as a place "in which a lewd priest sows the minds of girls and married women with lascivious suggestions." It was "an open way to damnation along which untold thousands of our sisters have traveled to hell." The Catholic confessional was pictured as a snare where there were made "secret confessions to unmarried Lotharios, parading as priests and enjoying themselves carnally with the choicest women of the earth." Watson betrays his own probable subconscious projection of debauchery to priests in his assertion that in the confessional "the priest finds out what girls and married women he can

---

[28] Dollard, *op. cit.*, 162 ff. and 324–334.

[29] Gustavus Myers, *History of Bigotry in the Unites States,* revised by Henry M. Christman (New York: G. P. Putnam's Sons, Inc., 1960), 92–103.

seduce. Having discovered the trail, *he wouldn't be human,* if he did not take advantage of the opportunity." [30] Watson assumed—projected—that what was "human" for him held true for others as well.

Not dissimilar charges have been directed against Jews and rabbis. Watson, fanning the flames of hate against Leo Frank, a Jew framed in the rape-murder of a White fourteen-year-old Georgia girl, wrote, "Leo Frank was a typical young Jewish man of business who lives for pleasure *and runs after Gentile girls.* Every student of sociology knows that the black man's lust after the white woman *is not much fiercer than the lust of the licentious Jew for the Gentile.*" [31] Frank was subsequently hanged by an armed mob of twenty-five or thirty men grandiosely styling themselves "a vigilance committee." In Europe it also has been a common practice to accuse Jews of gross sexual immorality. In Hitlerite Germany in particular, Jews were depicted as given to overindulgence, rape, and perversion. A special newspaper was formed for the purpose of warning the "chaste and innocent" Germans against alleged Jewish sexual perverts who ostensibly derived diabolical pleasure from raping "Aryan" women.[32] Yet it was precisely the Elite Guard of "Aryan" masculinity, the S.S., who were infamous for among other things raping Jewish women.

The Jews as Living Inkblots

Historically the Jew has represented a particularly suitable projection screen for man's conflicts. It is easy to project one's own unacceptable feelings upon an outer object that lacks a clear, sharp structure of its own. Psychologists employ this principle in various "projective tests" of which the Rorschach test is the best known. In the formless inkblot, people are capable of "seeing" an extraordinary number of things. In the process of interpreting inkblots, individuals project their intimate fantasy life and general personality pattern. Thus, projective tests are useful tools in psychology. Ackerman and Jahoda note that for the anti-Semite "the Jew is a living Rorschach inkblot." [33] The Jew is portrayed culturally as many

[30] Watson's *Jeffersonian,* March, 1911. Quoted in *Ibid.,* 195–196. Italics added.
[31] *Watson's Magazine,* January, 1915. Quoted in *Ibid.,* 203. Italics in the original.
[32] Rudolph M. Loewenstein, *Christians and Jews* (New York: International Universities Press, Inc., 1951), 45.
[33] Ackerman and Jahoda, *op. cit.,* 58.

things: as "successful" and as a "low class," as "capitalist" and as "Communist," as "clannish" and as "intruder into other people's society," as "oversexed" and as "impotent," as "strong" and as "weak." [34] Thus the image of the Jew is unstructured; he might be almost anything. As such, the Jew has constituted an especially suitable "inkblot" for the projection of traits and motives that one cannot acknowledge within oneself.

On the basis of an investigation of forty patients exhibiting anti-Semitism in psychoanalytic treatment, Ackerman and Jahoda concluded that not only do different people attribute different and mutually contradictory characteristics to Jews, but the same individual may make quite inconsistent accusations against them. One man asserted that Jews were degraded robbers and at still another time that they were too ethical. One woman contended that Jews are the incarnation of vulgarity but simultaneously they represented to her the symbol of a God figure.[35] Accordingly, Jews might represent almost anything and as such become a projection screen for inner conflict. One woman patient accused the Jews of being shams and fakers, capable of realizing high positions by unfair means. She herself was a highly successful business woman. Psychiatric analysis indicated that the woman continuously accused herself of having secured success without merit, by being a "faker" who "bluffed" her way into positions of prestige.[36]

Bettelheim and Janowitz suggest that prejudiced individuals are prone to project onto Jews those tendencies represented by the demands of the person's own conscience or superego.[37] Within America, failure to realize success goals is generally attributed to the individual's own shortcomings. Such alleged traits of Jews as "ambitious," "hard working," "cooperative" (clannish), "resolute," "perseverant," "shrewd," and "intelligent" remind the individual of his own failure to live up to societal expectations, expectations that have become an integral part of his conscience. But finding it too painful to admit his own shortcomings, the individual tends to excuse such shortcomings by blaming Jews for his failures.

[34] *Ibid.*, 58.
[35] *Ibid.*, 57.
[36] *Ibid.*, 59.
[37] Bruno Bettelheim and Morris Janowitz, *Dynamics of Prejudice* (New York: Harper & Row, 1950), 43.

Limitations of Projection Theories

Projection theories suffer from many of the same shortcomings that characterize the frustration–aggression theories. Most particularly they fail to explain why a particular minority is selected for the projection of specific traits when there are several minorities to choose from. Even assuming for the moment the merit of projection theories, how is it that the stereotypes of various minorities differ? Yet there is an even more severe problem with regard to these theories. They are premised upon inferences from observable facts, not upon the facts themselves. In short, the evidence for them is at best circumstantial.

The theories need to be subjected to rigid experimental test, yet such testing would pose considerable methodological problems. This is of course a problem central to testing various psychiatric and psychoanalytic theories. Therapy apparently gives some confirmation to such notions. However, the rigid experimental testing so essential to science has, for the most part, been lacking. One theory could be substituted for another, and there could be any number of theories to explain the same phenomenon. Does this mean, then, that the projection theories outlined earlier are of no value? Of course not. As was noted, psychiatric work gives some confirmation of them. Similarly, for some time the virus theory of disease was generally accepted even though the evidence for it was at best circumstantial; later, more powerful microscopes lent support to the theory. Thus, merely because a theory lacks experimental support, in the absence of contrary evidence, it need not be rejected. *Caution* needs, however, to be reserved in relation to it.

THE PREJUDICED PERSONALITY

A number of researchers have advanced the hypothesis that prejudice constitutes an ingredient that is closely and intricately bound to an *entire* personality structure. It is a property or symptom of a basic personality organization. This point of view is to be contrasted with that which holds that prejudice represents a more or less *isolated* trait to be found in almost any kind of personality. This latter position suggests that prejudice is an independent personality tendency that manifests itself as a specific response to a specific stimulus.

The prejudiced personality theorists dispute this. They argue that individuals differ in their susceptibility to anti-democratic propaganda and in their readiness to exhibit anti-democratic tendencies. The crucial factor determining such susceptibility and readiness is the personality organization. The personality organization or structure may contain contradictions as well as consistencies, but these aspects are *organized* in that they represent constituent parts of a larger whole.

To understand prejudice, these researchers insist, one must examine the total personality. Personality is seen as a more or less enduring organization of forces operating within the individual. These persisting forces of personality are largely responsible for the responses of an individual in various situations; they give consistency to behavior. Although the personality arises from a social environment, it is not, once developed, a mere object of this environment. A structure has been developed within the individual that is capable of self-initiated action upon the social environment. A selection of the varying impinging stimuli occurs on the basis of this relatively firmly established and unmodifiable structure.

The Authoritarian Personality

Perhaps the most ambitious and comprehensive effort to define a prejudiced personality type was undertaken by a group of University of California psychologists at Berkeley. Considerable attention has since been focused upon their findings, which appeared in 1950 in a book entitled *The Authoritarian Personality*.[38] The work represents a milestone in research in the field of dominant-minority relations. Particularly impressive were their efforts to develop a series of tests for the measurement of anti-Semitism (the A-S Scale), ethnocentrism (the E Scale concerned with attitudes towards "Japs," "Okies," "Negroes," Filipinos, zootsuiters, foreigners, criminals, and others), political and economic conservatism (the PEC Scale), and basic personality patterns (the F Scale). Together with these tests they employed detailed clinical interviews and projective tests on subjects who ranked among the highest 25 per cent and the lowest 25 per cent on the scale measuring anti-minority attitudes. The clinical interviews and projective tests were used to gain access to the con-

[38] T. W. Adorno, Else Frenkel-Brunswik, Daniel J. Levinson, and R. Nevitt Sanford, *The Authoritarian Personality* (New York: Harper & Row, 1950).

scious as well as unconscious aspects of the personalities of their subjects. The great majority of the subjects lived within the San Francisco Bay area and were drawn from the middle socioeconomic class. In addition, smaller groups of working-class men and women, inmates at San Quentin State Prison, and patients at a psychiatric clinic were studied.

The Berkeley group state the major premise upon which they based their theory and research in these terms:

> . . . the political, economic, and social convictions of an individual often form a broad and coherent pattern, as if bound together by a "mentality" or "spirit," and . . . this pattern is an expression of deep-lying trends in his personality.[39]

By employing the questionnaire associated with the F Scale (referred to as the Implicit Antidemocratic Trends or Potentiality of Fascism Scale and by many subsequent researchers as the Authoritarian Scale), the Berkeley group believed they could measure an individual's basic personality patterns. They grouped the thirty-eight items composing the F Scale under nine general characteristics. These characteristics define the antidemocratic or potentially fascistic syndrome. *Syndrome* is a word commonly used medically to refer to a collection of concurrent symptoms associated with a disorder or disease. Let us examine these nine characteristics, defining each and then illustrating each with two statements found in the questionnaire:

1. Conventionalism. Conventionalism involves a rigid adherence to conventional, middle-class values.

> *Example:* "Obedience and respect for authority are the most important virtues children should learn."
> *Example:* "If people would talk less and work more, everybody would be better off."

2. Authoritarian Submission. Authoritarian submission entails a submissive, uncritical attitude toward idealized moral authorities of the in-group.

> *Example:* "Young people sometimes get rebellious ideas, but as they grow up they ought to get over them and settle down."
> *Example:* "Science has its place, but there are many important things that can never possibly be understood by the human mind."

[39] *Ibid.,* 1.

3. Authoritarian Aggression.   Authoritarian aggression involves a tendency to be on the lookout for, and to condemn, reject, and punish people who violate conventional values.

> *Example:* "An insult to our honor should always be punished."
> *Example:* "Homosexuals are hardly better than criminals and ought to be severely punished."

4. Anti-Intraception.   Anti-intraception entails an opposition to the subjective, the imaginative, and the tender-minded.

> *Example:* "The businessman and the manufacturer are much more important to society than the artist and the professor."
> *Example:* "Nowadays more and more people are prying into matters that should remain personal and private."

5. Superstition and Stereotypy.   Superstition and stereotypy entail a belief that mystical determinants influence an individual's fate and a tendency to think in rigid categories.

> *Example:* "Some day it will probably be shown that astrology can explain a lot."
> *Example:* "Some people are born with an urge to jump from high places."

6. Power and "Toughness."   Power and "toughness" are viewed as a preoccupation with the dominance-submission, strong-weak, leader-follower dimension, an identification with power figures, an overemphasis upon conventional morality, and an exaggerated assertion of strength and toughness.

> *Example:* "No weakness or difficulty can hold us back if we have enough will power."
> *Example:* "Most people don't realize how much our lives are controlled by plots hatched in secret places."

7. Destructiveness and Cynicism.   Destructiveness and cynicism involve a generalized hostility toward and a vilification of humans.

> *Example:* "Human nature being what it is, there will always be war and conflict."
> *Example:* "Familiarity breeds contempt."

8. Projectivity.   Projectivity entails a disposition to believe that wild and dangerous things go on in the world and more generally the projection outward of unconscious emotional impulses.

Example: "Wars and social troubles may someday be ended by an earthquake or flood that will destroy the whole world."

Example: "Nowadays when so many different kinds of people move around and mix together so much, a person has to protect himself especially carefully against catching an infection or disease from them."

9. Sex.   Sex entails an exaggerated concern with sexual "goings-on."

Example: "The wild sex life of the old Greeks and Romans was tame compared to some of the goings-on in this country, even in places where people might least expect it."

Example: "Sex crimes, such as rape and attacks on children, deserve more than mere imprisonment; such criminals ought to be publicly whipped, or worse."

With the F Scale the Berkeley group hoped to identify a personality type that was potentially undemocratic and fascistic. Accordingly they expected F Scale scores to correlate with the scores realized from the Anti-Semitism, Ethnocentrism, and the Political and Economic Conservatism Scales. This indeed proved to be the case. For the first version of the F scale the mean correlation with A-S (the Anti-Semitism Scale) was .53, with E (the Ethnocentrism Scale) it was .65, and with PEC (the Political and Economic Conservatism Scales), .54. The Berkeley researchers revised the F Scale several times by dropping items that did not correlate with total scores or that were not predictive of A-S and E scores. On the final version of the F Scale, the mean correlation with an E Scale that included anti-Semitic items was .75. Hence the Berkeley group felt that its work convincingly demonstrated that prejudice and authoritarianism (as defined by the F Scale) often constitute closely interrelated personality characteristics.

Genesis of the Authoritarian Personality in Childhood

The Berkeley researchers did not limit themselves to defining the predominant personality patterns of those ranking high in prejudice. They were also concerned with the early childhood interrelationships within the family that they believed had fostered these patterns. In keeping with a predominantly Freudian approach, the

Berkeley group viewed early relationships with parents and siblings as of paramount importance in determining the basic personality organization. Hence the researchers undertook to identify a composite picture of the family patterns of the highly prejudiced. This picture emerged as an overview or abstraction taken from the total group. Accordingly, exceptions and variations could be noted in specific cases.

The home discipline of the prejudiced subjects was relatively harsh, arbitrary, and threatening.[40] One subject reported that his father "did not believe in sparing the rod for stealing candy or someone's peaches off the tree." Another stated, "But mother had a way of punishing me—lock me in a closet—or threaten to give me to a neighborhood woman who she said was a witch." [41] Within these families, relationships tended to be rather clearly defined in terms of roles of dominance and submission as opposed to equalitarian policies. As a result, the child developed an image of the parents as somewhat distant and forbidding. The child fearfully submitted to the demands of the parents and felt constrained to suppress impulses that were not acceptable to them. On the other hand, those low in prejudice tended to come from families placing less emphasis on obedience and greater emphasis on the unconditional giving of love and affection.

In a related study, children high in prejudice and children low in prejudice were asked to define the perfect boy. The highly prejudiced tended to define the perfect boy as being "polite," "having good manners," "being clean," whereas those low in prejudice tended to define the perfect boy in terms of "companionship" and "being fun." The tendency toward conformity in the prejudiced child found expression in frequent indorsement of such statements as "There is only one right way to do anything" and "Appearances are usually the best test." [42] The prejudiced children accepted the parental emphasis upon discipline, describing the perfect father in punitive and restrictive terms rather than in terms of love and understanding. Describing the perfect father, one child indicated, "He

[40] In this regard see: Donald Weatherley, "Maternal Responses to Childhood Aggression and Subsequent Anti-Semitism," *Journal of Abnormal and Social Psychology,* 66 (1963), 183–185.

[41] Adorno, *op. cit.,* 373.

[42] Else Frenkel-Brunswik, "A Study of Prejudice in Children," *Human Relations,* 1 (1948), 303.

spanks you when you are bad and does not give you too much money. . . ." Another reported, "When you ask for something he ought not to give it to you right away. Not soft on you, strict." [43] The children low in prejudice, on the other hand, were more likely to be treated as an equal and given the opportunity to express feelings of rebellion or disagreement.

The goals which the parents of the highly prejudiced sought to instil were highly conventional in nature. The parents fostered the adoption of a rigid and externalized set of values: "That which is socially accepted and helpful in climbing the social ladder is 'good,' and that which deviates and is socially inferior is 'bad.'" The parents of the unprejudiced, on the other hand, were less status-ridden and showed less anxiety with respect to conformity and less intolerance toward socially unacceptable behavior. Rather than condemning, they tended to provide more guidance and support, helping the child to work out his problems and feelings rather than continuously demanding that he suppress them.[44] Prejudiced subjects tended to feel themselves "forgotten," the victims of injustice who did not "get" enough of the things they deserved from parents.

The Berkeley researchers, then, stressed the part that severe parental discipline plays in the development of prejudice in children. In the previous chapter we outlined a somewhat different approach, namely that parents communicate their prejudices to children—in brief, that children learn their society's "people habits" in much the same manner that they take on its food habits.

Some recent research helps us to resolve some of these theoretical differences, and to integrate the divergent approaches. Epstein and Komorita, in their research involving young children, have found that childhood prejudice is related to an *interaction* between parental prejudice and punitiveness. Their work suggests that *moderate* discipline and high parental prejudice are most likely to foster the formation of childhood prejudice. They conclude that moderate discipline orients the child towards obtaining parental approval and serves to reduce the child's doubt regarding the appropriateness of his internalizing parental attitudes. Severe discipline, in contrast, encourages the child to avoid his parents while high permissiveness

---

[43] *Ibid.*, 301.
[44] Adorno, *op. cit.*, 385–388.

fosters excessive autonomy—in either events, the process of identification with parents and their prejudice is inhibited.[45]

Criticism of "The Authoritarian Personality"

Probably no other research in the field of race and ethnic relations has received greater attention than that of *The Authoritarian Personality*. Scores of studies have appeared criticizing, testing, refining, and qualifying the findings of the Berkeley group. By the end of 1956, six years after the publication of the volume, at least 230 publications appeared dealing with authoritarianism, an interest that continues unabated. Obviously, we are in no position here to review all the many criticisms of *The Authoritarian Personality*. We shall, however, note a number of the more vital ones.[46]

1. Many of the criticisms focus upon research methods. Critics point out, with some justification, that the sample of persons actually studied was not a representative or random sample of this population or of any other specifiable population. The subjects were primarily middle class and members of at least one formal organization (veterans' group, labor unions, Kiwanis clubs, etc.). Yet middle class people and members of formal organizations differ in many respects from other segments of the population. Similarly some critics suggest that the study's scales are inadequate, in fact faulty, and that many items are ambiguous. Asch goes even a step further and rejects "the assumption that one can deduct the content of psychological processes from the content of attitude items." [47]

2. Some writers have suggested that a tendency toward "acquiescence" can account for part of the apparent relationship between an

[45] Ralph Epstein and S. S. Komorita, "Parental Discipline, Stimulus Characteristics of Outgroups, and Social Distance in Children," *Journal of Personality and Social Psychology*, 2 (1965), 416–420; "Childhood Prejudice as a Function of Parental Ethnocentrism, Punitiveness, and Outgroup Characteristics," *Journal of Personality and Social Psychology*, 3 (1966), 259–264; and Prejudice among Negro Children as Related to Parental Ethnocentrism and Punitiveness," *Journal of Personality and Social Psychology*, 4 (1966), 643–647.

[46] For an extended evaluation of *The Authoritarian Personality*, see: Richard Christie and Marie Jahoda, eds., *Studies in the Scope and Method of "The Authoritarian Personality"* (New York: The Free Press of Glencoe, 1954), and John P. Kirscht and Ronald C. Dillehay, *Dimensions of Authoritarianism: A Review of Research and Theory* (Lexington: University of Kentucky Press, 1967).

[47] Solomon E. Asch, *Social Psychology* (Englewood Cliffs, N.J.: Prentice-Hall, Inc., 1952), 545.

authoritarian personality type and prejudice.[48] The items in the F
Scale are all "agree" items. A number of researchers have discovered
that some people have a marked tendency to agree with almost any
proposition, not only on the F Scale but on any and all scales, regardless of content. Conversely, other people disagree with practically
every proposition, regardless of its nature. Couch and Keniston
christen these types "Yeasayers" and "Naysayers" [49] :

The difficulty lies in the fact that every time you agree with an item on
the F-scale you chalk up a credit toward authoritarianism. If you agree that
"obedience and respect for authority are the most important virtues children
should learn," ping! you score one! If you agree that "to a greater extent than
most people realize, our lives are governed by plots hatched in secret by
politicians," ping! you score another point for authoritarianism. In other
words, all the items are unidirectional, so worded that agreement always signi-
fies authoritarianism. Only by disagreeing with every item can you obtain
a completely "democratic" score.[50]

3. The Berkeley group held that the association between authoritarianism (as measured by the F Scale) and a variety of the other
attitudes (including prejudice) argues for the existence of a unified
personality configuration. Not so, argue some critics. These writers
note that authoritarian tendencies increase as intelligence, education, and socioeconomic class status go down.[51] Hence, some insist,
the numerous components of authoritarianism are found together in

---

[48] There are many studies. See, for example, B. M. Bass, "Authoritarianism or
Acquiescence," *Journal of Abnormal and Social Psychology*, 51 (1955), 616–623;
S. Messick and D. N. Jackson, "Authoritarianism or Acquiescence in Bass's Data,"
Journal of Abnormal and Social Psychology, 54 (1957), 424–426; "Reply" by Bass
in the same volume, 426–427; N. L. Goge *et al.*, "The Psychological Meaning of
Acquiescence Set for Authoritarianism," *Journal of Abnormal and Social Psychology*,
55 (1957), 98–103. Also see: D. Peabody, "Attitude Content and Agreement Set in
Scales of Aunthoritarianism, Dogmatism, Anti-Semitism and Economic Conservation,"
Journal of Abnormal and Social Psychology, 63 (1961), 1–12. Peabody's conclusions
regarding acquiescence have been questional by F. Samelson, "Agreement Set and
Anticontent Attitudes in the F Scale: A Reinterpretation," *Journal of Abnormal and
Social Psychology*, 68 (1964), 338–342.
[49] A. Couch and K. Keniston, "Yeasayers and Naysayers: Agreeing Response Set
as a Personality Variable," *Journal of Abnormal and Social Psychology*, 60 (1960),
151–175.
[50] Gordon W. Allport, "Prejudice: Is It Societal or Personal?" *Journal of Social
Issues*, 18 (1962), 120–134.
[51] See, for example, H. H. Hyman and P. B. Sheatsley, " 'The Authoritarian Personality'—A Methodological Critique," in Christie and Jahoda, *op. cit.*, 50–122; W. J.
MacKinnon and R. Centers, "Authoritarianism and Urban Stratification," *American
Journal of Sociology*, 61 (1956), 610–620; and A. Kornhauser, H. L. Sheppard, and
A. J. Mayer, *When Labor Votes* (New York: University Books, 1956).

a person simply because they are the norms of people with little education and low socioeconomic class status:

> . . . there is the real possibility that *both* authoritarian beliefs and prejudices may be learned in the same way that we learn that the world is round (or flat, or held up on the back of a giant turtle). The association of both prejudices and personality items with formal education forces us to take seriously the possibility that widespread indoctrination, relatively independent of individual psychological needs, may account for at least a considerable part of the correlation of authoritarianism and prejudice. Thus, *both* authoritarianism and prejudice may tend to be characteristic of persons in economically and socially deprived positions in the social structure.[52]

Selznick and Steinberg take this criticism a step further. They argue that the authors of the *The Authoritarian Personality*, in common with many other researchers, were led astray by asking: Why do people *accept* anti-Semitic beliefs? In a society that culturally embodies anti-Semitism, an elaborate theory is not necessary: people acquire anti-Semitism through the normal processes of socialization. Rather we need to ask: Why in such a society do some people *reject* anti-Semitic beliefs. Phrasing the question in this manner directs our attention to the countervailing forces in American culture, those that run counter to the attitudes of the mass or common culture. These forces include attitudes of science, democracy, and humanitarianism that are transmitted chiefly through the educational system. Hence, it is the educated—especially the more highly educated—who reject not only anti-Semitism but also anti-intellectualism and anti-democratic attitudes.[53]

4. Some critics allege that authoritarianism may be spuriously related to prejudice through its association with status, anomie, or some other variable. Kaufman suggests, for example, on the basis of his study of 213 non-Jewish college undergraduates, that status is more closely related to anti-Semitism than is authoritarianism. By employing statistical measures, Kaufman undertook to determine the association between both authoritarianism and status and scores on the anti-Semitism scale. He attempted to discover through the use of partial correlations (statistical measures) the degree to which authoritarianism and status were each *independently* correlated with the anti-Semitism score. In other words, he measured the

---

[52] Robin M. Williams, Jr., *Strangers Next Door* (Englewood Cliffs, N.J.: Prentice-Hall, Inc., 1964), 90.

[53] Gertrude J. Selznick and Stephen Steinberg, *The Tenacity of Prejudice* (New York: Harper & Row, 1969), 136–169.

degree to which authoritarianism was correlated with anti-Semitism when the effect of status was allowed for, or to put it another way, was held constant. Smiliarly, he measured the degree to which status was correlated with prejudice when the effect of authoritarianism was allowed for. Since status and authoritarianism might go hand-in-hand, Kaufman wanted to look at the separate effect of each. The partial correlation of status and anti-Semitism was .48 (moderately high), while that of authoritarianism and anti-Semitism was .12 (quite low). Kaufman concluded that concern with status is the dominant dimension related to anti-Semitism and that the correlation he found of .53 between authoritarianism and anti-Semitism could be largely explained by their mutual relationship and concern with status. Thus, when the effect of status was held constant, the correlation between authoritarianism and anti-Semitism dropped to .12.[54]

Srole undertook to investigate the relationship of another variable, anomie, to prejudice. Anomie is a sociological concept derived from Durkheim which Srole used to designate a state of social malintegration within individuals, a state represented by disorganization, group alienation, and demoralization. In interviewing a sample of 401 white, native-born adults in Springfield, Massachusetts, Srole undertook to measure the association between both authoritarianism and anomie and scores on the prejudice scale. Using partial correlations, as did Kaufman, he was interested in discovering the degree to which authoritarianism and anomie each were *independently* correlated with the prejudice score. The partial correlation of anomie and prejudice was .35, while that of authoritarianism and prejudice was .12. On the basis of this sample, anomie appeared more closely associated with prejudice than authoritarianism.[55] Roberts and Rokeach, in a somewhat similar study of 86 adults, secured results differing from those of Srole. They found a correlation of .53 between authoritarianism and prejudice when anomic was held constant, and a correlation of .37 between anomic and

---

[54] Walter C. Kaufman, "Status, Authoritarianism, and Anti-Semitism," *American Journal of Sociology*, 62 (1957), 379–382. Also see: John D. Photiades and Jeanne Biggar, "Religiousity, Education, and Ethnic Distance," *American Journal of Sociology*, 67 (1962), 666–672.

[55] Leo Srole, "Social Integration and Certain Corollaries: An Exploratory Study," *American Sociological Review*, 21 (1956), 709–716. In this regard also see: Edward L. McDill, "Anomie, Authoritarianism, Prejudice, and Socio-Economic Status," *Social Forces*, 39 (1961), 239–245, and Kenneth G. Luttermann and Russell Middleton, "Authoritarianism, Anomia, and Prejudice," *Social Forces*, 48 (1970), 485–492.

prejudice when authoritarianism was held constant.[56] More definitive conclusions will have to await further research. Nevertheless, anomie appears to be a variable associated with prejudice.

5. A recurring criticism of *The Authoritarian Personality* deals with its tendency to equate authoritarianism tendencies with a right-wing (fascistic) political orientation. May we not find, suggest some critics, intemperate and exaggerated love-prejudice just as we find intemperate and exaggerated hate-prejudice? They ask: what about Communistic authoritarianism of the left? Indeed, can one be authoritarian even if one's attitudes are "on the side of the angels?"

Rokeach takes this kind of position. He criticizes the F Scale as being a measure of right-wing authoritarianism rather than a measure of authoritarianism in general.[57] Authoritarianism as described by the Berkeley group, Rokeach argues, is a subspecies of a more general personality syndrome which he calls "dogmatism." Whereas Communists score relatively low on the Berkeley F and prejudice scales, they score higher on Rokeach's Dogmatism Scale than most other political groups. Rokeach stresses that authoritarianism should be viewed as a mode of thought (a structure characterized by a "closed mind," dependence upon some absolute authority, and patterns of intolerance toward certain groups) rather than as a set of beliefs (for instance, the favorableness or unfavorableness of attiudes toward certain minorities). Hence what is crucial, according to Rokeach, is the tenacity with which beliefs are held, not the beliefs themselves; he views dogmatism as a stylistic personality attribute, relatively free from specific beliefs.

6. Finally, critics have often observed that the Berkeley group failed to give sufficient recognition to the role culture plays in prejudice. Where a society evolves elaborate definitions and norms governing interracial behavior, the mere presence of prejudice in a person tells us very little about his distinctive modes of personality. Under these circumstances prejudice and discrimination may constitute the characteristics of "normal" personalities. The matter is emphasized by comparative studies of prejudice in the southern and northern United States. Evidence abounds to support the fact

[56] Alan H. Roberts and Milton Rokeach, "Anomie, Authoritarianism, and Prejudice: Replication," *American Journal of Sociology*, 61 (1956), 355–358.

[57] Milton Rokeach, *The Open and Closed Mind* (New York: Basic Books, 1960).

that White southerners are typically more intolerant of Blacks than White northerners. Available research tends to indicate that this is primarily the product of sociocultural factors and not the product of a higher incidence of authoritarian personalities within the South.

Public-opinion polls have shown the South to be one of the least anti-Semitic regions in the nation. Prothro found that two-fifths of his White-middle-class sample in Louisiana harbored intensely *unfavorable* attitudes toward Blacks together with *favorable* attitudes toward Jews.[58] If an authoritarian personality type constituted the crux of the problem, the South should display *both* a high incidence of anti-Semitism and a high incidence of prejudice against Blacks. Further, we should expect to find a higher incidence of authoritarian personalities in the South than in the North. Yet Pettigrew could not find any higher incidence of authoritarianism in four small southern towns in Georgia and North Carolina than in four roughly matched communities in New England. From his data, which included a study of various sociocultural variables, Pettigrew concluded that it was the sociocultural and social adjustment factors that accounted for the sharp differences between the North and the South, not differences in personality.[59] Nor does the authoritarian personality theory take into account inconsistency in prejudice and discrimination, for example, tolerance of Blacks in one's union but not in one's neighborhood.

After reviewing *The Authoritarian Personality* and various criticisms of it, what can we conclude? Perhaps Robin M. Williams, Jr., summarizes the situation best in this appraisal:

> . . . there is every reason to accept the contention that authoritarianism, of the kind that is indexed by the F-scale, tends to enhance the likelihood of ethnic prejudice. But neither the authoritarian syndrome nor other related personality tendencies invariably constitute either a necessary or sufficient set of conditions for prejudice, much less discriminatory behavior.[60]

Hence, despite the lack of overall consensus on the study, the Berkeley research still commands considerable respect.

---

[58] E. Terry Prothro, "Ethnocentrism and Anti-Negro Attitudes in the Deep South," *Journal of Abnormal and Social Psychology*, 47 (1952), 105–108.

[59] Thomas F. Pettigrew, "Regional Differences in Anti-Negro Prejudice," *The Journal of Abnormal and Social Psychology*, 59 (1959), 28–36. Also see: J. Allen Williams, "Regional Differences in Authoritarianism," *Social Forces*, 45 (1966), 273–277.

[60] Robin M. Williams, Jr., *op. cit.*, 94.

SUMMARY

In this chapter we have considered a number of "personality-centered" approaches to racism. Although telling us little regarding the origins of racism, they are helpful in contributing to our understanding of how racism is maintained and even intensified. Probably the most popular of these approaches is the scapegoat theory. It holds that individuals often find themselves frustrated in realizing their needs. Frustration breeds aggression that is displaced upon weak victims. In turn, individuals evolve a variety of beliefs that rationalize their otherwise unacceptable hostile impulses. Although a number of studies have tended to confirm the scapegoat theory, still others have contradicted it. The predictive value of the approach is increased by taking into account a number of other variables including the personality of the displacer, the kind of frustration involved, the perceived qualities of potential targets, and the nature of a group's culture.

Another approach examines the part that projection plays in racism—the tendency of people to attribute to others motives or traits that they sense within themselves but that would be painful to acknowledge. In cultures characterized by a disapproval of sex, dominant groups not uncommonly project to minorities traits of inordinate sexuality.

Still another approach considers prejudice to be an ingredient bound to an entire personality structure. *The Authoritarian Personality* is illustrative of this orientation, conceiving of prejudice as associated with an antidemocratic or potentially fascistic syndrome. Since its appearance in 1950, scores of studies have appeared criticizing, testing, refining, and qualifying the findings of *The Authoritarian Personality*.

III

INTERGROUP RELATIONS WITHIN AMERICA

6

Conflict

In the previous three chapters, we focused our attention upon sources of racism. In this and the next three chapters, we shall examine some of the chief processes and patterns of intergroup interaction within American life, devoting one chapter each to conflict, segregation, stratification, and assimilation.

We tend to associate race and ethnic relations, for instance, Black–White, Jew–Gentile, Italian-native American relations, with "social problems." The fact that conflict often represents an important ingredient in such relations probably contributes to this viewpoint. And the feeling is compounded by our tendency to equate conflict with violence. While it is true that riots, lynchings, and related forms of violence may periodically emerge when differing racial or ethnic groups are in contact, conflict need not be expressed exclusively in violent terms. Boycotts, strikes, wade-ins, sit-ins, passive resistance, legal litigation, at times even wit and humor, not to mention many other mechanisms, represent forms of conflict in which violence may be absent. *Conflict may be thought of as a struggle over values and claims to wealth, power, and prestige in which the opponents aim to neutralize, injure, or eliminate their rivals.* In its most extreme expression it may eventuate in the total annihilation of a group, such as was the fate of a number of American Indian tribes.

CONFLICT AND THE SOCIAL ORDER

Conflict and Social Stability

It is not unusual for us to conclude that the absence of conflict in a relationship is an indication that the relationship is highly integrated, stable, and secure. Some married couples pride themselves on "never once having had a quarrel." It is assumed that this is a positive testimonial to the couples' love and happiness. Actually most marriage counselors and psychiatrists have come to a contrary conclusion. In any deep, intimate relationship such as marriage, some bickering is inevitable and its total absence is suggestive of the relationship's failure. The resolution of differences between people requires that some degree of quarreling and conflict ensue. Where all conflict is lacking, family stagnation is likely. The crucial issue in evaluating marital success is not the absence of conflict but how the couple quarrel, how often, over what they quarrel, and the intensity of the quarreling.[1]

Similarly, the absence of racial and ethnic conflict, in and of itself, is not necessarily suggestive of a stable, non-stressful relationship. It may merely mean that a dominant group has more or less successfully coerced and intimidated a minority. We find it easy to confuse peace with satisfaction and silence with consent. Where a relationship is stable, where people feel that it will not be endangered by conflict, conflicts are quite likely to emerge. In fact, under some conditions, conflicts in intergroup relations may represent an index of a better integration of the minority within the community. A minority group which feels that the bonds uniting it to the dominant group are unstable may lack the security that is needed to act out hostility and engage in conflict. On the other hand, overt conflict may be an indication that the minority feels sufficiently secure in its relationship with the dominant group to risk such expression, that is, the members feel the consensual bond between the groups is strong enough to withstand antagonistic action.[2]

Also, interestingly enough, the more the parties to conflict feel themselves integrated within society, the less likely will their conflict take a violent form. In other words, they will choose weapons that

[1] See: George Simpson, *People in Families* (New York: Thomas Y. Crowell Co., 1960), 202–206.

[2] Lewis A. Coser, *The Functions of Social Conflict* (New York: The Free Press of Glencoe, 1956).

will not permanently menace their common bonds; violent class or ethnic wars are likely to give way to less militant means, such as institutionalized strikes, demonstrations, or boycotts, in those societies that permit the integration of lower classes or ethnic and other minorities into the social order. On the other hand, where a people feel themselves more or less permanently excluded from participation in the society's benefits, they come to reject the very assumptions upon which the society is built, and, if they no longer accord legitimacy to the prevailing social order, they will tend to attack it through revolutionary violence.[3]

Social Consequences of Racial and Ethnic Conflict

The emphasis placed upon peace and harmony within the United States contributes to the popular conception that conflict is harmful. According to this view, any expression of conflict within a society or between groups is to be condemned. Where a value system defines most forms of human conflict as harmful and morally wrong, greater attention of course tends to be focused upon its negative aspects. Now it is true that conflict may reach a frequency and intensity whereby the social system is imperiled or undermined—hostility is a potentially destructive and disruptive force within human interaction. Racial and ethnic conflicts often drain and dissipate energy and resources that might otherwise find direction within more productive channels and cooperative activities. Similarly, fears and expectations of friction may lead to an inefficient and ineffective employment of manpower and individual talents and capabilities. And conflict may imperil institutional functioning, as, for instance, in some areas of the South where a number of school districts have undertaken to close public schools rather than permit their desegregation. It is not surprising, then, that societies usually take considerable care to regulate, suppress, and rechannel aggressive impulses.

Yet it is easy to overlook a good many other consequences of ethnic and racial conflict. First, some authorities suggest that ethnic and racial conflict may function as a "safety valve" for the society as a whole. They argue that racial and religious prejudice provides for the "safe" release of hostile and aggressive impulses that are culturally tabooed within other social contexts. By channeling hos-

[3] Lewis A. Coser, "Conflict: Social Aspects," in David Sills, ed., *International Encyclopedia of the Social Sciences* (New York: The Macmillan Co., 1968), 234–235.

tilities from within family, occupational, and other crucial settings onto permissible and less vital targets, the stability of existing social structures may be promoted. This is the well-known scapegoating mechanism.[4]

Second, a multiplicity of conflicts between large numbers of differing groups within a society (conflicts among racial and ethnic groups, labor vs. business, consumer groups vs. producer groups, business vs. business, etc.) may be conducive to a democratic as opposed to a totalitarian order. The multiple group affiliations of individuals contribute to a multiplicity of conflicts crisscrossing society—in brief, they make individuals participate in a variety of group conflicts so that those who are antagonists in one conflict are allies in another. Thus the individual's segmental participation in numerous groups, rather than total absorption by one group, results in a kind of balancing mechanism and prevents deep cleavages along one axis, for example, it prevents cleavage along rigid class lines eventuating in class struggle. In totalitarian societies, on the other hand, there is a maximum concentration of power in one institution —the monolithic state.[5]

Third, conflicts may prevent the ossification of social systems by exerting pressure for innovations; it prevents habitual arrangements from freezing into rigid molds and hence from progressively sapping the ability of people and groups to react creatively to new circumstances. In this sense, conflict may contribute to social vitality.[6] Although our discussion does not exhaust the social consequences of conflict, it does point up the fact that the impact of conflict is not necessarily or entirely negative.

SOCIAL VIOLENCE IN THE UNITED STATES

Although we like to imagine ourselves as a democratic, peace-loving, and rational people, in truth the United States has been a violent nation. Indeed, we prefer to forget that from the earliest settlement period Whites systematically subjected the indigenous Indian population to repeated assault. We also conveniently tend to forget about Shays' Rebellion in Massachusetts in 1787 and Pennsylvania's Whiskey Rebellion in 1794 or about our frontier and

[4] Coser, *The Functions of Social Conflict*, *op. cit.*, 39–48.
[5] *Ibid.*, 76–81.
[6] Coser, "Conflict: Social Aspects," *op. cit.*, 235.

vigilante tradition of violence. Similarly, we have forgotten about the Draft Riots of the Civil War, in which during a span of five days, nearly 2,000 people were killed. And again we like to forget that economic strife erupted countless times in various agrarian revolts and in such bloody affairs as the railroad strikes of 1877, the Homestead and Pullman strikes of the 1890s, and the steel strikes of the 1930s.[7]

We also tend to forget our record of social violence—assaults upon individuals or their property solely or primarily because of their ethnic, religious, or racial affiliations.[8] We are prone to forget the anti-Catholic riots—the anti-Irish riots—of the 1840s and 1850s, with an especially bloody outbreak in Philadelphia, the city of brotherly love, in 1844. We forget about the anti-Chinese riots in the closing decades of the nineteenth century that were extraordinarily cruel. And we forget the 1940s with the wartime attacks not only on the civil rights of, but also against the persons and property of Chicanos and Japanese-Americans.[9]

White—Black Violence

The American tradition of violence has likewise enshrouded White–Black relations, finding expression in at least six broad patterns: [10]

1. Suppression–Insurrection. This pattern of racial violence derived from the dominant-subservient or master–slave relationship. Underlying this relationship was the assumption that a master had the "right" to resort to violence in dealing with his slaves. Physical force became a means for insuring that this superior-inferior arrangement would be maintained. Slavery so completely disrupted Black institutions, culture, and communication that it was virtually impossible for Blacks to launch a serious challenge to their subjugation.

---

[7] See, for instance: Hugh Davis Graham and Ted R. Gurr, eds., *The History of Violence in America: Historical and Comparative Perspectives* (New York: Frederick A. Praeger, 1969).

[8] Allen D. Grimshaw, ed., *Racial Violence in the United States* (Chicago: Aldine Publishing Co., 1969), *passim*.

[9] John R. Spiegel, "The Tradition of Violence in Our Society," *The Sunday Star* (Washington, D.C.), October 13, 1968, p. G–3.

[10] The types of patterns that follow have been adapted from a paper by Jerome Corsi, Jeffrey Hadden, and Kenneth Seminatore on "Patterns of Racial Violence in American History" summarized in *Unscheduled Events*, 2 (Fall, 1968), 1–4, and Louis H. Masotti, Jeffrey K. Hadden, Kenneth F. Seminatore, and Jerome R. Corsi, *A Time to Burn?* (Chicago: Rand McNally & Co., 1969), Chapter 5.

Nonetheless, during the 18th and 19th centuries a number of attempts at slave rebellion occurred, of which the insurrections of Gabriel in Virginia (1800), Denmark Vesey in South Carolina (1822), and Nat Turner in Southhampton County, Virginia (1831), are among the most striking examples. Hundreds of other less well-known slave rebellions also took place, but they were universally unsuccessful.

2. Lynchings. Lynching has been commonly defined as mob action that summarily and illegally takes an individual's life. In lynchings the action is one-sided and directed against particular persons. Thus lynchings are to be contrasted with race riots where mob action is usually a two-way encounter in which violence is more or less indiscriminately and, to one degree or another, reciprocally directed by one racial group against another. Before the Civil War, the lynching of Blacks was rare except in insurrection conspiracies. The financial investment in Black slaves served to restrain mob action. But with the coming of Reconstruction and the disfranchisement of the White leadership together with "scalawag" and "carpetbagger" rule, lynching became a major instrument for "keeping the Black in his place."

It is possible to gain an estimate of the number of lynchings since 1882 from an annual summary made by the Chicago *Tribune* between 1882 and 1917 and from the statistics kept by Tuskegee Institute from 1889 until 1953. The largest number of lynchings occurred during the 1890s, when 420 Whites and 1,111 Blacks met death at the hands of lynch mobs. Since the 1890s, lynchings have progressively declined. In the 1900s there were 885 lynchings (94 Whites and 791 Blacks), in the 1910s 616 (53 Whites and 563 Blacks), in the 1920s 315 (34 Whites and 281 Blacks), and in the 1930s 131 (11 Whites and 120 Blacks). By the 1940s the figure had fallen to 32, and during the 1950s the practice became virtually nonexistent. Except for New England, lynchings have occurred in all sections of the nation but were most frequent in the South, including Texas.

Contrary to popular opinion, most Black lynch victims have not been charged with rape. However, southern efforts to justify lynchings have traditionally revolved about the assertion that such fearsome tactics were essential to control and frighten Blacks lest they undertake wholesale sexual attacks upon White women. South

Carolina Senator Cole L. Blease, defending lynching, told a political rally in 1930, "Whenever the Constitution comes between me and the virtue of the White women of the South, I say, to hell with the Constitution." Various studies have suggested that no more than 25 per cent of the Blacks lynched since 1882 were accused of rape or attempted rape. The Tuskegee statistics indicate that accusations of homicide were responsible for slightly better than 40 per cent of the lynchings. Robbery, theft, insulting White people, attempting to vote, not knowing "a Black's place," and related charges were of lesser significance in the total picture. In some instances the lynched victim was mistaken for another or was completely innocent of the alleged crime.

Lynchings have not infrequently involved considerable brutality and sadism. On occasion victims were tortured, mutilated, and burned alive. The Southern Commission on the Study of Lynching cites this case, occurrring before 1930, which bears marked sadistic overtones:

The sheriff along with the accused Negro was seized by the mob, and the two were carried to the scene of the crime. Here quickly assembled a thousand or more men, women, and children. The accused Negro was hung up in a sweet-gum tree by his arms, just high enough to keep his feet off the ground. Members of the mob tortured him for more than an hour. A pole was jabbed in his mouth. His toes were cut off joint by joint. His fingers were similarly removed, and members of the mob extracted his teeth with wire pliers. After further unmentionable mutilations, the Negro's still living body was saturated with gasoline and a lighted match was applied. As the flames leaped up, hundreds of shots were fired into the dying victim. During the day, thousands of people from miles around rode out to see the sight. Not till nightfall did the officers remove the body and bury it.[11]

Since lynchings involved strong elements of popular excitement, they offered otherwise disgruntled Whites an opportunity to express pent-up emotions and feelings. The hard core of most lynch mobs was drawn predominantly from young, propertyless, unemployed Whites, some of whom had court records.[12]

3. White-Dominated, Person-Oriented Rioting. White-dominated, person-oriented rioting, in contrast with lynching, is not an attack upon particular individuals. Rather, the violence typically takes the following course: the attackers are White; their victims are Black;

[11] Southern Commission on the Study of Lynching, *Lynchings and What They Mean* (Atlanta: 1931), 40.
[12] See: Hadley Cantril, *The Psychology of Social Movements* (New York: John Wiley & Sons, Inc., 1941), 106–110.

the violence originates with, and is directed and controlled by Whites; the Whites seek to inflict personal injury more-or-less indiscriminately upon the Blacks; the Blacks, as victims, do little seriously to fight back or to defend themselves. Traditionally racial violence of this sort resulted not from conscious policy decisions of Whites, but rather from White reactions to real or perceived assaults by Blacks upon the existing racial structure. In brief, if Blacks were seen as "staying in their place," there was little likelihood of violence.[13]

The model for this form of violence is the Springfield, Illinois, race riot of 1908. Feeling against Blacks had been running high in Illinois during this period because of the influx of Blacks to Chicago, Peoria, East St. Louis, and Springfield. In mid-August, 1908, the White community became enraged at the alleged rape of two White women by Blacks. On Friday afternoon, August 15th, a crowd of some 4,000 persons gathered outside the jail where the two arrested Black suspects were being held. Many were merely curious bystanders, others tourists and shoppers in town for the evening and anxious to see what the excitement was about, and still others youthful thrill-seekers; many, however, were motivated by race hatred and, in the case of immigrant White laborers, anxious to put the competing Blacks "in their place." The crowd's mood became progressively ugly. When the crowd learned that the two Black suspects had been secretly removed from the jail and taken to the state prison in Bloomington, two days of rioting, burning, and lynching were unloosed. Some 3,700 militiamen were called into Springfield and subsequently restored order. The Black reaction to this outbreak was one of terror and flight.[14] Such terrorizing of the Black community also occurred in the South during Reconstruc-

[13] Guy B. Johnson, "Patterns of Race Conflict," in Edgar T. Thompson, ed., *Race Relations and the Race Problem* (Durham, N.C.: Duke University Press, 1939), 146–147. Also see Stanley Lieberson and Arnold R. Silverman." Precipitants and Conditions of Race Riots," *American Sociological Review*, 30 (1965), 887–899; and Allen D. Grimshaw, "Lawlessness and Violence in the United States and Their Special Manifestations in Changing Negro-White Relationships," *Journal of Negro History*, 44 (1959), 52–72; "Urban Racial Violence in the United States: Changing Ecological Considerations," *American Journal of Sociology*, 66 (1960), 109–119; "Relationships among Prejudice, Discrimination, Social Tension and Social Violence," *Journal of Intergroup Relations*, 2 (1961), 302–310; and "Negro-White Relations in the Urban North: Two Areas of High Conflict Potential," *Journal of Intergroup Relations*, 3 (1962), 146–158.

[14] James L. Crouthamel, "The Springfield, Illinois Race Riot of 1908," in Joseph Boskin, ed., *Urban Racial Violence in the Twentieth Century* (New York: The Free Press of Glencoe, 1969), 8–19.

tion—indeed, "Reconstruction was in a sense a prolonged race riot";[15] the pattern continued in the 1890s and on into the first two decades of the 1900s in a number of cities: Wilmington, North Carolina (1896); East St. Louis, Illinois (1917); Washington, D.C. (1919); and Tulsa, Oklahoma (1921).

4. Racial Warfare, Person-Oriented Rioting. Blacks have not always remained relatively passive in rioting; in this fourth pattern both Blacks and Whites engage in attacks upon members of the other race. The model for this type of violence is the 1943 riot in Detroit, Michigan.[16] Within Detroit, a climate of racial tension had been building up for some years. Two years earlier, in the spring of 1941, Blacks and Whites were pitted against each other during a strike in Ford Motor's large River Rouge plant. Furthermore, Detroit abounded in White, extreme right-wing, hate groups.

During the early war years, a considerable influx of Blacks and Whites from the South had supplied smoldering embers which contributed to racial tension. Whites from Kentucky, Tennessee, Oklahoma, and Arkansas, many of them former sharecroppers, brought with them racist notions of Blacks. Within Detroit southern Blacks were able to secure jobs that gave them a wage and a sense of freedom that they had previously not known. Among southern White immigrants, for that matter many northerners as well, Detroit Blacks were seen as becoming too "uppity." The situation was compounded by Detroit's severe housing shortage that condemned thousands of both Whites and Blacks to live in slums, tents, and trailers.

Such were the setting and the diverse currents that provided the backdrop for the Detroit riot. The initial outbreak flared Sunday evening, June 20, at Belle Isle, Detroit's 985-acre playground and beach. Versions differ regarding the chief incident that precipitated the riot. Whatever the triggering event, the riot began on the bridge leading to the island, and within a short time some 200 White sailors were fighting with Blacks. A number of Blacks were severely kicked and beaten. Rumors quickly spread through the Black and White communities.

Within Paradise Valley, the congested Black ghetto, rioting broke out in the early morning hours of Monday, June 21. By 2:00

---

[15] Johnson, *op. cit.*, 138.
[16] This summary of the Detroit riot is based primarily upon Alfred McClung Lee and Norman Daymond Humphrey, *Race Riot* (New York: Holt, Rinehart & Winston, Inc.), 1943.

A.M. a White man had been stabbed in the chest, a policeman had suffered a possible skull fracture, and injured people were being taken into Detroit's Municipal Receiving Hospital at a rate of one a minute. Blacks stoned White workers inside a streetcar, and attacked Whites coming off from work at the Chevrolet Gear and Axle Plant. Large groups of Blacks started looting stores and destroying White property in Black districts. By 3:00 A.M. the situation appeared to be out of control, especially in Paradise Valley. An hour later Whites began ganging up on isolated Blacks along Woodward Avenue.

During the day the rioting continued. Gangs of Whites stopped and burned Black cars on Woodward Avenue, the city's main north-south thoroughfare. Although police took action against Black looters, there were numerous reports of their failure to protect Blacks from White attack. Humphrey gives this account of one such incident:

> There was an automobile burning on Woodward and up a side street a Negro was being horribly beaten. Eventually the mob let the Negro go, and he staggered down to the car tracks, and he tried to get on a streetcar. But the car wouldn't stop for him.
> The Negro was punch-drunk. There were policemen down the street, but they didn't pay any attention to him.
> I started shouting, "Hey, copper. Hey, copper." And I pointed to the Negro in the middle of the street. The policeman finally took notice of me, but instead of going in the direction in which I was pointing he walked over to his parked scout car. Then two huge hoodlums began to slug the Negro, and he hung there on the side of the safety zone, taking the punches as if he were a bag of sand . . .[17]

In the Black community, groups of Blacks looted White-owned or -operated stores.

By early evening, 10,000 surging, angry Whites had jammed the City Hall area. As the evening wore on, violence increased. White men stopped streetcars and removed and beat Black passengers. Automobiles were overturned in the street, and some of them were set on fire. A large White mob attempted to invade the Black slum, but it was momentarily stopped by police near the Frazer Hotel, a Black hostelry. Black snipers in the hotel opened fire on the police, and a pitched battle between the snipers and the police ensued. Police were peppered with bullets from hotel windows. They returned the fire, blazing away at windows and hurling tear-gas bombs.

[17] *Ibid.*, 32–33.

Later that evening Governor Harry F. Kelly made a formal, official request for federal troops. Shortly before midnight, President Franklin D. Roosevelt signed the proclamation requested by the governor, calling upon the "military forces of the United States" to put down the "domestic violence" in Michigan. The U.S. Army quickly restored order within Detroit and dispersed the mobs. Nevertheless, tension continued to prevail in Detroit for days thereafter.

In the rioting, 34 people had lost their lives (25 Blacks and 9 Whites). Twelve Blacks were shot to death by police while looting stores and three others after they reportedly had fired shots at the police. The City Receiving Hospital treated 433 riot victims of whom 222 were Whites and 211 Blacks. At least 101 riot victims were hospitalized.

5. Black-Dominated, Property-Oriented Rioting. In this type of riot, Blacks initiate the violence and direct their hostilities toward property rather than toward persons. Most of the property is White-owned but located within the Black ghetto. The violence seldom spreads outside the Black neighborhoods to White residential areas or to such neutral areas as downtown locations. The first major occurrence of this type of violence occurred in Harlem in 1935. On March 19, a Black youth was caught stealing a knife from a Harlem dimestore. The crowd that gathered outside the store gained the impression that White store personnel had murdered the youth. The rumor spread and Blacks roamed the streets of Harlem, breaking store windows and looting. With the exception of confrontations between police and looters, incidents between Blacks and Whites were at a minimum. The looting continued through the next day, but was finally brought under control through the efforts of police and local Black leaders.

In the summer of 1964, the 1935 Harlem riot pattern again emerged in Philadelphia, Rochester, and Harlem, and by 1970, it had appeared in the vast majority of major American cities. The National Advisory Commission on Civil Disorders, in its report on the 1967 riots, provided the following insights on the rioting: [18]

---

[18] This material is from the *Report of the National Advisory Commission on Civil Disorders* (Washington, D.C.: U.S. Government Printing Office, 1968). The Committee's findings are consistent with those of a wide variety of other studies. See: J. R. Feagin, "Social Sources of Support for Violence and Nonviolence in a Negro Ghetto," *Social Problems*, 15 (1968), 432–441; H. Edward Ransford, "Isolation,

Of 164 disorders reported during the first nine months of 1967, eight (5 percent) were major in terms of violence and damage; 33 (20 percent) were serious but not major; 123 (75 percent) were minor and undoubtedly would not have received national attention as "riots" had the nation not been sensitized by the more serious outbreaks.

In the 75 disorders studied by a Senate subcommittee, 83 deaths were reported. Eighty-two percent of the deaths and more than half the injuries occurred in Newark and Detroit. About 10 percent of the dead and 38 percent of the injured were public employees, primarily law officers and firemen. The overwhelming majority of the persons killed or injured in all the disorders were Negro civilians.

Violence usually occurred almost immediately following the occurrence of the final precipitating incident, and then escalated rapidly. With but few exceptions, violence subsided during the day, and flared rapidly again at night. The night-day cycles continued through the early period of the major disorders.

Disorder generally began with rock and bottle throwing and window breaking. Once store windows were broken, looting usually followed.

Disorder did not erupt as a result of a single "triggering" or "precipitation" incident. Instead, it was generated out of an increasingly disturbed social atmosphere, in which typically a series of tension-heightening incidents over a period of weeks or months became linked in the minds of many in the Negro community with a reservoir of underlying grievances. At some point in the mounting tension, a further incident—in itself often routine or trivial—became the breaking point and the tension spilled over into violence.

"Prior" incidents, which increased tensions and ultimately led to violence, were police actions in almost half the cases; police actions were "final" incidents before the outbreak of violence in 12 of the 24 surveyed disorders.

The typical rioter was a teenager or young adult, a lifelong resident of the city in which he rioted, a high school dropout; he was, nevertheless, somewhat better educated than his nonrioting Negro neighbor, and was usually underemployed or employed in a menial job. He was proud of his race, extremely hostile to both whites and middle-class Negroes and, although informed about politics, highly distrustful of the political system.

A Detroit survey revealed that approximately 11 percent of the total residents of two riot areas admitted participation in the rioting, 20 to 25 percent identified themselves as "bystanders," over 16 percent identified themselves as "counter-rioters" who urged rioters to "cool it," and the remaining 48 to 53

Powerlessness, and Violence: A Study of Attitudes and Participation in the Watts Riot," American Journal of Sociology, 73 (1968), 581–591; T. M. Tomlinson, "Determinants of Black Politics: Riots and the Growth of Militancy," Psychiatry, 33 (1970), 247–264; David Boesel, "The Liberal Society, Black Youths, and the Ghetto Riots," Psychiatry, 33 (1970), 265–281; David O. Sears and John B. McConahay, "Participation in the Los Angeles Riot," Social Problems, 17 (1969), 3–20; James A. Geschwender and Benjamin D. Singer, "Deprivation and the Detroit Riot," Social Problems, 17 (1970), 457–463; Eugene L. Loren, Economic Background—The Los Angeles Riot Study (Los Angeles: University of California Institute of Government and Public Affairs, 1967); David O. Sears and John B. McConahay, Los Angeles Riot Study: Riot Participation (Los Angeles: University of California Institute of Government and Public Affairs, 1967); and Raymond J. Murphy and James M. Watson, The Structure of Discontent: The Relationship between Social Structure, Grievance, and Support for the Los Angeles Riot (Los Angeles: University of California Institute of Government and Public Affairs, 1967).

percent said they were at home or elsewhere and did not participate. In a survey of Negro males between the ages of 15 and 35 residing in the disturbance area in Newark, about 45 percent identified themselves as rioters, and about 55 percent as "noninvolved."

What the rioters appeared to be seeking was fuller participation in the social order and the material benefits enjoyed by the majority of American citizens. Rather than rejecting the American system, they were anxious to obtain a place for themselves in it.

Although specific grievances varied from city to city, at least 12 deeply held grievances can be identified and ranked into three levels of relative intensity:

First Level of Intensity

1. Police practices
2. Unemployment and underemployment
3. Inadequate housing

Second Level of Intensity

4. Inadequate education
5. Poor recreation facilities and programs
6. Ineffectiveness of the political structure and grievance mechanisms

Third Level of Intensity

7. Disrespectful white attitudes
8. Discriminatory administration of justice
9. Inadequacy of federal programs
10. Inadequacy of municipal services
11. Discriminatory consumer and credit practices
12. Inadequate welfare programs

Social and economic conditions in the riot cities constituted a clear pattern of severe disadvantage for Negroes compared with whites, whether the Negroes lived in the area where the riot took place or outside it. Negroes had completed fewer years of education and fewer had attended high school. Negroes were twice as likely to be unemployed and three times as likely to be in unskilled and service jobs. Negroes averaged 70 percent of the income earned by whites and were more than twice as likely to be living in poverty. Although housing cost Negroes relatively more, they had worse housing—three times as likely to be overcrowded and substandard. When compared to white suburbs, the relative disadvantage is even more pronounced.

6. Black-Dominated, Person-Oriented Violence. By 1970, the nation's press had carried any number of stories telling of premeditated shoot-outs, snipings, and attacks by Black Power advocates and teen-agers upon police. The Lemberg Center for the Study of Violence at Brandeis University found these reports to be largely inaccurate and sensational.[19] Nonetheless, whereas previously many Blacks expressed their anger at police and Whites by burning and

[19] Terry Ann Knopf, "Sniping—A New Pattern of Violence?" *Trans-action* (July/ August, 1969), 22–29.

looting property in the comparative safe environment of their own community, some were becoming increasingly prepared to direct their anger at the person of Whites—snipers, for instance, to take aim at Whites who ventured into the Black community and bombers to single out White-owned businesses, police stations, and government buildings.

Black-dominated, person-oriented violence has in part been fed by the view that the Black ghettos constitute colonies of White America. The two-nation metaphor of "colony" and "colonizer" has suggested to some Black Power advocates the need of freeing one from the other—a conflict of interest best handled by making the separation more complete and violent. Viewed from this perspective the police and other armed agents of the state constitute "an army of occupation" protecting the interests of outside exploiters and maintaining White establishment domination over the ghetto. Some Black militants call for "a war of independence," and sympathetically identify with guerrilla warfare of the sort waged in Cuba, Vietnam, and Africa.

Sources of Black Militancy

The upsurge in Black militancy during the past decade or so has been associated with a broad crisis of legitimacy within American life. Draft resisters, student protesters, and liberated women have also come to question the legitimacy of the authority exercised by the military, college administrators, and males—authority that the latter had come to regard as being historically, if not biologically, under their jurisdiction. Indeed this denial of legitimacy has come to encompass traditional authorities in the family, the school, the church, the army, and even the national political system. Among the factors underlying the decline in legitimacy were our nation's involvement in the unpopular war in Vietnam, the widespread loss of credibility associated with the style and nature of the Johnson and Nixon Administrations, the traumatic impact of the political assassinations of a number of charismatic leaders, including the Kennedy brothers and Rev. Martin Luther King, Jr. (individuals who enjoyed the trust of the excluded and disaffected), and the attraction of current youth toward a more humanist, experimental, and relativistic world outlook.[20]

[20] Herbert C. Kelman, "A Social-Psychological Model of Political Legitimacy and Its Relevance to Black and White Student Protest Movements," *Psychiatry*, 33 (1970), 224–245.

Although Black unrest has been closely tied to the broader crisis of legitimacy within our society, any number of sociologists and psychologists have suggested that a variety of other factors have also been at work. Among these are the following:

1. The Relative Deprivation Thesis. Relative deprivation refers to the gap between what people actually have and what they have come to expect and feel to be their just due. According to this view, ghetto "riots" are bred by the discrepancy between the rapid escalation of Black expectations and what in fact Blacks have been able to attain. During the 1960s, civil rights leaders and top goverment officials promised a lot—a new day for Black Americans to be realized through civil rights legislation and the war on poverty (a Great Society)—but delivered little; Blacks were led to believe that they would be much better off, but little dramatic improvement occurred. At the same time television penetrated—indeed invaded—the Black ghettos, popularizing a cliched version of White middle-class life styles and feeding discontent.

Other forces also fed a sense of relative deprivation. With the migration of Blacks from rural areas to urban centers, the educational, occupational, and income gap between Blacks and Whites became exaggerated and magnified. Further, the early gains of the civil rights movement made credulous the notion that Blacks would rapidly gain a fair share of America's good things. Yet many Blacks found themselves much in the position of the underprivileged urchin who had his nose pressed against the window, longing for the goodies inside; in the past, segregation and discrimination barred him from entering the door—now he could enter the store, but he lacked the economic resources for securing the goodies. Hence, the new expectations went unfulfilled, or in any event were fulfilled too slowly. Such circumstances gave rise to a sense of relative deprivation—to frustration which then found expression in aggressive and violent outbursts (a variant of the frustration-aggression theory).[21] We shall consider this matter of relative deprivation at greater length in Chapter 12.

---

[21] Ted Gurr, "Urban Disorder: Perspective from the Comparative Study of Civil Strife," in Grimshaw, *op. cit.*, 371–383; James A. Geschwender, "Social Structure and the Negro Revolt: An Examination of Some Hypotheses," *Social Forces*, 43 (1964), 248–256; Thomas J. Crawford and Murray Naditch, "Relative Deprivation, Powerlessness, and Militancy: The Psychology of Social Protest," *Psychiatry*, 33 (1970), 208–223; and Carl F. Brindstaff, "The Negro, Urbanization, and Relative Deprivation in the Deep South," *Social Problems*, 15 (1968), 342–352.

2. Social Disorganization Thesis. Black rioting and militancy have also been attributed to a breakdown of consensual norms within society and to the inability or unwillingness of the agencies of social control to effect their restoration.[22] Such circumstances derive from massive social change—from such trends as industrialization, urbanization, and modernization that give birth to new classes and groups with new social perceptions and life styles. Accompanying these changes go anomie and alienation, conditions in which individuals no longer feel attached to or a part of the existing social and political order. When large numbers of people experience frustration and stress over an extended period of time, they become susceptible to courses of action not otherwise considered. As the Black population migrated to urban centers, the traditional structure of race relations, characterized by Black subordination and adapted to a feudal, rural environment, was no longer appropriate. Black rioting, then, may be viewed as an attack upon the traditional accommodative pattern of race relations.

As part of the larger breakdown of traditional patterns, Crane Brinton points to the disintegration of ruling elites as one factor underlying the four revolutions he studied, typified by the breakdown in Tzarist Russia of March, 1917: traditional elites find their cohesiveness undermined, their ruling effectiveness impaired, and their legitimacy questioned.[23] Something of this sort has occurred in the United States. In earlier decades the relative absence of Black violence in the South was partly the product of the well-founded fear by Blacks that severe retribution would be visited upon them. But as Black strength increased sufficiently in northern cities and Whites became troubled by brutal retaliation, it became safer for Blacks to translate their rage against White oppression into violence. Indeed, the faint stirrings of White conscience concerning their racist behavior may have had the paradoxical effect of legitimizing Black violence without simultaneously leading to actions that dramatically alter racist institutions. In the past decade or so, American society has widely disseminated the message that Blacks

---

[22] Don Bowen and Louis Masotti, *Riots and Rebellion* (Beverly Hills: Sage Publications, 1968); James W. Vander Zanden, *Race Relations in Transition* (New York: Random House, Inc., 1965); and Bryan T. Downes, "Social and Political Characteristics of Riot Cities: A Comparative Study," *Social Science Quarterly*, 49 (1968), 504–520.

[23] Crane Brinton, *The Anatomy of Revolution* (New York: W. W. Norton Co., 1938).

were and are being treated badly. This in turn has suggested that Blacks are justified in taking strong, even violent, actions to eradicate racism.[24]

3. Group Conflict Thesis. Civil violence has also been viewed as a product of a struggle for power among various groups within a society. As we observed in Chapter 3, some things defined as "good" are scarce and divisible, so that the more there is for the one, the less there is for the other. By virtue of their control of critical institutions, Whites were able to effect Black subordination and hence to lay claim to an unequal and larger share of the socially defined "good" things. The slogan—Black Power—reflects a demand by Blacks that the "good" things of American life be reallocated. Viewed from this perspective, rioting represents a "Black Revolt," a renunciation of allegiance and subjection to the White "Establishment."

Any number of sociologists have suggested that the looting accompanying racial outbreaks has constituted a bid for a redistribution of property: "It is a message that certain deprived sectors of the population want what they consider their fair share—and that they will resort to violence to get it."[25] In Watts, Newark, and Detroit, the main businesses affected were groceries, supermarkets, pawn shops, and furniture and liquor stores, while banks, utility stations, industrial plants, schools, hospitals, and private residences (except where the latter were burned as a by-product of being in or near vulnerable business establishments) were usually ignored. The looters generally received support from many people in their community and often worked together in pairs, as family units, or in small groups. Property redefinition typically passed through three stages: initial looting was often a symbolic act of defiance—an assault upon the White man's reverence for property; in the second phase, a more conscious, deliberate plundering developed, at times spurred on by the presence of delinquent gangs; and, in the third stage, looting became the socially *expected* thing to do (on occasion a "carnival spirit" coming to prevail). Widespread looting

[24] Aaron Wildavsky, "The Empty-Head Blues; Black Rebellion and White Reaction," *The Public Interest*, Spring, 1968, pp. 8–9.

[25] Russell Dynes and E. L. Quarantelli, "Looting in American Cities: A New Explanation," *Trans-action* (May, 1968), 14. Also see: E. L. Quarantelli and Russell R. Dynes, "Property Norms and Looting: Their Patterns in Community Crises," *Phylon*, 31 (1970), 168–182.

may then constitute a kind of mass protest against dominant American conceptions of property.[26]

4. Psychology of Violence Thesis. "At the level of individuals, violence is a cleansing force. It frees the native from his inferiority complex and from his despair and inaction; it makes him fearless and restores his self-respect."[27] These words were written by Frantz Fanon, a Black psychoanalyst from Martinique who served with the Algerian rebels. In his book, *The Wretched of the Earth*, he argued that violence is not only a political necessity for colonial peoples seeking their independence but a personal necessity for "colored natives" striving to be men. Because the systematic violence of colonialism deadened and degraded the natives, Fanon insisted, they could achieve psychic wholeness only by committing acts of violence against the White rulers and masters whom they wish to supplant.

Kenneth B. Clark makes a somewhat similar point. Discussing Black youth engaged in urban rioting, Clark, a Black psychologist, writes:

Direct observation of the young Negroes reveals that they are not only destructive, but in the process of destroying are seeking to affirm. They are affirming their power to destroy. In the act of rebelling they appear to be asserting the ability to rebel. Beneath the random and clearly destructive and irrational behavior, there remains the pathetic logic of asserting self-esteem and searching for a positive identity by exposing oneself to danger and even inviting death. This is the quest for the self-esteem of the truly desperate human being. This is the way those who have absolutely nothing to lose seek a pathetic affirmation of self even if it is obtained moments before death.[28]

Friedrichs also argues that Blacks need to pass through a period of emotional catharsis realized by aggression and social withdrawal if they are later to move on to full participation in American society.[29] Thus ghetto rioting is seen as a search for self-esteem and a positive group identity.

5. Riot Ideology Thesis. T. M. Tomlinson suggests that a "riot ideology" has become fashionable in Black communities and that a significant minority of Blacks have come to view civil violence as

[26] *Ibid.*, 180, and Dynes and Quarantelli, *op. cit.*, 9–14.

[27] Frantz Fanon, *The Wretched of the Earth* (New York: Grove Press, Inc., 1966), 73.

[28] Kenneth B. Clark, "The Search for Identity," *Ebony*, 22 (August, 1967), 42.

[29] Robert W. Friedrichs, "Interpretation of Black Aggression," *The Yale Review*, Spring 1968, 358–374.

a legitimate and productive mode of protest.[30] It is of interest to note that the idea that ghetto "riots" are "weapons" and "rebellions" only began to be publicized and to gain popular acceptance during the spring of 1966. The kind of behavior manifested in these later "riots," including those following Dr. Martin Luther King's assassination in the spring of 1968, were practically indistinguishable from that typical of the 1964 "riots" or the 1965 Watts "riot." What changed was the accompanying attitudes and interpretations. Hence, the McCone Commission report was probably correct in denying a political or revolutionary basis to the Watts disturbance. Further proof of this verdict is reflected in the post-riot lead article "Watts, L.A.: A First Hand Report, Rebellion Without Ideology," which appeared in the September, 1965, *Liberator*, and which explicitly stated that the riots lacked purpose, ideology, and organization. It took roughly a year-and-a-half after the 1964 "riots" for militant Black intellectuals—e.g., Stokely Carmichael and Rap Brown —to formulate the interpretation that the "riots" had a revolutionary message—that they were conscious political acts. It took another two years for this conclusion to be ratified by a significant number of rank-and-file Blacks.[31]

According to the "riot ideology" thesis, civil violence among Blacks is a response to frustrations experienced within a racist society and to *shared interpretations* of such frustration. Spilerman singles out a number of factors—the national government, television, and the development of Black solidarity—as having fostered these shared interpretations which cut across Black community lines.

[The federal government's] leadership in this area [civil rights and the war on poverty] has been marked by vacillation, compromise, expedient retreat, and unfunded promises, a situation which must provoke feelings of frustration and betrayal. In conjunction with this, the wide availability of television now brings the activities of the federal government into the home [TV sets expose Black viewers to the insensitivities of congressmen and the minimal impact of anti-poverty programs].

Television must also be credited with stimulating the development of racial consciousness in Negroes. Sights of the insurrection of black persons elsewhere, or of Negroes being set upon by dogs, beaten, or worse, have enabled them to share common experiences, witness a common enemy, and in the process develop similar sensitivities and a community of interest. Previously fragmented and isolated from one another by class and spatial boundaries, the

[30] T. M. Tomlinson, "The Development of a Riot Ideology Among Urban Negroes," *American Behavioral Scientist*, 2 (1968), 27–31.

[31] Howard Hubbard, "Five Long Hot Summers and How They Grew," *The Public Interest*, Summer, 1968, pp. 3–24.

impact of television has fostered a consciousness of identity which now transcends these divisions.[32]

Factors such as these, then, laid the groundwork for the formulation and mass dissemination of an ideology interpreting the riots as political events.

We have considered five views concerning the sources of Black militancy. Social scientists are not in agreement on this matter—some prefer to stress one factor, others another, and still others some combination of factors. Perhaps the most satisfactory approach would be one that would view the various interpretations as complementary—as adding an additional ingredient to our understanding —rather than as contradictory explanations.

SOME OTHER FORMS OF CONFLICT

Litigation

In those nations where there is recourse to courts of law, minority groups may seek to advance their status through this instrumentality. Conflict is then likely to find a legalized expression. The dominant and minority groups fight for their respective aspirations through legislation and litigation. The United States Constitution, especially since the adoption of the equality provisions of the Fourteenth Amendment, has provided an important weapon in the hands of racial and ethnic minorities.

An important part of the Black attack upon the American caste system has been waged within the legal arena. The vulnerability of Blacks especially in the southern rural setting where various informal and economic controls have traditionally prevailed, served for decades to limit the means by which the Black minority might advance its position. Accordingly, the National Association for the Advancement of Colored People focused its efforts primarily upon legal action. With the urbanization of large segments of the Black population, new means such as the ballot, boycotts, and sit-ins have come increasingly to the forefront as weapons in the Black arsenal.

The Supreme Court's school-desegregation ruling of May 17, 1954, was both a product of litigation and a source of subsequent litigation. By virtue of its unique position in the American govern-

[32] Seymour Spilerman, "The Causes of Racial Disturbances: A Comparison of Alternative Explanations," *American Sociological Review*, 35 (1970), 646.

mental system, the nation's highest court was able to unleash forces capable of initiating tremendous social and cultural change within the South. The upsurge in conflict ensuing since the ruling suggests that the South is moving toward a new social equilibrium in Black-White relations. The "separate but equal" doctrine formulated in 1896 in the famous case of Plessy v. Ferguson provided legal sanction to the southern normative system. In the 1896 decision the Supreme Court had held that laws requiring the separation of the races did not violate the Fourteenth Amendment so long as equal facilities were provided for Blacks. The court denied that the enforced separation of the races stamped Blacks with a badge of inferiority. "If this be so," the court said, "it is not by reason of anything found in the act [of separation], but solely because the colored race chooses to put that construction upon it." As Borinski observes, the Plessy v. Ferguson decision established an equilibrium in the southern social order by granting the Blacks formal equality in principle and the Whites separation in fact, in this manner preserving the caste order.[33] But, in a dynamic, ever changing society such as that in the United States, a social equilibrium established in 1896 could not be expected to prevail endlessly into the future. Within the 1896 adjustment there were elements of latent legal and social conflict. Southern Whites did not really accept the equality of the Blacks and the Whites did not really accept separation. As time progressed, circumstances altered. The May 17, 1954, ruling gave recognition to this fact and liquidated the old "separate but equal" doctrine.

The new Supreme Court ruling did not, however, provide for a sudden or immediate liquidation of the old arrangement, and hence cases of school desegregation are still being litigated in the 1970s. In its decree of May 31, 1955, implementing the desegregation ruling, the court provided for the gradual realization of school desegregation. The 1955 decree in essence invited further litigation. Concrete plans for local desegregation were left in the hands of federal district judges. Furthermore, if desegregation were to be realized, unless southern communities would desegregate without judicial compulsion, separate legal action would have to be instituted in virtually every school district. The Supreme Court's approach was widely interpreted as allowing for the gradual institu-

[33] Ernst Borinski, "The Litigation Curve and the Litigation Filibuster in Civil Rights Cases," *Social Forces*, 37 (1958), 142.

tionalization of social change without disrupting the social fabric through precipitous change.

Accordingly, the stage was set for acute legal conflict. Many southern states resorted to legal obstruction in hopes of frustrating desegregation. More than 200 new segregation laws were enacted. The strategy of the South was outlined in editorial candor in the influential and respected Richmond, Virginia, *News Leader* on June 1, 1955:

> To acknowledge the court's authority does not mean that the South is helpless. . . . Rather, it is to enter upon a long course of lawful resistance; it is to take advantage of every moment of the law's delays. . . . Litigate? Let us pledge ourselves to litigate this thing for 50 years. If one remedial law is ruled invalid, then let us try another; and if the second is ruled invalid, then let us enact a third.

On the other hand, the National Association for the Advancement of Colored People organized with considerable success to overturn through litigation these various legal devices. The courtroom thus became a major instrument of intergroup conflict. The Civil Rights Acts of 1957, 1960, 1964, 1965, and 1968 gave Blacks additional legal weapons with which to fight discrimination and segregation.

Sit-ins

As the Black movement for full equality expanded in the early 1960s, new weapons were introduced with which to wage the struggle. "Sit-ins" at Jim Crow lunch counters (later expanded to libraries and other facilities), "wade-ins" at segregated beaches and pools, "kneel-ins" at all-White churches, "stand-ins" at voter registration offices, and "freedom rides" to bus terminals with Jim Crow seating and eating facilities became a new note on the American scene. The lunch-counter demonstrations emerged first and served as an inspiration for the later tactics, hence let us consider them at greater length. The movement was launched on February 1, 1960, when four Black freshmen from North Carolina Agricultural and Technical College entered a Greensboro variety store and bought some merchandise.[34] About 4:30 in the afternoon, they sat down at a lunch counter reserved for Whites, but they had not been served by closing time an hour later. The movement did not take formal, organized shape until the next day, when some seventy-five A & T

[34] This material has largely been summarized from James W. Vander Zanden, "Sit-ins in Dixie," *The Midwest Quarterly*, 2 (1960), 11–19.

students inaugurated a "sit-in" at the same lunch counter. The movement quickly snowballed throughout the South, involving Black youth from at least thirty-nine colleges and White youth from another nine. "You sell us pencils, paper, toothpaste, and clothes," was the students' argument, "therefore you are inconsistent not to serve us meals." Black students undertook to sit at lunch counters despite their failure to be served. In this manner facilities were tied up and the stores lost business. Success was not long in coming to the movement. Within a year and a half at least 126 southern cities had some eating facilities desegregated.

The sit-ins had a number of ingredients that provided a special appeal to the participants. For one thing they presented an opportunity for individual participation and direct action. There was no need to go through the intermediary of a team of lawyers and a court. The issue was clear-cut, not bogged down in legal jargon. Furthermore, the activity had a flare for the dramatic; it was spectacular and quickly gained the attention of the media of mass communication. The participants could acquire considerable satisfaction from their involvement in the movement. Feelings of rapport, solidarity, and mutuality flourished in the crowded atmosphere of the lunch counters and served to reinforce determination and to provide a euphoric sense of strength and achievement. And, with the opposition economically vulnerable, victory promised to be immediate.

The Citizens Councils and "Economic Pressure"

On the heels of the Supreme Court's 1954 decision outlawing mandatory school segregation, the battle cry "Racial integrity—states' rights" once again loomed over the southern horizon.[35] The action of the Supreme Court confronted many southern Whites with a situation that they viewed as a distinct threat. In quick order more than 100 resistance organizations mushroomed across the South. Of these the most notable and successful were the Citizens Councils of the Deep South states and their sister organizations in Virginia, North Carolina, Georgia, and Tennessee.

The overwhelming bulk of the Citizens Council strength resided in the heavily Black-populated Black Belt counties of the Deep South. The region lies north of both the Gulf Coastal Plain and the long-leaf piney woods country, and south of the Piedmont. It is here

[35] This material has in large part been summarized from James W. Vander Zanden, "The Citizens Councils," *Alpha Kappa Deltan,* 29 (1959), 3–9.

where the heart of the "Old South" was located, where the old ways hang on with the greatest tenacity, where Black subordination has been most intense, and where yet today a considerable stake remains in the preservation of the traditional racial patterns. Speaking of this fact, State Representative J. S. Williams of Mississippi said:

> The citizens committee [Citizens Councils] of Mississippi is not a Ku Klux Klan, but our purpose is to give a direct answer to the National Association of [sic] Colored People. We have a heritage in the South for which we should ever be vigilant. . . . The NAACP's motto is "The Negro shall be free by 1962"—and shall we accept that?
> We can't have it, for if we do, it would ruin the economic system of the South. The men of the South are either for our council or against it. There can be no fence-straddling.

The Councils sprang up in the Black Belt as resistance organizations. Accordingly their fate was closely linked with the status of integrationist efforts. Mississippi Councils had shown success prior to the Supreme Court's 1955 school-desegregation-implementation decree. But they did not to "boom" until the decree was handed down and five NAACP petitions for immediate desegregation were filed in the state. Then the movement surged in growth in terms of both chapters and membership. The story was not too different in other Deep South states. When the NAACP launched its offensive in the summer of 1955 to win school desegregation throughout the Deep South, the Citizens Councils mushroomed in chapters and membership. But as the Councils succeeded in wiping out NAACP chapters and activity in the area, Council activity waned. Robert Patterson, leader of the Mississippi Councils, repeatedly asserted, "Organized aggression must be met with organized resistance." In short, *movement begets counter-movement.* The corollary has also tended to be true, namely, *if movement subsides, counter-movement tends to subside.*

Although no reliable figure on the Councils' membership has been available, it is probable that it never exceeded 250,000. The organization engaged in a great variety of activities: it backed a Black-college fund raising, sponsored segregation legislation, held mass meetings and rallies, combed voter-registration lists to disqualify Blacks, sponsored regular television and radio programs, and searched for "subversiveness" in schools and various civic organizations. Most controversial of Council activities and tactics were its alleged use of economic boycotts and sanctions. Some of its leaders publicly called for "economic pressure." Fred Jones, a Council

leader, declared, "We can accomplish our purposes largely with economic pressure in dealing with members of the Negro race who are
not cooperating, and with members of the white race who fail to
cooperate, we can apply social and political pressure." United States
Senator Herman Talmadge of Georgia, addressing an Alabama Council rally, recommended a social and economic boycott of "the scala-
wags and carpetbaggers who fail or refuse to join the fight to preserve segregation. Anyone who sells the South down the river—
don't let him eat at your table, don't let him trade at your filling
station and don't let him trade at your store."

AROUSAL AND RESOLUTION OF CONFLICT

Muzafer Sherif and his associates have conducted a number of
experiments designed to show how conflict typically arises between
two groups, and how, occasionally at least, hostility gives way to
cordial relationships.[36] For experimental purposes they employed
an isolated summer camp as the setting. For their subjects they
chose boys 11 or 12 years old, all of whom were healthy, socially
well-adjusted, somewhat above average in intelligence, and from
stable, white, Protestant, middle-class homes—in brief, boys with a
homogeneous background. This procedure was designed to rule
out from the beginning explanations of hostility or friendly intergroup attitudes in terms of differences in socioeconomic, ethnic, religious, or family backgrounds. The several stages of one experiment
were as follows:

1. During the first six days of the boys' stay in camp, Sherif and
his associates aimed to develop two separate groups, each having
high cohesiveness and each unaware of the other's existence. Although the two campsites were not far apart, they were out of sight
and earshot of each other; each group had its own facilities for swimming, boating, making campfires, and the like. Group cohesiveness
was fostered through the promotion of common and interdependent
activities characterized by goals integral to actual situations—cook-
outs, preparing campfires, improving swimming facilities, treasure
hunts, and so on. Before the end of the first stage each group had

[36] Muzafer Sherif, "Experiments in Group Conflict," *Scientific American,* 195
(1956), 54–58, and Muzafer Sherif, *et al., Intergroup Conflict and Cooperation:
The Robbers Cave Experiment* (Norman: University of Oklahoma Book Exchange,
1961).

adopted a name ("Eagles" and "Rattlers"), had developed a recognized status hierarchy among its members, had formulated individual role assignments, and had evolved various norms (e.g., concerning "toughness" and cursing).

2. The second six days, stage 2, consisted of experimental efforts to create friction between the Rattlers and the Eagles. The experimenters brought the two groups into competitive contact with one another through games and tournaments (baseball, touch football, a tug-of-war, a treasure-hunt, etc.) in which cumulative scores were kept for each group (not for individuals). The experimenters also devised situations designed to be frustrating to one group and perceived by it as caused by the other group—for instance, a ball field considered by the Rattlers to belong to them was pre-empted by the Eagles (as arranged by Sherif and his associates). Friction became commonplace. The Eagles, after a defeat in a tournament game, burned a banner left behind by the Rattlers; the next morning the Rattlers seized the Eagles' flag when they arrived on the athletic field. Other incidents of namecalling, scuffling, and raiding developed.

3. The third six-day period was designed as an integration phase. Sherif and his associates first undertook to test the hypothesis that pleasant social contacts between members of conflicting groups would reduce friction between them. The hostile Rattlers and Eagles were brought together for social events: going to the movies, eating in the same dining hall, shooting off firecrackers, and so on. But far from reducing conflict, these situations only provided new opportunities for the rival groups to berate and attack each other—for instance, in the dining hall, they would hurl paper, food, and vile names at each other.

Sherif and his associates then returned to a corollary of their initial assumption about the creation of conflict. Just as competition generates friction, they reasoned, working in common on a project should promote harmony. To test this hypothesis experimentally, they created a series of urgent, and natural, situations that challenged the boys. In this way superordinate-goal activities were introduced. One of these followed the shutting off of the common water supply by the experimenters, a development explained by the experimenters as the work of "vandals." A plan was formulated whereby the damage was repaired through a good deal of work on everyone's part. As the boys began to complain of thirst, Eagles and

Rattlers found themselves working side by side. A similar opportunity offered itself when the boys requested a movie. The experimenters told them that the camp could not afford to rent one. The two groups then got together, chose the film by a vote, jointly financed the venture, and enjoyed the showing together. In due course, intergroup frictions were virtually eliminated, new friendships developed between individuals across group lines, and the groups actively sought opportunities to mingle, entertain, and "treat" each other.

The Sherif experiments demonstrate the role that competition plays in generating hostility and prejudice. It also shows that the possibilities for achieving harmony are greatly enhanced when groups are brought together to work toward common goals. Hostility gives way when groups pull together to achieve overriding goals that are real and compelling to all concerned. This often occurs, for instance, in real life situations during wartime when various racial and ethnic groups rally together to pursue the war effort against a common national enemy.

SUMMARY

Conflict entails a struggle over values and claims to wealth, power, and prestige in which the opponents aim to neutralize, injure, or eliminate their rivals. The absence of conflict in a relationship is not necessarily evidence that the relationship is highly integrated, stable, and secure. Conflict at times reaches a frequency and intensity whereby the social system is imperiled or undermined. Yet conflict may also promote group formation, serve as a "safety valve" for the larger society, provide for a crisscrossing of loyalties fostering a democratic order, and prevent the ossification of social systems.

Although we like to imagine ourselves as a democratic, peaceloving, and rational people, in truth the United States has been a violent nation. We have, for instance, a long record of social violence—assaults upon individuals or their property solely or primarily because of their ethnic, religious, or racial affiliations. White–Black violence has found expression in at least six broad patterns: suppression-insurrection; lynchings; White-dominated, person-oriented rioting; racial warfare, person-oriented rioting; Black-dominated, property-oriented rioting; and Black-dominated, person-oriented violence.

The upsurge in Black militancy has been associated with a broad crisis of legitimacy within American life. But it has also been a product of other factors including a sense of relative deprivation, widespread social disorganization, group conflict over the allocation of scarce, divisible "good things," and a psychology of violence associated with the pursuit of self-esteem. Conflict may also find expression in boycotts, strikes, wade-ins, sit-ins, passive resistance, legal litigation, economic pressure, wit, and humor.

Muzafer Sherif and his associates have conducted research that points to the part that competition plays in generating hostility and prejudice. And it reveals how hostility may give way to harmony when groups pull together to achieve goals that are real and compelling to all concerned.

7

Segregation

Segregation may be thought of as a process or state whereby people are separated or set apart. As such, it serves to place limits upon social interaction. Segregation finds one form of expression in discrimination, where individuals are accorded differential treatment by virtue of their membership in a particular group. But discrimination should not be thought of as a practice exclusively limited to members of the dominant group; racial and ethnic minorities may discriminate against members of the dominant group, but their ability to do so is usually quite limited. Another form in which segregation finds expression is in physical or spatial separation. Through the operation of various ecological processes, contrasting types are sifted and sorted into different sub-parts of an area, as reflected in Chinatowns, Harlems, Little Italys, and ghettos in general.

AMERICAN INDIANS

In 1492 there were about 700,000 to 1,000,000 Indians in that area which now comprises the United States.[1] For the most part they were thinly scattered throughout the territory in hundreds of tribes, with numerous distinctive cultures, some of which were as different from each other as were the cultures of England and China of that period. In some cases the Indian groups were treated as alien nations that could be either enemies or allies against compet-

[1] Alfred L. Kroeber, "Demography of the American Indians," American Anthropologist, 36 (1934), 1–25.

ing European powers. Yet in due course, in the regions of earliest contact with Europeans—the area along the Atlantic seaboard and the Gulf of Mexico—the tribal territories of the Indians were appropriated and the aborigines were either annihilated or driven inland. Some made their way into the swamps, coves, and wooded mountains of these regions. Following the American Revolution, the new government followed a policy of negotiating treaties of land cession with the Indians. Where the Indians failed to agree, they were confronted with military force. Local groups of Whites often moved on their own against the Indians. When the Indians resisted White encroachments upon their lands, warfare ensued, the Seminole War in Florida and the Black Hawk War in the Illinois Territory being among the better known of the wars fought east of the Mississippi. Eventually, with the exception of portions of the Iroquois nations, the tribes signed treaties of cession and moved westward. Some went resignedly, others at bayonet point.

West of the Mississippi, the tragedy of defeat and expropriation was repeated.[2] With the discovery of gold in California, wagon trains of gold-seekers and emigrants began to rumble across the Plains. Western tribes were settled on reservations and issued rations in compensation for their loss of lands and hunting opportunities. At times bands of dissatisfied warriors rebelled—the uprisings in the Southern Plains in 1874, of the Sioux in 1876, the Nez Perce in 1877, the Cheyenne and the Bannock in 1878, the Utes in 1879, the Apache any number of times in the 1870s and 1880s, and farther west in northeast California the Modocs in 1872–1873. As in the East the aim of the frontiersmen was to get rid of the Indians, even to the point of massacring them. At Sand Creek in Colorado in 1864 militiamen descended upon an encampment of Cheyenne who had been guaranteed safe conduct, and slaughtered most of them. And in the frigid Plains winter of 1890, United States forces armed with Hotchkiss machine guns mowed down nearly three hundred Sioux at Wounded Knee, South Dakota. Yet it proved impossible to exterminate the Indians (in 1870 it was estimated that it cost the Federal Government about one million dollars for every dead Indian) and the stage was set for the formulation of a new policy.

[2] Heavy reliance was placed on the following sources in the discussion that follows: Robert F. Spencer and Jesse D. Jennings, *The Native Americans* (New York: Harper & Row, 1965), 496–506, and Vine Deloria, Jr., "The Cry is 'Indian Power'—The War Between the Redskins and the Feds," *The New York Times Magazine*, December 7, 1969, pp. 47, 82, 84, 86, 88, 92, 94, 96, 98, and 102.

Until 1871, the Federal Government treated the tribes as sovereign yet dependent domestic nations with whom it entered into treaty arrangements, a practice ended that year by Congress. This marked the beginning of a new phase in White–Indian relations, during which Indians were considered to be "wards" of the government. No longer was the aim one of extermination; in any event, it appeared at the time that the Indians were on the road to becoming a "vanishing race." The new policy was directed at "forced assimilation." Strenuous efforts were undertaken to eliminate Indian cultures, including the forced indoctrination of Indian children in Anglo-American ways at boarding schools far removed from reservation homes. And under the Dawes Act of 1887, the tribal lands were broken up and divided among individual Indians with the aim of making them small freehold farmers—the remaining tribal holdings were declared "surplus" and opened to non-Indian settlement. The net result was that within 60 years, 86 million acres of the best Indian lands were lost, and some 90,000 Indians were landless. The effect of individualizing the tribal estate (undertaken in the name of Indian "civilization") was the creation of massive poverty and poor health conditions, with Indians often existing in a slough of despondency.

In 1929 a new policy in Indian affairs was inaugurated, which was strengthened during the Roosevelt New Deal years. It reversed previous policy and encouraged the Indians to retain their tribal identifications and cultures, stopped all allotment of remaining Indian lands and sought to rebuild a land base for Indian communities, fostered tribal self-government, aimed to improve health and schools, returned to Indians their constitutional right of religious freedom, and encouraged native arts and crafts. But during the 1950s, this policy was again reversed, and the official aim of the Federal Government became one of accelerating the liquidation of governmental responsibility to the Indians as speedily as possible. This meant that Indians would lose any special standing they had under Federal law (in a sense, as dual citizens of their tribe and the United States [Indians were granted American citizenship in 1924]) the tax exempt status of their land was to be discontinued; federal responsibility for Indian social and economic well-being was to be repudiated; and the tribes themselves were to be effectively dismantled. Where applied (as among the Menominee of Wisconsin and the Klamath of Oregon) the "termination" policy led to the dissipation of tribal capital and the undermining of Indian communities. But termination fitted into the integrationist and Civil Rights thought of the period, so to many Americans it seemed the right thing to do. Not surprisingly the termination policy stirred up a storm among alarmed Indians who were confronted with the destruction of their institutions and who for the most part preferred the existence of their own self-governing communities. The program was slowed during the Kennedy-Johnson Administrations and then reversed by the Nixon Administration. Federal policy, then, has oscillated between separatist and assimilationist extremes.

Today there are some 500,000 Indians living on approximately 200 reservations in 26 states. In addition some 200,000 reside in cities and another 100,000 in scattered Eastern areas (the largest groups being the Eastern Cherokee in the Great Smoky Mountains, the Iroquois of Upper New York State, and the Seminoles in the Florida Everglades). Little more than 56 million acres remain in Indian possession. Forty-two per cent of Indian school children (almost double the national average) drop out before completing high school; nearly 60 per cent have less than an eighth-grade education. Unemployment reaches 40 per cent, nearly ten times the national average. Fifty per cent of Indian families have incomes below $2,000 a year, 75 per cent below $3,000. Overall, poverty is widespread (the oil-rich Osages of Oklahoma are the exception), making the Indians America's most deprived minority. Infant mortality is 36 deaths per 1,000 (at least 10 points above the national average) and average life expectancy is 44 years. Rates of tuberculosis, dysentery, enteritis, trachoma, pneumonia, and alcoholism are high. Even at present, more than 70 per cent of reservation Indians haul their drinking water a mile or more, often from unsanitary sources (and only the smallest fraction have indoor plumbing)—contributing to health problems.

Prejudice and discrimination tend to be strongest in the areas surrounding the reservations, where the frontier conception of Indians as shiftless and drunken inferiors tends to persist. Not infrequently, Indians are Jim-Crowed in towns near reservations and at times are subject to police abuse.

As with any minority, Indians have exhibited different responses to their disadvantaged circumstances. Some have "spun-off" into the larger community, becoming more or less assimilated. Others have chosen to stress their tribal identity and to undertake the development of effective self-governing communities. And still others have found appeal in "Pan-Indianism," the coming together of Indians regardless of tribal affiliation to realize common ends and to develop "an ethnic Indian" derived from a synthesis of diverse Indian cultures.[3]

BLACKS

It is quite likely that the first Black came to the New World with Columbus. During the period of exploration, Spain was a racial melting pot: the Moors had a considerable admixture of Black ancestry and Black slaves had also been brought to the country from central Africa. Hence, there is every reason to believe that some Blacks were among the Spanish explorers and colonists.

In 1619 English colonists at Jamestown, Virginia, purchased from a Dutch man-of-war twenty Blacks. Since there was no precedent in English law regarding slaves, it appears the Blacks initially assumed the status of indentured servants, much in the fashion of Whites. However, the Blacks' distinctive physical characteristics doubtless furthered their differential treatment from the beginning, and in time facilitated their enslavement.

The growth of Black slavery was closely tied with the development of the plantation system of agriculture that evolved within the South. Prior to the invention in 1793 of the cotton gin, slaves were primarily used in commercial agriculture based upon tobacco, rice, indigo, and naval stores. To supply the considerable demand for slaves, an elaborate trade system emerged. The voyage of the slaves from Africa to America, often referred to as the "Middle Passage," was a veritable nightmare, with overcrowding and epidemics common.

At the time of the first federal census, taken in 1790, there were 757,208 Blacks in the country (about 20 per cent of the total population), of which more than 90 per cent were concentrated in the South (in 1970, there were 22,580,289 Blacks, 11.1 per cent of the total U.S. population). However, it was not until Eli Whitney solved the problem of separating the cotton seed from the close-adhering lint that cotton became the major crop of the South. By 1815 the production of cotton had increased at a phenomenal rate.

[3] See: Robert K. Thomas, "Pan-Indianism," *Midcontinent American Studies Journal,* 6 (1965), 75–84.

This expansion of the cotton economy was accompanied by the growth of the slave population, reaching 1,771,656 in 1820.

In any event, and this is our primary concern here, even at the time of the Declaration of Independence, Black slavery was deeply entrenched and the idea of Black inferiority was well established. This fact was underlined when Southerners succeeded at the Constitutional Convention of 1787 in winning some representation on the basis of slavery, in securing federal support for the capture and rendition of fugitive slaves, and in preventing the closing of the slave trade before 1808. In truth the New Nation arose as a Greek-style democracy, where democracy was accepted, but only for a segment of the population. Indeed, until the last decade or so, Whites for the most part did not see democracy as extending to Blacks anymore than Americans generally see democracy as extending to children (for instance, in the realm of voting rights). The doctrine of Black inferiority or "differences" served to place the Black beyond the pale of the American democratic creed. And the notion persists at the present time among some segments of the population. This is illustrated by the experience of the author not too long ago while walking near a Black section in Augusta, Georgia. As he was passing a number of White children who were hurling stones and insults at a nearby group of Black children, he inquired of the former, "Why are you throwing stones at those children?" They replied, "Mister, they ain't children, they're niggers!"

Yet the dilemmas posed by racism within an egalitarian society have been a source of constant embarrassment. "It always appeared a most iniquitous scheme to me," Mrs. John Adams wrote her husband in 1774, "to fight ourselves for what we are daily robbing and plundering from those who have as good a right to freedom as we have." [4] Hence, from its earliest days a conflict has inhered in the American system between the dictates of its creed and its racial practice. The main norms of the American creed are centered in the belief in the common brotherhood of man as found in Christian teaching and the belief in equality and in the rights of liberty as found in the Declaration of Independence; it is a creed that "all men are created equal." [5] The contradiction between the American value system and the way in which Blacks have been treated has, if

[4] John Hope Franklin, "The Two Worlds of Race: A Historical View," *Daedalus*, 94 (Fall, 1965), 900.
[5] Gunnar Myrdal, *An American Dilemma* (New York: Harper & Row, 1944).

anything, forced many Whites to think even more harshly of the Black than they might if they lived in a more explicitly ascriptive culture.

There is little justification, then, to repress a group such as Blacks within an egalitarian society unless they are defined as a congenitally inferior race. According, Whites have been under pressure either to deny the Black's right to participate in the society, because he is inferior, or to ignore his existence, to make him an "invisible" man. The White South traditionally insisted on the first alternative. The North tried for many decades after the Civil War to take the second path.[6]

Racism has resulted in the victimization of Blacks. It has operated to deprive Blacks of many of the fruits of American life (products in part of Black labor), to use Blacks as a means for gaining White ends (economic, psychological, political, and sexual),[7] and to pose for many Blacks "identity problems" stemming from a curtailment of their autonomy and from a systematic assault upon their self-esteem. This has been reflected, for instance, in the "ghettoization" of Black life. Massive concentrations of Black populations in metropolitan areas exist North and South, and small town replicas are found throughout the nation, for the roots of racism lie deep in American history. In older southern towns slave quarters were transformed into Black residential areas after Emancipation—a few blocks here, a whole neighborhood there, often adjacent to White homes. In newer southern towns and cities a less secure, at times upwardly mobile, White population demanded a greater degree of segregation from ex-slaves and their descendants. Prior to World War I, the residential patterns did not vary greatly between North and South, but the great northward migration of Blacks beginning about 1915 expanded the small Black neighborhoods into massive Black Belts.[8]

Along with the influx of Blacks into the nation's major urban centers, there has been a migration of middle- and upper-class White families into the suburbs. The trend has served to transform large city areas into slums, with very large Black populations, ringed by

[6] Seymour Martin Lipset, *The First New Nation* (New York: Basic Books, Inc., 1963), 330.

[7] John Dollard, *Caste and Class in a Southern Town*, 3rd ed. (New York: Doubleday & Co., Inc., 1957).

[8] St. Clair Drake, "The Social and Economic Status of the Negro in the United States," *Daedalus*, 94 (Fall, 1965), 772–774.

more affluent White suburbs.[9] In recent years the growth of the Black suburban population has accelerated, but this growth appears concentrated in three types of areas: older suburbs that are experiencing population succession, new developments designed for Black occupancy, and some impoverished suburban enclaves. Despite this growth, however, city–suburban differences in the proportion of Black population are increasing, and patterns of residential segregation by race within suburbs are emerging that are similar to those found within central cities.[10]

A number of factors have contributed to the relative exclusion of Blacks from the suburbs. First, the sheer cost of suburban housing has placed it beyond the means of the great mass of Blacks, who, for the most part, are heavily concentrated in the lower income groups. Second, Whites often have made it clear that Blacks would be unwelcome in the suburbs, and rather than experience social isolation many Blacks have chosen to avoid such communities. Third, restrictive zoning and various subdivision and building regulations have been employed to keep Blacks out. Some communities, for example, have set a minimum of two or more acres for a house site or have required expensive street improvements but have waived these regulations for "desirable" developments while enforcing them for "undesirable" developments. Fourth, violence and coercion have occasionally been employed, such as the demonstrations that occurred before homes acquired by Black families at Levittown, Pennsylvania.[11] Fifth, real estate agents, bankers, and mortgage officials have often engaged in subterfuge to circumvent fair housing legislation, for instance, "warmly" welcoming Black prospects and showing them houses, but if they show real interest, "regretfully" informing them that earnest money has already been taken from another prospect. Sixth, many Blacks—like Irish, Germans, Scandinavians, Poles, Jews, and others who have often welcomed ethnic isolation—want to be near friends and relatives; this factor has gained greater significance with the emergence of the Black Power movement stressing Black pride and identity. Whites, of course, have often

[9] Leo F. Schnore and Harry Sharp, "Racial Changes in Metropolitan Areas, 1950–1960," *Social Forces*, 41 (1963), 247–252.

[10] Reynolds Farley, "The Changing Distribution of Negroes within Metropolitan Areas: The Emergence of Black Suburbs," *American Journal of Sociology*, 75 (1970), 512–529.

[11] Morton Grodzins, "Metropolitan Segregation," *Scientific American*, 197 (October, 1957), 33–41.

sought to rationalize their exclusion of Blacks from their neighborhoods by arguing that property values would be jeopardized. Yet scholars know from careful research that Blacks do not depress property values; however, White racist attitudes toward Blacks do.[12] So long as Whites view Blacks as a symbol of lower social status, proximity to them will be considered undesirable, a fact that finds reflection in the market place.[13]

Patterns of residential segregation are pronounced within American cities. Demographers have developed an index of urban residential segregation that ranges in value from 0 to 100. If each city block contains only Whites or only non-Whites, the index would assume a value of 100. On the other hand, if race plays no role at all in determining residential location, then any block chosen at random would have each racial group represented in the same proportion as in the city as a whole, and the index would assume a value of zero. Taeuber, computing indexes for 109 cities with Census data from 1940, 1950, and 1960, found that in each of these years between one-fourth and one-half of the 109 cities had index values above 90.0, and more than three-fourths had values above 80.0:

> Substantively, the most interesting finding of this research is the universally high degree of residential segregation between whites and Negroes within the cities of the United States. Whether a city is in the North, South, or West; whether it is a large metropolitan center or a suburb; whether it is a coastal resort town, a rapidly growing industrial center, or a declining mining town; whether nonwhites constitute forty percent of the population or less than one percent; in every case white and Negro residences are highly segregated from each other. There is no need for cities to vie with each other for the title of "most segregated city"; there is room at the top for all of them! [14]

With the exception of two regions, the Northeast and the West (which showed declines in the index values for the period 1940–1960), residential segregation appears to be increasing within the United States.[15]

The residential segregation of Blacks contributes to segregation

[12] See, for instance, Luigi Laurenti, *Property Values and Race* (Berkeley: University of California Press, 1960).

[13] Drake, *op. cit.*, 774–775.

[14] Karl Taeuber, "Negro Residential Segregation: Trends and Measurements," *Social Problems*, 12 (1964), 48.

[15] Using a somewhat different index, Cowgill comes to somewhat similar conclusions. See Donald O. Cowgill, "Trends in Residential Segregation in American Cities, 1940–1950," *American Sociological Review*, 21 (1956), 43–47, and "Segregation Scores for Metropolitan Areas," *American Sociological Review*, 27 (1962), 400–402). Also see, Reynolds Farley and Karl E. Taeuber, "Population Trends and Residential Segregation Since 1960," *Science*, 156 (March 1, 1968), 953–956.

in other spheres of life. Schools are commonly districted on the basis of neighborhoods, with the result that segregated facilities emerge. Although there is no legal segregation of Blacks within northern schools, some city officials have attempted to exploit the spatial separation of the races by drawing school-district lines so as to minimize the number of mixed schools and the number of Black children in predominantly White schools. Since elementary schools generally draw upon a smaller locality than high schools, segregation has been more prevalent in the former than the latter. Even where officials have the best of intentions, it is often difficult, if not impossible, to escape the consequences of segregated residential patterns in establishing school districts.

Chicago is a good illustration. The city's 530,000 public school pupils are essentially segregated as soon as they start school. Ninety per cent of the elementary students attend either all-White or all-Black schools; only 18 per cent of the high school students go to integrated schools. De facto segregation results from a neighborhood school policy under which children attend schools close to home. Surveys conducted by Robert J. Havighurst and Philip M. Hauser, both of the University of Chicago, reveal that Black schools are much more overcrowded than White schools, and served by the least experienced teachers. Even under ideal circumstances, it is more difficult to teach youngsters from slum environments. The Havighurst report observes:

> These children come to school pitifully unready for the usual school experiences, even at the kindergarten level. Teachers remark that some don't even know their own names and have never held a pencil. Their speech is so different from that of the teachers and the primer that they almost have a new language to learn. They have little practice in discriminating sounds, colors or shapes, part of the everyday experiences of the middle-class preschool child, whose family supplies educational toys and endless explanations.[16]

Patterns of spatial separation influence the development of separate Black social institutions and associations. Many factors contribute to the perpetuation of separate Black churches within northern cities, but the common role of the church as a neighborhood organization within American life cannot be overlooked as one such factor—coupled with a sense of Black pride and identity. The Black ghettos have provided the foundation for separate Black businesses, usually small establishments offering consumer goods or services. Social cliques and organizations often arise out of neighborhood

---

[16] Jack Star, "Chicago's Troubled Schools," *Look* (May 4, 1965), 59.

patterns and accordingly take on a segregated character. The same situation holds true in the use of various recreational facilities including parks, beaches, swimming pools, theaters, and bowling alleys and in the use of eating places.

Within employment, Blacks are disproportionately represented in the lower rungs of the job hierarchy and underrepresented in skilled, clerical, business, and professional positions. The years have witnessed a slow erosion of the color line, yet a job ceiling is still prevalent in Black employment, relegating Blacks chiefly to the less skilled, menial, or unpleasant jobs. Government employment, however, is usually open to them on a non-discriminatory basis. One of the major problems confronting Black workers is that they are usually the last to be hired, and accordingly, through the operation of seniority, the first to be fired. During economic recessions, their rate of unemployment generally runs more than double that of White workers. Similarly, their concentration within unskilled and semi-skilled jobs in industry, jobs particularly vulnerable to the vicissitudes of the business cycle, has rendered their position especially difficult. Long-term unemployment, the product of automation and other technological developments, has likewise had a lopsided effect upon Blacks. Anti-discrimination laws have been passed by a number of states, and anti-discriminatory clauses have been inserted in federal contracts offered to private industry, all of which have been designed to immunize Blacks against hiring bias. Still Siegel finds, employing Census data, that after making allowances for regional, educational, and occupational differences, it still costs Blacks roughly a thousand dollars a year just to be a Black.[17]

Even if bias could be erased, Blacks as a group would still tend to be handicapped. The critical problem of Black employment today has been accentuated by large-scale economic and technological changes involving the elimination of many unskilled and semi-skilled jobs. In brief, a serious problem is posed for those who have to work with their hands in a society that appears to have less and less work for people with only hands.

PUERTO RICANS

In 1898, Spain ceded Puerto Rico, a Caribbean island, 35 miles wide, 100 miles long, to the United States. Despite the rapid eco-

---

[17] Paul M. Siegel, "On the Cost of Being a Negro," *Sociological Inquiry*, 35 (1965), 41–57.

nomic and political changes that followed, Puerto Rico retains in language, religion, and many other aspects its Latin character. Since 1917, Puerto Ricans have been United States citizens, but until 1948 they did not elect their own governor. Although sending delegates to national party conventions, they do not vote for the President of the United States nor are they represented in Congress by voting members. Racial intermixture has been going on in Puerto Rico since the sixteenth century, and the variety of racial types ranges from light-skinned Caucasians to dark-skinned Blacks. While the Blacks were for the most part not discriminated against during Spanish occupancy, the Spanish Caucasians enjoyed a higher status, and whenever it was possible to do so Black ancestry was denied. Since 1898, Puerto Ricans have adopted in some part American patterns of race consciousness, with distinctions on the basis of skin color and physical appearance. Nevertheless, discrimination is only subtly apparent in social affairs and is infrequent in other spheres of life, including employment.[18]

Puerto Ricans have been migrating to the mainland of the United States for over a hundred years, but it is only since the end of World War II that the migration has taken on mass proportions. Since the early post-World War II years, however, there has been an increasing dispersion of Puerto Ricans throughout the United States. Whereas in 1950, 85 per cent of all migrants lived in New York City, by 1964, only 60 per cent were living there.[19] The main center of Puerto Ricans within New York has been east Harlem, but there are also large Puerto Rican communities elsewhere in Manhattan, the south Bronx, and Brooklyn. The best data we have on Puerto Rican migrants is contained in a study conducted by C. Wright Mills and his associates; its major drawback, however, is that the investigation is now over twenty years old and there is a real need for its replication. The study revealed that in "racial" composition, 64 per cent of the migrants were White, reflecting the predominantly White character of the island's population; 16 per cent were intermediate, including the *Indio*, those with copper cast to their skin and a tendency toward prominent cheekbones, and the *Grifo*, those with light complexions, blue or gray eyes, but kinky hair, or some

[18] C. Wright Mills, Clarence Senior, and Rose Kohn Goldsen, *The Puerto Rican Journey* (New York: Harper & Row, 1950), 3–6.

[19] Eva E. Sandis, "Characteristics of Puerto Rican Migrants to, and from, the United States," *The International Migration Review*, 4 (1970), 26.

other combination of diverse racial features; and 20 per cent were Black. The migrants were selected from the most productive age groups of the Puerto Rican population. Although less educated than the general population of New York, they were on the whole more educated than the average within Puerto Rico. Most of them had lived in the island's urban centers before coming to New York.[20]

A number of special institutions have grown up in Stateside Puerto Rican communities, most notably food shops, storefront churches, and travel agencies. The *bodegas*, the Spanish-American food shops, owe thir existence in part to the great difference between the island's food habits and those prevailing within the United States. The storefront churches have a strong evangelical, puritanical, and even Holy Roller cast and are making inroads upon the traditional Roman Catholicism of the Puerto Ricans. The travel agencies can be spotted by the sign "PASAJES" (passages) on their fronts and deal mainly in "thrift"-class plane tickets to Puerto Rico.[21]

The crucial motivating force in the migration appears to be the economic pull of New York; the island sources of information about the city are many and usually favorable. Population pressure on the island (the island is more densely populated than any Latin American country) has contributed to low living standards and a lack of jobs, which, when coupled with the city's reputation for economic opportunity, has served to stimulate out-migration. Many of the migrants also respond to the pull of relatives already settled in New York.[22] Language is one of the major problems confronting the immigrants. Spanish is the language of the island, and at least three-fifths of the migrants arrive in New York without a mastery of English adequate to make their way inconspicuously. Yet, to travel on subways or buses and to function in many other areas of life, some familiarity with English is necessary.[23]

The Puerto Rican migrants cluster primarily in the manufacturing and processing industries of New York, where some 50 to 60 per cent of those working find employment. Another 30 per cent are found in the service trades and domestic service. The jobs open to Puerto Ricans are restricted mainly to semi-skilled and unskilled jobs in the city's factories, hotels, restaurants, and other service trades. Some

---

[20] Mills, Senior, and Goldsen, *op. cit.*, 22–39.
[21] Christopher Rand, *The Puerto Ricans* (Oxford University Press, 1958).
[22] Mills, Senior, and Goldsen, *op. cit.*, 43–59.
[23] *Ibid.*, 142.

white collar jobs have opened in the past decade or so in banking. Although many migrants experience downward mobility in terms of their job level, their average earnings in New York are considerably higher than they enjoyed within Puerto Rico.[24] Only a small proportion of the women go into domestic work, while a considerable number find employment within the garment industry. Puerto Rico has an old tradition of fine needlework, and the Puerto Ricans are rated high within the garment industry in both "manual" and "finger" dexterity.[25]

It takes no discerning eye to see the sea of misery confronting Puerto Rican newcomers. In 1960, for instance, Puerto Rican median family income in New York City was considerably lower than even non-White median income—$3,811 against $4,437. This was 63 per cent of the median income for *all* New York City families. Further, unemployment runs consistently higher among Puerto Ricans than among the White and Black population.[26] This gap between Puerto Ricans and most other New Yorkers persists.

Puerto Ricans are concentrated in slum areas, finding housing in pre-World War I tenement buildings where apartments are at a premium. It is often necessary to "purchase" an apartment although ownership is not vested in the tenant, and monthly rent is collected. As a rule the apartments are self-contained, having from two to seven rooms, including a closet toilet. In some slum areas, however, a whole family may occupy only one room.[27] The slum buildings are often in a poor state of repair, but tenants are frequently afraid to report violations lest the whole building be abandoned or condemned. If this happens, new housing it difficult to come by. As a result a continuous deterioration of the buildings occurs. Further, the dwellings are frequently infested with vermin: rats, mice, cockroaches, and bedbugs. Leaking roofs, broken windows, and splintered steps are common.[28] Alleyways and streets are strewn with litter which remains to rot and decay. In winter, apartments that are equipped with central heating are often as cold as those without it. In summer, the sticky weather and the warmth exuded by hot-water pipes in the apartments combine with the smell of garbage

[24] *Ibid.*, 68–75.
[25] Rand, *op. cit.*, 9–10.
[26] Nathan Glazer and Daniel P. Moynihan, *Beyond the Melting Pot* (Cambridge: The M.I.T. Press and Harvard University Press, 1963), 116–117.
[27] Elena Padilla, *Up From Puerto Rico* (New York: Columbia University Press, 1958), 7, and Armando Rendon, "El Puertorriqueño: No More, No Less," *Civil Rights Digest*, 1 (Fall, 1968), 27–35.
[28] Mills, Senior, and Goldsen, *op. cit.*, 92–93.

and defective plumbing to push the residents into the streets, where the atmosphere is likely to be cooler and more fragrant.[29]

The schooling of Puerto Rican children has been a concern to both parents and educators. A significant proportion (about 40 per cent) of the children are Spanish-speaking, possessing little or no facility in English. The number of teachers who are bilingual does not begin to approximate the needs of the school system. As a result children often learn little in school, although kept in school and promoted. Even as late as 1968, little more than one per cent of Puerto Rican high school graduates received academic diplomas, about 8 per cent received vocational certificates, while 90 per cent were given general diplomas (merely in effect attesting to a student's class attendance).[30] The difficulties are often compounded by a sizable turnover of students during the school year, through parental shifts in residence. Some well-meaning educators have suggested that it might be desirable to set aside certain classes or even entire schools for Spanish-speaking pupils. However, Puerto Rican leaders and spokesmen for civil rights groups have generally opposed such proposals on grounds that segregation would inevitably result, and that, within any such split, Spanish-speaking pupils would end up with poorer facilities. Others have argued that New York City should inaugurate a bilingual program (in light of its sizable Spanish-speaking population) for *all* its school children.[31]

In Puerto Rico, race is subordinate to social class; in New York it is made central to Puerto Rican life. As viewed by American culture, the Puerto Ricans are not a single racial type. A third of them are perceived as having Negroid characteristics. The world into which these Negroid Puerto Ricans move within New York is largely a Black world, with all the restrictions commonly imposed upon it by the dominant White group.[32] It is particularly difficult for this group of Puerto Ricans, by virtue of racial barriers, to move out of the slums in Spanish Harlem, the south Bronx, and the lower east side.

The fair-skinned Puerto Ricans, if they so choose, can generally find their way into the larger White world; similarly, dark-skinned Puerto Ricans can often find their way into the Black group. But for those in the intermediate racial group the situation is more dif-

29 Padilla, *op. cit.*, 8.
30 Rendon, *op. cit.*, 29.
31 Rand, *op. cit.*, 111–116.
32 Mills, Senior, and Goldsen, *op. cit.*, 87.

ficult. The intermediate group distinguishes between itself and Blacks, a distinction that is recognized on the island. Within Puerto Rico it was their personal aspirations and achievements which served to influence their position within the social order. But in New York this margin of privilege is no longer acknowledged. To many continental Whites such individuals are Blacks. If they are to become assimilated, they must "become like" the Black. Traditionally this intermediate group tended to emphasize the desirability of whiteness in a society in which they were not considered White. They found they could hold only certain jobs, mix socially only with certain people, and for the most part live only in Puerto Rican or Black neighborhoods.[33]

Still, in truth, Puerto Ricans generally managed to maintain the pattern of a single ethnic community in which people mingled in social events of all kinds in disregard of the color marks that have affected American behavior. Fitzpatrick found confirming evidence for this conclusion in a survey of marriages in six Catholic parishes which revealed that 25 per cent of the Puerto Rican marriages involved people of noticeably different shades of color.[34] More recently, a Puerto Rican identity has been stressed and the alternative of becoming either White or Black has been increasingly rejected. One Puerto Rican leader states the issue this way:

> The blacks want us to be black and the whites want us to be white because they both want to use us. In terms of issues, I would have to side with the blacks—but I'm a Puerto Rican and no one has the right to tell me or want me to be black or white.[35]

On the whole Puerto Ricans have had an ambivalent attitude toward Blacks—sometimes seen as allies, sometimes as rivals. Further, a large percentage (perhaps more than half) of Puerto Rican families hope to return to Puerto Rico; in actual fact, however, very few of these families will be able to do so.

CHICANOS

What Americans of Mexican ancestry call themselves or prefer to be called is a matter of considerable sensitivity. The term "Chi-

[33] Ibid., 132–136, and Padilla, op. cit., 72–78.

[34] Joseph P. Fitzpatrick, "The Adjustment of Puerto Ricans in New York City," in Earl Raab, ed., American Race Relations Today (New York: Doubleday & Co., Inc., 1962), 176–177.

[35] Rendon, op. cit., 32.

cano" has gained considerable acceptance in recent years among the members of this ethnic group. The reason in part stems from its popular origin and the fact that it has been chosen by members of the group itself. As such it has not been imposed on the group by Anglo-Americans, as were such terms as "Mexican American" or "Spanish American" (a similar parallel exists between the differing uses and connotations of "Black" versus "Negro"). A lesser tendency has involved the use of "Brown" and "La Raza," both terms also denoting peoplehood—ethnic pride, identity, and solidarity.[36]

Following the conclusion of the Mexican-American War in 1848, Mexico ceded to the United States a vast territory that encompassed California, Arizona, New Mexico, Nevada, Utah, and portions of a number of other states, and also approved the prior annexation of Texas. The area was greater in extent than Germany and France combined, and represented one-half of the territory that in 1821 constituted Mexico. Under the terms of the Treaty of Guadalupe Hidalgo, all Mexican citizens in the territory were to become United States citizens if they did not leave the territory within one year. Very few returned to Mexico. At the time of the treaty, approximately 75,000 Spanish-speaking people lived in the Southwest: about 7,500 in California, roughly 1,000 in Arizona, perhaps 5,000 in Texas, and 60,000 in New Mexico. The overwhelming majority of these people were of mixed Spanish-Indian ancestry.[37] Many of them bear some of the proudest names of the Spanish explorers-soldiers-settlers who made this territory a part of New Spain in the 1500s and whose ancestors, mixing with the Indians, were third generation before the Pilgrims landed at Plymouth Rock.

In the early 1900s, a new group of Mexican immigrants began to enter the United States, migrating to work from their homes, during the cotton harvest, to the old cotton-producing sections of East Texas and then, after the harvest, returning to their homes. East Texas had long been a cotton-growing section in contrast with the cattle areas of South and West Texas. Although Blacks supplied the primary source of labor, Mexicans constituted a secondary source. About the turn of the twentieth century, cotton production started

[36] Fernando Penalosa, "Recent Changes among the Chicanos," *Sociology and Social Research*, 55 (1970), 47–52, and John H. Burma, ed., *Mexican-Americans in the United States* (Cambridge, Mass.: Schenkman Publishing Co., Inc., 1970), xiii–xv.

[37] Carey McWilliams, *North from Mexico* (Philadelphia: J. B. Lippincott Co., 1949), 51–52.

advancing into middle Texas and between 1910 and 1930 into West Texas, with the result that cattle were replaced in wide areas. In these new cotton-producing areas, landlords and overseers relied primarily upon transient Mexican labor.[38] As the years passed, many of the immigrants remained in the United States and became ancestral to much of the contemporary Spanish-speaking population of the Southwest.

By 1940 nearly 400,000 transient workers, two-thirds of whom were Mexicans, were engaged in following the "big swing" through the cotton-producing regions of Texas. Each year a vast army of migratory workers started harvesting cotton in the southern part of the state, moved northward into eastern Texas, and then proceeded into the central and western cotton-growing areas. The workers were organized by labor contractors and truckers. These latter individuals usually spoke English, knew the routes, dealt with the employers, and organized the expedition. They transported the workers in open or stake trucks, hired the crews out to employers, and oversaw the work.[39]

The conditions of life for transient workers was difficult. Writing in 1946, Kibbe observed:

> Generally speaking, the Latin American migratory worker going into West Texas is regarded as a necessary evil, nothing more nor less than an unavoidable adjunct to the harvest season. Judging by the treatment accorded him in that section of the State, one might assume that he is not a human being at all, but a species of farm implement that comes mysteriously and spontaneously into being coincident with the maturing of the cotton, that requires no upkeep or special consideration during the period of its usefulness, needs no protection from the elements, and when the crop has been harvested, vanishes into the limbo of forgotten things—until the next harvest season rolls around. He has no past, no future, only a brief and anonymous present.[40]

Sanitary facilities were especially inadequate and hygienic conditions were poor.

Beginning in 1942 Mexican nationals came to this country for migrant farm work under agreements entered into by the governments of Mexico and the United States. Prior to the program's termination in 1964, as many as 450,000 Mexicans annually entered the United States for this purpose. Another source of Mexican labor has been commuters who daily cross the border to work in and

[38] Ibid., 169–170.

[39] Ibid., 172.

[40] Pauline R. Kibbe, Latin Americans in Texas (Albuquerque: University of New Mexico Press, 1946), 176.

near nine border cities (numbering about 50,000 in 1970). Still another part of the Mexican immigration to the United States is illegal; Mexican nationals swim or wade across the Rio Grande (derogatorily referred to as "wetbacks") to fill the considerable demand for workers to harvest crops. The number of Mexican workers illegally in this country is unknown but estimates place it at about one million.

Historically employment opportunities for Chicanos have resided overwhelmingly in unskilled jobs. In agriculture, ranching, and mining, early industries of the Southwest, these were the people who served as laborers. And as we have noted, as crops needed cultivation or harvesting, these were the main body of field hands doing the chopping, thinning, and picking. When the railroads were laid, these were the section hands, and they serve them today as maintenance-of-ways workers. When irrigation works spread in the Southwest, these were the ditchers and irrigators; when fruits and vegetables needed sorting and packing, it was the Chicanos who manned the canning plants and packing sheds; when smelters were built, they handled the ore; and when construction boomed, they were the hod carriers and common laborers.[41] Outside of the Southwest there are also sizable Chicano populations in Chicago, Detroit, Gary, Kansas City, Omaha, and Denver. In Chicago, Chicanos first appeared as railroad laborers and later were employed in the steel mills, the packing plants, and the tanneries.

At the present time there are within the United States an estimated 5 million or so persons of Mexican descent, most of whom have either migrated to or been born in this nation since 1900. Their area of greatest concentration runs from the Gulf of Mexico across Texas, through New Mexico, up into Colorado, over through Arizona, and across California to the Pacific Ocean. In recent decades the Chicano population has been shifting from the eastern to the western states of the Southwest (with California replacing Texas as the state with the largest Chicano population).

In recent years, Chicanos, long ignored by the news media, have been catapulted into the national limelight as a result of such developments as the organization of California farm workers by Cesar Chavez and Reies Tijerina's crusade to regain the land indigenous Chicanos of New Mexico claim was illegally taken from them. Yet

[41] Fred H. Schmidt, *Spanish Surnamed American Employment in the Southwest* (Washington, D.C.: U.S. Government Printing Office, 1970), 8.

the news reports have served to reinforce nationally a false image of the Chicanos as a rural people.[42] While this was the case prior to World War II, today an estimated 80 per cent are urban (although some who reside in urban areas have agricultural jobs). Moreover, Chicanos do not form a homogeneous group with identical values, customs, or aspirations. They are divided along socioeconomic class lines from the affluent rancher, businessman, or public official to the migrant worker or relatively isolated farmer in the mountains of New Mexico. And they also differ in the extent to which they have become Anglicized and integrated into the larger society.[43]

Mechanization has been one factor contributing to the shifting in recent decades of Chicanos from agricultural to nonagricultural jobs. The switch from men to machines had considerable impact in the harvesting of cotton and more recently mechanical harvesters have been introduced for other labor-intensive crops like tomatoes, asparagus, grapes, and lettuce. But like Blacks, Chicanos within urban settings have been heavily concentrated in blue-collar jobs (less than 20 per cent of all employed Anglo males are in low-skill manual occupations as contrasted with nearly 61 per cent of all Chicano males) and have made only modest headway into the managerial, professional, clerical, and sales occupations (for instance, of all employed Chicano males, only 4.9 per cent are found in managerial and proprietor categories compared with 14.7 per cent of Anglo males). In craft occupations, on the other hand, Chicanos come close to parity with Anglos. In terms of income and the rate of unemployment, Chicanos are typically better off than Blacks but worse off than Anglos.[44]

In southwestern towns and cities with any sizable Chicano population, separate Chicano ghettos are prevalent. In smaller towns the Chicano section is usually set apart from the rest of the town by a railroad track, a highway, or a river. In larger communities, there is usually at least one section made up of Chicanos. Informal patterns of discrimination generally operate to maintain residential

[42] Leo Grebler, Joan W. Moore, and Ralph C. Guzman, *The Mexican-American People* (New York: The Free Press of Glencoe, 1970), 6.

[43] Burma, *op. cit., passim;* Fernando Penalosa, "The Changing Mexican-American in Southern California," *Sociology and Social Research,* 51 (1967), 405–417; and Joan W. Moore, "Colonialism: The Case of the Mexican Americans," *Social Problems,* 17 (1970), 463–472.

[44] Grebler, Moore, and Guzman, *op. cit.,* Chapters 8 and 9; Schmidt, *op. cit., passim;* and Walter Fogel, "Job Gains of Mexican-American Men," *Monthly Labor Review,* 91 (October, 1968), 22–27.

segregation and to bar Chicanos as renters or property owners from other neighborhoods. Nevertheless, the restrictions on Chicanos have been rarely as strict as those upon Blacks in the United States, especially in higher income areas, where the assumption frequently has been that if one can afford to buy, he probably is "Spanish" and hence "White," and if he is poor he is "Mexican" and hence "non-White," and cannot buy anyhow. Within Chicano ghettos there is a high degree of poor housing and overcrowding.

The level of formal education found among Chicanos tends to be low in terms of American standards. Thus they find themselves at a considerable disadvantage in the larger American society, where a premium is placed upon formal schooling and academic achievement. Their life, especially in the past, was geared by their cultural heritage to an agricultural tempo; conflicts between rural and urban values have served to complicate their adjustment to American life. Poor school attendance, limited average grade completion, and frequent school failures contribute to the situation.[45]

Until relatively recently, Chicano children were often segregated for purposes of instruction, either in separate buildings or in segregated classes within the same building. Nevertheless, there was no overall pattern for the segregation.[46] Throughout most of the Southwest, segregation of Chicanos was considered desirable but not absolutely essential, and in this way differed from the attitude of southern Whites toward the segregation of Blacks. In some communities segregation was strict and complete, in others there was a "Mexican" school, but a few favored children with Spanish surnames who came from the top socioeconomic level of the Chicano subcommunity would attend the White school. Still others, lacking separate segregated schools, maintained segregated classrooms in the "White" school. Some communities even fluctuated between segregation and non-segregation depending upon the current number of Chicano students.[47] On the basis of pedagogical considerations some educators insisted that it was a sound practice to separate Mexican

[45] Edward C. McDonagh, "Status Levels of Mexicans," *Sociology and Social Research*, 33 (1949), 449–459; and William Madsen, *The Mexican-Americans of South Texas* (New York: Holt, Rinehart & Winston, Inc., 1964), 106–108. Those readers who are interested in an anthropological treatment of the Mexican American subculture will find Madsen a valuable source.

[46] Kibbe, *op. cit.*, 95 ff.

[47] John Burma, "The Civil Rights Situation of Mexican Americans and Spanish Americans," Jitsuichi Masuoka and Preston Valien, eds., *Race Relations* (Chapel Hill: The University of North Carolina Press, 1961), 157–158.

children who spoke little or no English during the first few grades until they had acquired an adequate mastery of English. But a strong factor influencing local decisions to maintain either separate schools or intra-school segregation ("Mexican rooms") was the prevalence of racism. At the present time some communities have set up "opportunity," "second chance," or similarly labeled rooms for their "culturally deprived" children, but in practice these have often become the modern equivalent of the "Mexican room." [48] Broadly speaking, as Chicano children advance in age, the rate of dropouts from schools progressively increases. Further, schools with large Chicano enrollments tend to be characterized by overcrowding, inferior equipment and plant facilities, and less competent teachers.

A frequently mentioned complaint mentioned by both the Chicano community and school authorities concerns the issue of the use of Spanish in schools. Spanish is the language of La Raza, and is a binding factor in the community. Yet in many schools the speaking of Spanish is forbidden both in the classrooms and on the playground and not infrequently students have been punished for lapsing into Spanish. Chicano activists have demanded that Spanish be permitted and taught within the schools. Similarly some educators have called for the teaching of *both* Spanish and English in all schools of the Southwest (including those attended by Anglos). A great many Chicanos want their children to learn about the Anglo way of life, but not at the expense of the Chicano heritage and a knowledge of the Spanish language.[49]

CHINESE

It was during the gold-rush period in California that the first large scale immigration of Chinese to the United States occurred. Initially, Chinese were welcomed as a source of cheap labor. The American fortune seekers who came expecting to find gold had no intention of performing menial or laborious tasks, or of earning their money as common laborers. Under these circumstances, Chinese were readily sought. Governor John MacDougall, in addressing the

---

48 Grebler, Moore, and Guzman, *op. cit.*, 156.

49 See: Anthony Gary Dworkin, "No Siesta Mañana: The Mexican-American in Los Angeles," in Raymond W. Mack, ed., *Our Children's Burden* (New York: Random House, Inc., 1968), 408–439, and Arthur J. Rubel, "Some Cultural Aspects of Learning English in Mexican-American Communities," in Andreas M. Kazamias and Erwin H. Epstein, eds., *Schools in Transition: Essays in Comparative Education* (Boston: Allyn and Bacon, Inc., 1968), 370–382.

California legislature, in 1852, referred to the Chinese as the "most desirable of our adopted citizens" and recommended "a system of land grants to induce further immigration and settlement of that race."[50] Chinese were employed in building the Union Pacific, Northern Pacific, and Southern Pacific railroads; reclaiming swamplands; building levees and roads; mining; and a wide variety of manufacturing jobs.[51] By virtue of the shortage of women in the frontier West, Chinese men were also hired to do work usually done by women, such as cooking, washing, and gardening.

It was not long, however, before the speculative bubble of gold burst and Whites were thrown into the employment market. Increasingly, American labor began feeling the competitive economic pinch of the cheap Chinese labor. From a total of 758 Chinese in the continental United States in 1850, the number rose to 105,465 in 1880, most of whom resided in California. The competitive impact was intensified by the fact that the Chinese population in America was overwhelmingly male (between 1860 and 1900 the ratio of Chinese males per 100 Chinese females was exceedingly high: 1,858 in 1860; 1,284 in 1870; 2,106 in 1880; 2,678 in 1890; and 1,887 in 1900; numerical equality in the sexes was not achieved until the middle of the twentieth century).[52] In addition, the Chinese constituted a highly visible group. The newly arrived immigrant often shuffled along the street in a sort of dogtrot, displayed food habits different from those of the dominant Americans, dressed in oriental clothes, wore his hair in a queue, spoke a quite different language, and often believed in omens, good-luck signs, and practices that dominant Americans viewed as superstitious. Out of this situation involving competition for jobs and high social visibility there arose the cry "The Chinese must go." These factors were compounded by scapegoating following the business crash of 1876: business houses failed; banks and mines were closed; and a drought hit agriculture. The Chinese were severely persecuted, subject to violence, riots, bloodshed, pillage, and incendiarism. Within San Francisco it was not uncommon to see Chinese pelted with stones or mud, beaten or kicked, harassed on the streets, and tormented by having their queues cut. Under the leadership of Denis Kearney, an Irish labor

[50] R. D. McKenzie, *Oriental Exclusion* (Chicago: University of Chicago Press, 1928), 25–26.
[51] B. Schrieke, *Alien Americans* (New York: The Viking Press, Inc., 1936), 8–10.
[52] Stanford M. Lyman, "Marriage and the Family among Chinese Immigrants to America, 1850–1960," *Phylon*, 29 (1968), 321–330.

leader, the Workingmen's party was founded on a militant anti-Chinese program. It succeeded in electing candidates to major local and state offices.[53]

Some Chinese responded to this persecution by returning to China, but most responded by dispersing eastward throughout the United States. In 1880, some 22 per cent of the Chinese were in cities with a population of 25,000 and over, whereas 78 per cent were in less populated areas. But hand-in-hand with the dispersion of the Chinese went a trend toward greater urbanization. By 1890, 42.7 per cent were concentrated in urban centers having a population of 25,000 and over; by 1920, the figure had risen to 66 per cent.[54] Today at least 99 per cent of the Chinese are urbanites.

With the urbanization of the Chinese, Chinatowns made their appearance within various American cities. A Chinatown is a "ghetto" made up of Chinese, "a community within a non-Chinese community, having no independent economic structure but attached symbiotically to the larger economic, political, and social base."[55] Chinatowns arose both as voluntary and involuntary responses to common problems. The dominant group often erected barriers to Chinese entry into its lily-White neighborhoods. Further, meeting rebuffs in the larger society, many Chinese preferred to insulate themselves defensively from further rebuffs by residing in their own ethnic community. Kinship and clan ties, a desire to preserve meaningful and cherished Chinese cultural traditions and practices, and an inability to afford housing in other than low-rent areas also operated to attract Chinese to common urban settlements.[56]

The Chinatown of Philadelphia was perhaps not untypical of Chinatowns within the United States thirty or so years ago. In 1940, it occupied one square block in a blighted area of Philadelphia. The stores abounded with all kinds of decorations: Signs were made of wooden boards with Chinese characters; neon-light signs lit up the fronts of most restaurants; and the store windows were full of big Chinese vases, porcelain statues of "Milo," and strips of red paper

[53] Schrieke, op. cit., 14.

[54] Rose Hum Lee, "The Decline of Chinatowns in the United States," American Journal of Sociology, 54 (1949), 422–432, reprinted in Arnold M. Rose, ed., Race Prejudice and Discrimination (New York: Alfred A. Knopf, Inc., 1951), 146–160, and The Chinese in the United States of America (Hong Kong: Hong Kong University Press, 1960), chapters 3 and 4.

[55] Lee, "The Decline of Chinatowns," op. cit., 148.

[56] D. Y. Yuan, "Voluntary Segregation: A Study of New Chinatown," Phylon, 24 (1963), 260–262.

announcing the merchandise inside. Within Chinatown proper, there were eighteen stores, a curio shop, one needle manufacturing company, one barbershop, and ten or twelve gambling and opium houses and brothels (providing recreation and respite from the day's toil for single Chinese men).[57]

In 1940, some 922 Chinese resided in Philadelphia, of which about one-third lived in Chinatown proper. The occupational range of the Chinese in Philadelphia was very limited. In 1945, it was estimated that 400 were employed as laundry operatives, 100 in restaurants, 18 in grocery stores, 2 in art-goods and curio shops, 12 in engineering, 4 as typists, and 11 in scattered occupations.[58] Outside of Chinatown, Chinese laundries were more or less evenly scattered throughout the city and were generally operated by unmarried men who made their residence within the laundry building. The laundryman functioned as an "intimate stranger" within the White community—intimate since he lived within the community and was known derogatorily as "Charley Chinaman," yet a stranger since he tended to be culturally and socially isolated from the larger community. As such, he was often a lonely soul.[59] The Chinese restaurants were found in a number of sections of Philadelphia: the majority were concentrated in south Philadelphia where the Black population predominated; a number in west and north Philadelphia catered exclusively to White customers; and a few in Chinatown proper catered to the customers in the Chinese gambling houses.[60]

Since World War II, except for a few large cities, Chinatowns have largely disappeared from the American scene. Lee suggests that to survive, at least 360 Chinese must either be in the Chinatown itself or live within the same city or state where it is located. Although theoretically the ghetto is considered the "home" for the Chinese, many live outside of it for work or personal reasons. Once the Chinese population falls below the above figure, the Chinatown struggles vainly to survive—the population is not large enough to support separate economic and other institutions. Further, Chinatowns most often are located near central business districts. Urban expansion—with its attendant demolition of buildings, rezoning of land use, and widening of transportation arteries—together with the

[57] David Te-Chao Cheng, *Acculturation of the Chinese in the United States* (Philadelphia: University of Pennsylvania, 1948), 72–73 and 80.
[58] *Ibid.,* 80.
[59] *Ibid.,* 84–86.
[60] *Ibid.,* 90–94.

invasion of new immigrant groups have proved devastating to the continued maintenance of many American Chinatowns. In Pittsburgh, for instance, the Chinatown was totally obliterated by the building of a modern expressway. A population once dispersed seldom relocates, in toto, at a new site. Many Chinese utilize the opportunity to resettle elsewhere. The assimilation of second and third generation Chinese and the lowering of dominant group barriers have hastened the process.[61] With education, many younger Chinese have been able to acquire those skills that have enabled them to escape from the limited range of occupations previously open to Chinese—launderers, waiters, cooks, domestic workers, restaurateurs, and seamstresses—and to find their way into American middle class life.[62]

The Chinatowns of New York City and San Francisco, however, have obtained a new lease on life and have actually expanded in recent years as a result of sharp increases in immigration from Hong Kong and Taiwan (made possible by the passage of new immigration legislation in 1965 that did away with the old quota system under which only 105 Chinese were allowed entry a year). A good many of the some 25,000 yearly immigrants have settled in the New York and San Francisco Chinatowns, contributing to even greater overcrowding. A brisk demand has arisen for the blighted railroad flats and tenements in which four or five families share a common kitchen and bathroom. Within the Chinese community, cultural and social differences between American-born Chinese and recent immigrants have created new tensions. And though still a low-crime area, both Chinatowns have a growing teenage problem and some juvenile delinquency. A garment district is developing within the New York and San Francisco Chinatowns, employing primarily women immigrants (in contrast with Chinese immigration of the nineteenth century, family immigration now prevails resulting in a more normal sex ratio).

Within the United States, the Chinese have experienced a long tradition of discrimination. In 1882 Congress passed the first Chinese Exclusion Act suspending for ten years all Chinese immigration, save for a small group of scholars, ministers, and mer-

[61] Lee, *The Chinese in the United States of America*, op. cit., 65–68.
[62] See, for instance, D. Y. Yuan, "Division of Labor Between Native-Born and Foreign-Born Chinese in the United States: A Study of Their Traditional Employments," *Phylon*, 30 (1969), 160–169.

chants. In 1892 the Act was extended another ten years, and in 1902 the suspension of Chinese immigration was extended indefinitely. In 1943, under the impact of war conditions, President Roosevelt signed a law that provided for an annual Chinese quota of 105 and made Chinese aliens eligible for citizenship. Exclusion legislation contributed to the decline of the Chinese population in the United States from a high of 107,488 in 1890 to a low of 61,639 in 1920. Other factors contributing to the decline were the excess of departures from the United States over admissions, and the marked disproportion of the Chinese sex ratio within the United States.[63] Since 1920, the Chinese population has increased through internal growth and immigration and is now estimated to be in excess of 435,000.

California early enacted a series of anti-Chinese laws. Lawmakers successfully drove Chinese from mining activity within the state by a foreign miners' tax. An early legal decision prevented Chinese from testifying against a White man in court, a decision which placed them at the mercy of their persecutors. For a time, Chinese children were excluded from some public schools. San Francisco enacted various ordinances harassing Chinese laundries, including an act that made it a misdemeanor for any person on a sidewalk to carry baskets suspended on a pole across the shoulders, a typical Chinese practice. As late as 1952 the California constitution provided that corporations could neither directly nor indirectly employ Chinese; forbade the employment of Chinese in any state, county, municipal or public job; and empowered cities and towns to remove Chinese from within city limits. Most of this discriminatory legislation has either been repealed or declared unconstitutional.

JAPANESE

At the peak of the anti-Chinese agitation in the late 1870s and early 1880s, the Japanese population of the continental United States was virtually nil—the 1880 Census recorded only 148. By 1890 their number had risen to 2,039; by 1900, to 24,326; and by 1910, to 72,157 (by 1970, the figure was 591,290). The immigrants moved through the port cities of Seattle and San Francisco into the sur-

[63] In this regard see: S. W. Kung, *Chinese in American Life* (Seattle: University of Washington Press, 1962).

rounding areas and cities. As late as 1940 nearly 90 per cent of the Japanese population was concentrated in the Pacific Coast states— 74 per cent in California and 39 per cent in Los Angeles County. As with the Chinese, much of the initial impetus in anti-Japanese feelings came from workingmen's groups: in Seattle, the Western Central Labor Union; and in San Francisco, the Labor Council. The anti-Japanese movement initially gained momentum in 1900, and, as a result of the previous decades of agitation against the Chinese, mounted quickly. Pressure came from labor and patriotic groups for legislation to exclude Japanese in much the manner as the Chinese had been excluded earlier.

The first formal step taken against the Japanese was the action taken by the San Francisco School Board in 1906 which attempted to segregate Oriental students in separate schools. By virtue of protests from the Japanese government, President Theodore Roosevelt prevailed upon San Francisco authorities to rescind the measure. As a sequel to this settlement, Roosevelt took steps to check Japanese immigration through the "Gentleman's Agreement" of 1907. Under the agreement Japan undertook to refuse laborers passports to the United States unless they were coming to join a husband, parent, or child; to resume a formerly acquired domicile; or to assume control of a previously owned farming enterprise. The agreement did not end immigration or check the agitation against the Japanese, but it did serve to change the nature of the immigration and to relieve tension betweeen the United States and Japan.[64] Prior to the agreement most Japanese immigrants were males, but, following 1907, a considerable number of women entered to become wives of the men who had preceded them. Many of these were arranged marriages. Some 38,000 brides entered the United States until the "Ladies Agreement" was reached in 1920, the product of stepped-up American agitation against the "Yellow Peril," in which Japan agreed to end the migration. By 1920 the Japanese population within the United States stood at 111,010. Then in 1924 Congress enacted legislation barring Japanese immigration.

Prior to Pearl Harbor, 55 per cent of the Japanese within the United States were urban inhabitants. Within the cities they were largely concentrated in "little Tokyos," the result of various social and economic forces and restrictive covenants that prevented them

[64] Forrest E. La Violette, *Americans of Japanese Ancestry* (Toronto: Canadian Institute of International Affairs, 1946), 2–3.

from buying or renting housing outside their own areas. Similarly, informal restrictions served to bar them from occupations and professions for which their education had fitted them. Within Los Angeles, Japanese had established groceries, hotels, restaurants, fruit stands, barbershops, flower shops, nurseries, cleaning and dyeing shops, and similar establishments, most of which were small businesses run by a single family. Along the West Coast, Japanese were an important source of labor in lumber mills and fish canneries. They were also heavily concentrated in agriculture, often working on truck farms near urban centers. Immediately prior to American entry into World War II, Japanese raised about 42 per cent of the produce crops in California, including berries, onions, asparagus, celery, lettuce, peppers, tomatoes, cucumbers, spinach, and cauliflower. The bulk of the farmers operated as tenants, since state legislation forbade alien Japanese from owning land. In addition, there were about 1,600 Japanese-owned farms, the titles of which were vested in American-born Japanese (American citizens) in order to circumvent the proscription against alien Japanese.

While many Chinese reacted to native opposition with passivity, the Japanese tended to respond with assertiveness. They demanded better employment and housing conditions, violated contracts, struck when the strike would be least opportune for the farmers, and were eager to become landowners. Strong, in a sample of 1,457 first-generation newcomers, found that during their first five years in the United States 80.7 per cent were common laborers. Twenty years later only 46.1 per cent were in this group, the rest becoming owners, managers, or tradesmen.[65] As William Petersen observes, even in a country whose patron saint is the Horatio Alger hero, there is no parallel to the Japanese success story.[66] It is little wonder that the Caucasian stereotype of the Japanese came to be that of an aggressive, cunning, and conniving individual, a stereotype in some respects similar to that of the Jew. It was a stereotype in sharp contrast with that of the Chinese, who were commonly depicted as humble and ignorant.

The Japanese success in establishing themselves in small-scale farming resulted in native demands for the restriction of Japanese

[65] E. K. Strong, Jr., *Japanese in California* (Stanford, Calif.: Stanford University Press, 1933), 116.

[66] William Petersen, "Success Story, Japanese-American Style," *The New York Times Magazine*, January 9, 1966, pp. 20–21, 33, 36, 38, 40–41, and 43.

landownership and tenure. In 1913, California enacted the first anti-alien landownership law barring aliens who were ineligible for citizenship from owning agricultural land, or from leasing land for periods longer than three years. In 1920, and again in 1923, the law was revised, each time being made more severe. The ingenious feature of the act was that the prohibition ran against "aliens ineligible to citizenship." Until 1870, American naturalization laws had defined aliens eligible to citizenship as "free White persons." In 1870 the word "White" was removed, but it was added again in 1875, largely through the impact of the anti-Chinese agitation in California.[67] On this basis the Japanese as alien "non-Whites" were barred from citizenship. In 1922 the U.S. Supreme Court upheld this interpretation in the Ozawa case, declaring that a Japanese was not a "White" person and hence was ineligible to citizenship. Of course American-born Japanese still automatically became citizens by birth.

Prior to World War II, West Coast Japanese were commonly denied free access to many places of public recreation, including swimming pools and dance halls, although in Los Angeles motion-picture houses did not discriminate against them. Intermarriage with Caucasians was forbidden in most western states. In restaurants they often received less courteous treatment than White patrons. On the other hand, although with some exceptions, store clerks usually treated them in a courteous manner, they were permitted to use the public libraries, and there was no discrimination against them at public schools. Since World War II, most of the discriminatory and repressive measures aimed at the Japanese have been either repealed or declared unconstitutional. In 1952 the Supreme Court declared that citizenship could not be denied anyone on the basis of race. Similarly, the alien land laws have been declared unconstitutional, and Japanese are now eligible for admission to the United States under new immigration legislation.

With the Japanese attack upon Pearl Harbor on December 7, 1941, there occurred an intense upsurge in anti-Japanese feelings on the West Coast. Rumors (later proved false) circulated of Japanese sabotage and "fifth-column" activities. Suspicions were aroused by the facts that Japanese sometimes lived near airfields and some of their number engaged in coastwise fishing (to columnist Walter Lippmann the very lack of sabotage and espionage on the West

---

[67] Carey McWilliams, *Prejudice* (Boston: Little, Brown & Co., 1944), 47–48.

Coast was cause for alarm; he warned that such innocuous behavior was merely a ploy to disarm American suspicions). Japanese known to have strong loyalties to their mother country were quickly rounded up by the FBI. Out of the war hysteria that followed the early months of the war, a decision was made by military leaders to evacuate the Japanese population from the Pacific Coast states and place them in internment centers (interestingly enough, Hawaii's Japanese population—one-third of the total population of the island and 3,000 miles closer to Japan—was generally allowed to go about its business). Ten centers were established in the West and Middle West, to which, beginning in the spring of 1942, some 100,000 Japanese were sent (see Chapter 10). Nearly two-thirds of these were American citizens. This action by the government was racial rather than political since none of America's other so-called enemies-in-residence (e.g., Germans and Italians) were subjected to relocation.[68]

The relocation worked a considerable hardship upon the Japanese. Businessmen and merchants, within the space of a few weeks, had to sell or liquidate their business interests and properties. Buyers, as a rule, were unwilling to pay reasonable prices when fully aware of the commercial disadvantage of the Japanese in having to make quick sales. Farmers were in the worst bargaining position possible, as evacuation came after planting and fertilizing but before harvesting. Unable to harvest their crops, they had to make the best bargain available.[69] Bloom and Riemer estimate that the evacuated Japanese suffered an economic loss of $367.5 million. A sample survey of 206 families showed the median loss per family to be $9,870 in terms of the 1941 value of the dollar.[70]

Soon after the evacuation, some of the interned Japanese were resettled in non-western parts of the United States. Students were often given permission to attend college; employment permits were given for some agricultural and industrial workers; and church groups, through the establishment of hostels, aided those unable to find employment. In December, 1944, the military ban on returning to the West Coast area was lifted. Although the wartime reset-

[68] Ronald O. Haak, "Co-opting the Oppressors: The Case of the Japanese-Americans," *Trans-action*, 7 (October, 1970), 23–31.
[69] Dorothy Swaine Thomas and Richard S. Nichimoto, *The Spoilage* (Berkeley: University of California Press, 1946), 14–18.
[70] Leonard Bloom and Ruth Riemer, *Removal and Return* (Berkeley: University of California Press, 1949), 202–204.

tlement patterns entailed some dispersion of the Japanese through non-western portions of the United States, by 1950 some 80 per cent of the persons of Japanese descent within the country were living in western states. Initially, there was some opposition to the return of the Japanese to California and some serious incidents occurred. But the new storm raised a counter-reaction among the natives for fair play, and this became the dominant response. By virtue of the wartime evacuation, many formerly independent Japanese business establishments were disrupted and lost. Japanese farmers found it extremely difficult to re-establish themselves. The net result was the emergence of a new employment pattern, represented by a major shift from independent employment or employment by other Japanese to employment by non-Japanese employers.

JEWS

Within the United States there are an estimated 5.8 million Jews, about 45 per cent of the world's Jewish population. Of these, perhaps 2.5 million reside in the New York metropolitan area (roughly equal to the Jewish population of Israel). By virtue of their minority status, American Jews have experienced prejudice and discrimination, although it has diminished in recent decades. Political anti-Semitism—defined as a preoccupation with alleged Jewish power— has declined almost to the vanishing point (in 1938 as many as 41 per cent agreed with the statement that Jews have too much power in the United States; in 1945 it reached a peak of 58 per cent, but by 1962 had declined to 17 per cent and by 1964 to 11 per cent). "Conventional" anti-Semitism—beliefs in Jewish clannishness and unethical business practices—has declined less radically (in 1964, for instance, 35 per cent still believed that Jewish businessmen are so shrewd and tricky that other people don't have a fair chance in competition).[71]

In employment, Jews have long encountered discriminatory barriers, the nature and extent of which are suggested by a number of surveys. In a study conducted by Jewish organizations in Chicago between 1952 and 1955, it was found that, of 40,000 job orders placed with Chicago's commercial employment agencies, 8,800, or 22 per cent, were restrictive against Jews. Of the 5,500 firms cov-

[71] Gertrude J. Selznick and Stephen Steinberg, *The Tenacity of Prejudice* (New York: Harper & Row, 1969), 8.

ered by the survey, 1,500, or 27 per cent, specified restrictions against Jews, including such statements as "Protestants only, no Jews or Orientals"; "We have no religious preference as long as they are of the Nordic race"; "We're desperate, but not desperate enough to hire Jews"; and "We only employ high type Anglo-Saxons." [72] In 1956, the Institute of Industrial Relations of the University of California undertook a survey of job discrimination against Jews in the San Francisco Bay area. It reported that, of the 340 private employers in major industries interviewed, 75, or 22 per cent, acknowledged that they either barred Jews completely or limited their employment on a quota system. [73] Yet nationally the situation has improved since the 1950s and especially since the 1930s, when some employment agencies estimated that some 95 per cent of their job orders were closed to Jews.

Jews are conspicuously absent in the management teams of banks, public utilities, insurance companies, and certain large concerns in heavy industry (including the automobile industry). It has been estimated that Jews constitute one-half of 1 per cent of the total executive personnel in leading American industrial companies. Yet 8 per cent of all college graduates and 25 per cent of Ivy League college graduates are Jewish. [74] A 1966 survey of the nation's 50 largest commercial banks showed that only eight of the 632 senior officers were identified as Jewish; of 3,438 "middle management" jobs at the banks, just 32, or 0.9 per cent, were filled by Jews. Similarly, a 1965 survey of 26 large industrial, insurance, railroad, and food companies headquartered in Philadelphia revealed that of 530 top-level executives, only three were Jewish. [75]

Lewis B. Ward studied the hiring practices of 324 recruiters on college campuses for some 250 major companies. Sorting out the recruiters in terms of the ethnic backgrounds of the students they hired, 80 hired only Protestant students, 42 hired only Catholic students, 14 hired only Jewish students, and 188 hired students from more than one ethnic background. Those companies that hired only

[72] Albert Weiss, "Jews Need Not Apply," in N. C. Belth, ed., *Barriers* (New York: Friendly House, 1958), 44.

[73] *Ibid.*, 45.

[74] See: Benjamin R. Epstein and Arnold Forster, *"Some of My Best Friends . . ."* (New York: Farrar, Straus and Giroux, 1962); Lewis B. Ward, "The Ethnics of Executive Selection," *Harvard Business Review*, 43 (1965), 6–40; and "Anti-Jewish Bias Laid to Auto Men," *New York Times,* October 7, 1963, 32.

[75] Frederick C. Klein, "Religious Groups Push to Get Firms To Hire Jewish Executives," *Wall Street Journal,* October 26, 1966.

Protestants were viewed by their recruiters as discouraging the taking of risks, as downgrading ability, and as placing a premium on "being a good Joe." This contributed to a homogeneous environment that served to exclude Jews.[76]

It was not uncommon prior to 1948 to find "restrictive covenant" clauses in title deeds to property in fashionable sections of American cities. Restrictive covenants serve as instruments to bar particular religious and racial groups, usually specifying that the property could not be sold to any but "White Gentiles." These agreements were enforceable within the courts and were a means by which Jews were excluded from many neighborhoods. In 1948, the U.S. Supreme Court ruled that such covenants were no longer enforceable in the courts, as they violated the "equal protection" guaranty of the Fourteenth Amendment. Since then, new devices, of which "gentlemen's agreements" have become the most prevalent, have been resorted to in order to keep neighborhoods restricted. Some real-estate interests have also attempted to circumvent the high court's ruling through new legal devices. Real-estate promoters may establish clubs or corporations to which the landowner deeds his land, and, in turn, he is allowed the use of it; the owner cannot, however, sell the property without the consent of the club or corporation. Another scheme gives the community the option to purchase the land and to hold it for sale to an approved buyer in the event the owner decides to dispose of the property.[77]

Informal means may also be employed to exclude Jews from many communities. A case in Greenwich, Connecticut, is illustrative. A prominent real-estate broker in that community acknowledged to the Connecticut Commission on Civil Rights that she had written a memorandum to her sales staff warning against selling property to Jews. A part of the memorandum follows:

From this date on when anyone telephones us in answer to an ad in any newspaper and their name is, or appears to be, Jewish, do not meet them anywhere!

If it happens on Sunday, tell them we do not show on Sunday, take a phone number and throw it away!

If they walk into the office in answer to an ad we are running, screen them carefully . . .

We can do only one thing by cooperating with them [Jews] and that is to be liable to severe criticism by the board [Greenwich Real Estate Board]

[76] Ward, op. cit.

[77] Arnold Forster, "The Hidden Barbed Wire in Housing," in Belth, op. cit., 92–100.

and our fellow brokers, as these people are everywhere and just roam from one broker to another hoping to get into Greenwich.[78]

Within colleges and universities there has been evidence through the years that discrimination operated among some schools in the admission of Jews. At times "quota systems" were maintained in which a specified number of Jewish students were accepted, despite the fact that other Jewish applicants may have been more qualified than many of the accepted Gentile students. Medical schools in particular have had a long tradition of imposing quotas on the number of Jewish admissions. However, in higher education generally and medical education in particular, there has been a marked decline since World War II in discrimination based upon religion.[79] Similarly there has been a decline in fraternity bias.[80]

Country clubs, luncheon clubs, and related social clubs have represented an important area of discrimination directed against Jews. Exclusive clubs and informal gatherings of the "prestige classes" constitute strongholds of discrimination. A survey of the American Jewish Committee reveals that out of some 1,800 downtown men's clubs in the United States, roughly 80 per cent have no Jewish members.[81] This discrimination often has implications for the employment and promotion of Jews in the business world. One industrialist explained why he could not readily employ Jewish executives in his organization:

It is important for our business that our plant managers maintain a certain status in their communities. They must join the country club and the leading city club. Today, that's where the big deals are discussed and made. They must be socially acceptable to the banking and business leaders of the town. They must be able to maintain a free and easy association with the people who count. If we promote Jewish personnel into key, sensitive positions, we run a risk of social non-acceptability. We avoid this by picking someone else.[82]

While the influence of such clubs may be waning somewhat, they nonetheless are valuable centers where ideas are presented and major business transactions are informally handled. Hence, the failure of Jews to acquire social club membership seriously hampers their climb up the executive ladder in the world of business.

[78] *New York Times,* September 15, 1961, 35.
[79] Harold Braverman, "Medical School Quotas," in Belth, *op. cit.,* 74–77.
[80] Louis Krapin, "The Decline of Fraternity Bias," in Belth, *op. cit.,* 78–88.
[81] Elliot Carlson, "Negroes, Jews Press Efforts to Join Groups That Now Refuse Them," *Wall Street Journal,* September 10, 1969.
[82] N. C. Belth, "Discrimination and the Power Structure," in Belth, *op. cit.,* 11.

SUMMARY

We have seen that segregation often plays a major role within the United States in governing the relations between dominant and minority group members. The net effect of segregation is to place major limitations and restrictions upon social interaction between the members of these groups. It may find expression in discrimination where an individual's membership in a particular racial, ethnic, or religious group becomes the foundation for differential and unequal treatment. Accordingly, minority group members may find themselves disadvantaged in securing access to certain jobs, homes, health services, educational opportunities, and various public facilities and activities. Segregation similarly may find expression in spatial separation and the appearance of minority ghettos.

8

Stratification

Within any society, people are ranked in a vertical arrangement —a hierarchy—that differentiates them as superior or inferior, higher or lower. We refer to this differential ranking of people as *social stratification*. Broadly considered, it is questionable whether any society, even the simplest, lacks some form of stratification. In this sense, social inequality is universal—in certain socially important respects, all societies differentiate between and rank people. This fact finds expression in the unequal distribution among the members of any society of scarce, divisible values, namely, wealth, power, and status. Accordingly, stratification represents institutionalized inequality in the allocation of rewards.

CLASS, ETHNIC, AND RACIAL STRATIFICATION

Social Stratification and Types of Social Organization

In considering social stratification, it is useful to distinguish between three types of social organization. First, there is role differentiation, that is, a division of labor.[1] Early in human history it was discovered that a division of labor within society resulted in greater efficiency. The earliest and simplest expression of specialization was the division of labor between the sexes. With the growth in technology and societal complexity, the division of labor became increasingly specialized.

[1] Dennis H. Wrong, "The Functional Theory of Stratification: Some Neglected Considerations," *American Sociological Review*, 24 (1959), 773.

Second, there is the unequal distribution of rewards among the various roles making up the division of labor. Within any society there are certain essential social functions or tasks that have to be performed. These functions are indispensable to the continuing and orderly existence of the society. But not all the functions are equally pleasant to the human organism, nor are they all equally in need of the same ability or talent. If all functions were equally rewarded, it is clear that some might never be performed. If doctors were given the same material rewards, status, and power that were given unskilled laborers, it is questionable whether enough young men would be willing to undergo the expensive and burdensome training necessary to become doctors. Accordingly, over an extended period of time, societies tend to evolve a system of differential rewards in order to instill in some individuals the desire to fill certain positions; once in these positions, the individuals need to be motivated to perform the duties attached to them. It is this system of unequal reward distribution that constitutes the foundation of stratification.[2]

Third, there is the tendency for the positions themselves, or at any rate the opportunities whereby the positions are secured, to be passed on from one generation to the next, giving rise to enduring classes or strata monopolizing certain positions. By virtue of family and kinship loyalties, one generation attempts to pass on to the next its advantaged position so that through time there exists a high correlation between the initial social positions of individuals at birth and their adult social positions. Accordingly, there emerges some degree of relative stability and permanence of the classes or strata. This contributes to the appearance of a common style of life and common values and sentiments that tend to be shared by the members of any given class and to set it off from other classes.[3] Thus, within the United States, the major social classes—the working, middle, and upper classes—can be distinguished in terms of their attitudes toward education; their systems of morality; their political, family, religious, and recreational behavior; and their patterns of life in general.[4]

[2] Kingsley Davis and Wilbert E. Moore, "Some Principles of Stratification," *American Sociological Review*, 10 (1945), 242–249.

[3] Wrong, *op. cit.*, 773.

[4] James W. Vander Zanden, *Sociology: A Systematic Approach*, 2nd ed. (New York: The Ronald Press Co., 1970), 218–229.

A Multi-dimensional Approach to Class

Consensus among sociologists as to the best or most appropriate definition of social class has as yet not been achieved. Although in agreement that the concept deals with the stratification of a population into higher and lower categories, scholars are in disagreement as to just what differences are to be emphasized. Whether class stratification is to be viewed as based upon income, power, occupation, education, group identification, level of consumption, family background, cultural differences, status, or a combination of these is a matter on which there is no substantial agreement.

In recent years, a multi-dimensional approach to class has gained increasing recognition and support. Three dimensions of class are frequently singled out: the economic, the status, and the power aspects. The *economic* dimension refers to the position that individuals occupy in the social order as determined by income, property, access to credit, degree of dominance-subordination in employment relations, and degree of control over the determination of wages and prices of goods.[5] The *status* dimension refers to the relative standing or prestige enjoyed by individuals, based upon their position or role. The *power* dimension refers to the ability of individuals to influence or control the behavior of others. It can be seen that there are several analytically distinct dimensions of class, and that these are not necessarily identical; in fact, they may be disparate. Hangmen, prostitutes, and professional criminals are often paid exceedingly well, yet they may enjoy little status or power. University faculty members, while often ranking high in status, usually rank comparatively low in income and power. Some public officials may enjoy a good deal of power yet receive low wages and little status. On the whole, however, these three dimensions tend to hang together, feeding and supporting each other.

Stratification Based upon Racial and Ethnic Membership

Within American life there is, in addition to the stratification structure based upon social class, that based upon religious, ethnic, and racial membership. These two sets of stratification structures criss-cross. A general formulation of this principle is found in Hollingshead's statement that a social structure may be "differentiated

[5] Milton M. Gordon, *Social Class in American Sociology* (Durham, N.C.: Duke University Press, 1958), 240–243.

vertically along racial, ethnic and religious lines, and each of these vertical cleavages, in turn, is differentiated *horizontally* by a series of strata or classes that are encompassed within it. . . ." [6] Thus religious, ethnic, and racial groups are not arranged in a simple higher and lower ranking with respect to the class stratification system. Each of the religious, ethnic, and racial groups tends to span a range of higher and lower positions within the class structure, sometimes from the top to the bottom, sometimes within a narrower range. The most critical consequence of these two stratification structures is that members of a minority group who achieve mobility into a higher class are not accorded many of the benefits bestowed upon members of the dominant group of the equivalent class.

The two systems need to be kept conceptually separate in order to discover the nature of their interrelationships. An illustration will help to clarify the matter. How does A, member of the old-American group and the "working class," articulate his status attitude toward B, a member of the Jewish (or Italian or Polish or Black) group who has a high "middle class" status? In terms of the class hierarchy, the minority-group member would outrank the member of the old-American group. But, in terms of the ethnic or racial structure, the reverse situation would hold true. Reciprocally, the question becomes: How does B articulate his status attitude in relation to A? Do the attitudes of one stratification structure, either the ethnic and racial or class structure, tend to prevail? Do confusion and tension ensue from the criss-crossing of the two sets of patterns within specific behavior situations? [7]

The answers to these questions in part depend upon whether individual B is a member of the Jewish, Italian, Polish, or Black group. The resolution of the matter would quite probably be reversed in some circumstances in the case of an Italian, on the one hand, and a Black, on the other—the attitudes of the class structure tending to prevail in the former case, the attitudes of the racial and ethnic structure in the latter. Everett C. Hughes points to the dilemma of the Black professional man: "The dilemma, for those whites who meet such a person, is that of having to choose whether to treat him as a Negro or as a member of his profession." [8] Similarly, within this situation the Black professional faces a dilemma as to the choice

[6] August B. Hollingshead, "Trends in Social Stratification," *American Sociological Review,* 18 (1952), 679–686.

[7] Gordon, *op. cit.,* 252–253.

[8] Everett Cherrington Hughes, "Dilemmas and Contradictions of Status," *American Journal of Sociology,* L (1945), 357.

of his proper role. In the realm of social organization, such matters are likely to be avoided by an "elaboration of social segregation," where the Black professional man may serve only Black clients. Where a White client makes use of a Black's professional services, the contact is likely to remain purely professional and specific, rarely extended into a general social relationship.

The importance of keeping these two systems conceptually separate is seen in still another connection. It is known that family, clique, associational, and social relationships tend to be confined to members of one's own or closely adjoining classes. To what extent does the ethnic or racial factor divide the intimate group life of members of the same social class? By way of illustration, do middle-class Jews have more intimate social contacts with middle-class Gentiles or with lower-class Jews? The same question can be asked of Italians, Poles, and Blacks in relation to the old-American group. The matter again depends to a considerable extent upon the ranking of the ethnic or racial minority on the social-distance scale.[9]

The distinction between the two systems is similarly of importance in considering social mobility, that is, the movement of people up and down the stratification hierarchy. In situations where the accent falls on democratic relations, status ideally is determined by what an individual can *do*, not by what he *is*. A distinction can be made between these two types of status, that is, between *achieved* status and *ascribed* status. Ascribed statuses are assigned to individuals, without reference to ability, on the basis of such characteristics as sex, age, and family membership. Achieved statuses are acquired by individuals through competition and individual effort.[10] Within the ethnic and racial structure of stratification, status is ascribed to the individual by the society; it is not rooted in his own competitive or individual effort. On the other hand, within the class structure, there is greater room for the achievement of status, although complete achievement often is limited by inheritance and unequal access to opportunities, both of which tend to be associated with family membership. To the extent to which status is ascribed (e.g., on the basis of religious, ethnic, and racial membership), social mobility within a social order is impaired; to the extent to which status is achieved, social mobility is facilitated.

We have noted, then, that sociologists find it useful to distinguish

---

[9] Gordon, *op. cit.*, 253.
[10] Ralph Linton, *The Study of Man* (New York: Appleton-Century-Crofts, Inc., 1936), 115 ff.

between stratification systems based upon social class and those based upon racial and ethnic membership. But, we may ask, does racial and ethnic stratification differ significantly from forms premised upon class, age, or sex characteristics? Or is racial and ethnic stratification simply another form of general stratification? It indeed does appear that racial and ethnic stratification is distinctive—only racial and ethnic groups have the *potential* to carve their own autonomous nation from the existing state. In other words, political separatism offers a solution to disadvantaged groups in an ethnic stratification system that is not possible for disadvantaged class, sex, or age groups (in that the latter are not normally self-sufficient).[11]

Although the probability of a separatist movement and its chances for success vary enormously between nations with ethnic stratification, the underlying potential for such movements exists in most nations with diverse ethnic groups. The issue, then, unlike economic stratification, is not replacement of one party or elite by another or even a revolutionary change in the political system, but whether the ethnic segments will be willing to participate within the existing nation-state arrangement.[12] The new states of Africa and Asia provide a good illustration of this. Although there are many competing non-ethnic loyalties in the new states—ties to class, party, business, union, profession, or whatever—groups formed of these ties are seldom considered as possible self-standing, maximal social units, as candidates for nationhood. In contrast, competing religious, linguistic, racial, cultural, and related loyalties often threaten the state's very existence, as in the case of Nigeria (the secessionist Ibo state of Biafra) and the former Belgian Congo (the secessionist Katanga province). Geertz summarizes the matter as follows:

> Conflicts among them [e.g., conflicts between classes or economic interests] occur only within a more or less fully accepted terminal community whose political integrity they do not, as a rule, put to question. No matter how severe they become they do not threaten, at least not intentionally, its existence as such. They threaten governments, or even forms of government, but they rarely at best . . . threaten to undermine the nation itself, because they do not involve alternative definitions of what the nation is, of what its scope of reference is. Economic or class or intellectual disaffection threatens revolution, but disaffection based on race, language, or culture threatens partition, irredentism, or merger, a redrawing of the very limits of the state, a new definition of its domain.[13]

---

[11] Stanley Lieberson, "Stratification and Ethnic Groups," *Sociological Inquiry,* 40 (1970), 172–181.

[12] *Ibid.,* 175.

[13] Clifford Geertz, "The Integrative Revolution," in Clifford Geertz, ed., *Old Societies and New States* (New York: The Free Press of Glencoe, 1963), 111.

PATTERNS OF STRATIFICATION

Stratification in "Yankee City"

The community provides an excellent setting from which to gain a view of the operation of the two sets of stratification structures, the ethnic and racial on the one hand, the class on the other. One of the earliest investigations into the structure and social life of a specific community was undertaken in the 1930s by W. Lloyd Warner and his associates. Warner, an American social anthropologist, selected a small New England town of about 17,000 as the setting for his research. The resultant series of volumes on "Yankee City"—Newburyport, Massachusetts—became a major landmark in the field of social stratification.[14] Initially, Yankee City's economy rested upon shipping, shipbuilding, and fishing, but, beginning in the 1840s, the economic base was extended to manufacturing, chiefly shoes, silverware, and textiles.

The Class Structure of Yankee City. By the 1930s, Warner found a well-developed social class system within Yankee City, which he described as falling within a sixfold division: upper-upper, lower-upper, upper-middle, lower-middle, upper-lower, and lower-lower. We should note that Warner's classificatory system rests primarily upon the *status* ingredient and tends to neglect the power and economic dimensions of class.

The *upper-upper* class represents "an aristocracy of birth and wealth." [15] It is an "old-family" class whose members can trace their lineage and wealth through many generations that likewise participated in an upper-class way of life. The members are old not only to the community but also to the class. *Birth* is crucial for membership. Although the men of this level are gainfully occupied, usually as large merchants, financiers, or in the higher professions, family wealth is inherited. Ideally the wealth should stem from the colonial and early-American sea trade when the city's merchants and sea captains amassed large fortunes. Upper-upper class people tend to

[14] The "Yankee City" Series (New Haven: Yale University Press): W. Lloyd Warner and Paul S. Lunt, *The Social Life of a Modern Community* (1941); W. Lloyd Warner and Paul S. Lunt, *The Status System of a Modern Community* (1942); W. Lloyd Warner and Leo Srole, *The Social System of American Ethnic Groups* (1945); W. Lloyd Warner and J. O. Low, *The Social System of the Modern Factory* (1947); W. Lloyd Warner, *The Living and the Dead* (1959).

[15] The class characteristics are in part summarized from W. Lloyd Warner, Marchia Meeker, and Kenneth Eells, *Social Class in America* (Chicago: Science Research Associates, Inc., 1949).

be closely intermarried, either with members of the same class within Yankee City or with upper-uppers in Salem, Providence, Boston, or other New England cities. This group represented about 1.5 per cent of Yankee City's population.

The *lower-upper* class is in many respects similar to the upper-upper class in that the members of both live in large, expensive houses in exclusive residential sections and have somewhat similar patterns of participation in associations and informal social groups. In terms of wealth, the lower-uppers are able to meet the *means* test but they fail to meet the *lineage* test so essential for upper-upper class membership. Their wealth is as yet too new and too recently earned to have the sacred quality of wealth long present within a family line. Nevertheless, in term of wealth the lower-uppers have a slightly higher average income than upper-upper class members. Lower-upper class people tend to engage in conspicuous expenditure and fast living, behavior disdained by the upper-uppers. They aspire to upper-upper class membership, but they are barred by the absence of proper lineage. This group represented about 1.6 per cent of the population of Yankee City.

The *upper-middle* class comprises a group of substantial business-men and professionals—"solid, highly respectable" people but not "society." They often serve as leaders in civic affairs. They aspire to the classes above them and hope their good deeds and civic activities will win them acceptance by their social "superiors." About 10 per cent of the population of Yankee City is upper-middle class. The three higher classes, the two upper classes and the upper-middle, comprise what Warner calls the "level above the common man." Together they represent approximately 13 per cent of the total population.

The *lower-middle* class, the top of the common-man level, is made up of small businessmen, clerical workers, other lower-level white-collar workers, and a few skilled workmen. Their homes are small and neat, located in the "side streets." They are proper and conservative, careful with their money, concerned about respectability, and labeled "good common people." They made up 28 per cent of the population.

The lower-middle class tends to shade imperceptibly into the *upper-lower* class; the dividing line between the two is often difficult to establish with precision. Nevertheless, the two do not represent one class, the upper-lowers being distinguished as "poor but honest workers." The upper-lower class is made up of semi-skilled workers in factories, service workers, and a few small tradesmen. Its members live in the less desirable sections, have lower incomes, but are nevertheless viewed as "respectable." They represented 33 per cent of the population.

In contrast with the upper-lowers, the *lower-lower* class is not "respectable" and enjoys a "bad reputation" within the larger community. Its members are viewed as lazy, shiftless, and dependent, traits commonly viewed as opposite to "good middle-class virtues." They are thought to "live like animals," because it is believed that their sexual mores are not too exacting. They live in the least desirable sections of the community and comprise the largest proportion of individuals on relief. They made up 25 per cent of Yankee City's population.

Yankee City's Patterns of Ethnic Stratification. The Irish were the earliest of the ethnic groups coming to Yankee City, arriving in substantial numbers in the 1840s. However, factory positions were almost entirely filled by "natives" from within the city, since until the 1860s such jobs were commonly associated with middle-class status. Accordingly, Irish immigrants were able to find only unskilled employment as farm laborers, stevedores, carters, hod carriers, and domestics. In the 1860s the wage scales and working conditions within Yankee City were adversely affected, depressing the prestige value of factory work. This fact and the sharp decline in the city's maritime enterprises induced the movement of many middle-class "natives," especially young people, out of Yankee City in search of new opportunities elsewhere. Simultaneously the birth rate of the middle and upper classes began to decline. These two developments account for the fact that, in spite of only a slight expansion of the local economy since 1870, new immigrant arrivals have been able to find acceptance within the economic system. In the middle 1880s, French Canadians started arriving in Yankee City in some numbers. They were followed by Jews, Italians, Greeks, and Armenians, who in turn were followed by the Poles and Russians.[16]

At the time of Warner's study, there were 9,030 "natives" in Yankee City, 53.8 per cent of the total population. Of the ethnic groups, the Irish were by far the largest. There were 3,943 Irish, 1,466 French Canadians, 677 Poles, 412 Greeks, 397 Jews, 284 Ital-

[16] Warner and Srole, *op. cit.*, 31–32, and 46–47.

ians, 246 Armenians, 141 Russians, and 80 Blacks.[17] Table 8–1 gives
the percentage breakdown by social class of the respective ethnic
groups. Table 8–2 gives the percentage breakdown by ethnic groups
of the six social classes. These tables demonstrate the disproportionate concentration of the nine ethnic groups, when compared with
the native Yankee City group, in the level below the common man
—in the lower-middle and the two lower classes. The entire upper-
upper class and all but a small fraction of the lower-upper were
"native." More than four-fifths of the upper-middle class were
"native," but the proportion dropped to two-thirds in the lower-
middle. The ethnics, when compared with the "natives," were disproportionately concentrated in the two lower classes and, except
for the Jews and the Irish, in the lower-lower class.

TABLE 8–1   Percentage, by Social Class, of Yankee City
Ethnic Groups

Ethnic Group	Social Class *					
	UU	LU	UM	LM	UL	LL
Yankee	2.7	2.8	15.9	35.3	23.1	20.2
Total ethnic		0.2	3.5	20.4	44.3	31.6
Irish		0.3	5.9	27.5	53.7	12.5
French			1.0	13.1	40.3	45.6
Jewish			3.0	41.8	47.6	7.6
Italian			0.3	13.7	41.9	44.0
Armenian			1.2	17.9	50.8	30.1
Greek			2.2	5.4	35.8	56.6
Polish				0.7	9.8	89.5
Russian				4.3	25.5	70.2
Black						100.0
Unknown			19.7	7.9	36.8	35.5
Total	1.4	1.6	10.3	28.4	32.9	25.4

* UU—Upper-Upper; LU—Lower-Upper; UM—Upper-Middle; LM—Lower-Middle; UL—Upper-Lower; LL—Lower-Lower.
Source: L. Lloyd Warner and Paul S. Lunt, The Social Life of a Modern Community (New Haven: Yale University Press, 1941), Table 7, 225. By permission
of the publishers.

The tables also suggest that the average class status of an ethnic
group tended to be associated with the length of time it had been in
the city. The French Canadians and the Jews constituted the only
important deviations from this pattern. There were, however, other

[17] Ibid., 78.

Table 8–2   Percentage, by Ethnic Group, of Yankee
City Social Classes

Ethnic	Social Class *					
Group	UU	LU	UM	LM	UL	LL
Yankee	100.0	95.4	83.4	67.1	38.0	42.8
Irish		4.6	13.4	22.7	38.3	11.5
French			0.8	4.1	10.7	15.6
Jewish			0.7	3.5	3.5	0.7
Italian			0.1	0.8	2.2	3.0
Armenian			0.2	0.9	2.3	1.8
Greek			0.5	0.5	2.7	5.5
Polish				0.1	0.1	14.3
Russian				0.1	0.7	2.3
Black						1.9
Unknown			0.9	0.1	0.5	0.6
Total	100.0	100.0	100.0	100.0	100.0	100.0

* UU—Upper-Upper; LU—Lower-Upper; UM—Upper-Middle; LM—Lower-Middle; UL—Upper-Lower; LL—Lower-Lower.

Source: W. Lloyd Warner and Paul S. Lunt, The Social Life of a Modern Community (New Haven: Yale University Press, 1941), Table 7, 225. By permission of the publishers.

considerations which suggested that the correlation between the position of a group's status line and its length of settlement in Yankee City was less than perfect. The Armenians and the Greeks arrived in Yankee City during the same decade, yet the Armenians as a group had advanced their status position more than the Greeks. Furthermore, in terms of the time they had been in Yankee City and the status positions of more recently arrived groups, the Irish and the French Canadians did not enjoy the relatively high position that might be expected.[18]

In addition to the length of the group's establishment in Yankee City, certain secondary factors had contributed to the varying rates of mobility among the ethnic groups. One of the more important of these factors was the type of motivation which induced migration to the United States. For the Jews, Armenians, and Russians, migration was undertaken with a view toward establishing themselves permanently within this country. Thus they were anxious to strike roots that would enable them to adapt themselves to the dictates of American life. On the other hand, a substantial portion of the Italians, Greeks, and Poles migrated with the expectation of return-

18 Ibid., 98–99.

ing to their homeland. They hoped to secure sufficient funds to increase their landholdings and their economic status in their native
land. The number of those who actually repatriated themselves
was comparatively small, but, until the decision was made to remain
permanently in America, there was little impetus to meet any but the
minimal demands of this society.

Proximity to the homeland, as in the case of the French Canadians, also served to slow assimilation and, with it, the process of
status advancement. Living only a few hundred miles from Quebec,
the French Canadians were able to revisit their homeland easily.
The French Canadians' strong identification with the family (in
which initiative for mobility does not rest with the individual but
with the family as represented by the father) further served to retard
the group's upward mobility. A large group population (by facilitating the institutional retention of ethnic patterns) similarly impeded
a group's immersion within the larger society and thus served to impair upward mobility, e.g., the Irish and French Canadians. And
finally, as in the case of the Irish, status mobility may be retarded by
the fact that a group is the first in order of appearance among the
ethnic groups, arriving in a period of a fixed native population and
of relatively limited opportunities for advancement within the social
system. On the other hand, status mobility may be accelerated by
similarities between the ethnic ancestral society and the general
social-organization type of the "natives" (e.g., the Jews) [19] or by
similarities between the ethnic ancestral society and the religious
complex of the "natives" (e.g., the Armenians).[20]

The occupational histories of the ethnic groups in Yankee City
followed courses quite similar to one another. The workers of the
newly arrived groups started at the very bottom of the occupational
hierarchy and, through time, especially through generations, advanced upward to jobs with higher pay and increased prestige. To
a considerable degree, each new group repeated the occupational
history of the preceding one. Upon arrival, the Jews and Armenians
were absorbed by the shoe factories, while the other ethnic groups
were initially drawn into the textile mills. With the collapse of the
local textile industry, the ethnics tended to widen their industrial
representation, although for the most part they then moved into the
shoe factories.

---

[19] In this regard see: Mariam K. Slater, "My Son the Doctor: Aspects of Mobility
among American Jews," *American Sociological Review*, 34 (1969), 359–373.
[20] Warner and Srole, *op. cit.*, 99–102.

Warner divides the occupational classes into six groups and assigns numerical weights to each, as follows: (1) unskilled labor—1, (2) skilled factory—2, (3) skilled craft—2.5, (4) management-aid (e.g., foremen, secretaries, salesmen, clerks, etc.)—3, (5) management—4, and (6) professional—6. He was then able to secure an occupational index for each ethnic group—the absolute number in each of the classes in a given year is multiplied by the assigned numerical value of the class, and the sum of these products is then divided by the total employed population of the ethnic group. This quotient is a number between one and six and indicates the relative position of the ethnic group in terms of the occupational hierarchy. Table 8–3

Table 8–3 Occupational-Status Indexes of Yankee City Ethnic Groups (by Decades)

Group	1850	1864	1873	1883	1893	1903	1913	1923	1933
Irish	1.62	1.76	1.74	1.76	1.84	1.94	2.14	2.31	2.52
French					1.95	2.10	2.14	2.23	2.24
Jews							3.10	3.22	3.32
Italians							2.32	2.29	2.28
Armenians							2.46	2.51	2.56
Greeks								2.53	2.34
Poles								1.88	1.97
Russians									1.95
Total ethnics									2.42
Total natives									2.56

Source: W. Lloyd Warner and Leo Srole, The Social Systems of American Ethnic Groups (New Haven: Yale University Press, 1945), Table 2, 60. Reproduced by permission.

reveals the occupational-status indexes of the ethnic groups by decades. The Jewish occupational index in 1933 would probably have been above 3.75 if account were taken of the fact that about one-third of the mature members of the younger generation left Yankee City for the greater occupational opportunities of other cities.[21]

The Irish, with the longest history in Yankee City, passed through three phases: (1) 1850–1864—mobility moderate, (2) 1864–1903—mobility slight, and (3) 1903–1933—mobility rapid. Social mobility among the Irish served to split the group along class lines. With the scattering of the Irish through all but the topmost levels of the

21 Ibid., 59–61.

class hierarchy, class differences and antagonisms emerged that undermined the group's inner cohesion. The sharpest antagonisms existed between the lower classes (the lower-lower and upper-lower) and the higher classes (the upper-middle and lower-upper). The former referred to the latter as "lace-curtain Irish," a term not without reproachful connotations, while the latter referred to the former as "shanty Irish." [22] Warner observes that, by the 1930s, between the Irish and the natives of the two lowest classes, and between the Irish and the natives of the three highest classes, "there is a class solidarity greater than the group solidarity between the Irish of the lowest and highest classes or between the natives of the lowest and highest classes." [23]

The Norwegians of Jonesville

W. Lloyd Warner and his associates also undertook an investigation of the social stratification of a midwestern town of about 6,000, to which the pseudonym "Jonesville" (also called "Elmtown," "Prairie City," and "Hometown" in the several publications reporting the research) was given.[24] Jonesville (Morris, Illinois) was established in the 1840s, receiving its initial impetus from the completion of a canal that ran through the town and connected the Mississippi River and Lake Michigan. Several warehouses were built along the canal's banks, and barges could transport goods to and from the Jonesville vicinity. Surrounding agricultural areas used the canal as a means of shipping produce to market, and in time Jonesville became a commercial center for farmers. Several industries also located in Jonesville.

Jonesville is characterized by a five-class pyramid including an upper class, two middle, and two lower classes. In contrast with Yankee City, there is an absence of an "old-family" (upper-upper) class. See Figure 8–1. Two factors apparently have accounted for this situation. First, middle-western communities have been settled comparatively recently and thus for the most part have not had sufficient time to evolve an established old-family aristocracy based upon lineage. Secondly, the population of Jonesville has not been

[22] Ibid., 93.
[23] Ibid., 94.
[24] W. Lloyd Warner and Associates, Democracy in Jonesville (New York: Harper & Row, 1949). Also see: W. Lloyd Warner, Robert J. Havighurst, and Martin B. Loeb, Who Shall Be Educated? (New York: Harper & Row, 1944); and A. B. Hollingshead, Elmtown's Youth (New York: John Wiley & Sons, Inc., 1949).

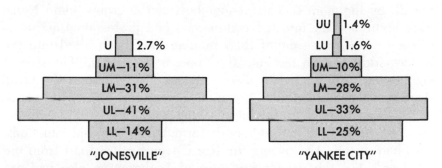

Fig. 8-1. Stratification Pyramids in "Jonesville" and "Yankee City." *Source:* Adapted from W. Lloyd Warner, *Democracy in Jonesville* (New York: Harper & Row, 1949), pages 24-25.

sufficient to make it possible for the older families to hold themselves aloof from the new rich and to organize their own exclusive group; there simply would not be enough people to make up a separate upper-upper class.[25]

The area surrounding Jonesville was settled in large numbers by Norwegians, who undertook farming as their main source of livelihood. After 1870, some of the Norse began to enter nearby towns including Jonesville, where they came into contact with people of other ethnic derivations. Within Jonesville the Norse were confronted with the fact that many of the local citizens viewed them as "foreigners" and looked down upon them as such. The Jonesville Norse found themselves at the bottom of the social and economic hierarchies as untrained and inexperienced laborers. Their subordinate position was the product of their relative lack of skill and the "foreigner" status assigned them by the "Americans." Also in the lower classes with the Norse at this time were the Irish and a mixed body of old Americans. In this early period the Irish and the Norse seem to have been in frequent conflict, numerous street fights and tavern brawls taking place between them. In marked contrast to their present strong opposition to the use of alcohol, the Norse were known as heavy drinkers. At the time of Warner's study, the Norse comprised 15 to 20 per cent of the total population of Jonesville.

In the seventy years since the entrance of the Norse into Jonesville, two types of change have altered their class position. By virtue of better educational opportunities and the accumulation of

[25] *Ibid.*, 25-26.

wealth by the more successful members of the group, some Norse have secured entry into the commercial and professional activities of the town. Thus some of their number have been lifted into the lower-middle class, a few into the upper-middle class. The second change has been related to their religious life. Through the years there developed among the Norse an increasingly strict observance of the moral rules of Lutheranism, along with a more rigid enforcement of these rules through both formal and informal sanctions. This had the effect of setting the Norse even further apart from the "natives." But the strict observance of Lutheranism also had another effect. It contributed to a shift of behavior away from rough, wild, "disreputable" activities to "respectability"—a shift from the lower-lower to the upper-lower class ("disreputability" and "respectability" being the distinction between the two groups).[26]

Their ethnic membership and the evolution of religious sectarianism have served to establish the Norse within Jonesville as a minority. Local Lutheranism has been extended and elaborated in a system of moral values that have placed the Norse beyond the mainstream of community life. Such relatively commonplace activities as dancing, card playing, smoking, and moviegoing are strenuously opposed. A Lutheran pastor cites this rationale for the disapproval of dancing: "It's not the dance itself that is sinful, it is what the dance leads to. You know that out of many a dance has come a fatherless child. I think that activities that are not sinful in themselves but will lead to sin should be stopped before the temptation of sin is placed before these boys and girls." [27]

The effect of these various taboos has been that the Norwegian Lutherans have been isolated from the usual patterns of community life. Their children are kept away from many school activities, and the ban on dancing serves to prevent their teen-agers from participating in much of the social life of their age group. Card playing, an avenue that is religiously barred to the Norse, constitutes a significant activity for bringing people into social contact and cliques. The taboo on drinking prevents the Norse from joining men's clubs or from participating in parties in which drinking is an accepted part of the ritual. These taboos interfere with Norse assimilation and close to them important avenues for upward mobility. In fact, social mobility appears to be the greatest threat to Lutheran sectari-

[26] *Ibid.*, 171–173.
[27] *Ibid.*, 185.

anism, in that mobility above the lower-middle class necessitates in large measure a rejection of some of the major elements in the sectarian ideology.[28]

Caste and Class in "Old City"

As part of their extended study of social stratification within American life, Warner and his colleagues initiated an investigation of a Deep South community of about 10,000, to which the pseudonym "Old City" was given.[29] Four social anthropologists, two White and two Black, lived in Old City (Natchez, Mississippi) for two years in an effort to gain an understanding of the social structure and customs of the community's Blacks and Whites. Old City was a trade center for the large plantations of the cotton counties that surrounded it. At the time of the study, Blacks represented more than half of Old City's population, and about 80 per cent of the population in the neighboring rural areas. Before the Civil War, the area comprised one of the most prosperous and flourishing cotton-growing areas of the South. Many of the planters amassed fortunes, built splendid, great homes, and lived in the manner of a White, feudal aristocracy. With the defeat of the South, the old social order of White master and Black slave was destroyed, although cotton continued to be raised.[30]

The most important factor about the social structure of Old City —for that matter, much of the South—is that it consists of a dual system of stratification, the class system on the one hand, the racial system on the other (patterns that still persist).[31] The latter system, that of race, is often referred to as a *caste* system. Warner and his associates view stratification as any system of ranked statuses by which all the members of a society are placed in superior and inferior positions. As a result of this ranking, privileges, duties, obligations, and opportunities are unequally distributed among the various strata. In this sense both class and caste systems are stratification structures. But castes are to be distinguished from classes by two ingredients: (1) castes are endogamous and (2) prevent vertical mobility (classes are not mandatorily endogamous and per-

[28] *Ibid.*, 173–176.

[29] Allison Davis, Burleigh B. Gardner, and Mary R. Gardner, *Deep South* (Chicago: University of Chicago Press, 1941).

[30] *Ibid.*, 3–4.

[31] See: Jerry W. Robinson, Jr., and James D. Preston, "Class and Caste in 'Old City,'" *Phylon*, 31 (1970), 244–255.

mit vertical mobility). In other words, a caste does not sanction marriage outside its own group and provides "no opportunity for members of the lower group to rise into the upper group or for the members of the upper to fall into the lower one." [32] On the other hand, a class permits its members to marry members of other classes and permits movement either up or down into higher or lower classes.

Warner and his associates suggest that, within Old City and the South generally, "there is a system of white and of Negro castes, and also a system of social classes *within each caste,* further stratifying groups and defining privileges." [33] The basis for determining membership in the respective castes is birth. Caste membership is an ascribed status, assigned to the individual on the basis of his parents' caste position. If both parents are defined by the community as Whites, the child automatically becomes a member of the White caste. If one or both parents are defined by the community as Black, the child automatically becomes a member of the Black caste. The important fact to be noted here is the role of the community definition of racial membership. *Biological* features in and of themselves do not determine such membership; it is rather a *social* definition. Thus a white-skinned man or woman may be *socially* defined as a Black by the community, on the basis of some previous Black ancestry. A relatively dark-skinned man or woman may be *socially* defined as a White by the community, on the basis of known White ancestry and the absence of known Black ancestry.[34]

The caste system within the South is organized to an important extent about the control of sex. Not only have interracial marriages been traditionally prohibited by law, but the severest informal penalties have operated to enforce the code. Offspring of intercaste sexual relations are accordingly born out of sanctioned wedlock. Where children ensue from such relations, the community refuses the child and its parents a recognized family position in the upper White caste and forces the child into the lower Black caste. Usually, the mother of a half-caste child is a Black and by social definition the child becomes a Black. But, if the mother is White, the community insists that all the child's family relationships be destroyed.

[32] Davis, Gardner, and Gardner, *op. cit.,* 9.

[33] Allison Davis and John Dollard, *Children of Bondage* (Washington, D.C.: American Council on Education, 1940), 12–13.

[34] Davis, Gardner, and Gardner, *op. cit.,* 7–8.

The child may be placed with a Black family, the father "run out of town" (or in the past lynched by community action), and the mother forced by social pressures to leave the community. In any event, the caste relationship is maintained by keeping all children who have a Black parent in the lower group and by refusing to recognize the relation of the White parent to the child.[35]

The belief system centering about "the purity of southern White womanhood" functions as one device through which a half-caste child is barred from becoming a member of the upper caste. It rigorously serves to block sexual relations between White women and Black men. But the ordinary double standard of American sexual mores continues to operate for White men within the caste situation. Sexual relations as "fun" are allowed to upper-caste men with the lower-caste women. But social condemnation would be the lot of a White man who would recognize the resulting offspring and accept the usual responsibility expected of an American father.[36]

The rank of the racial castes is determined by their privileges, duties, obligations, and opportunities in the society-at-large. This complex establishes the superordination of the White caste and the subordination of the Black caste. *Within each caste* there is a system of social classes further stratifying the society and defining privileges, duties, obligations, and opportunities. Within Old City, six social classes are identified within the White caste—two upper classes, two middle classes, and two lower classes, a division similar to that found in Yankee City. However, within the Black caste only a relatively slight differentiation by class has occurred, since segregation does not allow for the development of a sufficient occupational spread within the Black group. For the most part, Blacks are concentrated in those jobs near the bottom of the occupational hierarchy. Nevertheless, an incipient, as yet roughly defined, five-class pyramid is present in the Black community. The occupational status required to move into the Black upper and middle classes is lower than would be the case in White society, so that an upper class Black might be comparably ranked within the White class hierarchy as middle class.

Although there is no mobility *between* the two castes, there is internal class mobility *within* each caste. The development of class differentiation within the Black caste has had major consequences

[35] *Ibid.*, 6.
[36] *Ibid.*, 6–7.

for the pattern of American race relations. As Robert E. Park has noted, the castes were originally separated by a horizontal line, with all Whites above all Blacks. With the development of Black class differentiation, the situation has shifted.[37] The caste arrangement theoretically rests on the premise that *all* Whites are considered superior to *all* Blacks. Yet the class differentiation among Blacks has served to contradict this assumption, for not *all* Whites are superior to *all* Blacks in terms of various privileges, duties, obligations, and opportunities. Some Blacks rising to very high positions in the class hierarchy outrank in class status Whites on the lower rungs of the class hierarchy. Though inferior in caste to any White person, the upper-class Black is considered in social class to be superior to the lower-class White. Warner suggests that the caste line has shifted from its original horizontal position to one that is diagonal, so that higher class Blacks, although not equal to their White counterparts, are superior to lower-class Whites. This situation is illustrated in Figure 8–2.

Warner considers it probable that, as educational, occupational, and related opportunities for Blacks improve, the caste line will move from its present diagonal position (*AB*) to vertical position (*de*). Blacks and Whites would have similar class positions but would continue to be separated by the vertical caste line. He speculates that even more drastic changes might follow from such a development:

> It is possible that the ordinary social sanctions which apply to cross-caste "social" relations might finally be weakened with the increasing differentiation in the Negro community and the disappearance of caste differentials in power and prestige. Even the taboo on intermarriage might be relaxed. The children of such marriages would no longer necessarily be placed in the lower caste . . . the whole system of separate caste groups might disappear and new social forms develop to take its place.[38]

Time appears to be bearing out some of Warner's predictions, although it is still too early to determine whether the ban on intermarriage will be relaxed. In a study of "Crescent City" (a pseudonym for Durham, North Carolina—a textile and tobacco center), Burgess notes:

> It would be misleading to say that racial barriers have disappeared, or that Negroes are free to move within the community on the basis of equality with

[37] Robert E. Park, *Race and Culture* (New York: The Free Press of Glencoe, Inc., 1950), 243.
[38] Davis, Gardner, and Gardner, *op. cit.*, 11–12.

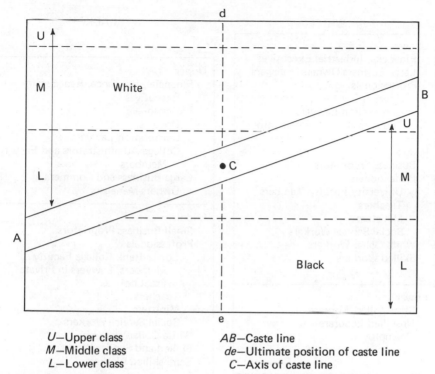

U—Upper class   AB—Caste line
M—Middle class   de—Ultimate position of caste line
L—Lower class   C—Axis of caste line

Fig. 8–2. Warner's Diagram of the Relationship Between the Caste System and the Class System in the Deep South. *Source:* Reprinted from *Deep South* by Allison Davis, Burleigh B. Gardner, and Mary R. Gardner, by the University of Chicago Press, 1941. All rights reserved.

whites. But change is occurring, and with increasing rapidity. The caste-like structure, now in a state of transition, is giving way to a dual-class system, and there are increasing contacts between class equals across color lines.[39]

Rohrer and Edmonson report changes similar to those noted by Burgess in their consideration of the class structure of New Orleans.[40] Figure 8–3 portrays the stratification structure that Burgess discerned in Crescent City.

A number of writers, particularly Oliver C. Cox, have criticized the use of the concept "caste" to describe the race structure of the

[39] M. Elaine Burgess, *Negro Leadership in a Southern City* (Chapel Hill: University of North Carolina Press, 1960), 28.
[40] John H. Rohrer and Munro E. Edmonson, *The Eighth Generation* (New York: Harper & Row, 1960), 26–27.

WHITE   BLACK

Upper
    Financial, Industrial Executives
    Large-Business Owners-Managers
    Professionals
        Doctors
        Corporation Lawyers
        Top University Administrators

Middle
    Business Proprietors
    Professionals
        University Faculty Members
        Teachers
        Ministers
        Social Service Workers
    White Collar Workers
    Skilled Workers

Lower
    Semi-skilled Workers
    Unskilled Laborers
    Unemployed
    Illegal

Upper
    Financial, Insurance, Real Estate
        Executives
    Professionals
        Doctors
        Corporation Lawyers
        College Administrators and Faculty
            Members
    Large-Business and Commercial
        Owners-Managers

Middle
    Small-Business Proprietors
    Professionals
        Lower-Rank College Faculty
            Members, Lawyers in Private
            Practice
        Teachers
        Ministers
        Social Service Workers
    White Collar Workers
    Skilled and Service Workers
    Semi-skilled Workers

Lower
    Domestic and Other Servants
    Unskilled Laborers
    Unemployed
    Illegal

Fig. 8–3. Stratification Structure of Crescent City. *Source:* M. Elaine Burgess, *Negro Leadership in a Southern City* (Chapel Hill: University of North Carolina Press, 1960), page 27. By permission.

South.[41] Cox, on the basis of a comparison of the caste system of India with the race patterns of the South, concludes that a number of ingredients inherent in a "genuine" caste system are lacking in the United States, including rituals relating to eating and avoidance, hereditary occupation, etc. It seems, however, that Cox errs in equating caste with the East Indian caste system. He fails to rec-

[41] Oliver Cromwell Cox, *Caste, Class, and Race* (New York: Doubleday & Co., Inc., 1948). Also see: Charles S. Johnson, *Growing Up in the Black Belt* (Washington, D.C.: American Council on Education, 1941), 325–327.

ognize that some non-Hindu practices are in essence truly caste and similarly that some Hindu practices are essentially non-caste.[42] There may be some point in referring to southern race patterns as "caste-like" rather than as "caste," but the latter concept has by now become rather embedded within the terminology of the field of race relations. Furthermore, it has been for sociologists a useful concept by which to distinguish between the racial (i.e., the caste) and the class systems of stratification.

MOBILITY

Upward Mobility Among Immigrant Stock in America

An integral element in "the American dream" has been the belief that any American who so wills can get ahead and make good. The saga of "from rags to riches" has contributed to an underlying faith in America and its capitalist democracy. The upward mobility of immigrant stock in the American status system has lent reinforcement to the belief. Since the Civil War, there has been a great excess in upward over downward mobility in American life. Immigrant groups have benefited from this fact and generally have been able to advance their position.

Insight as to the relative status and the upward mobility of ten nationality groups of European stock can be gained from Nam's analysis of census data.[43] Nam was able to secure data relating to the respective social statuses of foreign-born and second-generation populations. In measuring the status level of a nationality group, Nam employed a version of the Alba Edwards socioeconomic scale of occupations. Although there are several dimensions to social stratification, an individual's occupation is generally regarded by sociologists as the most reliable single-item measure of his social status. The data in Table 8–4 reveal the status indexes for the selected European nationality groups.

[42] Edward W. Pohlman, "Semantic Aspects of the Controversy over Negro-White Caste in the United States," *Social Forces,* 30 (1952), 416–419. For an excellent treatment of the controversy and a sound appraisal see Gerald D. Berreman, "Caste in India and the United States," *American Journal of Sociology,* 66 (1960), 120–127, and "Structure and Function of Caste Systems," in George DeVos and Hiroshi Wagatsuma, eds., *Japan's Invisible Race* (Berkeley: University of California Press, 1966), 277–307.
[43] Charles B. Nam, "Nationality Groups and Social Stratification in America," *Social Forces,* 37 (1959), 328–333.

TABLE 8–4   Socioeconomic Status Indexes * of Selected European Nationality Groups, by Generation, and of the Native White Population of Native Parentage for the United States, 1950

Native		Foreign-born		Second Generation	
				Russians	4.87
		Russians	4.47		
				Swedes	3.97
		English & Welsh	3.92	English & Welsh	3.92
				Norwegians } Irish	3.91
				Germans	3.78
		Germans	3.75		
Total	3.72				
				Austrians	3.70
		Austrians	3.55		
		Swedes	3.50		
		Norwegians	3.43		
				Czechs	3.41
				Italians	3.39
				Poles	3.24
		Czechs	3.08		
		Italians	3.04		
		Irish	2.99		
		Poles	2.97		

* Standardized for age and urban-rural residence; the age-by-residence distribution of the native white population of native parentage used as a standard.

Source: Charles B. Nam, "Nationality Groups and Social Stratification in America," *Social Forces*, 37 (1959), 330. By permission.

The level of socioeconomic status was generally much higher for the second generation than for the first. The group average of the status indexes for the ten nationalities was 3.81 for the second generation, compared with 3.47 for the foreign-born. The relationship, however, varied for specific nationalities. Thus the index for the English and Welsh remained the same for the two generations, while the Germans experienced an almost negligible generational difference. The second-generation Irish, on the other hand, had a substantially higher status level than the foreign-born generation. The different rates of generational status mobility of the various groups contributed to a shifting of status ranks, although the Russians ranked first and the Poles ranked tenth among both generations. The explanation for the higher position of the Russians probably rests in the fact that a sizable proportion of the migrants from Russia were Jews fleeing persecution and prejudice in Czarist Russia. The Swedes improved their position, ranking fifth in status among the foreign-born and second among the second generation, while the

Irish ranked ninth in status among the foreign-born and fourth among the second generation. Norwegians were likewise able to improve their rank on the status ladder.[44]

Group Characteristics Affecting Upward Mobility

Racial and ethnic groups have exhibited dissimilar rates of upward mobility. American Jews, for example, are cited by any number of social scientists as the group that climbed the social-status ladder more quickly and achieved middle-class status more widely than any other American ethnic group.[45] Within the Northeast, Greeks have similarly tended to attain middle-class stattus more rapidly than most other groups. In general, ethnic groups with Roman Catholic affiliation have witnessed less rapid upward mobility than non-Catholic groups.[46] Likewise, Black vertical mobility has been relatitvely slow.[47]

The factors responsible for these differential rates of upward mobility have varied with the group in question. Immigrant groups have differed in their possession of the various skills that are adaptive within an industrial setting. Many Jews came to America with occupational skills better suited to industrial living than those of their fellow immigrants.[48] Similarly, ethnic and racial groups whose

[44] *Ibid.*, 331.

[45] Nathan Hurvitz, "Sources of Middle-Class Values of American Jews," *Social Forces*, 37 (1958), 117; Edward P. Hutchinson, *Immigrants and Their Children, 1850–1950* (New York: John Wiley, 1956), 180, 189–190, and 253–254; Fred L. Strodtbeck, Margaret M. McDonald, and Bernard C. Rosen, "Evaluation of Occupations: A Reflection of Jewish and Italian Mobility Differences," *American Sociological Review*, 22 (1957), 546–553; and Fred L. Strodtbeck, "Family Interaction, Values, and Achievement," in David C. McClelland, *et al.*, eds., *Talent and Society* (New York: Van Nostrand Reinhold, 1958). The Duncans, however, raise some questions regarding this conclusion. See: Beverly Duncan and Otis Dudley Duncan, "Minorities and the Process of Stratification," *American Sociological Review*, 33 (1968), 356–364.

[46] See: Bernard C. Rosen, "Race, Ethnicity and the Achievement Syndrome," *American Sociological Review*, 24 (1959), 47; Gerhard Lenski, *The Religious Factor*, rev. ed. (Garden City, N.Y.: Doubleday & Co., Inc., 1963), 344–359; Albert J. Mayer and Harry Sharp, "Religious Preference and Worldly Success," *American Sociological Review*, 27 (1962), 218–227. For some qualifications on this conclusion see: Andrew Greeley, *Religion and Career* (New York: Sheed and Ward, 1963).

[47] Rosen, *op. cit.*, 47, and Otis Dudley Duncan, "Patterns of Occupational Mobility among Negro Men," *Demography*, 5 (1968), 11–12.

[48] Rosen, *op. cit., passim.* Glazer and Moynihan report, for instance, that less than one per cent of the nearly two million Southern Italians who came to the United States between 1899 and 1910 were in the professions, whereas roughly 77 per cent were farm workers or laborers. Nathan Glazer and Daniel P. Moynihan, *Beyond the Melting Pot* (Cambridge, Mass.: The M.I.T. Press and Harvard University Press, 1963), 184. Also see: William R. Aho, "Ethnic Mobility in Northeastern United States: An Analysis of Census Data," *Sociological Quarterly*, 10 (1969), 512–526.

cultures were rooted within rural, peasant surroundings are less likely to possess the cultural values appropriate to achievement in America than are those with experiences in urban environments. While most of the Roman Catholic immigrants from eastern and southern Europe and Blacks from the South came from rural communities, many Jews and Levantine Greeks came from small towns or cities. Upward mobility has likewise been related to the ability of ethnic and racial groups to organize effectively in order to protect and further their interests. Where the ethnic group had previous Old World experience in facing the problem of minority-group adaptation, it was often prepared, as were the Jews and Greeks, to develop more quickly effective community organization in America. The Jews had confronted a hostile Gentile world for centuries in Europe, and the Greeks had faced Turkish persecution. The attitudes and behavior of native Americans also played a part, influencing the nature and extent of the obstacles facing various groups. This can especially be seen in the case of Blacks, although it is less relevant as a factor in comparing Jews with southern Italians or French Canadians.[49]

Rosen suggests that a crucial factor in social mobility is the individual's psychological and cultural orientation toward achievement. Individuals differ in their psychological need to excel, their desire to enter the competitive race for social status, and their levels of educational and vocational aspiration. Rosen examines the differences in (1) motivation, (2) values, and (3) aspirations of six racial and ethnic groups in order to determine the role of these three factors in the dissimilar rates of social mobility found among them. Employing ethnographic, attitudinal, and personality data, he asserts that the groups differed, and to some extent still do, in their orientation toward achievement.

1. *Motivation.* Motivation is generated by at least two kinds of socialization practices: achievement training that teaches the child to do things well and independence training that teaches him to do things on his own. Achievement training fosters a strong valuation of high goals and the realization of such goals. Independence training promotes the development of self-reliant attitudes within the child and prepares him for relative autonomy in decision making. Rosen found that the various ethnic groups placed different emphases upon such training in the rearing of children. As a result,

[49] Rosen, *op. cit.*, 47–48.

achievement motivation tended to be more characteristic of Greeks, Jews, and White Protestants than of Italians, French Canadians, and Blacks. The Italians, French Canadians, and Blacks came from agrarian societies or regions in which opportunities for achievement were severely curtailed by the social structure and where habits of resignation and fatalism prevailed. Under such conditions children were not typically encouraged to be achievers.[50]

2. *Values.* The achievement motive by itself is not a sufficient condition of upward mobility. It provides the internal impetus to excel, but it does not impel the individual to take the steps essential for achievement. In addition the individual must be prepared to plan, work hard, make sacrifices, and be physically mobile. Whether or not the individual will understand the importance of these ingredients depends in part upon the values transmitted to him by his group. The cultures of White Protestants, Jews, and Greeks stand out as orienting their members in terms of this value system considerably more than do the cultures of Italians and French Canadians. Rosen's hypothesis that Blacks would score low in value orientations proved to be wrong; the Black score was not significantly different from those for White Protestants and Greeks although it was significantly lower than the Jewish score.[51]

3. *Aspirations.* Still a third element is necessary for social mobility: the individual's educational and vocational aspiration level. The elements of achievement motivation and values do not determine the areas in which the excellence and effort take place; they can be expressed in many kinds of behavior not conducive to social mobility, for example, deviant, recreational, or religious behavior. Thus, in addition, the individual needs to aim for high vocational goals and to prepare himself appropriately in order to move up the social ladder. Again the ethnic and racial groups differed in orienting their members toward vocational and educational preparation— the White Protestants, Jews, and Greeks enjoyed considerable advantage over Italians and French Canadians. In terms of educational aspirations, the Black score was comparable to those of Jews, White Protestants, and Greeks, although the vocational aspiration score of Blacks was the lowest of any of the six groups.[52]

[50] *Ibid.,* 50–53. For a discussion of Italian attitudes see: Herbert J. Gans, *The Urban Villagers* (New York: The Free Press of Glencoe, 1962), 124–136, and Aho, *op. cit.,* 518–524.

[51] Rosen, *op. cit.,* 53–57.

[52] *Ibid.,* 57–60.

The picture that emerges from Rosen's work and a number of other studies dealing with Black mobility aspirations is somewhat confusing. Examining differences between "aspirations" and "plans" of children of different social classes and races, Stephensen found no significant differences between White and Black ninth graders in occupational and educational aspirations. But despite the uniform level of occupational aspiration, the Black students tended to *plan* lower than White students at each occupational level. By "plans" Stephensen meant the realistic expectations regarding future occupation as opposed to idealistic "aspirations." [53] On the other hand, Holloway and Berreman found White fifth and sixth graders at both middle and lower class levels aspiring higher than comparably graded Blacks. Nor did Holloway and Berreman find Blacks scaling down their occupational plans below their aspirational level any more than White students. Hence, in large measure they failed to replicate Stephensen's findings.[54] Perhaps the age differences between the students in the Stephensen and the Holloway-Berreman studies played a critical role. The results of a study by Gist and Bennett still further complicates the picture. They found that among ninth and twelfth grade students the occupational aspirations of Blacks and Whites were roughly similar (a finding similar to that of Stephensen), but that Black educational aspirations exceeded those of White students.[55] Hence, although Black-White differences in mobility aspirations have received considerable attention from researchers, the studies have raised more questions than they have answered.[56]

Factors Favoring an Excess in Upward over Downward Mobility

In a relatively unchanging society in which the occupational structure is more or less stable and stationary through time, individuals may realize upward mobility chiefly through one of two

[53] Richard M. Stephensen, "Mobility Orientation and Stratification of 1,000 Ninth Graders," *American Sociological Review,* 22 (1957), 204–212.

[54] Robert G. Holloway and Joel V. Berreman, "The Educational and Occupational Aspirations and Plans of Negro and White Male Elementary School Students," *Pacific Sociological Review,* 2 (1959), 56–60.

[55] Noel P. Gist and William S. Bennett, Jr., "Aspirations of Negro and White Students," *Social Forces,* 42 (1963), 40–48.

[56] For a treatment of these matters see: "Motivation and Academic Achievement of Negro Americans," *The Journal of Social Issues,* 25 (1969). The entire issue is devoted to this topic.

means: (1) displacement of individuals in higher positions, forcing the latter into downward mobility, or (2) replacement of individuals in higher positions as the latter for one reason or another retire or withdraw from the labor market. The United States, however, especially since the Civil War, has been characterized by a somewhat different situation. A number of factors have contributed to a great excess of upward over downward mobility. This fact has had a major impact upon the occupational status of the various ethnic and racial minorities. To the extent to which upward occupational mobility has been related to overall class status as well as to the relative status position of the various ethnic and racial groups in relation to the native Americans, the minorities have been able to experience on the whole a betterment in their position within American life.

Changes in the Occupational Structure. Changes in the occupational structure within the United States have been a major factor contributing to an excess of upward over downward circulation in the class hierarchy. Developments within technology have appreciably reduced the proportion of the population engaged in the physical labor of producing and handling material goods, while simultaneously increasing the proportion in professional, business, and clerical occupations.[57] The technical-scientific nature of industry has called for constantly greater numbers of technical employees while the increasingly complex nature of production and distribution has called for growing numbers of managerial employees. The increase in consumer goods has resulted in an increase in employment in distribution and trade; and an increase in leisure, in an increased demand for professional and personal services. Between 1870 and 1940, the proportion of the population employed in the production of physical goods fell from around 75 per cent to 50 per cent, and the trend has continued since. Clerical employees have multiplied, while the growth in the economic functions of government and of public services has further increased the number of white-collar workers.[58] It is estimated that in 1930 alone some 9 million persons who were white-collar workers would have been engaged in manual labor if the occupational distribution of 1870 had persisted.

Glenn suggests that since the 1940s there have been continuing

[57] Elbridge Sibley, "Some Demographic Clues to Stratification," in Reinhard Bendix and Seymour Martin Lipset, eds., *Class, Status and Power* (New York: The Free Press of Glencoe, Inc., 1953), 381.

[58] Lewis Corey, "The Middle Class," in Bendix and Lipset, *op. cit.*, 373.

changes in the occupational structure of the United States that have favored an excess of upward over downward mobility. In general, the proportion of workers in the more highly rewarded occupations increased and the proportion in the less highly rewarded ones declined, although there were many specific occupations that were exceptions to the pattern. During this same period Black occupational differentiation increased, a fact reflected in their achieving relative gains in occupational position. The fact that within the nation as a whole there was more upward than downward occupational mobility probably facilitated these gains. In the absence of this favorable balance of upward over downward mobility, the upward occupational movement of Blacks would have resulted in about an equal amount of downward movement by Whites. Had this been the case, Black efforts at advancement would very likely have resulted in much greater White resistance. Thus a favorable balance of upward over downward mobility within a society is an important factor influencing the degree and nature of the resistance by a dominant group to a minority's advancement in status.[59]

Differential Birth Rates. Differential birth rates have also contributed to the excess of upward over downward mobility. The traditional pattern of an inverse relationship between fertility and social class (the higher the social class, the lower the fertility; the lower the social class, the higher the fertility) served to create a social vacuum within the upper strata. Recruits from the more prolific families of the level below the common man continuously flowed into the vacuum. The influence of this factor, however, has diminished since World War II with the increase in the fertility of the higher classes and a decrease in that of the lower classes.

Immigration and Mobility. The pattern of immigration similarly contributed to an excess of upward over downward mobility. Between 1900 and 1915, some 13 million to 14 million immigrants came to this nation. A disproportionate number of these were impecunious and unskilled when they arrived. Had these immigrants been distributed pro rata among the several social classes of the population, their arrival would have had no direct effect upon the rate or direction of vertical mobility. But this was not the case. Of the 642,724 immigrant workers admitted during the year ending June

[59] Norval D. Glenn, "Changes in the American Occupational Structure and Occupational Gains of Negroes During the 1940's," *Social Forces*, 41 (1962), 188–195.

30, 1914, 603,378 stated that they were engaged in manual occupations. Thus the immigrants included about 105,000 more blue-collar workers than would be found among an equal number of workers taken at random within the United States. If the same broad occupational distribution in the population were to be maintained, roughly an equal number of persons would have to have shifted from blue-collar to white-collar jobs during the same period.[60]

In some American cities the Irish were "helped" or "pushed" up the hierarchial ladder by the Italians who came after them and who displaced them in the lowest jobs. In turn, the Italians were "pushed" up the ladder by later arrivals from southeastern Europe and by Black migrants from the South. Within New York City the process appears to be currently repeating itself with the Puerto Rican displacement of Blacks in some of the positions at the bottom of the job hierarchy.

CONTROVERSIAL ISSUES

The Nature of Lower-Income Black Life

In 1965, the Office of Policy Planning and Research (Department of Labor) circulated in government circles a 78-page document, *The Negro Family*.[61] The "Moynihan Report," as it came to be known after its author, Daniel P. Moynihan, was confidential (labelled "for official use only"), but its contents soon leaked to the press and the document was subsequently "declassified." The report aroused a storm of controversy, angering many civil rights workers, Blacks, professionals, and social workers.[62] In it, Moynihan argued:

The evidence . . . is that the Negro family in the urban ghettos is crumbling. A middle-class group has managed to save itself, but for vast numbers of the unskilled, poorly educated city working class the fabric of conventional social relationships has all but disintegrated. . . .

At the heart of the deterioration of the fabric of Negro society is the deterioration of the Negro family.

It is the fundamental source of the weakness of the Negro community at the present time.[63]

[60] Sibley, *op. cit.*, 382–383.

[61] *The Negro Family: The Case for National Action* (Washington, D.C.: United States Department of Labor, 1965).

[62] For an excellent account of the "Moynihan Controversy" and a number of papers and articles evoked by the report see: Lee Rainwater and William L. Yancey, *The Moynihan Report and the Politics of Controversy* (Cambridge, Mass.: The M.I.T. Press, 1967).

[63] *Ibid., passim.*

The report was widely interpreted as saying that Black family instability (rather than White society) was a basic cause of Black inequality and of "the tangle of pathology" that is reflected in Black illegitimacy, welfare dependency, poor school performance, unemployment, and delinquency—and hence the document was labeled by some as "racist." This interpretation ran counter to the purported theme of the document, namely a call for a bold change in federal policy in which the government would identify itself with the Black Revolution and shift its programs from an emphasis on liberty to one on equality (a distribution of the "good things" of American life among Blacks in a proportion roughly comparable to that among Whites).

Moynihan portrayed a vicious cycle as operating in which Black men lack a stable place in the economic system; as a consequence, they cannot be strong husbands and fathers. Therefore Black families break up, and women must assume the task of rearing children without male assistance; often the women also have to assume the task of bringing in income—in brief, a matriarchal arrangement emerges. Since children do not grow up in a stable home environment and hence learn that they cannot look forward to a stable life, they are not able to achieve in school, leave school early, and therefore are in a very poor position to qualify for jobs that will produce a decent income; and so the cycle starts again.[64] Some read the report, then, as locating the source of the Black family's plight within itself—a variation of the *culture of poverty* thesis—rather than in external economic and social discrimination. In other words, poverty is essentially seen as breeding a distinct social ethos—a unique system of values and norms—which in turn is transmitted to successive generations.[65] Moynihan's thesis was hardly a new one; E. Franklin Frazier, a Black sociologist, among others, had advanced a somewhat similar view as early as 1932.[66]

Any number of social scientists, however, have challenged the

[64] *Ibid.*, 6.

[65] For a clear, forceful presentation of this type of argument see: Oscar Lewis, *La Vida: A Puerto Rican Family in the Culture of San Juan and New York* (New York: Random House, Inc., 1965), xlii–lii.

[66] E. Franklin Frazier, *The Negro Family in Chicago* (Chicago: The University of Chicago Press, 1932); *The Negro Family in the United States* (Chicago: The University of Chicago Press, 1939); and *The Negro in the United States* (New York: The Macmillan Co., 1949), Chapter 13. Also see: Hortense Powdermaker, *After Freedom* (New York: The Viking Press, 1939), and Charles S. Johnson, *Shadow of the Plantation* (Chicago: The University of Chicago Press, 1934).

"culture of poverty" thesis. Illustrative is the position of Elliot Liebow, a social anthropologist, who employed the participant–observer technique in studying a Black street-corner men's group in Washington, D.C.[67] Liebow portrayed the Black man, not as a carrier of an independent cultural tradition, but as very much immersed in and accepting of the broad culture of American life. He differs from other American men not in goals, Liebow argues—he too wants a stable marriage and job—but in his ability to realize these goals. Although he wants marriage, he fears his own ability to carry out the responsibilities of husband and father. His own father failed—had to "cut out"—and he has no evidence he will fare any better. Although he has attended school, he is illiterate (or almost so) and he is essentially unskilled: "Armed with models who have failed, convinced of his own worthlessness, illiterate and unskilled, he enters marriage and the job market with the smell of failure all around him." [68]

Liebow concludes that the similarities between Black father and son does "*not* result from 'cultural transmission' but from the fact that the son goes out and *independently* experiences the same failures, in the same areas, and for much the same reasons as his father." [69] The process only *appears* to be a self-sustaining cultural process. Valentine takes a similar position.[70] He too denies that lower-class people are socialized in a separate cultural design,[71] and maintains that many of the elements used to depict the poor (resignation, fatalism, low aspiration, hopelessness, and the like) are actually "secondary" attitudes *adaptive* to the circumstances of lower class life.[72] In brief, there is a distinction between people simply being poor on the one hand and on the other of being individuals characterized by a unique cultural tradition.

It may appear to the reader that this controversy is a trivial mat-

---

[67] Elliot Liebow, *Tally's Corner* (Boston: Little, Brown and Company, 1967).

[68] *Ibid.*, 211.

[69] *Ibid.*, 223. Italics added.

[70] Charles A. Valentine, *Culture and Poverty: Critique and Counter-Proposals* (Chicago: The University of Chicago Press, 1968).

[71] *Ibid.*, 129.

[72] A not dissimilar approach appears in a wide variety of papers. See, for instance: Seymour Parker and Robert J. Kleiner, "Social and Psychological Dimensions of the Family Role Performance of the Negro Male," *Journal of Marriage and the Family*, 31 (1969), 500–506; Lee Rainwater, "Crucible of Identity: The Negro Lower-Class Family," *Daedalus*, 95 (Winter, 1966), 172–216; and Lola M. Irelan, Oliver C. Moles, and Robert M. O'Shea, "Ethnicity, Poverty, and Selected Attitudes: A Test of the 'Culture of Poverty' Hypothesis," *Social Forces*, 47 (1969), 405–413.

ter, just another illustration of academic backbiting. Yet it has major policy consequences. If the alleged culture patterns of the lower classes are more important in their lives than the condition of being poor, then it is more important for the power holders of society to do away with these lifeways than to do away with poverty. Federal funds, then, should be diverted from the creation of more jobs, better housing, and good schools to programs having an individualistic, social work-psychiatric emphasis. Further, if Black lower-class society is "sick" and "disorganized," permitting Blacks to have significant decision-making powers in the allocating and administrating of poverty funds would be foolhardy—indeed, Vice President Spiro Agnew has said that control by the poor of poverty programs is analogous to permitting a sick patient to tell the doctor how to proceed with treatment.[73] The net effect of such a focus, then, is to divert effort from full implementation of civil rights legislation and "Great Society" progams; it turns attention away from the dominant social system to the poor Blacks themselves and their allegedly "defective culture" as the source of Black ills.[74]

Is a reconciliation between these divergent positions possible? The question of how best to view ghetto life—as the product of a cultural determinism internal to the ghetto (a "culture of poverty") or an economic determinism in the relationship between the ghetto and the wider society—may perhaps best be answered by saying ghettos are characterized by *both*, but in different ways. Black ghetto life is complicated. As Ulf Hannerz observes: "The socio-economic conditions impose limits on the kinds of life ghetto dwellers may have, but these kinds of life are culturally transmitted and shared as many individuals in the present, and many in the past, live or have lived under the same premises."[75] In brief, ghetto members share certain experiences in common deriving from the fact of their common poverty. But they do not exist in social vacuums or cultural limbos. The adjustments they make occur in interaction with one another—"it is hardly possible to invent new adaptations again and again, as men are always observing each other and interacting with each other."[76] Further, both camps are in

---

[73] Seymour Parker and Robert J. Kleiner, "The Culture of Poverty: An Adjustive Dimension," *American Anthropologist*, 72 (1970), 516.

[74] Valentine, *op. cit., passim.*

[75] Ulf Hannerz, "Roots of Black Manhood," *Trans-action* (October 1969), p. 21.

[76] *Ibid.* Parker and Kleiner also come to the conclusion that both extreme positions are not supported. See: Parker and Kleiner, "The Culture of Poverty," 516–

seeming agreement on at least one policy matter—employment opportunities for Black men are essential and such opportunities need to be broadened and strengthened.[77]

Black Problems in America: Product of Race or Class?

Any number of social scientists have advanced the argument that at bottom Black problems within America stem not from race but from their class position. James M. O'Kane takes this view:

> The Negro has been victimized not primarily by his color, not by his former slave status, but by his lower-class position. In this he remains no different from his Puerto Rican, Mexican-American, or Appalachian white counterpart. . . .
> Racial considerations add little to the analysis of these issues [the problems and tragedies of Blacks within America]; all too often they act as smoke screens which mask the real problems. . . . The gap exists between the classes, not the races; it is between the white and black middle class on one hand, and the white and black lower class on the other. Skin color and the history of servitude do little to explain the present polarization of the classes. . . . Class differentials, not racial differentials, explain the presence and persistence of poverty in the ranks of the urban Negro.[78]

John and Lois Scott take a somewhat similar position:

> Most racial antipathy in America is not "pure" racism but derives from the disdain of higher classes for those below them. The tragedy of race in this country (and many others) is that visible genetic differences, superficial in themselves, have become generally reliable clues to a person's class position—his education, his income, his manners. The present low position of black Americans is a legacy of centuries of living under a most extreme and brutal form of slavery and of strenuous efforts since legal emancipation to contain them socially as a subordinated caste. Events of the last 20 years have done much to modify the legal and political aspects of this subordination, but the more general social effects of the past remain: black Americans are disadvantaged and poor, and their culture—so much a "culture of poverty"—is offensive to more affluent classes.[79]

---

527. Likewise of interest is: Robert Blauner, "Black Culture: Myth or Reality?" in Norman E. Whitten, Jr. and John F. Szwed, eds., *Afro-American Anthropology* (New York: The Free Press of Glencoe, 1970), 347–366.

[77] In this regard see: Joan Adlous, "Wives' Employment Status and Lower-Class Men as Husband–Fathers: Support for the Moynihan Thesis," *Journal of Marriage and the Family*, 31 (1969), 469–476.

[78] James M. O'Kane, "Ethnic Mobility and the Lower-Income Negro: A Socio-Historical Perspective," *Social Problems*, 16 (1969), 309–311.

[79] John Finley Scott and Lois Heyman Scott, "They Are Not So Much Anti-Negro as Pro-Middle Class," *The New York Times Magazine*, March 24, 1968, 47 and 107. Also see: Leonard Reissman and Michael N. Halstead, "The Subject Is Class," *Sociology and Social Research*, 54 (1970), 301–304.

The above position by O'Kane and the Scotts runs counter to the argument that Black circumstances in America cannot be likened to those of European immigrant groups. Blauner insists, for instance, that Blacks find themselves in a condition of "domestic" or "internal colonialism." He singles out three features as differentiating Black circumstances from those of European ethnic groups:

First, the ethnic ghettos arose more from voluntary choice, both in the sense of the choice to immigrate to America and the decision to live among one's fellow ethnics. Second, the immigrant ghettos tended to be a one and two generation phenomenon; they were actually way-stations in the process of acculturation and assimilation. . . . But most relevant is the third point. European ethnic groups like the Poles, Italians, and Jews generally only experienced a brief period, often less than a generation, during which their residential buildings, commercial stores, and other enterprises were owned by outsiders. The Chinese and Japanese faced handicaps of color prejudice that were almost as strong as the Blacks faced, but very soon gained control of their internal communities, because their ethnic culture and social organization had not been destroyed by slavery and internal colonization.[80]

Hence Black problems are unique; they are larger and more incomprehensible than those witnessed by other groups in our history, and thus the old answers are irrelevant to an improvement in the Black situation.

Yet it is this very view that O'Kane challenges, namely the notion that Black circumstances are unique. He argues that the Irish, the Italians, and the Poles faced not dissimilar problems: they migrated from agrarian poverty to industrial slums and encountered economic and social ostracism in the new environment. Subject to prejudice and discrimination, they had to seek routes of upward mobility not entirely in keeping with the hallowed Horatio Alger path. Each of the groups employed three core modes of movement from the lower classes to the dominant society: (1) stable unskilled employment; (2) crime, gangsterism, and racketeeering; and (3) ethnic politics —the latter two frequently intertwined in corrupt machine-boss-politics. O'Kane finds that Blacks too are pursuing these same routes.[81] Yet he admits that unlike their predecessors, lower-income Blacks face one enduring fact—the progressive disappearance of unskilled occupations. Hence, "it only remains for American society to provide [Blacks with] the employment necessary to make the

[80] Robert Blauner, "Internal Colonialism and Ghetto Revolt," *Social Problems,* 16 (1969), 397.

[81] O'Kane, *op. cit.,* 303–311.

journey productive and rewarding." [82] Yet O'Kane's critics note that this in part is the crux of the problem, and one facet that indeed makes the Black situation unique.[83]

SUMMARY

We have seen that, within the United States, people are differentiated vertically along racial, ethnic, and religious lines and horizontally along class lines. The racial, ethnic, and religious structure crisscrosses with the class structure. Thus members from these groups tend to span a range of higher and lower positions within the class structure. However, minority-group members are generally disproportionately represented in the lower strata while members of the dominant group are generally disproportionately represented in the upper strata. Although regional and community differences exist in the particular stratification patterns that have come to prevail, common elements are to be noted throughout the United States.

Racial, ethnic, and religious membership also plays a part in influencing an individual's movement up or down within the stratification hierarchy. Groups differ in their cultural heritage and patterns—in those aspects of life that foster or impede adjustment to an urban–industrial environment. And the attitudes and behavior of dominant group members differ toward various minorities, and hence the nature and extent of the obstacles facing various minorities differ.

Controversy surrounds the matter of the nature of lower-income Black life—whether Blacks are simply individuals who are poor or poor individuals who are carriers of a unique cultural tradition (a "culture of poverty"). This issue has major policy consequences, that is, whether power-holders within American life should focus on the lifeways of the poor or on their poverty. Similarly, social scientists have been in disagreement on the issue of whether Blacks have been victimized primarily because of their color or because of their lower socioeconomic status.

[82] *Ibid.*, 311.

[83] For a further discussion of these matters see: Stuart L. Hills, "Negroes and Immigrants in America," *Sociological Focus*, 3 (Summer, 1970), 85–96; Raymond S. Franklin, "The Political Economy of Black Power," *Social Problems*, 16 (1969), 286–301; William K. Tabb, "Race Relations Models and Social Change," *Social Problems*, 18 (1971), 431–444; and Nathan Glazer, "Blacks and Ethnic Groups," *Social Problems*, 18 (1971), 444–461.

9

Assimilation

The concept "assimilation" has been used by sociologists for at least sixty years, particularly with reference to immigrant groups in the United States. Nonetheless, it is one of the most elusive concepts employed in the study of race and ethnic relations. For the most part the concept has been applied to changes of a *cultural* and *social* sort, generally with implied direction toward greater *homogeneity*.[1] We may view assimilation as *a process whereby groups with diverse ways of thinking, feeling, and acting become fused together in a social unity and a common culture*. Assimilation, then, is an inclusive concept that many entail both *acculturation* and *integration*.[2]

THE NATURE OF ASSIMILATION

For the purposes of analysis we find it useful to distinguish between the customs of a people—*culture*—and their *social* relationships. Culture generally supplies us with a set of relatively common understandings by which we map our behavior—by which we interpret our experience and guide our actions. Yet human behavior is not simply a mirror image of culture; we are not merely passive,

[1] Stanley Lieberson, *Ethnic Patterns in American Cities* (New York: The Free Press of Glencoe, Inc., 1963), 7–8.

[2] For a critical examination of a variety of concepts commonly employed in treating assimilation see: T. B. Rees, "Accommodation, Integration, Cultural Pluralism, and Assimilation: Their Place in Equilibrium Theories of Society," *Race*, 11 (1970), 481–490. Also see: John Rex and Robert Moore, *Race, Community, and Conflict* (London: Oxford University Press, 1967), 13–14.

mechanical absorbers of prevailing cultural demands and expectations. Hence, we also need to focus upon what people actually do (in contrast with what their culture says they ideally should do)— in brief, we need to examine the flow of interaction that occurs between people and groups of people (the social dimension). This distinction between a people's culture and their social relationships is reflected in the concepts of acculturation and integration.[3] Whereas the focus of acculturation is upon the customs of a people, the focus of integration is upon the people who are practicing the customs. We shall first consider acculturation and then turn our attention to integration.

Acculturation

Culture is hardly static; it undergoes change. Some changes in custom (in those standardized ways of feeling, thinking, and acting that people acquire as members of society) result from intergroup contact. We refer to changes in culture set in motion by the coming together of peoples with differing traditions as *acculturation*.[4] Acculturation may take any number of forms[5]:

1. Intercultural Transmission. Intercultural transmission involves the diffusion of elements or parts of culture from one group to another. It is a matter of historical fact that each culture contains a minimum of traits and patterns unique to it or actually invented by it. It is easy, for example, to minimize America's debt to other cultures. As an illustration, consider the following account of the

---

[3] In this text we distinguish between acculturation and integration. Sociologists have also used other terminology to refer to these phenomena. Eisenstadt and Fitzpatrick distinguish between *cultural assimilation* and *social assimilation;* Gordon treats *behavioral* (cultural) *assimilation* and *structural* (social) *assimilation;* and van den Berghe deals with *cultural pluralism* and *social pluralism*. S. N. Eisenstadt, *The Absorption of Immigrants* (New York: The Free Press of Glencoe, 1955); Joseph P. Fitzpatrick, "The Importance of 'Community' in the Process of Immigrant Assimilation," *International Migration Review*, 1 (1966), 5–6; Milton M. Gordon, *Assimilation in American Life* (New York: Oxford University Press, 1964), Chapter 3; and Pierre L. van den Berghe, *Race and Racism* (New York: John Wiley & Sons, Inc., 1967), Chapter 7.

[4] This orientation to acculturation is less inclusive than that found in some of the literature. See: Edward H. Spicer, "Acculturation," in David Sills, ed., *International Encyclopedia of the Social Sciences* (New York: The Macmillan Co., 1968), Vol. 1, pp. 21–27.

[5] See The Social Science Research Council Summer Seminar on Acculturation, "Acculturation: An Exploratory Formulation," *American Anthropologist*, 56 (1954).

cultural content of a "one hundred per cent" American written as satire by a distinguished anthropologist:

If our patriot is old-fashioned enough to adhere to the so-called American breakfast, his coffee will be accompanied by an orange, domesticated in the Mediterranean region, a cantaloupe domesticated in Persia, or grapes, domesticated in Asia Minor. He will follow this with a bowl of cereal made from grain domesticated in the Near East and prepared by methods also invented there. From this he will go on to waffles, a Scandinavian invention, with plenty of butter, originally a Near-Eastern cosmetic. As a side dish he may have the egg of a bird domesticated in Southeastern Asia or strips of the flesh of an animal domesticated in the same region, which have been salted and smoked by a process invented in Northern Europe.[6]

2. Cultural Creativity. Contact situations entail not only the borrowing or mixing of cultural traits. Many early anthropologists made the error of viewing culture as so loosely knit together that the main theoretical task of cultural analysis consisted in disentangling the various elements from their matrix and showing whence they came. Culture was seen as just so many patches and shreds. Increasingly, we have come to realize that the parts comprising culture are often closely interwoven in such a fashion that a change in one part has consequences for other parts and for the whole. Hence in considering acculturation it is essential that we view it not merely as a culture-receiving process but as a *culture-producing* process as well.

Illustrative are two cases from South America. The Caribs of Latin America borrowed chickens from Europeans, but they did not use them for meat, feathers, eggs, or cockfighting as in European cultures. Instead the chickens were employed as objects of conspicuous display; men took pride in them, boasting about them to others, and people sat about admiring and comparing the fowl of the various men. To cite another example, automobile tires are in considerable demand among some Indian peoples of Latin America. The Indians do not own or drive cars but rather cut up the tire casings to make sandals.[7]

Cultural creativity may also contribute to the emergence of a qualitatively new culture. This process can be seen in the fusion of the Indian and Spanish cultures to produce the Mestizo culture

[6] Ralph Linton, "One Hundred Per Cent American," *American Mercury*, 40 (1937), 427–429.
[7] John Gillin, *The Ways of Men* (New York: Appleton-Century-Crofts, Inc., 1948), 556.

of Latin America and in the fusion of the Norman and Saxon cultures to produce the English culture.

3. Cultural Disintegration. As a result of culture contact, rapid cultural change may be initiated that cannot be managed by the cultural system. The system may find itself overtaxed and disintegrate. This condition may be induced by the dominant culture forcing changes upon a people unprepared for them, an especially devastating development when accompanied by drastic shifts in demographic and ecological conditions—for instance, by virtue of massacres, the introduction of deadly new diseases, the depletion of wild life (as in the case of the buffalo), and the like. Similarly it may be the product of a people taking over great quantities of alien cultural material which their cultural system is unable to ingest and integrate into the whole. Vast disorganization has been particularly evident in situations where small, non-literate societies have come into extensive contact with Western peoples, a condition reflected among many American Indian groups.[8]

Integration

Integration entails alterations in the *relationships* between people, in the flow of interaction that characterizes people's daily lives. As we noted earlier in the chapter, the focus of acculturation is upon the customs of a people; the focus of integration is upon the people who are practicing the customs. Typically a racial or ethnic group develops a network of organizations and informal social relationships that permit and encourage its members to remain within its confines for the meeting of a wide variety of needs. Social cliques, in-group dating and marriage, common residential patterns—even common occupations, schools, and religious affiliations—may characterize its members.[9]

Integration involves the fusion of groups in the sense that social interaction is no longer predicated upon one's racial or ethnic identity. The descendants of the former minority group and the former dominant group no longer make "dominant-minority" group distinctions. Individuals thus find their place within the community without reference to ethnic or racial origins. Hence, integration em-

---

[8] Felix Keesing, *Culture Change: An Analysis and Bibliography of Anthropological Sources* (Stanford, Calif.: Stanford University Press, 1953).

[9] Gordon, *op. cit.*, 31–51.

braces the elimination of prejudice and discrimination. In this regard, Killian and Grigg observe:

> At the present time, integration as a solution to the race problem demands that the Negro foreswear his identity as a Negro. But for a lasting solution, the meaning of "American" must lose its implicit racial modifier, "white." Even without biological amalgamation, integration requires a sincere acceptance by all Americans that it is just as good to be a black American as to be a white American.[10]

Acculturation Without Integration

Institutional duplication (as opposed to society-wide functional differentiation and specialization) is characteristic of a society containing differing cultures—in brief, the society is compartmentalized into quasi-independent units, each of which has a set of homologous institutions and limited points of contact with the other units (for instance, limited to common participation in a money economy and subjection to a common political body). Put still another way, where there is cultural pluralism, there is also social pluralism. Hence, not only do the people of the society experience different cultural worlds but they move in different social worlds as well. In such a society, we cannot take a social phenomenon and trace its ramifications throughout the entire society.[11] If this is the case, then we can see that *acculturation is a necessary precondition to integration.*[12] In other words, people must come to share a relatively common cultural map or blueprint for life (common guideposts that serve to channel their life activities). Only under such circumstances does the possibility exist of their coming to interact within the *same* institutional order so that the flow of their social actions (their social relationships) will be unimpeded by sharp boundaries and distinctions.

The reverse proposition, however, does not hold. Acculturation can occur in the absence of integration. Blacks within the United States present a good illustration. Although sharing with Whites in the larger American culture, Blacks still experience much White prejudice and discrimination—barriers to the free flow of social interaction. American Judaism presents still another illustration of

[10] Lewis Killian and Charles Grigg, *Racial Crisis in America* (Englewood Cliffs, N.J.: Prentice-Hall, Inc., 1964), 108.

[11] Pierre L. van den Berghe, "Toward a Sociology of Africa," *Social Forces*, 43 (1964), 11–18.

[12] Charles Wagley and Marvin Harris, *Minorities in the New World* (New York: Columbia University Press, 1958), 288.

this. For many American Jews, traditional Judaism has been "de-judaized." In the realm of religion, there are congregations of the Orthodox, Conservative, and Reform varieties, named in order of their degree of adherence to the traditional rituals and practices. Synagogues and temples, particularly those of the Conservative and Reform persuasions, have made major acculturating adjustments to the standards of American life—for example, Conservative Judaism has introduced English into portions of the service and into the synagogue's business affairs, has altered the function of the rabbi, has abolished the segregation of the sexes in worship, has emphasized "decorum," and has cultivated the "multifunctional" synagogue with its age- and sex-graded recreational and educational programs.[13] Yet with the shift away from Orthodox Jewish cultural practices (acculturation), there has simultaneously occurred a strong desire for the preservation of a Jewish ethnic identity (opposition to total integration). Herbert Gans refers to this development as the emergence of "symbolic Judaism"—a kind of minimal adherence to specifically Jewish cultural patterns, in which emphasis is placed on a selection of nostalgic items of "Yiddish" background (for example, Yiddish culinary delicacies or Yiddish phrases), the possession in the home of tangible objects denoting Jewishness (for example, books or pictures with Jewish themes), a concern with "Jewish" problems, and a selection of festive religious traditions that help socialize the children into an awareness of and affection for a Jewish identity.[14] Hence we find acculturation taking place in the absence of complete integration.

Some Related Concepts

Assimilation is a social and cultural process that is to be distinguished from the biological process of *amalgamation*. Amalgamation involves the biological fusion of differing "racial" and "subracial" groups. Assimilation does not necessarily imply the absence of physical visibility between groups; populations differing in the

[13] Marshall Sklare, *Conservative Judaism* (New York: The Free Press of Glencoe, Inc., 1955).

[14] Herbert J. Gans, "American Jewry: Present and Future," *Commentary*, 21 (1956), 422–430, and "The Future of American Jewry," *Commentary*, 21 (1956), 555–563. Also see: Erich Rosenthal, "Acculturation without Assimilation? The Jewish Community of Chicago, Illinois," *American Journal of Sociology*, 66 (1960), 275–288. For a paper dealing with a somewhat similar phenomenon among Indians see: John H. Bushnell, "From American Indian to Indian American: The Changing Identity of the Hupa," *American Anthropologist*, 70 (1968), 1108–1116.

incidence of genetically transmitted racial characteristics may persist. Assimilation does imply, however, in terms of the end result, an absence of cultural and social distinctions based upon racial membership. Individuals, when assimilated, would no longer exhibit the cultural or social marks that identify them as members of an alien or out-group, nor would any racial characteristics that they possess function as the foundation for group prejudice or discrimination. Although for analytical purposes assimilation and amalgamation are two separate concepts, it should be noted that they usually go hand-in-hand. Assimilation promotes intermarriage and intermarriage promotes assimilation.

Assimilation also needs to be distinguished from naturalization and absorption. *Naturalization* refers to the acquisition of legal citizenship. *Absorption* is generally used to refer to the immigrant's ability to secure and sustain economic employment within the new country. The immigrant may adopt the occupational pattern of the new country or add to this pattern through the introduction of new economic activities and occupations. On the whole, absorption proceeds more rapidly than acculturation or integration, because fewer changes in roles and institutions are required in the former than in the latter case.[15]

DIFFERING CONCEPTIONS OF ASSIMILATION

The "Melting Pot" Orientation

Americans are by no means unanimous in their conception of how assimilation may "best" or "most desirably" proceed. Prior to World War I, the "melting pot" notion achieved considerable popularity, and it still enjoys currency in some quarters. According to this view, the multitude of Whites from various European nations (Blacks and Orientals were not included) would fuse together within America, producing a new people and a new civilization—a people and a civilization that would achieve unparalleled glory in the annals of human history. Zangwill, a proponent of this thinking, declared with considerable enthusiasm:

America is God's Crucible, the great Melting Pot where all the races of Europe are melting and reforming!—Here you stand good folk, think I, when

[15] W. D. Borrie, *The Cultural Integration·of Immigrants* (Paris: UNESCO, 1959), 101.

I see you at Ellis Island, here you stand, in your fifty groups, with your fifty languages and histories, and your fifty hatreds and rivalries. But you won't be long like that brothers, for these are the fires of God you come to—these are the fires of God. . . . Germans and Frenchmen, Irishmen and English, Jews and Russians, into the Crucible with you all! God is making the American! . . . The real American has not yet arrived. . . . He will be the fusion of all races, perhaps the coming superman. . . . Ah, Vera, what is the glory of Rome and Jerusalem, where all races and nations come to worship and look back, compared with the glory of America . . .[16]

Following World War I, the "melting pot" theory lost favor.[17] There developed a growing awareness of the persistence of the cultural traits that the immigrants brought with them. For many native Americans, the great "crucible" of assimilation, the "melting pot," was not working fast enough. Initially, northern Europeans had heavily predominated among the immigrants to the United States, peoples whose cultures were quite similar to that of the earlier settlers. But, by the turn of the twentieth century, the tide had shifted—migrants from southern and eastern Europe predominated. In 1882, some 87 per cent of the migrants had come from northern and western Europe, whereas only 13 per cent had come from southern and eastern Europe. In 1907 the situation had been reversed, the corresponding figures being 13 per cent and 81 per cent, respectively. Native Americans were inclined to view the new arrivals as "different," in some respects even as "unassimilable." This was coupled with a post-war intensification of the fear of aliens and an abject terror after the Bolshevik Revolution of the alien as a "radical" and "Red." A host of passions, prides, and prejudices surged to the foreground, and in 1921 Congress responded by passing the emergency quota law of 1921 and later the Immigration Act of 1924.

The "Americanization" Orientation

Within the context of the post-World War I situation, the "Americanization" movement gained momentum. Whereas the "melting pot" theory had viewed the United States as evolving a new cultural way of life through a fusion of European cultures, the "Americanization" viewpoint saw American culture as an essentially finished product on the Anglo-Saxon pattern. It insisted that the immigrants promptly give up their cultural traits and take over those of the

[16] Israel Zangwill, *The Melting Pot: Drama in Four Acts* (New York: The Macmillan Co., 1921), 33 ff.

[17] For a more extensive consideration of melting pot theories see Gordon, *op. cit.*, Chapter 5.

dominant American group. Differences were not to be long tolerated. Public schools, patriotic societies, business organizations,
among others, turned their attention to "Americanizing" the immigrants. All evidences of foreign heritage were to be quickly
stamped out—aliens were to cease being "aliens" and to become
"Americans." Other cultures were seen as "foreign"—as "peculiar,"
"inferior," and "a source of trouble." [18]

The "Americanization" notion found its reflection in academic
circles and was popularized by Henry Pratt Fairchild. Fairchild
viewed assimilation as closely analogous to the physiological process
whereby an organism secures nourishment. Foodstuffs are con-
sumed by the organism; ultimately the ingested food becomes an
integral part of the physical organism and in this sense is assimilated.[19] Fairchild saw the process as a one-way street in which no
reciprocal exchange is present; between human cultures, as between
the body and food, no blending of consequence occurs: ". . . it appears that in social assimilation, as in physiological, . . . the receiving body sets the pattern. . . . And the process of assimilation does
require that all foreigners . . . must be adapted to fit into an integrated whole without friction or disturbance." [20]

The Theory of "Cultural Pluralism"

Adherents of both the "melting pot" and "Americanization" concepts looked toward an essentially monocultural system. The former
thought this could be achieved through "melting down" the immigrants and natives into a common whole; the latter, through
divesting the immigrants of their "foreign ways" and remaking them
into Anglicized Americans. Opposed to these notions, there has
arisen another school of thought, that of "cultural pluralism," which
has won considerable favor since World War II among sociologists,
demographers, and social scientists generally. It aims at achieving
uniformity within a society through immigrant conformity in those
areas where this is felt to be necessary to the national well-being; yet
simultaneously it permits immigrants to maintain their own cultural
traits in other areas that are not felt to be as essential. It implies

[18] For a more extensive consideration of the "Americanization" orientation see
Ibid., Chapter 4.

[19] Henry Pratt Fairchild, *Immigration* (New York: The Macmillan Co., 1925),
396 ff.

[20] Henry Pratt Fairchild, *Race and Nationality* (New York: The Ronald Press
Co., 1947), 109–112.

conformity within a framework of cultural pluralism—an imperfect fusion of a number of diverse cultural ingredients within the framework of a larger society.[21] Through time many of the foreign-born, as well as succeeding generations, would come to share increasingly in the common core of American life, while simultaneously retaining certain cultural characteristics of their own groups.[22] The retention of various religious preferences constitutes the classic example of this type of phenomenon. In brief, then, pluralism involves a continuation of the minority as a distinct unit within the larger society.

The proponents of this viewpoint suggest that cultural traits are quite persistent. This persistence, they argue, is a reality that cannot be escaped; in fact, to attack group values—to undertake their suppression—is likely to strengthen them. In addition, a number of advantages may flow from a cultural pluralistic approach. First, immigrants' retention of many of the traits of their original culture may constitute a stabilizing link between their old way of life and the new. Second, it serves to avoid some of the dangers of social and personal disorganization that may follow from attempting to force the immigrants into a world that they do not understand and that oversimplifies the complexities of American social and cultural structures.[23] Cultural pluralism, then, enables the immigrant to incorporate elements of the American culture at a pace that muffles and makes bearable the shock of cultural collision. Third, ethnic groups that cut across other social groups—the most important of which are social classes—are an important factor in the maintenance of social solidarity and in the avoidance of class consciousness and class conflict. The pluralistic nature of American society functions to provide various sources for the consolidation of competing centers of power, a condition vital to the maintenance of the democratic process.[24] Where there is a maximum concentration of power in one institution, for example, the monolithic totalitarian state, there is a minimum degree of freedom. Where there are competing groups, institutions, and voluntary associations—competing centers of power—democracy can flourish. Thus America's diversity in ethnic groups may contribute to the maintenance of the American democratic order.

[21] Borrie, op. cit., 93.
[22] Ibid., 114. For a more extensive discussion of cultural pluralism see Gordon, op. cit., Chapter 6.
[23] Ibid., 92.
[24] Amitai Etzioni, "The Ghetto: A Re-evaluation," Social Forces, 37 (1959), 260.

The cultural pluralistic school of thought puts less emphasis upon the objective of assimilation in the sense of conformity in all social and cultural areas. It would accept cultural differences between immigrants and native Americans in certain areas and would insist upon the right of groups and individuals to be different so long as the differences do not lead to national disunity. The adjustment between the groups is viewed not as a one-way street but as a reciprocal process in which the immigrant stock and the native Americans would each integrate with the other. This orientation is to be distinguished from that of the "melting pot," in its inclusion of non-European cultures in the process and in its willingness to tolerate —in fact, to welcome—differences over an extended period of time.

A NATURAL HISTORY OF RACE RELATIONS?

The Cycle of Robert E. Park

The late Robert E. Park, one of America's outstanding students of race relations, suggested that, whenever and wherever different racial and ethnic groups continuously meet, they inevitably pass through a series of irreversible stages: The groups come into *contact;* invariably contact produces *competition;* from this competition some kind of adjustment or *accommodation* is realized; and, finally, there is *assimilation*.[25] Within the United States, Park saw the process unfolding in somewhat this fashion:

The newcomers typically came to America poor, the product of European peasant stock. They were largely uneducated, often ignorant of the English language, disillusioned by harsh treatment received at the hands of immigration officials, and bewildered by the strangeness, complexity, and tempo of city life. Accordingly, they found themselves largely isolated from the mainstream of American life. Condescendingly viewed as "greenhorns," they were exploited as cheap labor by natives, taken advantage of by loan sharks, and swindled by some of their own countrymen who already "knew the ropes." Within the labor market they were the victims of the business cycle—welcomed in the upturn, discharged and abused in the downturn. Ghettos arose—Little Italys, Chinatowns, Little Bo-

---

[25] Robert E. Park, *Race and Culture* (New York: The Free Press of Glencoe, Inc., (1949), 150 ff.

hemias, and Black-Belts—the product of a number of forces: First, the immigrants were poor and hence were forced by rentals into the least desirable areas of the city—the slums. Second, they tended to huddle together in spatially compact areas, as their cultural likeness in language and traditions gave them a sense of comfort, belonging, and security. And third, the hostility and antagonism of the native population barred them from other areas while simultaneously reinforcing their disposition to reside with their "own kind."

Within the labor force the newcomers found themselves in competition for jobs with the natives and earlier arrivals. Conspicuous by virtue of their speech, traditions, customs, and manners, they became a convenient foil for attacks by politicians searching for publicity and fame. Professional patriots, special interests, and anxious nationalists joined in the attacks. Sensational newspapers depicted a few crimes committed by immigrants as a "crime wave." In periods of economic depression their unpopularity was intensified by their disproportionate representation among the unemployed and those on relief. Their continuing influx within America and their tendency to have large families served to accentuate native fears of engulfment.

Although contact first contributed to competition and conflict, it eventually resulted in a division of labor and the establishment of a modus vivendi. Thus, in time, competition and conflict increasingly gave way to accommodation. English more and more replaced the mother tongue; some of the immigrants attended night school to learn English, the new customs, and new skills. Various "German-American," "Italian-American," "Polish-American," and other nationality newspapers grew up, bringing a wider knowledge of American affairs to those who could not read English. City political machines with their neighborhood ward bosses quickly gained an appreciation for the potential of the newcomers' votes. These party machines, often corrupt, contributed to the integration of newcomers within American political and civic life. Party functionaries were quite adept at performing personal favors, providing relief in hard times, "fixing up" matters when immigrants got in trouble with the law, providing "Christmas baskets," and in general displaying personal interest in the immigrants. The children of the foreign-born functioned as carriers of the English language and American customs from the schools to the homes. And with time the birth rate of the ethnic groups began to decline. As they learned new skills, they started to climb up the occupational hierarchy; simultaneously, more recently arrived ethnic groups "pushed" them up the status ladder. Increasingly they gained acceptance and in due course became assimilated.

Critique of Park's Theory

Park's natural-history model has won considerable acceptance, and the theory has been applied in a number of well-known studies including Louis Wirth's *The Ghetto*.[26] The scheme, however, has come under criticism on several points. Etzioni suggests that, like many natural-history theories, Park's theory is not sufficiently specified to be tested.[27] He argues that Park formulated his theory in such a manner that different and even contradictory data can be interpreted to support it. Etzioni in particular criticizes Park's frequent use of the term "eventually":

> When an ethnic group is assimilating, it is suggested that the hypothesis is supported; if an ethnic group is not assimilating, it is suggested that it has not yet reached the stage of assimilation. "Eventually," one can still hold, every ethnic group will be assimilated. As no time interval is mentioned and the sociological conditions under which the process of assimilation will take place are not spelled out, the whole scheme becomes unscientific.[28]

Park has also been criticized for his assumption that there is an inevitable and irreversible unilinear progression toward assimilation among differing groups. It appears that under some circumstances this does not occur. By way of illustration, some children of Jewish parents who have been converted to Christianity or who are of mixed Jewish-Christian marriages return to Judaism.[29] Similarly, the Nazi program in Germany served to reverse the long-run trend toward Jewish assimilation in that nation. Accordingly, Park's assumption seems to lack sound ground. The interaction between different racial and cultural groups takes many forms, and assimilation need not necessarily be the last stage. Indeed, the processes of competition, conflict, accommodation, and assimilation may more appropriately be viewed not as stages in a fixed sequence but as alternative situations. Furthermore, Park does not always make it clear as to

---

26 Louis Wirth, *The Ghetto* (Chicago: University of Chicago Press, 1928).
27 Etzioni, *op. cit.*, 255.
28 *Ibid.*, 255.
29 *Ibid.*, 261.

exactly what forces are responsible for bringing about the transition from one stage to another.[30]

THE RATE OF ASSIMILATION

Warner's Propositions on Assimilation

W. Lloyd Warner and Leo Srole, on the basis of the Yankee City research, suggest three propositions as useful in predicting the relative rank and the rate of assimilation of various ethnic and racial groups within American life:

1. The greater the difference between the host and the immigrant *cultures*, the greater will be the subordination, the greater the strength of the ethnic social systems, and the longer the period necessary for the assimilation of the ethnic group.

2. The greater the *racial* difference between the populations of the immigrant and host societies, the greater the subordination of the immigrant group, the greater the strength of the social sub-system, and the longer the period necessary for assimilation.

3. When the combined *cultural* and *biological* traits are highly divergent from those of the host society, the subordination of the group will be very great, their sub-system strong, the period of assimilation long, and the processes slow and usually painful.[31]

Warner and Srole employ the white "old-American" stock as the prototype of the host society. They then develop a scale by which to assess the position of any group in terms of its racial resemblance to the old American stock. See Table 9–1. Five categories are employed for analytical purposes:

1. Light Caucasoids
2. Dark Caucasoids
3. Mongoloid and Caucasoid mixture with Caucasoid appearance
4. Mongoloid and mixed peoples with a predominantly Mongoloid appearance
5. Negroes and all Negroid mixtures

---

[30] *Ibid.*, 255–256. For a review of the literature dealing with Park's cycle and a presentation which argues that Park's approach is still quite fruitful for the sociological enterprise when viewed as a developmental model see: Stanford M. Lyman, "The Race Relations Cycle of Robert E. Park," *Pacific Sociological Review*, 11 (1968), 16–22.

[31] W. Lloyd Warner and Leo Srole, *The Social Systems of American Ethnic Groups* (New Haven: Yale University Press, 1945), 285–286.

Table 9–1 Ethnic and Racial Assimilation

Cultural and Racial Type	Degree of Subordination	Strength of Ethnic and Racial Subsystems	Time for Assimilation	Form of American Rank
Racial Type I—Light Caucasoid				
Cultural Type 1 English-speaking Protestants Tests: English, Scotch, North Irish, Australians, Canadians	very slight	very weak	very short	ethnic group to class
Cultural Type 2 Protestants not speaking English Tests: Scandinavians Germans, Dutch, French	slight	weak	short	ethnic group to class
Cultural Type 3 English-speaking Catholics and other non-Protestants Test: South Irish	slight	moderate	short to moderate	ethnic group to class
Cultural Type 4 Catholics and other non-Protestants who do not speak English Tests: ("fair-skinned") French Canadians, French, Germans, Belgians	slight	moderate	short to moderate	ethnic group to class
Cultural Type 5 English-speaking non-Christians Test: English Jews	moderate	moderate	short to moderate	ethnic group to class
Cultural Type 6 Non-Christians who do not speak English Tests: ("fair-skinned") European Jews and Mohammedans from Middle East	moderate	moderate	short to moderate	ethnic group to class
Racial Type II—Dark Caucasoids				
Cultural Type 1	—	—	—	—
Cultural Type 2 Test: Protestant Armenians (other "dark-skinned" Protestants)	slight to moderate	weak	moderate	ethnic group to class
Cultural Type 3	—	—	—	—
Cultural Type 4 Tests: "dark skins" of Racial Type I, Cultural Type 4; also Sicilians, Portuguese, Near Eastern Christians	moderate	moderate to strong	moderate	ethnic group to class

TABLE 9–1 (Continued)

Cultural and Racial Type	Degree of Subordi- nation	Strength of Ethnic and Racial Subsystems	Time for Assimi- lation	Form of American Rank
Cultural Type 5	—	—	—	—
Cultural Type 6 Tests: ("dark-skinned") Jews and Mohammedans of Europe and the Near East	moderate to great	strong	slow	ethnic group to class

Racial Type III—Caucasoid Mixtures

Cultural Type 1	—	—	—	—
Cultural Type 2 Tests: Small groups of Spanish Americans in the Southwest	great	strong	slow	ethno- racial to class or color caste
Cultural Type 3	—	—	—	—
Cultural Type 4 Test: Most of the mixed bloods of Latin America	great	strong	slow	ethno- racial to class or color caste
Cultural Type 5	—	—	—	—
Cultural Type 6	—	—	—	—

Racial Type IV—Mongoloids

Cultural Type 1 Tests: Most American Chinese and Japanese	great to very great	very strong	slow	racial to semi-caste
Cultural Type 2	—	—	—	—
Cultural Type 3	—	—	—	—
Cultural Type 4 Test: Filipinos	great to very great	very strong	very slow	racial to semi-caste
Cultural Type 5	—	—	—	—
Cultural Type 6 Tests: East Indians, Chinese, Japa- nese	great to very great	very strong	very slow	racial to semi-caste

Racial Type V—Negroids

Cultural Type 1 Test: Most American Negroes	very great	very strong	very slow	racial to color caste

TABLE 9–1 (Continued)

Cultural and Racial Type	Degree of Subordi- nation	Strength of Ethnic and Racial Subsystems	Time for Assimi- lation	Form of American Rank
Cultural Type 2	—	—	—	—
Cultural Type 3 Test: Some American Negroes	very great	very strong	very slow	racial to color caste
Cultural Type 4 Test: Negroid Puerto Ricans, etc.	very great	very strong	very slow	racial to color caste
Cultural Type 5	—	—	—	—
Cultural Type 6 Tests: Bantu Negroes and West African Negroes	very great	very strong	very slow	racial to color caste

Source: W. Lloyd Warner and Leo Srole, *The Social Systems of American Ethnic Groups* (New Haven: Yale University Press, 1945), Table 7, pp. 290–292. Copyright © 1945 by Yale University Press.

A similar scale is constructed for assessing the position of groups in terms of cultural traits, of which religion and language are taken as being the most important for purposes of differentiation. This gives six parallel cultural types:

1. English-speaking Protestants
2. Non-English-speaking Protestants
3. English-speaking Catholics and non-Protestants
4. Catholics and other non-Protestants speaking an affiliated Indo-European tongue
5. English-speaking non-Christians
6. Non-Christians who do not speak English

Each of the five racial types has its six parallel cultural types. Thus the light Caucasoids can be divided into those who are English-speaking Protestants (English, Scotch, Northern Irish, Canadians, etc.), those who are non-English-speaking Protestants (Scandinavians, Germans, Dutch, etc.), and so on through the remaining six cultural types. As a group all six types of light Caucasoids rank above the dark Caucasoids. The dark Caucasoids, in turn, are divided into English-speaking Protestants (there is no actual group with these characteristics), non-English-speaking Protestants (Protestant Armenians), etc. The same process can be repeated down through and including racial type 5 (Negroes and all Negroid mixtures).

On the whole, Warner and Srole feel that their propositions (relating to the degree of ethnic and racial subordination, the strength of the ethnic sub-system, and the timetable of assimilation) are confirmed when the various ethnic and racial groups are placed on this ethno-social scale. Most of the peoples from the British Isles have experienced slight subordination, developed weak sub-systems, and gone through a very short period of assimilation. Irish Catholics take many generations to assimilate, whereas the Protestant Irish are almost immediately assimilated. Jews from Germany and England, who tend to be light-skinned and not appreciably different in physical appearance from the old-American stock, on the whole assimilate more rapidly than do their co-religionists in the dark-skinned Caucasoid group. The rate of assimilation for Negroid Puerto Ricans, Cubans, and West Indians is very slow, and there is no predictable time when they will disappear into the total population. Lighter-skinned peoples from these same islands, although possessing cultural traits similar to the Negroid populations, have a more rapid rate of assimilation.[32]

While there is unquestionable merit in the Warner-Srole conceptual scheme, it does suffer from a certain degree of rigidity. Thus it is questionable whether a Portuguese or Sicilian Catholic (placed among the dark Caucasoids in cultural type 4) would be more subordinate within the United States than a light-skinned German-speaking Jew (placed among the light Caucasoids in cultural type 6). Likewise, there may exist significant regional variations such that the Japanese in New York City may enjoy a higher position than those in California. Variables other than cultural and racial differences may also prove of importance. To these we now turn our attention.

Some Additional Factors Influencing the Rate of Assimilation

The rate of a group's assimilation within American society is a function of many variables. While social scientists are generally in agreement that assimilation is a complex phenomenon, they are not necessarily in agreement as to just what factors tend to be most crucial in influencing the speed with which a group is assimilated. The evidence relating to the various variables is incomplete and controversial. Here we will outline a number of propositions in

[32] *Ibid.,* 284 ff.

addition to those formulated by Warner and Srole. The propositions probably represent as good an "educated guess" as one can currently make.[33]

1. *The larger the ratio of the incoming group to the resident population, the slower the rate of assimilation.*[34] Where the ratio of the immigrant group to the native population is small, the natives tend to view the immigrants with both a disinterested aloofness and a patronizing air ("those quaint people"). But, as the ratio increases, the native population generally becomes more aware of their presence, often begins defining the immigrant group as a threat, and to one degree or another erects barriers to the new group's assimilation. One or two Chinese families within a community may for the most part be overlooked, yet simultaneously represent for the natives a passing focus for conversation ("those strange and interesting people"). The old-American stock may even derive considerable satisfaction and pride from their "open-minded," "tolerant," and "big-hearted" attitudes toward a few minority-groups members. It is not uncommon to hear the individual who feels guilty about his anti-Semitism declare, "Look! I don't hate Jews. Why one of my best friends is a Jew!" Similarly, a few Chinese or members of another minority may serve for the community much the same function as the "one Jewish friend": "Look! We don't hate Chinese or minorities. See what a tolerant community we are!" But as the number of Chinese increases, they are likely to be increasingly regarded as a threat and set off from the dominant group.

2. *The more rapid the influx of the incoming group, the slower the rate of assimilation.*[35] A rapid influx of immigrants is likely to arouse among the natives a fear of engulfment—a feeling that they are going to be overpowered, overwhelmed, and swallowed up. Accordingly, they are likely both to intensify their resistance to immigrant assimilation and to erect various segregating barriers. By

---

[33] The condition "all other things being equal" should be understood here. Since "other conditions" are rarely "equal," this is a rigorous limitation on the propositions. Further, assimilation does not always increase with the length of time that a person spends in the host country, but rather often reflects regressions, especially at the onset of old age and times of frustration or changed social life. See: Ronald Taft, *From Stranger to Citizen: A Survey of Studies of Immigrant Assimilation in Western Australia* (London: Tavistock Publications, 1966).

[34] Robin M. Williams, Jr., *The Reduction of Intergroup Tensions* (New York: Social Science Research Council, 1947), 58.

[35] *Ibid.*, 58.

the same token, the immigrants are likely to respond by taking refuge in an intensified ingroup coalescence.

3. *The greater the dispersion of the group especially in the same territorial pattern as the dominant group, the more rapid its assimilation.*[36] Where groups are concentrated in large numbers they tend to coalesce and perpetuate their native cultures. Where they are scattered, they are less capable of insulating themselves from the larger community and of preserving their native institutions, customs, and in-marriage patterns. Further, residential segregation has the effect of accenting the differences between groups by heightening their visibility.

4. *The higher the educational, income, and occupational levels of the incoming group, the more rapid its assimilation.*[37] To the extent to which a group's members are concentrated on the lowest rungs of the class hierarchy, they suffer the additional disadvantage of incurring various class prejudices and discrimination. Thus it is not uncommon to hear middle-class southern White parents declare, "I wouldn't mind if my kids would go to school with Ralph Bunche's kids, but I'd never let 'em go to school with our maid's or handy man's kids." In time an entire group may come to be stereotyped as menial workers and laborers, with a "job ceiling" emerging as that for Blacks. Similarly, the higher the immigrant's former occupational status, the more transferable tends to be his skill within an urban–industrial environment, and hence the greater the likelihood that he will be more rapidly assimilated.

5. *The greater the predisposition of the incoming group to change, the more rapid the rate of assimilation.*[38] Groups differ in the premium they assign to their traditional patterns as well as the

[36] R. A. Schermerhorn, *These Our People* (Boston: D. C. Heath & Co., 1949), 460 and Lieberson, *op. cit.*

[37] S. Alexander Weinstock, "Some Factors that Retard or Accelerate the Rate of Acculturation," *Human Relations*, 17 (1964), 321–340), and "Role Elements: A Link Between Acculturation and Occupational Status," *British Journal of Sociology*, 14 (1963), 144–149; Ronald J. Silvers, "Structure and Values in the Explanation of Acculturation Rates," *British Journal of Sociology*, 16 (1965), 68–79; and J. T. Borhek, "Ethnic-Group Cohesion," *American Journal of Sociology*, 76 (1970), 33–46. For a paper of related interest see: Harold L. Wilensky and Jack Ladinsky, "From Religious Community to Occupational Group: Structural Assimilation among Professors, Lawyers, and Engineers," *American Sociological Review*, 32 (1967), 541–561.

[38] Borrie, *op. cit.*, 94. Also see: Irwin D. Rinder, "Minority Orientations: An Approach to Intergroup Relations Theory Through Social Psychology," *Phylon*, 26 (1965), 5–17.

premium they place upon admittance to the old-American group. Whereas the southern Irish on the whole retained a steadfast adherence to Catholicism, the Czechs, on their arrival, were more nominally Catholic and their defection from Catholicism was rapid. This fact probably accounts in part for the rapid assimilation of the Czechs, such that their position as a minority has dwindled to the vanishing point.[39]

6. *The greater the predisposition of the receiving community to recognize differences, the more rapid the rate of assimilation.*[40] Campaigns such as that of the "Americanization" movement following World War I often contribute to a "boomerang" effect in which assimilation, rather than being promoted, is actually delayed. Where group differences are accepted, people interact in a "matter-of-course" fashion and are less resistant to taking on new ways of behavior. But where differences are not accepted and where demands are raised that people divest themselves of particular traits, accentuated "consciousness of kind" and group cohesion tend to emerge, together with an intensified resistance to change. To attack group values is likely to strengthen them.

7. *The greater the degree of economic competition between the native and immigrant groups, the slower the rate of assimilation.* Economic competition is likely to contribute to hostile feelings, an intolerance of differences, an accentuated "consciousness of kind," and group cohesion.

8. *The greater the proximity and access to the homeland, the slower the rate of assimilation.*[41] French-Canadian assimilation in New England and Mexican assimilation in the Southwest have been slowed by their respective geographical proximities to Quebec and Mexico. Proximity makes it relatively easy for immigrants to return to their original homes for periodic visits. Such visits may enable the immigrants to avoid deeply rooted ties and commitments within the new homeland. It also enables them to experience a reinforcement of previous cultural traditions and life patterns.

9. *In situations of continuous intergroup contact, subordinate migrants* (newcomers who are politically and economically domi-

[39] Schermerhorn, *op. cit.,* 457.

[40] Borrie, *op. cit.,* 94–95. For a treatment of this factor relevant to Jewish assimilation see: Marshall Sklare and Joseph Greenblum, *Jewish Identity on the Suburban Frontier* (New York: Basic Books, Inc., 1967).

[41] Warner and Srole, *op. cit.,* 100–101.

nated by an established indigenous population) *tend to be more rapidly assimilated than subordinate indigenous populations* (native peoples who are subjected to political and economic domination by a migrant group). On the other hand, conflict is more likely to occur in situations of migrant superordination (for a discussion of these matters see pages 93–95).[42]

MARGINALITY

"The Marginal Man"

Individuals not infrequently find the process of assimilation turbulent, stressful, and emotionally disruptive. As early as 1928, Robert E. Park called attention to the individual who is torn between the conflicting demands of two cultural traditions, and referred to him as "the marginal man." [43] The marginal man as conceived by Park "is one whom fate has condemned to live in two societies and in two, not merely different but antagonistic, cultures." [44] He is an individual caught in the conflict of cultures, an individual who lives in two worlds, yet actually belongs to none. As an Amish student at a non-Amish college observed, "I feel like I am a man without a country. I don't fit in at home too well, and I don't fit in at school."

A person occupying a marginal status is *an individual who has internalized to one degree or another the cultural patterns of a group that frequently functions as his reference group and to which he aspires to membership, but in which he does not find full or legitimate membership.* These conditions are likely to foster marginality:

1. Where two groups with differing cultures or subcultures are in intensive and continuous contact
2. Where some of the members of one group for one reason or another come under the influence of another group or come to place a premium upon membership in the other group
3. Where the barriers between the two groups are sufficiently permeable for members of one group to internalize the patterns of the other

[42] Stanley Lieberson, "A Societal Theory of Race and Ethnic Relations," *American Sociological Review*, 26 (1961), 902–910.
[43] Robert E. Park, "Human Migration and the Marginal Man," *American Journal of Sociology*, 33 (1928), 881–893.
[44] Everett V. Stonequist, *The Marginal Man* (New York: Charles Scribner's Sons, 1937), xv.

4. Where for one reason or another the patterns between the two groups cannot be easily harmonized or where cultural and/or racial barriers serve to block full and legitimate membership within another group.[45]

A marginal individual is confronted with numerous situations in which his role is ill defined. But individuals differ in their definitions of situations and in their adjustments to them. There are a number of diverse responses to marginal situations. Antonovsky, on the basis of a study of fifty-eight Jewish men in New Haven, suggests a number of these differing responses as they relate to Jews.[46]

1. *Active Jewish orientation.* These Jews identified themselves with things Jewish, were opposed to assimilation, tended to reject non-Jewish patterns and identifications, and felt strong solidarity with Jewish groups. One remarked, "If you're not Jewish, then you can't understand anyway. And if you are, you don't have to ask questions; you already know what we feel. And all Jews feel alike, there's no need to go around studying them." [47] Another observed, "You say hello, goodbye, to the *goyim* [gentiles], but don't mix." [48]

2. *Passive Jewish orientation.* This group, although its reactions were in some ways similar to that of the first, was not quite as involved in, or as enthusiastic about, being Jewish. Nevertheless, its members were oriented toward the Jewish group and accepted their membership within it as fundamental. They were not, however, characterized by a clear, articulate desire to see Jews continue and survive as a distinct group. One remarked, "I see little point to being Jewish, but that's what I am. And there's little point in trying to be something else." [49]

3. *Ambivalent orientation.* This group's relationship to both Jewish and non-Jewish groups was fundamentally unsatisfying and conflicting. It was reflected in this statement by a Jewish man, a statement which reflects his ambivalent identification in his references to Jews as "the Jewish people," "they," and "we": "*The Jewish people* can be their own worst enemy, by the so-called ghetto idea. I grant you that sometimes *they* have to band together in a so-called ghetto to have strength. But I feel that *we* must get along with our

[45] Alan C. Kerckhoff and Thomas C. McCormack, "Marginal Status and Marginal Personality," *Social Forces,* 34 (1955), 50.
[46] See: Aaron Antonovsky, "Toward a Refinement of the 'Marginal Man' Concept," *Social Forces,* 35 (1956), 57–62.
[47] *Ibid.,* 60.
[48] *Ibid.*
[49] *Ibid.*

fellow beings; this means taking both the good and bad of the gentiles." [50]

4. *Dual orientation.* This group looked toward a slow but steady integration within the larger society and saw no insurmountable obstacles to it. They felt that the rewards to be gained from such integration were substantial.

5. *Passive general orientation.* This group of Jews were indifferent to, and in the process of drifting away from, Jewish culture; yet they did not actively seek to shut themselves off from Jewish life. Their solidarity with the Jewish group was nominal; they were completely indifferent to Jewish group survival; yet they were also indifferent to assimilation. One remarked, "Being Jewish is the least of my worries." [51]

6. *Active general orientation.* This group felt no solidarity with the Jewish group and came as close to assimilation as possible without hiding or denying their Jewishness.[52]

Shuttling Between Social and Cultural Worlds

We have observed that the concept of the marginal man draws our attention to the fact that people may experience assimilation as a turbulent, stressful, and emotionally disruptive process. It provides us with a valuable theoretical advance over the simplified conception often found among many laymen of two distinct categories: those people who are assimilated and those who are not. But we need to take our analysis even a step further, and in a somewhat different direction, and tackle the notion of "levels of assimilation"— the idea that there exists a continuum of change wherein a given amount of "tribal (or immigrant) loss" is replaced in due course by a comparative amount of "Westernized (or Americanized) gain," and that at some point along the continuum people inevitably become "hung-up" or "lost" between two social and cultural worlds.

In considering this matter an illustration may prove helpful, that of the Blackfeet Indians of Montana of whom in 1960 there were 8,456 members. McFee's field study revealed that all live in houses, most drive cars, watch TV, dress in Western clothes, attend the regional schools and churches, and all but a few of the old people

50 *Ibid.* Italics added.
51 *Ibid.*, 61.
52 *Ibid.*, 61.

speak English.[53] Indeed, in many respects they are similar to their
non-Indian, rural Montana neighbors. Broadly speaking the Blackfeet can be divided into two contrasting *social* groups—the In-
dian-oriented group and the White-oriented group. The former are
Blackfeet who *want to be Indian*—individuals who participate in
such activities as bundle openings, Indian dances, song services,
encampments, and visiting and who measure worth in terms of help-
fulness and generosity to others, even to the point of self-impoverish-
ment. In contrast the White-oriented group measures social worth
by economic standards, scheduled work hours, formal education, and
accumulated capital and feel that, while generosity in theory is fine,
in practice it should not lead to the point where a man and his family
undermine their economic position. The population, then, is socially
and culturally bifurcated. Yet, strictly speaking, neither group constitutes "marginal men."

There are in addition some individuals who are Indian-ori-
ented—they live with and want to be accepted by the Indian group
and to maintain their Indian identity—yet who have received a good
education in White schools and have had a wide range of experiences
in various aspects of White culture. Such individuals seemingly
would be "marginal men." Yet they are not. They "shuttle" or
"commute" between the two social and cultural worlds.[54] Indeed,
the bifurcated nature of the Blackfeet milieu has actually created a
need for such individuals—mediators to mesh the forces of the two
social and cultural worlds. In brief, such individuals have learned
new ways without abandoning the old; they are, to use McFee's
conception, "the 150% man." Such individuals seemingly are well-
adjusted—they simply commute or shuttle between systems and are
not "marginal men" in the classical sense. It is not inevitable, then,
that people become "hung-up" or "lost" between two social and cultural worlds.

INTERGROUP MARRIAGE

Intergroup marriage represents an important means through
which both assimilation and racial amalgamation are realized. In

---

[53] The discussion that follows is adapted from Malcolm McFee, "The 150% Man,
a Product of Blackfeet Acculturation," *American Anthropologist*, 70 (1968), 1096–
1107.

[54] In this regard see: Pierre L. van den Berghe, "Toward a Sociology of Africa,"
op. cit., 15.

the United States, intermarriage between peoples of differing nationality groups is a frequent occurrence; religious intermarriage is somewhat less common; while racial intermarriage is infrequent.

Interethnic Marriage

Although evidence suggests that nationality is not as binding a force as race or religion in mate selection, it nevertheless operates as a restrictive-selective factor. Although there are only a limited number of studies dealing with the incidence of interethnic marriage, available evidence suggests that out-group marriage is on the rise. Bugelski, for instance, studied the rate of in-group and out-group marriage for Poles and Italians in Buffalo, New York, a city with sizable Polish and Italian populations.[55] In 1930, in-group marriages were the common practice with more than two-thirds of the marriages involving partners of the same group. By 1960, Bugelski found the pattern virtually reversed with more than two-thirds of the marriages involving partners from different ethnic groups. He concludes, "somewhere before 1975, the 'Polish Wedding' and the 'Italian Wedding' will be a thing of the past." [56] Studies of mate selection in New Haven show similar patterns,[57] while Wessel, in a study of ethnicity in Woonsocket, Rhode Island, found that the rate of outmarriage for the first generation was 9.6 per cent, for the second 20.9 per cent, and for the third 40.4 per cent.[58] And Mittelbach and Moore, in a study of marriages involving Chicanos in Los Angeles, found that the group's exogamy rate is roughly the same as that of the Italian and Polish ethnic populations in Buffalo a generation ago—indeed, second and third generation Chicanos are more likely to marry "Anglos" than to marry immigrants from Mexico.[59] A not dissimilar picture of out-group marriage emerges among Puerto Ricans in New York City.[60]

[55] B. R. Bugelski, "Assimilation Through Intermarriage," *Social Forces*, 40 (1961), 148–153.

[56] *Ibid.*, 151.

[57] Ruby Jo Reeves Kennedy, "Single or Triple Melting-Pot? Intermarriage Trends in New Haven, 1870–1940," *American Journal of Sociology*, 49 (1944), 331–339, and August Hollingshead, "Cultural Factors in the Selection of Marriage Mates," *American Sociological Review*, 15 (1950), 624.

[58] B. B. Wessel, *An Ethnic Survey of Woonsocket, Rhode Island* (Chicago: University of Chicago Press, 1931), chapter 8.

[59] Frank G. Mittelbach and Joan W. Moore, "Ethnic Endogamy—the Case of Mexican Americans," *American Journal of Sociology*, 74 (1968), 50–62.

[60] Joseph P. Fitzpatrick, "Intermarriage of Puerto Ricans in New York City," *American Journal of Sociology*, 71 (1966), 395–406.

Interreligious Marriage

In the United States, intermarriage among the various Protestant denominations—Baptists, Methodists, Lutherans, Episcopalians, etc. —is not uncommon, although probably not as common as is frequently assumed.[61] When the matter of religious intermarriage is raised, however, reference is usually made to the pattern involving Protestants, Catholics, and Jews. All three of these major religious groups encourage their members to marry within the fold, but they exhibit considerable variation in their respective attitudes (see Figures 9–1 and 9–2). Protestant churches tend to be the most flexible, Jews the most rigid, and the Catholic church falls somewhere in between. Provided certain stipulations are met, a Catholic priest will ordinarily marry a Catholic and a non-Catholic, but a Jewish rabbi generally will not marry a Jew and a non-Jew.[62] A study involving 42,624 marriages in Indiana revealed that interfaith marriages (Protestants, Catholic, Jewish, and "other"), in comparison with intrafaith, tend more to be by civil ceremony; they tend more to involve individuals who are members of religious minority groups, who have been previously married, who are older, who are in high-status occupations, who reside in urban areas, and who become pregnant before marriage; and they tend to show up with a slightly higher divorce rate.[63]

Intermarriage between Catholics and Protestants represents the most significant interreligious marital pattern within the United States. Unfortunately there are insufficient data on the number of mixed marriages not sanctioned by the Catholic church. A study by John L. Thomas revealed that, during the decade from 1940 to 1950, mixed marriages sanctioned by Catholic nuptials represented 30 per cent of all Catholic marriages in the United States.[64] He further investigated mixed marriages in 132 parishes distributed throughout the East and Midwest. Of 29,581 mixed marriages, 11,710, or 39.6 per cent, were not sanctioned by Catholic nuptials.[65] A sample sur-

[61] Andrew M. Greeley, "Religious Intermarriage in a Denominational Society," *American Journal of Sociology,* 75 (1970), 949–952.

[62] William M. Kephart, *The Family, Society, and the Individual* (Boston: Houghton Mifflin Co., 1961), 276.

[63] Harold T. Christensen and Kenneth E. Barber, "Interfaith Versus Intrafaith Marriage in Indiana," *Journal of Marriage and the Family,* 29 (1967), 461–469.

[64] John L. Thomas, "The Factor of Religion in the Selection of Marriage Mates," *American Sociological Review,* 16 (1951), 488.

[65] *Ibid.,* 488–491.

Question: Do you approve or disapprove of marriage between Catholics and Protestants?

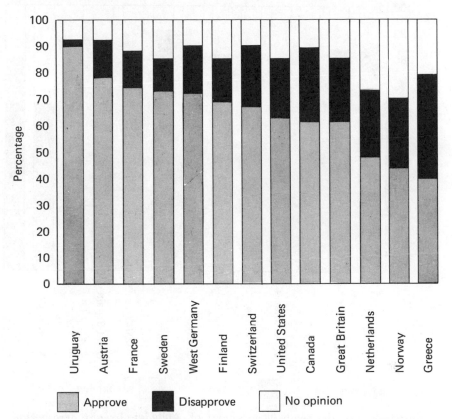

Fig. 9–1. A Thirteen-Nation Survey of Attitudes Toward Catholic–Protestant Marriage. *Source:* Adapted from Gallup poll, *The Washington Post,* November 10, 1968, page E4.

vey of the American population made by the Bureau of the Census in 1957 (based on 35,000 households) found a rate of *existing* Catholic mixed marriages of 21.6 per cent. The comparable figure for Protestants was 8.6 per cent.[66] These figures, however, underestimate the rate of interreligious marriage as they fail to include the rate of conversion of one spouse to the faith of the other. In fact, some data of Lenski's for Detroit White Protestants and White Catholics indicate how frequent the conversion process may be and

[66] U.S. Bureau of the Census, *Current Population Reports: Population Characteristics,* Series P-20, 79 (1958), 2 and 8.

Question: Do you approve or disapprove of marriage between Jews and Non-Jews?

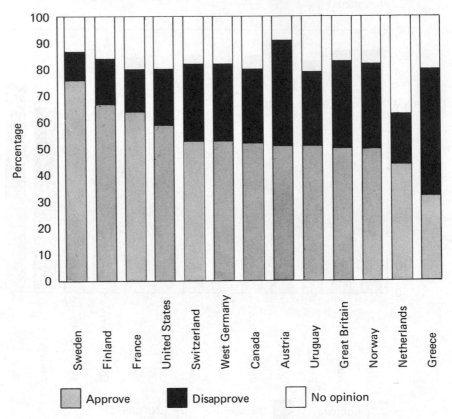

Fig. 9–2. A Thirteen-Nation Survey of Attitudes Toward Jewish–Non-Jewish Marriage. *Source:* same as Fig. 9–1.

how it may be trending. Of the combined Protestant-Catholic White sample, 85 per cent reported that they and their spouses were of the same major faith, but only 68 per cent had been reared in the same religion. Furthermore, among the members of the third generation, who had been born in the North and who had contracted a marriage with a person of another major faith, there appeared to be a greater tendency toward conversion of one spouse to the faith of the other than among the comparable first- and second-generation members of the sample.[67]

Probably the most accurate figures available on religious inter-

[67] Gerhard Lenski, *The Religious Factor,* rev. ed. (Garden City, N.Y.: Doubleday & Company, Inc., 1963).

marriage are to be found for the state of Iowa. Iowa marriage-application forms request each individual to cite his religious preference. In 1953, some 42 per cent of all Iowa marriages involving a Catholic party were mixed. For the same year, the Catholic Directory lists 30 per cent of all Iowa marriages that were sanctioned by the church as mixed. The state records reveal a much higher rate of Catholic-Protestant intermarriage, since the figures of the Catholic church do not include other-church and civil-ceremony marriages.[68]

Thomas suggests that three major factors influence the rate of Catholic intermarriage. First, where Catholics represent a relatively small proportion of the total population, rates of intermarriage tend to be high (provided that ethnic or other differences do not bar contacts between Catholics and non-Catholics). Thus, he found that mixed marriages sanctioned by the Catholic church constituted 70 per cent of the Catholic marriages in the dioceses of Raleigh, Charleston, and Savannah-Atlanta (dioceses with a small proportion of Catholics in the total population) but that they represented only 10 per cent of the marriages in the dioceses of El Paso, Corpus Christi, and Santa Fe (dioceses with a large proportion of Catholics in the total population). Second, the presence of cohesive ethnic groups within the community serve to put a check on interreligious marriage. Third, the higher the socioeconomic class, the higher the proportion of mixed Catholic and non-Catholic marriages.[69]

In its 1957 sample of 35,000 American households, the Bureau of the Census found that 7.2 per cent of the Jews contracted a marriage with a Gentile.[70] But here again the figure fails to note the rate of conversion. Further, it does not tell the *current* rate of interreligious

[68] Loren Chancellor and Thomas Monahan, "Religious Preference and Interreligious Mixtures in Marriages and Divorces in Iowa," *American Journal of Sociology*, 60 (1955), 237.

[69] Thomas, *op. cit.*, 488–491. Locke, Sabagh, and Thomes found that for each of the Canadian provinces in 1954 there was an inverse rank order correlation between the percentage of Catholic brides and grooms having interfaith marriages and the percentage of the total population of each province that was Catholic. Harvey J. Locke, George Sabagh, and Mary Margaret Thomes, "Interfaith Marriages," *Social Problems*, 4 (1957), 329–333. Apparently a somewhat similar factor applies to the rate of Jewish intermarriage. See: Eugen Schoenfeld, "Intermarriage and the Small Town: The Jewish Case," *Journal of Marriage and the Family*, 31 (1969), 61–64.

[70] U. S. Bureau of the Census, *op. cit.*, 2 and 8. However, estimates of the rate of Jewish intermarriages based on local studies of varied quality range as high as 17.2 per cent for San Francisco, 18.4 per cent for New York City, and 53.6 per cent for Iowa, and as low as 4.5 per cent for Providence. See: Sidney Goldstein and Calvin Goldscheider, *Jewish Americans* (Englewood Cliffs, N.J.: Prentice-Hall, Inc., 1968), Chapter 8.

marriage among Jews. Included in the figure were Jews who had taken their vows in Czarist Russian where intermarriage was forbidden as well as people who had married in the United States but who belonged to the virtually closed community of the immigrant generation. Hence, the current rate may well be double that of the Bureau's cumulative ratio. In this regard, Rosenthal, using a 1956 survey of Washington's Jewish population, found that 13.1 per cent of the households were characterized by a Gentile spouse. He also provided tabulations on the rate of intermarriage for successive generations: 1.4 per cent for the first generation, 10.2 per cent for the second, and 17.9 per cent for the third.[71] And a 1966 study by Rosenthal revealed a 30 per cent rate of intermarriage among third-generation, college-educated, American–Jewish males.[72]

Although only some 63 per cent are actual church members, Americans generally think of themselves as being part of a religious community (Protestant, Catholic, or Jewish). Various data suggest that some 95 per cent of the American population readily identifies itself with one of the major religious groups (roughly two-thirds with Protestantism, one-fourth with Catholicism, and 3 per cent with Judaism).[73] Moreover, a transfer of membership is quite uncommon; probably no more than five per cent of adults have shifted from the religious group of their birth to another of the three major religious groups.[74] Evidence such as this has led some writers to suggest that America has developed not a single but a *triple* melting pot. They argue that the sharpest reduction of differences appears to have taken place *within* each of the three major groups rather than between them, that is, barriers to interaction, cooperation, and intermarriage have been lowered between Irish Catholics and Italian Catholics, between German Jews and Russian Jews, and between English Protestants and Swedish Protestants. Ruby Jo Kennedy, in a study of intermarriage in New Haven, found that while there is a decreasing emphasis on national origins in choosing a mate, there is still a considerable tendency to marry within one's own religious group: "Irish, Italians, and Poles intermarry mostly among them-

[71] Erich Rosenthal, *Studies of Jewish Intermarriage in the United States* (New York: The American Jewish Committee, 1963). Also see: Marshall Sklare, "Intermarriage in the Jewish Future," *Commentary*, 37 (1964), 46–52.

[72] "Study Finds Steady Rise in Interfaith Marriages," *New York Times*, December 24, 1967.

[73] U.S. Bureau of the Census, *op. cit.*, 1..

[74] J. Milton Yinger, "Social Forces Involved in Group Identification or Withdrawal," *Daedalus*, 90 (1961), 249.

selves, and British-Americans, Germans, and Scandinavians do like-wise, while Jews seldom marry Gentiles."[75] Apparently religious considerations play a major role, as the Irish, Italians, and Poles have traditionally been Catholic, and the British, Germans, and Scandinavians Protestant. Yet not all evidence supports the triple melting pot thesis. We have already noted the rather high incidence of Catholic marriage with non-Catholics. Further, Heiss, with reference to a midtown Manhattan population sample, discovered that 21 per cent of Catholic, 34 per cent of Protestant, and 18 per cent of Jewish marriages were mixed.[76]

Interracial Marriage

The incidence of Black–White intermarriage within the United States is low. As late as 1970, 15 states still had laws that prohibited it, while the mores throughout the nation have generally functioned to limit its occurrence (see Figure 9–3). Interestingly enough, our knowledge of interracial marriage in the United States is fragmentary, inadequate, and fraught with contradictions.[77] Current information, nonetheless, leads us to the following tentative conclusions:

1. The rate of interracial marriages is on the increase.[78] Nearly two per cent of Philadelphia Black marriages, for instance, are currently interracial as compared to about one per cent in 1900.[79]
2. Most interracial marriages take place between Black men and White women. In Pennsylvania, two out of three mixed marriages involve non-White males, although the percentage varies from 52 per cent of such marriages in Philadelphia to 80 per cent in Pittsburgh.[80] In Iowa, in the 1962–1967 period, the Black male and Black female mixed marriage figures were respectively 13.9 per cent and 3.7 per

[75] Kennedy, *op. cit.*, 339. Also see: Charles H. Anderson, "Religious Communality among White Protestants, Catholics, and Mormons," *Social Forces*, 46 (1968), 501–508. For a paper of related interest see: Edward O. Laumann, "The Social Structure of Religious and Ethnoreligious Groups in a Metropolitan Community," *American Sociological Review*, 34 (1969), 182–197.

[76] Jerold S. Heiss, "Premarital Characteristics of the Religiously Intermarried in an Urban Area," *American Sociological Review*, 25 (1960), 47–55.

[77] In this regard see: Thomas P. Monahan, "Interracial Marriage: Data for Philadelphia and Pennsylvania," *Demography*, 7 (1970), 287–299, and "Are Interracial Marriages Really Less Stable?" *Social Forces*, 48 (1970), 462.

[78] Monahan, "Interracial Marriage," 289; John H. Burma, "Interethnic Marriage in Los Angeles, 1948–1959," *Social Forces*, 42 (1963), 156–165; David M. Heer, "Negro–White Marriage in the United States," *Journal of Marriage and the Family*, 28 (1966), 262–273; and Ann Q. Lynn, "Interracial Marriages in Washington, D.C.," *Journal of Negro Education*, 36 (1967), 428–433.

[79] Monahan, "Interracial Marriage," 289.

[80] *Ibid.*, 290.

Question: Do you approve or disapprove of marriage between Whites and Non-whites?

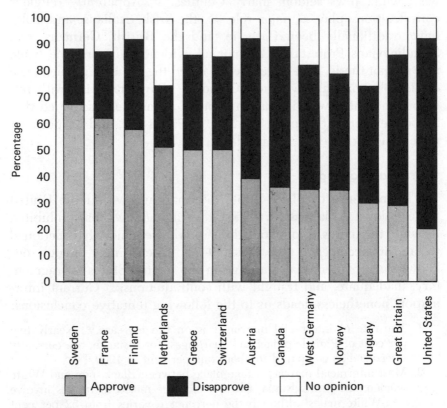

Fig. 9–3. A Thirteen-Nation Survey of Attitudes Toward Interracial Marriage. *Source:* same as Fig. 9–1.

cent; [81] in California, in 1959, 3.96 per cent and 1.16 per cent; and in Hawaii, in 1964, 20.3 per cent and 8.6 per cent.[82]

3. A considerable proportion of interracial marriages involve a foreign born or first generation White American. In Philadelphia, for example, one-third of the totality of Black–White marriages involved a foreign born mate, and one-half a mate of foreign parentage.[83]

[81] Monahan, "Are Interracial Marriages Really Less Stable?" 466.

[82] Heer, *op. cit.,* 266. Yet even on this matter the evidence is contradictory. 1960 Census data on married couples indicated that slightly more Black females in the United States had White spouses than Black males had White spouses. Monahan, "Are Interracial Marriages Really Less Stable?," *op. cit.,* 462.

[83] Monahan, "Interracial Marriage," *op. cit.,* 297. Also see: Joseph Golden, "Characteristics of the Negro–White Intermarried in Philadelphia," *American Sociological Review,* 18 (1953), 179, and Louis Wirth and Herbert Goldhamer, "The Hybrid and the Problem of Miscegenation," in Otto Klineberg, ed., *Characteristics of the American Negro* (New York: Harper & Row, 1944), 285–288.

4. On an area basis within a state, the rate of intermarriage tends to vary inversely with the concentration of the non-White population. The City of Philadelphia, for example, which has the highest concentration of non-Whites in Pennsylvania, has the lowest intermarriage rate in the state while the Northwestern and Northeastern counties have rates well above the state average, but low proportions of non-Whites in their populations.[84]

5. Interracial marriages involve approximately the same proportion of marriages between individuals of the same occupational status category or of adjoining categories as do intraracial marriages.[85] Hence, the prevailing lay view that higher status Black men marry low status, ignorant White women is not confirmed.[86]

6. Interracial couples marry as often under religious auspices as does the general population, but the proportion who have had a prior divorce experience is notably higher.[87]

Golden's study of Black–White marriages, based upon a Philadelphia sample, provides any number of insights regarding the problems interracial couples encounter in a society that for the most part disapproves of interracial marriage.[88] Commonly friends and relatives discourage the couple from getting married, and various pressures may be applied to compel them to discontinue the relationship. Unless they frequent interracial groupings, the couple find little opportunity to participate in larger groups. Each is an outsider to the racial group of the other. The Black partner is barred from places of entertainment that do not welcome Blacks, while the White partner is often viewed suspiciously in Black social circles. Since the community for the most part disapproves of interracial marriage and tends to view the couple during the courtship phase as maintaining an illicit relationship, many mixed couples carry on *sub rosa* courtship.

The couple often continue a pattern of concealment after marriage. Where the White spouse has carried on the courtship without the knowledge of his (or her) parents and siblings, the latter may not be notified of the marriage. In some instances the White

[84] Monahan, "Interracial Marriage," 290. Also see: Heer, *op. cit.*, 268–271.

[85] John H. Burma, Gary A. Cretser, and Ted Seacrest, "A Comparison of the Occupational Status of Intramarrying and Intermarrying Couples: A Research Note," *Sociology and Social Research*, 54 (1970), 508–519.

[86] This misconception was also reflected in the early literature on the matter. See: Kingsley Davis, "Intermarriage in Caste Societies," *American Anthropologist*, 43 (1941), 388–395, and Robert K. Merton, "Intermarriage and the Social Structure: Fact and Theory," *Psychiatry*, 4 (1941), 361–374.

[87] Monahan, "Interracial Marriage," *op. cit.*, 297.

[88] Golden, *op. cit.*, 177–183.

spouse tells the parents of the *fait accompli* and hopes they will become reconciled to it. But it is not uncommon for the White spouse's family to refuse any contact with the Black spouse. On the other hand, the family of the Black spouse is usually willing to have contact with the White spouse. It appeared that, among the Philadelphia couples studied by Golden, the Black spouse's family tended to respond to the White spouse in terms of the individual's merits and personal traits rather than as a violator of the mores. On the whole, the Black community took a similar point of view. While disapproving of Black-White marriage in general,[89] the Black community was generally prepared to view the White in terms of his (or her) personal qualities. Golden indicates that, although there was some reserve in the acceptance of the marriage, couples whose marriages had stood the test of time came to feel at home within the Black community. The child-production record of the inter-racial couples was rather small. This may have been in part the product of their higher median age at marriage (28.3 years) and in part the product of an unwillingness to invite the additional hazard of children within the context of a relatively difficult setting.[90]

Although an interracial marriage did not appear to impair the prestige of the Black spouse within the Black community of Phila-delphia, the White spouse for one reason or another was often avoided by former White friends. A number of White wives joined Black churches, while others attended White churches without their husbands. However, for the most part, they did not retain their previous organizational memberships. As with the children, the White spouses became Black socially. Their relations with the neighbors tended to be cordial but not intimate. Some of the Whites lost their jobs when their interracial marriages were discovered, while a number of others were careful not to let the fact of their intermarriage become known to their occupational associates.

A somewhat different picture of interracial marriage emerges

[89] Contrary to popular White stereotype, Bogue and Dizard, University of Chicago sociologists, found that very few Blacks report they would encourage their child to marry a White person. In a sample of 721 Black families in Chicago, about one-half of the Blacks said they would tolerate it, saying "It made no difference," while the other half indicated they would oppose it. D. J. Bogue and J. E. Dizard, *Race, Ethnic Prejudice, and Discrimination as Viewed by Subordinate and Superordinate Groups* (Chicago: Community and Family Study Center of the University of Chi-cago, 1964).

[90] Joseph Golden, "Patterns of Negro–White Intermarriage," *American Socio-logical Review*, 19 (1954), 144–145.

from Seattle, Washington, perhaps the product of differing sampling procedures, region, or period when the study was undertaken.[91] On the whole, interracial couples and their children in Seattle met few rebuffs. Some 57.8 per cent of the Black–White couples circulated freely among friends in both groups; for only a few did marriage end friendships. The greatest difficulty encountered was housing—63.1 per cent experiencing a problem, usually involving landlords. Fourteen per cent of the Black–White partners reported that interracial marriage had been a handicap in attempts to get or hold a job. For the children of Black–White couples, only "very minor incidents" occurred in school, such as the employment of derogatory names. The study concluded that the couples are "generally doing fine and meeting few problems based solely on marriage across the color line."

ASSIMILATION WITHIN HAWAII

Hawaii has often been referred to as a "polyracial paradise," "the showcase of American democracy," and "one of the most spectacular 'melting pots' in the world." [92] The ethnic breakdown is roughly as follows: 32.2 per cent are Japanese, 31.9 per cent Caucasian, 10.9 per cent Filipino, 6.0 per cent Chinese, and 18.1 per cent Hawaiian and Korean. Geographically, Hawaii is an archipelago composed of eight inhabited islands and a chain of uninhabited islets that runs to Midway.

At the time of their discovery in 1778 by the English navigator Captain James Cook, the Hawaiian Islands had an estimated population of 300,000. Racially the Hawaiians are kindred to the Samoans and the Maoris, belonging to the Polynesian stock. Between 1782 and 1796, Kamehameha, a powerful chieftain on the largest island, Hawaii, established his rule over the other islands and founded the Kingdom of Hawaii. From the beginning, Kamehameha pursued a policy of fair play and goodwill in his dealings with "the peoples and ships of all nations." This policy was continued by his

[91] The study was undertaken by the Seattle Urban League. Questionnaires were sent out to interracial couples, with a return rate of roughly one-half. "For Mixed Marriages, Some Expected Problems and Unexpected Receptions," *National Observer,* April 17, 1967, and "Mixed Marriages Found 'Doing Fine,'" *New York Times,* April 30, 1967.

[92] C. K. Cheng, "Assimilation in Hawaii and the Bid for Statehood," *Social Forces,* 30 (1951), 16.

successors, and through the years circumstances in the Islands have favored the process of racial and cultural fusion.[93]

Although there were an estimated 300,000 Hawaiians in the Islands at the time of Cook's discovery, the native population has since steadily declined. Civil wars, new diseases, the intemperate use of alcohol, and low fertility were contributing factors. In 1823 the number of Hawaiians stood at 142,505; by 1860 the figure had dropped more than 53 per cent to 66,984; by 1900 there were only 29,799 Hawaiians and 9,857 part-Hawaiians. Since 1900, the number of part-Hawaiians has increased and they represent more than 80 per cent of that group classified as "Hawaiian" by the census.[94]

Large-scale sugar-cane production was introduced to the Islands in 1835, and, in the decades that followed, the export of sugar became of increasing importance to the Islands' economy. The rise in the sugar export became phenomenal following the conclusion of the U.S.–Hawaii Reciprocity Treaty in 1875. In 1877 the total Hawaiian sugar export to the United States amounted to 30,600,000 pounds; by 1898, the year of the American annexation of Hawaii, it reached 499,800,000 pounds. The expansion of the sugar industry gave a marked impetus to the Islands' productive and business enterprises and encouraged Caucasian immigration. In 1900 there were some 8,547 Caucasians in the Islands; by 1920, the number had risen two and a half times to 19,708. In response to the growing demands for labor on the large sugar plantations, more than 100,000 Chinese, Portuguese, and Japanese arrived between 1877 and 1896. By 1900 there were approximately 25,700 Chinese, 18,200 Portuguese, and 61,100 Japanese in the Islands. Until the 1920s, Japanese migration continued in considerable numbers; Japanese laborers were augmented at different times by Puerto Ricans, Koreans, Portuguese, and Filipinos.[95]

Hawaii still gives the appearance of a racial and cultural conglomeration characteristic of a growing polyethnic community. Many of the immigrant generation cling to their native languages, religions, traditions, and customs. A number of those who have achieved financial success have undertaken to perpetuate the native patterns; they have sponsored foreign language schools, newspapers,

93 *Ibid.*, 16–17.
94 *Ibid.*, 18.
95 *Ibid.*, 20.

and radio programs and have organized national fraternal organizations.[96]

Although the Islands are often advertised as a "polyracial paradise," prejudices are by no means absent there.[97] Among the descendants of old Caucasian families and newcomers from the continental United States, there are those who seek to erect and maintain social barriers based upon racial origin. This has been most prevalent in rural areas. Similarly, prejudices are found among the non-Caucasian groups—the Chinese, Filipinos, and Koreans, for example, harboring antipathy toward Japanese because of the aggressive policies pursued by Japan in the fifty-odd years before 1945. Likewise, there are interracial and interethnic prejudices, the Japanese from Japan looking down upon Okinawans, the *Punti* Chinese feeling antagonism for the *Hakka* Chinese, and the old Caucasian families experiencing antipathy for the Caucasian newcomers. Still, racial and ethnic membership plays a relatively insignificant part in the larger institutional setting of Hawaii.[98] Japanese, Chinese, Hawaiians, and Caucasians have been elected to major public offices, and there is little evidence of bloc voting (although in the past decade or so the Japanese have come to be closely identified with the Democratic party of the state).

Assimilation is taking place rapidly, especially among second- and third-generation non-Caucasians. Among the latter, disparaging attitudes prevail toward the languages, religions, traditions, and customs of their forebears. In matters of dress, speech, expression, mannerisms, and behavior patterns, their break with the immigrant generation has been unequivocal. Individuals who are more closely identified with ancestral patterns often become the objects of ridicule. On the whole there is an emergent integration of the non-Caucasians within the host American society and culture.

The Chinese are one of the oldest ethnic groups within the Islands. With the American annexation of Hawaii (1898), Chinese

---

[96] *Ibid.*, 22.

[97] See, for instance: Frederick Samuels, "The Oriental In-Group in Hawaii," *Phylon*, 31 (1970), 148–156.

[98] Cheng, *op. cit.*, 22. Also see Andrew W. Lind, "Race Relations Frontiers in Hawaii," in Jitsuichi Masuoka and Preston Valien, eds., *Race Relations* (Chapel Hill: University of North Carolina Press, 1961), 58–77; and J. Milton Yinger, *A Minority Group in American Society* (New York: McGraw-Hill Book Co., 1965), 80–87.

inflow was largely shut off through the application of American exclusion laws. Since the turn of the twentieth century, Chinese assimilation has proceeded at a rapid pace. Chinese are active in politics and enjoy a number of high political positions. They are well established in practically all the professions—11 per cent of the total licensed lawyers and 18 per cent of the total licensed doctors in the Islands are of Chinese ancestry. Within Honolulu they own property far out of proportion to their number: 25.4 per cent of the city's rental units have Chinese landlords, whereas 32.2 per cent and 29.2 per cent of the units have Caucasian and Japanese landlords, respectively. The Chinese Americans react with the same heedlessness and indifference to the turn of events within China as do native-born Americans in the continental United States toward the countries of their immigrant forebears. Although often celebrating Chinese festivals, staging Chinese plays, and decorating their homes with Chinese antiques, they are not particularly concerned about China or its destiny.[99]

The reputation of Hawaii as "the world's most successful experiment in mixed breeding" is not without foundation. Table 9–2

TABLE 9–2   Percentages of Outmarriages in the Total Marriages of the Different Racial and Ethnic Groups in Hawaii

Group	1913		1941		1949	
	Male	Female	Male	Female	Male	Female
Hawaiians	17.4	38.4	65.0	75.5	78.1	80.8
Puerto Ricans	19.6	22.9	25.0	48.5	40.7	57.0
Caucasians	13.8	8.7	21.9	10.2	36.9	16.3
Chinese	48.8	6.1	24.9	32.2	41.1	40.3
Japanese	0.7	0.3	4.5	10.1	6.4	16.8
Koreans	31.3	—	37.5	57.1	56.8	67.3
Filipinos	15.4	2.1	44.0	7.6	40.2	23.9

Source: C. K. Cheng, "Assimilation in Hawaii and the Bid for Statehood," Social Forces, 30 (1951), 26. By permission.

presents figures which suggest that, through the years, racial and ethnic intermarriages have increased. In the decade between 1945 and 1954, a total of 110,696 persons of all racial and ethnic extractions were married in Hawaii. Of this number, 31,432, or 28.4 per

[99] C. K. Cheng, "A Study of Chinese Assimilation in Hawaii," Social Forces, 32 (1953), 163–167.

cent, married outside their own group. In absolute numbers, Caucasians and Hawaiians were the two groups most involved in intermarriage.[100]

MINIMUM ASSIMILATION: THE AMISH

Contact between groups does not inevitably result in assimilation. Groups may be in contact over a considerable period of time, yet assimilation may be held to a bare minimum. The "melting pot" does not always work. The Old Order Amish of Pennsylvania are a case in point. The Amish are a religious sect, an offshoot of the Mennonites. The group originated in Alsace and the upper Rhineland area of Germany and Switzerland during the Reformation conflicts of the sixteenth century. A schism occurred in the Mennonite movement in 1693, and Jacob Amman led his conservative followers, in time known as the Amish, from the larger group. The Amish were recruited from the peasantry and were both rural and lower class in background. The basic tenet of the group is that all practices and activities must be based upon a literal interpretation of the Bible, regardless of the laws or customs of the larger society. It appears that the movement originated as a revolt by a disadvantaged people against the culture of its day, a culture that had proved too punishing and too devoid of satisfactions to be followed longer. Because of religious persecution, the Amish migrated to Pennsylvania in the early 1700s. The group residing in Lancaster County is the oldest and most conservative of the Amish settlements in the United States.[101]

The Amish are a kin-oriented, rural-dwelling, religion-centered people. Although frequently living adjacent to non-Amish farm neighbors, all Amish households in a geographic area form a "church district." The Amish are highly successful as farmers, and their farms are acknowledged to be among the best in the world. Al-

---

[100] C. K. Cheng and Douglas S. Yamamura, "Interracial Marriage and Divorce in Hawaii," *Social Forces*, 36 (1957), 81. Also see: Margaret A. Parkman and Jack Sawyer, "Dimensions of Ethnic Intermarriage in Hawaii," *American Sociological Review*, 32 (1967), 593–607.

[101] This summary of the Old Order Amish is based primarily upon John Gillin, *The Ways of Men* (New York: Appleton-Century-Crofts, Inc., 1948), 209–220; and John A. Hostetler, *Amish Society* (Baltimore: Johns Hopkins Press, 1963). For an excellent account of another separatist people who have structured their society in terms of religious belief see: Calvin Redekop, *The Old Colony Mennonites* (Baltimore: The John Hopkins Press, 1969).

though very conservative generally, the Amish are not conservative in their farming techniques. They have adopted the new methods of rotating crops, applying fertilizer, and introducing new commercial agricultural products. While prohibiting the use of the tractor, they do employ some modern farm equipment including cultivators, sprayers, binders, and balers.

The Amish are oriented toward two major goals: (1) "the Christian way of life" as defined by the sect's interpretation of the Bible and (2) successful farming as defined by agricultural abundance rather than financial success. Their main objective in farming is to accumulate sufficient means to buy enough land to keep all the children on farms. To this end the Amish work hard, produce abundantly, and save extensively.

The Amish, far from being ashamed of their non-conformity, pride themselves on being a "peculiar people" who do not conform to the standards of the world. Non-conformity is held to be obligatory in those areas in which "worldly" standards are in conflict with those of the Bible. The sect members eschew the bearing of arms, going to war, public office, life insurance, and social security. Education beyond the eighth grade is opposed, since it is felt that higher education is both unnecessary and a danger in that it would draw the children away from the farm and the Amish way of life. They approve of elementary education in the "three R's," since literacy is required for reading the Bible. The fact that the Amish are trilingual contributes to their social isolation: Pennsylvania Dutch is the familiar tongue at home and in informal conversation; High German is used exclusively for services and ceremonials; and English (acquired in school) is employed with non-Amish Americans.

Their attire is distinctive. Men wear their hair long, cut in bangs, with low-crown, wide-brim hats on their heads. Their coats lack collars, lapels, pockets, and buttons (they are fastened with hooks and eyes). Trousers are plain and worn with homemade suspenders. Shirts are plain and worn without neckties. Married men wear a beard, but a mustache (considered the mark of a military man) is forbidden; unmarried men shave. Amish women wear plain, solid-color dresses with near-ankle-length skirts. Their stockings are of black cotton; their shoes are of a high-laced, low-heeled type; and their head covering is a homemade bonnet ("store hats" are forbidden). Within Amish society styles of dress become very important symbols of group identity. The symbols indicate whether people are fulfilling the expectations of the group, for instance, a young man who wears a hat with a brim that is too narrow is liable for punishment.

Amish conservatism extends to wide areas of life. Telephones, radios, television sets, automobiles, washing machines, and electric lights are all forbidden. They eschew all forms of "worldly" amusement including attendance at sporting events, movies, dance halls, and bars. Ornaments and jewelry are prohibited.

Marriage to outsiders is not permitted. Their marriages are very stable; divorces are unknown; and their families are large. All religious services are held in the homes of the members—the custom being for the meetings to rotate among the homes in each district. They lack a paid clergy and a formal bureaucratic church organization. They select their bishops, ministers, and deacons by election from among the married men. After the Sunday service (which may last for four hours), a large dinner is served for all sect members in the home in which the service was held.

A number of factors have operated to keep Amish assimilation at a bare minimum. First, competing customs have had little opportunity to be presented and tried out, by virtue of the group's nonconformity and isolation. The Amish are kept from contact with most stimuli or models by which they might learn other customs and practices. Second, the group supplies plentiful rewards for following Amish practices. In time of difficulty or when he is starting a new farm, the community comes to the individual's aid. The group also satisfies various personal needs, for instance, ego-satisfaction, affection, companionship, and security. In a word, the Amish community provides for all or most of the activities and needs of the people in it. Third, the fear of punishment is considerable. The members are taught that transgressions of God's will result, after death, in certain punishment in the fires of Hell. The group also excommunicates and "shuns" violators of its norms, withdrawing all social intercourse with the wrongdoer. No member may knowingly eat at the table with an expelled member or have normal work or domestic relations with him. If the case involves husband or wife, they are to suspend their usual marital relations. Shunning constitutes a powerful instrument for keeping the church intact and for preventing members from involvement in the wider society. Similarly it operates to keep the Old Order Amish socially isolated from innovators within their own group.

Yet Amish society has not been able to shut the door entirely upon social change. Indeed, the Amish search for improvement and innovation in the sphere of production contrasts with a tradition of resistance to change in the sphere of religion. This underlying contradiction generates considerable internal stress within the Amish social order, for innovations in production do not necessarily meet the test of religious criteria. As such, pressure continuously exists to compromise religious doctrine—to accommodate religion to the demand for excellence in farming. This has been a major source of schism within Amish groups; it has not been uncommon for entire congregations to break with Old Order orthodoxy. Among such groups, it is not unusual to find the members adopting tractors, automobiles, and meeting houses, trimming their hair and beards shorter and shorter, securing clothing more nearly resembling that of other Americans, and shifting to non-farm occupations.[102]

Among those who retain their Old Order allegiance, the individual may still eschew electric lights, rubber-tired farm implements, and telephones. Yet he may install propane gas on his farm, secure the latest style gas-range, a kerosene-burning refrigerator, and an automatic, gas water-heater with a gasoline engine to keep up the water pressure. His home may be lit with gasoline mantle lanterns. And although he does not have his own telephone, he may use that of a neighbor or a pay phone. Although still not buying a car, he may ride in a cab or in the automobile of a non-Amish neighbor. In order to sell Grade A milk, he may alter his barn, milk house, water supply, and his habits of working with farm animals. Hence, the Amish society is hardly static.

SUMMARY

We have seen that assimilation entails a process whereby groups with diverse ways of thinking, feeling, and acting become fused together in a social unity and a common culture. Americans have not been in agreement on how assimilation may "best" proceed, some adhering to the "melting pot" orientation, others to the "Americanization" approach, and still others to the position of cultural pluralism. Some scholars have suggested that contact between groups inevitably results in assimilation, a point of view that seems difficult to

---

[102] Daniel Yutzy, "The Decline of Orthodoxy among the Amish," *Sociological Focus*, 2 (1968), 19–26.

substantiate. Numerous variables influence the rate of assimilation, including the degree of racial and cultural differences that exist between the populations. Yet people do not change in a smooth synchronized manner—one in which a given amount of "tribal (or immigrant) loss" is replaced in due course by a comparable amount of "Westernized (or Americanized) gain." As a result of assimilation, individuals may find themselves occupying a marginal status in which they have internalized to one degree or another the cultural patterns of a group functioning as their reference group and to which they aspire to membership, but in which they do not find full or legitimate membership. And people may also commute or shuttle between social and cultural worlds and not be "marginal men" in the classical sense. We also considered trends in intergroup marriage within the United States and the contrasting cases of assimilation within Hawaii and the Old Order Amish of Pennsylvania.

IV

MINORITY REACTIONS TO DOMINANCE

10

Responding by Acceptance

How do minority group members think and feel about their subordinate status? How do they react to segregation, discrimination, disadvantaged conditions, and disparagement? What are their sentiments toward members of the dominant group? The answers to these questions are by no means simple. Any number of sociologists and anthropologists have attempted to classify minority reactions to dominance.[1] Yet none of these classificatory efforts has been entirely satisfactory. From these various approaches, however, we can identify four common patterns of reaction to dominance:

1. *Acceptance.* Minority-group members may come to acquiesce in—to accommodate themselves to—their disadvantaged and subordinate status.
2. *Aggression.* Minority-group members may respond to dominance by striking out against—engaging in hostile acts against—a status that is subordinate and disadvantaged.

[1] See, for example, Charles S. Johnson, *Patterns of Negro Segregation* (New York: Harper & Row, 1943), 244–315; M. R. Davie, *Negroes in American Society* (New York: McGraw-Hill, 1949), 434–457; George E. Simpson, "The Ras Tafari Movement in Jamaica: A Study of Race and Class Conflict," *Social Forces*, 34 (1955), 168–170; Robert B. Johnson, "Negro Reactions to Minority Group Status," in Milton L. Barron, ed., *American Minorities* (New York: Alfred A. Knopf, Inc., 1957), 210; Brewton Berry, *Race and Ethnic Relations*, 3d ed. (Boston: Houghton Mifflin Company, 1965), 380–403; Eric R. Krystall, Neil Friedman, Glenn Howze, and Edgar G. Epps, "Attitudes toward Integration and Black Consciousness: Southern Negro High School Seniors and Their Mothers," *Phylon*, 31 (1970), 109; and Donald L. Noel, "Minority Responses to Intergroup Situations," *Phylon*, 30 (1969), 367–374.

3. *Avoidance*. Minority-group members may attempt to shun—to escape from—situations in which they are likely to experience prejudice and discrimination.
4. *Assimilation*. Minority-group members may attempt to become socially and culturally fused with the dominant group.

We may view avoidance and assimilation as opposites, each constituting a pole on a continuum.[2] Each pole establishes an "outer

Avoidance   Assimilation

limit" or standard between which transitional or intermediate reactions can be located. Confronted with a potential intergroup situation, the minority individual may tend either to avoid contact with the dominant group or merge himself socially and culturally with it. The continuum reflects the fact that there are different degrees of avoidance and assimilation. A specific reaction is distributed somewhere along the continuum depending on the degree to which it constitutes avoiding or assimilating tendencies.

Similarly, we may view acceptance and aggression as opposites, each constituting a pole on a continuum. Confronted with an intergroup situation—with contact with dominant group members—the minority individual may either tend to acquiesce in his disadvantaged and subordinate status or strike out against it.

Acceptance   Aggression

These two continua pose choices that confront a minority individual within an intergroup situation.[3] First, he generally must either allow intergroup contact to take place or he must avoid (or, at least, minimize) such contact. Second, once in the contact situation, he must either acquiesce in his subordinate status or strike out against

2 *Ibid.*, 369–370.
3 *Ibid.*, 370.

it. In some situations, however, one or both decisions may remain
latent. Hence, if the minority person undertakes to assimilate and
succeeds, he need not choose between aggression and acceptance;
conversely, where contact is unavoidable and the dominant group

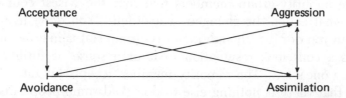

imposes inequality, the minority individual's only choice revolves
about the aggression-acceptance dimension.

Minorities never follow one exclusive pattern of response. Intergroup relations are much too complex for any one pattern to be
operative at all times. Rather, at times one pattern of reaction may
come into play, at still other times another, and frequently some
combination of responses may predominate. In this latter regard,
based upon our two continua, we can identify four mixed response
patterns: acceptance-avoidance, acceptance-assimilation, aggression-
avoidance, and aggression-assimilation. In order to gain a clear picture of minority reactions to dominance, we shall devote one chapter
each to acceptance, aggression, avoidance, and assimilation. In this
chapter we shall be concerned with acceptance.

Some Expressions of Acceptance

Acceptance involves the renunciation of protest against the circumstances of minority status and the organization of responses so
that instead accommodation appears. Daily life requires that humans accommodate themselves to various unpleasant situations. It
is necessary to accept, and make the best of, disagreeable aspects of
work, disagreeable traits in associates, disagreeable elements in the
weather, and disagreeable facts of disease and death, in fact all the
aspects of life that are limiting. Thus acceptance is not an adaptive
mechanism found exclusively among minority peoples. They may,
however, be required to employ it to an unusual degree. Here we
shall examine some of the more typical manifestations of acceptance
as it is reflected in minority-group adjustment to dominance. We

shall draw chiefly upon studies of Blacks, as the evidence here is more extensive than for perhaps any other minority.

Resignation

Some minority-group members feel that the wisest course is to accept what cannot be changed or avoided: "You don't like it, but what can you do?" Although minority-group status may be disliked, there is a conscious resignation to it or a sense of futility about changing one's lot. The minority member accepts his fate out of a feeling that there is nothing else to do. And some people feel that resignation serves to reduce the wear and tear on their personality. This was a common pattern of survival for Blacks during slavery times and continues to be followed by some, especially the older generation. A Black lower-class woman with six children said she instructed her children as her mother had instructed her: "When white folks don't treat you right, don't try to hit back. The Negro is weak—that what he is, and the white man is power. Vengeance is mine, says the Lord, and we gotta leave to Him to vengeance us. We are the underdogs." [4]

Internalization of Accepting Attitudes

It has been seen that some minority-group members *dislike* their disadvantaged status but become *resigned* to it. Others may go even further and *internalize* the attitudes associated with this status. They accept the existing order, neither questioning it nor doing anything about it. In essence they accept the dominant group's evaluation of themselves. They become indifferent to or even oblivious of their status. This is reflected in such statements as "I never think about it. I just take life as it comes, and go on from there." The attitude is typified by a Black Birmingham millworker during the 1930s:

No telling what I would do if I had to set down to the table and eat a meal with a white man. I wouldn't enjoy it. I would be wondering what everybody that sees us would say. I tell you it would be hard. I would much rather wait until they finish if I had to eat at the same place with them. They would feel better, and I know I would. [5]

---

[4] E. Franklin Frazier, *Negro Youth at the Crossways* (Washington, D.C.: American Council on Education, 1940), 49. By permission.

[5] Johnson, *Patterns of Negro Segregation, op. cit.*, 256. By permission of the publishers, Harper & Row.

His attitude was made clearer in his philosophy toward voting:

> I can't read and write, so I don't need to be voting just to be doing some-
> thing. Ain't much need of these Negroes getting in that voting business, any-
> how. The white folks running the country, and he [the Black] can't do no
> good. That's the way it looks like it is to me.[6]

An older Black lower-class woman in Harlem tells about her
earlier life in the South:

> To tell the truth, I never had no trouble down there. I heard of people
> being treated bad but it never happened to me. The people I worked for,
> we got along fine. When you live there you know where you're supposed to
> go and what you're supposed to do and if you mind your own business you
> won't have any trouble. It's like that wherever you be. The world is like a
> bunch of bees. If you stir them up you get into trouble. If you let things
> be you won't have no trouble, but if you go looking for trouble, you'll get it.[7]

In some instances, such accommodating attitudes were taken over
from those of parents and grandparents who had accepted the unequal status of the races as natural and inevitable. Frazier, in his
study of Blacks in Washington, D.C., and in Louisville, Kentucky,
during the 1930s, found such patterns most prevalent among lower-
class Blacks. A twenty-year-old Black youth of fifth-grade education
had accommodating attitudes impressed upon him by his parents.
When he lived in North Carolina his parents had taught him "to do
as we were told, be as courteous as possible to white people, don't
talk back to them, and do your work as well as possible. They said
'niggers' that are liked by white people are those who don't give any
trouble and don't ask for much." The youth indicated he thought
this advice was good and he had tried to "follow it to the letter."
He had not given "white people any trouble," but he had not "bitten
his tongue in asking for things." He had discovered that "if you can
act big enough monkey [clown], you can get almost what you
want."[8]

Minority Group Self-Hatred

Closely associated with the internalization of accepting attitudes
is the phenomenon of minority group self-hatred. The late social
psychologist Kurt Lewin suggests that a tendency exists among mi-

---

[6] *Ibid.* By permission of the publishers, Harper & Row.

[7] Abram Kardiner and Lionel Ovesey, *The Mark of Oppression* (New York:
W. W. Norton & Co., Inc., 1951), 146. By permission of A. Kardiner.

[8] Frazier, *op. cit.*, 42–43. By permission of the publishers, American Council on
Education.

nority group members toward self-hatred—an attitude toward one's own group characterized by aversion and dislike.[9] Such feelings of negative identification or rejection may have any number of sources:

1. Minority individuals may come to accept a large number of dominant group values by virtue of making the dominant group their reference group—the group that provides them with their standards for evaluating behavior. Included within the accepted values of the dominant group may also be the dominant group's evaluations and conceptions of the minority group. Accordingly, the minority-group member may come to agree with the dominant group's appraisal, seeing himself and his group through its eyes. This process may underlie assimilationist strivings and under some circumstances lead to the individual's absorption into the dominant group.

2. Since belonging to the minority group may produce disadvantages in meeting various social and psychic needs, some individuals attempt to disaffiliate themselves from the minority and move outward into the dominant society. Yet they are often blocked by the dominant group in this, and as a result build up frustration and finally aggression. Since the dominant group is seen as omnipotently powerful and statusful, this aggression may be turned inward upon the self and upon the minority group.[10]

3. Learning that one is a member of a minority, that one is a "Black," a "Jew," or a "Mexican," is part of the process of acquiring one's self-identity. The child learns his racial or ethnic role in much the manner in which he learns his other roles. Yet his racial or ethnic role is defined for him by the larger society as demeaning and inferior. The self-image, then, that he comes to acquire may have many negative and unfavorable properties promoting feelings of inferiority, a sense of humiliation, and a constriction of potentialities for self-development.[11]

---

[9] Kurt Lewin, *Resolving Social Conflicts* (New York: Harper & Row, 1948), 186–200.

[10] *Ibid.*, 193.

[11] In this regard see: Raymond G. Taylor, Jr., "Racial Stereotypes in Young Children," *The Journal of Psychology*, 64 (1966), 137–142; Ralph Epstein and S. S. Komorita, "Childhood Prejudice as a Function of Parental Ethnocentrism, Punitiveness, and Outgroup Characteristics," *Journal of Personality and Social Psychology*, 3 (1966), 259–264, and "Prejudice among Negro Children as Related to Parental Ethnocentrism and Punitiveness," *Journal of Personality and Social Psychology*, 4 (1966), 643–647; J. Kenneth Morland, "A Comparison of Race Awareness in Northern and Southern Children," *American Journal of Orthopsychiatry*, 36 (1966), 22–31,

Self-hatred, however, is seldom an open and uncomplicated reaction. Most of the time it takes the form of an indirect, unconscious self-hatred that may be accompanied by ambivalent feelings of superiority and chauvinism. Indeed, research suggests that Blacks who show the greatest prejudice towards Whites also tend to manifest the strongest rejection of their own group and themselves.[12]

Self-hatred finds reflection in anti-Semitism among some Jews; such individuals may expend considerable energy in an effort to dissociate themselves from Jewish group membership, even to the point of engaging in severe anti-Semitism. Ackerman and Jahoda, in their study of anti-Semitism, found a number of anti-Semitic Jews among their case studies. One individual changed his Jewish-sounding name and adopted Christianity, not because of religious conviction but in a desire to fortify himself against Jewish membership. He considered Jews inferior, disliked Jewish girls, and sympathized with Hitler's program against the Jews. Several individuals planned conversion to Catholicism, and one woman underwent a nose operation to alter her appearance so that she might pass as a Christian. To this end she wore a cross. She hoped to get married but never to a Jew—"Who wants to be a 'Mrs. Cohen'?"[13]

Other minorities may experience similar feelings. A Japanese-American student at a midwestern university observes:

I feel Whites are superior—up here [gesturing with her hand] and Japanese down here. They're [Japanese] just an inferior bunch of people—just passive. They aren't aggressive enough. They're in a rut. They're too complacent.

---

and "Race Awareness among American and Hong Kong Chinese Children," *American Journal of Sociology*, 75 (1969), 360–374; and A. James Gregor and D. Angus McPherson, "Racial Attitudes among White and Negro Children in a Deep-South Standard Metropolitan Area," *Journal of Social Psychology*, 68 (1966), 95–106. For a paper that questions the commonly held hypothesis that Blacks experience "crisis of identity" and exhibit low self-esteem see John D. McCarthy and William L. Yancey, "Uncle Tom and Mr. Charlie: Metaphysical Pathos in the Study of Racism and Personal Disorganization," *American Journal of Sociology*, 76 (1971), 648–672.

[12] See: Donald L. Noel, "Group Identification among Negroes: An Empirical Analysis," *Journal of Social Issues*, 20 (1964), 71–84; and R. D. Trent, "The Relation between Expressed Self-Acceptance and Expressed Attitudes toward Negroes and Whites among Negro Children," *Journal of Genetic Psychology*, 91 (1957), 25–31.

[13] Nathan W. Ackerman and Marie Jahoda, *Anti-Semitism and Emotional Disorder* (New York: Harper & Row, 1950), 79–80, 101, 105, 107, and 117. Also see Gerald Engel, Harriet E. O'Shea, Myron A. Fischl, and Geraldine M. Cummins, "An Investigation of Anti-Semitic Feelings in Two Groups of College Students: Jewish and Non-Jewish," *Journal of Social Psychology*, 48 (1958), 75–82.

I've assimilated White ways—I'm aggressive in getting what I want. The only way to get away from Japanese is to associate with Whites. I don't date Japanese or associate with them. I'm going to marry an American or else I will always be looked down upon.

By virture of American racism, some Blacks suffer considerably in terms of self-esteem and have every incentive for self-hatred. In many respects even good performance is an irrelevant factor in face of the fact that the Black frequently gets a poor reflection of himself from the behavior of Whites, regardless of what he does or what his merits are. To compensate for low self-esteem, some Blacks come to identify with Whites, even to the point of wishing to be white (frequently an unconscious response reflected, for instance, in the use of skin bleaches and hair straighteners).

Some Blacks, especially in previous decades, came to internalize White standards of beauty. Martin found this tendency in his study entailing the beauty ratings of 50 male American Blacks and 50 male American Whites. He asked his subjects to rank from most attractive to least attractive ten photographs of Black women differing in the degree to which they displayed Negroid to Caucasoid features. His data supports the proposition that American males, Black and White, share a common esthetic standard for judging beauty in which Caucasian features are considered to be more attractive than Negroid features. The Black and White males were in almost complete agreement on the most attractive and least attractive females; both groups judged the more Negroid females to be less attractive.[14] It is little wonder that White standards of beauty should have an impact upon the Black community since the communication media bombard every inhabitant of the land with this ideal via television, newspapers, magazines, and motion pictures. More recently, however, resistance has emerged within the Black community to such notions as reflected in the "Black is beautiful" movement. Indeed, with the development of Black self-identity and pride, the conventional symbolism has been reversed among many Blacks with black coming to be associated with goodness and beauty and white with badness and ugliness.

[14] James G. Martin, "Racial Ethnocentrism and Judgment of Beauty," *Journal of Social Psychology*, 63 (1964), 59–63. Also see: J. Richard Udry, Karl E. Bauman, and Charles Chase, "Skin Color, Status, and Mate Selection," *American Journal of Sociology*, 76 (1971), 722–733.

THE CASE OF THE RURAL SOUTH

A social system of White dominance and Black subordination survived the Civil War and the abolition of slavery within the rural areas of the South. In this arrangement there was little room for Blacks as large landowners or professionals. For the most part, a Black tenant population predominated, dependent upon White owners and planters. Farming was often carried on in large-scale units, plantations, that were subdivided into smaller units worked by tenants. The system operated in such a manner as to control practically the entire life of the families living within it. Work was seasonal and highly dependent upon such externally controlled factors as flood, drought, pests, and market prices. During the year, tenants were advanced credit by the landlords for living needs. By virtue of costly credit advances, low returns on labor, and dishonest bookkeeping, tenants realized little if anything in the way of a cash surplus. Following World War II, with the shift of southern agriculture from cotton to other crops, the large-scale introduction of cattle, the mechanization of agriculture, the unwillingness of landlords to share federal subsidy payments with tenants, the purging of Blacks who registered and voted, factors that were coupled with the growth in the attracting power of the cities and the North, Blacks left the rural South in large numbers. Today the sharecropping system is largely dead. Some of the older sharecroppers still farm, but as day laborers; others now depend on welfare and rent the shacks that dot the farm areas of the South.

The tenants under the sharecropping system had no stake in the land and no voice in determining what or how much would be planted or when and where the crop would be sold. By virtue of their position, the tenants were dependent upon the White landlords. As a result of this dependence and the southern race structure of White dominance, the landlord could exercise considerable influence and control over the lives of the Black tenants. Such control —reinforced by lynch law, White harassment, and extra-legal violence—constituted a potent weapon in the hands of Whites seeking to cope with any overt emergence of militant sentiment among tenants. Even as late as 1957, at the time of the Little Rock school desegregation disorders, a White Arkansas plantation manager pointed to the role of Black dependence when asked if Blacks on his plantation might seek integration: "I can take care of things out here. It gets down to this—in winter time, when the groceries run out, they come to me." [15]

Poverty prevailed among the Black tenants to a degree equal to, if not greater than, almost any other segment of the American population (the American Indians being another blatant case.) The houses were usually unpainted, small frame units of the "shotgun" type, typically resting on stones at each of the four corners. Underneath the home, a hound or two, a half-dozen chickens, and a few pigs not uncommonly found a sheltered place. Many of the homes were not equipped with glass windows; instead crude wooden shutters served as window coverings. The privy was found as standard equipment.

Where education was minimal and contact with the active currents of life were limited—where there was little communication with the larger world—traditional patterns of accommodation tended to prevail. Within the parochial, paternalistic, and oppressive context of the rural South, many Blacks went on from year to year without acute consciousness of race. Perplexed by their poverty when it became acute and taking such satisfactions as they might find from their group, they adjusted to life and the racial system as they found it. In this isolated setting, the racial situation usually was not generalized but conceived in terms of personal relationships with "good" or "bad" landlords. The "White folks" saw that they got "advances" for living, got out of trouble, and got attention (more often than not inadequate) when they were sick. Many Blacks did not consider the race issue important enough to discuss, or perhaps safe to discuss. A typical answer was "We get along fine with our White folks —but the poor Whites make a lot of trouble." [16] Among them there was widespread ignorance of, or indifference to, developments in the anti-segregation movement. In the contemporary world—where militancy is commonplace—it is often difficult to comprehend the emasculating impact of a repressive, exploitative social order upon a subject people. Rev. King clearly noted this when he observed:

Their minds and souls were so conditioned to the system of segregation that they submissively adjusted themselves to things as they were. This is the

---

[15] "Arkansas Man in the Street Has His Say About Little Rock," *U.S. News & World Report*, 43 (October 11, 1957), 45.

[16] Johnson, *Patterns of Negro Segregation, op. cit.*, 245.

ultimate tragedy of segregation. It not only harms one physically but injures one spiritually. It sears the soul and degrades the personality.[17]

Within the setting of the sharecropping South, a Black explains how he instructed his son:

When I goes to a white man's house I stands in the yard and yells, and he comes to the door. If he tells me to come then I goes up to the door to talk to him, and I don't go in unless he tell me. If he tell me, then I goes in, but I don't set down lessen he tell me. And I don't talk to white folks direct like I does to colored. I lets him do the talking, let him take the lead. That's what he wants, and if he says something to me that I don't like, I says, "Now, Mr. ———, don't you think I oughta do such and such a thing," and then mos' likely he say "yes," but you better not go straight at the thing with a white man, he'll think you're smart. Yes, suh, I tells my chillen to do lak that. That's the way to get along.[18]

The movement among Blacks for civil rights in the 1950s and 1960s did not typically stem from Blacks in the rural communities. Relatively isolated on the plantations through cultural and educational factors, and intimidated by the dominant Whites, they were generally removed from the mainstream of integrationist efforts. This is not of course an untypical situation. It is difficult to organize masses at the very lowest rungs of the society. It is among the urban and the more advantaged Blacks that the integrationist appeal found its initial and greatest reception. College students in particular, propelled into the mainstream of American life and into currents of social mobility, were often in the forefront of such endeavors. On the other hand, rural Blacks typically accommodated themselves to the prevalent racial and class structure or migrated from the countryside.[19]

THE CASE OF EVACUATED WEST COAST JAPANESE

Soon after the American entry into World War II, the United States undertook to remove all Japanese residents from the three West Coast states. Between March 2 and June 8, 1942, some 100,000 Japanese were moved into ten temporary relocation centers located

---

[17] Martin Luther King, Jr., *Stride Toward Freedom* (New York: Ballantine Books, 1958), 29.

[18] Johnson, *Patterns of Negro Segregation, op. cit.*, 247. By permission of the publishers, Harper & Row.

[19] In this regard see: Maurice Pinard, Jerome Kirk, and Donald Von Eschen, "Processes of Recruitment in the Sit-In Movement," *Public Opinion Quarterly*, 33 (1969), 355–369.

in the West and Middle West. The mass evacuation was undertaken as a wartime measure in what was alleged to be the interest of national security. In the years intervening since this action, considerable controversy has stirred within America as to the wisdom, legitimacy, and fairness of the expulsion of the Japanese from their homes. The relocation centers were largely arranged in army-camp style; the inmates were housed in barracks, and the camps were surrounded by barbed wire. Involved were men, women, and children, both citizens and aliens.

An excellent study is available on the relocation center at Poston, Arizona, where nearly 10,000 of the evacuees were retained.[20] Leighton discusses the reactions of the Japanese to the difficult and stressful situation they found themselves in within the camp. He classifies these reactions as (1) cooperation, (2) withdrawal, and (3) aggressiveness. Here we are concerned with the cooperative and accommodative response, although there were also strong overtones of withdrawal and aggressiveness.

Reactions to life in the camp was not the same for all the evacuees. One factor playing a major role in influencing their responses was their membership in the Issei and Nisei groups. The Isseis were first-generation immigrants who had come to the United States at about the turn of the century. They had not intended to make America their home but had hoped to acquire a little money and return to Japan. As a result they made no particular effort to learn English or to become part of the American community. Nevertheless, they did have contact with Americans through teachers of school-aged children, employers, and those ministers who took an interest in them. The Isseis were reluctant to give up their dream of returning to Japan, although they had gradually come to realize that its realization was unlikely. The war found them imbued with strong positive sentiments toward their native land of which they still were legally citizens. Yet, by the same token, they had lived a good portion of their lives in the United States and were tied to the fortunes of this nation. In this dilemma, the Isseis wanted Japan to win but simultaneously wanted no harm to come to America.

The Isseis came to Poston with a feeling that their lives' work had been wasted, and with bitterness, apathy, and fear. They felt that American declarations about equal rights and equal opportunity

[20] Alexander H. Leighton, *The Governing of Men* (Princeton, N.J.: Princeton University Press, 1945).

were pure fiction. They tended to mistrust and misinterpret much of what the officials of the relocation center did and said. They were not in the least interested in building a model community within the center. Nevertheless, for the most part, they obeyed the rules of the camp. They adjusted themselves to life in Poston, more or less resigned to their fate. They assisted their neighbors with odd jobs to promote mutual comfort, but they withheld themselves from more active participation in hard work.

The Niseis were the American-born, American-citizen, and American-raised children of the Isseis. Many of them spoke Japanese as their first language, but, from the age of six, when they entered school, they had become increasingly assimilated within American life. Many had become Christians, while others who remained Buddhists took on many characteristics of American religious behavior. In spite of social barriers, the Niseis had developed a fairly wide circle of American friends, and it was largely from these that they had acquired their goals and ideals, as well as their Americanized manners, language, and habits. In large measure they had grown away both from the customs of their parents and from their parents themselves.

Many of the Niseis came to the relocation center with burning feelings that "they can't do this to me!" They tended to be quite bewildered and at sea as to what they should do and what to expect. They were not particularly troubled or concerned with the future of Japan; rather their concerns revolved about a job, "three square meals," and what they would make of their lives. Although confused and suspicious, they still had faith in some American leaders. They came to the centers angry and discouraged, yet they were not without hope, "wanting to believe," "looking for a chance," and on the whole receptive to the ideas of community living entertained by the American officials. From among the Niseis came the active participants in community life.

On the whole, cooperation and accommodation were reflected among the evacuees in the development of self-government and liaison with the administration of the camp, in the maintenance of law and order, in obedience to regulations, in work on plans for community building, and, in short, in practically every aspect of daily living. Accommodation ranged from those who made outer and superficial adjustment to center life, making the best of a situation against which they internally rebelled, to those who, while preferring release from the camp, actively and willingly participated in the overall life of the camp. In addition, there were some instances of evacuees showing extreme dependence, and clinging to various American officials for support. Such evacuees were likely to agree to any proposal made by the American officials, even those that were ill advised, and would maintain that their food was satisfactory when by any normal standards it was inadequate.

APATHY AND REFORM MOVEMENTS

Acceptance and Black Group Protest

A common lament often heard among Blacks engaged in various reform activities is the considerable difficulty they experience in channeling and crystallizing Black resentment into sustained, organized movements of protest and for integration. In other words, merely because a group finds itself in a minority or disadvantaged position does not necessarily mean that it will actively organize to improve its lot. Its position may be quite unfavorable, as in slavery, yet sustained social cohesion to alter its condition may be minimal. In the United States there were only three slave rebellions of any consequence, involving small numbers of slaves. In each instance they were discovered through betrayal by house slaves. This is not to suggest that there was an absence of powerful and resourceful leaders among the slaves. Nor does it mean that the Blacks accepted their state of slavery with docility. There were numerous *individual* protests. But organized rebellion on a *group* basis was infrequent and failed for a variety of reasons, the primary factor being that the fabric out of which social cohesion is made was eroded by slavery. Social cohesion was undermined by severe White repression, by individual slave efforts to gain advantage with the master, by dependence upon Whites, by frequent identification with Whites as well as latent self-hatred, by in-group distinctions between house slaves and field hands, and by general resignation.[21]

Upon emancipation, the slave, previously a piece of property with no rights at all, attained the status of a human being, although an

[21] Kardiner and Ovesey, *op. cit.*, 359–361; and Hortense Powdermaker, "The Channeling of Negro Aggression by the Cultural Process," in Clyde Kluckhohn and Henry A. Murray, eds., *Personality*, 2d ed. (New York: Alfred A. Knopf, Inc., 1956), 600–603.

underprivileged one. But the proclamation of freedom was not capable in and of itself of eradicating the heritage of slavery. In the period following the Civil War, the ex-slave's illiteracy, his lack of capital and property, his habituation to the past, and the continuing authority and power of the Whites created new conditions for the continuance of dependence, techniques of self-ingratiation, self-hatred, and distinctions based on color, and for adjustments based upon acceptance of, and accommodation to, minority status. This is not to suggest that simultaneously other types of adjustments were not also made, but these will be discussed in subsequent chapters.

Vested Interests in Minority Status

Behind the walls of segregation barring Blacks from full participation in American life, there have grown up various institutions similar to those of the White community. These institutions are largely the product of segregation, and many of them would be jeopardized if segregation were to come to an end. A sizable proportion of upper- and middle-class Blacks secure their positions by virtue of the existence of these separate institutions. Prior to the Supreme Court's desegregation ruling, the existence of a dual school system in the South gave Black educators an exclusive monopoly in the education of Black children and guaranteed them positions that since have often been endangered by desegregation. Many Black entertainers benefit by the fact that large numbers of Whites stereotype Blacks as being unusually rhythmic and accordingly there is a strong demand for their services. Owing to their vested interests, some Blacks are placed in an ambivalent position with regard to segregation. On the one hand, they may be anxious to do away with their disadvantaged minority status; on the other hand, they may realize that success in the battle against segregation would wipe out their advantaged position.

Some Black institutions such as the separate church have grown up out of a long history. The segregated church has provided a field in which Black leaders could realize social and economic security. Many Black pastors feel a vested interest in ministering to the spiritual needs of Blacks. Because of the historic background and deep roots of the Black church, religious integration will probably follow rather than precede the breakdown of the secular color line.[22] Some Black religious leaders have been resistant to quite moderate proposals to undercut segregation. Frazier cites one such illustration:

. . . it was suggested in a midwestern city that as a means of breaking down segregation in churches, a white church might take on an assistant Negro minister. The suggestion was immediately opposed by the Negro ministers in the city. Seemingly, they feared that if the plan were carried out members of the segregated Negro churches would be drawn away, into the white church.[23]

Black vested interests in separate Black schools, libraries, hospitals, and welfare organizations offer in-group resistance to the breakdown of segregation. Separate schools traditionally freed Black educators from competition with White teachers, since Blacks enjoyed exclusive rights to employment and leadership within the segregated Black schools. Lamanna studied the reactions of teachers in 31 Black schools in North Carolina to the prospect of school desegregation. While only a very small minority of the teachers preferred segregation, Lamanna found that a majority expected some Black teachers to lose their jobs and that a significant minority expected to be adversely affected by desegregation.[24] Such fears and apprehensions take their toll of Black teachers prepared to give battle against segregation. Some Black physicians prefer to take advantage of a segregated practice and to have a primarily Black clientele.[25] Indeed, some advocate separate hospitals on grounds that in them they would have more opportunities to develop their skills and to serve their "own people"—this despite the fact that all-Black hospitals have generally been characterized by lower standards of medical care (there are of course exceptions; further, ghetto hospitals are for the most part notorious for the treatment accorded their patients). Similarly, Howard, in an attitudinal study of 100 male Black physicians, dentists, lawyers, and public school teachers, found ambivalence among Black professionals toward open competition with Whites; while they tended to accept the idea of open

[22] E. Franklin Frazier, "The Negro's Vested Interest in Segregation," in Arnold M. Rose, ed., *Race Prejudice and Discrimination* (New York: Alfred A. Knopf, Inc., 1951), 332–334.

[23] *Ibid.*, 334.

[24] Richard A. Lamanna, "The Negro Teacher and Segregation: A Study of Strategic Decision-Makers and Their Vested Interests in Different Community Contexts," *Sociological Inquiry*, 35 (1965), 26–40.

[25] Kurt W. Back and Ida H. Simpson, "The Dilemma of the Negro Professional," *The Journal of Social Issues*, 20 (1964), 60–70.

competition, they were considerably less than enthusiastic about it.[26]

Black business is especially vulnerable to a non-segregated world. The owners of a good many of these enterprises have attempted through the years to win mass Black support for themselves through appeals to "race pride." Often the patrons of these enterprises have to pay higher prices for the goods and services. Black restaurants in the Black ghettos of large American cities illustrate this point. Frazier observes that "not only are Negro patrons forced to pay higher prices than are charged in comparable White restaurants but they must often tolerate poor service and outright incivility on the part of the employees."[27] Black businesses, characterized as they are by the relatively modest nature of the enterprise, would find competition against large established White firms and chain stores difficult in a non-segregated society.

The class structure that has arisen in segregated Black communities has been the product of discrimination in employment and of the social isolation of the Black. As a result, occupations and incomes in the Black community do not have the same relation to social status as they do in the White community. Blacks whose jobs and resources would place them in the middle class or even the lower middle class in the White community may be upper class in the social pyramid of the Black community. Within the Black community these Black professional and white-collar workers are able to assume an upper-class style of life. A non-segregated society would bring about a deflation of their status and prestige.[28]

The ambivalent position of many middle- and upper-class Blacks in relation to segregation is part of a more general problem of minority-group leadership. Lewin, in his observations about Jews, speaks of the weaknesses of "leadership from the periphery," that is, leadership from minority-group members who are economically successful and who gain a degree of acceptance by the dominant group. These upper-class minority members can protect themselves to a certain extent from discrimination and prejudice. They can, for example, afford good housing and avoid slum living; their incomes are relatively high, enabling them to avoid discrimination in employ-

[26] David H. Howard, "An Exploratory Study of Attitudes of Negro Professionals Toward Competition with Whites," *Social Forces*, 45 (1966), 20–27.

[27] Frazier, "The Negro's Vested Interest in Segregation," *op. cit.*, 336.

[28] *Ibid.*, 337. Also see: E. Franklin Frazier, *Black Bourgeoisie* (New York: The Free Press of Glencoe, 1957), and Gary T. Marx, *Protest and Prejudice* (New York: Harper & Row, 1967), 64–67.

ment; they enjoy material comforts, prestige, and security; and they are sheltered from harsh day-to-day contact with members of the dominant group. Such individuals are frequently called upon for leadership by the minority group because of their status and power. But under such circumstances the minority tends to be led by leaders who are lukewarm toward the group, who may, under a thin cover of loyalty, be fundamentally eager to leave it. Minority upper-class leaders may thus be especially prone to soft-pedal any action that might arouse the antagonism of the dominant group.[29]

Displacement of Accommodating Leadership

The changes in American life following on the heels of the desegregation decision of the Supreme Court in 1954 have contributed to the emergence of new patterns of Black leadership in southern communities. High court decisions withdrew legal support from the traditional framework of segregation and gave impetus to various civil rights movements. Prior to these decisions, Black leadership within the South was predominantly of the "accommodating" or "compromise" type. These compromise leaders held their position primarily because they were acceptable to White leaders. Blacks tended to go along with such leaders because accommodation appeared to be the most practical and effective type of adjustment within a setting where segregation had legal and extra-legal sanction.[30]

Among accommodating Black leaders, Booker T. Washington (1856–1915) enjoys a preeminent position. Washington, president of Tuskegee Institute, gained instantaneous and nationwise recognition following his espousal in 1895 of a doctrine that came to be known as the "Atlanta Compromise." In a speech that year at the opening of the Atlanta Cotton States and International Exposition, Washington set forth the following position: "In all things that are purely social we can be as separate as the five fingers [in brief, segregated], yet one as the hand in all things essential to mutual progress." It was a doctrine that called upon Blacks to make their peace with a segregated social order. As Woodward, the noted historian, observes: "It was a time when the hope born of Reconstruc-

[29] Kurt Lewin, Resolving Social Conflicts (New York: Harper & Row, 1948), 195–197.

[30] Lewis M. Killian and Charles U. Smith, "Negro Protest Leaders in a Southern Community," Social Forces, 38 (1960), 253.

tion had all but died for the Negro, when disfranchisement blocked his political advance and the caste system closed the door to integration in the white world, when the North had abandoned him to the South and the South was yielding to the clamor of her extremists." [31]

Yet it would be a mistake to characterize Washington as an all-out accommodating leader. He never relinquished the right to full equality as an ultimate goal. For the time being, however, he gave up on social and political equality, and soft-pedaled the protest against inequalities in justice. He was quite willing to flatter Southern Whites and be harsh toward Blacks—*if* the Blacks were only allowed to work undisturbed with their White friends for education and business. But in both fields he accepted the White doctrine of the Blacks' "place." In education he pleaded for vocational training, a position that comforted Whites in their beliefs about what Blacks were good for and where they should be held in the occupational hierarchy. Washington believed that through patience, thrift, skill, industry, and good morals Blacks would gradually improve so much that, at a later stage, a discussion of equal rights could be taken up. [32]

Although Washington achieved a position of national fame by virtue of the acclaim afforded him by Whites, we should not overlook a long line of Black protest leaders—the leaders of local slave insurrections (Gabriel Prosser, Denmark Vesey, Nat Turner, and others), Black abolitionists (Sojourner Truth, Henry Highland Garnet, David Ruggles, Harriet Tubman, Frederick Douglass, and many others), and 20th century militants (W. E. B. DuBois, Stokely Carmichael, H. Rap Brown, Eldridge Cleaver, and others). Frederick Douglass (1817–1895) is a case in point. He was an outstanding Black abolitionist and one of this nation's best known orators—indeed, few anti-slavery leaders did so much to carry the case of the slave to the people of the United States and Europe. [33] In 1903, Kelly Miller contrasted the leadership afforded by Douglass and Washington for the readers of the *Boston Evening Transcript*:

The two men are in part products of their times, but are also natural antipodes. Douglass lived in the day of moral giants; Washington in the era of merchant princes. The contemporaries of Douglass emphasized the rights

[31] C. Vann Woodward, *Origins of the New South, 1877–1913* (Baton Rouge: Louisiana State University Press, 1951), 356.

[32] Gunnar Myrdal, *An American Dilemma* (New York: Harper & Row, 1944), 739.

[33] John Hope Franklin, *From Slavery to Freedom* (New York: Alfred A. Knopf, Inc., 1952), 249–250.

of man; those of Washington his productive capacity. The age of Douglass acknowledged the sanction of the Golden Rule; that of Washington worships the Rule of Gold. The equality of men was constantly dinned into Douglass's ears; Washington hears nothing but the inferiority of the Negro and the domi- nance of the Saxon. Douglass could hardly receive a hearing today; Washing- ton would have been hooted off the stage a generation ago. Thus all truly useful men must be, in a measure, timeservers; for unless they serve their time, they can scarcely serve at all. But great as was the diversity of formative influences that shaped these two great lives, there is no less opposability in their innate bias of souls. Douglass was like a lion, bold and fearless; Washing- ton is lamblike, meek and submissive. Douglass escaped from personal bond- age, which his soul abhorred; but for Lincoln's proclamation, Washington would probably have arisen to esteem and favor in the eyes of his master as a good and faithful servant. Douglass insisted upon rights; Washington upon duty. Douglass held up to public scorn the sins of the white man; Wash- ington portrays the faults of his own race. Douglass spoke what he thought the world should hear; Washington only what he feels it is disposed to listen to. Douglass's conduct was actuated by principle; Washington's by prudence. Douglass had no limited, copyrighted programme for his race, but appealed to the decalogue, the golden rule, the declaration of independence, the constitution of the United States; Washington, holding these great prin- ciples in the shadowy background, presents a practical expedient applicable to present needs. Douglass was a moralist, insisting upon the application of righteousness to public affairs; Washington is a practical statesman, accepting the best terms which he thinks it possible to secure.[34]

The Washington-type leader tended to dominate the American scene during the first half of the twentieth century (with a few notable exceptions, for instance, W. E. B. DuBois). Following 1954, however, militant Black leaders, reflecting the protest motive instead of the theme of patience and accommodation emerged with promi- nence on the southern horizon and gained considerable recognition. The late Rev. Martin Luther King, Jr., symbolized this new type of leadership. Whereas the compromise leadership had typically operated in a non-controversial and often clandestine manner, the militant leadership has been characterized by its controversial, pub- lic, and activist techniques.

Thompson, in his study of Black leadership in New Orleans, dis- tinguishes between three types of Black leaders [35]

1. *The Uncle Tom.* The most characteristic feature of Uncle Tom lead- ers is their acceptance of the subordinate status assigned Blacks by White supremacists. They never make demands in terms of "Black rights," but rather beg for favors. A New Orleans White lawyer describes one Uncle Tom leader whom he regards as a "great Negro

[34] Kelly Miller, "Washington's Policy," *Boston Evening Transcript,* September 18 and 19, 1903.

[35] Daniel C. Thompson, *The Negro Leadership Class* (Englewood Cliffs, N.J.: Prentice-Hall, Inc., 1963), Chapter 5.

leader": He came "hat in hand, stood at my desk, waiting for an invitation to be seated, as was his custom . . . as an humble, but great supplicant for the friendship of the white man for his race." [36] Uncle Tom leaders have tended to stress to other Blacks that they should "appreciate" what Whites have done for "our people."

2. *The Racial Diplomat.* Unlike the Uncle Toms, the racial diplomat leaders do not accept segregation as right, but as effective diplomats, they display an astute understanding of the "ways of the South." They generally have a strong feeling of belonging in the local community and a keen sense of community pride. They identify with the problems of the total community and, as one racial diplomat put it, talk about the welfare of human beings, not just about "what is good for the Negro." They undertake to interpret the peculiar needs of Blacks in terms of general community well-being.

3. *Race Man.* The race man provides militant leadership. Such leaders see the world through race-colored glasses and they give a racial interpretation to a good many community events. They harbor a good deal of bitterness toward Whites and accommodating Black leaders—in short, any who are able and qualified to help the civil rights struggle but refuse to do so.[37]

Within New Orleans, the Black community has increasingly come to reject Uncle Tom leaders, and since White men of power tend to refuse to do business with Black diplomats and race men, an impasse has developed in that city's race relations.

The north-Florida city of Tallahassee is another southern community in which a new pattern of Black leadership has emerged. A major challenge to the traditional race structure was posed when local Blacks initiated action against segregation on city buses. A boycott of the buses by Blacks followed. Out of this movement there emerged a new group of Blacks leaders in Tallahassee. Killian and Smith undertook a study of this shift in Black leadership.[38]

The new leaders of Tallahassee Blacks were closely identified with the bus Boycott. As a result of the developments stemming from, and revolving around, the boycott, these protest leaders replaced the old accommodating leaders, the latter having remained aloof from or in opposition to the movement. Although the boycott had failed of its purpose to force desegregation of city buses, these new leaders were emerging as permanent leaders of the Black community, not so much, Killian and Smith suggest, because of the attractiveness of their personalities or their skill at organizing but rather because they adhere to the form of militant leadership that is increasingly making

[36] *Ibid.,* 62.
[37] Robert Johnson, *op. cit.,* 207.
[38] Killian and Smith, *op. cit.,* 253–256.

its appearance among Blacks. The new leadership is not of the accommodating type. It aspires to gain its goals through formal
demands and requests, boycotts, sit-ins, lawsuits, and voting. The
protest leaders are not concerned, as were the old accommodating
leaders, with whether or not the Whites high within the power
structure know, like, or want to deal with them. Burgess also notes
the displacement of accommodating Black leadership in Durham,
North Carolina,[39] and Ladd a similar process in Winston-Salem,
North Carolina.[40]

Most of the Tallahassee White leaders are unwilling to deal with
the Black protest leadership, because of the latter's militancy and
uncompromising opposition to segregation. By the same token, the
accommodating leaders no longer could claim the support of the
Black population, no matter how acceptable they were to the Whites.
Killian and Smith conclude that, as long as this situation prevails,
"the structure of the situation seems to permit only one kind of communication between the Negro community and the white power
structure: formal, peremptory demands, backed by the threat of
legal action, political reprisal, or economic boycott." [41]

The rise over the past two decades of Black expectations, skills,
and political power (based on Black registration and voting), has
made possible a Black leadership whose effectiveness rests not on
White support or tolerance, but on support within the Black community. The new leadership is issue-oriented, and the dominant
issue is race. Ladd observes:

The sharper the competition and the greater the estrangement, rejection,
and isolation of the ethnic group in the political system, the more firmly will
such leadership be identified with the interests of the ethnic group *as* ethnic
group. The experience in the United States has been that as ethnic groups
are accepted, they have increasingly few interests ethnically defined, and their
leaders become differentiated by nonethnic considerations: they become Republican and Democratic leaders; upper-class, middle-class, and lower-class
leaders; business, social welfare, labor, and intellectual leaders. . . . Negroes
who are political leaders are *Negro* political leaders. Negro leadership in the
United States has been and remains issue leadership and the one issue that
matters is race advancement.[42]

[39] M. Elaine Burgess, *Negro Leadership in a Southern City* (Chapel Hill: University of North Carolina Press, 1960), Chapter 7.
[40] Everett C. Ladd, Jr., *Negro Political Leadership in the South* (Ithaca, N.Y.:
Cornell University Press, 1966), *passim*.
[41] Killian and Smith, *op. cit.*, 256.
[42] Ladd, *op. cit.*, 115.

The fact that race constitutes the one overriding issue in Black communities has consequences for the stability of Black leadership; where major racial confrontations ensue, the conflict of competing definitions becomes intense and inevitably some leaders must lose community support. Over the past two decades the Black revolution has tended to move "always to the left"; a demand recognized as more militant than the previous one has tended to find a hearing among Blacks since their problems are seen as so pressing and solutions to these problems are not immediately at hand. The content of the leadership styles then changes: new goals mean new demands that are recognized as more militant and that come to supplant those previously at the militant end of the continuum; as a result, everyone on the leadership continuum moves slighty toward the conservative pole.[43] This has been seen on the national level as well. During the 1950s the NAACP was commonly viewed as a "radical" organization; by 1970, if not earlier, it had been redefined as "conservative." The same held true for the late Rev. Martin Luther King, Jr., who, at the time of his assassination, had been displaced from the radical pole well toward the center of the continuum.

VARIABLES AFFECTING THE RESPONSE OF MINORITY-GROUP MEMBERS

Being a member of a minority group does not mean the same thing to every person but, rather, operates within the context of many variables. Social scientists have repeatedly pointed to the fact that Blacks and other minority-group members react in different ways to their status. But social scientists are not always in agreement on the role and relative importance of the variables that influence the selection of the varying responses. One frequently cited variable is that of socioeconomic class. It is generally agreed that attitudes of acceptance are most prevalent among lower-class Blacks. By virtue of such factors as their conditions of life, their minimal formal schooling, their greater isolation from divergent conceptions of the Black's position in American society, and their frequent de-

[43] *Ibid.,* 115–136; 320–321.

pendence upon Whites, they are more inclined toward acceptance patterns than are other socioeconomic groups.[44]

Age is another factor of importance in influencing minority reaction. Powdermaker found in her study of a Mississippi community that the older generation of Blacks were more inclined than younger generations to accept the doctrine of White supremacy and to display deference toward Whites.[45] Kramer and Leventman similarly point to generational differences in the responses of Jews in a midwestern community to the problems posed by minority status. The first generation—immigrants from Eastern Europe—experienced the problem of economic and social survival in an alien society. They responded economically through employment in the garment and retail trades, socially through the establishment of a ritualistically correct community in a segregated ghetto, and religiously through the acceptance of Orthodox Judaism and the acquisition of a secular ethic of self-improvement. The second generation's life situation was characterized by marginality, which resulted in tensions pressing for improvement of its social position. It sought upward mobility into middle-class occupations and professions. Socially it sought to resolve its problems through the establishment of acculturated but separate ethnic communities, while religiously it adapted Judaism to modern American life, reflected in Conservative and Reform Judaism. The third generation tended to accept the economic and religious resolutions of the second generation but rejected its social resolutions, namely, its isolation from the larger society. The third generation undertook to seek appropriate social status and acceptance in the community-at-large, e.g., movement to the suburbs.[46]

Variations in temperament and personality, sex, the nature of minority-dominant relations, the extent of the individual's experience in intergroup relations, and the distinctions made by a minority, e.g., in shades of color, are other relevant variables. The role of personality factors can be seen in this example of two Black brothers:

Two brothers, brought up in the same family and now in college, since their childhood days have shown marked differences in their modes of response

[44] See, for instance, Donald R. Matthews and James W. Prothro, *Negroes and the New Southern Politics* (New York: Harcourt Brace Jovanovich, 1966), 340–341, and Joseph L. Scott, "Social Class Factors Underlying the Civil Rights Movement," *Phylon*, 27 (1966), 132–144.

[45] Hortense Powdermaker, *After Freedom* (New York: The Viking Press, 1939), 325 ff. Also see: Matthews and Prothro, *op. cit.*, 340–341.

[46] Judith R. Kramer and Seymour Leventman, *Children of the Gilded Ghetto* (New Haven: Yale University Press, 1961).

to frustration by family authorities or the white world at large. The older one early began to conform to authoritative requirements and to resort to substitutive expression of his hostile impulses, while the younger one equally early developed the pattern of forcing his demands upon the environment by open and unrestrained expression of his feelings. Thus, the former invariably ran away from white boys when they came threateningly close to him; the latter, though younger, took almost every challenge without hesitation. At present one is literally engrossed in intergroup aggression, while the other seems to be relatively free from race feeling.[47]

A great many variables, then, come to bear upon an individual's and a group's response to their disadvantaged circumstances deriving from minority status.

SUMMARY

One minority response to dominance is acceptance—minority group members come to acquiesce in, to accommodate themselves to, their disadvantaged and subordinate status. Some minority group members display resignation to their unfavorable fate, feeling that they are powerless to alter their lot. Others engage in overt compliance with the dictates of a racist order but covertly assert their feelings of worth and dignity. Still others may internalize accepting attitudes, viewing themselves as inferior or degraded people, a phenomenon reflected in minority group self-hatred. Acceptance may be motivated in some cases by the stake some members of a minority group have in the continuance of racism, for instance, due to business or class advantage. Changes in American life in the past thirty years have drastically undercut acceptance as a mode of minority response; increasingly it has come to be defined as an inappropriate reaction to the enduring and aggravated frustrations of the racial order.

[47] Charles S. Johnson, *Patterns of Segregation*, op. cit., 240–241. By permission of the publishers, Harper & Row.

Responding by Aggression

Still another reaction to minority-group status is *aggression.* Some members of minority groups respond to dominance by striking out against—engaging in hostile acts against—a status that is subordinate and disadvantaged. Hostility represents an extremely common type of reaction to frustration. All individuals, not alone minorities, experience anger; they get "mad" from time to time. But the aggressive acting out of hostility is a potentially destructive and disruptive force within human interaction. Accordingly, societies undertake to regulate, suppress, and rechannel aggressive impulses. A major part of socialization is directed toward this end. It is easy to overlook the part that aggression plays in human life since it takes so many different forms. Not infrequently it becomes so well camouflaged as to be virtually unrecognizable. This chapter will undertake to explore aggression as a response to minority-group status.

THE EXPRESSION OF HOSTILITY

Aggression Against the Dominant Group

Minority-group members generally find it the better part of wisdom to suppress and contain aggressive impulses toward members of the dominant group, by virtue of the greater retaliatory capabilities and resources commonly enjoyed by the latter. As a result, passive acceptance and resignation may ensue. Hostile protest is driven underground, bottled up within the individual. Yet it frequently remains a lurking and latent force. It is not unusual to hear minority-group members indicating to one another how infuriated—how "mad"—they may get from time to time over some discriminatory or insulting action on the part of dominant group members. Occasionally some may really "get mad" and strike back in the fury of frustration.

The bitterness and resentment that some Blacks feel regarding their subordinate and disadvantaged status is reflected in these statements by two Harlem Blacks:

> The way the Man has us, he has us wanting to kill one another. Dog eat dog, amongst us! He has us, like we're so hungry up here, he has us up so tight! Like his rent is due, my rent is due. It's Friday. The Man wants sixty-five dollars. If you are three days over, or don't have the money; like that, he wants to give you a dispossess! Take you to court! The courts won't go along with you, they say get the money or get out! Yet they don't tell you how to get the money, you understand? They say get the money and pay the Man, but they don't say how to get it. Now, if you use illegal means to obey his ruling to try to get it—which he's not going to let you do—if you use illegal means to pay your bills according to his ruling—he will put you in jail.
>
> —Man, age 31

> The flag here in America is for the white man. The blue is for justice; the fifty white stars you see in the blue are for the fifty white states; and the white you see in it is the White House. It represents white folks. The red in it is the white man's blood—he doesn't even respect your blood, that's why he will lynch you, hang you, barbecue you and fry you.
>
> —Man, age about 35 [1]

Outright aggression on the part of Blacks against White persons tends to represent a point of considerable sensitivity in the United States, especially within the South. In fact, in wide areas of the South, direct aggression by a Black against a White traditionally posed a grave threat to the person of the Black. The taboo against physical assault upon Whites operated with its greatest severity in relation to adult Black men. Much more open antagonism was tolerated from Black women; they could often say and do things that would bring men a severe penalty. This probably was the product of the chivalry that our society expects of men toward women and of the lesser degree of fear commonly felt by Whites of

---

[1] Kenneth B. Clark, *Dark Ghetto* (New York: Harper & Row, 1965), 2 and 6. By permission.

aggression by Black women since it cannot take the form of sexual attack.[2]

Aggression may find many routes for expression. Although Blacks have traditionally been taught to hide their hostility toward Whites, one need not look far for examples of it. Hostility is attested to by a large number of derogatory words such as crackers, rednecks, white trash, lynchers, paddies, pinks, ofays, grays, cotton tops, peckerwoods, devils, buckras, whitey, charley, and honkeys. Hostility is more evident in the sporadic outpourings of violence toward Whites and White-owned property, reflected in the form of gang attacks upon Whites and in ghetto "rioting."[3] It may also find expression through secretive acts including the slashing of tires, setting fire to property, poisoning a valued dog, or "shooting from the bush" (murdering a White man under cover of night or from ambush). Gossipy tales may be spread that sooner or later reach the ears of Whites and endanger the reputation of a hated White.

A far safer form for the expression of hostility is vicarious aggression. A case in point is the Black community's adulation of Joe Louis several decades ago:

In the ring he was the picture of fury. As he demolished foe after foe, every black man could vicariously taste his victory. If his victims were white, the pleasure was even greater. He symbolized assertiveness and unbridled aggression for the black man. In watching him or reading about him, an entire community could find expression through him of inhibited masculine drives. As others have entered professional sports in later years, the heroes have served a similar purpose. Educated and sophisticated Negroes also participate in this hero worship, since all black men swim in the same sea.[4]

Hostility may find other channels for indirect expression. Automobiles may be used to this end. A Black furnace worker in Texas said of his own experience: "I drive in a way that makes it look like I'll run over them [Whites] if they walk in front of me when I have the right. I act like I don't see them. I have had some of them to curse at me for this, but I just laugh at them and keep on driving."[5]

---

2 John Dollard, *Caste and Class in a Southern Town*, 3d ed. (New York: Doubleday & Co., Inc., 1957), 289–290.

3 Gary T. Marx, *Protest and Prejudice* (New York: Harper & Row, 1967), 168.

4 William H. Grier and Price M. Cobbs, *Black Rage* (New York: Bantam Books, 1968), 57–58.

5 Charles S. Johnson, *Patterns of Negro Segregation* (New York: Harper & Row, 1943), 303.

Politeness itself may be used as a weapon, as in the case of a Black schoolteacher in Arkansas. Referring to White insurance men, she said:

Sometimes when they come here and act so smart—they always have some nasty joke to tell you—I make them stand out on the porch, and when it's cold it is not so comfortable. You know there is a way of being polite to white people that it is almost impolite. I say polite things, but I look at them hard and I don't smile, and while what I was saying is polite the way in which I say it isn't.[6]

Undercurrents of Hostility

In the previous chapter we observed that minority group members may come to acquiesce in—to accommodate themselves to—their disadvantaged and subordinate status. Yet despite overt, unaggressive accommodation to the racial structure, any number of writers note that Blacks harbor covert or latent aggressive impulses toward Whites. Guy B. Johnson observes that "no system of human adjustment which is based upon the subordination of one group or race to another and the restriction of free competition between them can operate with perfect smoothness. There may be mutual adjustment, good will, and a high degree of cooperation, but always beneath the surface there will be the subtle play of friction . . ."[7] In brief, the stifling and destruction of a people's self-pride and identity —termed by some "psychological castration"—tends to beget aggressive impulses.

These feelings of latent hostility and aggression are not always conscious. McLean observes from her psychiatric treatment of Blacks that deep-seated sources of hostility and fear may be unconscious: "The intense fear of the white man with its consequent

---

[6] *Ibid.*, 304. By permission of the publishers, Harper & Row.

[7] Guy B. Johnson, "Patterns of Race Conflict," in Edgar T. Thompson, ed., *Race Relations and the Race Problem* (Durham, N.C.: Duke University Press, 1939), 126. Also see John Dollard, *Caste and Class in a Southern Town*, 3d ed. (New York: Doubleday & Co., Inc., 1957), 252; Hortense Powdermaker, "The Channeling of Negro Aggression by the Cultural Process," in Clyde Kluckhohn and Henry A. Murray, eds., *Personality*, 2d ed. (New York: Alfred A. Knopf, Inc., 1956), 602–603; Robin M. Williams, Jr., *Strangers Next Door* (Englewood Cliffs, N.J.: Prentice-Hall, Inc., 1964), 300; Harry Stack Sullivan, "Memorandum on a Psychiatric Reconnaissance," in Charles S. Johnson, *Growing Up in the Black Belt* (Washington, D.C.: American Council on Education, 1941), 247–263; and Grier and Cobbs, *op. cit.*, *passim*.

hostility and guilt may not be conscious in the Negro, but from my own psychoanalytic experience in treating Negro men and women, *I have yet to see a Negro who did not unconsciously have a deep fear of and hostility toward white people.*" [8]

To deal with and handle these undercurrents of fear and hostility, strong counter-mechanisms of one sort or another are mobilized. Kardiner and Ovesey note, on the basis of a study of twenty-five cases employing psychoanalytic techniques, that Blacks are trained by experience from earliest childhood in the suppression of aggression. Although possessing plenty of aggressive impulses, Blacks tend to fail on the side of implementing these feelings in overt behavior. "Watchfulness over this aggression is a constant preoccupation with every Negro. He does not discharge it because he is afraid to do so." [9] Although there is considerable resistance to discharging aggression toward Whites, there is less resistance to discharge from Black to Black. Thus, most of the violence observed by Kardiner and Ovesey was of the beating-up variety, taking place largely between husbands and wives, and parents and children.

Karon, in a study of Black personality characteristics in a northern and a southern city, concludes that Blacks in the South develop strong mechanisms of denial with respect to aggression. Such mechanisms are generalized not only to the race situation but to the whole of life. Compared with the Blacks in the northern city, southern Blacks are characterized by an increase in the number of people whose whole emotional life is deadened by the struggle not to be angry.[10]

Thus evidence points to the fact that there exist among Blacks deep undercurrents of hostility and aggression toward Whites. Simultaneously, Blacks have been immersed in a cultural tradition calling for the suppression and repression of hostility and aggression toward Whites. Thus many Blacks find themselves in a dilemma. They are placed in race situations in which hostility is an inevitable product; life confronts them with circumstances that constantly stimulate aggressive thoughts and fantasies. Yet the expression of

[8] Helen V. McLean, "The Emotional Health of Negroes," *Journal of Negro Education*, 18 (1949), 286. Italics added.
[9] Abram Kardiner and Lionel Ovesey, *The Mark of Oppression* (New York: W. W. Norton & Co., Inc., 1951), 342.
[10] Bertram P. Karon, *The Negro Personality* (New York: Springer Publishing Co., 1958), 165–167.

hostile and aggressive impulses is dangerous and defined as morally "sinful." [11]

Within this setting, the program of non-violent resistance to segregation offered a strong appeal to southern Blacks. The program, closely identified with the leadership of the late Rev. Martin Luther King, Jr., had particular appeal in the early 1960s during the early phases of the "Black Revolution." King placed great stress upon non-violent means such as boycotts and sit-ins, and non-violent reactions in the face of attack. He gave articulate and forceful expression to the crosscurrents we have noted—the feelings of hostility toward Whites on the one hand, and the dictates requiring suppression of these impulses on the other—and posed a solution to the dilemma.

King told Blacks that they had long been abused, insulted, and mistreated, that they had been "kicked about by the brutal feet of oppression." In essence, he repeatedly stressed to his Black audiences, using such veiled euphemisms as "protest," that it was permissible and legitimate to feel hostility and to engage in aggressive activities against the existing racial order. Indeed, he emphasized the theme that Blacks have "a moral obligation" to fight segregation: "To accept passively an unjust system is to cooperate with that system; thereby the oppressed become as evil as the oppressor. Noncooperation with evil is as much a moral obligation as is cooperation with good." [12] He thus defined the traditional pattern of acceptance and resignation as immoral.

Simultaneously, King and his followers paid extensive homage to non-hatred and Christian love: "Love must be our regulating ideal. Once again we must hear the words of Jesus echoing across the centuries: 'Love your enemies, bless them that curse you, and pray for them that despitefully use you.'" In a sense, King's message to Blacks appeared to say that they could have their cake and eat it too; that they could protest but that really it was motivated not by animosity but by love. He aided Blacks to redefine as moral and acceptable what otherwise had been defined as immoral and unacceptable.

[11] James W. Vander Zanden, "The Non-Violent Resistance Movement Against Segregation," *American Journal of Sociology*, 68 (1963), 546. Also see: Jacob R. Fishman and Fredric Solomon, "Youth and Social Action: Perspectives on the Student Sit-In Movement," *American Journal of Orthopsychiatry*, 33 (1963), 872–882.

[12] Martin L. King, Jr., *Stride toward Freedom* (New York: Ballantine Books, 1958), 173.

An incident at a Knoxville rally in support of the "Stay Away from Downtown" movement (part of a campaign to win the desegregation of that city's lunch counters) is illustrative. After a number of bitter and militant speeches, the chairman of the meeting came back to the microphone and reassuringly indicated, "We're making a lot of noise, but that doesn't mean we're angry at anybody. If you have no love in your heart, stay at home." [13] The assembled Blacks were permitted to vent their hostility but then, fittingly enough, were comforted, "We're really not angry." Indeed, anger constituted an appropriate reaction, yet it was felt necessary to deny it. As the "Black Revolution" gained momentum, Blacks became more comfortable in expressing protest sentiment. The King appeal, then, mediated between the conflicting traditions of the accommodating Black and the militant Black. In some respects it marked a *transitional* phase in the civil rights movement between accommodation and the more militantly aggressive tactics of the late 1960s and 1970s.

The Hoodlum: Rebel Against Minority Status

For a lower-class boy who has internalized the glittering goals of "the American Dream" involving "the good life," his racial or ethnic background may be a formidable obstacle. Television and the movies have taught that American men should own convertibles and handsome clothes. A luxurious style of life is presented as within the grasp of every American. But as he gets into his teens he learns that his own prospects for "getting ahead" are poor. The role of the hoodlum offers one kind of response to this situation.

Many lower-class minority youths find themselves trapped at the bottom of the socioeconomic heap. Their racial or ethnic membership offers one obstacle, but there are also others. Sent to school because the law requires it and because their mothers may be anxious to get them out from underfoot, they regard the classroom as a kind of prison. Parents and friends, as contrasted with those in the middle and upper classes, usually do not hold education in awe, nor do they encourage strenuous efforts to learn. Accordingly, lower-class minority youth often lack the incentive for academic achievement, regardless of their intellectual potentialities. In time, many

---

[13] Merrill Proudfoot, *Diary of a Sit-In* (Chapel Hill: University of North Carolina Press, 1962), 118.

of them find themselves retarded in basic skills such as reading, and, whether promoted, "left back," or shunted into "slow" programs, others frequently define them as "dumb." School becomes still more unpleasant, and disinterest increases. By adolescence, the educational route no longer represents a realistic road to a higher standard of living.[14]

Lower-class minority youth confront still other problems in school. Many of their teachers have conceptions of them that work against effective education. For instance, a study of teachers in ten public schools located in depressed areas of a large northern city revealed that,

> . . . while there were some outstanding exceptions . . . the overwhelming majority of these teachers and their supervisors rejected these children and looked upon them as inherently inferior. For most, the teachers indicated that they considered these children to be incapable of profiting from a normal curriculum. The children were seen as intellectually inferior and therefore not capable of learning.[15]

Thus it is not uncommon for many middle-class teachers to communicate to their lower-class children the attitude and feeling that they are somehow unacceptable. Most American teachers, regardless of their social class origins, fit into middle-class life and share its outlook on such things as thrift, cleanliness, punctuality, respect for property, ambition, sexual morality, and neatness. Judged by such standards, lower-class youth at times come up short. Yet teacher disgust, horror, and discomfort regarding them are not easily hidden. In turn, many children, especially minority group children, turn out dull because their teachers *expect* them to be dull—a self-fulfilling prophecy.[16] Indeed, this is one of the structural subtleties of racism.

With the educational route to a higher standard of living blocked by poor scholastic performance, minority youth may quit school. But those who leave school find that unskilled work as a stock clerk, delivery boy, or soda jerk offers little chance for advancement. Dif-

[14] Jackson Toby, "Hoodlum or Business Man: An American Dilemma," in Marshall Sklare, ed., *The Jews* (New York: The Free Press of Glencoe, Inc., 1958), 544–545.

[15] Kenneth B. Clark, "Educational Stimulation of Racially Disadvantaged Children," in A. Harry Passow, ed., *Education in Depressed Areas* (New York: Teachers College Bureau of Publications, 1963), 148.

[16] For a discussion of these matters and a useful bibliography see: Ray C. Rist, "Student Social Class and Teacher Expectations: The Self-Fulfilling Prophecy in Ghetto Education," *Harvard Educational Review*, 40 (1970), 411–451. Also see: Annabelle B. Motz and George H. Weber, "On Becoming a Dropout," *Phylon*, 30 (1969), 125–138.

ficulties with teachers may be carried over to supervisors, and employment is recurrently changed. Uncommitted to school or job, such youth may start "hanging out" on street corners with other unsuccessful boys. The gang sets up a heroic rather than an economic basis for self-respect. The individual must demonstrate that he is not "chicken," and to do this he must display a reckless willingness to steal, to fight, and to indicate rebellion against conventional values. As Toby points out:

> He must repudiate the bourgeois virtues associated with school and job: diligence, neatness, truthfulness, thrift. He becomes known as a "loafer" and a "troublemaker" in the community. When family and neighbors add their condemnations to those of teachers and employers, all bridges to respectability are burned, and he becomes progressively more concerned with winning "rep" inside the gang.[17]

The role of the hoodlum comes to represent rebellion against, and compensation for, permanent low status in the community-at-large. Since the larger society has clearly rejected him, he rejects—or appears to reject—the values and norms of that society.

Ethnic groups differ in their attitudes toward academic achievement, a factor apparently related to the incidence of delinquency among them. Both Jews and Italians came to the United States in large numbers at the turn of the century and settled in urban areas. But the two groups are to be distinguished in their attitudes toward intellectual accomplishment. Eastern European Jews regarded religious study as of immense importance for an adult male. Life in the United States gave a secular reinforcement to the Jewish reverence for learning. Immigrants from southern Italy, on the other hand, frequently viewed formal education as either a frill or the source of dangerous ideas. Children were encouraged in neglect of schoolwork and in truancy.[18]

The Jews, through their emphasis upon academic achievement, tended to open a major route for the social ascent of their children. On the other hand, the Italian immigrants, with their conception of schools as of little worth, tended to deprive their children of the best opportunity for upward mobility. This factor may well be related to the disproportionately high incidence of delinquency among second-generation Italians and the low incidence of delinquency among second-generation Jews. Apparently, second-generation Jewish

[17] Toby, *op. cit.*, 545–546.
[18] *Ibid.*, 548.

youths had less reason to become hoodlums. As Toby observes, "Their parents kept legitimate channels of social ascent open for them by inculcating the traditional attitude of respect for education and by transmitting the business know-how gleaned from hundreds of years of urban life in Europe."[19]

In-group Aggression

The dictates and requirements of the social order may be such that minority-group members must of necessity contain and suppress a good many of their hostile impulses toward the dominant group. Some of the aggression that otherwise might be directed at the dominant group may be redirected, or displaced, against one's fellows. Studies of lower-class Black life have pointed to the relatively high incidence of internal aggression that tends to characterize the group (further, with the exception of robbery, 60 to 70 per cent of the victims of Black crimes are Black). It is quite likely that this aggression represents in some part hostility that is deflected from the White group. Since Whites occupy a powerful position by virtue of the racial structure, it is dangerous to vent aggressive impulses directly against them. It is safer to divert the hostility from the White group and focus it instead upon the Black group. But it should not be assumed that all the aggression found within a minority is displaced from the dominant group. A good deal of it is the product of interaction within the minority group itself.[20]

One of the most important sources of Black aggression against Black derives from sexual jealousy. Among lower-class urban and southern rural Blacks, violence stemming from jealousy is relatively frequent. Johnson writes of the plantation area:

Jealousy and the violent expressions of this passion are manifested by both men and women during the courtship period, by legally married couples and by companions in a common-law relationship. Because Ben Mason began courting Alice Harris' daughter another woman shot him five times. But Ben Mason had not himself the best reputation. A few years earlier he had accidentally killed one girl while shooting at another who had spurned his attentions.[21]

[19] *Ibid.*, 549.

[20] A similar situation apparently prevails in South Africa. See: C. R. Bagley, "Individual Fulfilment, Alienation, and Social Structure: A Case Study of South Africa," *Journal of Human Relations*, 17 (1969), 12–25.

[21] Charles S. Johnson, *Shadow of the Plantation* (Chicago: University of Chicago Press, 1934), 51.

Dollard, in his study of Southerntown, similarly notes the prevalence of encounters deriving from sexual jealousy. Razor blades, ice picks, and knives were used as weapons by both men and women who felt themselves "wronged" by a lover.[22]

Similar patterns prevail among lower-class Blacks in large cities.[23] Drake and Cayton cite the case of a Black night watchman who was employed at a junkyard. He would get home about seven o'clock in the morning and sleep during the day. One day, he woke earlier than usual and called his wife. Not finding her home, he dressed and went looking for her. He found her at her friend's house with two other men, consuming a bottle of whisky:

> We began to argue and a rap came to the door. A young man said, "Is this the place that ordered the beer?" My wife said, 'Yes, bring it in." She gave him a dollar bill and the boy was going to give her some change. She said, "It's on John"—meaning me. I got mad and I punched her. I chased the two men out and I grabbed her again. I told her to put her clothes on and get home. She was half drunk and she took a long time to get ready.
>
> When we got down in front of the house she began to call me dirty names. I hit her on the face and she fell. She began to bleed, but I didn't care. I was so mad I could've killed her.[24]

Gambling is another frequent occasion for the expression of violence, as is a type of aggressive banter and boasting that occurs among groups of men gathered together. The banter takes the form of competition between men in which insulting remarks are exchanged about the other person's status, his performance, and even about the virtue of his wife, sweetheart, or mother. Although beginning in jest, the activity sometimes goes over into violent assault.[25] Dollard notes that there seems to be an actual idealization of personal violence among lower-class rural Blacks. It is not dissimilar from the admiration felt during the period of the frontier for the individual who was physically or morally capable of taking care of himself. Under circumstances where the formal machinery of law takes care of Blacks' grievances much less adequately than those of the Whites, greater recourse is had to one's own competence in protecting and advancing one's interests.[26]

Violence may be a frequent accompaniment of family and marital

---

22 Dollard, *op. cit.*, 269 ff.

23 St. Clair Drake and Horace R. Cayton, *Black Metropolis* (New York: Harcourt Brace Jovanovich, 1945), 564 ff.

24 *Ibid.*, 588. By permission of the publishers, Harcourt Brace Jovanovich.

25 Dollard, *op. cit.*, 272–274.

26 *Ibid.*, 274.

conflict. An illustration is afforded from the case of a lower-class Black subject in the Kardiner and Ovesey study. One morning the subject, a woman, phoned prior to one of the interview sessions and said, "My father got drunk yesterday and beat me up. My face is all swollen. Should I come anyway?" The interviewer was agreeable, and she appeared quite drunk on arrival. She told this story of what had occurred:

> A friend of mine invited us over for drinks. When we got home my father hit my mother. He was kind of jealous she had gone. Well, naturally, I'm her daughter, so I hit him back and we started to fight. I wouldn't have gotten hurt if I hadn't been drinking myself. He bit me here. [She shows the teeth marks on her arm.] Then he kicked me here. [She displays a large bruise on her leg.] Then he tried to strangle me. . . . Then my husband came home. I told him he had to get me out of the house or I would kill my father. I'd kill him! Yet I love him in a way because he's my father; yet I hate him! I hate him!" [27]

Another day she phoned in tears, indicating her husband had beaten her up: "My face is still swollen, my arm is in a sling, and I can't hear out of one ear." [28]

Deflection of Hostility to Other Minorities

Not only may hostility be deflected from the dominant group and focused upon one's fellows, it may also be displaced upon other minorities. As was noted in Chapter 4, the social distance rankings of minority-group members are quite similar to those of dominant-group members. However, while the minority tends to retain the standardized social distance pattern, it moves its own ranking from one near the bottom of the scale to one at the top. Clearly the normative factor plays an important role in influencing the attitudes and behavior of one minority toward another. Simultaneously, hostility that cannot find direct expression against the dominant group may in some instances be rechanneled toward a permissive target, another minority. Other minorities are also weak, sometimes weaker than one's own group. Further, through aggression directed against another minority, the minority person borrows some measure of dominant group status.

Anti-Semitism among Blacks in the United States appears to be a development of relatively recent decades and in large measure is

[27] Abram Kardiner and Lionel Ovesey, *The Mark of Oppression* (New York: W. W. Norton & Co., Inc., 1951), 163. By permission of A. Kardiner.
[28] *Ibid.*, 165.

limited to urban settings. It has found fertile roots among Black businessmen, who often find themselves competitors of Jewish merchants.[29] Traditionally a large proportion of the White merchants who solicited Black trade and established their businesses in Black slums were Jews. Similarly, there were other areas of friction with Jews. Many of the housewives who hired Black domestic workers in large cities were Jews, and many of the property owners who were willing to rent or sell homes to Blacks were Jews. A Black owner of a small grocery store says:

When we first opened up, we had just as good a stock as any of them whites. But then the colored did not come in and buy and we went back. We had a struggle. A Jew across the street tried to move us out. But he's gone now. He tried to undersell us. Jews are dirty. He told the cake man and vegetable man that if they sold to me they could not sell to him.[30]

A recent study by Gary T. Marx suggests that 24 per cent of those Blacks who are anti-Semites are in positions where an economic explanation of the hostility they express toward Jews seems likely (and in another 42 per cent of such cases, economic factors could be relevant).[31]

Yet, contrary to popular opinion (and the expectations of the scapegoat theory of displacement), a good deal of Black anti-Semitism is directed at Jews not as Jews but at Jews as Whites. Indeed, Marx, in the survey referred to above, found that, to the extent Blacks distinguish between Jewish and non-Jewish Whites as merchants, landlords, and employers, they tend to prefer Jews: nationally, 20 per cent said Jewish store owners were better than other White store owners, seven per cent said they were worse, and 68 per cent said they were about the same; 34 per cent said they were better to work for, 19 per cent they were worse, and 10 per cent about the same (37 per cent replied, "Don't know"); 24 per cent said they were better landlords, seven per cent they were worse, and 32 per cent

[29] Harold L. Sheppard, "The Negro Merchant: A Study of Negro Anti-Semitism," *American Journal of Sociology*, LIII (1947), 96–99, and Nathan Glazer and Daniel P. Moynihan, *Beyond the Melting Pot* (Cambridge, Mass.: M.I.T. Press and Harvard University Press, 1963), 71–77. For a consideration of Black anti-Semitism also see: Richard L. Simpson, "Negro-Jewish Prejudice: Authoritarianism and Some Social Variables as Correlates," *Social Problems*, 7 (1959), 138–146; and J. S. Gray and A. J. Thompson, "Ethnic Prejudices of White and Negro College Students," *Journal of Abnormal and Social Psychology*, 48 (1953), 311–313.

[30] W. Lloyd Warner, Buford H. Junker, and Walter A. Adams, *Color and Human Nature* (Washington, D.C.: American Council on Education, 1941), 115. By permission.

[31] Marx, *op. cit.*, 166–167.

about the same (37 per cent replied, "Don't know"); and 45 per cent believed they were more in favor of civil rights than other Whites, three per cent they were less in favor, and 35 per cent about the same.[32]

PROTEST

Humor

A very prevalent way of expressing hostile feelings is through humor. When friction and antagonism exist within important areas of interaction, joking and teasing function to discourage the development of serious overt aggression. The following is an illustration of this phenomenon:

A factory hand in Cleveland, Mississippi, indicated that at the place where he worked the White foreman and the Black workers often exchanged jokes. One morning the foreman told one of the Blacks, "Hurry up there, you son-of-a-bitch. Your mammy must not have given you any breakfast." The Black youth retorted, "You skinny bastard, look like your mammy never gives you anything to eat." Then all laughed.[33]

Aggressive impulses that otherwise might not be tolerated find a permissive outlet behind the veil of joking. Hostility is often rendered harmless, or so it seems, through jest. But many a true word is said, and many genuine feelings are expressed, by means of the "joke." Thus, joking and teasing provide an important outlet for hostility.

Humor may also be a mechanism for expressing aggression toward the dominant group in the latter's absence. Through ridicule and sarcasm, hostile impulses are released. At times the jokes are so bitter as almost to lack humor:

It says in the white folks' newspaper that our women are trying to ruin the white folks' homes by quitting their jobs as maids.

Yeah. A lot of white women are mad because they have to bring up their own children.[34]

And this bitter joke in a message from H. Rap Brown:

That whole nonviolence thing was nothing but a preparation for genocide. At one point, not so long ago, the man could have sent a message to black people,

---

[32] *Ibid.*, Chapter 6.

[33] Adapted from Charles S. Johnson, *Patterns of Negro Segregation, op. cit.*, 308.

[34] Gunnar Myrdal, *An American Dilemma* (New York: Harper & Row, 1944), 961.

saying meet me at such and such a concentration camp and black people would
have been there—on time! [35]

Some of the jokes have a strong protest character:

I went into the store _____ to get some tobacco. I asked for "Prince
Albert" and the clerk said "see the man on that can. He's white. Say 'Mister
Prince Albert.'" I thought for a minute and then said "No thank you, sir;
I believe I'll just take Bull Durham; I don't have to 'mister' him!" [36]

As Dollard points out, many jokes that Blacks tell have a delicate
suppressed quality, in which the hostility is hard to locate but in
which the individual has the baffled general feeling that the Whites
have been lampooned without knowing quite how. He relates this
example in which the Black exerts his stubborn self-respect and in
which a fragile joke is had on the White man:

A Negro named George went into a white store to buy a hat. The clerk
said, "Well, *Bill,* what will you have?" The Negro guessed he would have
nothing. At the next store, "Well, *son,* what will you have?" He said nothing. And so on, through a list of names such as "uncle," "Mose," etc. Finally
he came to a store where the clerk said, "Well, *George,* what will you have?"
"A hat," he answered and bought it.[37]

Although such a joke may appear uproariously funny to some
Blacks, it would not appear at all humorous to most White persons.
More recently, jokes have appeared about Blacks who attempt
to pass as Whites that serve to improve Black self-attitudes and en-
hance racial pride:

An elegant Negro—wearing a Brooks Brothers suit, a Homburg, and gray
gloves—boarded a New York bus, sat down and began to read his copy of the
Wall Street Journal. His white seatmate leaned over and shouted, "Nigger!"
Whereupon the Negro leaped from the seat in total alarm and asked,
"Where? Where? Where?" [38]

Protest in Art

Through poetry, prose, and songs, racial and ethnic minorities
may find vehicles by which to voice protest. Some of the Black
spirituals suggest underlying symbolism with important elements
of protest hidden in them. A number such as "Go Down, Moses,"

[35] Sol Stern, "America's Black Guerrillas," *Ramparts,* 6 (September, 1967), 26–27.
[36] John H. Burma, "Humor as a Technique in Race Conflict," *American Sociological Review,* 11 (1946), 713–714.
[37] Dollard, *op. cit.,* 309.
[38] Irwin D. Rinder, "A Note on Humor as an Index of Minority Group Morale,"
Phylon, 26 (1965), 120.

"The Lord Delivered Daniel," and "Good News, Member" were vehicles by which to report the success of an escaped slave's flight via the Underground Railroad. "Heaven" and "Paradise" were often symbolic representations of freedom and the North.

Opinions differ considerably as to how much the spirituals represented a vehicle for Black hatred, revenge, and protest. A few authorities suggest that these elements were entirely lacking in the spirituals; others insist that they contained marked symbolic expressions of conscious protest; and still others are convinced that the spirituals represented a deep and profound sort of protest in which the meaning often was hidden from the singer himself in an unconscious form.[39] Whatever the case, the spirituals did represent a means of expressing the Black's grim dissatisfaction with his worldly status. The emphasis upon other worldliness was reflected in such songs as "Dere's a Great Camp Meetin' in de Promised Land," "Look Away in de Heaven, Lord," "Fo' My Soul's Goin' to Heaven Jes' Sho's Your Born," and "Heaven, Heaven, Everybody Talkin' 'Bout Heaven Ain't Goin' There." They typified the slaves' hope that life would be easier in the next world. In a sense they were "sorrow songs" molded by the hardships and suffering during slavery. "Nobody Knows" expressed such sentiment:

> Oh, nobody knows de trouble I've seen.
> Nobody knows but Jesus.
> Nobody knows de trouble I've seen.
> Glory hallelujah.
>
> Sometimes I'm up, sometimes I'm down,
> Oh, yes, Lord.
> Sometimes I'm almost to de groun',
> Oh, yes, Lord.
>
> Although you see me goin' 'long so,
> Oh, yes, Lord.
> I have my trials here below,
> Oh, yes, Lord.

The "blues" played a somewhat similar role in a later period, but they no longer appear to be in accord with the contemporary mood of ghetto Blacks, and "soul music" has tended to replace it as the

[39] John Greenway, *American Folksongs of Protest* (New York: A. S. Barnes & Co., Inc., 1960), 79. Also see: Sterling Broun, "Negro Folk Expression: Spirituals, Seculars, Ballads, and Work Songs," *Phylon*, 14 (1953), 45–61.

dominant form of musical expression. Bill Crane of WVON (a Chicago station oriented to a Black audience) observes:

> Years ago people identified with all this sadness, all sadness. . . . Now people don't feel so oppressed or depressed. They know that there's people that are against them but they're no longer canned up or nailed down. Y'see now we can move freely even though sometimes we can't express ourselves freely.[40]

In the concept of "soul," Blacks believe they can sing and dance and experience music in a way that Whites cannot.[41] Soul is an umbrella concept for a rather wide variety of definitions, but very broadly it has come to stand for the "essence of Blackness." Hannerz observes that "soul seems to be a folk conception of the lower-class urban Negro's own 'national character.' "[42]

Literature may also represent a vehicle for expressing protest. Among a group of Blacks during the decades between the first and second world wars, a literary movement emerged that has been variously referred to as the "Harlem Renaissance," the "Black Renaissance," and the "New Negro Movement." For the most part, the work was the product of a race-conscious group. Poetry and prose became instruments for crying out against social and economic wrongs. The writers protested against segregation and lynching; demanded higher wages, shorter hours, and better working conditions; and insisted upon full social equality and first-class citizenship. Among them were Claude McKay, James Weldon Johnson, Jean Toomer, Countee Cullen, Langston Hughes, Walter White, W. E. B. Du Bois, and Richard Wright. Probably the best known of these was Richard Wright, whose *Uncle Tom's Children* (1938), *Native Son* (1940), and *Black Boy* (1945) depicted with stark, tragic realism the frustrations of many Blacks.[43] More recently, LeRoi Jones, Eldridge Cleaver, Ralph Ellison, John Oliver Killens, among others, have emerged as powerful protest writers.

[40] Michael Haralambos, "Soul Music and Blues: Their Meaning and Relevance in Northern United States Black Ghettos," in Norman E. Whitten, Jr., and John F. Szwed, eds., *Afro-American Anthropology* (New York: The Free Press of Glencoe, 1970), 371.

[41] "The idea that Negroes have natural rhythm was originally used by whites to depreciate any musical creativity observed among blacks. Today this stereotype is embraced by black people and elaborated in the creation of a singular music which the white cannot create and which he can neither play nor understand." Grier and Cobbs, *op. cit.*, 106.

[42] Ulf Hannerz, "What Negroes Mean by 'Soul,' " *Trans-action* (July/August, 1968), 57.

[43] See: John Hope Franklin, *From Slavery to Freedom* (New York: Alfred A. Knopf, 1952), 489–511.

Irresponsible and Awkward Work

Finding themselves in a disadvantaged and relatively powerless position, it is not unusual for minority-group members to work slowly or awkwardly, and at times even leave a job entirely without notice. Inefficient and sluggish activity represents a means of striking back at the dominant group, without necessarily provoking retaliation. It becomes a subtle instrument by which to mock the dominant group: "You say we are inferior, lazy, and no-good. Well, we'll just show you by being ignorant, awkward, slow, and inefficient. We'll take your money but we'll deliver little." A generalized lethargic disposition may become a rooted way of life and a response to difficult circumstances.

Franklin indicates that one type of reaction of Blacks to slavery was loafing on the job, feigning illness in the fields and on the auction block, and engaging in an elaborate program of sabotage. Since the slave was hard on farming tools and not disposed to exercise care with them, special tools were developed for him. He drove the animals with a cruelty that suggested revenge, and he was often so ruthless in his handling of the crops that the most careful supervision was necessary to ensure their survival until the harvest. Self-mutilation and suicide were likewise employed. In order to render themselves ineffective workers, some slaves mutilated themselves and cut off their toes and hands.[44]

Not only may minority-group members express resentment through inefficiency and low motivation, they may also show hostility through high labor turnover. Whites frequently complain that their "Black help up and leave without so much as a word of notice." Quitting a job is a form of retaliation that exasperates Whites and thus becomes an instrumentality by which Blacks can express hostility. The disappearance of a Black domestic worker after a payday frequently involves some element of protest. It is as if the Black were saying, "I may seem inferior to you and you may have many advantages over me, but at least you do not own my body." [45]

VARIABLES AFFECTING THE RESPONSE OF MINORITY-GROUP MEMBERS

Socioeconomic-class membership plays a crucial role in influencing patterns of reaction to dominance. Tendencies toward the direct

[44] *Ibid.*, 206.
[45] Dollard, *op. cit.*, 302.

expression of aggression among Blacks are probably most prevalent in the lower class. Circumstances of life among lower-class Blacks may encourage an explosive resolution of intense hostile impulses. Children see considerable violence within their communities and families, and some are also the object of the violent behavior of their parents and immediate associates.[46] Furthermore, among the middle and upper classes respectability is stressed and fighting and squabbling are severely scorned.

By virtue of their relatively greater isolation, the product of their disadvantaged position and lower levels of education, lower-class Blacks have traditionally been less involved in civil rights activities and movements than have the other classes. The strength of the NAACP and Urban League has traditionally resided in the middle and upper classes. Covert expressions of hostility in the form of petty sabotage, quitting of jobs, gossip, and pseudo-ignorant malingering tend to be more prevalent among the lower class than among the middle and upper classes.[47]

Robert Johnson, in his study of 150 Blacks in an upstate New York community, found that aggression, as a response to dominance, was more prevalent among the less educated, the southern-born, youths and adults under forty-five, females, and those whose interracial contact was minimal.[48] Not infrequently, hostility was deflected toward other groups, especially the foreign born, who were resented for enjoying privileges on their first day in America that were denied Blacks who were lifetime residents. Hostility was most closely related to place of birth. Lifetime residents of the North were generally less hostile than the southern-born, a finding also confirmed by other studies.[49] Buried racial antagonisms arising from southern experiences often came to the foreground in the more permissive setting of the North.

The readiness to employ violence as a way of gaining Black rights is associated with age and sex,[50] a fact reflected in Figure 11–1. The disposition toward violence is also associated with those Blacks who are intensely dissatisfied, feel powerless to change their posi-

[46] E. Franklin Frazier, *Negro Youth at the Crossways* (Washington, D.C.: American Council on Education, 1940), 52.

[47] Johnson, *Patterns of Negro Segregation, op. cit.,* 302.

[48] Robert Johnson, "Negro Reactions to Minority Group Status," in Milton L. Barron, ed., *American Minorities* (New York: Alfred A. Knopf, Inc., 1957), 201.

[49] Marx, *op. cit.,* 186, and Johnson, *Patterns of Negro Segregation,* 310.

[50] Angus Campbell and Howard Schuman, *Racial Attitudes in Fifteen American Cities* (Washington, D.C.: U.S. Government Printing Office, 1968), 56.

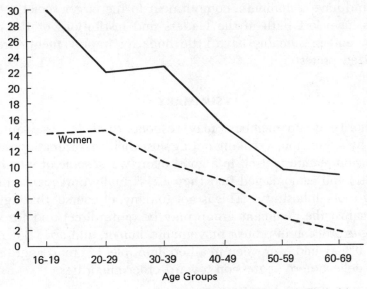

a. Percentage saying readiness to use violence is way to gain Black rights.

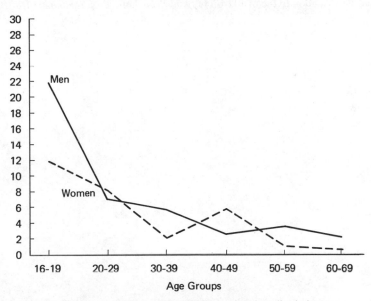

b. Percentage saying violence should be used against discriminatory
   shopkeeper if other methods fail.

Fig. 11–1. Relations of Age and Sex on Willingness To Employ Violence
(based on a survey of the perceptions and attitudes of Blacks in 15 major cities,
conducted on behalf of the National Advisory Commission on Civil Disorders).
Source: Angus Campbell and Howard Schuman, *Racial Attitudes in Fifteen
American Cities* (Washington, D.C.: U. S. Government Printing Office, 1968),
Figures V–a and V–c, page 56.

tion, and have a minimum commitment to the larger society; these Blacks have lost faith in the leaders and institutions of the community and presumably have little hope for improvement through organized protest.[51]

SUMMARY

Minority group members may respond to their disadvantaged status by aggression, a striking out against their subordinate position. Aggression manifests itself in a good many ways, some of which are so subtle and camouflaged that they are virtually unrecognizable as having roots in hostility. This is not to deny, of course, that aggression against the dominant group may be quite direct and forceful, finding expression in protest movements, humor, and art. But more subtly it may find expression in a hoodlum role, in-group aggression, or the deflection of aggression toward other minorities.

[51] H. Edward Ransford, "Isolation, Powerlessness, and Violence: A Study of Attitudes and Participation in the Watts Riot," *American Journal of Sociology,* 73 (1968), 581–591.

12

Responding by Assimilation

We noted earlier that avoidance may be viewed as the polar opposite of assimilation, and aggression as the polar opposite of acceptance. These two continua pose choices that confront a minority individual within an intergroup situation. First, he must either allow intergroup contact to take place or he must avoid (or, at least minimize) such contact. Second, once in the contact situation, he must either acquiesce in his subordinate status or strike out against it. Thus far we have considered acceptance and aggression. In this chapter we shall consider assimilation as a reaction to dominance. Much of our treatment will entail a consideration of Blacks, as the evidence is more extensive here than for perhaps any other minority.

As we noted in Chapter 9, assimilation is a process whereby groups with diverse ways of thinking, feeling, and acting become fused together in a social unity and a common culture. However, in contrast with Chapter 9, where we examined assimilation broadly as an *intergroup* process, in this chapter we shall consider assimilation more narrowly focusing not so much upon the interplay between dominant and minority individuals as upon the minority group itself. Hence, this chapter shall consider an approach or orientation found among some minority individuals that is characterized by a desire to lose their minority group identity and to become socially and culturally fused with the dominant group.

EUROPEAN IMMIGRANT GROUPS

Viewed over the long run, European immigrant groups within the United States have generally oriented themselves toward an assimilationist goal. Usually acculturation—alterations in a group's cultural practices in the direction of the dominant Anglo-American pattern—has proceeded more rapidly than integration—alterations in a group's network of formal and informal social relationships (in brief, in-group ties have tended to display greater strength than customs). Perhaps an actual case, that of the assimilation of southern Italians, may prove helpful. Certainly of the "new immigrants" —those arriving after 1880—the Italians deserve special emphasis. They constitute the second-largest ethnic group within the United States, nearly 5 million Italians having migrated to this nation since 1820. Their recorded immigration is exceeded only by that of the Germans. Today there are within the United States some 4.5 million individuals who were born in Italy or had at least one Italian-born parent. The peak years of the Italian immigration were 1907 and 1913. The pre-World War I migration, which had reached 300,000 in a single year, was reduced to 5,807 by the quota system of 1924 (although special laws often admitted more than twice as many non-quota immigrants). Prior to 1900, Italians from northern provinces represented more than two-thirds of the total migrants from Italy. By the time of the quota law, four-fifths of all the Italians within the United States were from southern Italy, a fourth of these being from Sicily.[1]

Background of Southern Italian Immigrants

The Italians from southern Italy and Sicily came from an agrarian, small-village background. In their native land the lot of the peasants had been one of economic hardship. The soil was not especially fertile and rainfall was inadequate. Remnants of the feudal order persisted, and the peasant renter often received little to support his family. Onerous mortgage debts, usurious interest, exploitation by landlords, and unemployment were among the hardships that made America seem attractive by comparison. The people were largely illiterate and ridden by superstition. Christianity had become in-

---

[1] Joseph Velikonja, "Italian Immigrants in the United States in the Mid-Sixties," *The International Migration Review,* 1 (1967), 25–37, and R. A. Schermerhorn, *These Our People* (Boston: D. C. Heath & Co., 1949), 235.

stituted by decree rather than conviction, and numerous ancient religious practices persisted, often taken over bodily into Catholic practice with little modification.[2]

The individual was closely and intimately linked with his family. The *famiglia*, the large family, included both blood relatives and in-laws up to the fourth degree. Family allegiance, solidarity, and affection were stressed. The *famiglia* represented a world within a world, in which obligation to family members was absolute. Outside of the family was a world of "strangers," and a benevolent act performed for a non-family member was often considered as a weak-headed deed. The individual's responsiblity was to his family rather than to the community, and friendships outside of the family generally were not intimate. To the South Italian, the government and everyone else outside his little village was suspect. For the most part, the Italian family was patriarchal, the men exercising authority. Nevertheless, the mother enjoyed a powerful position.[3]

Early Adjustments to American Life

By the turn of the twentieth century, the frontier and free lands had virtually vanished from the American scene. It was largely this fact that accounted for the settlement of the southern Italians within urban communities, especially those in the Northeast and on the Atlantic seaboard. New York City became the largest center of Italians in the United States, for that matter in the world, Rome not excluded. The introduction of the Italians to American life took place under difficult circumstances. In the cities they suffered from low wages, irregular and unskilled employment, child and woman labor, and poor housing in slum tenements. They were found in large numbers in the "sweatshops" of New York City; some earned their living as peddlers of vegetables and as pushcart vendors; and many others found work on the railroads, where they succeeded the Irish laborers.

In the earlier years of the immigration, males highly predominated among the migrants. Lacking relatives or friends in the United States and unfamiliar with the language, money, and customs, the

---

[2] *Ibid.*, 242.
[3] *Ibid.*, 237–240. Also see: Nathan Glazer and Daniel P. Moynihan, *Beyond the Melting Pot* (Boston: The M.I.T. Press and Harvard University Press, 1963), 194–198; and Edward C. Banfield, *The Moral Basis of a Backward Society* (New York: The Free Press of Glencoe, 1950).

migrants frequently secured employment through an intermediary the *padrone*. The *padrone* was usually an Italian who already "knew the ropes" and who found jobs for his fellow countrymen. Similarly he often made arrangements for room and board, banking, and other services. In some cases the *padrone* contracted for the labor of men in the old country and arranged for their passage to the United States. By virture of the *padrone's* position and the ignorance of the immigrants, exploitation was not unusual.[4]

Many of the men had expectations of returning to Italy once they had amassed sufficient funds for realizing a "comfortable" existence in their homeland. An appreciable number managed to return, but, for the most part, circumstances did not permit the great majority to do so.[5] Accordingly, it became a common custom for those in America to send for other members of their families in order to have as many of them together as possible. With the passing of time, the Italian communities in American cities were characterized by poly-nucleated groups with one street made up of villagers from a hamlet in Avellino, still another from a community in Basilicata, and so on.

In many cases, immigrants came from parts of Italy in which Italian nationalism had not yet taken firm hold. Many tended to think of themselves in terms of a section, province, or town. But in America, their circle of friends from the old area was too small to be self-sustaining. Moreover, members of the dominant group, con-fused by the multiplicity of place names, and accustomed to think-ing in national terms, tended to refer to them not by region—the region being unfamiliar—but rather by nation (Italy). Within the Italian-American community, collective action of any sort—social club, burial society, politics—was more effective if undertaken not by the people from this or that province, but by "Italians." But the "sense" had been generated in the United States. Immigrants from provincial and rural areas became conscious of their "national origin" only after a few years in the States. Indeed, Italian-Ameri-can immigrant organizations sometimes used their influence to trig-ger nationalistic movements in the Old Country.[6]

To a considerable degree, the immigrants were insulated from the larger American society. It was not unusual to find the dialect,

4 Glazer and Moynihan, *op. cit.*, 190–191.
5 Schermerhorn, *op. cit.*, 246–247.
6 Stuart Levine, "The Indian as American," *Midcontinent American Studies Jour-nal,* 6 (1965), 10.

cooking habits, and religious practices of the old country continuing without an appreciable break. "Little Italys" enabled the immigrants to cushion the shock of adjusting from a rural to an urban and from a foreign to an American society. By the same token the "Little Italys" offered them some shelter from the hostility and antagonism of the native Americans who viewed them as "wops," "dagos," and "guineas." [7] Yet it should not be overlooked that "Little Italys" seldom contained solidly Italian neighborhoods—indeed, it was unusual for the Italian population density to exceed 50 or 60 per cent. This mixing of nationalities made inevitable innumerable contacts with non-Italian peoples. And as a result, neither the Italian community nor its institutions were fully Italian in character; nor were they American.[8]

Mutual-aid societies, organized to reduce the ever-present risks of sickness, accident, and death, sprang up by the hundreds. In time their functions were broadened to include social activities; group mergers designed to overcome financial weakness contributed to an increase in their size and a decrease in their number. The Order of Sons of Italy of America, The Venetian Fraternal Order, and the Italo-American National Union were among the better-known fraternal insurance organizations. Similarly, a considerable number of Italian newspapers grew up within the United States. As late as World War II, there were some 130 Italian newspapers in this country, most of them weeklies. The press served as a kind of crutch for immigrants having difficulties in adapting to their new surroundings or those unable to break away from homeland traditions.[9]

Italian immigrants gained notoriety among Anglicized Americans (and the wrath of social workers) because their children were often not permitted to obtain adequate schooling. While complaining that their own lack of education kept them from getting better jobs, parents nonetheless sent their offspring out to work in order to supplement family income. Although in time most Italians complied with minimum requirements of compulsory education laws, they encouraged their children to take jobs after school hours. When Italian children reached the legal withdrawal age of fourteen, not infrequently they were withdrawn from school and put to work.[10]

[7] Schermerhorn, op. cit., 248.
[8] Humbert S. Nelli, "Italians in Urban America: A Study in Ethnic Adjustment," The International Migration Review, 1 (1967), 41 and 46.
[9] Ibid., 46–52, and Schermerhorn, op. cit., 249–252.
[10] Nelli, op. cit., 53.

Yet despite dire predictions that Italians were caught in a "cycle of poverty," by the early 1900s they had begun progressing from unskilled labor into commercial, trade, and professional classes, including printing, bricklaying, carpentering, import and export, banking, law, and medicine. Notwithstanding the complaints of reformers and the laments of social workers, financial success at this time did not absolutely require education; ambition and cunning could, and did, overcome the handicaps associated with illiteracy. Crime—one means of economic advancement independent of education, social background, or political connections—provided an avenue for quick and substantial monetary gain and at times social and political advancement as well. In time the "syndicate" (the Mafia), an illegal business operation reaping vast profits from the American community, offered almost limitless opportunities for a measure of upward social mobility. As a consequence, many Americans came to believe that Italians were "natural criminals" much in the same manner that the Irish were "natural politicians" (yet a comparison of Irish experiences in other parts of the world would have challenged this belief—Irish immigrants and their children, for instance, did not achieve political successes in London, Liverpool, or other English and Scotch cities comparable to their achievements in the States). The prominence of Italians in crime was due primarily to availability of opportunity rather than "inborn" characteristics, much in the fashion of Irish pre-eminence in political life and Jewish prominence in the clothing industry.[11]

The Children of Southern Italian Immigrants

For a large part of each day, the children of the immigrant Italians were immersed within the mainstream of American life by the public-school system. From their teachers and school companions they learned to esteem American ways and to look down upon Italian ways as "foreign" and "undesirable." They often developed contempt for their parents as stupid, "greenhorns," and unknowing of American ways. A conflict ensued within the families between two ways of life, the one American, the other Italian. Considerable misunderstanding and frustration existed between the parents and the children and threatened to destroy family stability. The children frequently expressed American values and expectations and attempted to transmit them to the family situation. On the other

[11] *Ibid.,* 53–54.

hand, the parents sought to reinforce the pattern of the old-country peasant family.[12]

Child, in a study of the Italian colony in New Haven prior to World War II, distinguishes three types of reaction among American-born children of Italian parents to their situation: the *rebel*, the *in-group*, and the *apathetic*.[13] The *rebels* responded by revolting against their parents and the old traditions. They wished to be considered Americans and attempted to dissociate themselves from everything Italian. In contrast, the *in-groupers* strongly identified themselves with Italian symbols and traits and sought to shun American ways. They preferred membership in the Italian sub-community to full participation in the larger American society. The *apathetic* group attempted to retreat from the stresses and strains of conflicts arising from the counter-pulls of the two ways of life. They undertook to avoid situations where nationality would be emphasized, and they minimized their membership within the Italian group. They attempted to get along both with the older generation and with their American associates, but their dual status often posed problems for them.

Acculturation of Southern Italian Immigrants

Today the families of the American-born children of southern-Italian immigrants tend to approximate the urban American family type. From the patriarchal, folk-peasant-type family of the Italian peasant, they have shifted toward the democratic and highly individualized pattern. Family solidarity has been increasingly undermined, and the small-family system—as opposed to the peasant large-family system—has come to prevail. Where previously the focus had been upon children living for their parents, among the American-born the situation has been reversed with the parents living for children. Families have become small in contrast to the relatively large families of the Italian immigrants. The age at marriage has risen; mates are no longer selected by parents; dowry rights are unrecognized; and a growing number of marriages are taking place outside of the Italian and Catholic groups. Few magical and superstitious notions persist in connection with pregnancy; during illness, increasing reliance is placed on physicians and specialists. Breast-

---

[12] Paul J. Campisi, "Ethnic Family Patterns: The Italian Family in the United States," *American Journal of Sociology*, LIII (1948), 443–449.

[13] Irvin L. Child, *Italian or American?* (New Haven: Yale University Press, 1943).

feeding of infants is now rare, and birth control is the rule. The value of chastity has declined; chaperonage is no longer practiced; and divorce has become permissible.[14] Italian names are slowly being Anglicized, while second-generation children named Giuseppe by their parents introduce themselves as Joseph and give only the English name to their children. A number of Italian patterns, however, have survived, the most visible ones being food habits. Nonetheless, the food is milder and less spicy than that eaten by their parents.

In a like fashion, acculturation occurred in the religious sphere. Italian newcomers found the Roman Catholic Church in America to be a cold and puritanical organization, controlled and operated by Irish clergy. Many churchmen feared that the degree and prevalence of immigrant antagonism toward the Church posed a serious threat to its future in the United States. This antagonism, however, has waned among the second and third generations. Indeed, the Italians of the second and third generations closely approximate the Irish in their attitudes toward parish priests and in their participation in parish activities. Unaccustomed to church donations and collections in Italy where the church was state-supported, the first generation contributed little to church support; the second generation, in contrast, seemingly has adopted the Irish pattern of generous support, a pattern continued by the third generation. Similarly, a considerable increase has occurred among third generation Italians in Catholic school enrollment.[15] As regards religious practices among Italian-Americans, the evidence is in keeping with the general finding of Lenski's Detroit study, namely, increasing church attendance among immigrant groups is associated with increasing Americanization.[16] Overall, then, acculturation has almost completely eroded Italian cultural patterns among the second generation, and is likely to erase the rest in the third generation.[17]

[14] Campisi, op. cit. Also see: Bartolomeo J. Palisi, "Ethnic Generation and Family Structure," Journal of Marriage and the Family, 28 (1966), 49–50; and Michael Lalli, "The Italian-American Family: Assimilation and Change, 1900–1965," The Family Coordinator, 18 (January, 1969), 44–48.

[15] Nelli, op. cit., 47–49, and Nicholas John Russo, "Three Generations of Italians in New York City: Their Religious Acculturation," The International Migration Review, 3 (1969), 3–17.

[16] Gerhard Lenski, The Religious Factor, rev. ed. (Garden City, N.Y.: Doubleday & Co., 1963).

[17] Herbert J. Gans, The Urban Villagers (New York: The Free Press of Glencoe, Inc., 1962), 32–34.

Integration of Southern Italian Immigrants

Integration—the disappearance of the Italian social system—has proceeded much more slowly than acculturation. Gans, in a study of an Italian section in Boston, notes:

> Indeed, the social structure of the West End . . . is still quite similar to that of the first generation. Social relationships are almost entirely liimted to other Italians, because much sociability is based on kinship, and because most friendships are made in childhood, and are thus influenced by residential propinquity. Intermarriage with non-Italians is unusual among the second-generation, and is not favored by the third. As long as both parties are Catholic, however, disapproval is mild.[18]

Glazer and Moynihan, in their study of New York City ethnic groups, make a similar observation about that city's Italians:

> Nor are these old Italian neighborhoods only shells of their former selves, inhabited exclusively by the older people. Many of the married sons and daughters have stayed close to their parents. Even the trek to the suburbs, when it does occur among Italians, is very often a trek of families of two generations, rather than simply of the young. And it is striking how the old neighborhoods have been artfully adapted to a higher standard of living rather than simply deserted, as they would have been by other groups, in more American style.[19]

This pattern—a lag of integration behind acculturation—has also been common among many other European immigrant groups.

PASSING

Undoubtedly one of the most complete forms of assimilation is leaving the minority group and "passing" as a member of the dominant group. This adjustment is a feasible alternative for those minority-group members who physically and culturally resemble the dominant group. The task is not particularly difficult for a German immigrant who decides to Anglicize his name and to become an Episcopalian rather than a Lutheran. Nevertheless, language accents, cultural differences, and community knowledge of his family background may in part frustrate his efforts. Still, his attempt to identify himself with the dominant group may meet with little resistance, in fact it may be actually welcomed by the larger community as part of a process of Americanization.

As the position of the racial or ethnic minority declines in relation

[18] *Ibid.*, 35.
[19] Glazer and Moynihan, *op. cit.*, 187.

to the social distance scale of the larger community, the possibility of successful passing becomes more difficult, especially when physical or cultural differences are discernible. Nevertheless, some minority-group members may succeed in the endeavor, as in the following case:

> I was a Jew, until a few years ago. Now, I am not!
>
> Many of you, the Jews whom I address, as well as many gentiles, may scoff at the notion of a Jew ever becoming a non-Jew. And my former people may blame me bitterly for changing.
>
> Fortunately, I cannot be reached. I have changed my name. I have changed my work. I have moved into a strange region and started afresh. My past is as finally sealed as though I had died and arisen with a new personality—for it is really necessary that a Jew change some important parts of his personality when he throws off his Jewishness.[20]

He changed his name and claimed to be descended from non-Jewish Adrianople Turks. He went west and "tried a variety of callings, but shunned the Jewish favorites." He later entered a western university and married. "I am now raising children who need never learn to endure snubs, who will never be tempted to retaliate against cruel discrimination. From this pleasant sunshine, I look back with horror at the somber world in which my race-proud kin persist on their ancient and unhappy course."

Broom, Beem, and Harris studied the characteristics of more than 1,000 persons in Los Angeles County who had petitioned to change their names. Although Jews constituted only 6 per cent of the population, 46 per cent of those petitioning to change their names were of Jewish origin. In comparison with non-Jewish petitioners, the Jewish group had a significantly higher percentage of foreign-born, married males, children included in the petition, older males, and residents in areas of high social rank and urbanization. The researchers concluded that the change in names probably represented a change in self-definition and group identification, especially by those who regarded their membership in the Jewish group as a barrier to further upward mobility.[21]

Where a sharp line is drawn on the basis of color, as in the case of Blacks, passing is open to only a small proportion. For those possessing light skin coloring and relatively Caucasian and non-Negroid

[20] Anonymous, "I Was a Jew," *Forum*, 103 (January, 1940), 8–9. Quoted by Brewton Berry, *Race and Ethnic Relations* (Boston: Houghton Mifflin Co., 1958), 489–490.

[21] Leonard Broom, Helen P. Beem, and Virginia Harris, "Characteristics of 1,108 Petitioners for Change of Name," *American Sociological Review*, 20 (1955), 33–39.

hair texture and facial characteristics, it is a feasible alternative. How many Blacks pass permanently into the White group? Estimates range from a few thousand to tens of thousands annually within the United States. But, since present methods of making such estimates are quite inadequate, the actual number is not known. Blacks and passers themselves are reluctant to give information about those who pass, and census data and vital statistics are too inaccurate to catch discrepancies from one period to another.

Seldom do people, regardless of the extent of their White features, grow up as Black and then suddenly make an intellectual decision to pass. Rather it is a step-by-step process in which emotional ties to the Black group are severed and new relationships with Whites achieved. Passing may initially be of the unintentional variety, but the realization that one can pass for White may lead to more adventurous passing for convenience or employement. As intimate relationships are established with White friends and fellow workers, the individual tends to be drawn gradually farther and farther away from his emotional attachments to the Black community. The final break comes when the irritations of trying to remain Black and the attractiveness of the White world outweigh his inner agitation.[22]

Some writers also attempt to explain why many Blacks who can pass do not do so. Among the factors frequently cited are these: (1) fear and anxiety concerning possible later exposure of Black identity; (2) race consciousness and pride; (3) loyalty to family and close friends; (4) a feeling of potential estrangement and loneliness as a White; (5) a perceived loss of status and esteem in the White world; (6) the considerable risks involved; and (7) a feeling that passing would entail too much well-thought-out and calculated planning.[23]

THE BLACK PROTEST—1955–1965: AGGRESSION–ASSIMILATION

As European immigrants to the United States became acculturated, they lost many of the identifying "marks" or "signs" that set them apart from the dominant group. By the second and third generations, their English was usually indistinguishable from that of other Americans, while their distinct ethnic mannerisms, dress, ges-

[22] St. Clair Drake and Horace R. Cayton, *Black Metropolis* (New York: Harcourt Brace Jovanovich, 1945), 166.

[23] James E. Conyers and T. H. Kennedy, "Negro Passing: To Pass or Not to Pass," *Phylon*, 24 (1963), 215–224.

tures, food habits, religious practices, and the like became less pronounced. In brief, their "visibility"—those conspicuous features differentiating them from the dominant group and so essential for maintaining in-group and out-group boundaries—became less apparent. Although integration generally proceeded less rapidly than acculturation, the slower pace of integration was in part the product of the immigrant group's own doing; many of its members simply preferred to make their own group the primary focus for their informal and formal social relationships.

American Blacks, however, have found themselves in somewhat different circumstances. Although for the most part culturally indistinguishable from dominant group Whites, the fact of race has served to make them quite visible. Barriers premised upon race pose major obstacles to Black integration. Yet despite experiencing persistent discrimination and segregation, evidence suggests that a substantial majority of Black Americans share an integrationist outlook—the goal of an open society.[24]

Blocked in realizing their integrationist aspirations, some Blacks responded with a social movement designed to break down the walls that barred them from full and equal participation within American life, a response reflected in the Niagara Movement in 1905 (which culminated in 1910 in the formation of the National Association for the Advancement of Colored People [NAACP]) and in the Southern Christian Leadership Conference (identified with the leadership of the late Rev. Martin Luther King, Jr.). This represented a combined *aggression–assimilation* response. It constituted a striking out against—a protest against—minority status; yet it also represented an assimilationist response reflecting a strong integrationist orientation.

The Aims of the Black Protest—1955–1965

The Black protest movement that unfolded in the 1950s and the early 1960s was not so much directed against major deprivations inherent in the American social system as against relative depriva-

---

[24] A 1965 *Newsweek* poll, undertaken by public-opinion analyst Louis Harris, showed that by 6 to 1 Blacks wanted integrated schools and by 10 to 3 preferred racially mixed to all-Black neighborhoods. "The Negro in America—1965," *Newsweek*, February 15, 1965, 24–28. A comparable 1969 poll conducted by The Gallup Organization for the same magazine revealed that 78 per cent of Blacks would rather send children to an integrated school and 74 per cent would rather live in an integrated neighborhood. "Angry—But They Still Have A Dream," *Newsweek*, June 30, 1969, 20.

tions or inequalities that Blacks experience as American citizens. One sociologist, writing in 1965 and prior to the emergence of the slogan "Black Power," observed of the movement:

> . . . its grand strategy is designed to achieve goals and effectuate values that are already acknowledged to be inherent in a political democracy and which are firmly established in our national culture. Consequently, Negro protest leaders do not advocate the overthrow of constitutional laws, changing the basic structure of our republican form of government, rearrangement of the American class structure, or the establishment of new political, economic, and ethical goals. Instead—except for a small extremist element—the Negro protest, itself, is a clear endorsement of the "American Creed" and a re-affirmation of the faith which the great majority of Negroes have in the essential goodness of the individual and in the democratic process.[25]

Yet in some respects, even in this early period, the Black protest resembled more typical revolutions. Its stressed direct action (demonstrations, sit-ins, boycotts, and the like), possessed broad objectives (the elimination of the segregated order), and entailed a genuine *mass* movement. And like revolutionary movements, it achieved a heightened militancy and urgency, a sense that "even yesterday was too late."[26]

Nevertheless, in a technical sense, this Black protest constituted a reform and not a revolutionary movement. As Pettigrew noted at the time:

> It aims to modify, not to overturn, the society it confronts; it seeks to amend, not to ravage. Negro Americans are so firmly rooted in and shaped by their land that their . . . [movement] is attempting merely to guarantee full participation in the society as it otherwise exists. In short, they do not wish to deprecate or destroy that which they wish to join.[27]

The "Old" and "New" Protests

A good many Blacks have always resented the disadvantaged and subordinate status assigned them in American society. However, they have been unable to do much about it, at least until recently, because they have been virtually powerless. Hence, acceptance in large measure constituted the principal Black reaction to dominance. Yet, even so, the decades have witnessed at least periodic ripples of Black protest. During slavery, over 200 slave plots and revolts were

[25] Daniel C. Thompson, "The Rise of the Negro Protest," *The Annals of the American Academy of Political and Social Science*, 357 (1965), 20.

[26] Thomas F. Pettigrew, *A Profile of the Negro American* (New York: Van Nostrand Reinhold Co., 1964), 193.

[27] *Ibid.*

recorded.[28] The Civil War and Reconstruction brought new strivings among segments of the Black population for equality, but these were crushed with the overthrow of the Reconstructionist regimes and more particularly by the evolution of a Jim Crow system in the 1890s.[29]

The twentieth century witnessed the formation of a number of civil rights organizations, the most important of which was the National Association for the Advancement of Colored People. The NAACP established a legal redress committee soon after its founding, and it won some important legal victories even in its early days —beginning with the Supreme Court decision against the "grandfather clauses" in 1915. It was this highly developed, selectively applied, legalistic approach on the part of the NAACP that led to the Supreme Court's overthrow in 1954 of the legal foundation of segregation. Yet it was an approach that entailed "tokenism"—a small gain here, and a small gain there involving usually a White university, park, or other public facility, railroad pullman cars, and the like, gains frequently realized by middle class Blacks *for* middle class Blacks and having little implications for the great mass of American Blacks. For the most part, the great majority of Blacks were merely spectators during the legal battle; extensive support in the local community was not needed since one or a few plaintiffs were sufficient to enable the NAACP lawyers to launch their legal attack and to pursue their strategy until at least a token victory was won.[30]

The Black protest of the 1960s is to be distinguished from these earlier protest activities in a number of respects: (1) the shift from primarily legal and educational means of protest to direct action (demonstrations, boycotts, sit-ins, wade-ins, and the like); (2) the shift in initiative from the hands of a relatively few professional desegregationists (e.g., NAACP lawyers and officials) to a large number of average citizens who were willing to confront the segregated system through direct action; (3) the broadening of objectives from a narrow attack upon a particular public facility (e.g., a particular

[28] Herbert Aptheker, *American Negro Slave Revolts* (New York: Columbia University Press, 1943), 162.

[29] C. Vann Woodward, *The Strange Career of Jim Crow*, rev. ed. (New York: Oxford University Press, 1957). See Chapter 15 of this textbook for a summary of Woodward's work dealing with the rise of Jim Crow.

[30] Lewis M. Killian, "Community Structure and the Role of the Negro Leader-Agent," *Sociological Inquiry*, 35 (1965), 73.

school, recreational center, etc.) to a full-scale attack against the entire segregated order; and (4) the expansion of the movement to assume a *mass* character that cut across divisions in the Black community and reached from coast-to-coast.[31]

The Montgomery Bus Boycott

The Montgomery bus boycott (1955–1956) marked a turning point in the Black protest movement. Here the narrowly circumscribed boundaries of legalistic tactics were broken, and large numbers of Blacks in Montgomery became active participants in the civil rights struggle. The Montgomery movement constituted a spontaneous confrontation of the White community by an aggrieved and aroused Black community. With Montgomery the Black protest moved from selective attack to mass confrontation.[32]

The Montgomery movement incorporated many specific tactics —mass meetings, nonviolent techniques, mass boycotts, and legal-judiciary measures—that became "standard operating procedures" for the civil rights movement of the 1960s. The success of the Montgomery movement projected upon the national horizon a new group of militant Black leaders represented by the late Rev. Martin Luther King, Jr.

The Montgomery movement was precipitated by an incident that occurred on December 1, 1955. Mrs. Rosa Parks, a forty-two-year-old Black seamstress employed at a downtown department store, was returning home in the evening on a city bus. At one stop, several white passengers boarded the bus, whereupon the driver instructed four Blacks to stand so that the Whites might sit. The bus driver was acting within his rights as prescribed by Alabama law. Three of the Blacks complied with the driver's instructions, but Mrs. Parks refused. The bus driver called a policeman, and Mrs. Parks was charged with violating the bus segregation law.

Word of Mrs. Parks's arrest spread throughout the Black community. Talk was heard among some rowdy elements of initiating physical reprisals against Montgomery bus drivers. But a non-violent direction was given to resentment by a group of Black ministers who called a one-day boycott of the buses for the day of the trial.

[31] See: James H. Laue, "The Changing Character of the Negro Protest," *The Annals of the American Academy of Political and Social Science*, 357 (1965), 119–126, and Pettigrew, *op. cit.*, 192–193.

[32] Killian, *op. cit.*, 73.

The protest plans received wide dissemination through announce-
ments at Black church services and through news stories carried in
the Montgomery press. On December 5, the day of the trial, a very
high percentage of Blacks, perhaps as many as 75 per cent of the
usual riders, stayed off the buses. Since Blacks represented about
70 per cent of the company's passengers, the protest was noticeable.

Mrs. Parks was fined $10 and $4 in costs. That evening a mass
meeting was held in the local Holt Street Baptist Church. Some
5,000 Blacks, including 47 ministers, and 1 White minister of a
Black congregation were present. The crowd engaged in hymn
singing and listened to attacks upon the Jim Crow system. A resolution was adopted continuing the bus boycott until such time as
city and bus-company officials would agree to (1) more courteous
treatment of Blacks, (2) seating on a first-come-first-serve basis, and
(3) the employment of Black bus drivers on predominantly Black
runs. The Montgomery Improvement Association was formed and
Rev. Martin Luther King, Jr., was elected chairman. Twenty-seven
years of age, King had secured his doctorate in religion from Boston
University prior to becoming pastor of Montgomery's Dexter Avenue
Baptist Church.

The Montgomery Improvement Association set up a car pool to
get Blacks to work. Unsigned and unidentified schedules were
posted on telephone poles and the sides of buildings. The city police responded to this challenge by becoming especially zealous in
enforcing traffic laws, attempting in this manner to interfere with
the operation through harassment.

Montgomery White leaders expected the movement to collapse.
But the boycott continued into 1956 with considerable effectiveness
—roughly 80 per cent of the usual Black riders stayed off the buses.
Exasperated, Montgomery Mayor W. A. Gayle issued a statement
on January 23 announcing that he and members of the city commission had joined the Citizens Councils, the militant White segregationist group. He stated that Montgomery Whites had "pussy-
footed around on this boycott long enough."

Within a month of Mayor Gayle's announcement of his intention
to take firm action, a grand jury returned indictments against some
ninety Blacks including twenty-four ministers. The action was taken
under an almost forgotten anti-labor law enacted in 1921. Blacks
were angered by this development, but King cautioned, "Even if
we are arrested every day, let no man drag you so low as to hate."

Despite police harassment, the boycott continued. The NAACP, at the request of Montgomery Blacks, undertook legal action challenging the legality of bus segregation in Alabama. During 1956 the case moved through the federal courts. On November 13, 1956, the United States Supreme Court upheld a lower federal court's ruling that invalidated the Alabama law and the city ordinance requiring bus segregation. The following evening some 2,000 Montgomery Blacks held another mass meeting and voted to end the eleven month-old boycott as soon as the Supreme Court's decree was delivered to Montgomery. This occurred on December 21, 1956. Once again Blacks rode Montgomery buses, but no longer on a segregated basis.

After Montgomery

The sit-ins of 1960 (see Chapter 6) unleashed the Black protest on a national scale. Cities across the nation—both North and South—became the scene for demonstrations, boycotts, sit-ins, and the like. In the course of these developments, the late Rev. Martin Luther King, Jr., and his associates evolved a fourfold set of tactics which King explained in these terms:

1. Nonviolent demonstrators go into the streets to exercise their constitutional rights.
2. Racists resist by unleashing violence against them.
3. Americans of conscience in the name of decency demand federal intervention and legislation.
4. The Administration, under mass pressure, initiates measures of immediate intervention and remedial legislation.[33]

In brief, Blacks needed "a crisis to bargain with"—and hence often had to create a crisis.

This fourfold strategy was effectively employed to secure passage of the Civil Rights Acts of 1964 and 1965. In the spring of 1963, Rev. King took the civil rights fight to Birmingham, Alabama, alleged to be the most segregated large city in the South, saying, "As Birmingham goes, so goes the whole South." He organized a siege of demonstrations against that city's segregation barriers (the first step). Over 3,000 Birmingham Blacks were arrested, while newspapers, magazines, and television stations beamed to the nation pictures of Blacks facing snarling police dogs and being bowled over

---

[33] Martin Luther King, Jr., "Behind the Selma March," *Saturday Review of Literature,* April 3, 1965, 16.

by high-pressure fire hoses (the second step). Although little was accomplished in Birmingham itself, the civil rights issue quickly became the number-one topic not just in the South, but over the entire nation (the third step). Demonstrations quickly spread across the nation, some 1,122 being recorded within a four-month period. The demonstrations culminated in August 28, 1963, in the "March on Washington" in which some 200,000 civil rights marchers demonstrated "for jobs and freedom." The wave of demonstrations spurred the Kennedy Administration to sponsor new civil rights legislation, legislation that was passed by Congress the following year (the fourth step).

The same strategy was employed in 1965 when many Black leaders became convinced that a much more stringent law was needed to protect Black voting rights. This time King took his campaign to Selma, Alabama. On Sunday, March 7th, some 520 Blacks prepared to march from Selma to Montgomery, the state capital, to dramatize their case to the nation (the first step). Television cameras recorded this scene: as the Blacks, marching two abreast, reached the Pettus Bridge crossing the Alabama River, Alabama state troopers unleashed a savage attack against the marchers with billy clubs and gas grenades (the second step). The nation was collectively outraged at this brutality. Soon thousands of sympathizers were bound for Selma, and the national spotlight was again focused upon the civil rights issue (the third step). The Johnson Administration responded with the Civil Rights Act of 1965 (the fourth step). Selma was the last of the classic southern nonviolent campaigns, and was followed two months later by Watts (the 1965 Los Angeles ghetto riot).

In the Montgomery and post-Montgomery civil rights movement, the late Rev. Martin Luther King, Jr., enjoyed a preeminent position among Black leaders—in both 1963 and 1966, for instance, some 88 per cent of Blacks approved of his leadership.[34] During this period he served for Blacks and Whites alike as the symbol of the direct action movement. King's influence and popularity centered on the fact that better than any other spokesman, he articulated the aspirations of Blacks; they responded to the cadence of his addresses, his religious phraseology and manner of speaking, and the vision of his dream for them and America. He intuitively adopted the style of the old fashioned Black preacher and restored oratory to its place

[34] William Brink and Louis Harris, *Black and White* (New York: Simon & Schuster, 1966), 54.

among the arts. Further, he effectively communicated Black aspirations to White America. His religious terminology and use of Christian symbols of love and nonviolence were reassuring to White America. In many ways, King gave the feeling to Whites that he was their good friend and posed no threat to them. He combined militancy with conservatism and caution and with a willingness to negotiate and bargain with White House emissaries. King, then, epitomized conservative militancy.[35]

Factors Underlying the Black Protest

We have noted that in the period between the overthrow of Reconstruction and the 1950s, the principal response of Blacks to their minority status was that of acceptance. This changed, however, during the 1950s and early 1960s as a number of forces were at work that made Blacks susceptible to a protest or militant approach against racial segregation. Let us examine a few of these factors.

, **An Emergent, New Black Self-Image.** Heightened Black self-respect and identity acted as a powerful stimulus to the protest movement. This improved Black self-image was partially fostered by an emergent redefinition of the Black's status within American life. The Supreme Court in particular played an important role in this development. The net effect of the Supreme Court's desegregation decisions was to advance in an authoritative, formal, and official fashion a new definition of the Black as a first-class citizen. In its 1954 school ruling, the Supreme Court overturned the "separate but equal" doctrine formulated in 1896 in *Plessy* v. *Ferguson*, a decision that had relegated Blacks to second-class citizenship and gave legal sanction to a segregated racial order.[36] Presidential statements and Congressional enactment of new civil rights laws reinforced the effect of the Supreme Court's decisions.

These developments were closely associated with another important stimulus to an improved Black self-image, the emergence of the new nations of Africa. Rev. Martin Luther King, Jr. observed:

. . . today he [the Black] looks beyond the borders of his own land and sees the decolonization and liberation of Africa and Asia; he sees colored

---

[35] August Meier, "On the Role of Martin Luther King," *New Politics*, 4 (1965), 52–59.

[36] James W. Vander Zanden, "The Non-Violent Resistance Movement Against Segregation," *American Journal of Sociology*, 68 (1963), 544–545.

peoples, yellow, black and brown, ruling over their own new nations. He sees colored statesmen voting on vital issues at the United Nations. . . .[37]

Such developments as these contributed to a new Black self-image in which accommodation no longer constituted for many Blacks an acceptable response to segregation. And the civil rights movement itself, once it got under way, offered a further impetus to heightened Black self-respect and identity.

The Anticipation of Victory.   Until the past decade, strong feelings of defeatism tended to characterize many Blacks. For those in the South in particular, the "road to a better life" appeared as an endless maze, with a mammoth White wall at every turn. Government officials, quasi-military personnel (e.g., the police), and business and educational leaders—in a word, the entire power structure— were usually lily-white. Concentrated largely in lower socioeconomic class positions many Blacks felt virtually powerless. The segregated order seemed impregnable. Indeed, segregation appeared to be—and in truth was—the "law of the land"; for example, the U.S. Army still had all-White and all-Black units at the time of the Korean War, *Plessy* v. *Ferguson* still had the force of law, and since the defeat of Reconstruction the nation had been more or less willing to allow the South a measure of sovereignty on the race issue. History reveals that movements for basic social change are unlikely to originate with people of despair. Demoralized people typically do not believe that an improved future is possible, and their sense of futility leads to apathy, not action, and to despair rather than demonstrations.[38]

In the 1950s, however, especially with the Supreme Court's 1954 school ruling, this picture was altered. The machinery and resources of the federal government became decisively committed for the first time since Reconstruction to an anti-segregation program. Where previously widespread despair and hopelessness prevailed, now the situation was progressively defined as one that could be altered. This prospect of victory created a climate conducive to struggle.[39]

A Sense of Relative Deprivation.   During World War II promotions were rapid and widespread in the Air Force and slow and piecemeal

[37] Martin Luther King, Jr., "Civil Right No. 1—The Right to Vote," *New York Times Magazine*, March 14, 1965, 26.

[38] Gary T. Marx, *Protest and Prejudice* (New York: Harper & Row, Inc., 1967), 85.

[39] Vander Zanden, *op. cit.*, 545.

in the Military Police. Most of us probably would be inclined to predict that the men in the Air Force would be more satisfied with their chances for promotion than the men in the Military Police since in absolute terms they were moving ahead faster in their careers. Yet research has demonstrated that the men in the Air Force were considerably more frustrated over promotions than those in the Military Police. Among the men in the Air Force it was not so much the *absolute* level of attainment that made for poor morale but a sense of *relative* deprivation—the dissatisfaction aroused by the discrepancy between what the Air Force men anticipated and what they attained. In contrast, the Military Police did not expect rapid promotions and they learned to live with relatively few advances in rank.[40]

In hindsight it is surprising that social scientists did not anticipate the Black protest. Yet at the time it was easy to conclude that Blacks should be more satisfied than in any previous time in American history: data revealed that employment opportunities for Blacks had gradually expanded, their median annual family income had increased 73 per cent between 1950 and 1960, and from 1940 to 1960 the number of Blacks who attended college had more than doubled. Yet many Blacks in 1960 found themselves in a position quite similar to the men in the Air Force. The prosperity of the World War II years and the 1950s gave Blacks a taste of "the good life," a taste of the affluent society. Blacks had gained enough to hope realistically for more. Hence barriers blocking their further advancement were felt as severely frustrating. Any number of observers have noted that revolutions are not made by persons who are utterly dispossessed and despairing, but by those who have already gained something, who hope for more, and who believe their aspirations to be legitimate and realistic.[41]

The mass media—radio, television, magazines, and the press—penetrate, indeed invade, the Black ghettos with the values and aspirations of the larger White-dominated society. Some nine out of ten Black homes have a TV set, and a TV set that juts out an

---

[40] Robert K. Merton and Alice S. Kitt, "Contributions to the Theory of Reference Group Behavior," in Robert K. Merton and Paul F. Lazarsfeld, eds., *Continuities in Social Research: Studies in the Scope and Method of "The American Soldier"* (New York: The Free Press of Glencoe, Inc., 1950).

[41] See, for example, Crane Brinton, *The Anatomy of Revolution* (Englewood Cliffs, N.J.: Prentice-Hall, Inc., 1952), 53; Eric Hoffer, *The True Believer* (New York: Harper & Row, Inc., 1951), 7; James C. Davies, "Toward a Theory of Revolution," *American Sociological Review*, 27 (1962), 5–19; and James A. Geschwender, "Social Structure and the Negro Revolt," *Social Forces*, 43 (1964), 248–256.

antenna that senses the White world and its ways as never before. Even a soap commercial can sow seeds of discontent if its setting is a modern suburban kitchen. Those who live in the congested Black ghettos of our large cities are aware that others are not so disadvantaged. The Black protest then has not so much been a product of despair as a protest fed by rising expectations. Indeed, recent surveys testify to the fact that most Blacks feel they are doing better than five years ago and expect to do even better all around five years from now.[42]

Yet Blacks face formidable obstacles and frustrating barriers in realizing their aspirations. If Blacks are to satisfy their expectations there must be a marked *closing* of the gap between Blacks and Whites as well as large *absolute* gains. At recent rates of change in the relative standing of Blacks, the income gap, as measured by the ratio of non-White to White median family income, would not close until 2410. And non-Whites would not attain equal proportional representation among clerical workers until 1992, among skilled workers until 2005, and among business managers and proprietors until 2730.[43] A sharpening Black awareness of these Black–White differentials—of the considerable and continuing gap between Blacks and Whites in education, jobs, and income—accentuates this sense of relative deprivation.

Additional Factors. We have examined a number of factors that made Blacks increasingly susceptible to the protest orientation. Still other factors were also at work. Among these we might note the "piling up" of Blacks in urban ghettos where communication and social movements can spread rapidly; the assumption by the movement during Rev. King's leadership of a strong religious flavor having a revivalistic impact; the exposure of many Blacks in the armed forces to a democratic and integrationist ideology; and the movement's early successes which begot pressures for still more change.

[42] William Brink and Louis Harris, *The Negro Revolution in America* (New York: Simon & Schuster, 1964), 234–242; "Report from Black America," *Newsweek,* June 30, 1969, 17–23; "The Black Mood: More Militant, More Hopeful, More Determined," *Time,* April 6, 1970, pp. 28–29; and Joel D. Aberbach and Jack L. Walker, "The Meanings of Black Power: A Comparison of White and Black Interpretations of a Political Slogan," *American Political Science Review,* 64 (1970), 378–379.

[43] Leonard Broom and Norval D. Glenn, "When Will America's Negroes Catch Up?," *New Society,* 25 (1965); Norval D. Glenn, "Some Changes in the Relative Status of American Non-whites, 1940 to 1960," *Phylon,* 24 (1963), 109–122; and Pettigrew, *op. cit.,* 188.

The Future

Barring a major war or economic depression it seems relatively safe to venture the prediction that the battle against formal and legalized segregation will probably be won in the foreseeable future. Recent civil rights legislation, judicial decisions, and presidential orders have indicated in a rather definitive manner that the United States as a whole will not tolerate direct, formal, and blatant segregation much longer. This is not to suggest that various individuals or sections of the nation will not attempt to "bootleg" segregation here and there, and perhaps with some measure of temporary success. Nor does it necessarily mean that there will be a *mass* entry of Blacks into formerly all-White schools, neighborhoods, or public accommodations. But the stigma of enforced legal segregation will be removed. In this sense, the battle for desegregation is being won; in many respects it represents primarily a "mopping up" operation—the principle having been established.

Integration, however, the genuine, fundamental acceptance of individuals in their own right without reference to their group identity, is at best an extremely distant goal, perhaps even a goal of a century or so, not of decades. Without question, prejudice and discrimination (especially in informal social relationships) will persist, both North and South. White America has to go a considerable distance before it accepts the idea that it is just as good to be a Black American as to be a White American—or for the meaning of "American" to lose its implicit racial modifier, "White." [44] For the foreseeable future, Blacks can expect that on the whole prejudice will no longer express itself in a direct, blatant, and frontal fashion. Rather prejudice will be of a more subtle, indirect variety, the kind experienced by Jews.

Further *de facto* segregation, separation that lacks explicit legal sanction, will persist, perhaps become even more prevalent in the immediate future. Residential-spatial patterning—the product of ecological processes through which contrasting types (e.g., different social classes, racial and ethnic groups, commercial and business activities, etc.) are sifted and sorted into different sub-parts of an area—will continue to contribute to *de facto* segregation in other spheres of life. Schools, churches, social cliques, recreational facili-

[44] Lewis Killian and Charles Grigg, *Racial Crisis in America* (Englewood Cliffs, N.J.: Prentice-Hall, Inc., 1964), 108.

ties, and the like, to the extent to which they arise out of neighborhood patterns, will bear the influence of this segregated patterning.

Obviously, a frontal civil rights attack based largely upon laws
cannot do the job of eliminating the more subtle, indirect varieties of
discrimination. Nor is an attack upon discrimination itself enough.
The problems that confront the great mass of Blacks will remain
for a good many years even if all discrimination—formal as well as
informal—were to end tomorrow. As James Q. Wilson, a political
scientist, observes:

> If every city and state adopts and enforces to the best of its ability laws
> preventing discrimination in employment, housing, public accommodations,
> and medical facilities; if every school district in the North and South were
> desegregated in fact as well as in name; if every level of government spent
> generously on welfare payments to indigent Negro families—if all these things
> occurred tomorrow, we would still be confronted with a social problem of
> considerable proportions.[45]

The heritage of Jim Crow lives on. For decades, indeed centuries, Blacks have been the victims of inequality and low status,
conditions that tend to become self-perpetuating through the structuring of the social order. Hence Blacks have become increasingly
concerned not merely with removing the barriers to full opportunity
but with achieving the fact of equality of results (a fair share of
America's good things), and achieving it now—bringing an end to
racist institutional arrangements.

Certainly there is little ground for believing that the Black protest will come to an end in the foreseeable future. Much depends
on whether the bottle is seen as half full or half empty; whether one
concentrates on what has been done or what remains to be done.
While many Whites see the bottle as half full, many Blacks see it as
half empty. We shall return to this matter in the next chapter when
we consider Black Power.

VARIABLES AFFECTING THE RESPONSE OF MINORITY-GROUP MEMBERS

Generational differences appear to play an important part in the
responses of minority individuals to their subordinate and disadvantaged status. Among European immigrants, the second and third
generations generally have displayed stronger assimilationist striv-

---

[45] James Q. Wilson, "The Changing Political Position of the Negro," in Arnold
M. Rose, ed., *Assuring Freedom to the Free* (Detroit: Wayne State University Press,
1964), 182–183.

ings, particularly with an integrationist emphasis, than the first generation. Further, the civil rights movement among Blacks in the early 1960s found particular strength among Black youth. Solomon and Fishman, in their study of student participants in civil rights activities, noted:

> Most of the young demonstrators whom we have been studying were at the threshold of their adolescence when the United States Supreme Court ruled unanimously that the segregated schools these youngsters had been attending were illegal. This public recognition of the desirability of desegregation and of its possible achievement in the near future was an experience in the adolescent development of these young people that was quite different from that of their parents and older siblings. Feeling that desegregation was now their right, the students experienced increasing frustration with the painful slowness of its implementation and with the seeming hypocrisy and helplessness of adults—white and Negro—who paid lip service to principles but took no risks for their realization.[46]

Similarly, assimilationist strivings have been particularly strong among middle class Blacks and European immigrants. Psychologically, such individuals have been quite prone to identify themselves with similarly situated dominant group members. Searles and Williams, in a study of Black college student participation in sit-ins during the early 1960s, concluded:

> Socialized to value respectability and achievement, educated to affirm their right of equal opportunity, legitimized in their expectations by civil rights legislation and an important body of opinion, living in a college environment where freedom from constraints and ease of communication facilitate the development of protest activity, these students have selected nonviolent protest as an acceptable means of demonstrating their anger at barriers to first-class citizenship. Far from being alienated, the students appear to be committed to the society and its middle class leaders.[47]

Indeed, for such youth, middle class White society functioned as a key reference group.

Gary T. Marx, in his study of the collective mood of the Black community in 1964, found that those Blacks who were militant over civil rights issues tended to be an elite within the Black community: they were better educated and more involved in voluntary organizations, more likely to vote, they had more friends, a more positive self-image, a higher morale, greater sophistication, and they were

---

[46] Fredric Solomon and Jacob R. Fishman, "The Psychosocial Meaning of Nonviolence in Student Civil Rights Activities," *Psychiatry*, 27 (1964), 91–99.

[47] Ruth Searles and J. Allen Williams, Jr., "Negro College Students' Participation in Sit-Ins," *Social Forces*, 40 (1962), 219. Also see: John M. Orbell, "Protest Participation among Southern Negro College Students," *American Political Science Review*, 61 (1967), 446–456.

less hostile toward Whites.[48] He suggests that high social status produces militancy to the extent that status produces hope which in turn makes militancy seem realistic. Militancy calls for at least some degree of hope, a belief that a new tomorrow is possible; a sense of futility, more prevalent among the less advantaged, seems to work against the development of the morale and hope required for a militant vision. Further, those who enjoy social privilege generally have the energy, resources, and self-confidence needed to challenge an oppressive and powerful system.[49]

SUMMARY

Minority group members may respond to their disadvantaged status by seeking to lose their minority group identity and becoming socially and culturally fused with the dominant group; in brief, they may seek assimilation. European immigrant groups typified this orientation, a case in point being the immigrants from southern Italy. Passing constitutes one form of assimilation. In the case of the Black protest of the 1950s and 1960s, an assimilationist orientation was linked with aggression—with a striking out against minority status in order to break down the walls that barred Blacks from full and equal participation within American life. The NAACP and the movement led by the late Rev. Martin Luther King, Jr., typify this type of response.

[48] Marx, *op. cit.*, 206.
[49] *Ibid.*, 68–69.

13

Responding by Avoidance

In the previous chapter we considered assimilation as a minority group reaction to dominance. In this chapter we continue our discussion by focusing upon a response that is the polar opposite of assimilation—avoidance. In avoidance members of a minority group attempt to shun—to escape from—situations in which they are likely to encounter prejudice and discrimination.

INSULATION

Avoidance of Direct Contact

Experiencing a variety of rebuffs from the dominant group, minority-group members may respond with efforts directed at withdrawal and isolation from the stresses of intergroup contacts. Withdrawal and avoidance represent a relatively frequent type of response. Robert Johnson, for instance, in his study some years ago of Black youth in Elmira, New York, found sentiment favoring insulation from Whites quite prevalent as represented by indorsement of the following statements:

"Negroes should live around their own people." (27% agree.)
"If I had a choice between an all-Negro club and a mixed club, I would join the all-Negro club." (50% agree.)
"I would find it a little distasteful to:
    Eat with a white person." (9% agree.)
    Dance with a white person." (17% agree.)

Go to a party and find that most of the people there were white." (21%
agree.)

Have a white person marry somebody in my family." (42% agree.) [1]

Black adults in the same community (based on a sample of 150)
showed similar patterns as reflected in their indorsement of the following statements:

"Negroes shouldn't go into business establishments where they think they're
not wanted." (64% agree.)

"Suppose you were downtown with a group of your Negro friends, and
they asked you to go with them into a restaurant that you were pretty
sure didn't serve Negroes—would you go?" (71% would not go.) [2]

Williams suggests that the pattern of avoidance and isolation found
among Elmira Blacks is influenced not only by the objective existence of prejudice and discrimination, but also by a distorted conception of the prejudice and discrimination that still remains—indeed, this distorted conception is itself partially the product of social
isolation (avoidance).[3] In-group bonds, pride, and loyalties may
operate toward a similar end.

The reluctance of some Blacks to take advantage of desegregated
facilities and the continuance of avoidance patterns often stems from
an uneasiness and uncertainty about the new situation. Lingering
fears from the past may lead some Blacks to expect that they will
be humiliated and mistreated even at officially desegregated facilities. This vicious circle is quite similar to what psychologists describe as "avoidance learning." If we construct an experimental
setting in which a subject's finger is repeatedly shocked electrically
immediately after the flashing of a light, he quickly learns to avoid
the painful shock by lifting his finger when the light comes on. But
what happens when the electric shock is no longer applied? How
can the subject acquire knowledge of the changed setting? As long
as he lifts his finger at the light, he can never learn that the light
is no longer associated with a shock. This is a critical element in
avoidance learning. Blacks, too, have learned to withdraw from

[1] Robert Johnson, "Negro Reactions to Minority Group Status," in Milton L. Barron, ed., *American Minorities* (New York: Alfred A. Knopf, Inc., 1957), 202. Also
see: Charles S. Johnson, *Growing Up in the Black Belt* (Washington, D.C.: American Council on Education, 1941), 295; Regina Mary Goff, *Problems and Emotional
Difficulties of Negro Children* (New York: Teachers College, Bureau of Publications,
Columbia University, 1949), 46–47; and P. H. Mussen, "Differences between the
TAT Responses of Negro and White Boys," *Journal of Consulting Psychology*, 17
(1953), 373–376.

[2] Robin M. Williams, Jr., *Strangers Next Door* (Englewood Cliffs, N.J.: Prentice-
Hall, Inc., 1964), 249.

[3] *Ibid.*, 250.

painful interracial settings. Even when these situations change and
the discomfort is removed, many Blacks are reluctant to test them
and discover the changes.[4]

Blacks cite a wide variety of factors as influencing their avoidance patterns. One of these is antipathy toward Whites and White
discrimination. This is how two Black youth recently stated the
matter in Mobile, Alabama:

> We know integration (I should say desegregation—the court always uses
> that word) desegregation has been going on for a long time now. That's why
> black folks have thirteen shades of color. But integration is playing out, it's
> played out. In Mobile integration just won't work because when we go to a
> white school they treat us like some dog. We never get to be the officers of
> the class so we'd rather just stay in our own schools.
> I think it's [integration] an impossibility at this time. How can you have
> integration when the white man is on the top of the pole? He controls every-
> think, he's the head of everything and he owns the power structure and we're
> at the bottom. We aren't equal in the white man's eyesight.[5]

In some cases there may be an absence of active antipathy toward
Whites, but Whites may be avoided because of possible conflict.
Such Blacks may be willing to have contact with Whites but consider it inexpedient. An Arkansas Black farmer explains this thinking in these terms:

> I found that the best way to get along with white folks is to just be pretty
> careful and come in contact with them as little as possible. There are times
> when you have to take a lot of things. Those things that you can avoid, you
> ought to. I am not a white folks' "nigger," and I try to keep out of trouble.
> I know, though, that I am in the South, and I know they can make it hard
> for me, so I just try to attend to my business and see if I can dodge a lot of
> trouble.[6]

Avoidance may be motivated by fear of discomfort or embarrassment and a desire to maintain self-respect. A Black carpenter in a
small North Carolina community reports such a situation:

> The white dentist here makes a difference between white and colored. He's
> the only one here who does it, and I guess he wouldn't if there was a colored
> dentist here. You know he has special hours for colored, and he lets them
> all know they're colored. He insults the colored women so that none of them
> won't even pass his door. He's crazy about colored women. One of the col-
> ored teachers here didn't know about him, and she went to get some work
> done. He told her he would do the work and she wouldn't have to pay him a

---

[4] Thomas F. Pettigrew, *A Profile of the Negro American* (New York: Van Nostrand Reinhold Co., 1964), 162–163.

[5] Betsy Fancher, *Voices from the South* (Atlanta: Southern Regional Council, Inc.,
1970), 18–19.

[6] Charles S. Johnson, *Patterns of Negro Segregation* (New York: Harper & Row,
1943), 269. By permission.

penny because she was just the girl he had been looking for. Of course she came away and told what he said. She was as mad as a hornet.[7]

Avoidance may take the form of developing towns or communities composed principally or entirely of minority-group members. Even when residential segregation is not initiated and enforced by the dominant group, minority-group members may prefer to live in their own communities. In this manner they endeavor to avoid the continuous harassment incident to living in the larger society. Mozell C. Hill reports on some all-Black communities in Oklahoma in which there is a positive feeling and consensus that the common welfare is best served by shunning social relations with Whites.[8]

Mound Bayou, an all-Black community in Mississippi, has fostered a tradition of race consciousness and avoidance of Whites. A fourteen-year-old youth in Mound Bayou asserts:

I like it here. I like it because it's an all-colored town. You don't have to be around white people. You can laugh if you want to here. Down in Marigold or some place like that the white folks would be saying, "Nigger, do this and do that," but here you can play ball right out here in the street and nobody will run you away.[9]

Within the South at the present time, any number of Black communities have undertaken incorporation, making them eligible for federal aid projects and opening the door to greater Black control. A 42-year-old steelworker who plans to move from Attala, Alabama, to nearby Ridgedale, a Black town, observes:

I can't make it in the white man's society, so I'm getting out. I can't be elected to anything. I can't serve on the white man's boards, and I'm sick of it. I'm going to where I can do anything I'm capable of doing.[10]

MIGRATION

Minority-group members may seek to deal with their disadvantaged position through migration. The stimulus to move may come

[7] *Ibid.*, 275–276. By permission of the publishers, Harper & Row.

[8] Mozell C. Hill, "Basic Racial Attitudes Toward Whites in the Oklahoma All-Negro Community," *American Journal of Sociology*, 49 (1944), 519–523. Also see: William E. Bittle and Gilbert L. Geis, "Racial Self-Fulfillment and the Rise of an All-Negro Community in Oklahoma," *Phylon*, 18 (1957), 247–260, and Everett Groseclose, "Oklahoma Town Finds Its Own Novel Remedy for Racial Disharmony," *The Wall Street Journal*, August 23, 1966.

[9] Charles S. Johnson, *Growing Up in the Black Belt*, 250. By permission of the publishers, American Council on Education.

[10] Neil Maxwell, "Negroes in Dixie Form Separate Municipalities in Bid To Improve Lot," *The Wall Street Journal*, November 11, 1968.

from conditions at home that they desire to escape or from conditions elsewhere that attract them. More frequently forces of both "push" and "pull" are present. This has been reflected in the mass migration of Blacks from rural communities of the South to northern and southern urban centers. Except for the movement of some 40,000 southern Blacks to Kansas shortly after the Civil War, there was no significant migration to the North or the West until 1915. In view of the harsh and frequently severe circumstances of discrimination in the South, this is somewhat difficult to explain; although large northern and western cities were hardly a racial paradise, they did offer Blacks the vote, considerable equality in justice, better schools, and public welfare benefits. Rose suggests that among the factors accounting for the virtual absence of migration were the lack of a tradition of migration, the lack of sufficient job opportunities in the North, the lack of contacts in the North to ease the adjustment period, the lack of train fare, low morale, and a general accommodation to minority status.[11]

In 1910 some 90 per cent of the nation's Black population was located in the South and 77 per cent in rural communities. Factors of both "push" and "pull" operated to encourage the first major strivings of migration about 1915. Within the South "White infiltration" into types of work formerly monopolized by Blacks, the relative shift westward of cotton growing, the ravages of the boll weevil, and the drought of 1916 and 1917 served as special stimuli to Black out-migration. World War I served as an added impetus. The draft moved a great number of Black men from their home communities. The draft of White workers, the stopping of European immigration, and conditions of war prosperity forced northern industry to turn actively to Blacks for new workers.

The history of Black migration during recent decades demonstrates clearly that the Black population moves primarily in response to strong economic incentives.[12] According to Census data, the growing inadequacy of employment opportunities in southern agriculture induced a net migration from the South of over 700,000 Blacks between 1920 and 1930. During the 1930s, when few job openings were beckoning, net Black migration out of the South fell

---

[11] Arnold M. Rose, *The Negro's Morale* (Minneapolis: University of Minnesota Press, 1949), 37–38.

[12] In this regard see: Donald R. Matthews and James W. Prothro, *Negroes and the New Southern Politics* (New York: Harcourt Brace Jovanovich, 1966), 449–455.

below 350,000. During the decade of World War II large numbers of job openings for unskilled workers at rising rates of pay led an unprecedented 1,200,000 Blacks to leave the South. The migration rate during World War II was higher for Black than for White men; it was particularly high among unskilled Black workers.[13] The migration of Southern Blacks to the North continued at high levels in the 1950s and 1960s. Although the South still contains 53 per cent of the Black population, the figure stood at 77 per cent in 1940. More than three-fourths of the 1.4 million Black migrants from the South during the 1960s went to five states: New York, California, New Jersey, Illinois, and Michigan. Since 1940, the Black population of the Northeast and North Central states has gone from about 11 to 20 per cent.[14]

SEPARATISM

Diametrically opposed to the assimilationist response to minority-group status is the separatist approach. Whereas assimilation implies the absorption of the minority by the larger society, separatism has an opposite aim, secession by the minority. Separatism undertakes to maintain or realize a separate group identity that is usually linked with efforts to achieve territorial separation from the dominant group. In this respect it is a form of withdrawal or avoidance. Separatism, however, seldom simply involves avoidance. Indeed, separatist movements may most aptly be described as constituting an *aggressive-avoidance* reaction. In this sense, it is a combined response, a fact that can be noted in a consideration of a number of separatist movements.

Zionism

The Zionist movement, arising in the nineteenth century among Jews and culminating in the establishment of the new nation Israel, represents one of the classic examples of a separatist movement. The movement constituted a reaction to the persecution that the Jews had experienced since their dispersion from their ancient homeland in Palestine. Theodor Herzl, great pioneer of Zionism, expressed the despair felt by many of the world's Jews in 1896 in a

[13] U.S. Department of Commerce, *Negro-White Differences in Geographic Mobility* (Washington, D.C.: U.S. Government Printing Office, 1964).

[14] Jack Rosental, "Negro Migration to North Found Steady Since '40's," *New York Times,* March 4, 1971, pp. 1 and 20.

book that became an ideological cornerstone of the Zionist movement, *Der Judenstaat* (*The Jewish State*):

> The Jewish question still exists. It would be foolish to deny it. It is a
> remnant of the Middle Ages, which civilized nations do not even yet seem
> able to shake off, try as they will. . . . The Jewish question exists wherever
> Jews live in perceptible numbers. Where it does not exist, it is carried by
> Jews in the course of their migrations. We naturally move to those places
> where we are not persecuted, and there our presence produces persecution.
> This is the case in every country, and will remain so, even in those highly
> civilized—for instance, France—until the Jewish question finds a solution on
> a political basis. The unfortunate Jews are now carrying the seeds of Anti-
> Semitism into England; they have already introduced it into America.[15]

For Zionists, assimilation was not the answer. In fact it was unwanted. Herzl wrote, "I referred previously to our 'assimilation.' I
do not for a moment wish to imply that I desire such an end. Our
national character is too historically famous, and, in spite of every
degradation, too fine to make its annihilation desirable." [16] Herzl's
answer to the Jewish question was "Let the sovereignty be granted
us over a portion of the globe large enough to satisfy the rightful
requirements of a nation; the rest we shall manage for ourselves." [17]

Many contemporary Jewish leaders are no less strong than Herzl
in rejecting Jewish assimilation. Dr. Nahum Goldmann, president of
the World Zionist Organization, has insisted that Jews intensify
their efforts in all spheres of life to combat assimilation and to
achieve a deepened identification with Israel as the center of Jewish
life and activity:

> We have become part and parcel of the life of the other peoples and with
> that we have lost the main basis of our separate existence. . . . The result
> is that we live in a period where a very large part of our people, especially
> the young generation, is threatened by an anonymous process of erosion, of
> disintegration, not as a theory or as a conscientious ideology but by the fact
> of this day-to-day life. This process, if not halted and reversed, threatens
> Jewish survival more than persecution, inquisition, pogroms and mass murder
> of Jews did in the past.[18]

And Dr. John Slawson of the American Jewish Committee asserts
that the "defense against assimilation" is even more urgent today
than "defense against discrimination." [19]

[15] Theodor Herzl, *The Jewish State* (New York: American Zionist Emergency
Council, 1946), 75.
[16] *Ibid.*, 91.
[17] *Ibid.*, 92.
[18] "World Zionists Beset by Doubt," *New York Times*, January 12, 1965, and
"Judaism in Peril Zionists Are Told," *New York Times*, December 31, 1964.
[19] "Nation's Jews Found Retaining Identity as Group," *New York Times*, April
30, 1964.

The chief Zionist aim, as set forth by Herzl, was to secure "the survival of the Jewish people" and to solve "the Jewish problem" by establishing the Jews in Palestine with all the attributes of a modern nation: land, language (Hebrew), and sovereignty. The dispersion of the Jews throughout the world was seen as an intolerable condition that could be solved only by the establishment of a Jewish nation. Zionists saw the root of the Jewish problem as residing in the fact that the Jews lived as unwelcomed guests in lands occupied and ruled by others. If this were the case, then the solution seemed obvious. The Jews needed to establish themselves in a land not occupied and ruled by others, a land in which they themselves would be the hosts.

Zionists thought that the mere existence of the Jewish state would in large measure serve to solve the Jewish problem. Anti-Semitism was viewed as a kind of ghost fear aroused among the Gentiles by the anomalous survival of the Jews despite their dispersion when, under similar circumstances, other peoples had become extinct or assimilated. In turn, anti-Semitism contributed to Jewish self-hatred and inferiority complexes. Zionists asserted that both types of problems could be solved by the creation of a Jewish nation to which world Jews could migrate. By the same token those Jews who continued to live in other nations would be benefited. Jewish rights could then be protected through international diplomatic channels. Since the Jews living in Palestine would enjoy status as a nation, the Jewish nation would occupy a position among the nations of the world and be in a position to advance the interests of world Jewry. In addition, Jews living outside of Palestine might derive a new sense of self-respect from the existence of a Jewish nation.[20]

Since the establishment of Israel in 1948, the world Zionist movement has found itself divided. Israeli Zionist leaders insist that, to be qualitatively a full Jew, a Jew must settle in Israel. They strongly argue that it is obligatory for all Zionists to migrate to Israel now that the doors of the Jewish state are open to them. On the other hand, Zionists from the free West find it quite unreasonable that they should be expected to go to Israel as a duty.[21] As a result many American Zionists find themselves suspended in a kind of limbo somewhere between the Israeli stand and the various non-Zionist positions. Israeli Zionists, in essence, are saying, "Come or you ex-

---

[20] Ben Halpern, *The Idea of the Jewish State* (Cambridge, Mass.: Harvard University Press, 1961).
[21] *Ibid.*, 232 ff.

communicate yourself"; non-Zionists are, in essence, urging, "Let us hoe our respective gardens." Many American Zionists find them-selves trapped between the two positions.[22]

Garveyism

Immediately following World War I, a mass movement emerged among American Blacks with a strong separatist appeal. It blos-somed under the leadership of Marcus Garvey, a Black West Indian, who possessed considerable gifts of leadership. His organization, The Universal Negro Improvement Association (UNIA), found a responsive setting for its appeal of Black nationalism among large numbers of southern Blacks who had migrated to northern cities during and following the war. Among the migrants, there existed considerable disillusionment with the city as a promised land and with race riots and racial discrimination in the North. They had been uprooted from traditional patterns of life and found themselves confused and disoriented within their new surroundings. An old way of life had been displaced, but a new way of life had not as yet been realized. Migration had brought with it a destruction of old rural values, a disruption of social roots, and an isolation from many traditional personal ties. Propelled into an urban industrial world, the migrants found themselves in an ambiguous position and status.

The setting provided a fertile ground for a mass movement with a blatant racial and nationalistic appeal. A central ingredient in Garvey's appeal was the glorification of blackness. He exalted every-thing black and exhorted Blacks to be proud of their distinctive features and color. He told his listeners, "I am the equal of any white man. I want you to feel the same way." [23] One enthusiastic delegate to the first UNIA convention, in 1920, served notice that "it takes 1,000 white men to lick one Negro." [24] Garvey catered to the darker Blacks. He laughed at the light-skinned Blacks, who, he asserted, were always seeking "excuses to get out of the Negro Race," and he scornfully accused his light-colored opponents, such as W. E. B. Du Bois, of the NAACP, of being "time-serving, bootlicking agencies of subserviency to the whites." [25]

Garvey angrily accused White scholars of distorting Black history

---

[22] Judd L. Teller, "American Zionists Move Toward Clarity," *Commentary*, 12 (1951), 444–450.

[23] Edmund David Cronon, *Black Moses* (Madison: University of Wisconsin Press, 1955), 172.

[24] *Ibid.*

[25] *Ibid.*, 191.

to make it appear unfavorable to Blacks. "Every student of history, of impartial mind," Garvey taught, "knows that the Negro once ruled the world, when white men were savages and barbarians living in caves; that thousands of Negro professors . . . taught in the Universities of Alexandria." [26]   He glorified Blacks and told how Whites were far below the darker race:

> When Europe was inhabited by a race of cannibals, a race of savages, naked men, heathens and pagans, Africa was peopled with a race of cultured black men, who were masters in art, science and literature; men who were cultured and refined; men, who, it was said, were like the gods. Even the great poets of old sang in beautiful sonnets of the delight it afforded the gods to be in companionship with the Ethiopians. Why, then, should we lose hope? Black men, you were once great; you shall be great again. Lose not courage, lose not faith, go forward. The thing to do is to get organized.[27]

Along with his efforts to build Black pride went a reorientation in religion as well. Garvey insisted that Blacks should end their subservience to the White man through the worship of a White God and worship instead a Black God. For him Christ was a Black.

Garvey advocated an aggressive philosophy of racial purity and social separation. He demanded that racial amalgamation end at once and warned that any member of the Universal Negro Improvement Association who married a White would be summarily expelled. Speaking to Whites, he indicated, "We do not seek intermarriage, nor do we hanker after the impossible. We want the right to have a country of our own, and there foster and re-establish a culture and civilization exclusively ours." [28]   It was a program of separation from Whites. He denounced other Black leaders as being bent on cultural assimilation, which he violently opposed. He viewed the National Association for the Advancement of Colored People as the worst offender because it "wants us all to become white by amalgamation, but they are not honest enough to come out with the truth." [29]

Garvey reassured Whites that they need have no fears of the aims of the Universal Negro Improvement Association. He declared the organization was stoutly opposed to "miscegenation and race suicide" and believed strongly "in the purity of the Negro race and the purity of the white race." [30]   He sought to warn the White world of

[26] *Ibid.*, 176.
[27] *Ibid.*, 176.
[28] *Ibid.*, 191–192.
[29] *Ibid.*, 192–193.
[30] *Ibid.*, 192–193.

the dangers lurking in social equality. "Some Negroes believe in social equality," he cautioned. "They want to intermarry with the white women of this country, and it is going to cause trouble later on. Some Negroes want the same jobs you have. They want to be Presidents of the nation." [31] Thus Garvey abandoned the fight for integration, a type of assimilationist appeal, and promoted racial compartmentalization, or separatism. His plans for the abdication of Black rights in America brought him the open support of White supremacists and the Ku Klux Klan, which was reactivated following World War I.

An integral aspect of Garvey's separatism was his program to lead Blacks back to their African homeland. With his customary flare for the dramatic he assured his followers that within a few years Africa would be as completely dominated by Blacks as Europe was by Whites. He believed a great independent African nation was essential for race redemption, and he was earnestly convinced that within Africa Blacks would achieve their destiny as a great people. Garvey warned Whites, "We say to the white man who now dominates Africa that it is to his interest to clear out of Africa now, because we are coming . . . 400,000,000 strong." [32] But it was never Garvey's intention that all New World Blacks should return to Africa. Like many Zionists he felt that, once a strong African nation was established, Blacks everywhere would realize new prestige, strength, and protection.

In 1921 he created the "Empire of Africa" and made himself provisional "President General." To assist him he created the positions of "Potentate" and "Supreme Deputy Potentate," and a nobility consisting of "Knights of the Nile," "Knights of the Distinguished Service Order of Ethiopia," and "Dukes of the Niger and of Uganda." Since the new nation needed a military arm, Garvey founded the Universal African Legion, the Universal Black Cross Nurses, the Universal African Motor Corps, and the Black Eagle Flying Corps —all with uniforms and officers. Great emphasis was placed upon ceremony, ritual, and pomp. He staged parades and consecrated a black, red, and green flag for his organization. Through the invention of social distinctions, honors, and pageantry, the Black was made a somebody in his existing environment. While Blacks had found a degree of self-magnification in fraternal orders and the

[31] *Ibid.*, 193.
[32] *Ibid.*, 184.

church, these organizations did not give the support to their ego-consciousness that Whites found in the Masons, Kiwanis, and especially the Klan.[33]

While the vision of a great Black nation in Africa thrilled many Blacks, probably few of them were really interested in returning to Africa. The prospect of a great African nation served to give the newly arrived migrants from the rural South a sense of identity in the face of the disorientation of urban industrial life. It helped to answer the question as to who they were, and it answered the question in terms that served to build up self-respect and a feeling of being significant, meaningful, and worthwhile. It identified Blacks as a people with a heritage and a promising future. In the transition from a rural to an urban way of life it provided a stopgap identity. And it simultaneously provided emotional escape and a release for protest feelings.

Garvey set up his organization in New York City, with local branches in Chicago, Philadelphia, Cincinnati, Detroit, Washington, and other cities. In 1924 he claimed 6 million members. This figure is undoubtedly exaggerated, although the UNIA may have had as many as 100,000 dues-paying members. The number of Blacks who, though not actual members, identified themselves with the Garvey program probably was considerable and gave the movement a mass character. He published the *Negro World* as the official newspaper of the movement. He organized cooperative enterprises including grocery stores, laundries, restaurants, hotels, and printing plants.

The movement collapsed after 1923, not because Garvey's followers were disaffected, but because Garvey became entangled in a series of long-drawn-out legal suits. He was imprisoned in 1925, following conviction on a federal charge of using the mails to defraud in connection with the sale of stock for his Black Star Line, a steamship company. After two years he was released and deported as an undesirable alien. As a consequence of these reverses, the movement declined and lost membership rapidly.

In many respects Garvey resembled Theodor Herzl, pioneer of Jewish Zionism. Rose points out that, in their early years, neither Garvey nor Herzl had been exposed to very strong anti-minority feelings. When they later came into contact with prejudice, their predilection was to escape to a land free of discrimination, rather

[33] E. Franklin Frazier, "The Garvey Movement," *Opportunity*, 4 (November, 1926), 346–348.

than to protest and to try to change the existing order. Both adopted a chauvinistic, even a religious nationalism, and both condemned amalgamation and assimilation. Both sought support from those groups most hostile to their own minority. There is no evidence, however, that Garvey was familiar with Herzl's *Judenstaat*. The similarity between the two reflects the frequent similarity in reaction of minorities facing extremely difficult circumstances.[34]

The Black Muslims

Sometime in the midsummer of 1930, a peddler—variously known as Mr. Farrad Mohammad, Mr. F. Mohammad Ali, Professor Ford, Mr. Wali Farrad, and W. D. Fard—made his appearance in the Black community of Detroit. Apparently he was an Arab, but his racial and national identity remains undocumented. In addition to peddling his silks and artifacts, he expounded a doctrine that was a hodge-podge of Christianity, Mohammedanism, and his own personal prejudices. As time passed, his teaching took the form of increasingly bitter attacks against the White race as well as the Bible. A number of people experienced sudden conversions and became his followers. Soon house-to-house meetings no longer could accommodate all those who wished to hear Fard. A hall was hired and named the Temple of Islam. With this, the Black Muslim movement was launched. Fard described himself to his followers as having been sent to awaken the "Black Nation" (American Blacks) to the full range of its possibilities in a world temporarily dominated by Whites—"blue-eyed devils." [35]

One of Fard's earliest lieutenants was Elijah Muhammad, born Elijah Poole in Sandersville, Georgia, in 1897, the son of sharecropping Baptist Black minister. The family had moved to Detroit early in his life. Muhammad left school at the age of nine and took odd jobs around Detroit, later drifting around the country. When he returned to Detroit, he was attracted to Fard and his movement.[36] Sometimes around June 1934, Fard mysteriously disappeared. Muhammad took over the leadership of "The Lost Nation of Islam," as the movement was known. In time Fard, no longer present, became

[34] Rose, *op. cit.*, 43–44.
[35] C. Eric Lincoln, *The Black Muslims in America* (Boston: Beacon Press, Inc., 1961), 10–14.
[36] William Worthy, "The Angriest Negroes," *Esquire*, 55 (1961), 102.

identified with the god Allah. Muhammad assumed the title of Allah's "Prophet" and, more often, the "Messenger of Allah." [37] Factionalism developed within the movement, and Muhammad withdrew to Chicago, where the headquarters of the organization remains. Renewed factionalism in 1964 led Malcolm X, east coast leader of the Black Muslims, to break with Muhammad. Intense hostility and feuding developed between the followers of Muhammad and those of Malcolm X, the latter attempting to provide the Muslims with a more adaptable ideology, a less rigidly separatist orientation, and a more political direction. On February 21, 1965, Malcolm X was shot to death while addressing a rally, apparently slain by followers of Muhammad.

The Black Muslims are not recognized as a legitimate Moslem group by any affiliate of the Federation of Islamic Associations in the United States and Canada nor by the world Islamic movement. Many of the teachings of the group are at variance with those of other Moslem groups.[38]

The Muslims do not consider themselves "Negroes." They resent and reject the word as no more than "a label the white man placed on us to make his discrimination more convenient." They prefer to call themselves Black Men. They rarely use the word "Negro" without the qualifier "so-called." Muslims assert that Blacks have been kept in mental slavery by Whites even while their bodies were free. Systematically and diabolically, Whites have estranged them from their heritage and from themselves. "They have been educated in ignorance," and their origin, history, true names, and religion have been kept secret from them.[39] They have been "absolutely deaf, dumb and blind—brainwashed of all self-respect and knowledge of kind by the white Slavemaster." They are little more than "free slaves." [40]

In the Garvey spirit, the Black past is extolled. In fact, Blacks are depicted as the original humans from whom all other races were made. In its earlier years the Muslims preached a virulent hatred of all Whites. As one Muslim minister stated: "A white man's head is made to be busted." [41] More recently, however, the movement

[37] Lincoln, *op. cit.*, 15–16.
[38] *Ibid.*, 72–73, 218–219.
[39] *Ibid.*, 68–69.
[40] *Ibid.*, 70.
[41] Worthy, *op. cit.*, 104.

has tended to tone down its anti-White racism and to stress instead the pro-Black character of its program.[42]

The Black Muslims stress the pursuit of a "righteous life." Their stringent code of morality prohibits the following: extra-marital sexual relations; the use of alcohol, tobacco, and narcotics; indulging in gambling, dancing, movie-going, dating, sports, long vacations from work, sleeping more than is necessary to health, quarreling between husband and wife, lying, stealing, discourtesy (especially to women), and insubordination to civil authority (except on the ground of religious obligation); and maintaining unclean personal habits and homes. Also prohibited are the eating of pork, cornbread, and kale (and generally any typical southern Black food), hair straightening, or hair dyeing, excessive makeup for women, and loud laughter or singing.[43] A number of observers have noted that these puritanical ethical prescriptions place the Black Muslims in the mainstream of the dominant American middle class value system.[44] Hence, ironically, the movement functions in part to socialize lower class Blacks in the value system of the rejected White world.

The Black Muslims demand the absolute separation of the White and Black races. In his booklet *The Supreme Wisdom*, Muhammad condemns integration as a kind of social opiate:

> The Slavemaster's children are doing everything in their power to prevent the so-called Negroes from accepting their own God and salvation, by putting on a great show of false love and friendship.
>
> This is being done through "integration," as it is called; that is, so-called Negroes and whites mixing together such as in schools, churches, and even intermarriage. . . . The poor slaves really think they are entering a condition of heaven with their former slaveholders, but it will prove to be their doom.[45]

The Black Muslims adamantly reject intermarriage. They remain convinced of their "superior racial heritage" and believe that admixture with whites would only serve to weaken the Black Nation physically and morally.[46]

[42] J. Milton Yinger, *The Scientific Study of Religion* (New York: The Macmillan Co., 1970), 338.

[43] E. U. Essien-Udom, *Black Nationalism* (New York: Dell Publishing Co., Inc., 1964), 28.

[44] *Ibid.*; James H. Laue, "A Contemporary Revitalization Movement in American Race Relations: The 'Black Muslims,'" *Social Forces*, 42 (1964), 315–324; Lawrence L. Tyler, "The Protestant Ethic Among the Black Muslims," *Phylon*, 27 (1966), 5–14; and Harry Edwards, "Black Muslim and Negro Christian Family Relationships," *Journal of Marriage and the Family*, 30 (1968), 604–611.

[45] Lincoln, *op. cit.*, 124.

[46] *Ibid.*, 89.

The Black Muslims demand an entirely separate Black economy. They argue that the Black cannot achieve genuine freedom until he is economically independent. They point out that the total annual income of the American Black is more than $20 billion, a sum greater than the total income of Canada. If this money were spent exclusively among Black businessmen and invested in Black enterprise, they argue that it would command the respect of every nation in the world. Their ideal would involve a complete economic withdrawal from the White community.[47]

Muslim statements about their political goals are couched in mystical and vague terms. But they do periodically call for "a separate nation for ourselves, right here in America" or "some good earth, right here in America, where we can go off to ourselves." Muhammad told a Washington audience, "To integrate with evil is to be destroyed with evil. What we want—indeed, justice for us is to be set apart. We want, and must insist upon an area in this land that we can call our own, somewhere we can hold our heads with pride and dignity without the continued harassments and indiginities of our oppressors." [48] Muhammad has called for "four or five states in America" to be turned over to him. Yet it is extraordinary that this demand for a national homeland has not been coupled with some sort of political program for its realization. Indeed, the Black Muslims have been an apolitical movement. And despite newspaper sensationalism, the Black Muslims have not been a violent group—indeed, one Chicago police official confides, "We don't regard them as a security risk." [49]

The size of the membership is not known, but estimates range from 5,000 to 200,000. Public opinion polls have shown that support for or approval of the Black Muslims and their most important leaders, Elijah Muhammad and the late Malcolm X, has ranged around five per cent of the Black respondents. The impact, however, of the Black Muslims, especially through Malcolm X, on later expressions of Black Power has been great.[50] The Muslim's chief temple is on Chicago's South Side, where Muhammad has also established a Muslim restaurant, cleaning business, barbershop, grocery, butcher shop, and department store. In nearly every city with a temple, the organization has launched some business establishments.

[47] *Ibid.*, 20 and 42.

[48] *Ibid.*, 95.

[49] "Negroes Building Farm Empire," *U.S. News & World Report*, September 21, 1970, p. 84.

[50] Yinger, *op. cit.*, 336.

In addition, the Muslims own large farms in Michigan, Georgia, Alabama, Florida, Mississippi, and Texas, and operate active parochial schools (known as "Universities of Islam") in a number of cities.

Through the years the Black Muslims have recruited their members primarily from among urban low-income groups with little schooling, many of them migrants from the rural South. Black nationalism has its roots in the frustrations, anxieties, and disillusionments of contemporary urban life that are complicated by segregation, discrimination, and poverty—by life within Black ghettos at the periphery of White society. Its members are often strangers not only to the White society but also to the urbanized Black community. The vast majority are the "unwanted from Dixie," who find themselves rejected by both the White society and by upward mobile and middle class Blacks who resent, fear, and despise the migrants as a threat to an improved "Black image." The result is a dual alienation giving rise to a sense of apathy, futility, and emptiness of purpose.[51]   E. U. Essien-Udom, a Nigerian who studied the movement, asserts:

In a psychological sense, many are lonesome within and outside their own group. They are rootless and restless. They are without an identity, i.e., a sense of belonging and membership in society. In this situation, there is neither hope nor optimism. In fact, most lower-class Negroes in these large cities see little or no "future" for themselves and posterity. This is partly because they have no faith in themselves or in their potential as black men in America and especially because important decisions which shape their lives appear entirely beyond their control.[52]

The Black Muslims offers its members a way out. The convert to the movement is no longer a member of a despised minority. He belongs, at least spiritually, to a larger whole where people are "dark, proud, unapologetic." The movement combines the attractions of religion, nationalism, and political "pies in the sky" with a sense of belonging and self-esteem.[53]

Black Power

The slogan, "Black Power," apparently was coined by Stokely Carmichael in 1966, but its connotations of racial pride, self-respect, and unity can be traced back to Marcus Garvey and indeed even

[51] Essien-Udom, op. cit., 16–17, 23–24, 26–27, 95, 201–203, and 297–298.
[52] Ibid., 354–355.
[53] Ibid., 317 and 362. Also see: Howard M. Kaplan, "The Black Muslims and the Negro Quest for Communion," British Journal of Sociology, 20 (1969), 164–176.

Booker T. Washington, or for that matter on further to Frederick Douglass and other Black abolitionists. The slogan has no sharply defined or agreed upon meaning. Whites tend to see it as an illegitimate, revengeful challenge; one study suggests that 57.2 per cent of Whites view it as a synonym for violence and destruction, racism, or even Black rule over Whites.[54] And among Blacks, it excites many different emotions and at times motivates Blacks to express their loyalty or take action for almost contradictory reasons.[55]

Indeed, no sooner did the slogan appear, then an acrimonious debate unfolded among Black leaders as to its true meaning. Initially it was a blunt battle cry symbolizing a break with the past tactics of the civil rights movement. Stokely Carmichael put it this way in one of his early speeches:

> The only way we gonna stop the white men from whippin' us is to take over. . . .
> We've been saying freedom for six years and we ain't got nothin'. What we gonna start saying now is black power . . . from now on when they ask you what you want, you know to tell them; black power, black power, black power! [56]

But speeches of this kind were not only a challenge to the White community; they threatened established Black civil rights leaders as well. The NAACP's Roy Wilkins responded swiftly, angrily, and negatively:

> No matter how endlessly they try to explain it, the term means anti-white power. . . . It has to mean going it alone. It has to mean separatism. Now separatism . . . offers a disadvantaged minority little except a chance to shrivel and die. . . . It is a reverse Mississippi, a reverse Hitler, a reverse Ku Klux Klan. . . . We of the NAACP will have none of this. We have fought it too long.[57]

This clash over meanings was partly fueled by a clash of personalities and ambitions, but more basically it reflected differences over the role of a Black minority in a White dominated society. Should the ultimate goal be complete assimilation, one in which a "color blind" society would arise; or should Blacks strive to build a cohesive, autonomous community, one unified along racial lines, in which Blacks would be in a position to extract fundamental concessions

[54] Joel D. Aberbach and Jack L. Walker, "The Meanings of Black Power: A Comparison of White and Black Interpretations of a Political Slogan," *American Political Science Review*, 64 (1970), 371.

[55] *Ibid.*, 367–388.

[56] *Ibid.*, 367.

[57] *Ibid.*, 367.

from Whites and perhaps even carve out politically separate enclaves? [58]

Black Power, then, has been interpreted in a great many ways. For some Blacks, the slogan has meant that Blacks should organize themselves politically (much as did the Irish and Italians in our nation's big cities in an earlier period) and economically ("Black capitalism"). Others, more radical and militant, have seen it as a rallying cry for the formation of paramilitary organizations, for instance, the Black Panthers. And on college campuses Black Power has at times encompassed a kind of cultural nationalism—the proliferation of Afro-American Associations or Black Student Unions, Black Studies programs, and Afro dress and hair styles. It should be noted, however, that among the great mass of Blacks within urban ghettos, the slogan has not meant the abandonment of integration as an ultimate goal, although there is considerable disagreement over how soon integration might occur—they tend to view Black Power as a call for a fair share (equal opportunity) and/or an appeal for racial unity.[59] Generally all Black Power groups (including many local Urban Leagues at the conservative end of the continuum) ascribe to a basic ideology of Black pride, Black unity, and economic and political power for the Black community, although each has its own ideological "bag," develops its peculiar style and stance, and "does its own thing." [60] Black Power, by calling on people to be, feel, think, and act Black has fostered a sense of community in Black ghettos, especially among the youth.

But why, we may ask, did the movement shift in the direction of Black Power? [61] The decade of the 1960s opened with the sit-ins and freedom rides and continued through Birmingham, the March on Washington, and Selma with the battle cry, "Freedom Now." Yet by 1964 and 1965, episodes of rioting began unfolding in the nation's Black ghettos; the rhetoric of protest became increasingly demanding, blanket charges of pervasive White racism were more common, and some Blacks began actively to discourage Whites from

[58] *Ibid.*, 368.

[59] *Ibid.*, passim.

[60] Luther P. Gerlach and Virginia H. Hine, "The Social Organization of a Movement of Revolutionary Change: Case Study, Black Power," in Norman E. Whitten, Jr., and John F. Szwed, *Afro-American Anthropology* (New York: The Free Press of Glencoe, 1970), 390–391.

[61] See: William J. Wilson, "Revolutionary Nationalism 'Versus' Cultural Nationalism Dimensions of the Black Power Movement," *Sociological Focus*, 3 (1970), 44.

participating in protest demonstrations and civil rights organizations. Probably nothing better symbolized the changing mood and style of Black protest than the change in the dominant symbol from "Freedom" to "Black Power." [62] A number of factors appear to have been at work in producing this shift.

First, many Blacks experienced considerable disappointment, disgust, and despair over the pace, scope, and quality of social change.[63] The millennium so eloquently promised by President John F. Kennedy, if only a civil rights program were enacted, did not come to pass. President Johnson successfully steered the program through Congress—additionally calling for an "unconditional war on poverty in America" and the building of a Great Society—yet the heritage of Jim Crow lived on. Probably the closest one can come to social dynamite is to promise people freedom and a Great Society and then delivery handouts.

For decades Blacks have been the victims of inequality and low status. The handicaps associated with poverty, high fertility, an absence of skills, inadequate education, and low job seniority were left untouched by civil rights legislation. Indeed, low status is self-perpetuating. President Johnson himself apparently came to recognize this fact, for, in a commencement address at Howard University in 1965, he asserted:

> You do not take a person who for years has been hobbled by chains and liberate him, bring him up to the starting line of a race and . . . say, you're free to compete with all the others, and still justly believe that you have been completely fair.

In brief, equality of opportunity (even if realized in America) could not get the job done; equality of opportunity does not necessarily produce equality of results: on the contrary, to the extent that winners imply losers, equality of opportunity almost insures inequality of results. Hence, Blacks became increasingly concerned not merely with removing the barriers to full *opportunity* but with achieving the fact of *equality of results*, and achieving them *now*.

The civil rights movement, however, despite its detractors, did open up genuine opportunities for a small minority of Blacks who were already middle class, highly educated, and relatively well off. But it was as if the color computer had been programmed to extend

---

[62] Aberbach and Walker, *op. cit.*, 367.
[63] See: Samuel Dubois Cook, "The Tragic Myth of Black Power," *New South* Summer, 1966), 59.

to selected Blacks of high accomplishment selected categories of privileges previously withheld from all Blacks.[64] Yet this was of little help to the vast majority of Blacks who were, after all, not discriminated against merely as *individuals*, but as a *group*. As we have noted, they were excluded from the system in a systematic, self-perpetuating fashion. Under such circumstances, a new generation of leaders recognized that Blacks would have to be brought into the system as a group, just as they had been excluded from it as a group. And thus the slogan of "Black Power" was born.[65]

Second, the whole emphasis of the civil rights movement had been one in which Whites should change *their* attitudes (the emphasis, for instance, of Rev. Martin Luther King's message being one of gaining White sympathy and appealing to the hearts and souls of Whites) and opening up avenues of access to opportunities under *White* control. Blacks were to enter the White world—be assimilated within it—but not the other way around. Yet this was a degrading, emasculating position. Stokely Carmichael put it this way:

> Integration today means the man who "makes it," leaving his black brothers behind in the ghetto as fast as his new sports car will take him. . . . Integration, moreover, speaks to the problem of blackness in a despicable way. As a goal, it has been based on complete acceptance of the fact that in order to have a decent house or education, blacks must move into a white neighborhood or send their children to a white school. This reinforces, among both black and white, the idea the "white" is automatically better and "black" is by definition inferior. This is why integration is a subterfuge for the maintenance of white supremacy.[66]

Further, the White world had, to a large extent deprived Blacks of their own ethnic identity, made them feel ashamed of their own culture, made them feel that they had no culture, no history, no roots, no art, no language—that they were merely a substandard version of general White American culture. And the role and contributions of Blacks in American life were played down in the school texts on which the White as well as the Black children were brought up; the American educational system inculcated racism. The slogan,

[64] C. Eric Lincoln, "Color and Group Identity in the United States," *Daedalus*, 96 (1967), 536.

[65] Herbert C. Kelman, "A Social-Psychological Model of Political Legitimacy and Its Relevance to Black and White Student Protest Movements," *Psychiatry*, 33 (1970), 235.

[66] Stokely Carmichael, "What We Want," *The New York Review of Books*, September 22, 1966, p. 6.

"Black Power," became a vehicle by which Blacks could foster a sense of self-awareness, pride, and identity.[67]

A third factor accounting for the shift in the direction of Black Power was the friction that developed between Black and White civil rights workers in the South. During the Summer Projects of 1964 and 1965, campaigns which brought many White students into Southern civil rights work, it became apparent that a crisis in Black–White relations was emerging. All civil rights organizations (including the Congress of Racial Equality [CORE] and the Student Non-Violent Coordinating Committee [SNCC]) had initially championed Black–White solidarity—indeed, the anthem of the movement, "We Shall Overcome," was rarely sung without including the stanza, *"Black and White together,* we shall overcome." Within the movement, idealistic young people tried to be exemplars of successful interracial living; most workers—both Black and White—set out with dedication to be "color-blind" and to accept all people as "just human beings." For their part, local Black people often went out of their way to accommodate the White students in their homes and their communities.

As the Blacks and Whites were drawn into working relationships, however, their latent feelings slowly began to emerge. They painfully learned that racism had affected their behavior in so many ways that normal human relations between the races were fraught with severe social and psychological difficulties. Blacks complained that in one way or another White volunteers acted as if they thought themselves superior to Blacks: within a week or so of their arrival, Whites often behaved like "experts" and "authorities" (dubbed the "White African Queen Complex" [in women] and the "Tarzan Complex" [in men]), doing most of the "talking" and very little "listening"; Whites were impatient and quickly began to "direct programs" and "run" the project offices, thus "taking over" from Blacks; and, in some instances, some Whites were anxious to show off how "free" they were around Blacks, flouting the moral and social standards of the Black community with unconventional behavior (as if to say "anything goes in the Black community"). The antagonism was compounded by sociosexual conflicts (resulting from Black male–White female and White male–Black female relationships). Increasingly Black workers became disenchanted and discouraged by the

[67] Kelman, *op. cit.*, 235.

problems that an integrated movement had presented. Frustrated, they began to theorize that the movement was not "ready" for White workers, and, further, they launched a drive "to get the Whites out!" This drive took many forms, but finally culminated in the slogan of "Black Power" which was widely interpreted as excluding Whites automatically from work in the Black community.[68]

Fourth, the slogan "Black Power" seemed to make White America pay heed to Black demands. Whites for the most part found the slogan threatening, conjuring up images of Black racism, violence, and destruction.[69] Paraphrasing the *Communist Manifesto*, Jerry Talmer of the *New York Post* aptly observed: "A specter is haunting America—the specter is Black Power." [70] According to some social scientists, it is the *threat* of violence, not violence itself, that gets one what one wants. With a vivid enough imagination, especially on matters where widespread ignorance prevails, it is possible to erect a creditably threatening facade of potential guerrilla warfare and violence, even though carrying out the threat might be self-defeating and hence irrational. Strictly speaking, this would constitute a Black bluff. Yet none of this is sufficiently calculable or controllable to be so calmly dismissed. And if someone has a reputation for being quite angry already, who is to say how rational he will be? Further, sufficiently bellicose talk creates a crisis atmosphere that increases the likelihood that incidents will escalate—a kind of "brinkmanship" that increases the risk of a shared disaster that few would deliberately initiate (this exercise in brinkmanship parallels the United States-Soviet threats of thermonuclear war over Berlin and Cuba which while seemingly irrational are taken very seriously).[71]

One Black student summarizes the matter in these terms:

If you have something I want, okay. I can ask you for it; I can beg you for it; I can demonstrate around it; I can sit in it. But as long as it's yours, it's

[68] Alvin F. Poussaint and Joyce Ladner, " 'Black Power': A Failure for Racial Integration—Within the Civil Rights Movement," *Archives of General Psychiatry,* 18 (1968), 385–391; Alvin F. Poussaint, "The Stresses of the White Female Worker in the Civil Rights Movement in the South," *American Journal of Psychiatry,* 123 (1966), 401–407; and "Problems of White Civil Rights Workers in the South," *Psychiatric Opinion,* 3 (1966), 18–24.

[69] Aberbach and Walker, *op. cit.,* 371.

[70] *New York Post,* June 19, 1967, p. 33.

[71] Howard Hubbard, "Five Long Hot Summers and How They Grew," *The Public Interest,* Summer, 1968, pp. 17 and 23.

yours. And the only way I'm going to get you to listen to me is if you think I can destroy you.[72]

Similarly Malcolm X made the tactical observation to a middle-of-the-road Black leader that without pressure from the extremists the moderates would get nowhere.[73] The rhetoric of Black Power, then, offered the promise of extracting White concessions where the rhetoric of nonviolence had failed.

In closing our discussion of Black Power, it is worth noting that many Whites tend to view Black Power as the antithesis of integration. This conception vastly oversimplifies the matter. It is one thing to want equality within American life—not only to enjoy equality of opportunity but equality of results (a fair share of the good things America has to offer). But it does not necessarily follow that all Blacks are opposed to the maintenance of a distinct Black community—be it defined merely as the preservation of Black consciousness and identity or more broadly as the preservation of ethnic enclaves and institutions—assuming of course that the onus of compulsory segregation is eliminated. Public opinion studies reveal that many Blacks are attracted to the positive aspects of cultural pluralism, the Campbell-Schuman study, for instance, concluding: "A substantial number of Negroes want *both* integration and Black identity." [74] In brief, a good many Blacks do not want to become totally immersed and lost within White society as just so many atomized individuals. Rather, they would prefer to nurture Black *group* pride, self-confidence, and identity. Black Power, then, may serve as a means for facilitating the group's entry into the broader system, without, at least for the present, relinquishing the benefits of pluralism.

Nativistic Movements

When societies with different cultures are in continuous contact, it is not unusual to find a situation of inequality existing between them. Under conditions of dominance whereby the one society holds the other in a subordinate and disadvantaged state, nativistic

[72] Lawrence Mosher, "Why Blacks Turn Backs to War Protest," *National Observer*, June 29, 1970, p. 12.

[73] Hubbard, *op. cit.*, 21.

[74] Angus Campbell and Howard Schuman, *Racial Attitudes in Fifteen American Cities* (Washington, D.C.: U.S. Government Printing Office, 1968), 6. Also see: Thomas F. Pettigrew, "Racially Separate or Together?" *Journal of Social Issues*, 25 (1969), especially 65–66.

movements have been known to emerge. These movements represent a conscious, organized effort on the part of the members of the subordinate society to revive or perpetuate selected aspects of their culture. A notable ingredient of nativistic movements is the attempt to resist assimilation by the alien society that surrounds them. Strong undercurrents of withdrawal are present in which members of the subordinate society undertake to separate themselves from various elements and patterns of the dominant group's culture and to advance various current or remembered elements of their own culture. Simultaneously, strong overtones of aggressive behavior may be present.[75]

Among the North American Indians, nativistic movements represented one type of reaction to conditions of widespread deprivation. Under the impact of the White culture, Indian societies were undermined and their members thrown out of adjustment with significant features of the social environment. Old sets of norms were weakened by contact with the White culture, and as a consequence there arose a prevailing sense of confusion and a loss of orientation. No longer did there exist a foundation for security. The impact of the White culture not only deprived the Indians of their customary sense of direction and usual satisfactions, but it added to their sufferings by introducing the effects of new diseases and intoxicating liquor. Epidemics of measles, grippe, and whooping cough served to decimate their numbers.[76]

One of the fundamental myths of the Indian nativistic movements was the belief that a culture hero would one day appear and lead the tribal members to a terrestrial paradise. Through the intervention of the Great Spirit or his emissary, a "golden age" was to be ushered in within a short time. There was to be no sickness or death, only eternal happiness when the golden age arrived. Some twenty such movements were recorded in the United States prior to 1890. In anticipation of the establishment of the millennium, believers were instructed to return to the aboriginal mode of life. Traits and customs symbolic of foreign influence were to be put away.

Probably the best known of these movements was the "Ghost

[75] Ralph Linton, "Nativistic Movements," *American Anthropologist*, 45 (1943), 230–240.

[76] Bernard Barber, "Acculturation and Messianic Movements," *American Sociological Review*, 6 (1941), 663–669.

Dance" which spread among the Plains tribes in 1890. The movement had gone through an earlier phase in 1870 but by 1875 had exhausted itself. Wovoka, a Paiute, who was known to the Whites as Jack Wilson, played a key role in the revived movement. During an illness Wovoka had experienced a trance that led him to believe he had been chosen by departed ancestors to initiate a movement among the Indians. His teachings were a composite of various beliefs and traditions long present in Indian life plus ingredients acquired from Christianity. Wovoka urged the Indians to live morally, to love one another, to live at peace with the world, and to prepare for a day when all Indians living and dead would be reunited in a state of everlasting happiness. A Messiah would appear in the future and would bring with him in bodily form their deceased ancestors. A great whirlwind would arise and all Whites would perish. The buffalo and other game would be restored. It was essentially a doctrine of hope. The golden age would be a world without Whites, in which once again Indians might attain stature. All this represented an effort to isolate the Indians from the disorganizing impact of White society.

Messengers went from tribe to tribe, bringing with them the new religion and teaching the dance. Some of the participants in the dance would wear a "ghost shirt," tailored in the Indian fashion and made of white cloth. The leader would carry red feathers, red cloth, and a "ghost stick" some six feet in length. Arrows with bone heads, bows, gaming wheels, and sticks found incorporation within the ritual. The dancers would shake with emotion and fall into hypnotic trances. During the trances, they would experience visions of departed Indians in the world beyond who were engaged in dancing, playing games, gathering for war dances, preparing for the hunt, and joining together in traditional fraternal organizations.[77]

VARIABLES AFFECTING THE RESPONSE OF MINORITY-GROUP MEMBERS

Robert Johnson, in his study of 150 Blacks conducted two decades ago in an upstate New York community of 60,000 persons, found the

[77] Brewton Berry, *Race and Ethnic Relations,* 3rd ed. (Boston: Houghton Mifflin Co., 1965), 398–399. Also see: Vittorio Lanternari, *The Religions of the Oppressed: A Study of Modern Messianic Cults* (New York: Mentor Books, 1965), especially Chapter 3.

withdrawing or insulating response most prevalent among women, the southern-born, the less educated, and older Blacks—the most significant variables associated with insulating attitudes being low education and southern origin.[78] More recently Campbell and Schuman found that this picture had altered somewhat with Black youths being the most inclined of all age groups to favor "separatist" policies (separatism here ranges from the "black power–community control" approach to that of the "separate nation" doctrine), as shown in Table 13–1.[79] Similarly, the Black Muslim movement has had its greatest appeal in recent years among race-conscious Black youth who have encountered racial barriers or frustrations on the path to a share of the status and economic rewards commonly enjoyed by Whites. Yet such findings may be deceiving. Among youthful Black supporters of the Black Muslims, the organization represents more an affirmation of Black manhood and solidarity than of racial separation—Muslim supporters do not markedly differ from other Black youth, for instance, in the belief that Blacks should require Whites to open their neighborhoods to Blacks and that Black organizations should not exclude Whites.[80]

As we noted in the chapter, the slogan Black Power has come to the forefront in the Black community since 1966. It has meant quite different things to various segments of the Black community—the most popular interpretations revolving about the concept of racial unity and a claim to a fair share of America's good things. Viewed in these terms, the appeal of Black Power has cut across age and socioeconomic lines.[81]

Aberbach and Walker, based on an attitude survey in Detroit, Michigan, found that the variable of age did not appreciably differentiate among members of the Black community with reference to a favorable interpretation of Black Power. Differences existed, not so much between the young and the old, but between those who grew up in Michigan and those who were born and grew up in the South. The data suggested that the further a Black was from life in the South, and the sooner he experienced life in a city like Detroit, the more likely he was to approve of Black Power. Life in the north-

---

[78] Robert Johnson, op. cit., 202–203.

[79] Angus Campbell and Howard Schuman, Racial Attitudes in Fifteen American Cities (Washington, D.C.: U.S. Government Printing Office, 1968), 18.

[80] Glen H. Elder, Jr., "Group Orientations and Strategies in Racial Change," Social Forces, 488 (1970), 459.

[81] Aberbach and Walker, op. cit., 374 ff.

TABLE 13–1　Percentage in Each Age Category Showing Separatist Thinking on Five Questions

	Black Men					
	16–19	20–29	30–39	40–49	50–59	60–69*
Believe stores in "a Negro neighborhood should be owned and run by Negroes"	28	23	20	18	14	18
Believe school with mostly Negro children should have mostly Negro teachers	22	15	13	6	5	15
Agree that "Negroes should have nothing to do with whites if they can help it"	18	14	6	12	4	13
Believe whites should be discouraged from taking part in civil rights organizations	19	12	8	6	3	5
Agree that "there should be a separate black nation here"	11	10	5	5	4	10
	Black Women					
Believe stores in "a Negro neighborhood should be owned and run by Negroes"	18	16	16	15	13	8
Believe school with mostly Negro children should have mostly Negro teachers	11	9	6	5	5	12
Agree that "Negroes should have nothing to do with whites if they can help it"	11	7	7	8	5	7
Believe whites should be discouraged from taking part in civil rights organizations	11	7	7	5	7	3
Agree that "there should be a separate black nation here"	9	3	2	6	4	3

* Campbell and Schuman suspect that the relatively high percentage of males in the 60–69 age bracket involves an irrelevant artifact.

Source: Angus Campbell and Howard Schuman, Racial Attitudes in Fifteen American Cities (Washington, D.C.: U.S. Government Printing Office, 1968), Table II–f, p. 18.

ern city apparently brought to bear on a Black forces which led him to reject the traditional, accommodating attitudes of the South; he was away from the parochial, oppressive atmosphere of the South, while being exposed within the North to a cosmopolitan, secularized culture. The new life in the promised lands of Detroit, New York, and Chicago was experienced as exciting and simultaneously disillusioning. It brought new hopes and the promise of a better life, yet disappointments when achievements did not live up to expectations.[82]

Similarly, support for Black Power cut across socioeconomic lines. For lower education Blacks, however, approval of Black Power was strongly influenced by dissatisfaction with their lot and pessimism about the future. For Blacks with higher levels of education, these factors proved of considerably less importance. Rather they were drawn to Black Power by their identification with the Black community—their feelings for the group.[83]

Dizard likewise found in his study of Black attitudes in Berkeley, California, that a positive attachment to Black identity cut across age and socioeconomic lines. Although occupational strata differed in attachment (see Figure 13–1), persons with a positive sense of Black identity were nonetheless widely distributed throughout the social structure of the Black community. Dizard contends that

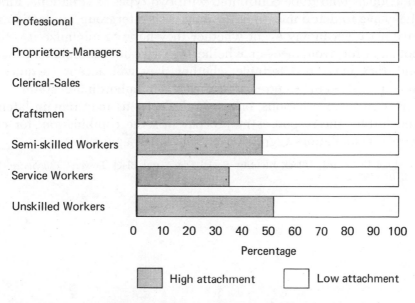

Fig. 13–1. Attachment to Black Identity, by Occupational Status. *Source:* Adapted from Jan E. Dizard, "Black Identity, Social Class, and Black Power," *Psychiatry*, 33 (1970), Table 2, page 202.

[82] *Ibid.,* 374–376.
[83] *Ibid.,* 379.

the growing attachment to Black identity has helped to obscure the lines of stratification within the Black community.[84]

SUMMARY

Avoidance is the polar opposite of assimilation, a response characterized by the attempt to shun or escape from situations in which a minority encounters prejudice and discrimination. Avoidance may find many forms of expression, from simple isolation to migration and separatism. In separatism, an aggressive response generally becomes linked with that of avoidance, reflected in Zionism, Garveyism, the Black Muslims, and some expressions of Black Power. Black Power, it should be noted, has been interpreted in a great many ways, although it tends to involve a theme of Black pride, Black unity, and economic and political power for the Black community.

Overall, we have indicated in the past four chapters that minority individuals tend to be confronted with two types of situation. First, they have to determine whether they wish intergroup interaction to take place (or in any event whether they hope to minimize it)—the potential for avoidance—or whether to strive for assimilation. Second, they have to determine whether they will accept (acquiesce in) or strike out (aggress) against their subordinate status. Of course in some situations, one or both decisions may remain latent, and further the responses may occur in some combination, for example, assimilation–aggression or avoidance–aggression.

[84] Jan E. Dizard, "Black Identity, Social Class, and Black Power," *Psychiatry*, 33 (1970), 195–207.

SOCIAL CHANGE

14

Minority-Dominant
Patterns in Transition

In a world in which prejudice and discrimination seem to abound, it is sometimes difficult to grasp the fact that minority-dominant relations actually change. Yet change is an integral and inescapable feature of social existence. All social systems are constantly in a state of flux, although at times the shifts may be slow and virtually imperceptible. Patterns of American dominant-minority relations have been no exception, undergoing continuous change. The dynamic nature of intergroup relations and the magnitude of the forces that have been an ever present feature of American life can perhaps best be appreciated by examining a number of these patterns through time.

THE EARLY YEARS

In contemporary America, where racial conflicts and antipathies are periodically caught within the swirling currents of publicity, controversy, and emotion, it is sometimes difficult to picture an America where the race issue was of relatively little consequence and where instead religious bigotry and persecution provided the principal focus of turmoil. Yet this was the setting of America during its early years. During the 1620s and 1630s, when James I and his successor, Charles I, of England were pursuing High-Church policies, thousands of Puritans migrated to America, locating in New

England. The Puritans stressed Low-Church practices and a Cal-
vinist tradition. In Massachusetts, the clergy dominated the government, and for this reason the colony has often been referred to as
a theocracy. Only a minority of the settlers had the privilege of
church membership, this being reserved for those who had expressed
repentance and had been officially admitted to the local congregations. Nevertheless, all residents of the colony were required to
conform to the faith. Separation of church and state was unknown
in Massachusetts. For more than fifty years no one who did not
belong to the Puritan church (in time known as the Congregational
church) could vote or hold office. Thus only about one-fifth of the
adult White males enjoyed the ballot.

Although they themselves had been the victims of religious intolerance in England, the Puritans had little sympathy for other
religious dissenters. Dissent was equated with damnation. Members of the Society of Friends, derisively known as "Quakers" because of their quaking motions and trembling mode of delivery,
were persecuted with fines, floggings, and banishment. Four Quakers who defied expulsion, one of them a woman, were hanged in Boston. Since the colonists were often at war with the Indians, Quaker
opposition to war intensified Puritan irritation. As have many other
peoples throughout history, the Puritans sought a scapegoat for their
difficulties. Among the charges they leveled against the Quakers
was that the latter incited Indians against them.

A sharp challenge to the authority of the Congregational clergy
came from some of the residents of Massachusetts, among whom
Roger Williams and Mrs. Anne Hutchinson were the chief spokesmen. The group was subsequently expelled from the colony, Williams for disseminating "newe & dangerous opinions" and Hutchinson as a "leper." Williams fled to the Rhode Island area, where he
founded Providence and Newport in the late 1630s. There he established complete freedom of religion, even for Jews and Catholics—
virtually unheard of at that time. No oaths regarding a person's
religious beliefs were required, nor were taxes to support a state
church or compulsory attendance at worship demanded. Simple
manhood suffrage was practiced from the start, although it was later
modified by property qualifications.

Stormy religious friction also characterized Maryland's early history. In 1632, Cecilius Calvert, the second Lord Baltimore, secured
a charter from Charles I to establish the colony. As a Catholic,

Calvert wanted to found a colony open to members of his faith. But Calvert did not exclude Protestants, since he was anxious to swell the number of settlers and thus make the venture profitable; in any case, the English government would have objected to an exclusively Catholic colony. It was not long before Protestants predominated in Maryland and, in keeping with the religious intolerance of the period, resented the presence of the Catholics. Bitterness was intensified by Jesuit activities and by the fact that the best offices in the colony were controlled by Catholics. By 1654, the Protestants had wrested control of Maryland from Calvert and had suppressed Catholicism. But, in 1657, with Oliver Cromwell's support, the supporters of Calvert regained control and restored religious tolerance. Religious friction persisted, and this together with economic difficulties contributed to a series of disorders and revolts. The result was that in 1691 England made Maryland a royal colony, and the Anglican church was established as the state church.

Whereas Maryland was founded by a Catholic, Pennsylvania was established by a Quaker, William Penn. The Quaker sect had arisen in England during the mid-1600s. Their "quaking" at religious services, their refusal to support the established Church of England with taxes, their use of thees" and "thous" instead of more conventional titles, their refusal to take oaths and to participate in military service, among other behavior, often embroiled them with government officials. Penn joined the sect in 1660 and, by virtue of the persecution to which he and his co-religionists were subjected, sought asylum in the New World. In 1681, he managed to secure from the King an immense tract of land in America, in consideration of a monetary debt owed by the Crown to his deceased father. Penn established an unusually liberal regime in Pennsylvania, in which freedom of worship was guaranteed to all residents. However, under pressure from London, Penn was forced to deny Catholics and Jews the privilege of voting or of holding office. By virtue of the freedom and tolerance prevailing within Pennsylvania, many Quakers and other religious dissenters were attracted to the colony.

In New Jersey and Delaware, Quaker influence was also strong; these colonies, like Pennsylvania and Rhode Island, had no official religion. In other colonies the state-church system prevailed. In New England, except for Rhode Island, the Congregationalists were dominant; elsewhere the established church was the Anglican, as in England.

A number of forces, however, were at work, which as the years passed contributed to the separation of church and state, religious freedom, and greater religious tolerance. Opposition to the established Anglican and Congregational churches arose among many ordinary farmers and tradesmen who objected to their aristocratic control. The leading clergy- and laymen were commonly drawn from the upper classes, a fact that irritated and angered many of the communicants. The popularity of the dissenting sects grew as dissatisfaction with the state churches intensified. Simultaneously, new immigrants contributed to the diversity of the religious beliefs within the colonies. The Great Awakening, in the 1730s and 1740s, led by such outstanding evangelists as Jonathan Edwards, George Whitefield, and John Wesley, fostered revivalistic fervor and leveling tendencies that did much to undermine the established churches and to further fractionize the American population religiously. The great multiplicity of faiths made intolerance impractical and disruptive of the social fabric.

SEGREGATION IN THE SOUTH

The Origins of "Jim Crow"

It has not been uncommon for White southerners and many other Americans to assume the "Jim Crow" system in the South—legalized segregation—always was that way. Or at any rate, if not always, then "since slavery times" or "since the Civil War" or "since Reconstruction." A good many of the discussions that have taken place over civil rights in recent decades have been premised on the assumption that southern segregationist practices are deeply rooted; from this assumption the conclusion was frequently drawn that segregationist practices are virtually ineradicable and not particularly amenable to change. Such notions are part of a prevalent myth that has viewed southern race patterns as having been virtually immune to change for over three hundred years, as having remained untouched by the passage of time until the past decade or so.

The myth persists despite the fact that southerners have probably been more familiar with the shifting fortunes of history than other Americans have been. Their own history has amply demonstrated that an old order and its institutions can perish quite quickly and rather completely. Following the Civil War, a new order was instituted that had behind it all the authority and confidence of a victorious North; and then again, within a span of ten years, this new order was to give way to still a third. Each successive regime in the South—slavery and secession, emancipation and reconstruction, redemption and reunion—had its characteristic economic organization, its system of politics, and its social arrangements. And in each the race patterns were quite distinct.[1]

C. Vann Woodward, a noted American historian, convincingly demonstrates the changing character of the southern racial structure in his study of the rise of Jim Crow. He suggests that the assumption is often incorrectly made that Reconstruction constituted an interruption of normal relations between the races in the South. According to this view, once the White southerners had overthrown the carpetbagger and scalawag regimes and established "home rule," while conceding that slavery was finished, they proceeded to restore to normality the disturbed relations between the two racial groups. This view overlooks the fact that segregation would have been impractical under slavery, as Black domestic servants participated quite extensively in the life and households of the White upper classes. Furthermore, the institution of Jim Crowism did not follow automatically upon the overthrow of Reconstruction but to a considerable degree was a development later in time.

Accounts written by both critics and friends of the South during the two decades following Reconstruction give ample testimony to the fact that Jim Crow was virtually absent from the region. Blacks generally received equality of treatment on common carriers, trains, and streetcars; were freely admitted to theaters, lectures, and exhibitions; and were served at the bars, restaurants, soda fountains, and ice-cream saloons patronized by Whites. When, however, there there was sufficient room, Whites avoided sitting with Blacks, and within restaurants were usually served at separate tables. Similarly, Blacks were not disfranchised immediately after the overthrow of Reconstruction. Although Blacks were often coerced and defrauded, they continued to vote in large numbers in most parts of the South for more than two decades after Reconstruction.

In South Carolina in 1898, when the movement for the institution of Jim Crow separation on railway cars was gathering momentum, the *Charleston News and Courier*, the oldest newspaper in the South,

---

[1] C. Vann Woodward, *The Strange Career of Jim Crow*, 2nd rev. ed. (New York: Oxford University Press, 1966). This account is summarized from this source.

editorialized against the measure in these terms: "As we have got on fairly well for a third of a century, including a long period of reconstruction, without such a measure, we can probably get on as well hereafter without it, and certainly so extreme a measure should not be adopted and enforced without added and urgent cause." The editor then called attention to what he considered the *absurd* consequences to which such a law might lead:

> If there must be Jim Crow cars on the railroads, there should be Jim Crow cars on the street railways. Also on all passenger boats. . . . If there are to be Jim Crow cars, moreover, there should be Jim Crow waiting saloons at all stations, and Jim Crow eating houses. . . . There should be Jim Crow sections of the jury box, and a separate Jim Crow dock and witness stand in every court—and a Jim Crow Bible for colored witnesses to kiss. It would be advisable also to have a Jim Crow section in county auditors' and treasurers' offices for the accommodation of colored taxpayers.[2]

What the editor of the Charleston papers obviously regarded as an absurdity became in a very short time a reality.

It should not be assumed that in the period between Reconstruction and the institution of the Jim Crow laws a golden age of race relations prevailed.[3] It was precisely in the eighties and nineties that lynching attained its most staggering proportions. The absence of formalized segregation did not mean that Blacks were accepted as social equals by Whites. Such acceptance was no more frequent before the introduction of the Jim Crow era than it was at the height of that era. Segregation probably entailed a further lowering of the Black's status, but it did not imply a fall from full equality. Evidence indicates that Blacks were often denied their civil rights and discriminated against before the era of genuine segregation which was introduced in the 1890s. In education in particular, custom dictated the separate education of Blacks and Whites. But after the 1890s the principle of segregation was consciously and deliberately applied to all possible areas of contact between the two groups and became a hard-and-fast dogma of southern life. Legalized Jim Crow, then, came to replace the increasingly inappropriate and ob-

---

[2] *Ibid.*, 67–68.

[3] In this regard also see: Joel Williamson, *After Slavery: The Negro in South Carolina During Reconstruction 1861–1877* (Chapel Hill: The University of North Carolina Press, 1965), especially Chapter 10. Also: August Meier and Elliott Rudwick, "A Strange Chapter in the Career of 'Jim Crow,'" in August Meier and Elliott Rudwick, eds., *The Making of Black America*, Vol. II (New York: Atheneum, 1969), 14–19.

solete mechanisms of social distance that had previously regulated White–Black interaction in a primarily informal fashion.

In the decades immediately following Reconstruction, the southern Bourbon regimes were predominantly characterized by a conservative philosophy on the race question. Blacks were viewed as belonging in a subordinate position, but the conservatives denied that this necessitated their being ostracized; similarly, they believed Blacks were inferior, but they denied that segregation must be the result. The conservatives looked with disapproval upon Whites who championed the cause of the Black, seeing such individuals as false friends who pretended friendship for the Black to advance selfish ends of party advantage and private gain. At the same time, they disapproved of the Negrophobe fanatics who proposed an aggressive war against the Blacks and a program of virulent racism. And then too the old Bourbon aristocracy sought to maintain its power in southern states by manipulating the Black vote against the poor Whites.

In contrast with the conservative philosophy, there arose in the 1890s another approach, worked out and expressed by the Populists. The Populists fancied themselves exponents of a new realism on the race issue, a realism that was neither the product of a liberal conscience on the one hand nor the product of a *noblesse oblige* paternalism on the other. It was the hope of an important segment of the Populist leadership that the great mass of southern White farmers and sharecroppers would join hands with their Black counterparts in a fight against want, poverty, and the large business and landed interests of the period. A Texas Populist expressed the position in these terms: "They [Blacks] are in the ditch just like we are." Populist leaders such as Tom Watson, before he became a virulent racist, preached that the identity of interests of the farming groups of both races transcended differences in race. Eventually disillusioned, the Populists assumed a leading role in promoting a strong Jim Crow program.

Prior to 1900, the only law of a Jim Crow type adopted by the majority of southern states was that applying to passengers aboard trains. South Carolina did not adopt such a measure until 1898, North Carolina not until 1899, and Virginia not until 1900. In the decade that followed, the application of mandatory segregation in new areas of life unfolded in fadlike fashion, each wave bringing additional laws. Across the South, law and custom dictated that "White Only" or "Colored" signs appear over entrances, exits, toilets, water fountains, waiting rooms, and ticket windows. Segregation became formally instituted in wide areas of life. Some southern communities even went to the extreme of enacting laws requiring the residential segregation of Blacks. Similarly, various measures were adopted to disfranchise Blacks. Mississippi was the first state to move in this direction, with South Carolina following in 1895, Louisiana in 1898, North Carolina in 1900, Alabama in 1901, Virginia in 1902, Georgia in 1908, and Oklahoma in 1910. These laws were aimed at nullifying the effect of the Fifteenth Amendment. Since Blacks could not be deprived of the right to vote on grounds of race, a whole battery of poll taxes, educational and literacy tests, white primaries, and grandfather clauses were evolved to achieve the same end.

Woodward suggests that the South's adoption of extreme racism was due not so much to a conversion as it was to a relaxation of the opposition. By the 1890s and early 1900s, there developed a general weakening and discrediting of the numerous forces that had hitherto kept racism in check. As the years passed, opinion in the North shifted away from liberalism, in many respects keeping pace with opinion in the South, and conceded one point after another, so that at no time were the sections very far apart on race policy. Within the South itself the position of the conservatives was weakened and undermined, and their willingness and ability to hold the Negrophobe fanatics in check were diminished. Although the conservatives had reaped enormous prestige by their overthrow of the Reconstruction regimes, an accumulation of grievances, financial scandals, and alliances with northeastern capital and conservatives served to undercut their popularity in the South. The Populists for their part found their biracial partnership dissolving in frustration and bitterness, with their opponents raising the cry of White supremacy against them. For a good many of the Populists it became easy to blame the Blacks for their defeat, to make him the scapegoat, and to vent their bitterness and hostility upon him. It was not long before former Populists were found in the forefront of many rabid anti-Black movements. With the capitulation of northern liberalism, the diminution of the strength of the southern conservative position, and the flight of the Populists from biracialism, racism triumphed.

The rise of the Jim Crow statutes in the South had the effect of tightening and freezing segregation and discrimination. In many instances these statutes actually served to instigate such practices. Prior to the enactment of these laws the Blacks could and did do many things in the South which he was subsequently prevented from doing. It is clear, then, that formalized segregation is relatively new in the South and that the southern race patterns have not been immune to social change.

The Second Reconstruction

By the early years of the twentieth century, the Jim Crow order was well established in the South. The sanction of law was lent to racial ostracism that extended to churches and schools, to housing and jobs, to eating and drinking, not to mention public transportation, sports, hospitals, prisons, asylums, and even funeral homes and cemeteries. As Woodward observes:

The new Southern system was regarded as the "final settlement," the "return to sanity," the "permanent system." Few stopped to reflect that previous systems had also been regarded as final, sane, and permanent by their supporters. The illusion of permanency was encouraged by the complacency of a long-critical North, the propaganda of reconciliation, and the resigned compliance of the Negro. The illusion was strengthened further by the passage of several decades during which change was averted or minimized.[4]

Since World War II, however, a new era of change set upon the South. Major assaults have been directed against segregation from a great many quarters, with demands that the South institute immediate reform. The stage was set for the new era with the May 17, 1954, school desegregation ruling. On that date, the Supreme Court, consolidating cases arising in Delaware, Kansas, South Carolina, and Virginia, unanimously ruled that the "separate but equal" doctrine, which had been used to bar Black children from White public schools, was unconstitutional. Mandatory school segregation was thus struck down. In so doing, the Supreme Court again demonstrated that it could change its mind. Fifty-eight years earlier, in the case of *Plessy* v. *Ferguson,* it held the contrary. In the years that followed the 1954 ruling, the Supreme Court moved toward outlawing legalized segregation in all areas of American life. In addition to the Supreme Court, pressures increased in other quarters. In the

[4] Woodward, *op. cit.,* 7–8.

past two decades, demands have mounted across America for congressional enactment of new civil rights legislation. Similarly, executive orders of presidents, policy decisions of federal agencies and the military, and actions by labor unions, professional groups, churches and others contributed to the assault upon Jim Crow. This new era of change is sometimes referred to as the "Second Reconstruction."

Movement and Countermovement. It is clear, then, that social change need not "just happen." It may occur because people undertake to *make* it occur. In brief, when people feel dissatisfied with the institutions or norms of their society, they may initiate social change. Through more or less persistent and organized effort —a social movement—they attempt to change a situation they define as unsatisfactory. And as we have noted elsewhere in this text, this is precisely what a good many Blacks have undertaken to do. Indeed the assault upon the southern Jim Crow order has also been joined by others, including the united AFL–CIO labor movement (although it has at times shown considerable resistance to the challenging of racist patterns within its own framework), the nation's major church bodies (although a few southern denominations have been at most only lukewarm supporters), the major political parties through their platform statements and the declarations of their spokesmen, many civic organizations, and, probably most formidable of all, the federal government via presidential executive orders, new congressional enactments, and judicial rulings.

Yet social movements do not initiate social change simply because they arise. Cultural persistence poses one formidable impediment to social reform. Once a pattern of social relationships has been established, it tends to carry on unchanged, except as the dynamics of other social forces operate to undermine it. Generally people find comfort, security, and a sense of well-being in old, familiar, and established ways. New forms of behavior, adjustments, and situational definitions often confront people with ambiguities and contradictions. For many individuals, efforts to resolve such ambiguities and contradictions would set up disturbing tensions that would in turn involve serious difficulties. Accordingly, it is frequently easier to go along with the old way of doing things, especially when no incentive for inaugurating the new way is seen. The situation is compounded when people assign strong emotional qualities to the old way, such as many White southerners assign to their traditional race patterns. Thus the fact of cultural tenacity has proved a major obstacle to the integrationist movement.

Another impediment to social reform may be the emergence of a counter-movement—a resistance movement. Movement frequently begets counter-movement. Between the two movements a dynamic interaction may ensue, involving a more or less prolonged struggle. Thus integrationist efforts to topple the Jim Crow order have stimulated the rise of a large-scale resistance movement. This movement has attempted to minimize the consequences of the various assaults upon the region's racial system, and to save the existing system intact.[5] Let us turn to an examination of the southern resistance movement and the progressive accommodation of Whites to desegregation.

Accommodation to Undesired Change.   The Supreme Court's decision of May 17, 1954, holding segregated public schools unconstitutional, confronted the South with the demand that mandatory school segregation be ended. Three more or less distinct phases can be noted in the resistance that unfolded within the region to this new demand for change. Here we will focus our attention upon Virginia, South Carolina, Georgia, Alabama, Mississippi, Louisiana, and Arkansas, where the resistance was most intense.[6]

The first phase, from May 17, 1954, through May 31, 1955, was generally characterized by two co-existing themes. The first theme was a prevailing disbelief, "It won't happen!" For the great mass of southern Whites the whole matter of desegregation appeared obtuse, one far off in Washington. It did not appear to them that desegregation could actually happen. Since the prospect of desegregation was a threatening, discomforting development, many southern Whites responded by magically denying the reality of the new situation. They reassured themselves that desegregation was unthinkable and thus would simply not take place. The second theme involved an attitude of "buying time." This orientation was most prevalent among state government leaders. It was widely believed among them that some desegregation would be inescapable. But if

---

[5] James W. Vander Zanden, "Resistance and Social Movements," *Social Forces*, 37 (1959), 312–315.

[6] Part of the account that follows is summarized from James W. Vander Zanden, "Accommodation to Undesired Change: The Case of the South," *The Journal of Negro Education*, 31 (1962), 30–35, and "Seven Years of Southern Resistance," *The Midwest Quarterly*, II (1961), 273–284.

it were inescapable, they nevertheless hoped to delay it, and delay became their major tactic. Overall, the southern scene was generally quiet and calm during the first year, with the region's leaders and newspapers reacting with restraint. Although new segregationist laws were added to the legal arsenal in hopes of delaying and circumventing the high court's ruling, their number was limited.

Then, on May 31, 1955, the Supreme Court handed down its decree *implementing* the ruling of the previous year. It declared that the federal district courts would have jurisdiction over lawsuits to enforce the ruling. It told the lower courts to be guided by "equitable principles" characterized by a "practical flexibility," but it warned that "constitutional principles cannot be allowed to yield simply because of disagreement with them." Defendant school districts were instructed that "a prompt and reasonable start toward full compliance" would be required and that admissions on a racially non-discriminatory basis must be made with "all deliberate speed."

The high court's 1955 decree initiated the second phase of the resistance, characterized by a marked tightening of sentiment throughout the Deep and mid-South. The National Association for the Advancement of Colored People immediately followed the decree with a new offensive. Some 170 school boards in seventeen states were confronted with petitions signed by local Blacks demanding immediate school desegregation. The fiction "It can't happen" was exploded. Angered, Whites inaugurated a policy of adamant resistance in which compromise was ruled out. Methods of resistance grew bolder. Within the heavily Black populated Black Belt areas, the White Citizens Councils mushroomed. Although these organizations had previously been limited to a handful of chapters, thousands now signed Council membership cards, and Council rallies were well attended. Newspapers published the names of Blacks who signed the petitions, and Whites applied sanctions and social pressures against them. On the government level, state leaders rushed into law more than 200 new acts, in a desperate effort to find some legal mechanism through which to circumvent the Supreme Court's ruling.

By the fall of 1956 the school-desegregation battle appeared stalemated, with the segregationists in the saddle. For integrationists the situation was bleak. Congressman Charles C. Diggs of Michigan, himself a Black, lamented, "We cannot point to one instance of submission by Mississippi, Georgia, South Carolina, or Alabama to the Supreme Court's three-year-old decision outlawing school segregation. There is little question that the Deep South has won the first round in the battle for compliance with the decision of May 17, 1954." It was within this context that the Little Rock drama unfolded in late 1957, setting the basis for the third phase in the southern resistance—a phase of progressive accommodation to desegregation that has continued through the present.

It is conceivable that history will show that Little Rock represented the key battle between school integrationists and segregationists, the turning point of the struggle. Arkansas Governor Orval Faubus had called out the National Guard in an effort to block the desegregation of Little Rock Central High School. As a result, a historic precedent was inevitable. The issue posed by Faubus was whether a state could use the National Guard, the ultimate coercive instrumentality at its command, to enforce segregation. The issue could not be compromised, since a state either could or could not use armed forces to defy the federal courts. As developments unfolded, President Eisenhower decisively intervened, broke the stalemate, and turned the tide in favor of desegregation.

Confronted by the new situation posed by the developments at Little Rock, the White South could in essence take only one of two possible alternative courses: Either it could intensify its resistance efforts and search for new weapons or it could begin the process of accommodation to school desegregation. The first course would have involved a continuation of the second phase, namely, adamant resistance and the rejection of compromise. Yet legal avenues for the total and more or less permanent blocking of desegregation had been effectively closed. Extralegal instrumentalities including violence and armed resistance would have offered still another means of blocking desegregation. But rioting, chaos, and violence would have jeopardized still other values. And Little Rock demonstrated that force would be met with force. If the South needed a reminder, memories of the Civil War still haunted the region, a war that demonstrated the folly of such an approach.

The South, accordingly, moved in the direction of the second alternative and began the process of accommodation to school desegregation. Virginia is a case in point. In Virginia, James Lindsay Almond, Jr., a fire-and-brimstone orator of the old school, became governor in January, 1958. Before his election as governor, Almond had served eight years as Virginia's Attorney General, and had been in the forefront of the fight to maintain the segregated order. It was a self-labeled program of "massive resistance" to desegregation. Campaigning for governor, Almond told Virginians, "There can be no surrender . . . I am willing to continue the fight to the last ditch, and then to dig another ditch. . . . If we yield one inch we are lost forever. . . . There can be no middle ground that will provide an avenue of escape. . . ."

Yet within thirteen months Almond stood before his 100-member House of Delegates and the 40-member Senate of Virginia, called into emergency session by him. "Massive resistance" had collapsed in the courts. Seven Virginia public schools had opened early in 1959 on a desegregated basis. Although his speech was elaborately embellished, paying homage to the cause of "massive resistance," Almond essentially declared that (1) the maintenance of completely segregated public schools was no longer possible in Virginia, (2) all legal avenues had been closed, and (3) the choice had become some integration if public schools were to be maintained or no public schools if total segregation was the goal. Significantly Almond cast his lot with the public schools and carried the state legislature with him. In subsequent speeches he explained, "I tell you now that we cannot overthrow the federal government, and we cannot reverse a final decree of a federal court." No mistake could be more costly than to "succumb to the blandishments of those who would have Virginia abandon public education and thereby consign a generation of children to the darkness of illiteracy, the pits of indolence and dependency and the dungeons of delinquency."

Defeated in their efforts to block school desegregation, southern leaders began to tell their constituents, "We have done everything possible to prevent desegregation. We can do no more. We are now in a situation where we will have to accept some Blacks in our White public schools. But we will do all in our power to see to it that the number of Black children is held to a bare minimum. We will maintain our southern way of life!" Although school desegregation was often little more than "token," involving small numbers of Blacks, the walls of school segregation were breached.

Southern leaders such as Virginia's James Lindsay Almond, Jr., served to make school desegregation palatable to the White citizenry. Their loyalty to "southern institutions" could not generally be questioned. They functioned to redefine school desegregation in terms that made it no longer equivalent to social equality. They reassured

Whites that southern traditions would carry on, that they need not feel alarmed or threatened. And, simultaneously, social change continued.

Yet despite signs that White southerners were progressively accommodating themselves to school desegregation, it was not until the introduction, debate, and enactment of the Civil Rights Act of 1964 that significant gains took place along the road toward ending formal segregation. The failure of southern Whites to block school desegregation and the passage of new civil rights legislation led many southern leaders to take the course of still further accommodation to desegregation. The late Senator Richard B. Russell, a longtime Senate power and leader of Senate anti-civil rights forces, called upon his fellow Georgians to live with the new law:

Violence and law violation will only compound our difficulties and increase our troubles. It is the understatement of the year to say that I do not like this statute [the 1964 Civil Rights Act]. However, it is now on the books. All good citizens will learn to live with the statute and abide by its final adjudication even though we reserve the right to advocate by legal means its repeal or modification. We put everything we had into the fight, but the odds against us mounted from day to day until we were finally gagged and overwhelmed.[7]

Within four months of the passage of the Civil Rights Act of 1964, a U.S. government survey of public accommodations in 53 cities in the 19 states which had no anti-Jim Crow public facilities' laws revealed that desegregation had been accomplished in two-thirds of the hotels in 51 cities and more than two-thirds of the motels in 46 cities; more than two-thirds of theaters in 49 cities; more than two-thirds of sports facilities in 48 cities; more than two-thirds of public parks in 50 cities; more than two-thirds of libraries in 52 cities; and more than two-thirds of chain restaurants in 50 cities (the largest downtown restaurants in major cities generally desegregated although neighborhood luncheonettes and taverns often remained segregated). All this did not mean that all southern Whites were bowing gracefully to desegregation, but that instances of accommodation more than offset instances of Whites who chose the course of continuing resistance. Nor did it mean that the use of public facilities once restricted to Whites had as yet become the pattern among southern Blacks.

In addition to the traditional judicial approach for ending formal

[7] "Rights Obedience Urged by Russell," New York Times, July 16, 1964.

school segregation, Title VI of the Civil Rights Acts of 1964 provided for an administrative remedy; federal officials were authorized to cut off funds to school districts practicing segregation. Under the Johnson Administration, school desegregation was pushed largely in this fashion, with the courts playing a complementary role in the process. The Nixon Administration, however, relied less on cut-off actions, deferring more to the courts and acting as an "adviser" to the courts in drafting desegregation plans.

By October, 1970, some 94 per cent of the South's 2,702 school districts were estimated by the Justice Department to be in compliance with constitutional and legal requirements for school desegregation. And on August 31, 1970, in Virginia, eleven years after Governor Almond had started the state down the path of accommodation to desegregation, another Governor, Linwood Holton, personally escorted his White 13-year-old daughter to a predominantly Black public school in Richmond to dramatize the duty of White people to act lawfully and constructively to make desegregation work.[8] On the same day in Georgia, longtime arch-segregationist and U.S. Senator, Herman E. Talmadge, was interviewed on television. Rather abruptly, he was asked whether he was a segregationist. "Well sir," Talmadge replied, "no sir, I'm not." After the program he mused, "It's just a *fait accompli*. There's nothing left to defend."[9] Indeed, in sixteen years the South had changed!

Yet, by the same token, the South's retreat from pure and simple segregation did not mean the obliteration of segregation. "Freedom of choice" and neighborhood schools (that is, schools not racially mixed by busing)—"northern-style" school segregation—came to the foreground. Further, desegregation did not necessarily mean integration, but rather the elimination of the old dual school system, one Black and one White. Thus, in some instances, Blacks went to the same schools as Whites, but attended virtually all-Black classes through "ability" segregation (by virtue of racism, Blacks as a group tend to do more poorly than Whites on ability and achievement tests). In addition more than 400,000 Whites fled mixed public schools for all-White private schools. And while Virginia's Governer Holton sent his daughter to a predominantly Black school,

[8] "A Southern Governor Dramatizes the Push for School Integration," *U.S. News & World Report*, September 14, 1970, p. 52.

[9] "Schools 1: Still a Long Way to Go in South," *New York Times*, September 6, 1970, p. 4E.

John Bell Williams, governor of Mississippi, not only counseled resistance but dramatized his objection to desegregation orders by placing his children in private school.[10] Accommodation, then, did not mean that a social revolution had occurred; nonetheless it did entail large-scale social change.

The Fate of the Second Reconstruction. By 1970, if not earlier, concern was increasingly being expressed among civil rights supporters that the Second Reconstruction was endangered—that the nation was again confronted with the betrayal of Black rights much in the fashion of 1877 (if one takes the "Compromise" and the withdrawal of federal troops from the last of the former Confederate states as the close of the First Reconstruction). The evidence for such a conclusion gathered as the new decade progressed. For one thing, there could be observed among some civil rights champions an erosion of commitment. Professor Alexander Bickel of the Yale University Law School, writing in *The New Republic* (February 7, 1970), in effect argued that the integration ordered by the Supreme Court in 1954 was an impossible dream. A month later, Daniel P. Moynihan—at that time serving as President Nixon's "liberal-in-residence"—suggested that on the issue of race the nation could benefit from "a period of 'benign neglect.' "

By October, 1970, Rev. Theodore M. Hesburgh, president of the University of Notre Dame, could issue the following statement as chairman of the United States Commission on Civil Rights:

> Our examination of various laws, executive orders, and judicial decisions has disclosed that there is indeed an impressive array of civil rights guarantees that provide protection against discrimination in virtually every aspect of life. . . . There is, however, a gap between what these guarantees have promised and what has actually been delivered.
>
> We are a result oriented nation. We judge the effectiveness of institutions on the basis of the results they achieve. By this yardstick, progress in ending inequity by the application of law has been disappointing. . . .
>
> The commission has examined the Federal civil rights enforcement effort and found it wanting. Each civil rights law that has been issued, and each court decision favorable to the cause of civil rights, has been viewed as another step along the road to full equality for all Americans.
>
> But perhaps what has been lost sight of is that these legal mandates in and of themselves cannot bring about a truly open society, that they must be implemented—and it is at this point that we have found a major breakdown.[11]

[10] Paul Gaston, "The South: Goal Still Distant, But Many Schools Go Well," *South Today*, 2 (December, 1970), 3.

[11] "Excerpts from Hesburgh's Statement on Rights Enforcement," *New York Times*, October 13, 1970, p. 28.

A similar failure had occurred after the First Reconstruction—a failure to enforce basic laws and decrees.

Noting developments such as those summarized by Rev. Hesburgh, some recalled the thesis of Professor Arthur Schlesinger, Sr., advanced in 1949, which argued that this nation from its earliest days has been dominated by alternating political attitudes: the conservative (Tory or Hamiltonian) philosophy and the liberal (Whig or Jeffersonian) philosophy. Liberal periods witnessed the accent on popular rights, programs of reform and efforts to share power with the unrepresented, as contrasted with the accent in conservative periods on property rights, safety first for the commercial classes, and efforts to perpetuate the power of the status quo. Schlesinger pointed out that "the chief liberal gains generally remain on the statute books when the conservatives recover power. They acquiese in the new status quo, though they may try to sabotage it by half-hearted enforcement and reduced appropriations while advancing their own special ideals by such methods as are still available to them." [12] It was not difficult for supporters of this pendulum theory to conclude that America had entered a new conservative era, especially in the realm of Black rights.

As the new decade was launched, then, many White Northerners seemed to be pulling back in a conservative direction, much in the fashion of their counterparts ninety years earlier. Some felt, as did Yate University's Alexander Bickel, that integration was made impractical by the flight of Whites to private schools or to the suburbs, that to pursue it was only to "fuel the politics of George Wallace," and that it was not worth the cost anyway. Others, including several national columnists, had adopted the view that forced integration was either disruptive or accomplished little and that more was to be gained by channeling energies into a drive to improve the quality of schools, whatever their racial composition. Many educators, North and South, became skeptical about the benefits of integration and were inclined to look with disfavor on plans that required the extentive reshuffling of students. And too, the decline of northern interest in desegregation suspiciously coincided with an attack upon segregation in northern schools, a tendency reinforced

[12] Bill D. Moyers, "The Negro Fears His Tide Is Ebbing," *Washington Post*, March 19, 1968, p. B1.

by the fears aroused by ghetto rioting and racial disorders and friction that occasionally occurred in desegregated school settings.[13]

Further, the First Reconstruction had failed because in part it was a "revolution from the top," directed by a segment of the dominant White group, with limited active support and push from the masses of the freedmen (at that time Blacks were too atomized, politically untrained, and unorganized to constitute a sustained, independent political force).[14] While Blacks today tend to reject any "junior partner" role in the drive for Black rights, doubts have grown within Black communities regarding the value of integration. Black leaders, such as Charles V. Hamilton, professor of political science at Columbia University, have expressed concern about placing Black children in "educationally racist" White classrooms, an apprehension also expressed by W. E. B. DuBois in the 1930s.[15] This concern has been coupled with increased demands within Black communities for "local [Black] control" of schools.

Remarkable parallels, then, can be found between the First and Second Reconstruction. Yet it would be easy to overlook the changes that had occurred during the 1960s. In 1963, 61 per cent of White southern parents objected to sending their children to schools in which even a few Blacks were enrolled; in 1970 the figure stood at 16 per cent, a shift described by the Gallup Poll organization as one of the most dramatic in the history of opinion sampling. Moreover, whereas in 1963 some 78 per cent said they would object to sending their children to schools where half the enrollment were Blacks, by 1970 the figure was reduced to 43 per cent (69 per cent still objected to sending their children to schools where more than half were Blacks compared with 86 per cent in 1963). Among northern White parents, 10 per cent opposed sending their children to schools with even a few Blacks in 1963 in contrast with 6 per cent in 1970 (however, 51 per cent in 1970 still opposed sending their children to predominantly Black schools compared with 53 per cent in 1963).[16] Perhaps the Second Reconstruction may not so much come to an end as it is likely to continue on a laborious pace.

[13] John Herbers, "National Push for School Integration Losing Momentum," *New York Times*, March 22, 1970.

[14] Pierre L. van den Berghe, *Race and Racism* (New York: John Wiley & Sons, Inc., 1967), 85.

[15] Herbers, *op. cit.*

[16] "Poll Finds Gains for Integration," *New York Times*, May 3, 1970, p. 53.

RACIAL INTEGRATION IN A NORTHERN TRANSITION COMMUNITY

Typically the in-migration of Blacks into previously White urban areas has led to eventual all-Black occupancy. During the transition period, however, some degree of cross-racial interaction flows from the mere fact of residential proximity. Within such biracial settings, various modes of interracial behavior emerge. "South Shore," a Chicago community some 67 blocks south of the Loop and along the lake front, provides a good illustration of this.[17] Traditionally, South Shore has conveyed the image of middle-class living, lakeside recreation, and well-kept lawns, homes, and buildings. Some 80 per cent of the 70,000 residents live in well-constructed apartments, usually of the walk-up variety, and built largely in the early 1930s. Between 1960 and 1966, the Black population of South Shore increased from about 152 to nearly 20,000, with Blacks coming to predominate in the northwestern sections, Whites continuing residency in the southeastern region, and mixed occupancy occurring in more central areas.

Overall, racial integration was very limited in frequency and intensity, despite biracial proximity. Racial retail shopping patterns generally coincided with racial residential patterns—in brief, stores and business blocks surrounded by predominantly Black residents were patronized almost exclusively by Blacks; those in White areas by Whites; and those in mixed areas by members of both races. Some exceptions nonetheless did occur. All barber and beauty shops, regardless of location, were segregated. Similarly, establishments catering to social and recreational needs were commonly segregated. This latter tendency became accentuated on Saturday evenings, hours commonly reserved for greater social intimacy, when segregation increased—indeed, even in the case of restaurants and groceries, there was a tendency toward increased segregation on Saturday nights in comparison with weekdays. Patterns of social segregation were pronounced in taverns, and, in some places, Black and White taverns alternated along a given block. Further, South Shore's two bowling alleys, integrated by day, became all-Black at night.

[17] This account is adapted from Harvey Molotch, "Racial Change in a Stable Community," *American Journal of Sociology,* 75 (1969), 226–238, and "Racial Integration in a Transition Community," *American Sociological Review,* 34 (1969), 878–893.

In still other spheres of life, patterns of segregation were also found. The community's parks were for the most part racially segregated (in one instance a park contiguous to both Black and White residential areas contained two tot lots, one of which was used by Blacks; the other by Whites). Schools operated on the "neighborhood" principle, and hence reflected racial residential patterns. Four of 16 Protestant churches held integrated church services, although church life, outside of worship services, was virtually completely segregated and completely White.

Integration of a thoroughgoing type—in which Blacks and Whites interacted freely and without racial distinctions—occurred in only a few settings, for instance, a peace group with a leftist political orientation and a human rights organization. Still another exception to the prevailing segregationist patterns was a fundamentalist Baptist church, located in a predominantly Black neighborhood, in which equal numbers of Blacks and Whites attended services; for the participants worship was a time of spontaneity and much animated social interaction.

On the whole, then, racial integration did not generally occur in South Shore settings in which interpersonal behavior was informal, spontaneous, or intense. Molotch, who studied the community, suggests that this fact resulted from the tendency of people to get "up tight" in the presence of others who are unknown, unproven, and thus, to them undependable—perhaps even dangerous. Hence people typically search for cues that bespeak similarity or the existence of some other personal tie (for instance, mutual friendship or a blood relationship) which would imply dependability and trustworthiness. Where such cues are absent, mutual avoidance or even hostility results.

This was reflected, for example, in the tavern, an intimate setting usually frequented by a small and stable group of "regulars" whose social lives revolved about the establishment. In brief, the tavern was a place where people "let their hair down." Accordingly, Blacks, who shared mannerisms, clothing tastes, and musical preferences at variance with those of Whites, were "outsiders" in the White environment, and vice versa. The mere presence of members of the "other" group thus served to inhibit the very kinds of interaction for which the tavern was sought.

Similarly, in the larger context of South Shore, Blacks and Whites tended to be set apart in speech and dialect, and even in manner of walk (many young Blacks utilized a swagger that was different in style from White school mates). And differences in economic status (Blacks lower), stage of life cycle (Blacks younger), and religion (few Black Catholics; no Black Jews)—commonly used bases for social differentiation—tended to coincide with and reinforce racial distinctions. The net results of these factors was that racial integration was minimal despite biracial proximity. On the other hand, racial transition in South Shore was *not* accompanied by a "flight" of Whites nor with a consequent abnormally high rate of property turnover.

TRENDS IN DESEGREGATION

We have observed that social change is an inescapable fact of social existence. Indeed, as Alfred North Whitehead, a noted English mathematician and philosopher, has noted, "the actual world is a process. . . ." [18] Every phenomenon of which man is aware—from galaxies to electrons, from human beings to amoebae, from societies to families, from philosophies to nursery rhymes—exists in a state of continual "becoming." There are no fixed entities; change is an ultimate fact.[19] And in this regard, dominant-minority relations are no exception, continuously changing, never completely static.

The rate of change, however, varies a great deal from one period to another. At times change proceeds slowly, hardly discernible from one generation to the next; at still other times change may be relatively rapid. It is this latter situation that has characterized American racial and ethnic patterns in recent years. Segregated institutions have been progressively undermined by a wide variety of forces. Indeed, the pace of change has quickened in the face of rising minority group militancy, urbanization, demographic shifts, judicial rulings, and new civil rights' legislation (Table 14–1 summarizes our nation's major civil rights laws). Let us now turn to an examination of some recent desegregation trends.

Education

The Supreme Court's 1954 decision outlawing mandatory school segregation gave rise to hopes in many quarters that school segrega-

[18] Alfred North Whitehead, *Process and Reality* (New York: The Macmillan Co., 1929), 33.
[19] Marvin E. Olsen, *The Process of Social Organization* (New York: Holt, Rinehart & Winston, Inc., 1968), 1.

TABLE 14–1   Major Civil Rights' Laws

Fourteenth Amendment. This amendment to the Constitution, adopted in 1868, declares that all persons born or naturalized in the United States are citizens, and provides that, if Congress chooses, a state's representation in Congress may be reduced if some citizens are denied the right to vote.

Fifteenth Amendment. This amendment, adopted in 1870, declares that "the right of the citizens of the United States to vote shall not be denied or abridged by the United States or by any state on account of race, color, or previous condition of servitude."

Legislation, 1865–1875. Of the many laws passed in this decade, six major laws survive, the others either struck down by Supreme Court decisions or repealed by Congress. These six laws restate the right of all citizens to vote regardless of race. Attempts to deprive anyone of any Constitutional right, interpreted as including voting, are made federal crimes, and guilty persons are also made liable for civil damage suits.

Hatch Act of 1939. Although not strictly a civil rights' law, this act makes it a crime to threaten, intimidate, or coerce voters in a federal election.

Civil Rights Act of 1957. This statute gives the Attorney General of the United States the power to enter court suits to protect the voting rights of any citizen in any election—federal, state, or local. A Civil Rights Commission was created and given subpoena powers to investigate violations of voting rights in any election.

Civil Rights Act of 1960. This statute makes defiance of court orders in voting cases a federal crime, requires preservation of all voting records for 22 months to prevent local officials from destroying registration forms and applications (these records are then available for court cases), and authorizes federal courts to appoint referees to see that qualified Negroes are allowed to register and vote should local registrars balk or resign to avoid complying with court orders.

Twenty-fourth Amendment. This amendment to the Constitution, adopted in 1964, abolishes the payment of poll taxes as a requirement for voting in federal elections.

Civil Rights Act of 1964. The voting rights section of this act applies to federal elections only. It provides that the same standards must be used in registering all voters; minor errors in applications cannot be used to disqualify registrants; a sixth-grade education is proof of literacy for voting purposes unless election officials can prove otherwise in court; literary tests must be given in writing, with copies available to applicants; and a three-judge federal court must be impaneled to hear any case in which the Attorney General of the United States charges voting discrimination, with right of direct appeal to the U.S. Supreme Court.

The statute prohibits discrimination or refusal of service on account of race in hotels, motels, restaurants, gasoline stations, and places of amusement if their operations affect interstate commerce or if their discrimination "is supported by state action"; requires that Blacks have equal access to, and treatment in, publicly owned or operated facilities such as parks, stadiums, and swimming pools; empowers the Attorney General of the United States to bring school desegregation suits; and authorizes the use of federal technical and financial aid to assist school districts in desegregation.

The act further provides that no person shall be subjected to racial discrimination in any program receiving federal aid, and directs federal agencies to take steps against discrimination, including—as a last resort, and after hearings—withholding of federal funds from state or local agencies that discriminate. It bans discrimination by employers or unions with 100 or more employees or members the first year the act is effective, reducing over four years from 100 or more to 25 or more. And the statute permits the Attorney General of the United States to intervene in suits filed by private persons complaining that they have been denied rights guaranteed to them by the Fourteenth Amendment.

Civil Rights Act of 1965. This act extends some of the provisions of the 1964 statute to cover state and local as well as federal elections, and simplifies the intricate time-consuming judicial procedures required for enforcing present voting laws.

Civil Rights Act of 1968. The act barred discrimination in the sale or rental of federally owned housing and multi-unit dwellings whose mortgages are insured or underwritten by the Federal Housing Administration and the Veterans Administration; effective December 31, 1968, barred discrimination in multi-unit housing, such as apartments and in real estate developments; and effective January 1, 1970, barred discrimination in single-family houses sold or rented through real estate brokers (owners selling their houses without the aid of brokers can discriminate but are not allowed to use discriminatory signs or other such advertisements).

The act also provides stiff federal penalties for individuals convicted of intimidating or injuring civil rights workers and Blacks engaged in schooling, housing, voting, registering to vote, jury duty, and the use of public facilities; makes it a federal crime to travel from one state to another with an intent to incite a riot; makes it a federal crime to manufacture, sell, or demonstrate the use of firearms, fire-bombs, or other explosive devices meant for use in a riot or other civil disorder; and extends broad rights to American Indians in their dealings with their tribal governments, the courts, and local, state, and federal governments.

---

tion would soon be on the way out as an American institution. On the surface of course a case might be made on behalf of the proposition that such hopes have in large measure been realized. By 1970, Justice Department officials could point to the fact that 90 per cent of Black youth in eleven southern states were in "desegregated systems." Yet as we noted elsewhere in the chapter, the White South has been able to minimize the reality of desegregation through a variety of circumventing techniques. Increasingly, southern school segregation has come to be of the *de facto* as opposed to the *de jure* variety. Whereas *de jure* segregation occurred by law, *de facto* segregation—"northern-style segregation"—derives in large measure from the familiar system of neighborhood schools in combination with residential concentrations of minority groups. These "ghettos" are not explicitly created by law. They arise in part because of the inability of minority group members to find housing elsewhere.

The South, then, has come to exchange *de jure* segregation for *de facto* segregation. Yet as Senator Abraham A. Ribicoff has observed:

> . . . Presidents, senators, sociologists and boards of education can debate the relative evils of *de jure* and *de facto* segregation all they want. But for the black child who is forced to suffer a segregated education, there is no difference.
>
> Whether you call it *de jure* or *de facto*, it is segregation—pure and plain. For the black child, it means white people don't think his life is as important as a white child's, or that he is good enough to associate with their children.[20]

Some educators believe that if the nation, North and South, capitulates to pressures for making peace with *de facto* segregation, it will be abandoning the most effective instrument known for improving the education of low-income Black youth—or for that matter all "disadvantaged" youth, be they Black or White. They base their arguments primarily upon the "Coleman Report," a monumental 1966 federal study of educational quality.[21] The massive study, supervised by sociologist James S. Coleman, found that all aspects of schooling combined are less important to a child's educational achievement than nonschool factors, especially family background. But of the strictly school-related factors, such as teacher–student ratios and the quality of buildings, integration, it found, is by far the most significant. Later studies also seem to suggest that integration is the only known educational mechanism to have significant impact on the "disadvantaged" Black child. In contrast, alternate approaches, such as compensatory education, in which spending is increased heavily in disadvantaged schools, show no evidence of consistent success. Such findings, of course, have been controversial, and with the emergence of the Black Power movement, many Blacks have come to reject the notion that to have a good educational system it is necessary to have mixing of Blacks and Whites.

In any event, *de facto* school segregation has been accelerating.

[20] Abraham A. Ribicoff, "Do Most Americans Secretly Want Segregation?" *Look*, September 8, 1970, p. 11.

[21] James S. Coleman, *et al.*, *Equality of Educational Opportunity* (Washington, D.C.: U.S. Government Printing Office, 1966).

In city after city, North and South, the story has been the same: Black urban in-migration and White out-migration to the suburbs have brought about a dramatic increase in the enrollment of Black pupils and a decrease in the enrollment of White pupils. For instance, the enrollment of Black children in the public schools of Baltimore rose from 34.6 per cent of the total in 1950 to 51.4 per cent in 1960 and to 65.1 per cent in 1968; in Washington, D.C., from 50.6 per cent (1950) to 79.5 per cent (1960) to 93.5 per cent (1968); and in Atlanta, from 31.8 per cent (1950) to 44.7 per cent (1960) to 61.7 per cent (1968). Desegregation tends to occur most rapidly in areas on the periphery of White neighborhoods into which Black families are moving. Once the process has begun, generally within a period of a few years, the racial composition of the neighborhood changes, and so does that of the school. Schools frequently go through a process of segregation, desegregation, and then *resegregation*—from White to mixed to Black. Figure 14–1 illustrates this phenomenon in Little Rock, Arkansas, in the period between 1950 and 1970—the net result being that not more than 25 per cent of the Little Rock School District's 8,661 Black students are in schools that can be called integrated by any objective standard; the rest go to schools that are all-Black or more than 75 per cent Black.[22]

To combat patterns of *de facto* school segregation, a number of. methods have been proposed including pairing systems, rezoning, busing, and educational parks. Let us examine each of these methods in turn. The *pairing* plan apparently was first adopted in Princeton, New Jersey, and soon after in a number of cities elsewhere in the country, including, on a limited basis, New York City. Where there are two nearby schools, one serving a White community and the other an adjacent Black community, the two schools are placed in a common zone, one to serve children in grades one through three, and the other to serve children in the higher elementary grades. The plan has the advantage over other methods of keeping all the children in the new common zone together on the same basis, without the onus of some children being regarded as "belonging" to the school and others coming in from the "outside." The pairing method, however, is seldom feasible with senior high schools, since they are usually geographically far apart, have few grades that can be split, and offer courses that are taught across grade levels. More-

[22] Roy Reed, "Resegregation: A Problem in Urban South," *New York Times,* September 28, 1970, pp. 1 and 46.

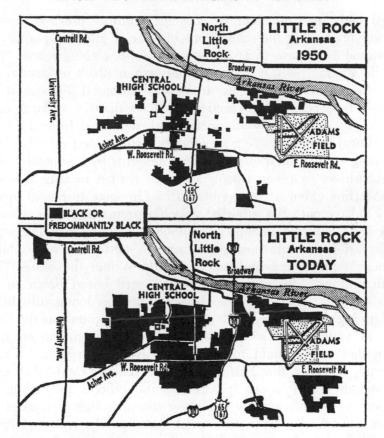

Fig. 14—1. Maps Showing the Expansion of Black Neighborhoods in Little Rock, Arkansas, over a Twenty Year Period. *Source:* © 1970 by The New York Times Company. Reprinted by permission.

over, the plan offers little promise of success in sprawling, densely populated cities in which sections of immense ghetto areas are remote from White schools.[23]

Rezoning involves the changing of geographic boundary lines in such a manner that school zones have a maximum of heterogeneity of population. Just as schools were often previously zoned to keep school populations homogeneous (all-White or all-Black), zoning now would be used for realizing desegregation. This method, however, also has a number of disadvantages. It exposes the school

---

[23] Arnold Rose, *De Facto School Segregation* (New York: The National Conference of Christians and Jews, 1964), 38–39; and Kenneth B. Clark, *Dark Ghetto* (New York: Harper & Row, 1965), 114.

board and superintendent to constant political pressure for the purpose of revising the school zone lines or of granting permits for individual exceptions in assigning students to a given school. And like the pairing plan, it is feasible only when Black residential districts are geographically close to White residential districts; it can scarcely be used for those sections of Black districts in large cities that are remote from White areas or are separated from the latter by political boundaries (e.g., separately incorporated suburbs).[24]

Busing entails the transportation of students by bus outside their neighborhood to other schools so as to realize racially balanced schools throughout a metropolitan area (in some instances involving a linkage with the suburbs). Such a program was launched in Berkeley, California, in September, 1968—the youngest Black pupils, kindergarten through third grade, were bused to the "hill" schools, formerly middle class and predominantly White; the older White children, fourth through sixth grades, were bused down to the "flats" section, where the schools were once predominantly Black. Underlying the Berkeley busing-to-integrate program was the thesis that, in a pluralistic society, mutual benefits accrue to *all* races when they are brought together for learning purposes.[25] Critics contend, however, that busing destroys a school's established identity and alters its relationship with its neighborhood, adds additional expense to already rapidly mounting school budgets, imposes unreasonable travel time upon a good many pupils, and contributes to additional traffic tie-ups during the morning rush hour period. Proponents in turn answer that more busing is currently going on in public education to maintain racially isolated schools within the United States than there is to eliminate racially isolated schools (and that few raise the argument of busing as a horrible thing when the function is to maintain segregated schools).

Of all the schemes proposed for desegregating urban schools, probably the boldest and most imaginative is the *educational park*. The rationale of the park rests on the premise that the effect on the school of pockets of segregated housing will be offset if an attendance area can be made large enough to include White and Black populations in balanced proportions. Hence, all the pupils of a greatly

[24] Rose, *op. cit.*, 39–41.
[25] Gertrude Samuels, "How School Busing Works in One Town," *The New York Times Magazine*, September 27, 1970, pp. 38–39, 44, 46, 48, 50, 52–53, 58, 60, and 62–63.

enlarged zone, perhaps in excess of 10,000, would be accommodated in a single site. Within the park, which might range all the way from a 100 acre-campus with many separate buildings to a single high-rise structure covering a city block, students would be assigned to relatively small units, each operated as a separate school in which teachers and pupils would work closely and continuously together. Beyond these general outlines, there is little agreement, however, on what an educational park should be. Some argue that the full grade range should be included, from nursery school to community college; others suggests that a park serve one or two levels, perhaps elementary and junior high schools. For their part, critics raise many of the same arguments against educational parks that they do against busing.[26]

Jobs and Income

A good deal of confusion exists as to whether non-Whites are actually moving toward equality with Whites in terms of jobs and income.[27] In 1965, President Johnson asserted that "For the great majority of Negro Americans—the poor, the unemployed, the uprooted and the dispossessed . . . the walls are rising and the gulf is widening." [28] And Carmichael and Hamilton have insisted that America's Black communities are becoming more and more economically depressed.[29] Yet most of the available statistics suggest that Blacks are making substantial progress in most fields.

The 1960s witnessed some substantial gains for non-Whites. In the first eight years of the decade, Black family income increased faster than White family income—the median annual income of non-White families as a percentage of White family income stood at 63 per cent in 1968 as contrasted with 55 per cent in 1960. Although the dollar gap between White median family income and non-White median family income increased since 1947, the proportionate increase was greater for non-Whites (see Table 14–2). And in 1968 about one third of all non-White families had incomes of $8,000 or more, compared with 15 per cent in 1960. By the same

[26] John H. Fischer, "Race and Reconciliation: The Role of the School," *Daedalus*, 95 (Winter, 1966), 33.

[27] Erdman Palmore and Frank J. Whittington, "Differential Trends toward Equality Between Whites and NonWhites," *Social Forces*, 49 (1970), 108.

[28] Commencement address at Howard University, June 4, 1965.

[29] Stokely Carmichael and Charles V. Hamilton, *Black Power* (New York: Random House, Inc., 1967).

TABLE 14–2 Distribution of Families by Income
in 1947, 1960, and 1968
(in 1968 dollars)

	Non-White			White		
	1947	1960	1968	1947	1960	1968
Number of families (in millions)	3,717	4,333	5,075	34,120	41,123	45,440
Total percentage	100%	100%	100%	100%	100%	100%
Under $3,000	60	41	23	23	16	9
$3,000 to $4,999	23	23	22	28	16	11
$5,000 to $6,999	9	16	17	23	21	14
$7,000 to $9,999	5	13	18	15	26	24
$10,000 to $14,999	} 3	{ 6	15 }	} 11	{ 17	26
$15,000 and over		{ 2	6 }		{ 7	16
Median income	$2,514	$3,794	$5,590	$4,916	$6,857	$8,937

Source: The Social and Economic Status of Negroes in the United States, 1969 (Washington, D.C.: U.S. Government Printing Office, 1970), 16.

token, during the same period, the percentage of non-White workers in the more highly skilled, well-paying jobs increased much more sharply than the percentage of White workers in these jobs; simultaneously, the percentage decrease in the number of persons employed in laborer and farm occupations was much greater for non-Whites than for Whites (see Table 14–3). Accompanying this

TABLE 14–3 Net Change in Employment by Occupation, 1960–1969

	Percentage	
	Non-White	White
Professional and technical	+109%	+41%
Managers, officials, and proprietors	+ 43	+12
Clerical	+114	+33
Sales	+ 61	+ 9
Craftsmen and foremen	+ 70	+17
Operatives	+ 41	+17
Service workers, except private household	+ 26	+32
Private household workers	− 28	− 9
Nonfarm laborers	− 8	+ 8
Farmers and farm workers	− 56	−31
Total	+ 21%	+18%

Source: The Social and Economic Status of Negroes in the United States, 1969 (Washington, D.C.: U.S. Government Printing Office, 1970), 41.

development was the fact that Black high school graduates had increased by two-thirds and Black college enrollment had doubled.[30]

Palmore and Whittington have evolved an equality index that measures the proportion of non-Whites who are equal to the same proportion of Whites—in brief, the overlap in the distributions of the two populations in terms of income, occupation, or education.[31] It can be viewed as the per cent of complete equality, since 100 would mean that there is complete identity or similarity, and 0 would mean that there would be no overlap between the two distributions. As reflected in Figure 14-2, non-Whites have made substantial progress in recent decades toward equality in income, occupation, and education. And if the annual rates of change remain roughly comparable to what they were in this recent period, Palmore and Whittington estimate that non-Whites could reach equality in income and occupation in some thirty or forty years and in education in about ninety years.

Lieberson and Fuguitt, employing a Markov chain model, also attempt to estimate the time span necessary for Blacks to attain parity with Whites in occupation and education.[32] They distinguish between those disadvantages resulting from current discrimination and those disadvantages deriving from the unfavorable position Blacks occupy in the stratification structure, largely the product of earlier discriminatory patterns. They estimate that had racially based discrimination in the job market ended in 1960, it would nonetheless take about eighty years before Blacks could achieve virtual occupational parity (the most rapid decline in inequality taking place during the first generation). Operating on similar assumptions, the educational gap would for the most part be closed at the end of about 60 years. Hence, even if discrimination had been totally eliminated in 1960—which of course was not the case—and by assuming both races followed mobility patterns found to prevail in the total population, occupational and educational differences between Blacks and Whites would become negligible only after about 60 or 80 years. In brief, the heritage of Jim Crow would live on for a number of generations—the handi-

[30] The Social and Economic Status of Negroes in the United States, 1969 (Washington, D.C.: U.S. Government Printing Office, 1970).

[31] Palmore and Whittington, op. cit., 108–117.

[32] Stanley Lieberson and Glenn V. Fuguitt, "Negro-White Occupational Differences in the Absence of Discrimination," American Journal of Sociology, 73 (1967), 188–200.

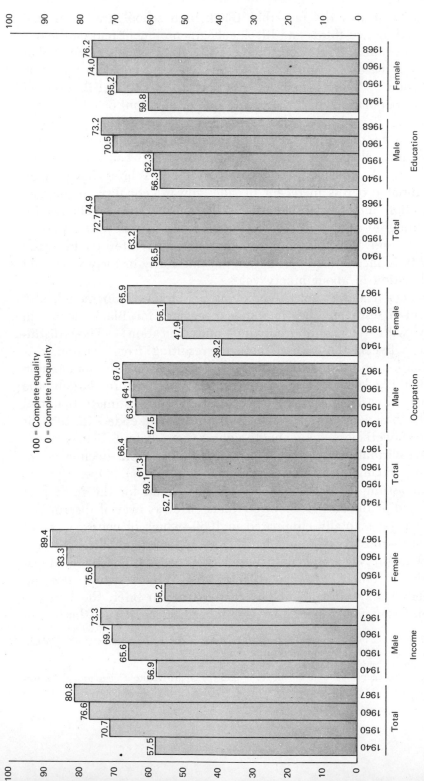

Fig. 14–2. Equality Indexes from 1940 to Present by Sex (the proportion of the White and Non-white percentage distributions that overlap each other). *Source:* Adapted from Erdman Palmore and Frank J. Whittington, "Differential Trends Toward Equality Between White and Non-Whites," *Social Forces,* 49 (1970), Table 1, page 112.

100 = Complete equality
0 = Complete inequality

caps and disadvantages sown by racism could not be overcome immediately by simply opening the gates of opportunity.

The Armed Services

With a few exceptions, the armed services of the United States practiced a policy of segregation until the post-World War II period. On July 26, 1948, President Truman issued an executive order calling upon the armed forces to put "into effect as rapidly as possible" a policy of desegregation. Two years earlier the Navy had initiated a policy of desegregation as a result of experiments with a number of desegregated ships during the war. It was not, however, until 1952 that the armed forces launched desegregation in a full-scale fashion (all-Black units, for instance, still served in the early phases of the Korean War).[33]

Although Blacks constituted in 1970 about 11.2 per cent of the total U.S. population, they made up only 9.3 per cent of the armed forces.[34] Within the armed services, they constituted 10.3 per cent of the enlisted men, 13.6 per cent of the non-coms, 2.1 per cent of the officers, 10 per cent of the forces in Southeast Asia, and 12.7 per cent of the Vietnam military fatalities.

Any number of problems confront Black servicemen. Lower-ranking Black enlisted men and officers not uncommonly encounter discrimination in civilian housing and schools (due to the shortage of government housing on military reservations). And a good many younger Blacks complain that Black soldiers are on the wrong end of a double standard at many installations in terms of job assignments, promotions, and the dispensation of military justice (Blacks, for example, usually make up at least 50 per cent of the inmates in military stockades and receive at least 25 per cent of the battalion-level punishment).

During the late 1960s and early 1970s, racial tensions mounted in the armed forces, as many Black servicemen refused to allow the regimentation and isolation of the military to lessen their identification with the struggle for Black rights—in some instances, deaths and injuries resulted from clashes between Blacks and Whites that had

[33] See: Richard J. Stillman II, *Integration of the Negro in the U.S. Armed Forces* (New York: Frederick A. Praeger, 1968), and "Negroes in the Armed Forces," *Phylon*, 30 (1969), 139–159.
[34] "Armed Forces: Blacks Don't Feel They Get a Fair Shake," *New York Times*, November 29, 1970, p. 3E.

racial overtones. At times competition for local women also sparked racial antipathies; many overseas Whites, for example, objected to Blacks fraternizing with European women. And although Blacks and Whites worked closely together during duty hours, and most often without overt hostilities, the two groups usually separated in off-hours, pursuing their relaxation and entertainment with members of their own racial group.

Voting

In the period since World War II, Black registration to vote in the South has climbed steadily. In 1947 there were an estimated 595,000 registered Black voters in the South; in 1952, 1,008,614; in 1958, 1,303,627; in 1964, 2,174,200; and in 1969, 3,248,000 (see Table 14-4). By 1969, some 65 per cent of all Blacks within the

TABLE 14–4   Southern Black Voting Registration

	Blacks Registered To Vote		Percentage of Voting-Age Blacks Registered	
	1964	1969	1964	1969
Alabama	111,000	295,000	23.0%	61.3%
Arkansas	105,000	150,000	54.4	77.9
Florida	300,000	315,000	63.7	67.0
Georgia	270,000	370,000	44.0	60.4
Louisiana	164,000	313,000	32.0	60.8
Mississippi	28,500	281,000	6.7	66.5
North Carolina	258,000	296,000	46.8	53.7
South Carolina	144,000	203,000	38.8	54.6
Tennessee	218,000	289,000	69.4	92.1
Texas	375,000	475,000	57.7	73.1
Virginia	200,000	261,000	45.7	59.8
Total	2,174,000		43.8	64.8

Source: Voter Education Project, Southern Regional Council.

South who were of voting age were registered to vote (more than 80 per cent of all White southern adults were registered, however, and White voters outnumbered Black voters in the area by a wide margin—16,169,900 to 3,248,000). The mid-1960s voter registration drives, the development of political organization by Black communities, and the 1965 Voting Rights Act (which among other things provided for the creation of a corps of federal examiners who were subsequently sent to at least 58 counties in five southern states) fermented the process of political activization of the Black community. Some evidence suggests that the greatest gains in Black voter registration since 1965 occurred in "Black Belt" counties with sizeable Black populations, contradicting the old aphorism that "The more Blacks, the fewer are registered." Daniel's investigation in Alabama, for instance, found that counties with a large Black population had a higher percentage of registered Black voters in 1966 than counties containing relatively few Black residents. Such variables as non-White socioeconomic status, as well as rates of poverty, tenancy, and agricultural employment, that had been *negatively* correlated with Black voter registration in 1960 were *positively* related to Black registration in 1966.[35]

This trend of increased Black registration had enabled Blacks to take advantage of the structure of American federalism that often has enabled relatively small groups in the electorate to command decisive majorities within specific localities and to use their local victories as a basis for gaining influence within larger political jurisdictions or organizations. In brief, Blacks had apparently established the foundation for the use of the Black vote as a "veto," a "balance of power," or a component part of a coalition with other segments of the electorate.[36]

Black political activity yielded some significant gains. By 1970, some 1,500 Blacks held elective offices (including 48 mayors, 575 other city officials, 362 school board members, 168 state legislators, 114 judges, and 99 other law enforcement officials), 38 per cent of which were in the South (despite the increase, however, Black elected officials made up only three-tenths of one per cent of the more than 500,000 elected officials across the country).[37] By serving as a foundation for political experience and ambition, these offices formed a basis from which Black politicians could launch campaigns for higher public offices, for significant modifications in national party platforms, and for launching third party ventures.[38]

---

[35] Johnnie Daniel, "Negro Political Behavior and Community Political and Socioeconomic Structural Factors," *Social Forces*, 47 (1969), 274–280.

[36] Joe R. Feagin and Harlan Hahn, "The Second Reconstruction: Black Political Strength in the South," *Social Science Quarterly*, 51 (1970), 42–56.

[37] John Herbers, "Nearly 1,500 Negroes Hold Elective Public Office," *New York Times*, March 31, 1970, pp. 1 and 16.

[38] Feagin and Hahn, *op. cit.*, 56.

Housing

Segregation in housing remains one of the most persistent areas of discrimination within American life. Racial discrimination in housing has taken many forms. Prior to 1948, the restrictive covenant constituted a widespread practice. Restrictive covenants are agreements between parties to the sale of real estate in which the purchaser agrees not to rent or sell his property to members of specified races, nationalities, or religions. In 1948 the Supreme Court held that restrictive covenants could not be enforced in courts of law; however, if the agreements were carried out by voluntary adherence to their terms, no violation of the Fourteenth Amendment was involved. Various other practices nevertheless operated to continue segregated housing: Mortgage lenders commonly refused to make loans to Blacks in an area in which "racial infiltration" had occurred or was threatened; Blacks at times were asked to pay more than the usual interest rates; building permits or the extension of utilities were on occasion withheld from Blacks seeking to build in particular areas; real-estate brokers often refused to show Blacks real estate in White neighborhoods; and club membership and various leasehold systems were also employed. The Civil Rights Act of 1968 was designed to eliminate most of these practices.

As we have already noted, patterns of residential segregation are pronounced within American cities. In our large central cities, Black population continues to grow while White population declines. Meanwhile the suburbs, most of them segregated along racial lines, grow at a rapid rate. Within a generation, if present trends continue, many of our largest cities will have populations more than 50 per cent Black. Any strategic program for desegregation that fails to explore the implications of such facts invites acute disappointments and boomerang effects. Indeed, American urban renewal and housing programs have actually operated to reinforce segregated housing. Such programs have typically meant the creation of *new* slums by pushing relocatees into areas that then have become overcrowded and have deteriorated rapidly; Blacks have been especially victimized in the process. Although Blacks occupy only about one-fourth of the substandard dwelling units in the nation, nearly 70 per cent of the dwelling units condemned for urban renewal projects have been Black residences. This has led some to refer derisively to urban renewal efforts as "Black removal programs"—in brief, programs that have operated to remove Blacks from the vicinity of central business districts in the interests of the White establishment.[39]

Historically, lower-income groups have tended to live in central cities, a residential pattern that in part has resulted from employment opportunities and structure. But with the accelerating pace of suburbanization of industry and jobs, this is no longer necessarily the case. Blacks are found in central cities primarily because of race and not because of income.[40] For instance, the median rent that Blacks pay in the Cleveland area ($82) is, in fact, slightly higher than the median rent that Whites pay ($76). Nor do Black people pay significantly less to own a house in the ghetto (13,100 median value), than Whites pay for houses outside it (13,900 median value). Black people live in the ghetto, then, not because it is cheaper but in the main because they find it difficult to buy or rent housing outside of it.[41]

SUMMARY

In this chapter we have stressed that American patterns of dominant-minority relations have undergone continuous change. Although many Americans assume that race relations within the nation and the South have "always been that way," we have noted that this is simply not the case. Legalized segregation, for instance, is a relatively recent development of the late nineteenth and early twentieth centuries. Moreover, especially in recent years, formal segregation has been progressively challenged and undermined.

[39] For critical appraisals of the urban renewal program see: Scott Greer, *Urban Renewal and American Cities* (Indianapolis: Bobbs-Merrill Co., Inc., 1966); Jerome Rothenberg, *Cost-Benefit Analysis of Urban Renewal* (Washington, D.C.: The Brookings Institution, 1964); Martin Anderson, *The Federal Bulldozer: A Critical Analysis of Urban Renewal, 1949–1962* (Cambridge: M.I.T. Press, 1964); Herbert J. Gans, "The Failure of Urban Renewal—A Critique and Some Proposals," *Commentary*, April, 1965; Don J. Hager, "Housing Discrimination, Social Conflict, and the Law," *Social Problems*, 8 (1960), 80–87.

[40] John F. Kain and Joseph J. Persky, "Alternatives to the Gilded Ghetto," *The Public Interest*, 14 (Winter, 1969), 74–87.

[41] "Roundup of Current Research," *Trans-action*, May, 1969, p. 7.

15

Toward Lessening
Racism

We have seen that, through the years, American race and ethnic relations have undergone considerable change and alteration. Social institutions change not only through the operation of a vast number of impersonal and non-deliberative forces but because men may deliberately set out to change them. This has been the case as well with various patterns governing American ethnic, racial, and religious interaction. Racism of course conflicts with the assumptions underlying the American democratic creed, a creed stressing the dignity and worth of each individual and the right of each to enjoy equality and the privileges of liberty. Accordingly, many Americans have sought to bring this nation's race and ethnic patterns in line with the democratic creed.

With the growing recognition that sociological findings can be applied in an effort to channel and change human behavior, sociologists have been increasingly called upon to contribute scientific knowledge that would be useful in realizing this goal. A value premise is of course implicit, namely, racism is undesirable and should be combated. In response to these various demands, a body of sociological literature has emerged dealing with means by which democratic goals may be advanced. In this chapter our attention will be focused upon some of these findings.

SOME PRELIMINARY CONSIDERATIONS

Before proceeding, however, with our consideration of techniques for combating racism, it would be well to recognize the existence of a number of issues pertinent to a consideration of this sort. First, individuals and groups may display considerable diversity in the goals that they are pursuing. Some are oriented toward a "melting pot" approach in which the end desired is the fusion of the differing groups within one common American culture; others are directed toward an "Americanization" focus in which ethnic and racial minorities are asked to divest themselves of their distinctive traits and assume the ways of the dominant group; still others favor an approach of cultural pluralism in which conformity would be realized in crucial areas but differences would be welcomed and tolerated in less essential areas; and finally there are those who prefer separation—not only some members of the dominant group but those "nationalists" among minorities who seek autonomy and self-determination. Sociology cannot answer the question as to which of these orientations is the most desirable—or, for that matter, if any of them are desirable. But it can shed light on the likely consequences of pursuing any one of them. This diversity in goals complicates the task of formulating an action approach for the lessening of racism.

Second, as we observed in Chapters 3, 4, and 5, the sources of racism are not a simple matter to untangle—racism feeds from many springs, all of which are interrelated and reinforce one another. By virtue of the great complexity that characterizes intergroup behavior and the multiplicity of factors involved, an attack upon racism must involve a many-sided approach. Moreover, social scientists are not in agreement as to the key factors that underlie racism. And, by virtue of their own predilections as well as the limited nature of our contemporary knowledge, they are often in disagreement on how best to tackle the problem. Furthermore, our knowledge of the causes of racism furnishes us merely with cues for action. These cues or suggestions with regard to the methods best suited for lessening racism need to be evaluated in their actual application by research.

Third, prejudice and discrimination are not the same phenomenon. It will be recalled that prejudice involves a state of mind whereas discrimination entails overt behavior. Attitudes and behavior are not to be equated. A considerable gulf—even a conflict—may exist between the two. Accordingly, one technique may be quite effective in combating prejudice but may be of little value in combating discrimination, and vice versa. Education may be useful in altering attitudes, but the normative system dictating discrimination may continue to prevail. Or discriminatory behavior may be punished via legal sanctions, and thus be minimized, yet prejudice may persist. And all these matters are further reinforced and complicated by institutional racism—the fact that society itself is structured and saturated with built-in patterns that impose more burdens and give less benefits to the members of one racial or ethnic group than to another.

Fourth, racism is not a phenomenon, as is sometimes implicitly assumed, that can be dealt with by focusing exclusively upon the dominant group. While there is probably good foundation for placing emphasis upon changing the attitudes and behavior of dominant-group members, racial and ethnic patterns are in some measure reciprocal. The antagonism between various racial and ethnic groups is not a one-way street in which the dominant group has a monopoly in adverse and negative feelings, ideas, and actions. Accordingly, rounded action programs need to deal with both sides of the racial or ethnic equation.

This chapter will focus attention upon a number of strategies commonly suggested for combating racism. We will be particularly interested in considering evidence dealing with the effectiveness of these strategies.

PROPAGANDA

Propaganda in Combating Prejudice

For many people propaganda has gained a sinister connotation. They frequently equate propaganda with lies, deceit, and fraud. This view became especially prevalent during World War II, when propaganda was commonly identified with the hate and racist appeals of Nazi Germany. More recently it has become associated with Communist and anti-American elements. However, as commonly used within the social sciences, the term has no necessary relation to truth or falsity. It merely refers to a deliberate attempt to influence opinions or behavior to some predetermined end.[1] Symbols are the vehicles by which propaganda is transmitted, be they written, printed, spoken, pictorial, or musical.

A major problem faced by those who would employ propaganda as a tool in fighting prejudice is the difficulty in reaching people who are not already in favor of the view it presents. Communications research has pointed up the fact that many people avoid points of view that are at odds with their own by simply not exposing themselves to such views. Those whom the propagandist would most like to influence by certain communications are often the least likely to be reached by them. People tend to listen only to ideas agreeing with their own opinions. It has been found, for example, that political propaganda within the United States which aims to win support from those who ordinarily give their allegiance to another party is usually unsuccessful. For one thing, Republicans, by and large, listen only to Republican speakers; Democrats expose themselves to Democratic speeches. A similar problem exists in the area of race relations. During World War II the government sponsored a weekly radio program, *Immigrants All, Americans All.* Each week the program dealt with the contribution of a specific nationality group within American life. Public-opinion research revealed that, when the program dealt with Italians, the great majority of listeners were Italians; when the Poles were presented, mostly people of Polish descent listened. Similarly, anti-prejudice propaganda is likely to reach a considerably smaller proportion of the prejudiced group than the non-prejudiced.

With the increasing role that motion pictures and television play in American recreational life, the potentialities for mass influence have been greatly enlarged. Accordingly, a number of studies have concerned themselves with the possible impact of these media upon racial and ethnic prejudice. The evidence suggests that motion pictures portraying an ethnic or racial group in adverse terms may function to increase prejudice. Peterson and Thurstone found, in their pioneer study of the phenomenon, that schoolchildren who saw *Birth of a Nation*, a film depicting Reconstruction from a White southern view, tended to exhibit a slight increase in prejudice toward Blacks.[2] On the other hand, a number of studies have revealed

[1] *Propaganda: How To Recognize It and Deal with It* (New York: Institute for Propaganda Analysis, Inc., 1938), 31.

[2] Ruth C. Peterson and L. L. Thurstone, *Motion Pictures and the Social Attitudes of Children* (New York: The Macmillan Co., 1933).

that movies with an anti-prejudice theme tend to reduce the expression of prejudice among these exposed to them.

Illustrative of these latter studies is Middleton's investigation of the impact of the movie *Gentleman's Agreement* upon the attitudes of a group of university students.[3] This film, which won the 1947 Academy Award, carries a strong message against anti-Semitic prejudice and sets forth an appeal for brotherhood, equality, and democracy. Middleton selected an experimental group and a control group of students, the latter of which did not see the movie. Both groups completed an attitude questionnaire: the experimental group before and again after the movie; the control group before and again after the intervention of a comparable period of time. The control group was introduced into the study to check for any attitude changes that might result from the mere fact of taking the "test." It was conceivable that any changes noted in the attitudes of the experimental group after they had seen the film might be due not to the film but rather to the test itself. Thus the differences between the before and after scores of the experimental group might reflect not the influence of the movie but that of the intervening variable, the questionnaire administered the second time.

The results presented in Table 15–1 reflect the wisdom of having introduced the control group, as both the control and experimental groups displayed attitude changes. Nevertheless, the evidence strongly suggests that the film played a major role in reducing the

TABLE 15–1 Degree of Change in Expressed Anti-Semitism Following the Showing of *Gentleman's Agreement*

Degree of Change in Anti-Semitism-Scale Scores	Experimental Group		Control Group	
	Number	Per Cent	Number	Per Cent
−11 or more	52	15.8	4	3.4
−4 through −10	112	34.0	27	23.3
No change or change of 3 points or less	112	34.0	49	42.3
+4 through +10	39	11.9	28	24.1
+11 or more	14	4.3	8	6.9
Total	329	100.0	116	100.0

Source: Russell Middleton, "Ethnic Prejudice and Susceptibility to Persuasion," *American Sociological Review,* 25 (1960), 682. By permission.

[3] Russell Middleton, "Ethnic Prejudice and Susceptibility to Persuasion," *American Sociological Review,* 25 (1960), 679–686.

expression of anti-Semitic prejudice. Subjects in the experimental group were five times more likely to display a reduction of eleven or more scale points than those in the control group. Reductions of four to ten scale points were also found to be more extensive among those in the experimental group. Yet the fact should not be overlooked that some 50 per cent of the individuals in the experimental group did not experience an appreciable diminution in expressed anti-Semitism; some even displayed an increase.

In connection with the use of anti-prejudice films, the question arises as to how well the effects of the film are retained over a period of time. Our knowledge on this matter is still far from adequate. However, the evidence presently available suggests that there is usually a regression in attitudes—after the intervention of time, opinions tend to slip back toward the original view, but not all the way.[4] But such regression does not occur in all cases. Hovland, Lumsdaine, and Sheffield show that some opinion changes in the direction of the propagandist's position are larger after the lapse of time than immediately after the communication.[5] They refer to this as the "sleeper effect." They suggest that individuals may be suspicious of the motives of the propagandist and initially discount his position. Thus these individuals may give little or no evidence of an immediate change in their opinion. But with the passage of time they may remember and accept *what* was communicated although they may not remember *who* communicated it. Consequently they may be more inclined to agree with the position at a later date than immediately after it was presented.

The Evasion of Anti-prejudice Propaganda

The anti-prejudice propagandist faces a major task in confronting prejudiced individuals with his point of view. As we have noted, people are inclined to avoid communications that are contrary to their established beliefs. But what happens when prejudiced people are involuntarily confronted with anti-prejudice propaganda? It might be inferred that they would either fight the propaganda or give in to it. But often many people are unwilling to do either: They prefer to *evade* the implications of ideas opposed to their own. It is often much easier simply not to understand or to twist and to

---

[4] See, for example: Peterson and Thurstone, *op. cit.*

[5] Carl I. Hovland, Arthur A. Lumsdaine, and Fred D. Sheffield, *Experiments on Mass Communication* (Princeton, N.J.: Princeton University Press, 1949).

misinterpret a message than to defend oneself or to admit error. While educational level is related to the understanding of anti-prejudice communications, more people who are prejudiced are apt to misunderstand the message than comparably educated unprejudiced people.

Cooper and Jahoda [6] have assembled a convincing array of evidence which suggests techniques that prejudiced individuals may employ in order to avoid understanding anti-prejudiced messages:

1. *Identification avoided—understanding "derailed":* Individuals may undertake to extricate themselves from facing the implications of the message through misunderstanding the point of the communication. Although initially grasping the message, individuals may then disassociate themselves from it, and in the process lose the original understanding that they had. The process is reflected in a number of typical reactions to a series of cartoons lampooning a character dubbed Mr. Biggott. Mr. Biggott is depicted as a rather prudish figure with exaggerated anti-minority feelings. In one cartoon, Mr. Biggott, lying sick in bed, says to a somewhat startled doctor, "In case I should need a transfusion, doctor, I want to make certain I don't get anything but blue, sixth-generation American blood!" In another cartoon, Mr. Biggott says to a humble American Indian, "I'm sorry, Mr. Eaglefeather, but our company's policy is to employ 100 per cent Americans only!" The producers of the cartoons had hoped that the following process would occur: The prejudiced individual would see that Mr. Biggott's ideas about minorities were similar to his own, that Mr. Biggott was an absurd character, and that to have anti-minority ideas was to make one appear as ridicuolus as Mr. Biggott. Presumably the individual would then reject his own prejudice in order to avoid identification with Mr. Biggott.

Yet a study of reactions to the cartoons showed quite a different result. Prejudiced individuals may first identify themselves with Mr. Biggott, as did one respondent who indicated, "I imagine he's a sour old bachelor. [laughing] I'm an old bachelor myself." He also appeared to be aware of Mr. Biggott's prejudices. But this did not end the matter. Criticism and disapproval of prejudice were implicit in the cartoons; Mr. Biggott had been made to appear ridicu-

[6] Eunice Cooper and Marie Jahoda, "The Evasion of Propaganda: How Prejudiced People Respond to Anti-prejudice Propaganda," *The Journal of Psychology,* 23 (1947), 15–25.

lous for holding such beliefs. Thus it was not uncommon for individuals to invent means by which to disassociate themselves from Mr. Biggott without necessarily surrendering their prejudice. Some people accomplished this task by making Mr. Biggott appear as an intellectual inferior, a Jew, a foreigner, a member of the lower class, etc. The net result was that they ended up losing the original understanding of the message. The "bachelor" in the above illustration finally concluded that the purpose of the cartoon was "to get the viewpoint of people to see if they coincide with the artist's idea of character and all." Clearly the issue of prejudice had become completely sidetracked.

2. *The message made invalid:* In other cases, individuals admitted understanding the message to a degree that did not permit their distortion of it. For them the process of disidentification often led to a more rationalized argument. They accepted the message on the surface but maintained the message was invalid for themselves. This was accomplished in one of two ways. Individuals might admit the general principle but conclude that exceptions existed which entitled them to their prejudices. One cartoon in the Cooper-Jahoda study concluded with a variant of the Golden Rule, "Live and let live." Prejudiced persons frequently expressed acceptance of the Golden Rule but would add, "But it's the Jews that don't let you live; they put themselves outside the rule." The second type of distortion involved an admission that the message was convincing in itself, but with the qualification that it did not contain a correct picture of usual life situations involving the minority group discussed. A case in point was a radio dramatization entitled *The Belgian Village.* In the story a Jewish couple in an occupied Belgian village were saved by the loyal support of the villagers who hid them from the Gestapo. The story was followed by an appeal for sympathy and tolerance toward the Jews. Many prejudiced individuals refused to admit the applicability of this dramatic story to other situations. They called it an "adventure story," "a war story," etc.

3. *Changing the frame of reference:* In some cases the perception of the prejudiced individuals was so colored by their prejudice that the message of the cartoon escaped them. They saw the issues that the cartoon presented in a frame of reference different from that which had been intended. One cartoon depicted a congressman who had native fascist, anti-minority views. He was shown in his

office, interviewing an applicant who had with him a letter of recommendation saying that he had been in jail, had started race riots, and had smashed windows. The congressman was pleased and said, "Of course I can use you in my new party." Some prejudiced individuals imposed upon the cartoon their own ideology and made it appear that "bad politics" was the sole issue. One respondent observed, "It's about a strike . . . about trouble like strikes . . . He is starting a Communist Party." Still another, "It's a Jewish party that would help Jews get more power."

4. *The message is too difficult:* This type of evasion takes the same form as misunderstanding by unprejudiced people. Some individuals stated that "they didn't get the point." This was often due to the respondents' intellectual and educational limitations or to defects in the propaganda.

Limits on the Effectiveness of Propaganda

It has been seen that individuals may consciously or unconsciously modify the stimuli they perceive from propaganda according to their own predispositions. Accordingly they may fail to understand the message contained in anti-prejudice propaganda. For somewhat similar reasons propaganda may "boomerang"—it may produce a result directly opposite to that intended by the propagandist. Instead of lessening prejudice, anti-prejudice propaganda may actually serve to promote it.[7] Some psychologists, for instance, have suggested that there may be a boomerang effect in films showing cruelty against minority groups. Many prejudiced persons, far from being repelled, may actually be attracted by cruelty. Films depicting the persecution of minority-group victims may permit these prejudiced individuals to secure vicarious gratification for the very same sadistic impulses—in the process bringing hidden desires to the foreground.

Another problem with propaganda is that the impact of a single program may be quite limited. Public-opinion experts stress that a single program may be relatively ineffective in reaching the public with a particular message. One program is not enough. A campaign is necessary. Several related programs often are capable of producing effects even greater than could be accounted for in

---

[7] Eunice Cooper and Helen Dinerman, "Analysis of the Film 'Don't Be a Sucker': A Study in Communication," *Public Opinion Quarterly,* 15 (1951), 243–264.

terms of simple summation. Multiple exposure tends to produce a pyramiding stimulation.

Overall, it appears that propaganda has a very limited direct effect in combating prejudice. This is not to suggest that there is no value in pro-democratic propaganda. Some authorities suggest that its effectiveness cannot be counted only in terms of winning the prejudiced over to a non-prejudiced view. Propaganda may strengthen the attitudes of those who are unprejudiced and make them less susceptible to pro-prejudice propaganda. Anti-prejudice propaganda may also give the impression to anti-Semites, segregationists, and others that public sentiment is against them. Accordingly, although continuing to hold their prejudiced attitudes, they may be less disposed to engage in discriminatory behavior.[8]

EDUCATION

"Give People the Facts!"

One of the prevalent assumptions underlying a good deal of the work in the area of intergroup relations is that prejudice will disappear if people are given the facts. The appeal to "education" as a cure-all for the most varied social problems is deeply rooted in the ideology of American life. Thus, within the setting of racial and ethnic relations many intergroup workers believe that their primary task is to teach the facts about minority groups, and prejudice will be reduced. This view assumes that (1) people are predominantly rational beings and (2) prejudice is the product of ignorance. If people are rational and if prejudice is due to "distorted stereotypes" and "warped social perception," then "correct" facts can be expected to change their hostile feelings. The naïveté of this view is apparent in terms of both the complexity of human behavior in general and prejudice in particular.

The assumption that education is a powerful cure-all for prejudice was one of the first premises within the field of minority relations to be subjected to the scrutiny of scientific investigation.

[8] For an overview review of the literature dealing with the impact of propaganda upon attitude change generally see Arthur R. Cohen, *Attitude Change and Social Influence* (New York: Basic Books, Inc., 1964); Bernard Berelson and Gary A. Steiner, *Human Behavior: An Inventory of Scientific Findings* (New York: Harcourt Brace Jovanovich, 1964), Chapter 13; and Paul F. Secord and Carl W. Backman, *Social Psychology* (New York: McGraw-Hill Book Co., 1964), Chapters 3, 4, 5, and 6.

Teachers in courses in race and minority relations were especially anxious to measure the impact of their courses upon their students' prejudices. The results were quite discouraging, especially as many of the teachers were highly motivated to curb prejudice. On the whole the studies coming out during the late 1920s and the 1930s generally revealed that education at best had negligible effects. By 1948, R. M. MacIver could conclude in his survey of strategies useful in combating prejudice, "All we can claim for instruction of a purely factual kind is that it tends to mitigate some of the more extreme expressions of prejudice." [9]

Today specialists in race relations tend to take a rather dim view of the effectiveness of anti-prejudice education. It suffers from many of the same problems as those of anti-prejudice propaganda. Individuals selectively perceive and interpret "facts" and protect themselves against facts they do not wish to believe.

Experimental evidence indicates that people most readily learn materials with which they agree. When given the experimental task of learning statements, individuals who favored segregation learned plausible pro-segregation statements and implausible anti-segregation statements much more readily than they did plausible anti-segregation and implausible pro-segregation statements. Individuals opposed to segregation showed the corresponding reverse tendencies. [10]

Still another limitation of education is its failure to penetrate beyond the level of verbal expression to overt conduct, i.e., to become translated into nondiscriminatory behavior. It is axiomatic that in learning situations rhetorical exhortations have little chance of success when they are in battle against actual behavior patterns. For example, a child will not tend to be honest because his father tells him to be (although he may mouth honest platitudes) if the same father is constantly engaged in dishonest practices himself.

Prejudice and Level of Education

Education is commonly looked upon in the United States as a source of liberation—as a means of freeing people from narrowness

[9] R. M. MacIver, *The More Perfect Union* (New York: The Macmillan Co., 1948), 222.

[10] E. E. Jones and R. Kohler, "The Effects of Plausibility on the Learning of Controversial Statements," *Journal of Abnormal and Socila Psychology*, 57 (1958), 315–320.

and provincialism. Since education stresses rational processes, it is often assumed that it causes people to control or reject the irrational and absurd. From this, many have concluded that education has value in and of itself as an instrument for eliminating prejudice. On the surface these surmises appear to be borne out by research. Researchers have consistently reported finding a negative correlation between prejudice of all kinds and amount of formal education, that is, the higher the level of education, the less the prejudice.[11] Illustrative are the findings of Selznick and Steinberg, based on a national sample, which are partially summarized in Figure 15–1.[12] Moreover, Selznick and Steinberg interpret these and other findings of their study as support for the view that education is an "enlighten-

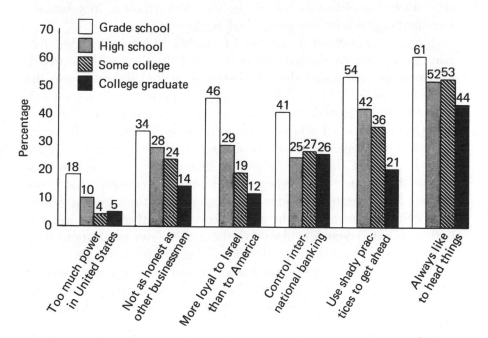

Fig. 15–1. Acceptance of Anti-Semitic Beliefs by Formal Education. *Source:* Adapted from Gertrude J. Selznick and Stephen Steinberg, The tenacity of Prejudice (New York: Harper & Row, 1969), Table 18, page 71.

[11] J. Harding, "Prejudice and Ethnic Relations," in G. Lindzey, ed., *Handbook of Social Psychology* (Reading, Mass.: Addison-Wesley Publishing Co., Inc., 1954), II, 1039.

[12] Gertrude J. Selznick and Stephen Steinberg, *The Tenacity of Prejudice* (New York: Harper & Row, Inc., 1969).

ing" process, leading to a rejection of anti-Semitism, anti-intellectual and anti-democratic attitudes, superstitions and rigidities, and provincial and particularistic orientations.

Yet any number of researchers have raised questions regarding such interpretations. Charles H. Stember, for instance, insists that most studies tend to understate the prevalence of prejudice among the educated.[13] His research lends support to the critics of attitudinal studies on race issues who allege that educated groups, because of intellectual sophistication, are reluctant to state prejudiced sentiment since it runs contrary to the norms of the American democratic creed. Stember suggests that the educated tend to express their prejudices more subtly. When responding on attitude tests, they are capable of recognizing and avoiding the trap set with rather obviously biased clichés. Nevertheless, in substance they may agree with the prejudiced position.[14]

Stember assembled a number of studies of prejudice that had been previously conducted and reanalyzed the data with appropriate controls. He found that the better educated differed from the less educated in (1) their beliefs and perceptions concerning minorities, (2) their attitudes toward discrimination, and (3) their acceptance of personal relationships with minority groups. In terms of beliefs and perceptions of minorities, the better educated were more likely than the less educated to give credence to certain anti-Jewish stereotypes: that Jews are a threat to the country, that many of them are Communists and racketeers, and that they are less willing than non-Jews to serve in the armed forces. On the other hand, the better educated were less likely to believe that Jews are unscrupulous in business, dishonest in public office, and too powerful or too demanding. Thus, although the less educated appear more likely to hold *traditional* stereotypes, the better educated nonetheless may hold certain highly charged and derogatory stereotypes of minority groups.

Stember found that discrimination as a matter of policy or insti-

---

[13] Charles H. Stember, *Education and Attitude Change* (New York: Institute of Human Relations Press, 1961).

[14] Also see: James W. Vander Zanden, "Voting on Segregationist Referenda," *Public Opinion Quarterly*, 25 (1961), 92–105; Melvin Tumin, *Desegregation: Resistance and Readiness* (Princeton, N.J.: Princeton University Press, 1958), Chapter 2; Michael Rogin, "Wallace and the Middle Class: The White Backlash in Wisconsin," *Public Opinion Quarterly*, 30 (1966), 98–108; and John M. Orbell and Kenneth S. Sherrill, "Racial Attitudes and the Metropolitan Context," *Public Opinion Quarterly*, 33 (1969), 46–54.

tutional practice is less acceptable to the educated than to the less educated, particularly in terms of such issues as systematic job discrimination, school desegregation, desegregation of public transportation, admission of refugees to the United States, and acceptability of a Jewish candidate for the presidency. However, in terms of *informal* discrimination, it appears that the educated do not take as strong a position as they do on more formal discrimination. Stember found that a similar, more definite picture emerges with regard to issues of personal acceptance. The better educated are more inclined to accept casual relationships with minority-group members, but they appear less willing to accept contacts that verge on the more intimate aspects of life. Thus one study revealed that persons of the middle educational level are more likely than others to reject Blacks as guests in their homes.

And Selznick and Steinberg, despite their conclusion that education has intrinsic value as an instrument for eliminating anti-Semitism, found that college graduates are the most likely of all educational groups to defend social club discrimination and that education is unrelated to attitudes toward intermarriage. They observe:

> Considering their frequent acceptance of anti-Semitic beliefs, the uneducated are relatively tolerant in the private areas of intermarriage and social clubs. But this must be set against their greater tendency to express their anti-Semitism in the political realm. On the other hand, the failure of the college educated to be especially tolerant in private areas must be set against their greater rejection of traditional anti-Semitic beliefs and greater opposition to political discrimination and political anti-Semitism.[15]

It would appear, then, that the issue is not so much one of which group—the educated or the uneducated—is the most anti-Semitic; rather the matter might be more appropriately phrased in terms of the ways the two groups either converge or differ in anti-Semitic tendencies and behavior.

On the basis of his survey, Stember concludes that the impact of education is limited: "Its chief effect is to reduce traditional provincialism—to counteract the notion that members of minorities are strange creatures with exotic ways, and to diminish fear of casual personal contact. But the limits of acceptance are sharply drawn; while legal equality is supported, full social participation is not." [16]

[15] Selznick and Steinberg, *op. cit.,* 90–91.
[16] Stember, *op. cit.,* 171.

Robin M. Williams, Jr., in his summary of the findings of Cornell sociologists, came to somewhat similar conclusions as Stember. He noted that the better educated tend to have more complex attitudes on issues since they have access to more facts, to divergent opinions, and to more subtle distinctions. Better educated people—in contrast with the less educated—are inclined to react to a more differentiated social world. Their prejudice, when it exists, may in some ways be harder, colder, more polite and more thoroughly buttressed by rationalizations, but it is less likely to be global, diffuse, and all-or-none in character.[17] However, as have other researchers, the Cornell sociologists found that in terms of some types of behavior, education, appears to play no part, for example, it is not associated with willingness to have a member of one's family marry a Jew.[18] Hence, the relationship between education and prejudice and between education and discrimination is quite complex.

CONTACT

Interracial Contact and Prejudice

"Bring differing racial and ethnic groups into contact and their prejudices will wither away." This counsel is manifest in a good many current activities to combat racism—indeed, an almost mystical faith resides in "getting to know one another" as a solvent of racial tensions. The view assumes that contact makes for intergroup friendliness. The simplified argument runs as follows: People in their daily lives are creatures of habit. They more or less continually follow a beaten path—a path that leads from home to work, then back home, then to a lodge meeting, back home, on Sundays to church and back, and occasionally on a visit to relatives and friends. Accordingly, people are exposed to few new social environments and few contacts with people of other racial and ethnic groups. Their lives are limited and they lack real experience with members of minority groups. But this does not prevent them from forming stereotypes and impressions about these groups. If people with differing racial and ethnic origins are brought together, their stereotypes and impressions will be challenged. They will see that the

[17] Robin M. Williams, Jr., *Strangers Next Door* (Englewood Cliffs, N.J.: Prentice-Hall, Inc., 1964), 374–375.
[18] *Ibid.*, 56.

minority groups are not in fact the people of the stereotypes. They will then tend to give up their prejudices and engage in harmonious interaction.[19]

Proponents of this view go on to argue that segregation has an impact opposite to that of contact in that segregation serves to promote distance and racism. Whites see Blacks living under conditions in which the latter are assigned inferior positions. It is not too difficult for the Whites to conclude that Blacks are indeed inferior and undesirable. Segregation thus operates to reinforce prejudice. By the same token, segregation serves to limit White opportunities for interacting with Blacks of similar status. The net effect is that it shields Whites from having to check their prejudiced beliefs against reality. Racism, then, is institutionalized; it is *bred* by the structuring of social relationships within our society—and in turn becomes self-perpetuating.

Racial isolation has still other consequences. It prevents each group from learning of the common beliefs and values that they in fact do share.[20] In Chapter 3 we observed that people tend to be attracted to others who hold beliefs and attitudes similar to their own and to experience aversion toward people with dissimilar beliefs and attitudes. We reviewed Rokeach's thesis that White Americans are motivated to reject Blacks less by racial considerations than by assumed belief and value differences.[21] And we further noted that a variety of studies reveal that Whites typically accept in a social situation a Black with beliefs that are similar to their own over a White with different beliefs—especially in more formal matters of general personal evaluation and social acceptance.[22]

Segregationist patterns, then, whether of the *de jure* or *de facto* variety, bar those forms of interaction that might otherwise undermine a racist social order—that would enable Blacks and Whites to discover their shared attitudes and provide a basis for mutual attraction. Hence, it is probably not surprising that the U. S. Com-

[19] John P. Dean and Alex Rosen, *A Manual of Intergroup Relations* (Chicago: The University of Chicago Press, 1955), 9.

[20] Thomas F. Pettigrew, "Racially Separate or Together?" *Journal of Social Issues,* 25 (1969), 48–57.

[21] For a review of Rokeach's work in this area see: Milton Rokeach and Louis Mezei, "Race and Shared Belief as Factors in Social Choice," *Science,* 151 (January, 1966), 167–172.

[22] In this regard see: David D. Stein, Jane Allyn Hardyck, and M. Brewster Smith, "Race and Belief: An Open and Shut Case," *Journal of Personality and Social Psychology,* 1 (1965), 281–290.

mission on Civil Rights, in its study of *Racial Isolation in the Public Schools*, found that both Black and White adults who as children had attended interracial schools were more likely today to live in an interracial neighborhood and hold more positive racial attitudes than comparable adults who had known only segregated schools.[23] And further, the "Coleman Report" suggests that White students who attend public schools with Blacks are the least likely to prefer all-White classrooms and all-White "close friends"; this effect is strongest among those who began their interracial schooling in the early grades.[24]

Selective Perception and Exemption

In and of itself, however, contact does not necessarily dispel prejudice. In fact, superficial contact is often a means by which prejudice is increased. A White having casual contact with a Black generally comes to the relationship possessing a well-formulated set of stereotypes. To a considerable extent the Black he "sees" is the Black of his stereotypes. Stereotypes *sensitize* individuals to signs that serve to confirm and reinforce the stereotyping process. The net result is that perception tends to be *selective*—indeed, even distorted. What in other relationships may be taken to be a normal lack of knowledge on a matter is taken by many a White in interaction with a Black to be evidence of Black "ignorance" and "inferiority." Similarly, what may be otherwise taken to be appropriate aggressiveness is taken by many a Gentile in interaction with a Jew to be evidence of Jewish "assertiveness" and "unbridled gall." When a Black or Jew engages in behavior remotely resembling the Black or Jewish stereotype, the incident "registers." [25]

When interacting with a member of a racial or ethnic minority, one has a tendency consciously or unconsciously to scrutinize the individual for behavior conforming to the stereotypes of his particular group—one is sensitized to the traits. In interaction with others, the trait would be overlooked or dismissed as a trait unique to the

[23] *Racial Isolation in the Public Schools* (Washington, D.C.: U.S. Government Printing Office, 1967), Vols. I and II.

[24] James S. Coleman, *et al.*, *Equality of Educational Opportunity* (Washington, D.C.: U.S. Government Printing Office, 1966). In this regard also see: Martha W. Carithers, "School Desegregation and Racial Cleavage, 1954–1970: A Review of the Literature," *Journal of Social Issues*, 26 (1970), 25–47.

[25] In this regard see: Alice B. Riddleberger and Annabelle B. Motz, "Prejudice and Perception," *American Journal of Sociology*, 62 (1957), 498–503.

individual and not characteristic of a larger racial or ethnic group. Casual interaction does not usually lead to a challenging of stereotypes, as the contact is not sufficiently intimate to permit people to assess other individuals in a way other than the traditional manner based upon racial identity. Thus the character of the individual as a unique human does not necessarily penetrate the armor of the racial mythology.

Intergroup contact may fail to challenge stereotypes for still another reason—*exemption.* Occasionally an individual meets a member of another racial or ethnic group who fails to fit that group's stereotype. But instead of altering or eliminating the stereotype, he makes the individual an exception—for example, a Black who is remarkably energetic, hardworking, and self-disciplined may be excluded from the stereotype as an exception, as "not really" a Black. Through exemption, an individual may retain his prejudice while circumventing discriminatory patterns for some particular purpose, for example, accepting a particular Black in his social clique.[26]

There is also substantial agreement among social scientists that contact between members of groups holding very different social and economic status is likely to increase prejudice, whereas contact between groups having the same or a nearly equal status tends to reduce prejudice.[27] When White middle-class individuals have contact with only lower-class Blacks, the stereotype that Blacks are "dirty," "dumb," and "shiftless" is reinforced. Class prejudices are readily activated in unequal-status contacts. An individual's perception of an ethnic or racial group may be influenced by his class antagonisms.[28] On the other hand, individuals possessing a common status tend to share common values and goals. Experiences along equal-status lines are more likely to run counter to the stereotypes of prejudiced individuals than are those that run along unequal status lines.

Evidence Relating to the Effects of Interracial Contact

A number of studies are suggestive of the effects of contact upon prejudice. One of the earliest studies employing a carefully planned

[26] Williams, *op. cit.,* 40–41 and 337–345.

[27] Gordon W. Allport and Bernard M. Kramer, "Some Roots of Prejudice," *Journal of Psychology,* 22 (1946), 9–39.

[28] In this regard, see: Hubert M. Blalock, Jr., *Toward A Theory of Minority-Group Relations* (New York: John Wiley & Sons, Inc., 1967), 199–203.

experimental methodology was undertaken by F. Tredwell Smith.[29] Smith administered a battery of tests measuring attitudes toward Blacks to 345 students at Columbia University's Teachers College. Without reference to the test or experimental purpose, he obtained by invitation an experimental group of 46 students. A control group of 46 students closely paired with the experimental group by individual scores and approximately comparable in age, sex, and geographical origin was likewise secured. The experimental group was exposed to a four-day tour of Harlem, in which the members of the group visited with Blacks, saw a good deal of the community, and heard a number of lectures. Ten days later the original 345 students were retested, and Smith found that the control group (the group that had not been exposed to the tour) had not altered its attitudes. The experimental group, on the other hand, experienced a marked increase in favorable attitudes toward Blacks. Eleven months later, 40 members of the experimental group were retested, and most of them continued to display significantly more favorable attitudes than they had on the first test. Twenty-five members maintained all their original gains or increased them. The study lends support to the hypothesis that contact which provides for some depth in interaction will function to reduce prejudice.

A number of limitations must be noted, however, in appraising the Smith study. First, the Blacks involved in the contact situation tended to be of relatively high status—equal or superior to the social status of the participants. Second, the contact situation was "artificially" created—the participants did not *happen* to engage in contact with Blacks; rather the interaction was arranged. It is conceivable that group norms arose in this special setting in which prejudiced attitudes were defined as inappropriate and that it was this factor and not necessarily the contact which accounted for the attitude changes. In the "real" world such favoring circumstances might well be the exception. Third, the study measured changes in responses to verbal tests—attitude changes—and not behavior changes. To what extent such changes in attitudes were implemented in intergroup interaction is not known.

With the growth of public housing since World War II, a particularly fruitful laboratory was provided social scientists for examining the impact of interracial apartment living upon racial attitudes

---

[29] F. Tredwell Smith, *An Experiment in Modifying Attitudes Toward the Negro* (New York: Teachers College, Bureau of Publications, Columbia University, 1943).

and behavior. Interracial housing affords an unusual opportunity for intimate and prolonged contact between individuals of differing racial groups. Two studies have appeared, utilizing sophisticated methodological procedure, that have supplied valuable insights on interracial residential contact. The first study, by Deutsch and Collins, investigated four low-rent public-housing projects—two integrated interracial projects in New York City and two similar segregated biracial projects in Newark—for the purpose of determining the social and psychological effects of the two occupancy patterns upon race relations and attitudes.[30] In the two integrated housing projects, Black and White families were assigned to apartment buildings regardless of race; in the two segregated biracial projects, Blacks were assigned to buildings that were area-separated from those of the Whites. Deutsch and Collins selected the projects in the two cities so as to match them in terms of Black-White ratios and other relevant variables. Some 100 White housewives were intensively interviewed in each of the four projects.

Deutsch and Collins found marked differences between the two types of projects in racial relations and attitudes. Compared with the segregated biracial projects, the integrated interracial projects were characterized by

1. A higher incidence of friendly, neighborly contacts between the two racial groups
2. A social atmosphere more favorable to friendly interracial associations
3. An ascription of a higher incidence of favorable stereotypes and a lower incidence of unfavorable stereotypes to Blacks
4. A higher rate of acceptance of the interracial character of the project and of recommendations for an integrated occupancy pattern for future projects
5. A far greater proportion of those who reported they had undergone favorable attitude change toward Blacks as a consequence of living in the project

Similarly, as indicated in Table 15–1, the White residents in the integrated projects were more likely than those in the area-segregated projects to hold Blacks in the project in high "esteem." Considerably more of the housewives in the integrated projects made such statements as: "They're very nice; they have beautiful homes"; "A lot of them are nicer than the white people; when I was sick the

---

[30] Morton Deutsch and Mary Evans Collins, *Interracial Housing* (Minneapolis: University of Minnesota Press, 1951).

TABLE 15–2   Percentage of Housewives Who Hold the Negroes in the Project in Different Degrees of Esteem

Degree of Esteem	Integrated Interracial Projects		Segregated Bi-racial Projects	
	Koaltown	Sacktown	Bakerville	Frankville
Respect Negroes living in the project; view them as equal to white people in the project	72%	79%	43%	39%
Feel Negroes are inferior; characterize them as low-class, childish, primitive, etc.	11	13	37	35
Neutral or ambivalent	17	8	20	26

Source: Morton Deutsch and Mary Evans Collins, *Interracial Housing* (Minneapolis: University of Minnesota Press, 1951), 82. By permission.

lady across the hall came in and cooked soup"; "They're just the same as the white people here; except for color, there's no difference." On the other hand, many more women in the segregated projects made statements which implied Blacks were inferior.[31]

A second study confirmed the major findings of the Deutsch and Collins research. Employing a comparable research design, Wilner, Walkley, and Cook were able to verify the findings in a setting outside the metropolitan area of New York City.[32] The authors concluded that, the more intimate the contact between Blacks and Whites, the more favorable the attitudes of the Whites toward Blacks. Similarly, the more favorable the perceived social climate surrounding interracial contact, the more favorable were the White attitudes. These studies suggest that contact, under the favorable conditions prevailing in the interracial public-housing projects, provides concrete experiences that test the White resident's pre-existing stereotypes and encourage the development of friendly relations and feelings.[33] Works replicated these studies among Black tenants in a single housing project that was partly desegregated and partly seg-

[31] *Ibid.*, 82–83.
[32] Daniel M. Wilner, Rosabelle Price Walkley, and Stuart W. Cook, *Human Relations in Interracial Housing* (Minneapolis: University of Minnesota Press, 1955).
[33] Meer and Freedman came to a similar conclusion regarding the impact of Black neighbors on White home owners in a middle-class neighborhood. Bernard Meer and Edward Freedman, "The Impact of Negro Neighbors on White Home Owners," *Social Forces*, 45 (1966), 11–19.

regated and found that anti-White prejudice is also diminished through intimate and interracial contacts between status equals.[34]

Some Limits to the Effectiveness of Interracial Contact

Interracial contact has a number of limitations as a means of combating prejudice. One of the most frequently encountered of these limitations is the failure of many individuals to generalize their favorable attitudes toward particular minority-group members so as to include the whole minority group. In this way the experiences acquired within one specific context are not carried over into other interracial situations. Harding and Hogrefe investigated the attitudes of White department-store employees toward their Black co-workers, for the purpose of determining whether or not the attitudes acquired within the one context would carry over into others.[35] For purposes of the study, they secured the cooperation of two leading eastern department stores that had been employing Blacks in white-collar jobs. The study revealed that equal status job contact produced a large increase in the willingness of the White employees to work with Blacks on an equal basis. The White employees were also willing to continue this pattern in a new situation of the same type. But there was no significant change in their willingness to accept Blacks in *other* relationships—in sitting next to Blacks in buses or trains, sitting down with a Black in a lunchroom or cafeteria, living in a new apartment building or housing project which contained both White and Black families, and having a Black for a personal friend. Thus the White employees tended to "compartmentalize" their experience of working with Blacks and did not generalize the experience to other situations involving Blacks.

A not too different kind of situation has prevailed in the coal fields of McDowell County, West Virginia. Within the coal mines the Black and White miners work together as equals in a spirit of general goodwill. In a number of instances, Blacks work in superior status positions as motormen on mine lorries or as company physicians without any friction. The community outside the mine, however, constitutes an environment in which the spirit of integration dissolves and the White miners again become members of a supe-

---

[34] Ernest Works, "The Prejudice-Interaction Hypothesis from the Point of View of the Negro Minority Group," *American Journal of Sociology,* 67 (1961), 47–52.

[35] John Harding and Russell Hogrefe, "Attitudes of White Department Store Employees Toward Negro Co-workers," *Journal of Social Issues,* 8 (1952), 18–28.

rior caste. The boundary line between the two communities is the mouth of the mine. Here management assists the miners in recognizing their entrance into the outside world by providing separate baths and locker rooms. About one-fifth of the White miners behave in a consistently prejudiced fashion and another one-fifth in a consistently unprejudiced fashion both inside and outside the mine. The remaining three-fifths tend to shift their role and status upon passing from the mouth of the mine into the world-at-large. Thus, many miners handle their dual role and status through a certain degree of fractionation or segmentation of their personality. In this manner they escape the necessity of instituting a total reorientation in their attitudes and behavior toward Blacks.[36]

Deutsch and Collins and Winner, Walkley, and Cook, in their respective studies of the effects of interracial housing upon interracial attitudes and behavior, found some evidence for the generalization of attitudes.[37] Nevertheless, there was a considerable gulf between the favorableness of attitudes toward the specific Blacks in the contact situation and the acceptance of the particular interracial experience, on the one hand, and the generalizing of favorable attitudes to Blacks as a group, on the other. Generalization to other non-White minorities was not significant.

When intergroup contacts do occur, the less prejudiced individuals, on the average, are most likely to develop those close associations and friendships that contribute to a further reduction of prejudice.[38] Nevertheless, even for those individuals who are highly prejudiced, intergroup contact on the whole tends to reduce prejudice.[39] Some of the conditions under which contacts between dominant- and minority-group members are most likely to result in a considerable change in the behavior and the attitudes of the prejudiced person seem to be:

1. The contact takes place between status equals.
2. The behavior of the objects of prejudice is at variance or does not conform with the beliefs of the prejudiced individual, e.g., the Blacks

---

[36] Ralph D. Minard, "Race Relationships in the Pocahontas Coal Fields," *Journal of Social Issues*, 8 (1952), 29–44. For still other studies pointing to the fact of compartmentalizing and the failure to generalize to other situations see R. H. Gundlach, "Effects of On-the-Job Experiences with Negroes upon Racial Attitudes of White Workers in Union Shops," *Psychological Reports*, 2 (1956), 67–77; E. B. Palmore, "The Introduction of Negroes into White Departments," *Human Organization*, 14 (1955), 27–28; and Meer and Freedman, *op. cit.*, 11–19.
[37] Deutsch and Collins, *op. cit.*, 103; and Wilner, Walkley, and Cook, *op. cit.*, 69.
[38] Williams, *op. cit.*, 201.
[39] *Ibid.*, Chapter 7.

with whom the prejudiced has contact are not "lazy," "ignorant," "delinquent," etc.[40]

3. The contact is of sufficient duration and intimacy to sufficiently challenge the stereotypes of the prejudiced individual.[41]
4. The prevailing social norms dictate that prejudiced attitudes and behavior are inappropriate.[42]
5. The members of the differing racial groups within the contact situation have a common interest, goal, or task that is the focus of the interaction.[43]
6. The individuals involved are personally secure and have low aggressive needs.[44]
7. Positive support for change is forthcoming from reference groups outside the specific contact situation.[45]

PSYCHOLOGICAL TECHNIQUES

Since prejudice is often deeply embedded in the functioning of the entire personality, some authorities insist that an effective program for combating prejudice must aim at reducing or rechanneling those elements within the personality that feed racial and ethnic antipathies. Focusing their attention upon the deep-seated anxieties, insecurities, and fears that frequently underlie and accompany prejudiced personalities, these specialists take a rather dim view of efforts that fail to come to grips with an individual's basic personality structure. The authors of *The Authoritarian Personality* are representative of this orientation. They suggest that educational approaches which employ rational arguments cannot be expected to have deep or lasing effects upon a phenomenon that is as intrinsically irrational in nature as is prejudice. Similarly, appeals to sympathy may backfire when they are directed toward people characterized by a deep fear of being identified with weakness or suffering. Nor can closer contact with members of minority groups be expected to influence an individual when his basic personality organization impairs or even precludes him from establishing a deep or meaningful relationship with anybody, regardless of racial or ethnic mem-

[40] Deutsch and Collins, *op. cit.*, 128.

[41] In this regard see: Barry S. Brown and George W. Albee, "The Effect of Integrated Hospital Experiences on Racial Attitudes—A Discordant Note," *Social Problems,* 13 (1966), 324–333.

[42] Also see: *Ibid.*

[43] See I. N. Brophy, "The Luxury of Anti-Negro Prejudice," *Public Opinion Quarterly,* 9 (1949), 456–466.

[44] J. Allen Williams, Jr., "Reduction of Tension through Intergroup Contact: A Social Psychological Interpretation," *Pacific Sociological Review,* 7 (1964), 82.

[45] *Ibid.*

bership.[46] What then can be done about prejudice? Adorno and his associates suggest that, ideally, psychological techniques need to be employed to change personality.[47]

Individual Therapy

Individual therapy is oriented toward the readjustment of individuals who are psychologically maladjusted. By means of therapy secured from a psychiatrist or trained counselor, an individual may undertake to cope with his emotional problems—his feelings of insecurity, inadequacy, and anxiety—and to find socially acceptable outlets for the expression of his needs. Clearly, individuals do not seek out a therapist for the express purpose of altering their attitudes toward minorities. However, in the process of gaining insight into the nature of their problems, their emotional need for racial prejudice and discriminatory behavior may be lessened. As they become increasingly capable of dealing with their problems and feelings on a mature, objective level, they will have less need to find immature, artificial, outlets.

The man who, to compensate for his inner feelings of weakness and inadequacy, obsessively and relentlessly strives for a sense of power may desperately clutch at his membership in the dominant group (e.g., the White race) to provide himself with a sense of strength. To give himself the power he otherwise lacks, he may incessantly search out opportunities to vilify and humiliate Jews and Blacks. In the process he seeks to reassure himself, "I am powerful." The minority, being weak and helpless, gives him a sense of contrasting strength. But the power he realizes is not genuine, since it is external and not rooted in the personality itself. He has to constantly reassert and demonstrate his power in order to prove to himself and the world that he really is powerful. Accordingly, his involvement in racist behavior becomes a preoccupation. Through therapy he may come to realize an inner sense of strength and adequacy. As a result he will have less need to find some external, artificial bulwark for his sense of well-being.

As a means of combating prejudice, individual therapy has a number of obvious limitations. First, therapy usually takes a con-

---

[46] T. W. Adorno *et al.*, *The Authoritarian Personality* (New York: Harper & Row, 1950), 973.
[47] *Ibid.*, 974.

siderable period of time and arduous work, often encompassing more than two hundred hours distributed over a number of years. Second, the number of trained therapists is small and even inadequate for dealing with the number of individuals who might benefit from such services. Third, highly prejudiced individuals are frequently char- acterized by personality types that are relatively unresponsive to psychotherapeutic methods. And finally, available empirical evi- dence raises serious doubts whether short-term individual psycho- therapy (for instance, therapy averaging three times weekly for nine weeks) contributes much in the way of prejudice reduction,[48] while little is known on the impact of long-term individual psycho- therapy.

Group Therapy

Group therapy has aims similar to those of individual therapy, but the former is organized about groups of maladjusted individuals. With the growing recognition of the role that groups play in the lives of human beings, increasing use has been made of therapy in a group situation. It offers a means by which individuals may over- come their feelings of isolation and rejection, and gain a sense of acceptance by other persons. Within the group, patients can find helpful new experiences and new insights that enable them to cope better with their problems and difficulties. Through the free, unin- hibited atmosphere fostered within the group by the psychiatrist or counselor, individuals are led to break down barriers and to realize corrective emotional experiences.

The indirect effects of group therapy upon prejudice are suggested in a study by Morris and Natalie Haimowitz.[49] As a part of a train- ing program in counseling, at the University of Chicago, twenty- four individuals participated over a six-week period in thirty-five hours of group therapy in which they discussed their personal prob- lems. These individuals ranged in age from twenty-five to sixty, had a master's degree or its equivalent in psychology, and had at least three years of professional experience. Before and after the six-

[48] David Pearl, "Psychotherapy and Ethnocentrism," *Journal of Abnormal and Social Psychology*, 50 (1955), 227–229.

[49] Morris L. Haimowitz and Natalie Reader Haimowitz, "Reducing Ethnic Hos- tility Through Psychotherapy," *Journal of Social Psychology*, 31 (1950), 231–241.

week training period, the members were administered the Bogardus social-distance test.

On the basis of the Bogardus test results, the individuals were classified as "friendly," "mildly hostile," or "strongly hostile" in their attitudes toward minority groups. The study revealed that, after the group-therapy experience, the number of individuals rated as "friendly" increased. The group designated "hostile" remained fairly constant. The changes that occurred took place among those who came to the therapy experience mildly hostile. There were no cases where a friendly individual became mildly or strongly hostile on the second test, and only one individual who had been strongly hostile on the first test displayed a shift on the second.

The authors suggest that the higher incidence of those classified as "friendly" after group therapy lends confirmation to the hypothesis that, with improved adjustment, hostility to minority groups declines. Through therapy, the individual becomes better able to cope directly and effectively with the source of his frustrations. He becomes less hostile in his reactions and has less need to displace whatever tensions do emerge. The authors conjecture that, for those individuals who are strongly hostile to minorities, prejudice assumes a more salient and basic part of their personalities. Since the therapeutic experience was relatively brief, it was not of sufficient duration to have an impact upon more deeply rooted patterns.

Two years later a follow-up study was made of seventeen of the twenty-four subjects in the study. The changes that had occurred between the pre- and post-therapy tests were maintained. Furthermore, there was a continued, though smaller, change during the succeeding two year period toward greater friendliness toward minorities. Yet evidence is also suggestive that individuals who were classified as "friendly" on the pre-test were not necessarily "tolerant" personalities. Although friendly toward racial and ethnic minorities, some of them indicated marked hostility toward Ku Klux Klansmen, Nazis, and Fascists. Thus one individual classified as "friendly" indicated that anyone associated with the Ku Klux Klan should be hung without trial. It appears that, in some cases of friendly disposition toward minorities, deep-lying hostility may be diverted into other channels.

Rubin also found that participants in a two-week sensitivity training program (akin to group therapy) displayed significant increases in self-acceptance and decreases in prejudice. Further, he found that a significant positive relationship existed between changes in self-acceptance and changes in prejudice.[50]

Pearl, in still another study, came to somewhat less optimistic conclusions regarding the value of group psychotherapy as an instrument for combating prejudice. He administered a series of attitude and personality scales (the same questionnaires utilized in *The Authoritarian Personality* studies) to 21 male, neurotic, hospitalized patients before and after psychotherapeutic treatment. A control group of seven randomly selected male tuberculous patients was given the same scales but not exposed to psychotherapeutic treatment. Pearl found no significant difference between the effectiveness of brief group therapy (12 hours of treatment) and intensive group therapy (60 hours of treatment) in reducing prejudice. But of even greater significance, the magnitude of the changes realized through group therapy was generally too small to be of great practical importance:

> Statistically significant shifts which yet leave highly ethnocentric individuals with strong ethnocentric ideology do not support the hope held by some that group psychotherapy may become a major technique for combating group prejudice. It would appear rather, that while psychotherapeutic treatment may play a role in any program designed to reduce ethnocentrism, it is not a panacea and must be utilized in conjunction with other approaches.[51]

Perhaps we shall want to reserve our judgment on the effectiveness of group psychotherapy, in light of the conflicting evidence, until such time as more research is available.

Prejudice Reduction Through Self-Insight

Katz and his associates have undertaken experiments dealing with the reduction of prejudice through the arousal of self-insight.[52] They suggest that an individual's attitudes (including prejudice) reflect deep motivational roots. Hence, to modify an individual's attitudes, Katz argues, it is necessary to produce self-insight into the associated

[50] Irwin M. Rubin, "Increased Self-Acceptance: A Means of Reducing Prejudice," *Journal of Personality and Social Psychology*, 5 (1967), 233–238.

[51] Pearl, *op. cit.*, 229.

[52] D. Katz, C. McClintock, and I. Sarnoff, "The Measurement of Ego Defense as Related to Attitude Change," *Journal of Personality*, 25 (1957), 465–474; D. Katz, I. Sarnoff, and C. McClintock, "Ego-Defense and Attitude Change," *Human Relations*, 9 (1956), 27–45; I. Sarnoff and D. Katz, "The Motivational Basis of Attitude Change," *Journal of Abnormal and Social Psychology*, 49 (1954), 115–124; and E. Stotland, D. Katz, and M. Patchen, "The Reduction of Prejudice through the Arousal of Self-Insight," *Journal of Personality*, 27 (1959), 507–531.

underlying motivations. His experiments show that individuals holding negative stereotypes toward Blacks—and otherwise resistant to positive information about Blacks—modify their attitudes through materials that give them insight into the dynamics of prejudice.

In the experiments, subjects read a case history designed to give self-insight into the psychodynamics of prejudice. This was followed by a threefold approach: (1) self-activity or self-involvement in which subjects were asked to order in logical sequence statements about the psychodynamics of prejudice; (2) the involvement of the subjects in making the materials that they read directly relevant to prejudice against Blacks; and (3) an appeal to the rationality and attitudinal self-consistency of the subjects. No significant changes occurred immediately after the experiment but significant change did appear several weeks later. This latter fact was assumed to result from a "sleeper effect" associated with internal restructuring— that is, an incubation period was necessary for the personality to integrate change.

THE LEGAL APPROACH

Can Laws Be Effective?

It is often said, "You cannot legislate against prejudice." This notion that laws are ineffective weapons against prejudice and discrimination is a frequently heard argument used against the enactment of various civil rights measures. Senator Barry Goldwater expressed this sentiment in the 1964 Presidential campaign: "I am unalterably opposed to . . . discrimination, but I also know that government can provide no lasting solution. . . . The ultimate solution lies in the hearts of men." [53]

According to this assumption laws must follow rather than precede social change and cannot by themselves change the norms of a society. The view was stated in classic fashion at the turn of the twentieth century by William Graham Sumner, a sociologist, who declared that "stateways [laws] cannot change folkways." Sumner believed that, when laws moved ahead of the customs or mores of the people, they were inevitably doomed to failure.[54] The dismal failure of Prohibition in barring the manufacture, transportation,

[53] *New York Times,* November 1, 1964, p. 1.
[54] William Graham Sumner, *Folkways* (Boston: Ginn & Co., 1906).

and sale of alcoholic beverages is commonly cited as proof of the position. Yet interestingly enough, many Americans believed that they *could* legislate inequality; and they proceeded to do precisely that, as we observed in the previous chapter. Beginning in the late nineteenth century, one southern state after another enacted Jim Crow laws and revised suffrage provisions so as to disfranchise Black voters.[55]

Although the Sumner-type argument against legislation sounds plausible, it is based upon a misunderstanding of the nature of laws and fails to distinguish between prejudice and discrimination. Laws can have little direct effect upon prejudice, since a state of mind— attitudes and feelings—is involved. But laws can prove effective weapons against overt acts of discrimination. Similarly, laws against murder and theft do not attempt to root out the desire to kill or steal; they seek to prevent these desires from becoming translated into overt acts. Laws are effective to the degree to which they act as deterrents to certain kinds of behavior, and therefore in part to the extent to which they are enforced. The fact that laws against murder and theft do not always succeed is no more evidence for the uselessness of such laws than is discrimination in employment evidence against fair-employment-practices acts. Many people feel that the fight against discrimination and segregation is more important than the fight against prejudiced attitudes and feelings. The former affect the right of an ethnic or racial minority to realize equality and freedom of opportunity. The latter may be considered a private matter. MacIver summarizes this position in these terms: "No law should require men to change their attitudes. . . . In a democracy we do not punish a man because he is opposed to income taxes, or to free school education, or to vaccination, or to minimum wages, but the laws of a democracy insist that he obey the laws that make provisions for these things. . . ."[56]

Evidence on the Effectiveness of Laws

Probably one of the clearest instances of the effectiveness of authoritative methods in combating discrimination and segregation is the current undermining of southern Jim Crow institutions through

[55] John Hope Franklin, "The Two Worlds of Race: A Historical View," *Daedalus*, 94 (1965), 908.

[56] Robert M. MacIver, "Forward," in Morroe Berger, *Equality By Statute* (New York: Columbia University Press, 1954), viii.

legislative, executive, and judicial action. The federal government has undertaken a monumental project in the field of social engineering, and it is an unquestionable fact that it is succeeding. Although in some instances contributing to a higher incidence of interracial friction, federal action has compelled the South to alter its traditional patterns in the direction of desegregation. Similarly, desegregation in the nation's armed forces was realized through the authoritative intervention of a presidential executive order. And state laws against discrimination, where enforced, have proved effective—for instance, action by New Jersey compelled Levitt and Sons, the nation's largest homebuilders, to sell housing on an open basis (the firm, finding that this had no ill effect on its sales, adopted a cooperative attitude towards fair housing laws; indeed, Mr. Levitt testified before Congress in 1966 in favor of a national fair housing law).[57]

A study by Saenger and Gilbert provides insight into the impact that laws may have against discrimination.[58] The law in question was New York State's act against discrimination in job hiring. The study focused attention upon the reaction of White customers to Black sales personnel in establishments that had hired Blacks in response to the law. Since the law did not apply to customers, they could withdraw their trade from the integrated stores if they so desired. Saenger and Gilbert compared the attitudes of White customers buying from Black clerks with attitudes of White customers buying from White clerks in a large New York department store. Trained interviewers were stationed near those sales counters where Black and White clerks worked side-by-side. In this manner, customers who dealt with Black clerks were distinguished from those dealing with neighboring White clerks. Both the customers of Black clerks and those of White clerks were then followed out of the store and interviewed. Since the customers were not told that they had previously been observed, it was possible to compare their actual behavior with their attitudes.

In the interviews, the White customers were asked to express their sentiments on the employment of Black clerks. At least 20 per cent indicated that they would not buy in stores which hired

---

[57] Mark Bonham Carter, "Measures Against Discrimination: The North American Scene," *Race*, 9 (1967), 1–26, and John H. Denton, "The Effectiveness of State Anti-Discrimination Laws in the United States," *Race*, 9 (1967), 85–92.

[58] Gerhart Saenger and E. Gilbert, "Customer Reactions to the Integration of Negro Sales Personnel," *International Journal of Opinion and Attitude Research*, 4 (1950), 57–76.

them. Another 20 per cent gave limited approval provided Black salesgirls were not used in departments handling food or clothing. The study revealed, however, that there was no relationship between what people said and what they did. No difference was found in prejudice between customers who had dealt with Black clerks and customers who had dealt with White clerks. In both groups 38 per cent either disapproved of Black clerks or wanted them excluded from some of the departments within the store. In fact, a number of women who had insisted a short time previously that they would not buy from Blacks were later observed buying from Black clerks.

Saenger and Gilbert suggest a number of factors as contributing to the discrepancy between what White people said and how they acted in relation to the Black clerks. First, the prejudiced individual was caught in a conflict between two contradictory motivations: his prejudice on the one hand and his desire to shop where he found it most comfortable and convenient on the other. The individuals in the study tended to resolve the dilemma though acting contrary to their prejudice and completing their shopping as quickly and expediently as possible. Second, prejudiced individuals were caught in still another conflict: whether to follow the dictates of prejudice or whether to live up to America's democratic ideals. Either of these attitudes may be activated, depending upon the prejudiced individual's definition of the situation. Third, a desire to conform with prevailing public opinion may be uppermost in the individual's mind. He may prefer to translate his prejudice into overt action but, nevertheless, yield to local custom. The fact that Blacks were found in the stores as clerks tended to suggest to many individuals that the public approved of their presence. Individuals who are strongly prejudiced are often insecure and, accordingly, frequently have a deep need to conform. Thus, where they have the impression that others do not share their thinking, they are less likely to defend their prejudices and less likely to translate them into discriminatory behavior.

Killian, in his study of the adjustment of southern White migrants to life in Chicago, came to similar conclusions. Evidence gathered from employers and the migrants themselves revealed that southern Whites were able to make a peaceful accommodation to the norms governing interracial situations within Chicago. Not only did they work in plants with Blacks, but they shared the same rest rooms and dressing rooms. The South continued as their principal reference group and they followed its practices of racial segregation when it was conveniently possible. When confronted with situations in which these ways could not be adhered to without personal sacrifice, they tended to make the necessary behavioral adjustments although attitude changes did not necessarily occur.[59] There are probably also instances of the opposite, that is, verbal expressions of tolerance accompanied by discriminatory behavior, although they are not as well documented—the flight of White, liberal, middle-class families from the cities to the suburbs may be a case in point.[60]

Studies such as those we have cited show that what people do in intergroup situations seems to be almost independent of how they feel or what they think. The *social setting* appears to constitute the chief factor. As Allport notes, "Segregationists act like integrationists where social prescription requires; integrationists behave like segregationists when it is socially appropriate to do so."[61] Hence laws may play an important part in defining the social setting for individuals.

Two types of individuals appear to be particularly susceptible to the influence of anti-discriminatory laws: first, those who are themselves not prejudiced but who find it expedient or profitable to stand by silently or to give passive support to discrimination; second, those who are prejudiced but who are not prepared to pay a significant price for translating their attitudes into behavior, preferring instead the easier course of conformity. For these two groups, laws against discrimination frequently provide an impetus for overcoming previous patterns and for instituting non-discriminatory behavior; thus, the laws act as deterrents to discriminatory behavior. Taken together, these two groups probably make up a sizable majority of the population, the militant integrationists and militant segregationists representing smaller segments of the total population.

In evaluating the effectiveness of laws, we have stressed that they can play an important part in combating discrimination—overt behavior. But what about prejudice—a state of mind? The matter is by no means simple. As we have noted, at least in the short run, laws may have relatively little impact upon prejudice. Indeed, it is

[59] Lewis M. Killian, "The Effects of Southern White Workers on Race Relations in Northern Plants," *American Sociological Review*, 17 (1952), 327–331.

[60] John Colombotos, "Physicians and Medicare: A Before–After Study of the Effects of Legislation on Attitudes," *American Sociological Review*, 34 (1969), 319.

[61] Gordon W. Allport, "Prejudice: Is It Societal or Personal," *Journal of Social Issues*, 18 (1962), 123.

even conceivable that legally compelled desegregation may for a time intensify feelings of hostility and hence increase prejudice. Viewed from the long run, however, prejudice in some cases may be decreased. Evidence suggests that *specific* attitudes shape themselves to overt behavior. In considering intergroup contact, we observed that Whites who actually work with Blacks, especially as equals, tend to develop favorable attitudes toward working with Blacks. Although this sentiment may not be generalized to other interracial situations, it nevertheless points to specific attitude change —to the lessening of prejudice in at least one sphere.

Some, however, also see law exerting a *direct* influence on attitudes, without necessarily changing overt behavior first. Bonfield argues: ". . . the mere existence of the law itself affects prejudice. People usually agree with the law and internalize its values. This is because considerable moral and symbolic weight is added to a principle when it is embedded in legislation." [62] In brief, law sets the moral atmosphere in which society exists, and in its own right it is a powerful instrument of education.[63] A case in point is physicians' attitudes toward medicare. Seldom has a law been more bitterly opposed by any group than was medicare by the medical profession. Yet with respect to their attitudes, the proportion of physicians in favor of the main part of medicare, the hospitalization program for the elderly, jumped from 38 per cent before the law was passed to 70 per cent ten months after it was passed, even before it was implemented, and then to 81 per cent six months after it was implemented. Hence, some laws may influence attitudes without first changing overt behavior.[64]

Some Limits to the Effectiveness of Law

In recent years, sociologists have increasingly come to recognize that laws can be effective instruments for reducing discrimination. But law, especially in a non-totalitarian society, is not all-powerful. Moreover, informal, indirect, subtle discrimination is much less susceptible to legal remedies than formal, direct, and blatant discrimination.

Moreover, civil rights legislation often functions as a tool with an

---

[62] Arthur Earl Bonfield, "The Role of Legislation in Eliminating Racial Discrimination," *Race*, 7 (1965), 108–109.

[63] Carter, *op. cit.*, 6.

[64] Colombotos, *op. cit.*, 318–334.

essentially negative character—it prescribes "thou shall nots." At still other times it may contribute to at best a "grudging acceptance" of minorities. Hence, although realizing desegregation, integration may remain a still distant goal. Accordingly, positive measures designed to promote intergroup goodwill are also called for.[65]

Then too, laws are likely to be effective to the extent that they are enforced; and of course authorities within the United States—both North and South, locally and nationally—have not always been committed to enforcing fully civil rights laws.[66] Still another problem is that very often the victims of discrimination are ignorant of the laws or reluctant to make complaints under them, patterns most frequently encountered among those segments of minority groups most susceptible to discrimination, namely poorly educated, low-income groups.[67] The New York City "fair housing" ordinance is a case in point. New York City was the first community to enact a "fair housing" or "open occupancy" ordinance banning discrimination in the sale or rental of all housing except owner-occupied duplexes and rooms in private homes. Yet, the effect of the law appeared to be limited. In the first three years of its operation, the New York City law adjusted slightly more than two hundred complaints to the satisfaction of the Black complainant. While this indeed constituted a gain, it is small when viewed in the perspective of New York's nearly one million Blacks. Most of the Black complainants were middle-class Blacks in white-collar or professional occupations; lower-class Blacks, for whom the housing problem is perhaps most severe, hardly participated in the benefits of the open-occupancy law at all. And finally, nearly half of the complaints were from Blacks who already were living in areas that were predominantly White—Blacks who had already broken out of the ghetto.[68] It is perhaps somewhat unfair, however, to view a law's effectiveness in terms of the number of complainants benefiting from

[65] See Arthur Shostak, "Appeals from Discrimination in Federal Employment: A Case Study," *Social Forces,* 42 (1963), 174–178.

[66] In this regard see: Morris Davis, Robert Seibert, and Warren Breed, "Interracial Seating Patterns on New Orleans Public Transit," *Social Problems,* 13 (1966), 298–306.

[67] Gerhart Saenger and Norma S. Gordon, "Influence of Discrimination on Minority Group Members in Its Relation to Attempts to Combat Discrimination," *Journal of Social Psychology,* 31 (1950), 95–120.

[68] Harold Goldblatt and Florence Cromien, "The Effective Reach of the Fair Housing Practices Law of the City of New York," *Social Problems,* 9 (1962), 365–370. Also see: Leon H. Mayhew, *Law and Equal Opportunity* (Cambridge, Mass.: Harvard University Press, 1968).

it. A good many landlords conceivably may have "fallen into line" with the law once it appeared on the books. These types of gains are difficult to measure.[69]

SUMMARY

By virtue of the great complexity of intergroup behavior and the multiplicity of factors involved, it is clear that an attack upon racism must involve a many-sided approach. Indeed, there appear to be no easy answers or quick solutions. If we consider our goal to be desegregation, the elimination of barriers, we are concerned mainly with social controls and institutional arrangements, in which case laws assume considerable importance. If we have integration (personal acceptance) as our goal, then the effectiveness of personal controls and the content of attitudes become central, in which case propaganda, education, contact, and psychological approaches (and under some circumstances laws) assume importance.

[69] See, for instance, Denton, *op. cit.*, 86.

Author Index

Aberbach, Joel D., 372, 394, 396, 399, 403
Adams, Walter A., 342
Adlous, Joan, 255
Adorno, T. W., 84, 142–53, 470
Aho, William R., 245, 247
Albee, George W., 469
Allison, Anthony C., 61
Allport, Floyd H., 128
Allport, Gordon W., 131, 133, 135, 149, 463, 478
Ames, Richard G., 102
Ammons, R. B., 116
Anderson, C. C., 74
Anderson, Charles H., 289
Anderson, Martin, 445
Antonovsky, Aaron, 280
Aptheker, Herbert, 364
Asch, Solomon E., 148
Atkins, Ruth Davidson, 99
Axebrod, Sidney, 56

Back, Kurt W., 320
Backman, Carl W., 455
Bagby, James W., 103
Bagley, C. R., 339
Baker, Paul T., 38
Banfield, Edward C., 353
Barber, Bernard, 401
Barber, Kenneth E., 284
Barnicot, Nigel A., 38, 39
Barron, Milton L., 13, 348, 378
Bass, B. M., 149
Bastide, Roger, 78
Bates, Alan P., 5
Bauman, Karl E., 312
Beem, Helen P., 360
Belth, N. C., 217, 218, 219
Bendix, Reinhard, 249
Benedict, Ruth, 73, 74
Bennett, William S., Jr., 248
Berelson, Bernard, 455
Berkowitz, Leonard, 125, 128, 129, 132
Berreman, Gerald D., 9, 243

Berreman, Joel V., 248
Berry, Brewton, 6, 7, 68, 305, 402
Bettelheim, Bruno, 140
Biblarz, Arturo, 8
Bickel, Alexander, 426
Bierstedt, Robert, 6, 7, 93
Biesanz, John, 110
Biggar, Jeanne, 151
Birdsell, Joseph B., 61–62, 63
Bittle, William E., 380
Bixenstine, V. Edwin, 74
Black, Donald J., 55
Black, Percy, 99
Blake, Robert R., 81
Blalock, Hubert M., Jr., 81, 87, 463
Blauner, Robert, 255, 256
Bloom, Leonard, 215
Blumer, Herbert, 90
Boesel, David, 168
Bogardus, Emory S., 22, 100–3
Bogue, D. J., 292
Bonfield, Arthur Earl, 479
Borhek, J. T., 277
Borinski, Ernst, 177
Borrie, W. D., 264, 267, 277, 278
Boskin, Joseph, 164
Bowen, Don, 172
Boyd, William C., 35
Brady, Tom P., 58
Braly, K. W., 22
Braverman, Harold, 219
Breed, Warren, 480
Briar, Scott, 56
Brindstaff, Carl F., 171
Brink, William, 368, 372
Brinton, Crane, 172, 371
Britt, S. H., 125
Broom, Leonard, 360, 372
Brophy, I. N., 469
Brown, Barry S., 469
Brown, H. Rap, 343
Brown, Sterling, 345
Bruner, Edward M., 76
Buettner-Janusch, John, 31

Bugelski, B. R., 283
Bugelski, Richard, 127
Burgess, M. Elaine, 241, 326
Burma, John H., 201, 204, 205, 289, 291, 344
Burns, Haywood, 56
Bushnell, John H., 263
Byrne, D., 74

Campbell, Angus, 348, 349, 400, 403, 404
Campisi, Paul J., 357, 358
Cantril, Hadley, 163
Carithers, Martha W., 462
Carlson, Elliot, 219
Carmichael, Stokely, 28, 397, 437
Carter, Dorothy Jean, 79
Carter, Mark Bonham, 476, 479
Cash, W. J., 132
Caspari, Ernst, 50
Catton, William R., Jr., 73, 75
Cayton, Horace R., 340, 361
Centers, Richard, 149
Chambliss, W. J., 56
Chancellor, Loren, 287
Chase, Charles, 312
Cheng, C. K., 293, 296, 297
Cheng, David, 209
Child, Irvin L., 357
Christensen, Harold T., 284
Christie, Richard, 110, 131, 148, 149
Christman, Henry M., 138
Clark, Kenneth B., 174, 331, 337, 435
Cobb, William Montague, 136
Cobbs, Price M., 332, 333, 346
Coffmann, Thomas L., 22, 25
Cohen, Arthur R., 455
Coleman, James S., 44, 433, 462
Collins, Mary Evans, 465–66, 468, 469
Colombotos, John, 478, 479
Comas, Juan, 41
Congdon, Clyde S., 128
Conner, Caryl, 44
Conyers, James E., 361
Cook, Samuel Dubois, 396
Cook, Stuart W., 466, 468
Coon, Carleton S., 31, 61–62
Cooper, Eunice, 452–54
Copeland, Lewis C., 78
Corey, Lewis, 249
Corsi, Jerome, 161
Coser, Lewis A., 158, 159, 160
Côté, A. D. J., 74
Couch, A., 149
Cowen, Emory, 128
Cowgill, Donald O., 193
Cox, Oliver C., 18–19, 241–43
Crawford, Thomas J., 171
Cretser, Gary A., 291

Cromien, Florence, 480
Cronon, Edmund D., 385
Crouthamel, James L., 164
Cullen, Countee, 346
Cummins, Geraldine, 311
Cutright, Phillips, 92
Czekanowski, Jan, 31

Daniel, Johnnie, 443
Davie, M. R., 305
Davies, James C., 371
Davis, Allison, 237–41
Davis, David Brion, 91
Davis, Kingsley, 222, 291
Davis, Morris, 480
Dean, John P., 461
DeFleur, Melvin L., 27
DeFriese, Gordon H., 27
Degler, Carl N., 91
Deloria, Vine, Jr., 186
de Neufville, Richard, 44
Deniker, Joseph, 31
Dennis, Rutledge, M., 27
Denton, John H., 476, 481
Deutsch, Morton, 465–66, 468, 469
DeVos, George, 243
Dillehay, Ronald C., 148
Dinerman, Helen, 454
Dizard, Jan E., 292, 405–6
Dodson, Dan W., 7
Doise, Willem, 75
Dollard, John, 86, 125, 127, 135, 138, 191, 332, 333, 340, 344, 347
Dobzhansky, Theodosius, 35, 36, 60, 63
Douglass, Frederick, 323–25
Dowd, Douglas, 9
Downes, Bryan T., 172
Drake, St. Clair, 191, 193, 340, 341
Dreger, R. M., 51, 53
DuBois, W. E. B., 323, 346, 385
Duncan, Beverly, 245
Duncan, Otis Dudley, 245
Dunham, Frances Y., 79
Dunn, L. C., 60
Dupertuis, C. Wesley, 33
Dworkin, Anthony Gary, 206
Dynes, Russell, 173–74

Edmonson, Munro E., 241
Edwards, Harry, 391
Eells, Kenneth, 227
Eisenman, Russell, 126
Elder, Glen H., Jr., 403
Ember, Melvin, 13
Engel, Gerald, 311
Epps, Edgar G., 305
Epstein, Benjamin R., 217
Epstein, Erwin H., 206

Epstein, Ralph, 128, 132, 148, 310
Essien-Udom, E. U., 391, 393
Etzioni, Amitai, 267, 271
Evans-Pritchard, E. E., 15

Fairchild, Henry Pratt, 266
Fancher, Betsy, 379
Fanon, Frantz, 135, 174
Faris, R. E. L., 118, 132
Farley, Reynolds, 192, 193
Feagin, Joe R., 167, 443
Fendrich, James M., 27
Ferdinand, Theodore N., 56
Feshbach, Seymour, 128, 130
Fischer, John H., 437
Fischl, Myron A., 311
Fishman, Jacob R., 335, 375
Fitzpatrick, Joseph P., 200, 259, 283
Flowerman, Samuel, 76–77
Fogel, Walter, 204
Ford, W. Scott, 27
Forster, Arnold, 217, 218
Fortes, M., 15
Fuguitt, Glenn V., 439
Francis, E. K., 70
Franklin, John Hope, 190, 323, 341, 475
Franklin, Raymond S., 257
Frazier, E. Franklin, 252, 308, 309, 320, 321, 348, 388
Freedman, Edward, 466
Freeman, Ellis, 125
Frenkel-Brunswik, Else, 142–53
Friedman, Neil, 305
Friedman, Samuel, 28
Friedrichs, Robert W., 174

Gans, Herbert J., 247, 263, 358, 445
Gardner, Burleigh B., 237–41
Gardner, Mary R., 237–41
Garn, Stanley M., 35, 36, 38, 61–62
Garrett, Henry E., 51
Garvey, Marcus, 385–89
Gaston, Paul, 425
Geertz, Clifford, 226
Geis, Gilbert L., 380
Gergen, Kenneth J., 72
Gerlach, Luther P., 395
Geschwender, James A., 168, 171, 371
Gilbert, E., 476–77
Gilbert, G. M., 22, 25
Gillin, John, 124, 260, 297
Gist, Noel P., 248
Glass, Bentley, 63
Glazer, Nathan, 198, 245, 257, 342, 353, 354, 359
Glenn, Norval, 92, 250, 372
Goge, N. L., 149
Golden, Joseph, 290, 291–92

Goldhamer, Herbert, 290
Goldmann, Nahum, 383
Goldscheider, Calvin, 287
Goldsen, Rose Kohn, 196, 197, 198, 199
Goldstein, Sidney, 287
Goodman, M. E., 116
Goody, Jack, 16
Gordon, Milton, 223, 224, 225, 261, 265
Gordon, Norma S., 480
Gouldner, Alvin W., 6, 7, 8
Gove, Walter R., 10
Graeber, Isacque, 125
Graham, Hugh Davis, 161
Gray, David J., 7
Gray, J. S., 342
Grebler, Leo, 204, 206
Greeley, Andrew M., 245, 284
Green, Edward, 55
Greenblum, Joseph, 278
Greenway, John, 345
Greer, Scott, 445
Gregor, A. James, 116, 311
Grier, William H., 332, 333, 346
Grigg, Charles, 262, 373
Grimshaw, Allen D., 83, 161, 164, 171
Grodzins, Morton, 192
Groseclose, Everett, 380
Guilford, J. P., 102
Gundlach, R. H., 468
Gurr, Ted R., 161, 171
Guzman, Robert C., 204, 206

Haak, Ronald O., 215
Hadden, Jeffrey, 161
Hager, Don J., 445
Hahn, Harlan, 443
Haimowitz, Morris L., 471
Haimowitz, Natalie Reader, 471
Hallowell, A. Irving, 103
Halpern, Ben, 384
Halstead, Michael N., 255
Hamblin, Robert J., 81
Hamilton, Charles V., 28, 437
Handlin, Mary, 91
Handlin, Oscar, 91
Hannerz, Ulf, 254, 346
Haralambos, Michael, 346
Harbin, S. P., 79
Harding, John, 457, 467
Hardyck, Jane Allyn, 74, 461
Harris, Louis, 262, 368, 372
Harris, Marvin, 10, 12, 262
Harris, Virginia, 360
Hartley, Eugene, 102
Havighurst, Robert J., 234
Hawkins, Gayle, 74
Heer, David M., 289, 290
Heiss, Jerold S., 289

Hendrick, Clyde, 74
Herbers, John, 427
Hernton, Calvin C., 135
Herzl, Theodor, 382–84
Hesburgh, Theodore M., 425
Hess, Charles, 63
Hill, Mozell C., 380
Hills, Stuart L., 257
Himmelweit, H., 129
Hine, Virginia H., 395
Hinkle, G. J., 5
Hinkle, R. C., Jr., 5
Hoffer, Eric, 371
Hogrefe, Russell, 467
Hollingshead, A. B., 224, 234, 283
Holloway, Robert G., 248
Hong, Sung Chick, 75
Hooton, Earnest A., 31, 32, 33, 34
Horney, Karen, 83
Horowitz, Eugene L., 104, 117
Horowitz, Irving, 9
Horowitz, Murray, 81
Horowitz, Ruth E., 104
Hostetler, John A., 297
Hovland, Carl I., 451
Howard, David H., 321
Howze, Glenn, 305
Hubbard, Howard, 177, 399, 400
Hughes, Everett C., 224
Hughes, Langston, 346
Humphrey, Norman Daymond, 83, 165
Hurvitz, Nathan, 245
Hutchinson, Edward P., 245
Hyman, H. H., 149

Ingle, Dwight, 45, 50

Jackson, D. N., 149
Jahn, Elso F., 63
Jahoda, Marie, 110, 130, 131, 139–40,
    148, 149, 311, 452–54
Janowitz, Morris, 140
Jenkins, William Sumner, 91
Jennings, Jesse D., 186
Jensen, Arthur R., 45–46, 50
Johnson, Charles S., 83, 242, 252, 305,
    308, 314, 315, 329, 332, 333, 339,
    343, 348, 378, 379
Johnson, Guy B., 164, 165, 333
Johnson, Robert, 325, 348, 378, 403
Johnson, Robert B., 305
Jones, E. E., 456
Jordon, Winthrop D., 77, 91
Junker, Buford H., 342

Kain, John F., 445
Kaplan, Howard M., 393
Kardiner, Abram, 309, 318, 334, 341

Karlins, Marvin, 22, 25
Karon, Bertram P., 334
Katz, D., 22, 473
Kaufman, Walter C., 151
Kazamias, Andreas M., 206
Keesing, Felix, 261
Kelly, William H., 97
Kelman, Herbert C., 170, 397, 398
Keniston, K., 149
Kennedy, Ruby Jo Reeves, 283, 289
Kennedy, T. H., 361
Kephart, William M., 284
Kerckhoff, Alan C., 280
Key, V. O., Jr., 85
Kibbe, Pauline R., 202, 205
Killian, Lewis M., 110, 262, 325–26,
    364, 365, 373, 477–78
King, Martin Luther, Jr., 315, 335, 367,
    370
Kirk, Jerome, 315
Kirkpatrick, Clifford, 134
Kirscht, John P., 148
Kitt, Alice S., 371
Klein, Frederick C., 217
Kleiner, Robert J., 253, 254
Klineberg, Otto, 48–49, 53, 290
Kluckhohn, Clyde, 97, 318, 333
Knopf, Terry Ann, 169
Kohler, R., 456
Komorita, S. S., 148, 310
Kornhauser, A., 149
Kramer, Bernard M., 20, 463
Kramer, Judith R., 328
Krapin, Louis, 219
Kroeber, Alfred L., 185
Krystall, Eric R., 305
Kung, S. W., 211
Kunstadter, Peter, 15
Kwan, Kian M., 5

Ladd, Everett C., Jr., 326
Ladinsky, Jack, 277
Ladner, Joyce, 399
Lalli, Michael, 358
Lamanna, Richard A., 320
Landes, Judah, 128
Lanternari, Vittorio, 402
LaPiere, Richard T., 26–27
Lasker, Gabriel W., 63
Laue, James H., 365, 391
Laumann, Edward O., 289
Laurenti, Luigi, 193
LaViolette, Forrest E., 23, 212
Lazarsfeld, Paul F., 371
Leach, Edmund R., 14, 15
Lee, Alfred McClung, 83, 165
Lee, Everett S., 49
Lee, Rose Hum, 208, 210

Lehman, F. K., 15
Leighton, Alexander H., 316
Lenski, Gerhard, 245, 286, 358
Lerner, Michael, 20
Lesser, Gerald S., 130
Leventman, Seymour, 328
LeVine, B. B., 76
LeVine, R. A., 76
Levine, Stuart, 354
Levinson, Daniel J., 142–53
Lewin, Kurt, 310, 322
Lewis, Oscar, 252
Lieberson, Stanley, 93–95, 164, 226, 258,
    277, 279, 439
Liebow, Elliot, 253
Light, Robert E., 36
Lincoln, C. Eric, 389, 390, 391, 397
Lind, Andrew W., 295
Linders, F. J., 34
Lindgren, Ethel John, 72, 80
Lindzey, Gardner, 128, 457
Linn, Lawrence S., 27
Linton, Ralph, 97, 98, 225, 260, 401
Lippmann, Walter, 22
Lipset, Seymour Martin, 121, 191, 249
Livingstone, Frank B., 36, 61
Locke, Harvey J., 287
Loeb, Martin B., 234
Loewenstein, Rudolph, 139
Lohman, Joseph D., 110
Loren, Eugene L., 168
Low, J. O., 227
Lubasch, Arnold L., 3
Luchterhand, Elmer G., 56
Lumsdaine, Arthur A., 451
Lundborg, H., 34
Lunt, Paul S., 227, 230, 231
Luttermann, Kenneth G., 151
Lyman, Stanford M., 207
Lynn, Ann Q., 289

McCarthy, John D., 311
McClelland, David C., 245
McClintock, C., 473
McConahay, John B., 168
McCormack, Thomas C., 280
MacCrone, I. D., 135
McDill, Edward L., 151
McDonagh, Edward C., 205
McDonald, Margaret M., 245
McFee, Malcolm, 282
McGurk, Frank, 51
MacIver, R. M., 114, 456, 475
Mack, Raymond W., 206
McKay, Henry D., 56
McKenzie, R. D., 207
MacKinnon, W. J., 149
McLean, Helen V., 334

McPherson, D. Angus, 116, 311
McWilliams, Carey, 201, 214
Madsen, William, 205
Mann, John H., 20
Manton, Jane S., 81
Markmann, Charles Lam, 135
Martin, James G., 312
Marx, Gary T., 321, 332, 342, 348, 370,
    375–76
Masuoka, Jitsuichi, 90, 205, 295
Masotti, Louis, 161, 172
Matthews, Donald R., 328, 381
Maxwell, Neil, 380
Mayer, Albert J., 149, 245
Mayer, Kurt, 17
Mayhew, Leon H., 480
Mead, Margaret, 36, 45
Meeker, Marchia, 227
Meer, Bernard, 466
Meier, August, 369, 414
Meltzer, H., 102
Merton, Robert K., 9, 77, 86, 111, 291,
    371
Messick, S., 149
Mezei, Louis, 74, 75, 461
Middleton, Russell, 151, 450
Miller, Kelly, 324
Miller, K. S., 51, 53
Miller, Neal E., 127
Mills, C. Wright, 196, 197, 198, 199
Minard, Ralph D., 468
Mittelbach, Frank G., 283
Moles, Oliver C., 253
Molotch, Harvey, 428–30
Monahan, Thomas P., 287, 289, 290, 291
Montagu, Ashley, 36, 38, 41, 53
Moore, Joan W., 204, 206, 283
Moore, Robert, 258
Moore, Wilbert E., 222
Morland, J. Kenneth, 116, 117, 310
Morse, Nancy C., 128
Mosher, Lawrence, 400
Motz, Annabelle B., 337, 462
Moyers, Bill D., 426
Moynihan, Daniel P., 198, 251–55, 342,
    353, 354, 359
Munch, Peter A., 73
Murdock, George P., 14
Murphy, Raymond J., 168
Murray, Henry A., 318, 333
Mussen, P. H., 378
Myers, Gustavus, 138
Myrdal, Gunnar, 114–115, 190, 323, 343

Nadel, S. F., 14, 76
Naditch, Murray, 171
Nagasawa, R. H., 56
Nam, Charles B., 243–45

Nelli, Humbert S., 355, 358
Newcomb, Theodore M., 124
Newman, Marshall T., 35
Nichimoto, Richard S., 215
Nicolaus, Martin, 7
Nisbet, Robert A., 9
Noel, Donald L., 67, 72, 79, 305–7, 311

O'Kane, James M., 255–57
Oppenheimer, Martin, 93
Orbell, John M., 110, 375, 458
O'Shea, Harriet E., 311
O'Shea, Robert M., 253
Ovesey, Lionel, 309, 318, 334, 341

Padilla, Elena, 198, 199
Page, Richard, 23
Palmore, Erdman, 437, 439, 468
Park, Robert E., 240, 268–71, 279
Parker, Seymour, 253, 254
Parkman, Margaret, 297
Parsons, Talcott, 125
Passow, A. Harry, 337
Pastore, N., 128
Patchen, M., 473
Peabody, D., 149
Pear, T. H., 129
Pearl, David, 471, 473
Pearlin, Leonard I., 107
Penalosa, Fernando, 201, 204
Persky, Joseph J., 445
Petersen, William, 68, 213
Peterson, Ruth C., 449, 451
Pettigrew, Thomas F., 55, 56, 99, 153,
    363, 365, 372, 379, 461
Photiades, John D., 151
Piliavin, Irving, 56
Pinard, Maurice, 315
Podain, Simon, 78
Pohlman, Edward W., 243
Poussaint, Alvin G., 399
Powdermaker, Hortense, 252, 318, 328,
    333
Preston, James D., 237
Price, A. Grenfell, 94
Prothro, E. Terry, 153
Prothro, James W., 328, 381
Proudfoot, Merrill, 336

Quarantelli, E. L., 173, 174
Quinn, Olive Westbrooke, 119–21

Raab, Earl, 121, 200
Rabbie, Jacob M., 81
Radke, Marian J., 117–18
Rainwater, Lee, 251, 253
Rand, Christopher, 197, 198, 199
Ransford, H. Edward, 167, 350

Razran, Gregory, 105
Reed, Roy, 434
Reissmann, Leonard, 255
Reitzes, Dietrich C., 110
Rendon, Armando, 198, 199, 200
Rex, John, 258
Ribicoff, Abraham A., 433
Riddleberger, Alice B., 462
Riemer, Ruth, 215
Ries, T. B., 258
Rinder, Irwin D., 277, 344
Ripley, William Z., 31
Rist, Ray C., 337
Roberts, Alan H., 152
Robinson, Jerry W., Jr., 237
Rogin, Michael, 458
Rohrer, John H., 49, 103, 241
Rokeach, Milton, 74–76, 152, 461
Rose, Arnold M., 14, 208, 374, 381, 389,
    435, 436
Rosen, Alex, 461
Rosen, Bernard C., 245, 246, 247
Rosenberg, Pearl, 117–18
Rosenblatt, Paul C., 73
Rosenthal, Erich, 263, 288
Rosenthal, Jack, 382
Rothenberg, Jerome, 445
Rubel, Arthur J., 206
Rubin, Irwin M., 473
Rudwick, Elliott, 414
Rule, Brendan Gail, 129
Russo, John, 358

Sabagh, George, 287
Sacks, Milton S., 63
Saenger, Gerhart, 76–77, 476–77, 480
Samelson, F., 149
Samuels, Frederick, 295
Samuels, Gertrude, 436
Sandis, Eva E., 196
Sanford, R. Nevitt, 142–53
Sarnoff, I., 473
Sartre, Jean-Paul, 43
Sawyer, Jack, 297
Scarpatti, F. R., 55
Schaet, Donald E., 128
Schaffer, Albert, 119
Schaffer, Ruth C., 119
Schapera, I., 16
Schermerhorn, R. A., 11, 81, 94, 277,
    278, 352, 354, 355
Schlesinger, Arthur, Sr., 426
Schlesinger, Lawrence E., 107
Schmidt, Fred H., 203, 204
Schnore, Leo F., 192
Schoenfeld, Eugen, 287
Schrieke, B., 207, 208

Schuman, Howard, 348, 349, 400, 403, 404
Scott, John Finley, 87, 255
Scott, Lois Heyman, 87, 255
Scott, Joseph L., 328
Seacrest, Ted, 291
Searles, Ruth, 375
Sears, David O., 168
Secord, Paul F., 455
Seibert, Robert, 480
Seidenberg, Robert, 137
Selznick, Gertrude J., 105, 150, 216, 457, 459
Seminatore, Kenneth, 161
Senior, Clarence, 196, 197, 198, 199
Sharp, Harry, 192, 245
Shaw, Clifford R., 56
Sheatsley, P. B., 149
Sheffield, Fred D., 451
Sheppard, Harold L., 149, 342
Sherif, Carolyn W., 106, 111
Sherif, Muzafer, 81, 103, 106, 109, 111, 181–83
Sherrill, Kenneth S., 110, 458
Shibutani, Tamotsu, 5
Shils, E. A., 131
Shockley, William, 45, 50
Shostak, Arthur, 480
Shuey, Audrey, 51
Sibley, Elbridge, 249
Siegel, Paul M., 195
Sigall, Harold, 23
Sills, David, 159, 259
Silverman, Arnold R., 164
Silvers, Ronald J., 277
Silvert, K. H., 23
Simpson, George, 158
Simpson, George E., 305
Simpson, Ida H., 320
Simpson, Richard L., 342
Singer, Benjamin D., 168
Singer, Robert, 128
Sklare, Marshall, 263, 278, 288
Slater, Mariam K., 232
Slawson, John, 383
Smith, Carole R., 74
Smith, Charles, 325–26
Smith, F. Tredwell, 464
Smith, Luke M., 110
Smith, M. Brewster, 74, 461
Solomon, Fredic, 335, 375
Speier, Hans, 75
Spencer, Robert F., 186
Spicer, Edward H., 259
Spiegel, John R., 161
Spier, Rosalind B., 56
Spilerman, Seymour, 176

Srole, Leo, 151, 227, 229, 233, 271–75, 278
Stagner, Ross, 128
Star, Jack, 194
Stein, David D., 74, 461
Steinberg, Stephen, 105, 150, 216, 457, 459
Steiner, Gary A., 455
Stember, Charles H., 458, 459
Stephenson, Richard M., 55, 248
Stern, Sol, 344
Stevenson, Harold W., 116
Steward, Edward C., 116
Stillman, Richard J., II, 441
Stonequist, Everett V., 279
Stotland, E., 473
Stricker, George, 128
Strodtbeck, Fred, 245
Strong, E. K., Jr., 213
Sullivan, Harry Stack, 333
Sumner, William Graham, 73, 474
Sutherland, Jean, 117–18
Swanson, G. E., 14
Swartz, Marc J., 73
Szwed, John F., 255, 346, 395

Tabb, William K., 257
Taeuber, Karl, 193
Taft, Donald R., 54, 56
Taft, Ronald, 276
Talmadge, H. E., 58
Taylor, Raymond G., Jr., 116, 310
Teller, Judd L., 385
Thomas, Dorothy Swaine, 215
Thomas, John L., 284
Thomas, Robert K., 189
Thomas, W. I., 40, 111
Thomes, Mary Margaret, 287
Thompson, A. J., 342
Thompson, Daniel C., 324, 363
Thompson, Edgar T., 78, 83, 164, 333
Thurstone, L. L., 449, 451
Tobach, Ethel, 36
Toby, Jackson, 337, 338
Tomlinson, T. M., 168, 175
Toomer, Jean, 346
Trent, R. D., 311
Triandis, Harry S., 23, 102
Triandis, Leigh Minturn, 102
Tucker, Richard D., 79
Tumin, Melvin M., 51, 110, 458
Turnbull, Colin M., 16
Tyler, Lawrence, 391

Udry, J. Richard, 312

Valentine, Charles A., 253, 254
Valien, Preston, 90, 205, 295

van den Berghe, Pierre L., 93, 259, 262, 282, 427
Van Den Haag, Ernest, 51
Vander Zanden, James W., 87–89, 172, 178, 179, 222, 335, 369, 370, 419–24, 458
Vassilious, V., 23
Velikonja, Joseph, 352
von Eickstedt, Egon, 31
Von Eschen, Donald, 315

Wagatsuma, Hirsohi, 243
Wagley, Charles, 10, 12, 262
Walker, Jack L., 372, 394, 396, 399, 403
Walkley, Rosabelle Price, 466, 468
Walters, Gary, 22, 25
Ward, Lewis B., 217, 218
Warner, Lyle G., 27, 100
Warner, W. Lloyd, 227–41, 271–75, 278, 342
Washburn, Sherwood L., 62
Washington, Booker T., 323–25
Watson, James M., 168
Watson, Tom, 138–39
Weatherley, Donald, 128, 146
Weber, George H., 337
Weiner, J. S., 38
Weinstock, S. Alexander, 277
Weiss, Albert, 217
Wessel, B. B., 283
West, Louis J., 135
Westie, Frank R., 27, 118, 121, 132
White, Walter, 346
Whitten, Norman E., Jr., 255, 346, 395
Whittington, Frank J., 437, 439

Wiercinski, Andrzej, 31
Wildavsky, Aaron, 173
Wilensky, Harold L., 277
Williams, J. Allen, 153, 375, 469
Williams, John E., 79
Williams, Robin M., Jr., 12, 70, 80, 110, 150, 153, 276, 333, 378, 460, 463, 468
Williamson, Joel, 414
Willis, R. H., 74
Wilner, Daniel M., 466, 468
Wilson, James Q., 374
Wilson, William J., 395
Wirth, Louis, 16–18, 270, 290
Wolfgang, Marvin E., 56
Wong, T. J., 74
Woodward, C. Vann, 87, 364, 412–17
Works, Ernest, 467
Worthy, William, 389, 390
Wright, Richard, 346
Wright, Sewall, 63
Wrong, Dennis H., 221, 222

Yamamura, Douglas S., 297
Yancey, William L., 251, 311
Yates, Aubrey J., 125
Yerkes, Robert M., 48
Yinger, J. Milton, 288, 295, 391, 392
Young, Donald, 82
Yuan, D. Y., 208, 210
Yutzy, Daniel, 300

Zangwill, Israel, 264–65
Zawadzki, Bohdan, 128, 131

Subject Index

Acceptance, as a minority reaction, 305–29

Acculturation, 259–61

Aggression, as a minority reaction, 330–50

Amalgamation, 263

American Indians, 185–89

Americanization orientation, 265–66

Amish, assimilation of, 297–300

Anti-Semitism
  concept of Jews as a race, 40–43
  in employment, 216–17
  in housing, 218
  as Rorschach inkblots, 139–41
  in social clubs, 219

Assimilation
  absorption, 264
  acculturation, 259–61
  acculturation without integration, 262–63
  amalgamation, 263 64
  Americanization orientation, 265–66
  among the Amish, 297–300
  defined, 258
  within Hawaii, 293–97
  integration, 261
  intergroup marriage, 282–93
  marginality, 279–81
  melting pot orientation, 264–65
  and migrant subordination, 93–95
  as minority reaction, 351–76
  natural history approach to, 268–71
  naturalization, 264
  passing, 259–61
  rate of, 271–79
  shuttling between worlds, 281–82
  among Southern Italians in America, 352–59
  theory of cultural pluralism, 266–68

Authoritarian personality, 141–53

Avoidance, minority responding by, 377–406

Blacks
  aggression against Whites, 330–33
  art, 344–46
  Black Muslims, 389–93
  Black Power, 393–402
  criminality among, 54–57
  deflection of hostilities to other minorities, 341–43
  displacement of accommodating leadership, 322–27
  and early English contact, 77–79
  fear of Black rape, 137–38
  families, 251–55
  Garveyism, 365–89
  the hoodlum response to dominance, 336–39
  humor, 343–44
  in-group aggression, 339–41
  insulation from Whites, 377–80
  intelligence, 43–51
  internalization of racism, 308–9
  interracial marriage, 289–93
  irresponsible work among, 347
  migration from rural South, 380–82
  mobility aspirations among, 245–48
  movement among of Rev. Martin Luther King, Jr., 334–36
  Moynihan Report on, 251–55
  notions of inordinate sexuality of, 134–36
  passing among, 359–61
  Protest, 1955–1965, 361–74
  Protest, post-1965, 393–402
  resignation among, 368
  in the rural South, 313–14
  segregation of, 189–95
  self-hatred among, 309–12
  sexuality of, 134–36
  sources of oppression, 255–57
  sources of recent militancy, 170–76
  undercurrents of hostility toward Whites, 333–36

Blacks—*continued*
  variables affecting responses of, 327–
    29, 347–50, 374–76, 402–6
  vested interests in segregation, 319–22
  violence in relations with Whites, 161–
    70
Black Muslims, 389–93
Black Power
  and fair share, 400
  and integration, 400
  origins of, 393–94
  sources of, 395–400
  various interpretations of, 394–95
Black Revolution
  after Montgomery, 367–69
  aims of, 1955–1965, 362–63
  factors underlying, 369–74
  Montgomery Bus Boycott, 365–66
  movement of Rev. Martin Luther King,
    Jr., 333–36
  NAACP, 363–65
  old and new protests, 363–65
Busing, 436

Caste, 237–43
Chicanos
  employment, 202–4
  housing, 204–5
  intelligence of, 43–51
  schooling, 205–6
  segregation of, 200–6
Chinese, 206–11
Citizens Councils, 179–81
Civil Rights Acts, 431–33
Combating racism
  education, 455–60
  intergroup contact, 460–69
  laws, 474–81
  propaganda, 448–55
  psychological techniques, 469–74
Competition, 79–92
Conflict
  arousal of, 181–83
  defined, 157
  and economic pressure, 179–81
  and group conflict, 173–74
  litigation, 176–78
  and psychology of violence, 174–75
  resolution of, 181–83
  and riot ideology, 174–76
  sit-ins, 178–79
  social consequences of, 159–60
  and social disorganization, 172–73
  and social stability, 158
  social violence in U. S., 160–76
Contact
  in combating racism, 460–69

early English contact with Blacks, 77–
    79
  and origins of racism, 67–70
Cultural pluralism, 266–68
Culture
  cultural creativity, 260–61
  cultural disintegration, 361
  defined, 97–98
  intercultural transmission, 259–60
  in learning prejudice, 115–22, 147
  and perception, 103–5
  of poverty, 251–55
  and projection, 133–34
  in racism, 97–106
Culture of poverty, 251–55

Desegregation
  armed services, 441–42
  and Civil Rights Laws, 423–24
  in education, 430–37
  housing, 444–45
  income, 437–41
  jobs, 437–41
  in a northern community, 428–30
  in Virginia, 421–22
  voting, 442–43
Detroit 1943 riot, 165–66
Discrimination; *see also* Segregation
  definition of, 26
  lessening, 446–81
  and prejudice, 26–27
  and structural racism, 28–29
Dogmatism Scale, 152

Education, level of and prejudice, 456–60
Educational parks, 436–37
Ethnic groups in Yankee City, 227–34
Ethnocentrism
  and belief dissimilarity, 74–75
  connotative meanings of color names,
    77–79
  and English, 77–79
  in-group virtues become out-group
    vices, 76–77
  nature of, 73–74
  out-group viewed as deviant, 75–76

Freedom rides, 178–79

Garveyism, 385–89
Genetic drift, 63
Group conflict thesis, 173–74
Group therapy, 471–73

Harlem 1935 riot, 167
Hawaii, assimilation within, 293–97
Hybridization, 64

Integration, 261–63
Intelligence, 43–51
Intermarriage; *see* Marriage
Isolation, 62–63

Japanese, 211–16, 315–18
Jews; *see also* Anti-Semitism
    generational differences in adaptation,
        328
    as a race, 40–43
    segregation of, 216–19
Jim Crow, origins of, 412–16

Kerner Report, 3, 168–69
Ku Klux Klan, 87–89

Laws, in combating racism, 474–81
Little Rock, 1957, 420–21
Litigation, 176–78
Lynchings, 162–63

Marginality, 279–81
Marriage
    interethnic, 283
    interracial, 289–93
    interreligious, 284–89
Melting pot orientation, 264–65
Mexican-Americans; *see* Chicanos
Migration
    of Blacks from South, 381–82
    free, 69
    forced, 68–69
    impelled, 68–69
    mass, 70
    migrant subordination, 93–95
    migrant superordination, 93–95
Minorities
    characteristics of, 10–12
    definition of, 12
    relativity of membership in, 12–13
    types of, 16–19
    on the world scene, 13–16
Montgomery Bus Boycott, 365–66
Movement and counter-movement, 418–
    19
Moynihan Report, 251–55
Mutations, 59–60

Nativistic movements, 400–2
Natural selection, 60–62
Norwegians of Jonesville, 234–37

Pairing, 434–35
Prejudice
    acquiring, 115–22
    and authoritarianism, 141–53
    and competition, 79–92
    and contact, 67–70

and culture, 97–106
definition of, 19–21
and discrimination, 26–27
and ethnocentrism, 72–79
frustration and aggression, 125–33
lessening, 446–81
and power gains, 83–86
and projection, 133–41
and reference groups, 106–10
social conformity, 98–100
social distance, 100–2
and social visibility, 70–72
and status gains, 86–89
and structural racism, 28–29
and vested interests, 90–92
and unequal power, 92–95
Propaganda, 448–55
Power, and origins of racism, 92–95
Projection theory, 133–41
Psychology of violence thesis, 174
Puerto Ricans
    intelligence of, 43–51
    segregation of, 195–200

Race
    breeding population school of, 35–36
    conceptions of, 31–40
    defined, 30–31
    fixed type school of, 31–35
    formation of, 59–64
    and intellectual superiority, 43–51
    and intermixture, 57–59
    and Jews, 40–43
    and morality, 53–54
    no-race school of, 36–39
    and personality, 52–53
Racism
    defined, 29
    lessening, 446–81
    maintenance of, 97–123
    origins of, 67–96
    personality bulwarks of, 124–54
    structural, 28–29
Reconstruction, Second, 417–30
Reference groups, 106–11
Relative deprivation thesis, 171, 370–72
Religious strife, 409–12
Rezoning schools, 435–36
Riot ideology thesis, 174–76
Riots, 163–76

Scapegoat theory, 125–33
Science
    ethical neutrality, 5–10
    knowledge for what, 5–8
    knowledge for whom, 8–9
    pure and applied science, 9–10
    the pursuit of objectivity, 4–5

Segregation
  American Indians, 185–89
  Blacks, 189–95
  Chicanos, 200–6
  Chinese, 206–11
  de facto, 430–37
  de juro, 430–37
  Japanese, 211–16
  Jews, 216–20
  Puerto Ricans, 195–200
Self-fulfilling prophecy, 111–15
Self-hatred, 309–12
Separatism, 382–402
Sit-ins, 178–79
Social change, 409–45
Social class
  and caste, 237–43
  definition of, 223
  in Jonesville, 234–37
  mobility of immigrants, 243–45
  in Old City, 237–43
  and social mobility, 243–51
  in Yankee City, 227–34
Social disorganization thesis, 172–73
Social distance, 100–2
Social mobility
  and caste, 237–43
  degree of, 248–51

  group characteristics affecting, 245–48
  of immigrants, 243–45
Social visibility, 70–72
Socialization, 115–22, 145–48
Springfield riot, 164–65
Stereotypes
  definition of, 21–22
  denial of, 23–26
  persistence of, 23–26
Stratification
  based on race and ethnicity, 223–26
  and Black families, 251–55
  among Blacks, 251–55
  defined, 221
  and definition of class, 223
  differs from other forms, 225–26
  in Jonesville, 234–37
  and mobility, 243–51
  in Old City, 237–43
  and types of social organization, 221–23
  in Yankee City, 227–34

Thomas theorem, 111–15

Vicious circle theory, 113–15

Zionism, 382–85